BY ARTHUR SCHLESINGER, JR.

The Letters of
Arthur Schlesinger, Jr.

The Letters of Arthur Schlesinger, Jr.

EDITED BY

Andrew Schlesinger and
Stephen Schlesinger

RANDOM HOUSE

New York

Published in the United States by Random House, an imprint of
The Random House Publishing Group, a division of
Random House LLC, a Penguin Random House Company, New York.

RANDOM HOUSE and the HOUSE colophon are registered trademarks of Random House LLC.

Grateful acknowledgment is made to the following for permission to reprint letters:
ESTATE OF JOSEPH W. ALSOP, V: One letter written by Joseph Alsop, copyright © 2012
by Estate of Joseph Alsop, V. Used by permission.
GROUCHO MARX PRODUCTIONS, INC.: One letter written by Groucho Marx.
Reprinted by permission of Groucho Marx Productions, Inc.
CYNTHIA HELMS: One letter written by Richard Helms. Reprinted by permission of Cynthia Helms.
DR. HENRY A. KISSINGER: Three letters written by Dr. Henry A. Kissinger.
Reproduced with permission of the copyright owner, Dr. Henry A. Kissinger.
Further reproduction prohibited without permission.
ANN ROSTOW: One letter written by Walt Rostow. Reprinted by permission of Ann Rostow.
JOAN BURESCH TALLEY: Two letters written by Allen Dulles.
Reprinted by permission of Joan Buresch Talley.

LIBRARY OF CONGRESS CATALOGING-IN-PUBLICATION DATA
Schlesinger, Arthur M. (Arthur Meier), 1917–2007.
[Correspondence]
The Letters of Arthur Schlesinger, Jr. / edited by Andrew Schlesinger and Stephen Schlesinger.
pages   cm
Includes index.
ISBN 978-0-8129-9309-7
eBook ISBN 978-0-679-64463-7
1. Schlesinger, Arthur M. (Arthur Meier), 1917–2007—Correspondence.   2. Historians—United
States—Correspondence.   3. United States—History—1945–   4. United States—Social life
and customs—1945–1970.   5. United States—Social life and customs—1971–
6. United States—Politics and government—1945–1989.   7. United States—Politics and
government—1989–   I. Schlesinger, Andrew.   II. Schlesinger, Stephen C.   III. Title.
E175.5.S38A4 2013   973.91092—dc23   2012049922
[B]
Printed in the United States of America on acid-free paper

www.atrandom.com

2   4   6   8   9   7   5   3   1

First Edition

Book design by Jo Anne Metsch

For Alexandra Schlesinger

Contents

Introduction

The historian Arthur Schlesinger, Jr., was an influential man. He wrote more than sixteen books concerning American history and politics, winning two Pulitzer Prizes and two National Book Awards. He was an adviser to President John F. Kennedy and a leader of the liberal wing of the Democratic Party. His judgments and opinions were sought after by editors of *The Wall Street Journal, The New York Times,* and the leading magazines of the day. The publication of his *Journals* after his death in 2007 was a bestseller.

Schlesinger was an inveterate letter writer. He communicated by mail with hundreds of friends, acquaintances, critics, and fans. His associations ranged widely, from presidents of the United States to Supreme Court justices, powerful public officials, celebrated intellectuals, notable literary figures, Hollywood actors and directors, members of the news media, fellow scholars, and religious leaders.

For the most part, what brought him together with these individuals were his political beliefs. The abiding theme of his correspondence over a sixty-year period is his preoccupation with liberalism and its prospects. He was always in some way promoting and advancing the liberal agenda; it was his mission, purpose, and justification.

What did the liberal credo mean to Schlesinger? As he wrote in his much acclaimed book, *The Vital Center,* published in 1949: "The job of liberalism [is] to devote itself to the maintenance of individual liberties and to the democratic control of economic life—and to brook no compromise, at home or abroad, on either of these two central tencts." For him, liberalism was "a fighting faith." In *The Cycles of American History* (1986) he noted that liberals do not see the unfettered marketplace as an "infinitely sensitive, frictionless, impartial, self-equilibrating mechanism." Instead, he wrote, "The liberal believes that the mitigation of [economic] problems will require a renewal of affirmative government to redress the market's distortion and compensate for its failures—but affirmative government chastened and reformed, one must hope, by stringent review of the excesses and errors of [past] centuries."

On September 14, 1960, Senator John F. Kennedy, accepting the New York Liberal Party's presidential nomination, proclaimed his liberalism in words Schlesinger helped craft, saying: "If, by a 'Liberal' they mean someone who looks ahead and not behind, someone who welcomes new ideas without rigid reactions, someone who cares about the welfare of the people—their health, their housing, their schools, their jobs, their civil rights, and their civil liberties—someone who believes we can break through the stalemate and suspicions that grip us in our policies abroad, if that is what they mean by a 'Liberal,' then I'm proud to say I'm a 'Liberal.' "

This is what liberalism meant to Schlesinger. These letters from the inside of the movement provide a quasi history of American liberalism and its struggles through the crucial decades from 1945 to 2005, from Franklin D. Roosevelt to George W. Bush.

After Schlesinger's death in 2007, the New York Public Library acquired his papers, which fill some 526 separate cardboard boxes. The boxes contain not only thousands of his letters, but also research materials, clippings, awards, data, transcripts, oral testimonies, scrapbooks, photographs, financial records, legal documents, and sundry other papers. From this rich hoard, one becomes aware of being in the presence of a communicator extraordinaire. We estimate the number of letters we reviewed in the archives approached 35,000.* Schlesinger may indeed be one of the last of the old-fashioned breed of American figures for whom letters were the paramount means of communication—a phenomenon that seems oddly archaic in a digital age.

---

*We also found letters at the John F. Kennedy Presidential Library, the Franklin D. Roosevelt Presidential Library, the Library of Congress, the Seeley G. Mudd Manuscript Library at Princeton University, and the Sterling Memorial Library at Yale.

How did we choose the letters in this book? What sort of criteria did we use? As noted, we focused principally on Schlesinger's intellectual and political development as one of the nation's leading liberal voices. Given that his missives ranged from brief notes to lengthy essays and included sober reflections on policy issues, humorous notations, book blurbs, eulogies, business correspondence, family exchanges, regrets at the deaths of friends, and replies to admiring fans, we determined to select those that best articulated his essential beliefs and reflected the movement of the times.

The letters trace the evolution and adjustments of his thinking over the decades: his fight against isolationism before the U.S. entry into World War II, his campaign to preserve liberalism from a Communist threat in the 1940s and 1950s, his work to awaken his country to a liberal revival in the 1960s, his struggles against the Vietnam War and American imperialism in the 1970s, and his push for a progressive presidential administration in the 1980s and 1990s.

Schlesinger wielded his pen as a literary weapon—for criticism, for influence, for humor, for chiding, for self-advancement, for righting wrongs, and for waving the flag of progressivism. He told the powerful what he thought and what they should think. He did not discriminate between his famous friends and anonymous correspondents, treating them with the same respect and offering the same bracing candor. As he seemed incapable of writing a bad sentence, he dispatched letters that invariably exerted an impact. (Nor did he falter in his letter writing in old age, though his notes grew shorter and his signature frailer.) And he was always conscious that potential readers (and history) were watching him, for he often initialed by hand the recipient's name and the date of the letter so the letter's context would remain clear.

Contained herein are letters to John and Robert F. Kennedy, Jacqueline Onassis, Lyndon B. Johnson, George H. W. Bush, Bill Clinton, Eleanor Roosevelt, Harry S. Truman, W. Averell Harriman, Adlai Stevenson, Hubert H. Humphrey, Jr., Al Gore, Jr., Henry Kissinger, John Kenneth Galbraith, Daniel Patrick Moynihan, Katharine Graham, Marietta Tree, Reinhold Niebuhr, Felix Frankfurter, Walter Lippmann, Joseph Alsop, William F. Buckley, Jr., Bill Moyers, Isaiah Berlin, George Kennan, McGeorge Bundy, Rebecca West, Robert Lowell, Gore Vidal, Bianca Jagger, William Styron, Art Buchwald, and others.

Schlesinger never regretted what he wrote. He told a correspondent in 1993: "I sometimes shudder a bit when I read what I wrote privately in years past, but it is all part of the record, and as a historian, I can hardly claim immunity that historians routinely deny to the dead."

This book is a testament to Schlesinger's unvarnished, elegant, and provocative correspondence over a six-decade period.

Andrew and Stephen Schlesinger, editors

Prologue

Precocious Beginnings

Arthur Schlesinger, Jr.'s paternal grandfather, Bernhard, was born in 1846 in Königswalde, a small town in East Prussia, and came to America in 1860 to join an older brother working in the leather business in Newark, New Jersey. Bernhard made knapsacks for Union soldiers during the Civil War and afterward settled in Xenia, Ohio, where he met Kate Feurle, an Austrian girl from the village of Kennelbach in the Tyrol. He was Jewish and she was Roman Catholic, and they married in the German Reformed Church. Her father ran a tavern for German-speaking travelers, complete with a grapevine-covered beer garden with sturdy wooden tables and benches.

Bernhard made a modest living as an insurance agent. Like many German Americans, he had a keen interest in public education. From 1881 to 1919—for nearly forty years—he served on the Xenia School Board, a body chosen by popular vote. He had three sons and two daughters. His youngest child was born on February 27, 1888, at the time Grover Cleveland was preparing to run for reelection to the presidency. Bernhard, an ardent Democrat, wished the infant to be named Grover Cleveland Schlesinger, but his daughters vetoed the idea. He was named Arthur. The daughters, Olga and Marion, were both schoolteachers. The three boys went to Ohio State University in Columbus. The oldest brother, Hugo, became a lawyer, and the middle brother, George, a civil engineer. Arthur's ambition was to become a newspaperman, but Ohio State offered no courses in journalism, and he turned to history, finding his lifetime vocation. He graduated in 1910.

Arthur met his wife at Ohio State. Elizabeth Bancroft was born in Co lumbus in 1886. Her father, a newspaperman named Arthur Bancroft, was evidently a charming man whose irregular work habits, especially with regard to hours and to drink, displeased his severe and strong-minded wife. After three children were born, the marriage broke up, leaving Elizabeth with faint but abiding memories of a much-loved father. A pretty coed with dark hair and chestnut brown eyes, she had returned to college after two years of teaching in a one-room school in order to earn the money to complete her education. Arthur and Elizabeth were married in 1914 by a Congregationalist minister and honeymooned in Atlantic City.

When Arthur was eight years old, during the 1896 presidential campaign, he had been in the crowd that greeted William Jennings Bryan at the Xenia railroad station, twice lining up and shaking the hand of the "Boy Orator of the Platte." In 1912, he heard Bryan speak at the chapel of Columbia University in New York City where he was studying as a graduate student in American history. "A person could not have a higher ideal than to live a life such as [Bryan] has,—one of purity, unselfishness, wholehearted devotion to the cause of the people," he wrote to his betrothed. "I hope I may contribute my mite some day."

Elizabeth was an enthusiastic suffragette and prodded him into watching the great women's rights parade on Fifth Avenue in the spring of 1912. He conceded that it was "an impressive spectacle," women walking four and sometimes eight abreast with bands and banners and flags and mottoes in a procession that took an hour and a half to pass. But he did not think that female suffrage was an issue of consequence. "I hope equal suffrage comes quickly so that people may devote themselves to the real issues," he wrote to her, adding, "I don't object to your being a suffragette as long as you aren't too militant." He cast his first presidential ballot in November 1912 for Woodrow Wilson. He never thought his commitment as a scholar abrogated his conscience as a citizen.

After two years at Columbia, Arthur returned to Ohio State as an instructor in American history and began his campaign to broaden the study of American history to include not only government, politics, war, and diplomacy, but also the social and cultural factors so potent in the development of a nation. He believed that the study of the habits and customs of the American people—examining how they worked, played, loved, ventured, suffered, and died—would help explain what it is to be an American. He imagined women's history, immigration history, labor history, ethnic history, urban history, and intellectual history one day being taught in universities across America. He was appointed chairman of the history department at the University of Iowa in Iowa City in 1919. In addition to his course "New Viewpoints in American History," he offered one called "The Social and Cultural History of the United States," the first of its kind at any university.

Arthur and Elizabeth's first child, Katharine, was born in September 1915 in Columbus and died of an intestinal ailment ten months later. A boy was born on October 15, 1917, and named Arthur Bancroft Schlesinger. Another boy, Thomas Bancroft, was born in Iowa City on June 9, 1922.

In 1924, the Schlesinger family moved to Cambridge, Massachusetts, when Arthur (Sr.) joined the history faculty of Harvard University. The boys attended the local public schools. Young Arthur went to the Peabody School, a few blocks from their house on Gray Gardens East. The instruction at Peabody was "not at all bad," he said later. He was pushed ahead rapidly, skipping the second and fourth grades. Condemned to eyeglasses by myopia and astigmatism, he was a "four eyes" in the school slang of the period. But he was happy to escape the boredom and stultification of a slower track.

His father worked in his book-lined study in the back of the house overlooking the garden, wearing a green eyeshade of the kind once familiar in newspaper offices and smoking a pipe while reading at his desk or typing. He was old-fashioned in many habits. He carried a gold Elgin pocket watch on a chain from which dangled his Phi Beta Kappa key. He applied lather with a brush and shaved with a straight razor stropped on a band of leather. On crisp, smoky fall days, he and his sons joined the crowd streaming over the bridge across the Charles River to the football stadium and returned in the dusk to Harvard Square. He usually stopped by Leavitt & Peirce, the tobacconist, where the results of football games across the country were chalked up on the blackboard. He was sentimentally attached to the fortunes of Ohio State and Iowa in the Big Ten.

The family shifted its tenuous religious allegiance from the Congregationalists to the Unitarians, domiciled in the First Parish Church across from Harvard Yard.

Of all childhood pastimes, reading was young Arthur's passion. His mother read aloud to him, exciting a quest for literature. He read every book he could find by G. A. Henty, author of more than a hundred historical novels for boys. He read all fourteen of L. Frank Baum's *Oz* books. He was fascinated by Mark Twain's *Huckleberry Finn.* He considered Alexandre Dumas, author of *The Three Musketeers* and *The Count of Monte Cristo,* supreme in the historical vein.

What he read spurred him to try his hand at writing. Juvenilia carefully preserved by his mother show an early preoccupation with history. He wrote stories about pirates in the Spanish Main and desperadoes in the American West, as well as "Alice's Adventures in Cambridge." While staying with friends at Squam Lake in New Hampshire and rereading Henty's *Under Drake's Flag,* the story of a brave English teenager sailing and fighting with Sir Francis Drake in the sixteenth century, he wrote one of his first letters, to his father, dated August 1926: "Every morning before breakfast Ed and I go out in the canoe. I can row and paddle. Ed and I pretend we're Francis Drake and his men. We have a rock which we call 'Panama.' Cotton's Cove is the 'Pacific Ocean.' Ed's house is 'Valparaiso.' We have a wharf where we captured two galleons and defeated one galley."

Professionally and personally, Professor Schlesinger was concerned that the United States was increasingly dominated by predatory businessmen and fanatical fundamentalists who were undermining freedom of thought with their insistence on orthodoxy and conformity. "We are in danger of becoming a nation of parrots," he said in 1926, delivering the commencement address at Ohio State. Standardization was now a principle of American society, he asserted. "The typical American today may be pictured as a man wearing a Knox hat, an Arrow collar, a Manhattan shirt, a Hart, Schaffner and Marx suit, and a pair of Walkover shoes, seated in a Ford car with a *Saturday Evening Post* under his arm on his way to the monthly meeting of the National Association for the Banishment of Privacy from the American Home." The forces making for the suppression of individuality—the fundamentalists, the super-patriots, the large corporations—were growing stronger.

Meanwhile, the free drinking habits of Cambridge rather shocked Arthur and Elizabeth. They had come to terms with the Eighteenth Amendment in bone-dry Iowa, yet nearly everywhere they were invited they were served alcoholic beverages and, not wanting to offend, found themselves imbibing, even though they scrupulously furnished none to their own guests. The situation became ludicrous. One day when a neighbor about to motor across the Canadian border to replenish his own supply offered to obtain some for the Schlesingers, Arthur (Sr.) succumbed. Young Arthur watched Bernard De Voto unloading bottles from the trunk of his car in the driveway, believing the distinguished writer was the family bootlegger.

The boy immersed himself in each year's *World Almanac*. At his parents' Sunday afternoon teas, he liked to quiz guests on the populations of the world's major cities and then implacably reveal them. He was equally in command of baseball batting averages. His father called him "a fiend at crossword puzzles." He collected stamps and autographs.

Arthur (Sr.) supported Governor Alfred E. Smith of New York against Herbert Hoover in the presidential election of 1928. He found the objections to Smith's Catholicism offensive as violating the constitutional principle of the separation of church and state. Smith, the slangy son of the polyglot city, was "wet," which no longer bothered the professor in view of the evil fruits of Prohibition in practice. In any case, the Republican Hoover had proven unduly friendly to business as secretary of commerce.

Arthur (Sr.) was by now an active supporter of women's rights. When Margaret Sanger came to Boston and was forbidden by Mayor Curley to speak out on birth control, Arthur, as toastmaster at a banquet in her honor, ceremoniously placed a gag on her mouth and proceeded to read aloud her speech.

In the spring of 1929, Elizabeth took young Arthur on a grand trip to New York and Washington. They traveled from Boston by night boat and stayed at the Hotel Bristol on West Forty-Eighth Street. The next morning, Arthur climbed to the top of the Statue of Liberty. Then they went to the Woolworth Building, the world's tallest. "This is one of the things I've dreamed about doing," he confided to his mother in the elevator. They visited Broadway, Wall Street, the Metropolitan Museum, the Museum of Natural History, Grant's Tomb, FAO Schwarz, and the Roxy Theatre. In Washington, they went to the Capitol and heard Senator Tom Heflin of Alabama shout an hour-and-a-half tirade against the pope and his minions. Arthur visited the White House for the first time, viewing the Blue and Green rooms.

Arthur graduated from the Peabody School in June 1929. He moved on to the Cambridge High and Latin School, where his parents' faith in public education fell under increasing strain. One day in his sophomore year when he came home and reported that his civics teacher had informed the class that the inhabitants of Albania were called Albinos and had white hair and pink eyes, that finished it for his father, who forthwith called a friend, the treasurer of Phillips Exeter Academy in New Hampshire, and entered Arthur as an upper middler (or junior) for the autumn of 1931. It was about this time that Arthur changed his middle name and became Arthur Meier Schlesinger, Jr.

Exeter was a big, impersonal school with a first-class faculty and a highly competitive student body of nearly seven hundred boys. Tuition was $350 a year, plus another $300 or so for room and board at $9 a week. Most of the students were from Republican families. Arthur's first-semester grades included Ds in Latin, French, and English, and a C in mathematics. For one who pulled down As without effort in public school, the shock was salutary. He set to work in earnest.

Both daily chapel and Sunday church were compulsory—an edict that transformed Arthur's indifference to religion into active hostility. "Compulsory church," he wrote to his grandmother Bancroft, "is an invention of the devil. Certainly it is bringing more souls to his side." In a more pensive mood, he wrote to his mother, "One thing more. When I die, and if services are held over me, please do not have religious stuff read. Just read some poetry, Gray's *Elegy* or something from Byron."

In Arthur's senior year, when Governor Franklin D. Roosevelt of New York ran against President Hoover, Arthur was among a tiny band committed to the cause of FDR. "Republican propaganda has tried to show Hoover as a demi-god and Roosevelt as a demagogue. According to all indications, however, the people refuse to be fooled," he wrote in a school essay. To his parents he wrote in October 1932:

> This school is filled with the most conservative, illiberal, intolerant, narrow-minded bunch of fellows which were ever brought together. There are about 125 people who are not dead dry conservatives, and don't think that Socialists and Reds should be shot at sight, that there is the slightest possibility that any nation is anywhere as good as the U.S.A., and that the Sacco-Vanzetti case was not a triumph for justice. Most think that all Jews are inferior and poisonous to touch and taste, Hoover is the greatest man of the century, Cal Coolidge and Dawes being close seconds, and that Woodrow Wilson was a poor president. That the Democrats were responsible for every bad thing that Hoover did, that Roo-

sevelt is controlled by Tammany, Hearst, Garner, Gene Tunney, and Marian Davies. etc. etc.

The majority of the school remained unshakably conservative. In the campus straw poll, Hoover received 494 votes to 84 for Norman Thomas of the Socialist Party and 80 for Roosevelt. But Arthur wrote home predicting that "Frank will win by 8,000,000 votes in the country"; the actual margin was seven million. Four months later, Arthur sat with a small group around a radio in the common room of Phillips Hall, listening to FDR in his inaugural address say that the only thing we had to fear was fear itself. "I heard Frank's speech. I thought it was pretty good," he wrote to his mother.

Whatever defects Exeter may have had, the standards were high, and the intellectual training was superb. Arthur thrived, winning many prizes on graduation day. But his parents believed he was too young at fifteen to matriculate at Harvard and in a burst of imagination decided to take a year off and travel with the boys westward around the world to England, where Arthur, Sr., was scheduled to give the Commonwealth Lectures at the University of London in February–March 1934. They visited Japan, China, Vietnam, Cambodia, Burma, India, Egypt, Greece, Italy, France, and England, where Arthur, Jr., saw sixteen plays. Fancying a future as a drama critic, he filled a notebook with reviews. Then they visited Switzerland, Austria, Belgium, and, briefly, Nazi Germany.

Arthur entered Harvard College in September 1934, a member of the class of 1938. Tuition was $400 a year. Room and board added another $700. After Exeter, the transition to Harvard was easy. In his sophomore year, he chose his field of concentration, American history and literature. Perry Miller was his tutor in his sophomore and senior years; F. O. Matthiessen, in his junior year. Arthur lived in Adams House. His chief extracurricular interest was the *Harvard Advocate,* the undergraduate literary magazine, where he served as a drama critic. He was a regular at the Colonial, Shubert, and Wilbur theaters in Boston.

Like his parents, he was an ardent New Dealer. The battles of the thirties shaped his politics—loyalty to the Democratic Party and recognition of the political shortsightedness, stupidity, and greed of American business leadership. He had no doubt that FDR and the New Dealers could work things out and do so within the system. He chose not to join the new Harvard chapter of the American Student Union, a Popular Front organization. "I am not joining because of a firm conviction that any spare time I have in college should be spent in enlarging my intellectual horizons rather than in messing about with pseudo-political organizations that will never do anything very effective," he recorded in his journal.

It was in those years that he embraced the bow tie. Many men he admired wore bow ties: FDR, Winston Churchill, Groucho Marx. He found the bow tie not only neat and suggestive of insouciance; for sloppy eaters its special advantage was the implausibility of spilling anything on it. Dry cleaning never restored any tie to its primal innocence.

In May 1937, he met the woman who would become his first wife, Marian Cannon, a lively, intelligent, twenty-four-year-old brunette, an artist and a Radcliffe graduate who had traveled in China and lived in New York City. Marian was one of four daughters of Walter Bradford Cannon, a distinguished physiologist at the Harvard Medical School, and Cornelia James Cannon, a novelist and all-purpose reformer. Courtship had its vicissitudes. Arthur was immature (according to his own later estimation); Marian was doubtful; they both had strong egos. They fought, parted, and came together again.

Arthur graduated from Harvard summa cum laude in June 1938. His senior thesis about the nineteenth-century American intellectual Orestes Augustus Brownson was accepted for publication by the Boston firm Little, Brown. In early September 1938, he left for England to take up his Henry Fellowship at Peterhouse College in Cambridge, arriving in Plymouth just as the crisis over the partition of Czechoslovakia was heating up. Prime Minister Neville Chamberlain went to Munich on September 29 and approved an agreement allowing Hitler to seize the Sudetenland. Arthur found the agreement "chilling and cause for indignation." Yet, like most Americans, he was a stout isolationist and supposed that the United States was immune from European convulsions.

"I suspect," he wrote home on October 4, 1938, "that in six months Germany and Russia will make a non-aggression pact. When Germany prepares to fight again, it will whip Great Britain and France unless the United States steps in. And, if I thought the Chamberlain government was at all representative of the English people, I should hope most strongly that the U.S. keeps out." But Arthur had mixed feelings about Britain and was a soft touch for British high style.

Peterhouse had been founded in 1284, and the great hall, though altered through the years, was six and a half centuries old. The stately court and its gabled buildings and oriel windows, completed in the eighteenth century, were filled with history and charm. Arthur dined very well in the hall, and college servants brought around excellent luncheons when he wished to entertain. The wine cellar lived up to advance notices. He made a lifelong friend in Charles Wintour, who roomed next door, "a man after my own heart, i.e., inquiring, skeptical, sensitive to relationships among people and politically adept at influencing them, flexible, vigorous." Arthur wrote articles and film reviews for *Granta,* the undergraduate weekly that Charles edited. Arthur even found himself directing plays for the Amateur Dramatic Club.

Hitler's howls on the radio provoked much hilarity among the scholars, but nervous laughter barely concealed deep anxiety. On a Saturday night in London in January 1939, Arthur walked out of a movie in Piccadilly Circus into a crowd of young men shouting "Mosley, Mosley" and "Down with the Jews" and singing about "building the Fascist state." These were Blackshirts, followers of Sir Oswald Mosley and his British Union of Fascists. They surged suddenly through the Circus, catching and beating people of Jewish appearance. "The most alarming feature was the attitude of the crowd," Arthur wrote home. "Some people were terrifically angry and went around swearing to themselves, but most seemed to regard the thing as a spectacle and stood amiably on the sidelines. . . . I have never seen such a mob at work before. My opinion of mankind has somewhat fallen."

In March 1939, despite the Munich Agreement, Hitler's armies overran all of Czechoslovakia. "Czecho-Slovakia has exploded like a bomb, and the skies have darkened considerably in Cambridge," Arthur wrote his parents on March 16.

It all crept up on me. For some reason, probably because the English newspapers played it down, I was but vaguely aware of a crisis in Czecho-Slovakia, and certainly expecting nothing more. Then yesterday, as I was listening to the radio while waiting for some one to come to lunch, I was suddenly shocked by a news bulletin with the word that Czecho-Slovakia had disappeared. It has plunged most of the people I know into a deep gloom. Late last night there was a bottle party at the *Granta.* Most of the people there were despairing of England and picturing themselves as refugees to the United States or prisoners in concentration camps. Charles Wintour left today, more depressed than I have ever seen him. I have just come from coffee with a Yugoslavian friend . . . who had just talked by 'phone with his family and found them filled with a kind of tormented fatalism about the situation. He is desperately gloomy. An Australian in Peterhouse with whom earlier in the year I used to argue the merits of England told me tonight that he was bitterly disillusioned and spoke of the imperial bond as a chain linking his country to a corpse. The hunting-shooting set in Peterhouse, who have always had placid confidence in the infallibility of England and the virtue of Chamberlain, are now bewildered and upset; a couple of them whom I talked to are openly cursing out Hitler. *The Telegraph* came through with a fine outspoken leader (much better than any of the radical papers), condemning the Chamberlain policy on the admirable ground that it is futile to try and appease a boa-constrictor. Even the Times has declared the business to be "a most reprehensible act." Chamberlain, of course, has been grotesque. I have never heard such an achievement in understatement as his recent remarks—"a shock to confidence," "not in accord with the spirit of the Munich agreement," "I am bitterly regretful." . . .

It is my impression that America has gone through two stages since Munich: 1) the immediate reaction of great indignation accompanied by the feeling that all moral obligations to England and France were dissolved; and 2) a second stage, where, with all moral considerations put aside, the case was rested on purely realistic grounds and the argument arose that the menace of Fascism is so great that it would be to our interest to help England and France as much as possible in order to save us further trouble in the future (e.g., "America's frontier is on the Rhine"). This second stage has (I think fortunately) not yet been wholly triumphant, but the collapse of the isolationist bloc in the Congress, apart from the few professional isolationists, suggests that it is growing rapidly. Is this impression at all correct? I hope not, and I am very suspicious of all the arguments about the necessity of fighting Germany in France to avoid fighting it in South America. . . .

Well, there'll be no war this year anyway; and probably none at all until Hitler tries to move in on Yugoslavia, Belgium, France or possibly Roumania. Elmer Davis's theory that England might try to purchase immunity by giving their fleet to Germany strikes me as horribly possible.

The English would somehow succeed in presenting such an act to themselves as highly moral and creditable behavior.

With war in the back of all minds, Arthur later remembered, the gaiety of May Week (taking place, as always, in June) was never more sustained, more riotous, more enchanted, or more desperate—the last fling before Armageddon. Arthur's year at Cambridge had been one of the most exhilarating years of his life, and he was sorry to see it end.

Marian Cannon came over in time for Wimbledon. The reunion was not an immediate success. "She does seem considerably older than you in her behavior," wrote Charles Wintour after seeing them together. "Whenever there was any kind of a dispute between you, even if her position was weak, she seemed more in control of the situation and was certainly less irascible about it than you. . . . It seems damn priggish advice to tell anyone that they're not old enough to marry."* After travel to France and Italy and to Dubrovnik on the Adriatic, Arthur and Marian returned to the United States in August 1939, their future unresolved.

Then everything changed. The Soviet Union signed a surprise nonaggression pact with Nazi Germany on August 23, 1939, and a week later German armies attacked Poland, prompting Britain and France to declare war on Germany. The Soviet Union invaded eastern Poland. Once rabidly anti-Nazi, the Communist party line in the United States whipped around 180 degrees to oppose American intervention in "imperialist wars" abroad.

A few weeks later, Arthur began a three-year fellowship as a member of Harvard's Society of Fellows, an institution providing stipends for young scholars to pursue their interests without professional obligations, "suited to the encouragement of the rare and independent genius." Preoccupied with the issues of economic power and the dilemmas of democratic capitalism, Arthur deepened his study of the Jacksonian period and began questioning the orthodox view that the western frontier was the driving force of Jacksonian democracy. His research suggested that the East as much as the West shaped the Jacksonian upheaval, that the struggle over control of the state—between the business community (represented by the Bank of the United States) and the rest of society—fully engaged the po-

* Quoted in Arthur M. Schlesinger, Jr., *A Life in the Twentieth Century: Innocent Beginnings, 1917–1950* (Boston: Houghton Mifflin, 2000), 215.

litical energies of the working men and small business owners of the Eastern cities. And Eastern intellectuals such as Orestes Brownson and George Bancroft had their stake in the movement. If Jacksonian democracy represented only the eruption of uncouth backwoodsmen, Arthur wondered, why were so many leading writers and artists of the day ardent Jacksonians: Nathaniel Hawthorne, James Fenimore Cooper, William Cullen Bryant, Walt Whitman, Washington Irving, Horatio Greenough, Edwin Forrest?

But much of the winter of 1939–40 was spent in inner turmoil over the war. The isolationism he had brashly expressed in England seemed increasingly hollow, even false. Hitler's spring blitzkrieg shattered his own internal Maginot Line. "The invasion of Holland and Belgium finally awoke me to Nazism," he wrote in his journal on May 23, 1940. "Hitler is not a mere imperialist conqueror, somewhat nastier and gaudier than the Kaiser, but moved essentially by economic needs and governed by considerations of expediency. His war is not a war for markets and colonies. It is a revolution and a crusade.... [Hitler] is the prophet of a new religion, and like all prophets is out to convert or destroy. It is democracy or Nazism."

Most Americans did not believe that the United States had a vital interest in preventing Hitler's conquest of Europe. When the Nazis overran France in June 1940 and only Britain remained to resist, Harvard president James Bryant Conant went on nationwide radio and urged that the United States take "every action possible to ensure the defeat of Hitler"—and was rewarded with a flood of abusive letters. At commencement, the class orator denounced aid to the Allies as "fantastic nonsense." But many influential faculty members joined the American Defense, Harvard Group to make the case for aid to Britain. Arthur gave some fifty broadcasts for the Harvard Group over Boston's WRUL, the most powerful shortwave radio station in the United States.

In August 1940, Arthur and Marian were married on the Cannons' hill in Franklin, New Hampshire, by the local Unitarian minister, and the young couple honeymooned on Cape Breton Island.

The British fought alone against the fascists—in Greece, in Norway, in Yugoslavia, in North Africa, in West Africa, in Iraq, in the Atlantic, in the Mediterranean, in the skies over Britain and Germany. President Roosevelt's proposal to lend and lease military aid to Britain, opposed vociferously by the isolationists (and the Communists), passed Congress in March 1941.

Arthur's research was beginning to bear fruit. In May 1941, he and Marian set out for New York, where he examined manuscripts and newspapers at the public library and the New-York Historical Society and attended the theater in the evenings. They went on to Washington to look at the papers of Jackson, Martin Van Buren, Roger B. Taney, and other Jacksonians at the Library of Congress. While he was entangled in the nineteenth century, the twentieth century exploded around him. On June 22, Hitler's armies invaded the Soviet Union. Communists and their sympathizers wheeled around once again and clamored for a second front in Europe.

Back in Cambridge, Arthur began to write. He had accumulated several shoe boxes of notes painstakingly inscribed in pen on four-by-six-inch cards. In advancing his interpretation, he was conditioned by the passions of his time, he later admitted in his autobiography. Conservatives in the angry thirties fulminated against the New Deal as "un-American." He wanted to show that FDR was acting in a robust American spirit and tradition. Jackson's war against Nicholas Biddle and the Second Bank of the United States constituted a thoroughly American precedent for the battles FDR waged against the "economic royalists" of his day.

On Sunday, December 7, 1941, Arthur and Marian returned from luncheon with his parents at Gray Gardens East. As they entered their Harvard Street apartment, the telephone began to ring. In a single gesture Arthur flicked on the radio to the New York Philharmonic live from Carnegie Hall and picked up the phone. Radios took a few seconds to warm up in those days. As he heard an agitated Avis De Voto shout over the phone that something terrible had happened in Pearl Harbor, the radio suddenly blared out the unbelievable news.

The next day FDR asked Congress to recognize a state of war between the United States and the Empire of Japan. Four days later Germany declared war on the United States. "The forces endeavoring to enslave the entire world now are moving toward this hemisphere," FDR told the American people. "Never before has there been a greater challenge to life, liberty, and civilization."

Victory was far from preordained. Democracy, demoralized by depression, unnerved by war, was for the moment a fragile hope. Arthur's bad eyesight kept him out of the draft. He was grappling with his manuscript on Jacksonian democracy, which had grown to more than fifteen hundred pages of typescript. His three-year term in the Society of Fellows was ending. His wife was pregnant.

Marian gave birth to twins on August 17, 1942. A week later Arthur accepted a job in the Writers Division in the Domestic Branch of the U.S. Office of War Information in Washington, D.C. The director of OWI was the celebrated newscaster Elmer Davis. The writers' mission was to provide "a full knowledge of what we are fighting for," in the words of Archibald MacLeish, the librarian of Congress, temporarily attached to the division. Arthur's assignments included ghostwriting official speeches and composing low-level White House messages for FDR's signature, and he made a fact-finding trip to army camps in the South that exposed him to some dark realities of American life. Growing up in a liberal family, he had always been aware of racial injustice. But he had not appreciated the true horror of the black predicament until he crossed the Mason-Dixon Line.

"I was pretty depressed by the South, particularly by the bitterness and obvious widespread tension over the Negro problem," he reported to his parents in November 1942.

> Only in a few older people did I come on the old paternal attitude toward them. Most people seemed just extremely scared of the Negroes, and the only policy they favored was one of absolute intransigence. Several people defended lynching, even of innocent people, on the ground that only such measures would keep the Negro in his place. The southerners are so frightened that they dare not relax their hold in the slightest.
>
> For the first time I developed some sympathy with the Negro attitude toward the war. It seems to me almost the literal truth that they could not be worse treated by Hitler than they are by the southerners today. On one unforgettable evening at Biloxi, Mississippi, we were taken by a couple of armed military policemen on a tour of the Biloxi colored district. I have never seen such misery and wretchedness. But that fact is less shocking and hopeless than the passionate conviction on the part of many southerners that terrorism and repression are the only policies open to them. It left [me] feeling deeply depressed.

The Schlesinger family lived in a rented house in northwest Washington where Arthur devoted evenings and weekends to the revision of the now gigantic Jackson manuscript. In January 1943 he sent the typescript, 330,000 words, more than thirteen hundred pages, to his father, who helped edit it and cut it down to publishing size.

Meanwhile, empowered by the results of the midterm elections of November 1942, Congressional Republicans intensified their campaign against the Office of War Information as a propaganda vehicle for FDR and the New Deal. Within OWI, the head of the Domestic Branch, Gardner Cowles, Jr., publisher of the *Des Moines Tribune* and *Look* magazine, hatched a plan to employ New York advertising men to "sell" the war like selling cigarettes or soft drinks, using well-honed Madison Avenue techniques. This was something MacLeish had feared: the use of "ballyhoo methods," as opposed to "the strategy of truth." MacLeish resigned in January 1943 and returned to the Library of Congress. Arthur persevered until April.

"No one would deny advertising men a place in an overall information program; but they are not equipped by their standards or by their experience for the somewhat arduous job of disseminating unadorned facts," he wrote Elmer Davis. "My own contacts with them in OWI have led me to conclude that they regard the plain recital of facts as exhibiting somehow a lack of proper ingenuity, and hardly worth doing. . . . This act of mine is not the result of hasty impulse. But the facts of the case declare irresistibly that the job of supplying people with honest news about the war, above the newspaper level, is through in the Domestic Branch."

• Arthur took a job in the Research and Analysis Branch of the Office of Strategic Services, the secretive new intelligence agency led by the dashing Colonel William J. ("Wild Bill") Donovan. Arthur was made editor of the *PW Weekly,* a classified journal distributed in numbered copies throughout the government. *PW* stood for "psychological warfare," championed for its alleged magical effectiveness, but Arthur was skeptical and steered the journal into political analysis. He made the rounds of the regional desks every few days, chatting up section chiefs, inquiring about studies in preparation, suggesting new topics, collecting completed studies, and later condensing and rewriting them for the *Weekly*. But he was desperate to serve abroad, to have a larger share of the "passion and action" of his time, and requested assignment to the London office.

In the spring of 1944 he completed the revision of the Jackson book, cutting fifty-eight chapters down to thirty-seven and 330,000 words to 260,000. At Benny De Voto's suggestion he submitted the manuscript to Little, Brown, which accepted it

June 6, 1944, D-Day, came and went. A few days later, Arthur finally received orders to ship out on June 19 from Brooklyn. He paid a sad farewell to the twins, now twenty-two months old, and took the train with Marian to New York City. In the evening they saw Billie Holiday sing at the Onyx at 57 West Fifty-Second Street, her "blue voice" floating huskily above the music filled with heartbreak. The next day, he embarked on the RMS *Queen Elizabeth*.

The Research and Analysis Branch of OSS was established in a handsome Georgian mansion at 68 Brook Street, in London, kitty-corner from Claridge's. Large windows gave Arthur an excellent view of incoming buzz bombs. The V-1 attacks continued through the summer with 150 bombs or so every day. These rudimentary cruise missiles killed 8,800 people in the following months. Then the Nazis introduced the far more destructive V-2, with its one ton of explosives. London was pitted with wrecked buildings and empty lots, mostly left over from the Battle of Britain four years earlier, compounded by the new bombs. "My own job is exhausting, time-consuming and not altogether satisfactory," he wrote to Marian in mid-August 1944. "I am going stale on the matter of putting out a weekly magazine, which I have now done for about 75 weeks without much vacation; I feel, as each weekly rat race recommences, like the Chinese prisoner tortured by the implacable drop of water."

He kept up with American news by reading periodicals in the library at the American Embassy. He read an article in the June 17, 1944, *New Yorker* by John Hersey about a young fellow he distantly remembered from Harvard named John F. Kennedy, class of 1940. The article was entitled "Survival" and told an amazing story of endurance and heroism in the South Pacific after Kennedy's PT boat was rammed and sunk by a Japanese destroyer.

The chief of the Secret Intelligence Branch of OSS was a New York lawyer named William Casey. In October 1944, Casey took command of the Paris office at 79 Champs-Elysées, and Arthur went along as a deputy for political intelligence.

Back in New York, a friend of the Schlesinger family, Gardner "Pat" Jackson, a labor reporter for the New York newspaper *PM,* was set upon with brass knuckles, badly beaten, and permanently blinded in one eye by Jack Lawrenson, a vice president of the Communist-controlled National Maritime Union, and other NMU thugs. Distraught, Arthur wrote to Pat on November 3, 1944:

I have just received the *PM* clipping about your recent terrible experience. It is one of the most miserable and shocking things I have ever heard; and I hope the people involved are punished as severely as the law allows.

It will be interesting to see whether those persons who are so profoundly shocked when anything happens to a Communist are shocked correspondingly when the Communists commit such an outrage. This episode reinforces everything I have seen on this side: that fifth columns and totalitarianism are pretty much the same, whether marching under a swastika or a hammer and sickle. I intend to devote a good deal of my energy in the next few years to fighting against the attempts of these people to gain a foothold in our country.

I am in Paris now; the electric current has just failed, which accounts for the aberrations of the typing. Pat, I cannot say how horrified I am about this business, and how my heart goes out to you and Dode. I can only hope it will open the eyes of enough people to do a little good.

By this point, eyesight requirements for the draft had been lowered, and the Cambridge draft board included Arthur in its October call. His location in Paris created difficulties. On March 7, 1945, he was inducted into the army, yet he continued to work at OSS. The authorities deemed it inappropriate for someone dressed as a buck private to deal with colonels and higher, as Arthur did every day, and ordered him into civilian clothes.

On Friday, April 13, 1945, Arthur heard the news of FDR's death. He wrote to Marian: "It was a beautiful day, and I strolled by the kiosk where I ordinarily buy the morning paper on my way to the metro. I took up *Combat,* noted vaguely the headline ('Roosevelt est mort') and then did a complete double-take and glanced wildly at the other papers, all of which said the same thing. It plunged me into a bad depression, which recurs whenever I am reminded that FDR is out of the picture; though most of the time, of course, I simply cannot believe it. What a dreadful thing to happen; any others of the three could have been much better spared. I have been disgruntled enough over the President the last couple of years; but his death leaves me a kind of awful vacancy which it will be hard to get over. The very real gallantry and grace of spirit which he had at his best are what I think of now."

Hitler committed suicide in his Berlin bunker on April 30, 1945. Fascism was not the wave of the future after all. Victory had vindicated the cause of liberal democracy.

The Letters of Arthur Schlesinger, Jr.

Schlesinger observes Paris in October 1944 from the roof of 79 Champs-Élysées, headquarters of the Office of Strategic Services.

Postwar Ambitions

1945–52

The date of the formal surrender of the Nazis was May 8, 1945: Victory in Europe Day.

To the Family*

9 May 1945

[Paris, France]

Dear Family:

What a two days! It is just as well that world wars are so few. I don't know how many peace celebrations I could stand per generation, especially in Paris.

It all began Monday afternoon, when the newspapers hit the street around six with the AP story announcing that the surrender had been signed at Reims at 2:41. . . . There had been an air of expectancy all day, and of course for the several days preceding, though Paris had never been victimized by false peace rumors of the Tom Connally type.† After dinner crowds began to flock up and down the Champs Elysees, while planes were flying very low over the center of the city.

---

* Addressed to his parents at 19 Gray Gardens East in Cambridge, the letter was to be shared with relatives in the vicinity.

† On April 29, 1945, Senator Tom Connally (D-Texas), U.S. delegate at the San Francisco UN conference, declared that Germany had surrendered and an official announcement was expected "momentarily." President Truman in Washington quashed the rumor, too early by a week.

Around nine thirty I was sitting at a sidewalk cafe along the Champs with Captain Gilpatric,[*] just over from London, and a gal named Ledlie Rial. Suddenly a plane swooped-down and dropped a flare; then others came, dropping white, red and green flares. The floodlights opened up on the Arc de Triomphe and soon on the Obelisk at the Place de la Concorde. After a time rockets began to go up. More and more people came on to the streets, milling around, singing La Marseillaise or It's a Long Way to Tipperary[†] (definitely the no. two song in the Paris peace celebrations). Impromptu parades would start up in the French manner. Sometimes two parades going in opposite directions would meet, whereupon each would chant, "AVEC NOUSE, AVEC NOUS," until one would dissolve and merge into the other. Trucks, jeeps and civilian cars, jammed with American and French GIs and girls, whizzed around. One soldier shouted from the top of a car, "CHANTEZ, CHANTEZ, LA GUERRE EST FINIE."

It was a lot of fun, though rather diffuse and I thought somewhat anti-climactical. But it was really only a dress rehearsal for Tuesday, about which there was nothing anti-climactical.

I worked more or less through the morning, until three o'clock, at which time De Gaulle,[‡] Churchill[§] and Truman[¶] made their speeches. The De Gaulle effort was broadcast through open microphones on the streets, while we heard Truman's clear and banal little voice from a radio of our own and watched the crowds on the Champs Elysees below. After a time a group of us went out to mingle in the crowd and wandered around for the rest of the afternoon. The crowd was really wonderful—good-natured, happy, spontaneous, enthusiastic.

---

[*] Chadbourne Gilpatric (1914–89). Harvard class of 1937; OSS; CIA; Rockefeller Foundation, 1949–72.

[†] "It's a Long Way to Tipperary," a British music hall song from 1912 about a longing to return to Tipperary in Ireland, was popular as a marching song among soldiers in World War I.

[‡] Charles de Gaulle (1890–1970). French general; leader of the Free French Forces; head of two provisional governments, 1944–46; president of France, 1959–69.

[§] Winston Churchill (1874–1965). Soldier; journalist; author; politician; British prime minister, 1940–45, 1951–55.

[¶] Harry S. Truman (1884–1972). Senator (D-Mo.), 1935–45; thirty-third U.S. president, 1945–53.

Last week I had got tickets for Tuesday evening for Maurice Chevalier,[*] who is making his first commercial appearance at the ABC music hall. He was in excellent form, and the crowd was most responsive. (Except for constant cracks in *Le Canard Enchaine*[†] there is not much bitterness against Chevalier on the collaborationist business. Louis Aragon[‡] and the Commies even claim that he did not collaborate and that, in fact, he worked with the resistance, though others say that the CP attempt to whitewash Maurice is not unconnected with a heavy gift he is supposed to have made to Front National, the Commie-front resistance organization. In any case the whole question of collaboration is much more complicated in Europe than it apparently is in the offices of the *New Republic*;[§] and there is a general disposition to forgive actors, with which I am in complete agreement.)

The ABC is located in the Boulevard Poissonnieres. We got out a little before eleven and strolled down toward the Opera. The boulevards were jammed with the same noisy, happy, cheerful crowds; I have never seen so many people. The Opera was illuminated and bedecked with flags and made a very stunning picture. We got there just as bands on the steps of the Opera were playing the various national anthems. It was very moving to stand in that crowded square while thousands of people sang La Marseillaise. Then we walked on down to the Madeleine, also illuminated. From the steps of the Madeleine you could see the flood-lit fountains playing in the Place de la Concorde and in the background the Chamber of Deputies, also under lights. We started walking down toward the Place de la Concorde. For the first time the crowd got a bit rough. The Rue Royale was packed, not only with people but with cars and trucks, and the crowd got a bit panicky and pushed wildly, jamming people against the automobiles

---

[*] Maurice Chevalier (1888–1972). Singer and entertainer who remained in Paris during the German occupation performing at Le Casino de Paris and kept a house near Cannes in Vichy where his partner, Rita Raya, a Jew, and her parents lived.

[†] *Le Canard enchaîné,* a weekly newspaper featuring investigative journalism and satirical takedowns of the elite; shut down during the Paris occupation until it ended in August 1944.

[‡] Louis Aragon (1897–1982). French poet and novelist; longtime member of the Communist Party.

[§] *The New Republic,* a liberal opinion journal published weekly in New York City, founded in 1914 by Willard Straight, Herbert Croly, and Walter Lippmann; now published in Washington, D.C.

and the buildings. It soon appeared futile to try to reach the Place de la Concorde, so we hopped on a US jeep, along with about eighty French people, and finally shook loose from the log-jam to career around Paris madly for a while. The ride ended near the Champs Elysees, still crowded, with the Arc lit up and the magnificent vista from the Etoile to the Concorde.

I finally got to bed around four o'clock. There were still crowds on the Champs. The fountains were going on the Rond Point, and GIs were sleeping in the grass behind the Theatre Marigny. I slept on the top floor of the Elysees Park Hotel, and I shall never forget the magnificent panorama of Paris with the great buildings lit up, from Sacre Coeur past the Opera, the Madeleine, Notre Dame, the Place de la Concorde, the Chamber of Deputies, the Invalides, around to the Arc de Triomphe, with the fountains playing in the Rond Point below and little groups of people singing La Marseillaise faintly in the distance.

So much for the end of the European war. I hope we are not such damned fools as to permit another. San Francisco is not encouraging.[*] Molotov[†] and Stettinius[‡] do not strike me as quite the types to solve the problems of the world. . . .

I hate to think of poor Dad's having to sit down and read that damn book again.[§] I will guarantee to stay in the country after my next book.

All my love,
A

---

[*] Representatives of fifty Allied governments had been meeting in San Francisco since April 25, 1945, to create the United Nations, an international organization to prevent wars and maintain world peace.

[†] Vyacheslav Molotov (1890–1986). Soviet foreign minister, 1939–49, 1953–56; negotiated the Nazi-Soviet nonaggression pact that kicked off World War II; led Soviet delegation at the San Francisco UN conference.

[‡] Edward R. Stettinius, Jr. (1900–1949). Former chairman of U.S. Steel; secretary of state, 1944–45; chief of U.S. mission to the San Francisco UN conference.

[§] Arthur Schlesinger, Sr., was proofreading the galleys of The Age of Jackson.

To the Family

21 May 1945

[Paris, France]

Dear Family:

We are all getting very depressed about the news these days. I had never imagined that post-war would change to pre-war so quickly. . . . If some one chooses to shoot somebody over Bornholm or Trieste,* we could be well started on the third world war in a couple of weeks. So far as I can see, a hell of a lot of people in Europe are convinced that it is inevitable.

I am not convinced that it is inevitable, but I am not very sure that the present leadership either American or Russian can avoid it. I feel that the policy of appeasement is not going to eradicate Russian suspicions nor strengthen the "moderates" in the Kremlin; appeasement always strengthens the sword-brandishers. But we should pick our spots. Obviously we must throw the Yugoslavs out of Trieste; obviously the British were essentially right in their Greek policy, though they bungled badly in its execution and confused the issue by their idiotic passion for the Greek king.† On the other hand, I think Stettinius' brand of toughness at San Francisco is criminally unsound. I can imagine no quicker way to unsell the USSR on the idea of international organization than to demonstrate that you can outvote it and then use your voting superiority to humiliate the USSR on inessential issues.‡ Molotov will return considerably more browned off on

---

*After liberation from the Nazis, Bornholm, a Danish island in the Baltic Sea, and Trieste in northeastern Italy were points of contention between Western Europe and the Soviet Union.

† King George II of Greece spent World War II in exile in Great Britain; after liberation, the prospect of his return caused dissension, especially among leftist partisans who had led the Greek resistance movement. The Allies saw to the establishment of a republican-dominated government. King George returned to Greece in 1947.

‡ To guarantee Latin American support for the seating of Belarus and Ukraine, the United States supported UN membership for Argentina (governed by a military junta with pro-Nazi sympathies), but Molotov threatened to protest unless Poland (under a pro-Soviet government) was admitted as well. Stettinius marshaled the votes to beat Molotov on Argentina. Columnist Lippmann regarded Stettinius's naked use of bloc politics as "dangerous" with the potential to "diminish" the United Nations. Poland, with its Communist dominated government, was admitted to the United Nations in July 1945.

international cooperation than Wilson[*] was after Versailles, and Molotov is reputed to be pretty much on the isolationist side anyway. Why do they leave Stettinius in? . . .

I don't want to sound alarmist, but the situation looks damn bad from here. The spread of the totalitarian police state on the Soviet model is most alarming. Tito's[†] Yugoslavia is no more of a democracy than Hitler's Germany.

Life in general goes on as usual. No further elucidation on my own plans.

Sunday I went to Chartres and had a very pleasant day. The windows are not yet back in the Cathedral. It was Pentecost—hence special services.

Two delicious and superbly chosen boxes arrived the other day—one with chicken and triskets, the other with lobster, cocoa, fruit juice and vitamin pills. All items rang the bell. Thank you ever so much.

Package request: a repeat on any of the above selections, with powdered coffee rating high priority if obtainable (regular coffee if not, and I will try to barter it). . . .

All love,
Arthur

---

[*] Woodrow Wilson (1856–1924). Professor of government; president of Princeton University, 1902–10; Democratic governor of New Jersey, 1911–13; twenty-eighth U.S. president, 1913–21. At the end of World War I, Wilson attended the peace conference at Versailles to promote his idea of a League of Nations to maintain world peace through collective action. The league was established but the Senate vetoed American participation.

[†] Josip Broz Tito (1892–1980). Communist revolutionary who became president of Yugoslavia for four decades; broke with Stalin and became one of the leaders of the nonaligned nations.

To Bernard De Voto[*]

[July 1945]

[Wiesbaden, Germany]

Dear Benny:

I have been intending to write for some time, but I have pretty well abandoned all correspondence except the minimum required to get food packages from my wife and family. This letter is precipitated by the fact that I have run several times into an old friend of yours named George Ball,[†] who reports that he read *The Year of Decision* with great delight in Hamburg and requests me to convey his regards to you. He is over here for USSBS (Strategic Bombing Survey).

I am located at a place called Biebrich, a suburb of Wiesbaden, in a champagne factory. The champagne is not very good, but we have to drink it because the water is suspect. Life in the army of occupation can be described adequately only by John O'Hara;[‡] we completed the local adaptation by opening an officers' club here last week. Necessarily our tight little community life discovers release only in drinking and gambling, or boating in the Rhine, or jeep trips to Frankfurt, 20 miles away, to eat ice cream and cold cuts in the SHAEF[§] snack bar (a cafeteria straight out of Howard Johnson). I came up here about three weeks ago after eight very pleasant months in Paris.

Cambridge, of course, is never far away. I had lunch today with Perry

---

[*] Bernard ("Benny") De Voto (1897–1955). Writer; conservationist; author of *The Year of Decision: 1846* (1943) and other histories of the American West; longtime columnist for *Harper's Magazine* ("The Easy Chair"); Pulitzer Prize winner. In May–June 1940, Schlesinger accompanied De Voto in his Buick on a research trip following the historic trails of the West.

[†] George Ball (1909–94). Chicago lawyer and New Dealer; director of the U.S. Strategic Bombing Survey that appraised the effects of the air war against Germany, 1944–45 (he debriefed Albert Speer, Nazi minister for armaments and war production, with John Kenneth Galbraith in May 1945); undersecretary of state in the Kennedy and Johnson administrations.

[‡] John O'Hara (1905–70). American writer of novels and short stories.

[§] SHAEF. Supreme Headquarters Allied Expeditionary Forces.

(Major) Miller,[*] Hugh (Captain) Cunningham[†] and Paul (Lieutenant) Sweezy.[‡] Perry, who wears a helmet still, is a field man looking with great scorn on us of the rear echelons. He spoke today of getting out of the army (on his 87 points) and going back to Cambridge, but I believe this mood to be the product of his hang-over. After a good night's sleep Widener[§] will seem as revolting as ever to him. I should not be nasty; Perry is a very good guy, going through a very difficult period, and Cambridge will be even more difficult. I met his girl several times in London. She is considerably more attractive than his wife. . . .

My feelings about Germany are mixed, but not very much. First you have the strange contrast of the giddy life we all lead against the background of desolation and rubble. Life in the Army of Occupation, as I said before, is very gay, and the flypaper has not yet begun to smother the flies. Some of my colleagues who have spoken to Germans are coming to regard them somewhat in the category of liberated peoples; but I cannot get over the fact that two months ago these sons-of-bitches were trying to kill every American they could find, and that continues to color my reactions. They seem to me a sullen, thick-headed race, lacking in charm, and every one of them over 16 deserves what is coming to them. Under sixteen everything breaks down, however. The children are cute as hell and a bit heart-breaking. The other day, when I was lunching at the casual officer's mess at Heidelberg, I happened to sit next to a window outside of which a collection of small German children soon gathered to beg for bread. After a time an MP[¶] in a very nice way shooed them away, but it was an experience I could take only by reminding myself forcibly of the condition of the French children last January and February when we froze to the marrow in Paris.

I have been over a year now. It is long enough, and I am possessed of a great desire to see my wife and family before they forget me completely. Of course, my initiation into that great fraternity the Army of the US, which took place about six weeks before the end of the war in Europe, has some-

---

[*] Perry Miller (1905–63). American intellectual historian; Schlesinger's Harvard tutor, 1935–36; OSS.

[†] Hugh Cunningham (1913–2000). Yale, 1934; OSS; CIA, 1947–77; one-time director of Clandestine Services.

[‡] Paul Sweezy (1910–2004). Harvard-trained Marxist economist; OSS.

[§] Widener Library: Harvard's main library since 1915.

[¶] Military police.

what hampered my freedom of movement. My army career has been absurd. I wore a uniform, as civilians had to in Paris, until I was inducted, when I promptly went into civilian clothes. I spent my first month in the Army as member of a Hospital Detachment located near Paris, but the Hospital returned me to OSS on temporary duty as soon as they signed me up, and I missed hardly a day at my desk. I could not come to Germany in my true guise as an EM,* because my job cannot be discharged by an EM in uniform, and civilian clothes are not permitted in Germany. Consequently I am now back in paramilitary uniform, disguised as a civilian and enjoying officers' prerogatives (after two months in Paris of eating with the cooks in a back room behind the E's mess along with the other strange characters who were in civvies). Thus I am temporarily relieved of the social disabilities, but the economic remain, as I am reminded with some force, having just received my monthly pay check of thirty one dollars. The financial side really hurts.

But with luck maybe I will be back by Christmas. I have seen *Harpers* [*Magazine*] occasionally, generally about four months late, and have been pleased to note that the Easy Chair is as lively as ever. Marian has also sent on news of you and Avis.† But in general I feel pretty much out of touch. Do drop a line when you have a moment, give my love to Avis and my stern military regards to Bunny, Mark, Lewis and Clark.‡

Yours ever,
Arthur

* Enlisted man.
† Avis De Voto (1904–89). Book reviewer; editor; accomplished cook; wife of Bernard; instrumental in getting Julia Child's first cookbook published.
‡ Gordon ("Bunny") and Mark were De Voto's sons; De Voto was editing a version of the journals of Lewis and Clark.

To Marian

8 August [1945]*

[Wiesbaden, Germany]

Dearest sweet:

The *Stars and Stripes* this morning is crammed with tales of the atomic bomb, including Conant[†] squatting with Vannevar Bush[‡] in the New Mexico desert and I am beginning to feel like a character out of J. Verne.[§] I am just as glad that the Germans never hit upon it—think of the howl we would have set up if they had. I have a certain sympathy for the Vatican point of view[¶] on the matter, though it is to be noted that papal solicitude was very much lacking when the Germans were trotting out their weapons of devastation.

I have now evacuated my job and my desk and am awaiting my orders—that inevitable process which appears to take three or four days here. I may not get away till the end of the week. If the sun would come out in the meantime, I could go out to the swimming pool, but it has turned cold and rainy today.

Monday, after a long drought, I got five letters, including a long one (5 single spaced pages) from Benny De Voto, filled with extravagant praise of the book. He is going to review it for the *Herald Trib,* which should be a help. . . .

I shall certainly be glad to move on to the big city. The local facilities are now pretty well exhausted so far as I am concerned. Tonight I am going over to Bad Nauheim for dinner at the palatial mansion shared by George

---

* Two days after the United States dropped an atomic bomb on Hiroshima.

† James Bryant Conant (1893–1978). Chemist; president of Harvard, 1933–53; chairman of FDR's National Defense Research Committee to mobilize civilian science for war; witnessed the first explosion of an atomic bomb in Alamogordo, New Mexico, on July 16, 1945.

‡ Vannevar Bush (1890–1974). MIT engineer; director of FDR's Office of Scientific Research and Development, 1941–46; oversaw the Manhattan Project, which developed the atomic bomb.

§ Jules Verne (1828–1905). French writer called "the father of science fiction"; author of *Twenty Thousand Leagues Under the Sea* (1870), *Around the World in Eighty Days* (1873).

¶ The first report on August 7 in *L'Osservatore Romano,* the Vatican City newspaper, that the use of the atomic bomb "created an unfavorable impression on the Vatican" was retracted the next day when Pope Pius XII denied authorizing any expression of the Vatican point of view.

Ball and Ken Galbraith.* I hope to spend a couple of days in Paris and get to London by the first of the week. . . .

Be sure to send me copies of your book† and, god damn it, some pictures of you.

It seemed to me that there were other things I had to tell you, but they have slipped away. I need not say that I love you desperately and think of you unremittingly and can only hold on till I see you again. It cannot be too long, dearest, particularly in the day of the atomic bomb. I love you so very much.

All love,

A

After sixteen months abroad, Arthur returned to the United States in early October 1945. His reunion with his family in Cambridge was joyous. The twins were now more than three years old, walking and talking and apparently delighted to greet their father.

President Truman shut down OSS after the Japanese surrender, and research and analysis was transferred to the State Department. Arthur received an honorable discharge from the army. On December 4, 1945, his resignation was accepted at the State Department. He was a free man.

He was no longer anonymous. The Age of Jackson *came out in September 1945 while he was still in London; rave reviews commanded the front pages of the Sunday book sections of both of New York's major newspapers. Allan Nevins‡ of Columbia University wrote in the* Times, *"a remarkable piece of analytical history, full of vitality, rich in insights and new facts, and casting a broad shaft of illumination over one of the more interesting periods in our national life." Benny De Voto concluded in the* Herald Tribune *that the book "overturns fundamental historical ideas."*

Though a book about the past, The Age of Jackson *carried implications for the future; it was "a study of the action of democracy in crisis to the end*

---

*John Kenneth ("Ken") Galbraith (1908–2006). Canadian-born American economist; deputy head of the Office of Price Administration (OPA), 1941–43; member of the U.S. Strategic Bombing Survey, 1944–45; longtime Harvard professor; author of *The Affluent Society* (1958); JFK's ambassador to India; Schlesinger's Cambridge neighbor and best friend.

† Marian Cannon, *Twins at Our House* (New York: Lothrop, Lee, and Shepard, 1945).

‡ Allan Nevins (1890–1971). Historian and journalist.

that we might foresee how it would act in crises to come," wrote De Voto. Critics called the book a defense of the New Deal disguised as a history of the age of Jackson. By May 1946 the book was in its eighth printing and had been on the bestseller list for twenty-five weeks. That spring it won the Pulitzer Prize for history. It sold ninety thousand copies in its first year.

Arthur juggled several career opportunities. Barry Bingham* asked him to write editorials for the Louisville Courier-Journal. Eugene Meyer† offered what seemed like a lot of money to write a history of The Washington Post, of which Meyer was the owner and publisher. Arthur enlisted instead as a free-lancer with Fortune magazine, where his friend Ken Galbraith was ensconced as a writer and editor gathering inside information on the corporate world. Arthur also accepted an offer as an associate professor of history at Harvard University beginning in September 1947.

To Eugene Meyer

13 April 1946

[Chevy Chase, Maryland]

Dear Mr. Meyer:

I should have written you long before this, but I have been living a harried life in the past three weeks—trying to move my family down to Washington and at the same time to complete a complicated magazine piece—and I have barely had a free moment. We are now located in Chevy Chase as of last week and are on our way to being settled.

After my conversation with you last month, Robert Van Gelder‡ published an interview with me in the *New York Times* which mentioned my intention of writing a book on *The Age of Roosevelt*. This stimulated the interest of various foundations in the project, and I have recently been accorded a grant by the Guggenheim Foundation and another by the American

---

* George Barry Bingham, Sr. (1906–88). Liberal publisher of the Louisville *Courier-Journal*.

† Eugene Meyer (1875–1959). Financier; former chairman of the Federal Reserve; publisher of *The Washington Post*; father of Katharine Graham.

‡ Robert van Gelder (1905–52). Book critic at *The New York Times*; editor in chief of Crown publishers.

Academy of Arts and Letters. These grants will enable me to work directly on the New Deal book over the next year or so before I return to Harvard.

The opening up of these unexpected facilities, combined with the misgivings I expressed to you in my last letter, led me to conclude that I would best serve your own purposes as well as my own if I turned down the *Post* offer. This decision did not come without soul-searching, which is why I have been slow to communicate with you; but, after hard and agonized thinking on the subject, I feel that this is the best decision I can make.

I am more grateful than I can say for your original interest and for your consideration in allowing me to weigh matters for so long. I hope it has not complicated matters for you. I know that the story of the *Post* is worth doing, and I am only sorry that I cannot do it myself.

I am writing this on the eve of going to New York for a week or so; otherwise I would come and see you. Please show this letter to Phil,[*] and tell him I will call him up when I get back. I hope that I will be able to talk to you occasionally about the New Deal book.

Thank you again for your many kindnesses. May I also add a word of gratitude for the campaign the *Post* has been carrying on to awaken the country to the food crisis.

Very sincerely yours,
Arthur M. Schlesinger, Jr.

The Schlesinger house was on the top of a hill just over the District line. An ample backyard had swings and a sandbox for the twins. Marian was again pregnant, and the baby was due in November 1946. Washington was filled with young couples happily reunited after the war, mingling carefree postwar gaiety with purposeful postwar ambitions. Arthur wrote articles for Fortune *on the Supreme Court and the Good Neighbor Policy, and for* Life *magazine on the U.S. Communist Party and the Roosevelt family.*

Georgetown was within easy striking distance. There were dinner parties at Joseph Alsop's house on the 2700 block of Dumbarton Avenue. Alsop[†] wrote

---

[*] Philip Graham (1915–63). Harvard law school; clerk to Supreme Court justice Felix Frankfurter; married to Katharine Meyer, 1940; publisher of *The Washington Post*, 1946–63; purchased *Newsweek* magazine in 1961; committed suicide.
[†] Joseph Alsop V (1910–89). Great-nephew of Theodore Roosevelt; Groton School;

an influential thrice-weekly syndicated column named Matter of Fact with his brother Stewart. *Joe was thirty-six years old in 1946 and an enterprising host. In his living room, with its elegant Chinese screens and Sung scrolls, Arthur met the great men of the day.*

To Arthur and Elizabeth Schlesinger

[1946]

[Chevy Chase, Maryland]

Dear Family,

Present were Averell Harriman,† Paul Porter,‡ Wilson Wyatt,§ Herbert Bayard Swope,⁵ Clark Clifford,** Leslie Biffle,†† FDR Jr.,‡‡ Jimmy Wechsler,§§ Stew Alsop. It was very entertaining. I sat next to Harriman at dinner

---

Harvard, 1932; columnist. Matter of Fact was syndicated in two hundred newspapers by the *New York Herald Tribune.* Stewart Alsop left the column in 1958; Joe Alsop continued it until 1974.

* Stewart Alsop (1914–74). Great-nephew of Theodore Roosevelt; Groton; Yale; OSS; co-columnist of Matter of Fact; *The Saturday Evening Post,* 1958–68; *Newsweek,* 1968–74.

† W. Averell Harriman (1891–86). Politician; businessman; diplomat; son of rail magnate E. H. Harriman; lend-lease coordinator, 1941–43; ambassador to the Soviet Union, 1943–46; secretary of commerce 1946–48; governor of New York, 1955–59; State Department, 1961–68.

‡ Paul Porter (1904–75). Lawyer; deputy administrator of the OPA; chairman of the Federal Communications Commission, 1944–46; Arnold and Porter law firm.

§ Wilson Watkins Wyatt (1905–96). Lawyer; Democratic mayor of Louisville, 1941–45; Truman's housing expediter for returning troops, 1945–46; first national chairman of Americans for Democratic Action, 1947–48; Adlai Stevenson's 1952 campaign manager; lieutenant governor of Kentucky, 1959–63.

⁵ Herbert Bayard Swope (1882–1958). Editor of the New York *World;* credited with coining the phrase "Cold War."

** Clark Clifford (1906–98). Lawyer; counselor to Presidents Truman, Kennedy, Johnson, and Carter; secretary of defense in 1968; persuaded LBJ to de-escalate the Vietnam War and initiate peace negotiations.

†† Leslie Biffle (1889–1966). Secretary of the Senate.

‡‡ Franklin D. Roosevelt, Jr. (1914–88). FDR's fifth child; lawyer; representative (D-N.Y.), 1949–55; JFK's undersecretary of commerce; first chairman of the Equal Employment Opportunity Commission, 1965; businessman and farmer.

§§ James ("Jimmy") Wechsler (1915–83). Journalist; member of the Young Communist League in the 1930s until "eye-opening" trip to the Soviet Union; national editor

and was quite favorably impressed by him. Young Roosevelt looks astonishingly like his father and has adopted many of his mannerisms. He talked very sensibly and is certainly strongly anti-Communist.

[1946]

Saturday night we went to Joe Alsop's for dinner. The [Henry Cabot] Lodges,* the Mike Monroneys,† and Jack Kennedy‡ were there. We both liked Mrs. Lodge very much. She is exceedingly attractive and somewhat more liberal than her husband. Mike Monroney is a nice and able person. Kennedy seemed very sincere and not unintelligent, but kind of on the conservative side.

[1946]

I had an entertaining evening at Joe Alsop's with Mrs. Alice Longworth§ and the Chip Bohlens.¶ To my surprise Mrs. Longworth is really quite witty and entertaining.

All love,
Arthur

Arthur and his friends were concerned about the waning of New Deal liberalism. In January 1947, a meeting was held at the Willard Hotel in Washington

---

of *PM* (a New York City daily published 1940–48); editor of the *New York Post*, 1949–61; editorial page editor until 1980; hired Schlesinger as columnist in the early 1950s.

*Henry Cabot Lodge, Jr. (1902–85). Senator (R-Mass.), 1937–44 and 1947–53 (defeated by JFK); ambassador to the United Nations, 1953–60; ambassador to South Vietnam, 1963–67.

† Almer Stillwell ("Mike") Monroney (1902–80). Representative (D-Okla.), 1939–51; senator, 1951–69.

‡ John F. ("Jack") Kennedy (1917–63). Representative (D-Mass.), 1947–53; senator, 1953–60; thirty-fifth U.S. president, 1961–63.

§ Alice Lee Roosevelt Longworth (1884–1980). Theodore Roosevelt's oldest child; married Representative Nicholas Longworth, an Ohio Republican and Speaker of the House, 1925–31; led an unconventional and controversial life; known for her witticisms.

¶ Charles E. ("Chip") Bohlen (1904–74). U.S. diplomat and Soviet expert; FDR's interpreter at Tehran and Yalta conferences; ambassador to the Soviet Union, 1953–57; to the Philippines, 1957–59; to France, 1962–68.

to create a new political organization to promote the liberal agenda and liberate the democratic left from Communist manipulation. The turnout was impressive, including Eleanor Roosevelt and her son Franklin, Jr., Reinhold Niebuhr,† Francis Biddle,‡ Walter Reuther,§ Hubert H. Humphrey, Jr.,¶ Joseph Rauh, Jr.,** James Wechsler, Barry Bingham, Stewart Alsop, Elmer Davis,†† Wilson Wyatt, Chester Bowles,‡‡ David Dubinsky,§§ Walter White,¶¶ Leon Henderson,*** John Kenneth Galbraith, Arthur Schlesinger, Sr., and Arthur, Jr. The new organization was christened Americans for Democratic Action. (ADA incorporated the Union for Democratic Action, founded in 1941 by Niebuhr and James Loeb††† as a pro-union, interventionist political organization.) ADA*

---

*Eleanor Roosevelt (1884–1962). Theodore Roosevelt's niece; married FDR, 1905; First Lady, 1933–45; helped draft the Universal Declaration of Human Rights in 1948; U.S. delegate to the UN General Assembly, 1949–52, and 1961; author and columnist.

† Reinhold Niebuhr (1892–1971). Theologian; writer; teacher; foreign policy realist; broke with the Protestant establishment in 1941 to found the publication *Christianity and Crisis* as an alternative to *Christian Century,* which preached neutralization and editorialized against an FDR third term. Niebuhr was based at the Union Theological Seminary in New York from 1928 to1960.

‡ Francis Biddle (1886–1968). Philadelphia lawyer; New Dealer; attorney general, 1941–45; chief American judge at the Nuremberg trials, 1945–46; chairman of Americans for Democratic Action (ADA), 1950–53.

§ Walter Reuther (1907–70). President of the United Automobile Workers, 1946–70; powerful liberal force in the Democratic Party; killed in an airplane crash.

¶ Hubert H. Humphrey, Jr. (1911–78). Mayor of Minneapolis, 1945–48; senator (D-Minn.), 1949–64 and 1970–78; U.S. vice president, 1965–69.

** Joseph ("Joe") Rauh, Jr. (1911–92). Civil rights and civil liberties attorney; represented the United Auto Workers and the Brotherhood of Sleeping Car Porters; defended victims of overzealous anticommunist investigations, including the playwright Arthur Miller; helped lobby for the Civil Rights Acts of 1964 and the Voting Rights Act of 1965.

†† Elmer Davis (1890–1958). Journalist; radio broadcaster; head of OWI, 1942–45.

‡‡ Chester Bowles (1901–86). Onetime advertising executive; administrator of the OPA; Democratic governor of Connecticut, 1949–51; ambassador to India, 1951–53, 1963–69.

§§ David Dubinsky (1892–1982). President of the International Ladies' Garment Workers Union, 1932–66.

¶¶ Walter White (1893–1955). Civil rights activist; secretary of the National Association for the Advancement of Colored People, 1931–55.

*** Leon Henderson (1895–1986). Businessman; New Dealer; administrator of the OPA; second national chairman of ADA.

††† James Isaac Loeb (1908–1992). Teacher; political organizer; newspaperman; ADA

rejected "*any association with Communism or sympathizers with commu-nism in the United States as we reject any association with fascists or their sympathizers. Both are hostile to the principles of freedom and democracy on which the Republic has grown great.*"

The founding of ADA marked a crucial breach in liberal ranks between the anticommunist liberals[*] and the membership of the Progressive Citizens of America, formed in December 1946, which welcomed Communists in its ranks and leadership, believing that the best hope for peace was a continuation of the wartime alliance with the Soviet Union.

As autumn 1947 approached, Arthur and Marian completed plans for a return to Cambridge. They purchased a large Victorian frame house at 109 Irving Street, an eight-minute walk from Harvard Yard. William James[†] had lived at 95 Irving Street; E. E. Cummings[‡] at 104. Arthur's study was on the second floor overlooking a spacious backyard. Marian, a painter, had a studio on the first floor; the three children had rooms of their own. Christina, born on November 19, 1946, was now almost one year old.

Arthur, Sr., had taught a Harvard course for many years on American so-cial and intellectual history. He now generously refashioned his famed History 63 (later 163) as "American Social and Cultural History," surrendering intel-lectual history to his son. History 169, "American Intellectual History," became young Arthur's account of the way ideas shaped American politics, religion, literature, and life. He also offered seminars for graduate students and han-dled his quota of undergraduate majors.

Arthur had returned from the war bearing copies of George Orwell's Ani-mal Farm, *recently published in England. At a luncheon given by Little, Brown, Arthur urged the editors to publish the satiric barnyard fable about the Soviet Union, but he met resistance from one editor who turned out to be a faithful follower of the Communist party line. Little, Brown quickly turned down* Animal Farm. *Thinking it over, Arthur decided that he did not want to be published by a house that had a fellow traveler as an important editor.* Animal Farm *instead became a bestseller for Harcourt, Brace.*

---

national director, 1947–51; ambassador to Peru, 1961–62, and to Guinea, 1963–65.

[*] ADA accepted Hollywood actor Ronald Reagan as a member in October 1947.

[†] William James (1842–1910). Influential psychologist and philosopher; Harvard professor; renowned for his writings on pragmatism; author of *The Varieties of Reli-gious Experience: A Study in Human Nature* (1902).

[‡] Edward Estlin Cummings (1894–1962). American poet.

To Alfred McIntyre[*]

21 December [19]47

[Cambridge, Massachusetts]

Dear Mr. McIntyre,

I wrote you two weeks ago requesting formal release from my contract with Little, Brown. I have not yet had the courtesy of an acknowledgment or a reply.

Each day increases my sense of shame at ever having been associated with your house. I would never have signed up in 1939 if one of your leading members had been an active pro-German and pro-Nazi; and I have no more intention of being published by Little, Brown today when one of your leading members is taking an active part in opposing the democratic effort to check the spread of Soviet totalitarianism.

Sincerely yours,
Arthur M. Schlesinger, Jr.

A pro-Soviet coup in Czechoslovakia in February 1948 completed the division of Europe.

On March 17, 1948, President Truman addressed a joint session of Congress asking for passage of the European Recovery Program—the Marshall Plan[†]—to rebuild war-devastated Europe while undermining the Communists. By speeding recovery and increasing employment, income, and productivity, aid would reduce communism's appeal to the working classes and revitalize democratic Europe. The bill sailed through the House and Senate.

Truman selected W. Averell Harriman to administer the Marshall Plan in Europe, and Harriman surprised Arthur by proposing that he come over for a few months as his special assistant to help with information policy. Liking Harriman and loving Paris—and having a professional interest in watching history in the making—Arthur said yes. He fit the assignment in during Harvard's summer recess.

[*] Alfred R. McIntyre (1886–1948). President of Little, Brown.
[†] Secretary of State George C. Marshall proposed the European reconstruction plan at the Harvard commencement on June 5, 1947. Over four years, the United States contributed from 6 to 9 percent of the federal budget to European recovery.

Meanwhile, at the 1948 Democratic National Convention in Philadelphia in July, President Truman lambasted the "do-nothing 80th Congress" and Hubert H. Humphrey, Jr., made a brave speech calling for action on civil rights.[*] But Truman's nomination proved so contentious that two breakaway factions established themselves as independent parties and nominated their own presidential candidates. The States' Rights Democratic Party, also known as the Dixiecrats, chose Governor Strom Thurmond[†] of South Carolina, who campaigned against federal efforts to end segregation; the Progressive Party selected former vice president Henry Wallace[‡] of Iowa, who ran against the Marshall Plan and Truman's containment policy. The Republican nominee was Governor Thomas Dewey[§] of New York, considered the favorite.

Truman's lonely gallantry, his increasingly liberal message, and his rollicking whistle-stop campaign raised Arthur's enthusiasm if not his hopes. On election night, he and Marian called in friends to mourn the anticipated result together.

[*] Humphrey: "There are those who say to you we are rushing this issue of civil rights. I say we are one hundred and seventy-two years late. There are those who say this issue of civil rights is an infringement on states' rights. The time has arrived for the Democratic party to get out of the shadow of states' rights and walk forthrightly into the bright sunshine of human rights."

[†] Strom Thurmond (1902–2003). Antiblack Democratic governor of South Carolina, 1947–51; senator, 1954–2003; switched to the Republican Party in 1964 in opposition to the Civil Rights Act; later moderated racist views. He is the only senator to reach the age of one hundred while still in office.

[‡] Henry Wallace (1836–1916). U.S. vice president, 1941–45; dropped as VP by FDR in 1944; secretary of commerce, 1945–46, fired by Truman over foreign policy differences; editor of The New Republic, 1946–48. Jimmy Wechsler's articles in the New York Post exposed Communist infiltration in the Progressive Party and the Wallace campaign.

[§] Thomas Dewey (1902–71). Liberal Republican; governor of New York, 1943–55; candidate for president, 1944, 1948.

To the Family[*]

4 November 1948

[Cambridge, Massachusetts]

Dear Family:

We are still stunned, overwhelmed and delighted by the events of the last 48 hours. The election, as you can imagine, was very exciting. We gave a party; and a miscellany of people gathered round—the Joe Caseys,[†] the Coxes,[‡] the Eliots,[§] Ballantines, Gilmores,[¶] Galbraiths, [Perry] Millers, etc. For the first part of the evening, we derived pleasure from the good fight Truman seemed to be making and from the Democratic successes in the Senate. When we went finally to bed at 4:30 AM, it looked as if there might well be a Democratic Congress; but I still had no serious expectation that Truman would win. When we got up the next morning, Truman was still holding a substantial lead in the electoral votes. I then began to believe that the election would go to the House. Suddenly, at 11:15, Dewey conceded.[**]

No one in America, except for Truman himself, thought he was going to win. The pollsters and political writers are in complete confusion. I enclose Scotty Reston's[††] mea culpa in the *Times,* and you will have seen Elmo Roper's[‡‡] very candid piece in the Paris *Herald Tribune.* No one knows how it all

[*] Elizabeth and Arthur, Sr., were in Holland in 1948–49; he was visiting professor at the University of Leyden.

[†] Joseph Casey (1898–1980). Lawyer; representative (D-Mass.), 1935–43; and his wife, Constance.

[‡] Gardner Cox (1906–88). Portrait painter; and his wife, Phyllis.

[§] Thomas H. Eliot (1907–91). New Deal lawyer; a drafter of the Social Security Act; representative (D-Mass.), 1941–43; OSS; chancellor of Washington University in St. Louis, 1962–71; and his wife, Lois.

[¶] Myron P. Gilmore (1910–78). Renaissance scholar; Harvard professor of history; and his wife, Sheila.

[**] Truman received 49.6 percent of the popular vote; Dewey, 45.1 percent; Thurmond, 2.4 percent; Wallace, 2.4 percent; Norman Thomas, the Socialist candidate, 0.3 percent.

[††] James ("Scotty") Reston (1909–95). Influential Scottish-born American journalist; national correspondent, Washington bureau chief, executive editor, and columnist for *The New York Times,* 1939–89.

[‡‡] Elmo Roper (1900–1971). Pioneer pollster; OSS deputy director; founded the Roper Center for Public Opinion Research.

happened. A man named Stouffer[*] in the Social Relations Department had given a talk to the Nieman Fellows election day in which he began by recalling Crum's experience in Adams House[†] before the 1936 election and then said: "But now we really have developed polling methods into an exact science. If any of you think that there is a chance that this election will be close, you are deceiving yourself."

My own view is that this is now a New Deal country—it is Democratic today as it was Republican from 1868 to 1930. It simply mistrusts the business community; and the disposition it had to reject Truman was killed by the record of the 80th Congress. I should like to inquire particularly how the author of *Paths to the Present*[‡] reconciles the evident appetite of the American public for the militant radicalism of Truman's campaign with the prediction of the conservative swing. If there is a good answer to this, maybe you should cable it to MacMillan and they could insert it as a footnote somewhere. . . .

All ADA calculations are at sea for the moment, Jim Loeb is coming to Boston next Wednesday, and maybe then the thinking will be more advanced. We are still all in a state of shock and exultation. Even the Republicans do not seem very mad—just involuntarily delighted by the triumph of rural virtue over the city slicker. My favorite crack of the campaign: "I would rather vote for the haberdasher than for the tailor's dummy in the window."

Love from us all,
Arthur

---

[*] Samuel Stouffer (1900–1960). Harvard sociologist and developer of survey research techniques.

[†] William Leonard Crum (1894–1967). Harvard economics professor. Predicted victory by the Kansas Republican governor Alf Landon over FDR in 1936; FDR won by a landslide.

[‡] Arthur Schlesinger, Sr., *Paths to the Present* (New York: Macmillan, 1949), included a chapter on the cycles of conservatism and liberalism in national affairs.

To Max Lerner*

November 15, 1948

[Cambridge, Massachusetts]

Dear Max:

I was somewhat concerned by your column in the Sunday *Star* calling for a resumption of direct talks between Russia and the U.S.[†] It would seem to me that if the experience of the years since the war suggests anything it suggests that agreements with the USSR are futile in advance of the underlying political and economic conditions which alone can guarantee the agreements. Do you seriously believe that any conceivable paper agreements with the USSR would deter it from pressing its disruptive activities in Western Europe so long as conditions in Western Europe give Communist disruption the slightest hope of success? My own belief is that the time for useful direct negotiations with the Russians will come only after solid foundations for such negotiations exist in the economic recovery, political independence, and military strength of Western Europe.

When the Marshall Plan will have brought about a strengthening of Europe politically, economically and militarily to the point where it becomes relatively immune to Communist activity, then we can perhaps hope for a stable agreement with the USSR. But to argue that we can get such an agreement now, that somehow an international miracle can be achieved by two men sitting around a table which would relieve America of the grim task of working for peace the hard way is to play into the hands of both the isolationists and the Communists. Surely we are in this for a long haul; there is no one-shot solution; and columns about the alleged magic which a Truman-Stalin meeting would work only serve to distract people from the continuing vigilance and responsibility which I know you will agree are essential for peace. . . .

My own belief—and, I suspect, that of the State Department—is that the raising of hopes by an agreement and the subsequent dashing of hopes

* Maxwell ("Max") Lerner (1902–92). Journalist; editor, *PM* and *New York Star* (*PM*'s short-lived successor); debuted his long-running *New York Post* column in 1949; moved rightward and supported Reagan in 1980.

† Lerner hoped that the wartime alliance could somehow be maintained; he felt it was important that opinion-makers continue to portray the Soviet Union in a favorable light.

when the Russians violate it will do more harm to the cause of peace than the postponement of talks until we have a solid basis on which to negotiate.

Sincerely,
Arthur

Republican Representatives Karl Mundt of South Dakota and Richard Nixon[†] of California were trying to pass a bill requiring members of the Communist Party of the United States (CPUSA) to register with the attorney general; also, no Communist Party member could be a federal employee or get a passport. The Mundt-Nixon bill, also called the Subversive Activities Control Bill, passed in the House but failed in the Senate when first introduced in 1948.*

With the reintroduction of the bill in 1949, despite opposing it, Arthur felt compelled to warn fellow liberals against supporting the National Committee to Defeat the Mundt Bill, organized by members of the CPUSA, which Arthur believed was a Trojan horse, actually designed to antagonize indifferent senators into pushing for the bill and generating a propaganda coup for the Soviet Union. Arthur was concerned that good liberals were being deceived by the Communist tactics and that the liberal movement was endangered.

To Professor Zechariah Chafee, Jr.[‡]

June 22, 1949

[Cambridge, Massachusetts]

Dear Professor Chafee:

Thank you for your note and also for sending along your very powerful brief on the new Mundt Bill. . . .

On the larger questions you raise, I do believe that the liberal objection

---

* Karl Mundt (1900–1974). Educator; right-wing representative (R-S.D.), 1939–48; senator, 1948–73.

† Richard Milhous Nixon (1913–94). Whittier College class of 1934; Duke University Law School, 1937; representative (R-Calif.), 1947–51; senator, 1951–53; U.S. vice president, 1953–61; thirty-seventh U.S. president, 1969–74.

‡ Zechariah Chafee, Jr. (1005–1957). First Amendment scholar; Harvard Law School professor.

to the National Committee to Defeat the Mundt Bill is something more than just "not liking the ideas" of those who set the committee up and control it. These ideas do not seem to me "just a matter of taste," as Molotov said of Nazism in his speech on the Stalin-Hitler pact; they represent a body of thought fundamentally and dynamically opposed to democratic society. This does not mean that people who advocate these ideas should not be allowed to form committees and fight for their ideas. But it does make it difficult for many of us to see why liberals can collaborate with them.

One great reason, I believe, that liberalism has lost vitality in recent years has been its tendency to surrender its own libertarian principles in the fantastic enterprise of regarding the Soviet Union as infallible and apologizing for its totalitarian monstrosities. We can recapture the vitality of our liberal principles only by believing in them—by insisting on their application both to the reactionary right and to the totalitarian left. . . .

As a moral matter, collaboration with Communists is an inconsistent and futile thing for liberals to attempt. As a practical matter, collaboration with Communists and fellow-travelers is disastrous. It has never worked. You say, "When there is a big fire raging, I do not inquire meticulously into all the political and economic views of the man who is carrying a bucket of water beside me." But you certainly would inquire what his attitude was toward having the house burn down; you would not work with him, for example, if he kept punching holes in the buckets. I urgently call your attention to the previous record of the Committee to Defeat the Mundt Bill—a record which suggests very strongly that its basic desire is not to defeat the bill at all but to blow it up as an issue and very possibly indeed to have the bill enacted.

You will recall the fight over the Mundt-Nixon bill in the 80th Congress. The Republican leadership in the Senate announced in the press over the weekend of May 29, 1948, that it would give three other bills priority for Senate action in the few days remaining before adjournment. This meant that the Nixon-Mundt bill was dead, so far as the 80th Congress was concerned. The Communists promptly swung into action. On May 31 they organized the Committee to Defeat the Mundt Bill. On June 2 they staged a march on Washington. The object of these tactics was unmistakable. The Communists hoped by organized intimidation to antagonize indifferent Senators and annoy those on the fence into reviving a dead bill. As Alan Barth[*] of the *Washington Post* (whom you may have known this year as a Nieman Fellow)[†] put it, "It is plain as any hidden intent can be that the Communists want to get the Mundt-Nixon bill enacted into law." Enactment would have given [Henry] Wallace a new and appealing issue; it would have provided the USSR with a potent weapon in the psychological war. Fortunately, in spite of the extreme irritation of some members of the Judiciary Committee, the Senate was not to be stampeded into the Communist trap. Now they are doing their best again to goad the Judiciary Committee into reporting the bill favorably. . . .

The distinction you drew in your Phi Beta Kappa address between "irreconcilable Communists" and confused persons of good will who become Communists out of a concern for social injustice was a true distinction for the twenties and the thirties. But I do not think you will find many people who know anything about the Communist movement who would regard it as true today. Any person who has survived the Moscow trials, the Stalin-Hitler pact and the transformation of the Russian Revolution into this monstrous police despotism is an "irreconcilable Communist" and has nothing in common with decent liberals.

I trust you will forgive my writing at such length and in a manner which can only seem an intrusion on your personal affairs. I have ventured to take this liberty because I know that many people share my sense of regret over seeing your great name in this present company.[‡]

Very sincerely yours,
Arthur M. Schlesinger, jr.

---

[*] Alan Barth (1906–79). Author, longtime editorial writer at *The Washington Post*, focusing on civil liberties.

[†] Nieman Fellowships, established in 1938, provided a year of study at Harvard University for working journalists.

[‡] Senator Pat McCarran (D-Nev.) rewrote the Mundt-Nixon bill, which over Truman's veto became the Internal Security Act of 1950, establishing a Subversive Activities Control Board to monitor Communist activities in the United States.

To W. Averell Harriman

December 12, 1949

[Cambridge, Massachusetts]

Dear Averell,

Since, as a Harvard man I suppose I am not entitled particularly to have opinions about the presidency of Yale, the subject of this letter is not strictly my business. But I am vitally interested in preserving liberal education in this country, and I feel that the kind of man chosen president of Yale may have a significant effect on the future direction of higher education.

As you know, the recent trend in choosing college presidents has been toward men like Eisenhower* and Stassen†—men who have many virtues but conspicuously lack any interest in or understanding of the educational process. The choice of such men is ordinarily dictated by the business office anxious to have a good front for fund-raising purposes; but the effect on the faculties is likely to be calamitous, as has been demonstrated already at Columbia and Pennsylvania. The presence of a college president indifferent to educational values or problems has, as you would well imagine, seriously demoralizing consequences for the total intellectual life of the university. It is most improbable that universities under such leadership, or lack of it, will become vital intellectual centers. In contrast, we at Harvard are extremely fortunate in having in Jim Conant a man who is keenly concerned with educational and intellectual issues.

The Yale corporation, I am informed (from sources within the corporation), tends to split into two groups on this question. One group—more or less, the academics, the politicians (Acheson,‡ Bowles), the clergymen—feel that Yale should have as president some one like Conant who will work to

---

*Dwight David Eisenhower (1890–1969). West Point, class of 1915; commander in chief of Allied forces in Western Europe, 1943–45; president of Columbia University, 1948–53; supreme commander, NATO forces in Europe, 1951–52; thirty-fourth U.S. president, 1953–61; a Republican.

† Harold Stassen (1907–2001). Republican governor of Minnesota, 1939–43; president of the University of Pennsylvania, 1948–53; sought Republican presidential nomination twelve times.

‡ Dean Acheson (1893–1971). Lawyer; diplomat; Groton; Yale, class of 1915; clerk to Supreme Court justice Louis Brandeis; Truman's secretary of state, 1949–53; author of the Pulitzer Prize–winning *Present at the Creation: My Years in the State Department* (1969).

restore Yale's intellectual vitality and leadership. The other group—mainly the businessmen ([Prescott] Bush,* Irving Olds†) and Bob Taft,‡ of course— feel that Yale should have a businessman who will be successful in raising money. (On this fundraising point, it should be pointed out that a man like Conant, who knows what he is selling, is generally much more successful in persuading people to give money than an Eisenhower or Stassen, who are obviously delivering prepared sales talks).

My own hope had originally been that some vigorous younger man, like Dick Bissell,§ might have been chosen. But Dick has apparently made too many enemies. In any case, as things developed, Philip Jessup¶ emerged as the chief candidate of the education-minded group; but unfortunately, when sounded out, he said that he was not interested. The business-minded group has succeeded in vetoing other suggestions from the first group. But in recent weeks great strength has developed behind Dr. Reinhold Niebuhr as a possible candidate.

I myself think that Yale could not make a more distinguished choice. I am sure you know Niebuhr; he is one of the great personal and intellectual leaders of our age. Moreover, he is vitally interested in the crucial problems of an intellectual community. As president, he would attract to Yale the ablest and brightest men in the country, both on the faculty and in the student body. The choice of a man like Niebuhr would revitalize the cause of liberal education in the United States.

I am writing this all to you partly because you are a Yale man and have a legitimate interest in this; and partly because I understand that [Prescott] Bush of Brown Brothers, Harriman has been the leading figure in opposing the suggestions from the education-minded group. If you agree with any of the things

* Prescott Bush (1895–1972). Yale, class of 1917; Wall Street executive; senator (R-Conn.), 1952–63; father and grandfather of U.S. presidents.

† Irving Olds (1887–1963). Yale, class of 1907; chairman of U.S. Steel.

‡ Robert Taft (1889–1953). Son of President William Howard Taft; Yale, class of 1910; senator (R-Ohio), 1939–53; leading conservative opponent of FDR's New Deal; known as "Mr. Republican."

§ Richard Bissell (1909–94). Groton; Yale, class of 1932; economist; Marshall Plan administrator; CIA's deputy director for plans, 1958–62; developed U-2 high-altitude spy plane; ousted over failed 1961 Bay of Pigs invasion of Castro's Cuba.

¶ Philip C. Jessup (1897–1986). Hamilton College; Yale Law School, 1924; taught international law at Columbia Law School, 1925–61; UN delegate, 1943–45; judge at the International Court of Justice, 1961–70.

I have said, and if you feel yourself that Niebuhr would be a good president of Yale, I hope that you may send word to somebody connected with the situation; because I am certain that favorable advice from you would be of inestimable help in relieving the anxieties of the potential opposition. I know you have many other urgent problems on your mind; but I am sufficiently concerned about the long-run effects of the example Yale will set by its next presidential choice that I do not hesitate to bring the matter to your attention. . . .

Give my very warm regards to Marie.[*]

Sincerely yours,
Arthur

From W. Averell Harriman

February 13, 1950

[Paris]

Dear Arthur,

I got your letter of December 12th just before I went away for a Christmas-New Year's skiing vacation in Austria. It was to have had my most immediate attention on my return, but whether it was the let-down of the vacation, or the intricacies of knowing how to write my friends on the Yale Corporation, I kept putting it off until I learned they had reached a decision which was today announced.[†]

I am now about to embark on another adventure in Washington in connection with the ECA renewal.[‡] Is there any chance of your being down there? It would be grand to see you and there is much I want to talk over.

Warm regards.

Sincerely,
Averell

---

[*] Marie Norton Whitney Harriman (1903–70). Art collector who left her husband Cornelius Vanderbilt Whitney to become Averell Harrimans's second wife in 1929.
[†] The new president of Yale was A. Whitney Griswold (1906–63); Yale, class of 1929; American historian.
[‡] The Economic Cooperation Administration (ECA) was established in April 1948 to implement the Marshall Plan.

Back in Washington, Harriman received a new assignment, special assistant to the president for national security affairs, just in time for the North Korean invasion of South Korea, which began on June 24, 1950.

To W. Averell Harriman

July 19, 1950

[Cambridge, Massachusetts]

Dear Averell:

I was sorry to have missed you in Paris; but glad that you were to be on hand during the crisis in Washington. The Berlin Congress[*] was very useful, I think, and, properly developed, could become an invaluable instrumentality in combatting the Communist "peace" drive in Europe and in fighting neutralism in general. The next step is in the hands of an executive committee consisting of [Arthur] Koestler, [Ignazio] Silone, Irving Brown, David Rousset and a German (either Carlo Schmid or Eugen Kogon, the novelist). They have behind them potentially the richest intellectual resources of Europe.

Nicolas Nabokov[†] and I took advantage of our Berlin stay to talk with some Russian escapees. One point was made to us several times; and it seemed of such interest that we had hoped to have a talk with you and Chip [Bohlen] about it in Paris (only to find that you both had departed). According to these Russian escapees, Soviet indoctrination has been sufficiently successful to give the Russian people as a whole a profound conviction that any American initiative is ultimately a mask for American expansion. They feel, however, that this conviction could be countered in part by solemn and binding statements by our government renouncing any purpose of territorial or economic aggrandizement. We pointed out that

---

[*] The Congress for Cultural Freedom, a gathering of anticommunist intellectuals, convened in West Berlin's Titania Palace on June 26, 1950; American delegates included Schlesinger, philosopher Sidney Hook, writer James Burnham, novelist James T. Farrell, playwright Tennessee Williams, actor Robert Montgomery, and chairman of the Atomic Energy Commission David Lilienthal.

[†] Nicolas Nabokov (1903–78). Russian-born composer and writer; first cousin of novelist Vladimir Nabokov; secretary-general of the Congress for Cultural Freedom, 1951–67.

Roosevelt and Truman had made such statements innumerable times. But they insisted that these statements had never been sufficiently solemn or specific, or perhaps never sufficiently publicized; and that some such general statement in connection with Korea would put our action there in a much more favorable context.

I mention this only because it came to us from several different sources. It might well be worth checking to see whether this is a widespread apprehension. It seems likely, for example, that the Asians themselves have doubts and misgivings about American intervention which a powerful statement of disinterestedness and self-denial might assist in dispelling. It certainly could do no harm.

In this connection, I hope that we are moving ahead in working out our own long-range intentions in Korea. Obviously the restoration of the status quo is no answer; for one thing, it would impose no penalty for aggression. Surely aggression against the UN can be adequately punished only by the reduction and detention of the aggressor regime. This raises the problem of a change of government in North Korea. On the other hand, the behavior of the South Korean army is one more evidence of the rottenness and incompetence of the Syngman Rhee[*] regime; and it would be politically disastrous in the rest of Asia if the result of our intervention was simply the extension of the power of Syngman Rhee over all Korea. The best solution, it seems to me, would be the establishment of some form of UN protectorate or trusteeship, into which the Syngman Rhee regime could be absorbed through some face-saving formula. I think too that the UN solution might solve difficult questions if it were to be applied to Formosa.

Obviously, the more that the weak points in the periphery around the Soviet Union are turned over to the UN, the less the Soviet Union can expand without arraying the whole world against it. It seems to me therefore distinctly to our advantage to involve the UN in the policy of containment wherever our military position is weak and uncertain. I had a chance to talk this problem over a night or two ago with Abe Feller[†] (Lie's general counsel). He indicated that Lie[‡] felt definitely that it was nonsense to stop at the

---

[*] Syngman Rhee (1875–1965). First president of South Korea, 1948–60.

[†] Abraham Feller (1904–52). New Deal lawyer; UN general counsel, 1947–52; hounded by congressional investigations on communism; committed suicide.

[‡] Trygvie Lie (1896–1968). Norwegian foreign minister, 1941–46; first UN secretary-general, 1946–52.

38th parallel—that North Korea must, of course, be reduced. Feller also commented that the UN trusteeship solution was entirely possible technically, if some form of UN guard could be developed. You will remember that Lie and Feller agitated for the development of a UN guard some years ago; General Marshall* liked the idea, but most of the State Department did not, and it never got anywhere.

Feller said, by the way, that Lie was particularly worried over Iran. The UN feeling seems to be that this is likely to be the next point of Soviet aggression. I hope our military planners are preparing to meet the problems of logistics which action in Iran would involve. . . .

Yours ever,
Arthur

To W. Averell Harriman

November 13, 1950

[Cambridge, Massachusetts]

Dear Averell:

The [midterm] elections were a sad disappointment.[†] I hope that the White House knows where things went wrong and plans to move in a positive way to remedy them. The fact that the Republicans may not have done so badly in any off-year election since 1934 is, to my mind, inadequately consoling. The fact remains that the Republicans have not had so poor a case—so few legitimate issues—in any recent off-year election. They made their gains, in other words, in the face of their own evident programmatic bankruptcy; they made them in spite of (one might almost say, because of) their obvious political desperation. I do not see how the elections can be honestly interpreted except as a triumph for McCarthyism.[‡]

---

* George C. Marshall (1880–1959). U.S. Army chief of staff, 1939–45; secretary of state, 1947–49; secretary of defense, 1950–51.

† The Democrats lost five seats in the Senate and twenty-eight seats in the House of Representatives; their majorities were narrowed to 49–47 in the Senate, 235–199 in the House.

‡ Joseph McCarthy (1908–57). Wisconsin Republican senator 1947–57. McCarthy announced in February 1950 that he had a secret list of hundreds of Communists work-

What went wrong? I have no confident answer to this; but I do have a few suggestions to toss into the pot. I cannot but feel that the basic failure is a failure in political education. The American people a few years ago went through the agony of a great world war. Today a bare five years after the conclusion of that war, they find themselves on the verge of another war. They cannot understand how such a dreadful situation could have developed so quickly. Consequently they tend to attribute it, not to historical necessities, but to bungling and to conspiracy. They feel that the administration in power must somehow be responsible for having "let" things go so sour so fast—either through its incompetence or through the sinister power within of Communist agents. It is this anxiety and confusion, I believe, which McCarthyism has exploited (and, in exploiting, has increased); it is this situation, in my judgment, which was basically responsible for the Republican gains.

How to cure this situation? If this analysis is right, the anxiety and confusion are, in a sense, the backwash of isolationism. It is not the old conscious isolationism of the thirties, which regarded an isolated America as tenable national policy; that, I believe, is dead. It is rather the psychology and the emotions which lay behind the isolationist policy and which have survived the death of the policy. While people are becoming aware of the fact that America cannot live by and to itself, they still resent and fear the necessity of protracted and indefinite responsibilities and involvements abroad. Because they will not accept these involvements (and the sacrifices required by these involvements) as part of the new historic position of the U.S. as the leading power in the free world, they can respond to the McCarthys who blame it all on a set of bunglers or conspirators within the government.

This state of mind is reflected in another way in the widespread conviction that we can unravel all our difficulties by one more action—whether that action be a preventive war or a new conference with Stalin.* This

---

ing in the State Department, reviving his faltering political career. The term "McCarthyism"—the exploitation of the fear of Communism for corrupt and vicious purposes—was coined by *Washington Post* cartoonist Herblock in a March 29, 1950, cartoon. The word became synonymous for demagoguery, baseless defamation, and mudslinging. McCarthy was censured by the Senate in 1954 and died in office in 1957, a hopeless alcoholic.

* Joseph Stalin (1878–1953). Soviet dictator; leader of global Communist movement; ally of U.S. during World War II; seized most of Eastern Europe at war's end, respon-

"one-shot" theory of international relations really proceeds, I think, from a deep isolationist faith that, if only we could do that one more thing, if only we could pull an international miracle, then we could relax and never worry again about the affairs of the world. The preventive-war theory and the sit-down-with-Stalin theory may be politically opposite, but they are psychologically akin. This is shown by the fact that a man like Stassen can advocate both approaches within a month of each other.

As you know, I am entirely in agreement with the administration's foreign policy and have written many articles and given many speeches in its support. Our failure has not been a failure in policy; it has been a failure in persuading the people of the moral and historical necessities which underlay the policy and which explain the present state of world affairs. Somehow we must do more than we have done to educate the American people in a few fundamental facts; for example, (1) that the roots of Soviet expansionism (as in China and in Eastern Europe) lie in profound historical movements, not in mistakes by the American government; (2) that we could not hope to rally the free peoples against Soviet expansionism until the USSR demonstrated beyond any doubt the nature of its objectives (as you put it in your *Herald Tribune* speech, "The strength of our moral position today rests upon the fact that we made every effort to reach an understanding with the Soviet Union."); (3) that our present policy has been soundly designed, not only to protect the free world in the present crisis but to get at the fundamental economic and political conditions which invite Soviet expansion; (4) that the logic of the Republican policy is either to divest us of all our allies overseas or else to sacrifice Europe in favor of an unlimited and hopeless military commitment in China.

How is this job of political education to be undertaken? I am confident that President Truman on his tremendous record of performance will go down into history as a great president; it is no criticism of him that he does not have the special qualities of a Churchill or a Wilson or a Roosevelt. But we do need a much more considered and positive effort to make the nation understand where it stands amid the great subterranean tides of world history; and I hope that the President will hit hard at this point in the future. Dean [Acheson's] speeches have been brilliant; but I wish that he had started

---

sible for the deaths of millions through periodic purges and collectivization campaigns.

making them a year earlier; and they are sometimes too abstract and intellectual for ready popular comprehension. Your own *Herald Tribune* speech was excellent and exactly in the right vein.

Until the American people reconciles itself to a future of protracted responsibilities and indefinite crisis, we will continue to have a feedback of McCarthyism; the people will continue to blame individuals for conditions for which they ought to blame history. But the job of education can only be done by persistent hammering away at the fundamentals of the situation. . . .

I will be in Washington toward the end of next week and will plan to drop by for a chat, if you have a moment. I am sorry to have written at such length; but the elections were a great shock.

Yours ever,
Arthur

Senator Robert Taft of Ohio challenged the Truman administration's legal right to send more American troops to Europe without the advance approval of Congress in a speech in the Senate on January 5, 1951. Taft was a staunch noninterventionist before Pearl Harbor, opposed the North Atlantic Treaty Organization as unnecessary and provocative, and questioned the constitutionality of the U.S. intervention in Korea.

To the Editor of *The New York Times*

January 6, 1951

[Cambridge, Massachusetts]

Sir:

Senator Taft in his speech on January 5 made the flat statement that President Truman "had no authority whatever to commit American troops to Korea without consulting Congress and without Congressional approval"; and, further, that he "has no power to agree to send American troops to fight in Europe in a war between the members of the Atlantic Pact and Soviet Russia." When he sent troops to Korea, Senator Taft continued, "the President simply usurped authority, in violation of the laws and the Constitution."

Senator Taft's statements are demonstrably ignorant and irresponsible. The public is entitled to know what provisions of the law or of the Constitution have been violated by President Truman in sending troops overseas. From the day that President Jefferson ordered Commodore Dale and two-thirds of the American navy into the Mediterranean to repel the Barbary pirates, American presidents have repeatedly committed American armed forces abroad without prior Congressional consultation or approval. In 1836 John Quincy Adams wrote, "However startled we may be at the idea that the Executive Chief Magistrate has the power of involving the nation in war, even without consulting Congress, an experience of fifty years has proved that in numberless cases he has and *must have* exercised this power. . . . Defensive war must necessarily be among the duties of the Executive Chief Magistrate."

In the century after 1812 there were at least *forty-eight* separate occasions of the use of our armed forces abroad without formal declaration of war. Indeed, our present intervention in Korea is not our first: it is our fourth, having been preceded by similar "unauthorized" interventions in 1871, 1888 and 1894.

Until Senator Taft and his friends succeed in rewriting American history according to their own specifications, these facts must stand as obstacles to their efforts to foist off their current political prejudices as eternal American verities.*

Yours sincerely,
Arthur Schlesinger, jr.

The commander in chief of UN forces in Korea was General of the Army Douglas MacArthur,[†] who had served as supreme commander of the Allied powers in the Southwest Pacific during World War II. On October 15, 1950, at

---

* Schlesinger had more appreciation for Taft's words twenty years later, after the Vietnam debacle. "By bringing the nation into war without congressional authorization and by then successfully defending his exercise of independent presidential initiative, Truman enormously expanded assumptions of presidential prerogative," Schlesinger wrote in *The Imperial Presidency* (1973).

† Douglas MacArthur (1880–1964). West Point, class of 1903; supreme commander for the Allied powers, Southwest Pacific Area, in World War II; commander in chief of UN forces in Korea, 1950–51.

a meeting with President Truman on Wake Island, MacArthur avowed that the war would be over by Thanksgiving and that the chances of Chinese intervention were "very little." But on November 26, some two hundred thousand Chinese Communist soldiers crossed over to North Korea and drove the UN forces back to South Korea and far down the peninsula.

From his headquarters in Japan, MacArthur let it be known publicly that he disagreed with Truman's decision to limit the war to Korea and forbid attacks on Chinese bases in Manchuria. MacArthur favored escalation: the blockade and nuclear bombing of China and the entry of Nationalist China. But Truman feared escalation could lead to World War III.

To W. Averell Harriman

April 8, 1951

[Cambridge, Massachusetts]

Dear Averell:

Just a note to say that I hope you are all giving the most serious consideration to cracking down really hard on MacArthur this time. I imagine that he feels that the Administration is politically in so precarious a position that it dare not do anything about him; therefore he feels free to invade the realm of foreign policy, to defy restraining orders, to traffic with the opposition leaders, etc. I am not so sure, however, that his recall at this point would not be greeted favorably as evidence that the Administration is moving to recapture control of the situation. It might well be the act which would break through the present miasmic atmosphere and reestablish the sense of presidential leadership and initiative.

I imagine that no general has so systematically lobbied and intrigued against his commander-in-chief since McClellan.[*] Lincoln[†] bore with McClellan's politicking and with his messiah complex for a long time; but he finally relieved McClellan of his command. The parallels are not exact,

---

[*] George McClellan (1826–85). Removed by President Lincoln from command of the Army of the Potomac during the Civil War; ran as Democratic Party candidate against Lincoln in 1864.

[†] Abraham Lincoln (1809–65). Lawyer, representative (Whig-Ill.), 1847–49; sixteenth U.S. president, 1861–65; a Republican; considered one of America's greatest presidents.

since MacArthur is a better general than McClellan was. But the real issue here is orderly government: we can only have one commander-in-chief at a time. It is odd how the same people . . . who get so upset when the Treasury and the Federal Reserve Board make conflicting statements demand full right of utterance for General MacArthur.

I do not think that the substantive issue—the question whether all-out war with Red China serves U.S. interests—has been adequately defined either. I hope that some senators next week may follow Senator Kerr's[*] example and sketch in concrete detail the implications of the MacArthur policy.

I am writing partly to say that my guess is that the President would get considerable support for disciplinary measures against MacArthur; and partly to suggest that something might be worked out of the McClellan parallel for press conference purposes.

Yours ever,
Arthur

Truman fired MacArthur for insubordination a few days later on April 11, 1951. The decision caused an outburst of public indignation that reached its apex on April 19 when MacArthur, back in the United States for the first time in fourteen years, addressed a joint session of Congress. Senator Taft wanted Truman impeached. But the uproar faded after a few weeks.

To W. Averell Harriman

May 24, 1951

[Cambridge, Massachusetts]

Dear Averell:

Just a note to thank you for your generous hospitality last weekend. I trust that an explanation of my non-appearance Saturday night has reached you. It is not that I am a gay dog who stays out all night; but that I foolishly

[*] Robert S. Kerr (1896–1963), Senator (D-Okla.), 1949–63, supported Truman on MacArthur controversy.

forgot to provide myself with a key and, not succeeding in rousing anyone, returned to the Grahams. . . .

We had a most interesting session with the President Monday night.[*] He was very alert and lively, seemed full of beans and fight, and pleased us all very much. It was a very useful meeting.

I have the impression that we have a great opportunity in the next few weeks. The Administration is coming back fast, as MacArthurism fades away; and it ought to be prepared to do much more than merely accept passively this restoration of confidence. It ought to have a positive program of action which would intensify and consolidate the resurgence of confidence. . . .

It was a great pleasure, as always, to see you. I hope to get down to Washington again before too long.

Yours ever,
Arthur

To Mr. Donner[†]

17 October 1951

[Cambridge, Massachusetts]

Dear Mr. Donner:

I have been uncertain whether to answer your letter of September 5 because it was hard to tell whether it was written by a crackpot or in good faith.

On the assumption that you were writing in good faith, may I state to you that your letter is a tissue of absurdities and falsehoods.

You state, "You have cooperated, collaborated, associated and/or affiliated with red fascist organizations, fronts and individuals." This statement

---

[*] Schlesinger, Reinhold Niebuhr, Francis Biddle, Joseph Rauh, Jr., and Hubert H. Humphrey, Jr., met with President Truman on May 21, 1951. "The worst thing I ever did was to give the order which killed all those people over there [Hiroshima]," Truman told them. "It was terrible; but I had no alternative; and I would give such an order again if it ever became necessary. But we must not let it become necessary." (Schlesinger, *Life in the Twentieth Century*, 351–52.)

[†] Robert Donner of Colorado Springs, Colorado.

is a lie. I have never associated with or been affiliated with any Communist organizations.

You state that I called John Reed[*] and Lincoln Steffens[†] "the warmest-hearted, most out-giving souls that ever lived." This is a lie. The statement you quote is from William C. Bullitt.[‡] You accuse me of having known John Reed. This is lie; John Reed died in 1920, at which time I was three years old. You call me a Marxian Socialist, which is another lie. Indeed, your whole letter strikes me as the outpouring of a disordered mind.

I imagine that there are few people in the country with as clear a record of outspoken anti-Communism for years as myself. At the very time that you were sending me your fantastic letter, I was under severe attack from the *New York Daily Worker* and the *New York Compass* (see, for example, the editorial in the *Compass* on September 16, 1951, entitled " 'Liberal' Cowards Do McCarthy's Dirty Work"). The attack in the *Worker* was only the most recent of a series of vicious attacks against me in that newspaper over the last five years.

I do not see how any responsible person can have any doubt about my position toward Communism. I would suggest that you glance at my book *The Vital Center*,[§] which was published in 1949, especially chapters III to VI. In 1947, I severed my connection with Little, Brown rather than continue to be published by a firm employing a pro-Communist editor; you will find that story in detail in the *New York Herald Tribune* of September 18, 1951, in the *New World Telegram* of September 17, and in *Time* Magazine of October 1, 1951, pages 20–21.

In the spring of 1946, I wrote one of the first full-length exposes of the American Communist Party. It appeared in *Life* on July 29, 1946. Even my book *The Age of Jackson,* published in 1945, though fundamentally a historical study, made amply clear my attitude toward Communism: I would call your attention, for example, to pages 432–433, 508 (where Commu-

---

* John Reed (1887–1920). Harvard, class of 1910; journalist and Communist activist; author of *Ten Days That Shook the World* (1919).

† Lincoln Steffens (1866–1936). Muckraking journalist; author of *The Shame of the Cities* (1904).

‡ William C. Bullitt (1891–1967). Progressive writer and diplomat, first U.S. ambassador to the Soviet Union, 1933–36; ambassador to France, 1936–41; became a Republican in 1948 and was a rabid anticommunist.

§ Arthur Schlesinger, Jr., *The Vital Center: The Politics of Freedom* (Boston: Houghton Mifflin, 1949). A defense of liberal democracy against communism and fascism.

nists are described as people "trumpeting their love of democracy and liberty, mainly in order to gain the power to destroy it"), 509, 522. This book, I should point out, though delayed by the paper shortage till 1945, was written in 1942 and 1943, at a time when many Americans were discovering virtues in Communism; I delivered the manuscript to the publisher before I went overseas in the spring of 1944. I might call your attention too to the review of the book in *Time*—a review written, as he subsequently told me, by Whittaker Chambers.[*]

I should add that my opposition to fascism and to its follow-travelers is as strong as my opposition to Communism, and it derives from the same impulse. I have no use for people who deal in false accusations and vicious insinuations. If your letter was the product of sincere misunderstanding, the facts I have cited should relieve your mind. If not, I can only commend you to the nearest psychiatrist.

Sincerely yours,
Arthur Schlesinger, Jr.

Arthur teamed up with Richard Rovere[†] of The New Yorker *to spin out an instant book on the Truman-MacArthur controversy, which was published in October 1951.[‡] President Truman approved.*

---

[*] Whittaker Chambers (1901–61). Former member of the Communist Party and Soviet spy who renounced communism and testified against Alger Hiss; senior editor of *Time* magazine, 1939–48; author of *Witness,* 1952.

[†] Richard Rovere (1915–79). Journalist; wrote Letter from Washington for *The New Yorker,* 1948–79; author of *Senator Joe McCarthy* (1959).

[‡] Richard Rovere and Arthur Schlesinger, Jr., *The General and the President, and the Future of American Foreign Policy* (New York: Farrar, Straus and Young, 1951), with cartoons by Herblock.

From President Truman

> November 5, 1951
> The White House
> *Personal*

Dear Doctor Schlesinger:

George Elsey[*] handed me the first copy of *The General and the President* and I appreciate very much your thoughtfulness in sending it to me. Sometime when it is convenient I would like very much to have you and your co-author write an inscription in it.

I had read the *Saturday Review of Literature*'s article about it and had also read the review of the *New York Times* and the *New York Herald Tribune*. The *Saturday Review* was fair, the other two were very much slanted—the *Times* particularly so. The editors of these great dailies are like the editor of *Look*—anybody who says the President is right is "wrong."

I wanted to write you about the articles in *Look* but I had been told you were at work on this book and I didn't want any sign of an attempt on my part to cause you to veer from an objective statement of the facts. You have stated the facts as they are.

When I made the 14,400 mile flight to meet the General at Wake Island, I left there under the impression there was a complete understanding and there would be no more trouble. He evidently got the impression, after the Chinese entrance into Korea, when he had very plainly told me they would never come in, that he had to do something to redeem his reputation. Like all other egotists do, he wanted to place the blame as far from himself as possible.

I think you analyzed the situation just as it is and I certainly appreciate your kindness in sending me a copy of the book.

> Sincerely yours,
> Harry Truman

Arthur was greatly impressed in the winter of 1940–41 when he first heard Reinhold Niebuhr preach at Harvard's Memorial Church, providing a Chris-

---

[*] George Elsey (b. 1918), Assistant to President Truman.

tian rationale for interventionism. Man is flawed and sinful, said Niebuhr. But even sinful man has the duty to act against evil in the world.

Arthur saw Niebuhr's conception of original sin as a brilliant metaphor for the human condition. Niebuhr summed up his philosophical argument for Arthur in a single mighty sentence in his 1944 book, The Children of Light and the Children of Darkness: *"Man's capacity for justice makes democracy possible; but man's inclination to injustice makes democracy necessary."*

In 1951, Niebuhr asked Arthur to review the manuscript of his latest book, The Irony of American History, *a study of the curious amalgam of virtue and vice in the American experience; "the ironic tendency of virtues to turn into vices when too complacently relied upon."*

To Reinhold Niebuhr

November 10, 1951

[Cambridge, Massachusetts]

Dear Reinhold:

Ursula* said that you were about to deliver the mss. of your book to the publishers; so I thought I would airmail my reactions, for whatever value they may have. I will return the mss. itself the first thing next week.

It occurs to me that the comments are valueless without page references. . . . I am not sure that I grasp with precision the larger design of the book (since I have not seen the first and last chapters); but this torso is splendid,—wise, valuable and illuminating. I only wish that you had put in more direct comment on the American experience. So many of your observations are good—as the one, for example, stressing the similarities between the Calvinist and Jeffersonian analyses—that I wish you had let yourself go in this field more often.

One irony deserving comment somewhere perhaps is the relationship between our democratic and equalitarian pretensions and our treatment of the Negro. This remains, as John Quincy Adams called it in 1820, "the great and foul stain upon the North American Union"; and I think you might consider mentioning it.

---

* Ursula Niebuhr (1908–97). Theologian and founder of the department of religion at Barnard College; wife of Reinhold.

A few specific comments: Actually the Jeffersonians were willing to increase the power of state governments; their unrelenting opposition was to the increase in the central power. The Jeffersonian tradition had strong tendencies toward local control of economic life.

Moreover, I am troubled here (and later) by the use of the phrase "our traditional theory." What you mean is "the traditional theory of the American business community" or "the Whig-Republican theory." Actually the Jackson-Populist-Progressive-New Deal tradition calls for a considerable measure of state intervention and control. The present political climate lays emphasis on the anti-statist elements in the American political tradition; but there are considerable statist elements which should not be overlooked because of their current neglect. . . .

Yours ever,
Arthur

To President Truman

28 November 1951

[Cambridge, Massachusetts]

Dear Mr. President:

I am deeply grateful for your recent letter about *The General and the President*. We felt that the facts ought to be placed squarely on the record; and we are gratified indeed to know that you did not find our analysis too far off the beam. I have no doubt at all how history will regard the episode: the relief of MacArthur will go down, I am confident, as one of the wisest and most courageous of the many wise and courageous decisions of your administration.

Very sincerely yours,
Arthur Schlesinger, jr.

Arthur first met Adlai Stevenson * *on a train from Washington to Chicago in 1948. Stevenson had recently returned from London, where he served as a U.S. delegate to the UN Preparatory Commission, and was contemplating a political career. They talked and drank in the club car till well past midnight. Arthur was delighted with Stevenson's wit, his wide range of reference, his shrewd, slightly cynical insight into people, and his belief in high standards of public service. He was a liberal and an internationalist, too.*

Stevenson was elected governor of Illinois in 1948.

In January 1952, he announced that he was running for reelection. "I cannot run for two offices at the same time," he said, addressing questions of his presidential availability. He prized the governorship and thought the presidency could wait. But pressure was coming from all directions, including the White House, where Truman considered his options; his approval ratings had sunk to 23 percent.

To Adlai Stevenson

March 25, 1952

[Cambridge, Massachusetts]

Dear Adlai:

I cannot say what a pleasure it was to see you here in Cambridge. I am only sorry there was no chance for you to come out and meet my wife. When I told her later about seeing you, she reported that she had been at the hairdressers that afternoon and that the talk had turned to the New Hampshire primaries.[†] The tough Irish girl who does Marian's hair made a series of disillusioned remarks about Kefauver, so Marian asked her who she was for. She replied, "Adlai Stevenson, of course," whereupon an expen-

---

* Adlai Ewing Stevenson (1900–1965). Grandson of Vice President Adlai Ewing Stevenson (1835–1914); New Deal lawyer; special assistant to secretary of the navy Frank Knox; U.S. spokesman at 1945 San Francisco UN conference; Democratic governor of Illinois, 1949–53; two-time Democratic presidential nominee, 1952 and 1956; ambassador to the United Nations, 1961–65.

† Senator Estes Kefauver of Tennessee made a run against Truman in the New Hampshire Democratic presidential primary. Truman did not campaign. The results of the March 11, 1952, election gave Kefauver all eight delegates and an important symbolic victory. Eisenhower beat Taft in the Republican presidential primary.

sively dressed woman in the next chair said, "Why I'm for Stevenson too." It looks as if you could count on support in all classes.

I saw Bob Sherwood* yesterday in New York. He expressed some concern over the way things are going. He feels, in particular, that if the President runs, it will really tear apart the Democratic party, which may have incalculable consequences in the future; and that, on the other hand, any retreat from the President's platform to appease the southerners would be even more fatal. You appear the only solution. I did my best to explain the reasons for your reluctance; but I fear that I am much less convincing at that than you are. . . .

This note is not to bring further pressure; but to say how much fun it was to see you, and also to say that, while I appreciate better the complexity of your position, I still hope like hell that you can see your way clear to becoming a candidate. Please don't bother to answer this letter.

Yours ever,
Arthur

On March 29, 1952, President Truman announced that he would not be a candidate for reelection. This is what Arthur had been waiting to hear—the door was open to Stevenson. But the governor resisted renewed pressure. After winning the April 8 Illinois gubernatorial primary, he issued a statement effectively closing the door on any presidential nomination. Yet no other person would emerge to fill the leadership vacuum in the Democratic Party over the next few months.

---

*Robert E. Sherwood (1896–1955). Playwright, screenwriter, and speechwriter; winner of a Pulitzer Prize for *Roosevelt and Hopkins: An Intimate History* (1948).

To Joseph Rauh, Jr.

June 10, 1952

[Cambridge, Massachusetts]

Dear Joe:

As you know, Reinhold Niebuhr suffered this spring a cerebral thrombosis.* While he is now on the mend, it is a long haul and he will be convalescent for many months. It occurred to Jim Loeb, Gertrude Scheft† and myself that it might ease his inactivity and enable him better to follow the political excitements of the summer if he were to have a television set; and it also occurred to us that many of his ADA friends would like to join with us in presenting him with a set as an expression of our appreciation of his years of leadership in the liberal movement and of our hope for his full and rapid recovery.

I am accordingly sending this note around to National Board members who might like to help. Jim, Gitty and I all know that there are many good causes this summer; but, if anyone would like to join in this one, simply send along a check (not more than five or ten dollars) to me.

Sincerely yours,
Arthur

The 1952 Democratic National Convention was held in Chicago at the end of July. Governor Stevenson, having professed no interest in the presidential nomination, accepted a draft by the convention, winning on the third ballot. Senator John Sparkman‡ of Alabama was chosen as the vice presidential nominee. Arthur signed on as head of the research and writing staff based in Springfield, Illinois, not far from the Executive Mansion.

---

*Niebuhr suffered a stroke that lamed his left side and impaired his speech. He was sixty years old. He was eventually able to use an electric typewriter and continue writing.

† Gertrude ("Gitty") Scheft (b. 1923), of Brockton, Massachusetts. Member of the ADA national board; sister of Schlesinger's friend Herbert Warren Wind, the golfing writer at *The New Yorker*.

‡ John Sparkman (1899–1985). Representative (D-Alabama), 1937–46; senator, 1946–79; Democratic Party vice-presidential nominee in 1952; chairman of the Senate Foreign Relations Committee, 1975–79.

To Ursula and Reinhold Niebuhr

August 6, 1952

[Cambridge, Massachusetts]

Dear Ursula and Reinhold:

I am back in Cambridge to order my affairs before going back almost immediately to Springfield. I have agreed to work fulltime for Stevenson until college begins.

The convention, as you can imagine, was most exciting. I think that the liberals were absolutely right in forcing the issue on the loyalty pledge.[*] One trouble was that the pledge was misrepresented, by both sponsors and opponents, as binding all delegates to support the candidates—which would have been intolerable. Actually all it did was to bind the delegates to see that the candidates got on the ticket on the Democratic line; once they had done this, the delegates would be perfectly free to do anything they wanted. In the end, the liberals won on the substance of the issue, and should probably have settled for substantial compliance instead of insisting on the letter of the pledge. Their refusal to do this permitted the bosses (led by Arvey)[†] and the Southerners to administer what appeared to be a smashing defeat to the liberals—though in fact the liberals won on the substance issue. The resentments of this defeat, exploited by the Kefauver[‡] people, almost turned many of the liberals against Stevenson. Fortunately Humphrey and Harriman stopped this and prevented Stevenson from emerging as the Dixiecrat candidate.

My admiration for Harriman increased steadily throughout the convention. He played a gallant and selfless role; made a clearcut stand on the issues; and gave the liberal position a dignity and a strength it might otherwise have lacked. I saw a good deal of him in his most intimate and

[*] The fight over the so-called loyalty oath split the convention. In reaction to the desertion of Southern Democrats to the Dixiecrats and Strom Thurmond in 1948, delegates were obligated to support the nominees of the convention and see that they appeared on their state ballots. The Virginia, South Carolina, and Louisiana delegations refused to sign any oath, yet were seated, averting a meltdown.

[†] Jacob Arvey (1895–1977). Chairman of the Cook County Democratic Party; powerful Chicago Democratic leader.

[‡] Estes Kefauver (1903–63). Liberal Tennessee Democrat; representative, 1939–49; senator, 1949–63.

troubled moments; and he behaved with a dignity, a decency and a clear-sightedness which were most impressive.

I think there are great possibilities in the Stevenson nomination. He is the one person in either party who speaks with an authentically new voice. Where Eisenhower,* for example, utters the cliches of the right, and Harriman the cliches of the left, Stevenson speaks with his own fresh voice. One has the sense of a personal vision which may lift us above and beyond the increasingly sterile party debates of the past generation and move us into a new political climate. I believe that Stevenson bears the imprint of an original political personality and has great creative possibilities. On the other hand, it must be admitted within the family that he is much less good on most issues than Harriman. Still [Woodrow] Wilson, for example, was a "good-government" governor of New Jersey, rather conservative on national issues, until necessities educated him; and I have the feeling about Stevenson that he is entirely educable.

I have put a discretionary label on this letter because I am most anxious that my views do not get into circulation. Stevenson naturally expects full loyalty from his staff, and will get it from me; the expression of reservations might destroy my usefulness at Springfield. Thus I would be grateful if you would not mention any of this to Frankfurter,† MacLeish,‡ etc.

One trouble is that Springfield is terribly isolated. If you have any ideas about what we should be doing, please write me at the Stevenson Campaign Headquarters, Springfield.

Of all the many idiotic reviews of Reinhold's book, the most idiotic is probably the one I enclose (from *The Freeman*—John Chamberlain's§ reactionary magazine).

We hope that Reinhold continues to mend. Why teach at all in the fall?

---

* At their convention in Chicago in early July, the Republicans selected General Eisenhower as their presidential nominee and Senator Nixon of California as his running mate.

† Felix Frankfurter (1882–1965). Harvard Law School professor; FDR confidant; U.S. Supreme Court justice, 1939–62.

‡ Archibald MacLeish (1892–1982). Lawyer; poet and writer; New Dealer; librarian of Congress, 1939–44; Harvard professor, 1949–62; three-time Pulitzer Prize winner.

§ John Chamberlain (1903–95). Right-wing journalist; author; editor of *The Freeman* magazine; syndicated columnist, 1960–85. The review, entitled "Incitement to Surrender," by Lawrence R. Brown, appeared on July 14, 1952.

Far better to read, think and write! Anyway, have a good rest this summer; and *let me have all possible ideas, suggestions, etc., at Springfield.*

Marian joins me in sending the best of love to you both.

Devotedly,
Arthur

PS: Adlai had all 6 of us to dinner when we were at Springfield. He could not have been nicer, and Stephen and Katharine were wordless with excitement. Wilson Wyatt (who is doing a good job [as campaign manager]) was also present. Chrissie, less impressed, asked her mother on the way home: "Which one was Stevenson?"

In her syndicated column of September 20, 1952, Eleanor Roosevelt wrote: "[Colonel McCormick* of the Chicago Tribune*] is frightened about Governor Stevenson's advisors and says they are a Socialist brain trust. Somehow, I never thought of Arthur Schlesinger Jr. as Socialist. Did you?"*

To Eleanor Roosevelt

October 2, 1952

[Springfield, Illinois]

Dear Mrs. Roosevelt,

Your column of September 22d has just caught up with me. I want to thank you for your generous defense of the Stevenson "brain trust."

This is obviously going to be a very dirty campaign. But I think that in the end Governor Stevenson's superiority in intelligence and character will make itself felt to the American people.

Very sincerely yours,
Arthur

---

* Robert R. McCormick (1880–1955). Owner and publisher of the *Chicago Tribune;* anti-intervention, anti–New Deal, anti–Fair Deal, anti–United Nations.

Little known outside Illinois at the beginning of the campaign, Adlai Stevenson quickly established himself as a brilliant, literate, and eloquent candidate. But the Republican themes of "Korea, Communism, and corruption" were crudely effective. The Republican vice presidential candidate Richard Nixon referred to Stevenson as "Adlai the appeaser . . . who got a Ph.D. from Dean Acheson's College of Cowardly Communist Containment." Senator McCarthy spoke on national television a week before the election and charged Arthur,* De Voto, MacLeish, and Wechsler with being pro-communist, and referred to Adlai as "Alger" before correcting himself.

On Election Day, November 4, 1952, Eisenhower won a smashing victory, garnering 54.9 percent of the popular vote to Stevenson's 44.4 percent, and 442 electoral votes to Stevenson's 89.

After sixteen years of progressive Democratic governance it was time for a change.

To Marie and W. Averell Harriman

November 20, 1952

[Cambridge, Massachusetts]

Dear Marie and Averell:

I cannot say how grateful the Schlesingers are to you for the Hobe Sound[†] interlude. I feel a new man as a result of the sun and the surf and the rest. In fact, I feel almost capable of coping with the New Era.

We had a good time with the Grahams. There was a certain initial tension, but we are all too old friends to keep it up for long. I find it easy to get mad at Phil and hard to stay mad at him. I think he deceived himself terribly during the election,[‡] but that he will be on the right side in most of the fights in the years ahead.

---

* McCarthy said Schlesinger "thought Communists should be allowed to teach your children" and was against religion.

† Hobe Sound, Florida, north of Palm Beach.

‡ Philip Graham supported Eisenhower for president and even campaigned for him a few times. (Katharine was solidly for Stevenson.) Graham was infuriated by Herblock cartoons at odds with the *Post*'s editorial line and dropped Herblock from the paper during the campaign's last weeks, although the cartoons appeared in syndication. He later acknowledged to Herblock that he had made a mistake.

I stopped off briefly in Washington on Tuesday. I was surprised to discover that Stewart Alsop shared our pessimism about McCarthy and agrees that the Republicans may well try in the next four years to put the Democrats out of business permanently by an orgy of investigation and slander to "prove" that the Democratic party is honeycombed with communism and treason. Unfortunately, just when I was about to ask him how he squared this thesis with his earlier view that the election of Eisenhower would weaken McCarthyism, I had to rush away to catch a plane [to] New York.

We saw the eminent pundit Mr. Lippmann[*] in Cambridge last night. He was more optimistic about the future and would not take seriously the prospect of McCarthyism run rampant. This makes it seem all the more probable that total pessimism is justified!

From our gray New England November, we look back with nostalgia on the sun and sea of Florida. But you have enabled us to survive the winter, and we cannot thank you enough.

Marian joins me in sending love to you both,
Arthur

To Adlai Stevenson

November 21, 1952

[Cambridge, Massachusetts]

Dear Adlai:

My present view, for what it is worth, is that the great danger in the next four years will lie not so much in the field of policy as in the field of politics. I don't think that the Republicans will make any very radical or drastic departures in foreign affairs; instead, we will probably have a dreary period in which the fabric of international security, as it is, will slowly unravel because the U.S. government will never supply enough money or send enough troops or do anything with boldness or generosity. Similarly, in domestic policy, I think things will deteriorate, not with bangs, but whimpers.

[*] Walter Lippmann (1889–1974). Influential liberal journalist and political commentator; author; a founder of *The New Republic* in 1914; editor of the New York *World* in the 1920s; wrote long-running column *Today and Tomorrow*, syndicated by the *New York Herald Tribune*.

Where the real immediate trouble will come, I think, will be in the accentuation of McCarthyism. I suspect that some Republicans believe that they can put the Democrats permanently out of business by persuading the nation that the Democratic party is so honeycombed with communism and treason that it can never again be trusted with power. This is precisely what the Republicans did after the Civil War, of course. By "waving the bloody shirt," they kept before the people the image of the Democratic party as the party of disloyalty—and it worked for the better part of two generations. . . .

I stopped a day in Washington on the way back [from Hobe Sound] and saw many friends and admirers of yours—Chip Bohlen, David Bruce,* Joe Rauh and others. All were filled with admiration for the campaign, grief for the results and apprehensions for the future.

Lippmann last night did make one interesting suggestion about your own activity. He pointed out that Roosevelt, as a private citizen and an invalid, managed to make himself a powerful national figure within the Democratic party by the simple process of correspondence. Through exchanging letters, he was in constant contact with Democrats all over the country, winning their support, confirming their loyalty, eliciting their opinions and influencing their views. I know you will do this anyway, and I think it could be a valuable technique. But I wish to hell you could get control of the *Pantagraph*!† . . .

I hope you had a good rest in Arizona, I look forward to seeing you before too long.

Yours ever,
Arthur

Arthur was greatly intrigued by the word "egghead" as applied to himself and other Stevensonians during the campaign. Stewart Alsop had first used the word in his column of September 26, 1952, after visiting the Stevenson headquarters in Springfield.

* David K. E. Bruce (1898–1977). OSS; chief of the Marshall Plan in France, 1948–49; ambassador to France, 1949–52, to West Germany, 1957–59, to the United Kingdom, 1961–69; first U.S. emissary to the People's Republic of China, 1973–74; U.S. envoy to NATO, 1974–76; married to the former Evangeline Bell.

† *The Daily Pantagraph* of Bloomington, Illinois, was founded by Jesse W. Fell in 1837. Fell's granddaughter married Lewis Stevenson, Adlai's father. The Stevenson family lost control of the *Pantagraph* in 1927.

The word had rather an Ivy League connotation—an A.B. degree, button-down collars, tweeds and flannels, pipes and crew cuts, with a lively but amateur interest in politics and a belief that reading books was not necessarily anti-American. Stevenson was amused by the usage. But what started out as an affable and friendly term quickly acquired uglier implications. An "egghead" was a "person of intellectual pretensions, often a professor or the protégé of a professor . . . superficial in approach to any problem . . . feminine . . . supercilious . . . surfeited with conceit . . . a doctrinaire supporter of middle European socialism . . . a self-conscious prig . . . an anemic bleeding heart," as Louis Bromfield* wrote in the conservative publication The Freeman. *After Stevenson's defeat, this meaning seemed to take hold.*

Arthur decided to write a piece in defense of the highbrow in American politics and contacted John Alsop,[†] from whom Stewart Alsop had picked up the term.

From John Alsop

December 29, 1952

Avon, Conn[ecticut]

Dear Arthur:

Thank you for your letter of December 16, which gave me a chuckle. I fear that such assistance I can give you in your quest is largely negative. For instance, as far as I know, the term "egghead" is not local, nor is it my own invention (as I feel sure I have heard it somewhere); but its application to the nation's intellectuals is probably my responsibility.

As he probably told you, Stewart happened to be in Connecticut with Mr. Stevenson during the early part of the campaign; and he called me on the telephone to discuss the situation here. During the course of the conversation, he pointed out that certain intellectuals who tended to support Eisenhower up to the Convention were deserting him. This made me rather angry because I knew that it was true, so I dredged up the derogatory term from my subconscious.

---

* Louis Bromfield (1896–1956). Writer; author of the Pulitzer Prize–winning novel *Early Autumn* (1926).

† John Alsop (1916–2000). The third Alsop brother; Groton; Yale; OSS; insurance company executive; veteran of Connecticut Republican politics.

My brothers have since accused me of anti-intellectualism, one of the many forms of discrimination to which they particularly object. I am not guilty! My comment was simply an expression of my political estimate that the visceral rather than the intellectual reaction is what wins the election. I think Truman was elected in 1948 on this basis; and I expected, as eventually transpired, that Eisenhower would win the same way (I hope, however, with better results).

I suppose if one were to analyze the term, one would say that it is a visual figure of speech, tending to depict a large, oval head, smooth, faceless, unemotional, but a little bit haughty and condescending.

To be honest with you, I thought very highly of Mr. Stevenson. I am satisfied that he was defeated by forces wholly beyond his own control. I trust that this letter has confused you sufficiently! Best regards.

Sincerely yours,
John Alsop

The Battle for Influence

1953–56

To Marietta Tree[*]

Inauguration Day [January 20, 1953]

[Cambridge, Massachusetts]

Dearest Marietta:

I feel so depressed today—first the Inauguration[†] itself (I watched it with morbid interest on TV; among other things, the new government *looks* so terrible), and then today, and then, darling, your disappearance from the country at the moment of its (and my) need. What a tough day it must have been for Adlai! And yet I imagine that he was superb, at least so far as the public face is concerned.

I shall send him a letter in a day or so with afterthoughts on the *Life*

The novelist Edwin O'Connor, author of *The Last Hurrah;* Philip Graham, publisher of *The Washington Post;* John Hersey, author of *Hiroshima* and *A Bell for Adano,* and his wife; and Schlesinger exchange ideas at his Cape Cod cottage.

piece.* These afterthoughts will be shamelessly plagiarized from you, as usual; but it seemed the quickest way of getting them to him.

Everything is going to be so dreary. The last time the bus[iness] community was in power there was at least great artistic exuberance and release. Now not even that. The next 4 years are going to be the 20s without the Jazz Age; *Babbitt* without Sinclair Lewis,† etc.

However, I am being silly. Doubtless we shall never have had it so good. Marietta darling, I can only reiterate well beyond the point of boredom what fun it has been seeing you these last weeks, how much I count on it, and how much I love & miss you. Take good care of yourself, and send me a note so that I shall know you are alive.

Much, much love,
Arthur

To Marietta Tree

January 31 [1953]

[Cambridge, Massachusetts]

Dearest Marietta:

I am just back from New York, where I went to attend a couple of meetings. I flew down with McGeorge Bundy,‡ who is (for the moment) entirely rueful and chastened about the Eisenhower administration. Then I went to Averell's for the meeting of the FDR Foundation.§ There was an excellent

---

* "*Life* Goes to a Party for Adlai's Sons," *Life* magazine, January 19, 1953: Stevenson gives a "lame duck" dance for his three sons at the Executive Mansion in Springfield before exiting the governorship.

† Sinclair Lewis (1885–1951). Writer; in 1930, became the first American to win the Nobel Prize for Literature; his novel *Babbitt* (1922) satirized American business culture and boosterism.

‡ McGeorge Bundy (1919–96). Groton; Yale; Republican; dean of faculty at Harvard, 1953–61; national security adviser, 1961–66; president of the Ford Foundation, 1966–79.

§ The Franklin D. Roosevelt Foundation was established in 1939 to develop and sustain the Franklin D. Roosevelt Library at Hyde Park, New York, the first official presidential library.

turnout (FDR jr, [Walter] Reuther, Leon Henderson, Tom Finletter,* Anna Rosenberg,[†] Ed Barrett,[‡] Elmo Roper, Frank Graham,[§] as well as Harriman, Sherwood, Rosenman,[¶] etc; but where was Mrs Tree?—elected "to serve until the Annual Meeting in January 1955") and a fairly fruitful discussion. Reuther, as usual, was most sensible and impressive. Afterward we had a number of drinks and bitched about the Eisenhower administration. (I now begin to understand how Republicans lived in the thirties.) And then I spent the evening with Mary McCarthy,** Dick Rovere and an egghead group who want to start a new magazine; and then caught the midnight back to Boston. I must report my complaint, dear, that you have spoiled New York for me. It is such a waste to come down and not to see you.

Your letter arrived and lit the day. What a wonderful time you must all be having![††] Your account of the ultramarine sea and the glistening waves is all the more irresistible (and hard to endure) against the background of Cambridge fog and slush. I am fascinated by the details of your life, and by your thoughts about Adlai; so please do not stop. You are quite right about his Calvinism. It operates in politics too; he cannot bear to have things come easy or to say things which please anybody. I think he feels that he has to pay a price for them later. I have always imagined that all this went back to his childhood catastrophe[‡‡] and to the everlasting journey of expia-

---

* Thomas Finletter (1893–1980). Lawyer; secretary of the air force, 1950–53; ambassador to NATO, 1961–65.

† Anna Rosenberg (1902–83). New Dealer, first female assistant secretary of defense, 1950–53.

‡ Edward W. Barrett (1910–89). Journalist; OWI; editorial director of *Newsweek*, 1946–50; assistant secretary of state for public affairs, 1950–52; dean of the School of Journalism at Columbia University, 1956–68.

§ Frank Porter Graham (1886–1972). Progressive president of the University of North Carolina, Chapel Hill, 1930–49; Senator (D-S.C.), 1949–50.

¶ Samuel I. Rosenman (1896–1973). Lawyer; judge; adviser to FDR and Truman.

** Mary Therese McCarthy (1912–89). Novelist; critic; teacher; liberal activist; author of *Memories of a Catholic Girlhood* (1957) and *The Group* (1963); sister of actor Kevin McCarthy; married to writer and critic Edmund Wilson, 1938–46.

†† The Trees were entertaining Adlai Stevenson, the Finletters, and the Barry Binghams at their lavish house, Heron Bay, on the west coast of Barbados in the Caribbean. Stevenson, Ronnie Tree's old Chicago friend, had arrived on January 20, 1953, for rest and recovery. He would begin a world trip in March.

‡‡ On December 30, 1912, twelve-year-old Stevenson accidentally shot and killed Ruth Merwin, a distant cousin and friend of his sister, Elizabeth ("Buffie").

tion to which it must have condemned him. As for the unselfconsciousness, I loved your story. He is curiously "free" in that sense; really an "inner-directed" type (have you read Dave Riesman's* *The Lonely Crowd*?); but, of course, doomed to the self-questioning, conscience, Calvinism, etc., which also goes with this type; so, that the "freedom" is superb when attained, but either comes at the end of a struggle or else breeds feelings of guilt. . . .

As for the Eisenhower administration, no one could have imagined that it would have dissipated its power and prestige so quickly. Of course, by the time you get this Ike may have recaptured the initiative by his State of the Union message; but I doubt it. These people simply have no idea at all; it is really a case of intellectual bankruptcy. They can't think of anything to do which would be much different from what Truman has been doing. But there is terrific pressure on them to have "new" ideas; and the danger is that they will be goaded into having them—into doing things for the sake of doing things—and the results may be disastrous.

The Dulles† speech, of course, was a sad flop. It is discouraging to think of JFD and Stassen‡ wandering about Europe lousing up our relations with our allies. I take it you get the *Times* (NY) and saw Scotty [Reston's] testy piece about the speech. The Alsops are writing about the administration in very impatient tones, as if Ike had personally let them down. (Joe, by the way, is quite sick—jaundice.)

About the only thing the new regime has done is to issue a flock of idiotic edicts—e.g., secretaries cannot smoke in the White House corridors; anyone leaking to the press after Cabinet meetings will be fired (my own belief is that the anti-leaking edict is a desperate attempt to conceal the fact

---

* David Riesman (1909–2002). Harvard Law graduate; clerk to Supreme Court justice Louis Brandeis; taught sociology at the University of Chicago and Harvard; author of *The Lonely Crowd* (1950) with Nathan Glazer and Reuel Denney, on the pressures toward conformity in American life.

† John Foster Dulles (1888–1959). Lawyer, Sullivan and Cromwell; Republican foreign policy specialist; adviser to the US mission at the San Francisco UN conference; secretary of state, 1953–59. In a speech on January 27, 1953, he identified the main concern of U.S. foreign policy as the "deadly serious" threat of "encirclement" by the Russian Communists and their allies.

‡ Harold Stassen was the newly appointed director of the Mutual Security Agency, overseeing foreign aid.

that none of them have anything to say). Brownell's[*] first executive order was that all Department of Justice employees stay at their desks all day; Benson's[†] that all Dept of Agriculture employees should do a full day's work, if they want a full day's pay. Etc; Tom F[inletter] will give you other sordid details. Marian says that it is government by common scold.

Life here is back to routine. I am lecturing this term, plus a seminar; so I live the academic life, with squash twice a week, a certain amount of work on the FDR book, etc. I went to Philadelphia last week to deliver a lecture—an event which both Philadelphia and I survived. We went to lunch last week at Burden Mullers[‡] for Lady Jebb.[§] I sat next to Alice James[¶] who enchanted me by telling me what you were like at the age of 17. . . .

But I have gone on enough. It was wonderful to hear from you. Write soon again. I miss you so much.

Much love,
A.

To Marietta Tree

February 9, 1953

[Cambridge, Massachusetts]

Dearest Marietta:

I have just come from a most discouraging talk with an old State Department friend. He says that things are far worse than one could imagine; that Eisenhower and Dulles do not seem to have any idea of the implications of what they are doing; that Dulles consults with almost no one in the

---

[*] Herbert Brownell, Jr. (1904–96). Lawyer; Republican activist; U.S. attorney general, 1953–57.

[†] Ezra Taft Benson (1899–1994). Republican secretary of agriculture, 1953–61; thirteenth president of the Church of Jesus Christ of Latter-day Saints, 1985–94.

[‡] Rowland Burden-Muller (1891–1980). Englishman who lived in Boston; connoisseur of the arts.

[§] Cynthia Jebb (1898–1990). Wife of Gladwyn Jebb; permanent representative of the United Kingdom to the United Nations, 1950–54.

[¶] Alice James (1887–1957). Cambridge hostess; wife of William ("Billy") James, son of the philosopher William James.

Department (and especially not with Chip [Bohlen] and George);* and that the chief hope of avoiding the war into which we are heading is that our allies will break with us and thereby make it impossible for us to fight. This comes from a most level-headed, unemotional person. And it came on top of a typically melodramatic phone call from Joe A[lsop], in which he said that, given the state of mind of the Eisenhower administration, the only possible alternatives are Louis-Johnsonism† or preventive war, and that the second seems far the more likely.

All this is concealed under the blanket of eulogy in the press which continues to be provoked by every act of the administration. But the Alsops, Lippmann, Reston, etc., are all privately disturbed, even if they continue to join in the public flattery. The best hope now is for the British to take a firm line. Churchill is perhaps the one man who might appeal to the American people over the head of Eisenhower. Joe thinks that the administration is deliberately courting war; my State Dept friend doubts this and thinks that they are just bungling into it. You ask what people think about Dulles. I regret the answer!

However, good wisecracks emerge, as that Dulles has given Europe sixty days to get out of town. . . .

I have been living my usually pointlessly active life. I went out to Detroit last weekend to speak to a Roosevelt Day dinner, along with Reuther and Dick Dilworth‡ (from Philadelphia). Dilworth gave a very rousing and effective speech; he seemed quite a good guy. As you probably know, Adlai wired me to meet him in NY on Friday (or did you instigate it?—he concluded his wire, largely a complaint about non-progress on his various projects, with the incriminating statement, "Sleeping here is excellent"). This I plan to do, and Averell has invited Marian and me to be his guests at the 100 buck a plate dinner, so we shall stay over for it. I wish to hell that Adlai would bring you back with him. I really miss you so much and would give anything for a few moments' sight of you.

---

* George Kennan (1904–2005). Historian; diplomat; Soviet expert; State Department, 1926–53; expounded policy of containment, 1947; Institute of Advanced Studies, Princeton, 1956–74; ambassador to the Soviet Union, 1952; ambassador to Yugoslavia, 1961–63.

† Louis Johnson (1891–1966). Secretary of defense, 1949–50; fired after Korean War began for his efforts to pare the Pentagon budget; a particular target of the Alsop brothers.

‡ Richardson Dilworth (1898–1974). Liberal Democratic mayor of Philadelphia 1956–62.

Sam Behrman* was in town last week and took us to the opening of a new play (*Picnic,* by Wm Inge,† who wrote *Come Back, Little Sheba* or whatever it was called). We had dinner with the Josh Logans‡ (josh was directing). The play was not bad. Then Sam came to dinner with us, and the Gardner Coxes and the Perry Millers for a most entertaining evening. He really is a delight. Much talk about Laski, who was a good friend of both Behrman's and Miller's. We all have been reading the Holmes-Laski letters, a quite extraordinary volume§ which rather raises my opinion of Laski. I saw most of him in the forties, when he was tired and doctrinaire and gave me a pain in the neck. But there was obviously much more to him than I thought; and the letters show an intelligence and exuberance which explains why men like Holmes¶ and John Morley** and Haldane†† were so delighted by him. It was an intellectual catastrophe for him to shift from pluralism to socialism. As long as he was a pluralist, he had a bright, various, creative mind. When he turned to socialism, it narrowed and then atrophied his intelligence. The process is visible in the letters. Of course, you never know what to believe in Laski's letters; but the stories are good nonetheless. He read prodigiously, and must have actually read a good deal of what he claimed to have read since he appended so many intelligent comments. These portions of his letters quite depressed me, since in the midst of my life I seem to find time to read practically nothing. I feel Middle Age creeping up, and am only partially consoled by your comforting rationalizations.... Anyway both Holmes and Laski could be destroyed on the

---

* S. N. Behrman (1893–1973). Prolific American playwright, screenwriter, and author.

† William Inge (1913–73). American playwright; his *Picnic,* directed by Joshua Logan, won the Pulitzer Prize.

‡ Joshua Logan (1908–1988). American stage and film director; *Annie Get Your Gun, Mister Roberts, South Pacific* (show and film), *Camelot* (film).

§ Oliver Wendell Holmes, Jr., *Holmes-Laski Letters: The Correspondence of Mr. Justice Holmes and Harold J. Laski, 1916–1935,* ed. Mark De Wolfe Howe (Cambridge, Mass.: Harvard University Press, 1953).

¶ Oliver Wendell Holmes, Jr. (1841–1935). Influential U.S. Supreme Court justice, 1902–32.

** John Morley (1838–1923). Writer; newspaper editor; statesman; Liberal MP, 1883–95, 1896–1908.

†† Richard B. Haldane (1856–1928). Lawyer and philosopher; Liberal MP, 1885–1911; helped found the London School of Economics in 1895; served as secretary of state for war, 1905–12; lord chancellor, 1912–15, 1924.

basis of their exchange of letters, but I think the fair-minded critic may give them both slight credits on it. . . .

Academic life proceeds as always. This seems to be my Indian year. Unfortunately a book of mine (*The Vital Center,* or as it was called in England *The Politics of Freedom*—the one I sent you) was a great failure in England; when it was remaindered, a great many copies were bought by some Indian bookseller and evidently sold cheap to Indian intellectuals. As a result, I have a vast following in India. In the last 2 weeks, three visiting Indians have come to see me as a consequence of having read the book. Unhappily I visited India at an impressionable age (in 1934) and came away with an indelible image of the insolubility of all problems; and, in the years since, my anti-Indian instincts have been confirmed by my brushes with Indian intellectuals, all of whom seem abstract, irrelevant and futilely argumentative to the extreme. The present crop, on the whole, is a little better. But I am not the ideal American for Indian contacts.

I hope you have received some letters from me. You should have got two by now, at least. I have two from you. I don't think that Adlai is really as much a basic worrier as he must have seemed in the BWI.[*] He is a literary worrier—i.e., he talks about it all the time, and he worries particularly over his writing, since he prides himself so much on it. He is, I think, less of a worrier over administrative decisions. . . . Marietta darling, may I say again that I miss you dreadfully and long to see you before too long. Write when you can, because your letters are avidly awaited and read. Much, much love,

A.

To Marietta Tree

March 7, 1953

[Cambridge, Massachusetts]

Dearest Marietta:

I cannot say how much pleasure your letters give me. I am not the world's most faithful correspondent; in fact, it has been a long time since I have written so regularly to anybody; but I so enjoy hearing from you.

[*] British West Indies.

Though letters are an inadequate substitute for the real thing: *when* are you coming back?

I have less news this time, since I have spent most of the week in bed. I guess that the accumulated fatigue of the last months and years struck all at once; and I had a fairly wretched few days, largely in a kind of unrestful semi-doze. But now it is all gone, and I really feel OK again. Harvard is still absorbed in its own troubles. One member of the faculty—an obscure and unknown physicist named Wendell Furry*—refused to answer questions before the House Un-American Activities Committee on the ground of self-incrimination. He was plainly (on the testimony of 4 witnesses, including Granville Hicks)† a party member in the late 30s; and, judging by his testimony, he is a fellow-traveler today. The problem is: should he be fired for refusing to say whether he was or is a party member? Conant, in a loose remark before the Senate Foreign Affairs Committee, said that a professor refusing to answer should be fired; and the Corporation has taken this position. But Paul Buck,‡ the acting president, has heroically taken the line that each case should be decided on its merits. In the meantime, Joe Alsop has become furiously mobilized in the cause. He thinks it would be terrible to fire Furry and he threatens to resign from the Board of Overseers, with a public letter of denunciation, if this is done. In the meantime, he harangues members of the Corporation§ over the telephone, stirs up dissent among the Overseers and writes powerful letters in defense of academic freedom. It is Joe at his best. I take the Buck-Alsop position because I shudder at the effect through the country if Harvard, of all universities, should take the lead in this sort of thing.

This local contretemps has, of course, quite overshadowed such non-Cambridge events as the death of Stalin. My own view is pessimistic. I

---

* Wendell Furry (1907–1984). Harvard physicist; member of a Communist "cell" of Harvard tutors and instructors in 1938–39.

† Granville Hicks (1901–82). Writer; educator; Marxist literary critic; member of Harvard Communist "cell"; left CPUSA in 1939 after Hitler-Stalin pact.

‡ Paul H. Buck (1899–1978). American historian; Harvard provost.

§ The Harvard Corporation, established in 1650, is the ruling body of the university, made up of six members and the college president; vacancies are filled by vote of members of the corporation. The board of overseers, elected among the alumni, approves the decisions of the corporation.

think Malenkov,* like John Foster Dulles, will try to start off by securing his domestic base, which means that he will appease the McCarthys of the Soviet Union, which means that everything will get worse. I aggravated my sickness, by the way, by watching the McCarthy investigation of the Voice of America over television. God knows that the VOA needs overhauling; but the McCarthy way of doing it really has to be seen to be believed. I heard most of the Reed Harris† interrogation. It was really terrible. Part of the time Harris sounded like a prisoner in the Moscow dock recanting his past faith in Trotsky;‡ in 1932 he had written a book called *King Football*, about subsidized athletics, which he had interlarded in a Menckenian§ way with cracks at the American Legion, the reverend clergy, etc—before McCarthy, Harris would keep protesting that he didn't really mean what he had said about the American Legion, that he regarded the American Legion as one of the finest institutions in America, and so on. Then McCarthy would goad him beyond endurance, and he would finally fight back—rather effectively at times. Those two great liberals Stu Symington¶ and Scoop Jackson** meanwhile sit silently by while McCarthy runs amuck. And Dulles, of course, crumpled up every time Joe shakes a finger. And Eisenhower occupies himself with more important matters, such as bringing his golf game down below 90 and finishing a portrait of Bobby Jones.†† Be sure to read the Washington Letter in the current

* Georgy Malenkov (1902–88). Premier of the Soviet Union, 1953–55; ousted by Nikita Khrushchev.

† Reed Harris (1909–82). Writer; editor; Federal Writers Project; OWI; Voice of America; target of McCarthy investigation.

‡ Leon Trotsky (1879–1940). Russian Marxist revolutionary; founder of the Red Army; lost power struggle to Stalin in the 1920s; assassinated in Mexican exile.

§ H. L. Mencken (1880–1956). Journalist; magazine editor; satirist; acerbic critic of American life and culture.

¶ Stuart Symington (1901–88). First secretary of the air force, 1947–50; senator (D-Mo.), 1953–76; candidate for president in 1960.

** Henry M. ("Scoop") Jackson (1912–83). Representative (D-Wash.), 1941–53; senator, 1953–83; neoconservative Democrat known as the "Senator from Boeing" for his fierce support of hometown company; favored Vietnam War; pro-Israel; pro–civil rights; distrusted U.S.-Soviet arms treaties; leader of conservative wing of Democratic Party.

†† Bobby Jones (1902–71). Lawyer; brilliant amateur golfer; won the Grand Slam in 1930; creator of Augusta National Golf Club.

New Yorker. Dick Rovere tells about Raymond Aron's[*] reaction to the McCarthy investigations.

Well, I continue gloomy. Barbara Ward[†] will be in Boston this week and I trust that she will cheer me up. Also, I have to go down to New York on Thursday and debate Jim Burnham,[‡] who has just written an idiotic and dishonest book called *Containment or Liberation.* Chip Bohlen, by the way, outdid himself before the Senate Foreign Affairs Committee. They called him up when they were considering his nomination for the Moscow job and quizzed him about Yalta. Chip pulled no punches and went straight down the line in defense. It is pleasant to have occasional displays of courage and honor in the current Washington squalor.[§]

I must tell you about young Franklin and Dulles, when Dulles read the text of the Eisenhower resolution at the House session on secret agreements.[¶] Dulles said that the Democrats had never made such a statement. Franklin said that he had been considering the question and had some language he would like to read. Dulles said it was fine—perhaps better than his own—could he see it? FDRjr handed it to him so he could read it. Dulles read it and said it was fine, an improvement really, it expressed all the ideas

---

[*] Raymond Aron (1905–83). Influential French philosopher and journalist; edited the wartime newspaper *La France Libre* from London; columnist for *Le Figaro;* taught at the Sorbonne, 1955–68.

[†] Barbara Mary Ward, also Baroness Jackson of Lodsworth (1914–81). English economist interested in the problems of developing countries.

[‡] James Burnham (1905–87). Former Marxist and Trotskyite turned rabid anticommunist; led Political and Psychological Warfare division at OSS; a founding editor of *National Review.*

[§] Joe McCarthy called Bohlen's years at the State Department "an ugly record of betrayal" and linked him with W. Averell Harriman, whom he called "that elusive statesman of the half world whose admiration for everything Russian is unrivaled outside the confines of the Communist party." In a rebuke to McCarthy, the Senate approved Bohlen as ambassador to the Soviet Union by a vote of 74 to 13.

[¶] Robert Taft and other conservative Republicans conceived of the "Secret Agreements" Resolution, condemning the 1945 Yalta agreements, but the administration opposed it, not wanting to undermine wartime pacts that were almost ten years old. Eisenhower offered a new resolution accusing the Russians of having "perverted" secret wartime agreements as a means to subjugate free peoples and declaring that the people of the United States "are never acquiescent in such enslavement." Yalta was not mentioned, much less repudiated, infuriating Republican conservatives. After Stalin's death on March 5, 1953, the resolution died in committee.

and expressed them well. Then Franklin told him that the language was taken from Truman's State of the Union message two years ago.[**]

I must stop. I need not say how much I look forward to your return. But I can well see how difficult it must be to consider leaving your island paradise for the clamors and confusions of Eisenhower's America. I think you have adopted the only possible solution for these appalling times. In the meantime, write.

All love,
A.

To Joseph Alsop

March 17, 1953

[Cambridge, Massachusetts]

Dear Joe:

I find that I will be in Washington on the 28th (a Saturday). Will you be around then?

I have one footnote on your recent epistle to Marbury.[††] In the fall of 1948, shortly after Marbury had been elected to the Corporation, he paid a visit to me one day in my office in the bowels of Widener. Without preliminaries, he told me that Dean Acheson had told him that I was denouncing Alger Hiss[‡‡] at every cocktail party in Washington, and that he, as Hiss's

[**] At the meeting of the House Foreign Affairs Committee on February 26, 1953, New York representative Franklin Delano Roosevelt, Jr., showed Dulles a passage from Truman's March 1947 message proposing immediate U.S. assistance to Greece and Turkey to prevent their falling into the Soviet sphere. Proclaiming the Truman Doctrine, the president had said it would be "the policy of the United States to support free people who are resisting attempted subjugation by armed minorities or by outside pressures."

[††] William L. Marbury (1901–88). Maryland lawyer; member of the Harvard Corporation, 1948–70; represented Alger Hiss in his libel case against Whittaker Chambers, 1948–49.

[‡‡] Alger Hiss (1904–96). Harvard Law School; clerk to Supreme Court justice Oliver Wendell Holmes, Jr.; State Department official at Yalta; acting secretary-general of the San Francisco UN conference; accused by Whittaker Chambers of spying for the Soviet Union, served three and a half years in jail for perjury.

lawyer, wanted to know on what basis I was making these remarks. He then went into a long song-and-dance about his own absolute conviction of Hiss's innocence.

I need not state my astonishment and dismay over the action of a member of the Harvard Corporation seeking, in the interests of one of his clients in private law practice, to bring pressure on a member of the Harvard faculty. In any case, he did not get very far.

Nor does it appear that he was even telling the truth about Acheson. I later wrote to Acheson, stating what Marbury had said Acheson had told him, and adding that I was sure he knew that I had done no such thing. Acheson replied (October 27, 1948): "I am sorry that you got the impression from Bill Marbury that I thought that you had been going around Washington denouncing Alger Hiss as a communist. I did not intend to give him such an impression and certainly did not have it myself."

It is somewhat ironic to note how people, who five years ago were beating their breasts over Hiss and regarding oneself as a dangerous red-baiter, are today thirsting for the blood of a fool professor,* and regarding all those less bloodthirsty as dangerously soft on the Communist issue. It is particularly odd when one remembers that Communism was an internal political threat in 1948 while it is wholly negligible today.

The one thing consistent about Marbury, though, I guess, is his self-righteousness!

Yours ever,
Arthur

Arthur believed that a true democracy thrived on the free exchange of ideas and that good ideas will drive out bad ideas if exposed to the light of day. He was particularly concerned by attacks on free speech on college campuses.

---

* A reference to Wendell Furry, who testified before McCarthy's Permanent Subcommittee on Investigations about his party activities but refused to name party associates. Furry was cited for contempt and indicted by a federal grand jury but never prosecuted. He was made a full professor in 1962.

To the Editor of *The Harvard Crimson*

April 10, 1953

[Cambridge, Massachusetts]

Sir:

What in the world has gotten into the students of Harvard? I note in the *Christian Science Monitor* of April 9 that (a) the Law School Forum has cancelled the participation in a debate of Howard Fast,* the Communist novelist, and (b) some other unnamed organization has cancelled a film starring Paul Robeson,† the Communist actor. What are the students so frightened about? Is their faith in themselves and in democracy so feeble that they fear subversion from the dreary imbecilities of Howard Fast or from the cavortings of Paul Robeson as the Emperor Jones?‡

A year ago I had a no-quarter debate with Howard Fast before the Yale Political Union. I am happy to report that the Yale undergraduates seem to have survived the sight of Mr. Fast without fatal contamination; that their sharp and intelligent questions showed how clearly they saw through his arguments; and that they felt by a whopping majority that the anti-Communist side had the best of the debate. I can add that Mr Fast said nothing that evening that my ten year old son could not handle on a bad day (and I suspect that Mr Robeson impersonating the Emperor Jones would hardly be a danger to my four year old).§ What has happened to this generation of Harvard men that they should flee in panic before such hopeless bores as the Fasts and the Robesons?

---

* Howard Fast (1914–2003). Novelist; OWI; Voice of America; joined CPUSA in 1943; jailed for contempt of Congress in 1950 for three months; author of *Spartacus* (1951); awarded Stalin Peace Prize, 1953; broke with CPUSA; author of *April Morning* (1961), a novel about the 1776 battle of Lexington and Concord as seen through a teenager's eyes.

† Paul Robeson (1898–1976). Scholar; professional football player; stage and film actor; concert singer; lawyer; political activist; his passport was revoked in 1950 under the McCarran Act. In 1952, Robeson was awarded the International Stalin Prize, which he accepted in New York City. He was allowed to travel outside the United States in 1956.

‡ *The Emperor Jones,* a 1920 play by Eugene O'Neill about an African American man who sets himself up as an emperor on a Caribbean island; Robeson starred in both the play and the 1933 film.

§ Andrew Bancroft Schlesinger was born in Boston on November 16, 1948.

I gather that in these cases the students acted on their own, without orders or even hints from the faculty. It is a stirring commentary on the courage of this new generation that the faculties and governing bodies of a university should be more in favor of free speech than the students.

Four years ago, when the Communist agent Gerhart Eisler[*] spoke at Harvard, Dean W. J. Bender[†] said, "The world is full of dangerous ideas, and we are both naive and stupid if we believe that the way to prepare intelligent young men to face the world is to try to protect them from such ideas when they are in college. Four years spent in an insulated nursery will produce gullible innocents, not tough-minded realists. . . . If Harvard students can be corrupted by an Eisler, Harvard College had better shut down as an educational institution."

Eisler was at least a top party dialectician, and Harvard survived. Now the students refuse to expose themselves to second-rate actors and third-rate novelists. What am I to say to my friends in New Haven, who took Howard Fast a year ago without scuttling and running when they ask what is frightening the students at Cambridge?

I ask again, what are Harvard men so scared about?

Sincerely yours,
Arthur Schlesinger, jr.

---

[*] Gerhart Eisler (1897–1968). German politician; lifetime member of the Communist Party.

[†] Wilbur J. Bender (1904–69). Dean of Harvard College, 1947–52; dean of admissions and financial aid, 1952–60.

To Eugene Meyer[*]

April 13, 1953

[Cambridge, Massachusetts]

Dear Mr. Meyer:

You write that you suspect that I do not understand McCarthy "and therefore cannot understand Eisenhower's handling of the situation."

I may not understand everything about McCarthy, but I understand enough to know that Eisenhower's method of general appeasement is not going to transform McCarthy into a decent, law-abiding citizen, or even into a reliable player on the Republican team.

You probably agreed with the *Post* when it said editorially a year ago, "It is this newspaper's hope and belief that McCarthyism would disappear overnight if Eisenhower were elected." I would bet a great deal that the methods which Eisenhower is following today toward McCarthy are hardly those which you would then have advised or predicted!

Sincerely yours,
Arthur Schlesinger, jr.

To Rebecca West[†]

May 29, 1953

[Cambridge, Massachusetts]

Dear Miss West:

As an old admirer of your work, I am taking the liberty of writing you about your *Sunday Times* articles on "McCarthyism," which, as you know,

---

[*] Meyer had written Schlesinger on April 8, 1953: "In response to your suggestion that I might have welcomed a more Trumanesque attitude toward McCarthy from the White House, I have only this to say: What I suspect is that you do not understand McCarthy and therefore cannot understand Eisenhower's handling of the situation. Moral indignation fits some situations and not others, but I haven't got time to explain and I doubt if you would agree if I tried to."

[†] Rebecca West (1892–1983). English journalist; novelist; literary critic; feminist; author of *Black Lamb and Grey Falcon* (1941); longtime paramour of H. G. Wells.

have just been reprinted here by *U.S. News and World Report.*[*] These articles have caused considerable surprise and dismay in the United States. As one who vigorously shares your conviction of the danger of Communist conspiracy and your alarm over democratic complacency in face of this danger, I want to explain why I share too this surprise and dismay over your articles.

Let me provide a little background (and also supply some of my own credentials). When I got out of the Army in 1945, I was deeply convinced that we were headed for post-war trouble with the Soviet Union, and that the American Communist Party was a conspiracy basically hostile to American liberalism and American freedom. These were not new views on my part; indeed, I had been much disturbed by the complacency which existed in London in the summer of 1944 over post-war prospects (one of the few exceptions I found among your fellow countrymen, oddly enough, was Aneurin Bevan,[†] who then had a vivid sense of the dangers of Soviet expansion and of the incompatibility between Communism and democracy)—as, I must confess, I remain disturbed today over the continued British complacency before the cases of Fuchs[‡] and Pontecorvo[§] and Burgess and Maclean.[¶]

Holding these views, I did what I could to call public attention to what seemed to me the Communist threat. One opportunity was provided me by *Life Magazine,* which asked me in the spring of 1946 to do a piece on the American Communist Party. In the course of research for this piece, I talked to many persons who had knowledge of the Communist movement. One such person was Whittaker Chambers, then a *Time* editor, who had written a favorable review of a book of mine (*The Age of Jackson*) for *Time,* and who told me in detail about the Communist underground in Washington, while

[*] *U.S. News and World Report,* May 22, 1953. West defended Senator McCarthy and the various congressional committees investigating Communist activities in schools, government, and the military.

[†] Aneurin ("Nye") Bevan (1897–1960). Welsh trade union activist; Labour MP, 1929–60; minister of health in the Attlee government, 1945–51; organized the National Health Service in 1948.

[‡] Klaus Fuchs (1911–88). German-British theoretical physicist and Soviet spy convicted in 1950 of passing atomic secrets to the USSR while working on the Manhattan Project in Los Alamos; sentenced to fourteen years in prison.

[§] Bruno Pontecorvo (1913–93). Italian-born nuclear physicist active in Canadian and British nuclear programs; a Soviet spy who defected to Russia in 1950.

[¶] Guy Burgess (1911–63) and Donald Maclean (1913–83). Burgess was a British intelligence officer, Maclean a British diplomat; members of the Cambridge Five spy ring; both defected to Russia in 1951.

stipulating that I could not use the detail in the article. Another man I consulted was Charles E. Bohlen of the Department of State, one of the coolest and most brilliant of our official experts on international Communism, a man who had informed our government for years about the Communist threat, and who indeed had been denounced by *Time* Magazine during the war as excessively anti-Soviet (*Time,* October 18, 1943). Another was James Wechsler, a leading anti-Communist newspaper man, who had been briefly in the Communist movement as a youth and who had just led a mass resignation from the newspaper because of its persistent pro-Communist slant. The result of these and other interviews and research was the first full-length exposure and indictment of the American Communist Party to be published in a national magazine after the war (*Life,* July 29, 1946).

It should perhaps be noted that, in this period, while men like Chambers, Bohlen and Wechsler were trying to rouse an apathetic public opinion about Communism, Joseph R. McCarthy, running against the veteran anti-Communist liberal, Robert M. La Follette jr.,[**] in the Wisconsin Republican primary election, had no hesitation about accepting Communist support. When questioned about this by reporters, McCarthy slyly replied, "Communists have the same right to vote as anyone else, don't they?"

In these years the American government and the American people slowly began to awaken to the nature of the Communist threat. In 1947 President Truman instituted the loyalty program to screen Communists and their agents or dupes out of the federal government. In the same year, the anti-Communist liberals began the fight against their bedizened or treacherous brethren by founding the anti-Communist organization Americans for Democratic Action. In the same year also, the fight against Communists within the Congress of Industrial Organizations (CIO) began to gather steam; it would end with the expulsion of the Communist unions and the election of the anti-Communist leader Walter Reuther as the CIO's president.

In 1948 and 1949 similar acts followed. Alger Hiss was prosecuted and convicted. The leaders of the American Communist Party were prosecuted and convicted under the Smith Act (signed by President Roosevelt in 1940). Coplon[††] and Gubitchev were arrested, and the case against the atomic spies

[**] Robert M. La Follette, Jr. (1895–1953). Progressive senator (R-Wis.), 1925–47; defeated by Joe McCarthy.
[††] Judith Coplon Socolov (1921–2011). Employed in the internal security section of the U.S. Justice Department; arrested in 1949 for passing secret documents to Valen-

was brought near completion. And the activities of the American Communist Party, in opposing the Marshall Plan and sponsoring the Wallace third-party movement of 1948, as well as the behavior of the Soviet Union itself, had left little doubt, except in the minds of the hopelessly bemused, about the sinister intentions of the Stalinist conspiracy. Any American who by January 1940 was not aware of the Stalinist threat was either in a condition of total stupor or else was in the service of the enemy—a fool or a knave. And this awareness and the isolation of Communists in our political and intellectual life had been gained on the whole, by constitutional methods, within our traditional democratic and libertarian framework.

And during all this period, it should be added, Joe McCarthy had nothing at all to say about Communism. It was not until after the fight had been won—in his Wheeling speech on February 9, 1950—that McCarthy publicly recognized Communism as an issue. You portray McCarthy in your articles as a talented but uncouth individual, genuinely devoted, if in a lamentably undisciplined way, to rooting Communists out of positions of power. Nothing could be farther from the truth. He is no more genuinely anti-Communist than the Communists themselves were genuinely anti-fascist. As the Communists exploited anti-fascism as a means of dissolving liberal restraint and rationality and of injecting liberalism with a turbulent madness, so McCarthy today exploits anti-Communism as a means of transforming conservatism into a mad, brutal and unrestrained fanaticism. An American conservative who collaborates with McCarthy's brand of anti-Communism, like a German conservative who collaborated with Hitler's anti-Semitism, becomes thereafter capable of anything.

The greatest fraud perpetrated on the American people in recent years is McCarthy's success in persuading some of them that nothing was done about Communism until he came along. This illusion I think you avoid. But you do fall victim, it seems to me, to the next greatest fraud—that is, the theory that McCarthy is genuinely interested in exposing Communism. I beg you to look at the names of the people on whom he has launched his main attack. The two most recent, for example, have been Charles Bohlen and James Wechsler—the very men who had been fighting Communism for years while McCarthy was accepting Communist support. Yet in McCar-

---

tin Gubitchev, a KGB agent working undercover at the UN Secretariat. Coplon's espionage conviction was reversed on appeal on technicalities.

thy's eyes they become security risks when they refuse to endorse his theory of Yalta or his investigative methods.

Look at some of the other men recently attacked by McCarthy: General George C. Marshall (whom McCarthy rather drastically described as the key figure in "a conspiracy so immense and an infamy so black as to dwarf any previous such venture in the history of man"): or Dean Acheson; or Philip C. Jessup; or Wilson Wyatt, Governor Stevenson's campaign manager and the first national chairman of the anti-Communist organization Americans for Democratic Action; or Bernard De Voto, who, as editor of the *Saturday Review,* had mercilessly ridiculed and attacked the Stalinist attempts to dominate the literary world in the thirties; or Leon Keyserling,[*] chairman of the Council of Economic Advisers; or Archibald MacLeish, the poet; or David D. Lloyd[†] of President Truman's staff; or, for that matter, myself.

Do you really regard this scatter-gun denunciation as useful in the fight against Communism? Or, can you really excuse it as merely amiable ignorance on McCarthy's part of how he is to use (as you perhaps over-delicately put it) "his gifts in harmony with the established practice of civilization"? If so, Goebbels and Zhdanov[‡] had the same disarming failings.

George Orwell used to criticize men on the left for their attempt to be anti-fascist without being anti-totalitarian. It is necessary today, I believe, to criticize equally those on the right who would attempt to be anti-Communist without being anti-totalitarian. We must continue to expose and identify Communist activity, without hesitation or sentimentality; but we would be fools if we swallowed every nostrum hawked under the "anti-Communist" label. In America today, the sentiments and emotions which McCarthy incites and symbolizes are far more dangerous to our freedom than any threat from the political action of American Communists.

George Kennan—along with Bohlen, our closest student of the Soviet tyranny—warned the other day at Notre Dame against the tendency in our own land to make the definition of social conduct a matter of fear in the face

---

[*] Leon Keyserling (1908–87). Lawyer; economist; New Dealer; helped draft the Social Security Act; chairman of President Truman's Council of Economic Advisers.

[†] David D. Lloyd (1911–62). Lawyer; assistant to President Truman, 1951–53; director of the Harry S. Truman Library, 1952–62.

[‡] Andrey Zhdanov (1896–1948). Soviet cultural czar.

of vague and irregular forces, rather than a matter of confidence in the protecting disciplines of conscience and the law. I would know of no moral or political authority for this sort of thing. I tremble when I see this attempt to make a semi-religious cult out of emotional-political currents of the moment, and particularly when I note that these currents are ones exclusively negative in nature, designed to appeal only to men's capacity for hatred and fear, never to their capacity for forgiveness and charity and understanding.

Both McCarthy and the Communists take the fanatic's eye view of the world; they are the crusaders of Either-Or; we must all be for one, or we are for the other. Obviously it is to the advantage of each to break down the robust, thoughtful middle, the vital center, on which freedom and dignity depend—to redefine politics so that every one is herded into one or the other camp. Each thinks his side will benefit by the drawing of the line. Insofar as you minimize the problem of McCarthy, and seek to discredit those who attack McCarthy, you inevitably support the joint Malenkov-McCarthy attempt at redefinition. If that redefinition should ever succeed we are all lost—except, of course, the fanatics and the totalitarians.

I am sorry to write at such length; and sorry too that, having written at such length, I must not trespass on your patience further by pointing out the large number of factual slips which somehow found their way into your pieces. I wholly agree with you that the fight against the Communist conspiracy deserves our most serious attention—and that it has not always received that attention. But I hope you will reconsider your evident belief that this fight can be helped by excusing and prettifying all those who seize the banner of anti-Communism to sanctify their own passion for destruction and their own lust for power.[*]

Sincerely yours,
Arthur Schlesinger, jr.

---

[*] On receiving this letter, West furiously dashed off a telegram: "Unable understand motive behind grossly offensive letter you have had the impertinence to send me.... My record entitles me regard your remarks regarding prettification and excuse of McCarthy and implying defence of scattergun denunciations as smears worthy Goebbels." This was followed by a five-page, single-spaced typed letter denouncing Schlesinger. Years later they became friends, and Schlesinger became the brother-in-law by marriage of Anthony West, Rebecca's son by H. G. Wells.

To Marietta Tree

August 9, 1953

[Cambridge, Massachusetts]

My dearest Marietta:

Your wonderful letter about Adlai at the Salisburys[*] has arrived. I read it with complete delight, liking particularly the story about Adlai's robbery. How did the English visit go off as a whole? The *Sunday Times* piece seemed to me excellent. The *New Statesman* is quite querulous about AES this week, however—a long, disappointed piece by Dick Crossman[†] (possibly because Adlai weekended with the Salisburys),[‡] and a most adverse TV review. Prosecuting my campaign to promote good Anglo-American relations, I have sent a cross letter to Dick, particularly about his view that Adlai could not defend the New Deal heritage because he was anti-Communist and pro-containment. Not that writing to Crossman will do any good; and in any case he will probably be writing the opposite in another six months. I can remember his telling me a few years back how Henry Wallace had betrayed the New Deal by his pro-Soviet positions. I am glad that the Gov. appears happy and cheerful. . . .

We came back sadly from the Cape about a week ago. It was really an extremely good month—relaxing, amusing and generally beneficial. I did very little work, but got caught up on sleep, sun, swimming and my children. And there were a large number of pleasant people about. The latest to enter our lives was Montgomery Clift,[§] the actor, who turns out to be a nice,

---

[*] Near the end of his world tour, Stevenson stopped in England and spent the weekend of July 26–27, 1953, at Hatfield House as a guest of Lord Salisbury, acting foreign secretary, and Lady Salisbury. Others of the party were William McCormick Blair, Jr., who accompanied Stevenson on his trip, and Marietta and Ronald Tree, who were visiting England.

[†] Richard Crossman (1907–74). Socialist intellectual; Labour MP, 1945–74; assistant editor of the *New Statesman,* 1939–55, editor, 1970–72; held cabinet positions in Harold Wilson's government; edited *The God That Failed* (1949) about the failure of Communism.

[‡] Schlesinger suggests that Crossman was irritated that Stevenson accepted the hospitality of a Conservative politician and leader in the House of Lords.

[§] Montgomery Clift (1920–66). Acclaimed American stage and film actor; he had just finished shooting *From Here to Eternity* with Burt Lancaster, Deborah Kerr, and Frank Sinatra, based on the novel by James Jones, directed by Fred Zinnemann.

confused, aspiring and quite likable person. Terribly young in all ways, including chronology: made me feel about 45. (I.e., on the verge of old age.) But now I am back; Marian and the children have gone off to Franklin (the ancestral Cannon family place in N.H.); my beautiful deep tan is fast giving way to Widener pallor (libraries are something like prisons); and soon I will begin to feel as if I had never been away.

I have a feeling that, with the end of the Korean War,* we are entering a new political phase here. Korea has really been the dominant fact in our politics in the last three years, even if many of its effects have been concealed and indirect. I suspect that it accounts more than anything else for the difference between the Democratic victory in '48 and the defeat in '52. And I think that it was really the bitter, protracted frustration over Korea which, along with the Hiss case, made McCarthy possible—or at least which made him the voice of more than the crackpots. As long as Americans were getting killed by Communists in Korea, under conditions in which we were unable to win a decisive victory, people began to get in a lynch-mob mood about Communists at home. They needed an outlet for violent emotions. They wanted to hit back—somehow—at the Communists. They could not get too excited over possible harm to innocent people. Korea, in short, created a climate of anger and anxiety in which McCarthy could thrive.

The truce would seem to change all that. I suspect that the fundamental reason for the stiffening against McCarthy is the end of the war. And, as the emotions stirred by the war recede, McCarthy will be more and more alien to the popular mood and more and more reduced to his lunatic fringe following. I think that this time he may be really on the skids.

If this theory is correct, the death of Taft may not make much difference, because the Republican extremists, no longer sustained by the frustrations of Korea, will have much less sense of popular support and will be much more careful about opposing Eisenhower. So, though Knowland† is

---

* Peace talks had begun in July 1951, but the fighting continued. In November 1952, President-elect Eisenhower visited Korea. On July 27, 1953, UN and North Korean officials signed an armistice with the ceasefire line at the 38th parallel, where the war began. Some thirty-three thousand Americans died in the war. Of the total casualty figure of about four million, half were Korean civilians.

† William F. Knowland (1908–74). Senator (R-Calif.), 1945–59; known as the "Senator from Formosa" for his strong support of Chiang Kai-shek; elected Senate majority leader on Robert Taft's death in 1953; his family controlled the *Oakland Tribune*.

much less a figure than Taft, he will also probably have much less of a tough assignment. And the people in the White House have learned enough in this first session to force Ike into taking a little more initiative.

All this puts me in a fairly pessimistic mood. I suspect that it may take the historians to discover what a bad president Eisenhower was. After all, every one agrees now that Grant* was a terrible president, but he was triumphantly reelected in 1872 and probably could have got a third term in 1880 if he had been able to get the nomination. Given the state of the press, it will take years for an understanding of the new mess in Washington to seep through; and even then it will be blamed for a long time on everybody but Eisenhower. In short, I see no reason why the Republicans should not stay in indefinitely, pending, of course, some bad economic jolts. My personal economic advisors (Seymour Harris† and Ken Galbraith) assure me that one is coming; a lot of economists, like Edwin Nourse,‡ think so, and a lot, like Leon Keyserling, think not. Personally I suspect that there will be enough military spending in the next few years, even with the budget cuts, to take up the slack. (And my pessimism is fortified, I need not add, by the evident determination of the New Yk City Dem. party to commit public hara-kiri. I fear you will have to end up voting for Halley,§ the liberal Roy Cohn.)¶

I felt rather sorry about Taft's death for a while. He really behaved in a gallant way in the last few months. But, as usual, everyone overdid it; people declared that he was the greatest statesman since Henry Clay;** he was

---

* Ulysses S. Grant (1822–85). Commanding general of the U.S. Army at the end of the Civil War; eighteenth president of the United States, 1869–77; a Republican.

† Seymour Harris (1897–1974). Harvard professor of economics, 1945–63; chairman of the economics department at the University of California, San Diego.

‡ Edwin Nourse (1883–1974). Economist, Brookings Institution; first chairman of the Council of Economic Advisers, 1946–49.

§ Rudolph Halley (1913–56). Lawyer; chief counsel to the Kefauver Committee investigating organized crime; the committee's hearings in April 1951 were televised nationally, making Halley a celebrity. He was elected president of the New York City Council in 1951 and ran for mayor on the Liberal Party line in 1953.

¶ Roy Cohn (1927–86). McCarthy crony and chief counsel on the Senate Permanent Subcommittee on Investigations, 1953–54; flamboyant defense lawyer and right-wing fixer in New York Republican politics.

** Henry Clay (1777–1852). Kentucky lawyer; Democratic Republican representative, 1811–14, 1815–21, 1023–25; Speaker of the House for ten years (three different times); senator 1806–7, 1810–11, 1831–42, 1849–52; secretary of state, 1825–29;

the 12th American to have a state funeral in the Capitol; etc. Even for obituaries, most of the writing about him was really awful. I used to know him slightly; and I think that the popular impression of him was almost diametrically wrong. People thought that he was a man of no charm but of great intellectual integrity. The fact is that he was a man of considerable charm and of little intellectual integrity (though this latter was obscured by the fact that he had real strength and integrity of character). Still, in this characterless age, one regrets to see characters disappearing.

I had dinner with Sam Lubell[*] the other night (you remember—the political expert who didn't come to your seance last spring). This deepened my gloom. Sam has a fresh, challenging, realistic approach to these matters which I always find bracing and useful. For him, people and ideas hardly matter at all in politics; he reduces everything to underlying moods and forces (suburbia; racial and religious origins; Korean frustrations, &c), and makes out a good case for this approach in terms of the statistics. He overdoes it, but it corrects my own tendencies in the opposite direction. He doesn't see much immediate hope for the Democrats. And he did say that he thinks Kefauver would have done better than AES last fall—that people could identify with K. much more easily, and that AES didn't register much with the man in the streets. I think he is wrong on this, but nonetheless he has been right on too many things recently.

For the rest, I have been getting quite a lot of work done. But I really hate living alone. I work too much; I can't get to sleep; and I find myself engaged in a futile, sanguinary and losing struggle with the house. A little while ago I pursued a mosquito into the bathroom; it flew to the ceiling out of my reach, so I got on the clothes hamper in order to make the kill. Needless to say, I struck, the hamper fell over, I was catapulted to the floor, my leg going through the hamper and wrecking it; and now I am sore all over, in a number of senses of the word. This kind of thing goes on all the time. Last night I decided to try and cook a steak in the kitchen. I managed to do everything, including setting the steak on fire, ruining it, filling the kitchen

---

three-time candidate for president; proponent of the American System economic plan: high tariffs to foster U.S. industry, federal funding for roads and highways, and a strong national bank. On the slavery issue, he helped broker the Missouri Compromise of 1820 and the Compromise of 1850.

[*] Samuel Lubell (1911–87). Journalist; OWI; public opinion analyst and political pollster.

with smoke, etc.—total fiasco. Also, after the pleasant novelty of the first two days, I don't like being by myself. . . .

I envy you Venice. It is a city I have always greatly liked. I hope you are having a happy and restful time. I also hope you get this letter—I feel it is rather like a message in a bottle. And I look forward so much to your return.

Much, much love,
A

To Marietta Tree

August 16 [1953]

[Cambridge, Massachusetts]

Dearest Marietta:

I have no confidence that this letter will ever reach you, but will send it along nevertheless and thus maintain theoretical contact. This has been a notable week for me, since, after all these years, I have finally begun seriously to write the Roosevelt book. I fear that I will not make the deadline (spring 1956), but it is a tremendous relief to be at last under way.

This is the first piece of serious writing that I have done for a long time, and I had forgotten what it was like. For years I have simply sat down and dashed things off in the expectation that they would meet the day's need and afterward could be forgotten. But this is different; and I had forgotten the *tension* of this kind of writing. It is terribly exciting, when things click, and dismal when they don't (thus far no trouble—fingers crossed), and exhausting all the time. I am aiming to bring it in at around 500,000 words (i.e., slightly longer than *Roosevelt and Hopkins*),* which means that, with luck, I should be able to finish a first draft sometime next summer. Enough of this—I really hate talking about my work most of the time—but I am so astonished and delighted at having finally begun that I had to tell you.

Our boy [Adlai] returns on Thursday. I have to go up to Canada (Lake Couchiching—a Canadian Broadcasting Corporation conference) to give a lecture on that day, so I will be away a good part of the week. I got a pleased

---

* Robert E. Sherwood, *Roosevelt and Hopkins: An Intimate History* (New York: Harper, 1948) was 979 pages, plus illustrations.

letter from Averell saying that Adlai had said he wanted to see him when he came through; so Averell is getting up to meet the 6:45 AM plane! I am glad to see that AES is missing no tricks.

Your analysis of him is so shrewd—especially his technique of saying something so that people (women) will tell him that he can't do that and must do what he intends to do anyway. E.g. here is an excerpt from a letter from a friend in Washington who had just seen Mrs. Roosevelt. "She talked about her conversation with Stevenson in London. Apparently he spoke to her about his willingness to step aside for Symington or Lyndon Johnson[*] or whoever could do a better job of leading the party. For this he got a good scolding from Mrs R. She told him in effect it was hard enough to win when you had the will to win and impossible when you did not. He also reiterated his distaste for the job of rebuilding the Democratic Party in various states and she reported that she had advised him that this was not his job personally but should be delegated to responsible Democratic leaders in Congress and in the states." Really! Do you suppose that marriage would help, or only compound the trouble?

I have seen a couple of State Dept friends this week. The picture continues to be one of unrelieved gloom. One of them said that he had never seen a body of people so united and dedicated in a common purpose as the State Dept employees are in their hatred of John Foster Dulles. There are a good batch of new Dulles stories. The best—evidently a perfectly true one—is about his swearing in the new Ambassador to Canada (another contribution of breakfast food—I believe Quaker Oats—to American diplomacy). "I have had to swear in a number of people in recent months," Dulles informed the new ambassador, "but rarely have I sworn in anyone with such peculiar pleasure. It is very gratifying to have the occasional opportunity to swear in a man who is going to a decent country." This remark was evidently received with something less than peculiar pleasure by the Washington diplomatic corps.

So far as I can see, we have no policy at all for the forthcoming political conference, except to keep attendance and agenda as limited as possible. The basic trouble, I think, is that the administration cannot decide whether

---

[*] Lyndon B. Johnson (1908–73). Representative (D-Texas), 1937–49; senator, 1949–61; senate majority leader, 1955–61; U.S. vice president, 1961–63; thirty-sixth U.S. president, 1963–69.

it should accept Communist China or seek to destroy it. A formidable body of opinion, possibly led by Admiral Radford* (new chairman of the JCS), believes that China will inevitably be an aggressive and expanding power, implacably hostile to the West, and that we had better work to overthrow the regime in these last remaining moments of its weakness. This group has a clearcut policy, redolent with "realism," and Dulles lacks the guts to go against it in any decisive way, probably because of internal politics. So his function is to fuzz everything up which he does with admirable skill.

I have no sympathy for what seems to be a prevalent British viewpoint that Communist China will be a virtuous nation, dedicated to land reform, city planning and the arts; and that we owe her immediate admission to the UN. But the Dulles position that admission to the UN is inconceivable, if not blasphemous, seems to me equally silly. It is all this abstract moralism which has always confused our thinking about foreign policy. The question of admission, it seems to me, depends entirely on what we can get in exchange. I don't think that most Americans are very doctrinaire about this question, and most would go along with a pragmatic approach. But no effort is being made by any one (except Bill Douglas,† to whom no one listens) to counteract the China boys on this point. The voice we hear is that of Bill Knowland, saying that we will leave the UN if China enters. . . . I hardly blame our allies if they begin to think that the US has begun to become a satellite of Syngman Rhee's. (However, I hope to hell the Europeans understand the differential treatment of prisoners of war. Evidently the English were treated well. Not all the Americans were—see clipping.)

I saw a wonderful movie the other night—*The Band Wagon*,‡ with all the old tunes, Fred Astaire,§ Jack Buchanan,⁋ a marvelous new dancer

---

* Arthur W. Radford (1896–1973). Hawkish U.S. Navy admiral; chairman of the Joint Chiefs of Staff, 1953–57.

† William O. Douglas (1898–1980). Liberal U.S. Supreme Court justice, 1939–75; following a mountaineering trip to Asia, he issued a statement in August 1953 calling for recognition of the People's Republic of China.

‡ *The Band Wagon*. MGM musical comedy directed by Vincente Minnelli; screenplay by Schlesinger's latter-day friends Betty Comden and Adolph Green.

§ Fred Astaire (1899–1987). Acclaimed American film and stage dancer; choreographer; singer; actor; starred in *Top Hat, Shall We Dance,* and *Easter Parade.*

⁋ Jack Buchanan (1891–1957). Scottish film and stage actor; singer; producer; director.

named Cyd Charisse,* all done with Minnelli dash and splendor. It is perfect for our generation, and I left drenched with nostalgia. There is something about Astaire which evokes a whole period of my life and of world history for me. I saw both Astaire and Buchanan in shows in London twenty years ago. They seem no older today. Not, alas, true for me.

I trust that you are loving Venice. I have come to feel that you have been gone too long and ought to come back. You don't know how much you are missed.

Much much love,
A.

To James Wechsler

August 28, 1953

[Cambridge, Massachusetts]

Dear Jimmy:

I had hoped we might have a word about the New York mayoralty situation. I have been somewhat disturbed over the failure of the [New York] Post to give any support to Wagner.† I recognize that you are committed to Halley but, within the framework of that commitment, it would still be possible to give Wagner a good deal of support in the Democratic Primaries.

The reason I feel so strongly about this is not that I give a damn who is mayor of New York, but that I care a lot about the future of the Democratic party. The New York Democratic party is the greatest—and almost only—stronghold of liberalism in the national Democratic party. Men like Lehman‡ and Harriman, as you well know, have been the most outspoken Democrats in the country on the issues you care about. The struggle in the Democratic primaries is a struggle for the control of the New York party. If Wagner wins, it means Harriman as the gubernatorial candidate in 1954,

---

* Cyd Charisse (1922–2008). American actress and dancer; appeared in *Singin' in the Rain* and *Silk Stockings*.

† Robert F. Wagner, Jr. (1910–91). Lawyer; son of Senator Robert F. Wagner (D-N.Y.); Manhattan borough president, 1950–53; mayor of New York, 1954–65.

‡ Herbert H. Lehman (1878–1963). Partner of Lehman Brothers; Democratic governor of New York, 1933–42; senator, 1950–57.

Finletter as the senatorial candidate in 1954, a liberal delegation in the 1956 convention, and New York as a powerful liberal voice in the national Democratic party. If Impellitteri[*] wins, it means that Farley[†] will take over. It will mean a succession of Lynches and Cashmores[‡] as state candidates; it will mean a conservative delegation in the 1956 convention; and it will mean that New York will speak with an essentially Dixiecrat voice in national party councils.

These are heavy stakes. Why not give Wagner against Impellitteri some support now; and then, if you want to, back Halley later? What troubles me is the obvious fact that some of the Liberal wiseacres almost certainly are calculating that, if Impellitteri wins the primary, then Halley will inherit most of the Wagner vote; whereas, if Wagner wins, Impellitteri will run as an independent and the decent vote will be split. Therefore, let's lick Wagner immediately. I should hate to see the *Post* connive in this kind of Alex Rose[§]–type calculation. I think that Halley will be elected anyway; but it is more important, in my books, to have a liberal Democratic party in the nation than to have a sharpie Liberal party running New York City.

So how about saying something about the Democratic primaries?

Yours ever,
Arthur

On September 15, 1953, Adlai Stevenson delivered a report to the nation about his world trip, televised from the Civic Opera House in Chicago. "A trip like mine is a sobering experience. It is more than a privilege, it is a responsibility to be an American in this world. It isn't one world, it's more like three worlds—the allied world, the Communist world, and the uncommitted world," he said. *"The ideological conflict in the world doesn't mean much to the masses. Anti-Communist preaching wins few hearts. They want to know what we are for, not just what we are against."*

[*] Vincent Impellitteri (1900–1987). Lawyer; mayor of New York, 1950–53; independent Democrat.

[†] James A. Farley (1888–1976). Businessman; New York political boss; FDR's postmaster general, 1933–40; Coca-Cola executive, 1940–73.

[‡] John Cashmore (1895–1961). Brooklyn borough president, 1940–61.

[§] Alex Rose (1898–1976). Leader of the Liberal Party of New York for more than thirty years.

To Adlai Stevenson

September 20, 1953

[Cambridge, Massachusetts]

Dear Adlai,

Just a line to say that the reactions to the speech around here have been terrific. Everyone felt that this was what had to be said, and is glad and grateful that you said it. Even Dulles seems to have taken some of it to heart.

I heard it near Philadelphia at a conference of Christian Action, an organization of Protestant clergymen of the Niebuhr school. This group, after having been put fairly effectively to sleep by an hour of oratory from me, began to wake up when the television set was wheeled into the room and applauded spontaneously and vigorously when your image came on the screen. But that was nothing to their applause at the conclusion of the speech. . . .

I hope you are making some progress in solving the problems of location and occupation. I still think the best thing would be for you to open law offices with Carl,[*] Bill [Blair],[†] Newt Minow[‡] (to do the work), and one or two other people. Law is the best of all covers for writing or for politics; and I think you could hold down your participation in the tedium of law to a minimum.

Yours ever,
Arthur

---

[*] Carl McGowan (1911–87). Lawyer; counsel to Governor Stevenson, 1949–53; judge of the U.S. Court of Appeals for the District of Columbia, 1963–81.

[†] William McCormick Blair, Jr. (b. 1916). Lawyer; Democratic Party activist; close associate of Adlai Stevenson; ambassador to Denmark, 1961–64, and to the Philippines, 1964–67.

[‡] Newton N. Minow (b. 1926). Attorney; author; chairman of the Federal Communications Commission, 1961–63; famous for calling television "a vast wasteland"; former chairman of PBS board of governors; partner in Chicago law firm Sidley Austin; recruited Barack Obama for a summer associate position.

To Robert Watson[*]

December 16, 1953

[Cambridge, Massachusetts]

Dear Bob:

I was glad to see that your office did not veto the proposal that Owen Lattimore[†] be invited to speak at Harvard. I must say, however, that I was disappointed to read that you had tried to persuade the United Nations Council not to invite Lattimore. I have no use for Lattimore myself; but I think the damage his presence might do to Harvard is far less than the damage that Harvard can do to free education by seeming to waver at all in its defense of the free exchange of ideas.

I think that sometimes we tend to view Harvard's problems too much in terms of Harvard alone. In such a context, considerations of "unfavorable publicity to the College" perhaps bulk too large. The people who want to attack Harvard will attack it whether or not the Lattimores are permitted to speak; nor will official discouragement of such invitations convince them of anything except the fact that the administration is on the run and can be pushed around.

What is really important is the extent to which colleges and universities through the country look to Harvard as the citadel of academic freedom. As the oldest, the best, the richest, and the most independent of American universities, Harvard is in a unique position to say to hell with those who

---

[*] Robert B. Watson (1914–2000). Harvard associate dean; first dean of students, 1958–70; athletic director, 1970–77.

[†] Owen Lattimore (1900–1989). Scholar; teacher; writer; an authority on the history and culture of East Asia with special knowledge of Mongolia; raised in China; served as editor of *Pacific Affairs* (publication of the Institute for Pacific Relations); advised Chiang Kai-shek, 1941–42; ran the Pacific operations of the OWI, 1942–44; taught at Johns Hopkins University, 1936–63. In 1950, Senator McCarthy named Lattimore the top Soviet espionage agent in the United States, a wild accusation that Lattimore fought vigorously. He was eventually exonerated by a Senate committee; federal perjury charges were dismissed in 1955. Lattimore had published an article in *Pacific Affairs* in 1938 praising Stalin's purges, then defended the article, saying of the Moscow trials, "That sounds to me like democracy." Schlesinger considered Lattimore politically befuddled, but no criminal. "I think that the persecution of him . . . has been outrageous," Schlesinger wrote to Lattimore's attorney Paul Porter.

would have us curtail our traditional faith in the free market of ideas. Whenever a Harvard official seems to falter or retreat under pressure, it inevitably weakens the nerve and undermines the position of academic administrators who would like to resist these things, but feel that, if Harvard won't stand up for them, they have little chance of fighting the issues through in the sticks.

In short, I commend your decision; but I feel that, in the present atmosphere, you should have exulted in it rather than to have publicly stated regret that the student organization was persisting in an unwise course against your advice.

I honestly don't see that anything since 1949 has rendered obsolete Bill Bender's classic statement about the importance of exposing undergraduates to the clash of ideas.

Sincerely yours,
Arthur

In a letter to The New York Times, *Robert F. Kennedy[*] attacked the Yalta agreements and supported a proposal to amend the Constitution to limit the "treaty power" of the executive, giving Congress greater control over foreign policy. Arthur found these positions absurd and unacceptable.*

To the Editor of *The New York Times*

February 4, 1954

[Cambridge, Massachusetts]

To the Editor:

Robert F. Kennedy's letter, published Feb. 3, is such an astonishing mixture of distortion and error that it deserves comment. In attempting to rebuke the *Times* for arguing that the trouble at Yalta lay not with the

---

[*] Robert F. ("Bob") Kennedy (1925–68). Lawyer; assistant counsel of the Senate Permanent Subcommittee on Investigations, 1952–53; chief counsel of the Senate Select Committee on Improper Activities in Labor or Management Field (the labor rackets committee), 1957–59; attorney general, 1961–64; senator (D-N.Y.), 1965–68; Schlesinger's close friend by the 1960s.

agreements but with subsequent Soviet violations, Mr. Kennedy suggests that the Yalta Far Eastern agreement gave Manchuria to Soviet Russia. The fact is that the Soviet Union, under the Yalta agreement, pledged that "China shall retain full sovereignty in Manchuria" and further pledged that by China it meant "the National Government of China." Obviously, the Soviet Union, in order to achieve its purposes in the Far East, had thus to break the Yalta agreement. The *Times* was correct in making this point, and Mr. Kennedy is evidently wrong when he attempts to contend otherwise. . . .

Mr. Kennedy's larger point is apparently that the Bricker Amendment* would be a fine thing, because it would subject Executive actions like the Far Eastern agreement at Yalta to Congressional debate. . . . Does Mr. Kennedy really think that so delicate a military matter should have been made the subject of an open debate in Congress? Does he really believe that in the future we should conduct our foreign policy by exposing our most secret and crucial plans to the enemy?

By his own illustration he thus convicts the Bricker amendment of absurdity and danger. Indeed, he shows quite convincingly how very little could be better designed than this amendment to render an alert and flexible foreign policy practically impossible.†

Arthur Schlesinger Jr.

The columnist Joseph Alsop was full of doom and gloom concerning the hydrogen bomb, Communist China, and the security of the United States. He believed that the United States risked "losing" all of Asia to the Communists if the local uprising in Vietnam were allowed to succeed. "Indo-China has already taken on the role of an Asian Czechoslovakia—the position that cannot be let go without disastrous consequences," he and his brother Stewart wrote in one of their columns. He feared that the Russians would have intercontinental ballistic missiles capable of carrying nuclear weapons before the United States possessed these missiles. He believed that the United States was a weakling in

---

* A proposal by Senator John W. Bricker (R-Ohio) to amend the Constitution to limit the "treaty power" of the Executive branch; opposed by the Eisenhower administration, failed by one vote in the Senate on February 26, 1954 (two-thirds majority was required).

† The exchange amused John F. Kennedy, who told Schlesinger: "My sisters are very mad at you because of the letter you wrote about Bobby."

*the world struggle and should pump massive amounts of money into defense
spending.*

*Yet he was excellent in his contempt for McCarthy and McCarthyism, and
he was an old friend, so Arthur respectfully listened him out. "The Alsops regarded communism as a danger* to *America but not a danger* in *America," he
used to say.*

To Joseph Alsop

June 1, 1954

[Cambridge, Massachusetts]

Dear Joe:

I read the article and the columns which you were kind enough to
send. They are excellent and qualify you for whatever gloomy awards
Cassandras deserve. I am sure you are right, both about the emergence
of China as a great new power, and about the inherent feebleness of
the western alliance. As China becomes the more pressing threat, the
alliance will no doubt disintegrate even more—both because Soviet
Russia will appear increasingly amiable, and China will appear increasingly irresistible—unless we suddenly come up with a caliber of leadership which we will not be likely to come up with (at least, not before
1956!)

All these things are true and justify despair (and desperate measures).
Yet I find myself increasingly disturbed by the "preventive showdown" view
which you have sometimes considered in conversation and which is appearing more and more often in the column.* Let me make myself clear: I
am not raising at this point any moral objections to the "preventive showdown" (though I think I have some). If I could be convinced that a "preventive showdown" would really improve matters, I would be prepared to
consider it. But I am convinced that it wouldn't work and that, for this
reason if for no other, it would be gross folly to attempt it.

The only argument for preventive war, it would seem to me, would be

* See, for example, the Alsop brothers' Matter of Fact column of May 28, 1954, in
which they reported that "apologetic yet quite serious talk about a 'preventive showdown' with the Soviet bloc is beginning to be heard in high quarters."

on the supposition that such a war would be a swift, surgical operation, laying the enemy low in a relatively limited period, with a limited expenditure of our own manpower and resources. A preventive war which did not knock out the enemy would only set off a protracted war, infinitely more destructive than any previous war in history; the nation which provoked such a war would operate under insuperable political and moral handicaps; and obviously no nation could emerge in any very convincing sense as the victor. A "preventive showdown," to justify itself, must surely issue in something a little better than *The Shape of Things to Come.*[*]

I do not believe for a moment—nor can I find any atomic scientist around here who does—in the notion that we could launch a knockout blow against either Russia or China. And anything less would surely be fatal (you remember Emerson: "When you strike at a king, you must kill him").

If these propositions are true, then the preventive—or provoked—war thesis is a blind alley. An all-out war today against Communist China, for example, would seem to me (a) a war we could not win in the sense of achieving the unconditional surrender of the Communist regime without a fantastic exertion of our national strength, and (b) a war which, by tying down the bulk of our strength, would expose us to more dangerous aggressions elsewhere ("the wrong war in the wrong place," etc.). This does not mean that we should not try and punish Chinese aggression as we can. But such action would be a response to aggression, and not a preventive showdown; limited and not unlimited in its objectives.

Perhaps I am wrong, but I see no future in this kind of talk, and I see many perils. This is why it disturbs me to see you, who are deservedly one of the influential makers of opinion in America, give this kind of talk currency and even a shading of support. If there is more in it than I think, and if my objections are shallow and irrelevant, I think that such objections at least deserve extended discussion and refutation. It would be a hell of a thing for us to back into preventive war.

You may well ask what alternative there is. I know nothing better than to resume the old policy of building strength and unity where we can in the free world; securing defenses; pushing weapons development; and trying to gain a little political and moral initiative. I want us to have the best radar-net

---

[*] H. G. Wells, *The Shape of Things to Come* (New York: Macmillan, 1933), speculates on future events to the year 2106.

in the world, the most potent Strategic Air Command, the most advanced guided missiles, the most ghastly atomic weapons, the strongest and most prosperous allies, and everything else. If we have these things, we may well deter the enemy from war long enough for the whole relationship to pass into another historic phase. I would rather aim at trying to get these things, remote as present possibilities and present leadership make them; I would rather try to develop a public opinion that would demand them; than to excite false hopes about easy solutions through preventive showdowns.

This is a long and contentious letter, and all I can say is that you brought it on yourself by sending along the article and columns, with most of which I so strongly agree. We hope you will stay with us during Commencement week, and perhaps we can talk some of these things over further then.

Yours ever,
Arthur

From Joseph Alsop

June 4, 1954

[Washington, D.C.]

Dear Arthur:

Thank you for your good letter. I share your revulsion from the hideous thing that I have been writing about; but one must not permit one's human instincts to rule one's reason in this inhuman age. The position is as follows:

First, the geographical-strategic balance between the Soviet and free halves of the world is about to break down for good in Indochina. (The President has decided on a Munich at all costs.) When Indochina is abandoned, all the consequences that we sought to avoid when we went into the Korean war will fall upon us with redoubled force. Throughout Asia, the Middle East and Europe, the demonstration of Soviet strength and Western weakness will discourage our friends, enflame our enemies, and bring the doubters down on the other side. One cannot foretell the precise events or tempo of the process that lies ahead; but I think it will go fast, will go very far, and will be very terrible.

Second, the weapons-balance is turning against us. Today we still retain, if not supremacy, at least decisive superiority in the vital field of air-atomic striking power. Why your scientific friends think we cannot destroy the Soviet Union, when they maintain so stoutly that this country can be destroyed by Soviet air-atomic attack, I really don't understand. At any rate, I don't agree with them. Over a rather short-period, however, this decisive superiority which is now ours will slip away from us. In the next stage, the theoretical threat will be approximately equal, 'though in practice greater to us because of the greater freedom of attack that the Soviets enjoy, the advantage always conferred by surprise, and the greater Soviet investment in protection against attack. In the second stage ahead—and not very far ahead either—decisive superiority is likely to pass to the Soviet Union. That is the meaning of the guided missile picture. There is no time, either, to reverse this trend.

Third, the effects of these two great changes that are now going on are already apparent among our allies. Churchill's reaction to the Indochina crisis is the best case in point, as I wrote the other day.* The totality of peril which already exists for our allies, and will soon exist for us, must dissolve any alliance. Total peril must lead to a universal policy of *sauve qui peut*. And if you think this is a theoretical conclusion, bear in mind the two practical facts. On the one hand, there is no device I know of that can halt the process of disintegration that the loss of Indochina must touch off. On the other hand, there is no way I know of to prevent the rapid turn against us of the weapons-balance. In these circumstances, it is ludicrously unrealistic to talk about reverting to the old policy of building strength. Too much time has been lost, too many opportunities have been wasted. That policy cannot be made to work again.

Fourth, with these prospects before us—and I have never been more filled with that horrible Cassandra-like certainty that these truly *are* the prospects before us—what are we to do? Before one answers this question, certain others must first be answered.

A. The strategic balance and weapons balance together compose the world power balance. If the power balance turns decisively against us, can we escape the fate of all other nations caught in this desperate historical

* The Eisenhower administration was ready to act to help the French in Indochina if U.S. allies went along, but Prime Minister Churchill and the British cabinet vetoed air strikes to relieve French troops besieged at Dien Bien Phu, scuttling the plan. See the Alsops' column of May 17, 1954, entitled "Long Step Nearer to War."

predicament? I say No. In this predicament, there is only Neville Chamberlain's[*] choice, between making a war of despair, and going on your knees to ask terms of the enemy.

B. Are we then to allow ourselves to fall into this predicament? Again, I say No. In the present world circumstances, there are logical arguments for surrender. But I should prefer to be destroyed. There are no logical arguments for the war of despair, combining all the horrors of modern total war with the further horror of surrender to top off.

C. How then are we to avoid Chamberlain's choice? If my analysis is correct, as I believe it is, there is no alternative except to act *before* the final and decisive turn of the power balance. That means preventive action, preventive war if you like.

I know of no escape from this chain of logic except by changing the assumptions, which I believe it is unrealistic to do. I now strongly hold the view that the great error of the Truman administration was the long refusal to face the meaning of the new weapons, and to examine the desirability of a preventive showdown in a clear-minded, realistic manner. Before the Soviets possessed a serious stock of atomic weapons, a preventive showdown was not easy, certainly, but entirely possible. Now, if Indochina goes, there will be no remaining expedient except a preventive attack—for we cannot invite a showdown in such a way as to give them the possibility of attacking first. So there you are.

Tell me where I am wrong if you can. I should like to be convinced; but I will not be persuaded to hope against hope, to play Micawber,[†] or to pretend to myself the facts are not what I know them to be. It has occurred to me that the Governor ought to be acquainted with this line of thinking, which I strongly suspect already dominates our JCS. So send him this letter if you like, with such searing and scathing comments as you may choose to attach to it.

Sincerely,
Joseph Alsop

---

[*] Neville Chamberlain (1869–1940). Conservative British politician; prime minister, 1937–40; signed the Munich Agreement in 1938 conceding the Sudetenland region of Czechoslovakia to Germany; known for his failed appeasement policy.
[†] A reference to Wilkins Micawber, a character in *David Copperfield* (1850) by Charles Dickens, who, despite being poor, lived in expectation of better fortune, believing always that "something will turn up."

To Richard Rovere

[July 1954]

Wellfleet, Mass[achusetts]

Dear Dick:

We are down at Wellfleet* again, surrounded by writers. Last time I looked at the beach I saw Alfred Kazin† and Saul Bellow.‡ Also the old standbys—Mary [McCarthy], Edmund W.,§ [Francis] Biddles, Kahns,⁵ Duffys, etc. Plus Harry Levin,** Gilbert Seldes†† and other anomalous & ill-assorted types.

We do not have nearly so snappy a house as last year, though much more convenient to the beach (in fact, right on it) and reasonably isolated. I have been spending my time since arrival reading the Oppenheimer‡‡ tran-

---

* The town of Wellfleet, Massachusetts, near the tip of Cape Cod, with its Atlantic shoreline and wide sandy beaches, was a summer haven for writers, academics, artists, actors, architects, and psychoanalysts. The Schlesingers had a small house on Slough Pond in a wooded area now part of the Cape Cod National Seashore.

† Alfred Kazin (1915–98). Liberal writer; literary critic; cultural historian; author of *On Native Grounds* (1942).

‡ Saul Bellow (1915–2005). Canadian-born American novelist; author of *The Adventures of Augie March* (1953), *Herzog* (1964), and *Humboldt's Gift* (1975), winner of the Nobel Prize for Literature in 1976.

§ Edmund Wilson (1895–1972). Writer; critic; noted man of letters; long association with *The New Yorker;* author of *To the Finland Station* (1940), *Patriotic Gore* (1962); married to novelist Mary McCarthy, 1938–46.

⁵ E. J. Kahn, Jr. (1916–94). Writer at *The New Yorker*.

** Harry Levin (1912–94). Harvard professor of comparative literature.

†† Gilbert Seldes (1893–1970). Influential writer and social critic; author of *The Seven Lively Arts* (1924); father of actress Marian Seldes.

‡‡ J. Robert Oppenheimer (1904–67). Brilliant, controversial left-wing American theoretical physicist; professor at the University of California, Berkeley, in the 1930s; led scientists of the top-secret Manhattan Project in Los Alamos, New Mexico, building the atomic bombs dropped on Hiroshima and Nagasaki in 1945; served as director of the Institute for Advanced Study at Princeton, 1947–66. Oppenheimer was a key postwar adviser on nuclear issues and argued against development of the hydrogen bomb, prompting some to question his loyalty, or his judgment, especially his fellow physicist Edward Teller of the Manhattan Project and the Lawrence Livermore National Laboratory, known as "the father of the hydrogen bomb." Teller was considered Stanely Kubrick's inspiration for the character of Dr. Strangelove in the 1964 movie *Dr. Strangelove or: How I Learned to Stop Worrying and Love the Bomb.*

script[*]—992 pages, fine print, nothing like it since the Moscow trials. I consider the verdict, after due brooding and contemplation, as really the most outrageous miscarriage in this whole age of madness. I cannot for the life of me see how reasonable men could have reached the conclusion they did on the basis of the record.

I shall speak at Bard on the morning of Aug 3 (Tues) and shall count on staying with you Monday night (Aug 2), if that is convenient. Must be in NY City Tues night. Let me know if this is not OK. It is too long since we have held the necessary autopsies on our times.

Best to all Roveres.
Yrs ever,
Arthur

To Estes Kefauver

August 19, 1954

[Cambridge, Massachusetts]

Dear Estes:

Just a line to send my warmest congratulations and thanks for your vote [against] the bill making membership in the Communist party a federal crime.[†] It is an action which you will look back on with pride at a time

---

[*] *In the Matter of J. Robert Oppenheimer: Transcript of Hearing Before Personnel Security Board* (United States Atomic Energy Commission). After AEC hearings in April and May 1954, Oppenheimer was stripped of his security clearance. Teller testified that, so far as loyalty was concerned, he saw no reason to deny clearance, but "if it is a question of wisdom and judgment as demonstrated by actions since 1945, then I would say one would be wiser not to grant clearance." The AEC concluded Oppenheimer had maintained "imprudent and dangerous associations" and exhibited "substantial defects of character," Schlesinger reported in *The Atlantic Monthly* of October 1954. President Kennedy awarded Oppenheimer the Enrico Fermi Award as a gesture of political rehabilitation in 1963.

[†] Senator Humphrey in a last-minute move to defeat a more pernicious Republican proposal and reestablish Democratic bona fides on the Communist issue before the November 1954 elections (he was running for a second term) had brashly conceived of the Communist Control Act, outlawing the Communist Party. The bill passed the Senate 81–1; only Kefauver voted against it. The sponsor in the House was the notorious Martin Dies, Jr., the Texas congressman who was the first chairman of the House Un-American Activities Committee (HUAC).

when many of your liberal colleagues will look back at their cowardice with shame.

One of the worst results of their foolishness is to kick away one of our best campaign issues—the Democratic party as the party of responsible and constructive opposition. After the childish performance of the last few days, it will be hard for Democratic orators to claim to be much more responsible than the Republicans themselves. This is a fearful price to pay for a few moments of visceral satisfaction.

Very sincerely yours,
Arthur

To Hubert H. Humphrey, Jr.

September 14, 1954

[Cambridge, Massachusetts]

Dear Hubert:

I went to Central America for a fortnight just as Congress was adjourning, and have only now returned to find, among other things, a pile of correspondence provoked by a column I wrote for the *New York Post* just before I left. This column had to do with the so-called Communist control bill; in it I expressed my objections both to the bill and to the manner in which it was passed. Most of the correspondence agreed with my viewpoint, but some of it rather shocked me by the virulence of its criticism of you. I have accordingly written to these people that a man with your record of courage and achievement in public service and in the liberal cause has a right to be judged by his total record, and not by a single (as it seems to me) aberration; and that your return to the Senate must continue to be a major liberal goal in the fall elections.

I have reread my own column, which was written in haste and under stress; and I find there certain regrettable phrases* about you which may

---

* "A fine record on the serious issues of this session has largely been kicked away by a collection of hot heads running wild like kids after their first glass of beer on a picnic," Schlesinger wrote in his History of the Week column in the *New York Post* of August 22, 1954. Humphrey and other liberal Democrats will "look back on their behavior with shame and wonder."

have piled fuel on the anti-Humphrey fire and which I would not now write again. I must confess, however, that I continue to be dismayed by the bill itself and by the manner in which it was bulled through the Senate. Had I been in the country, I would have written you at length at the time. But I do not think it is too late now to set forth my own doubts about this performance. I don't hope to persuade you of anything; but I do think you should know what many people who have respected you in the past—and who still respect you and ardently desire your reelection—nevertheless think about the anti-Communist bill.

In the first place, this bill represents a unique and unprecedented act on the part of the Congress. Never before in history has a political party been outlawed. Obviously so spectacular a departure from our previous customs and traditions should have been accorded the most sober congressional consideration. If we ever needed to employ the usual apparatus of committees, hearings, reports, and so on, this was the time. The most routine bills receive this treatment; why should so drastic and unusual a bill as this not get the same treatment? Surely no one could argue that the threat was so great that the republic would have been overthrown if this action had been delayed until the next session of Congress. I really can see no justification for this kind of legislation-by-stampede.

I also have grave doubts about the substance of the bill. I should first make clear, however, that I do not think that outlawing the Communist party necessarily presents a civil liberties issue. If I lived in Costa Rica, for example, where I have just been, I would support the action of President Figueres* who outlawed the Communist party in 1948. I do not put much stock in the argument that driving the C.P. underground makes it harder to deal with. I feel that if the Communist conspiracy inside America presents any kind of substantial threat which can be more effectively dealt with by outlawing the party, I would be for it.

But I do not favor this outlawry as a gratuitous act, simply because I do not feel that any contraction of our freedoms should be encouraged in this period unless the facts overwhelmingly require it. It is absurd to say that the Communist Party presents a greater threat today than it did in 1946, when

*José Figueres Ferrer (1906–90). President of Costa Rica, 1948–49, 1953–58, and 1970–74. During his first term, he abolished the army, nationalized the banking sectors, outlawed the Communist Party, and granted women and blacks the right to vote.

you and I in our various ways were trying to awaken the liberal community to the Communist danger. It is absurd to say that the Communist Party presents a greater threat today than it did in 1936. Yet the republic survived without resort to drastic measures in the thirties and the forties; and I do not think that the exercise of combatting Communist candidates, Communist arguments, Communist agents and Communist spies has weakened America. We licked a strong Communist movement to a frazzle by democratic means. For us now to say before the world that we no longer can cope with Communism by these means, that we dare not have the party operate or permit it access to the ballot or the mails—at a time when U.S. Communism has faded to a whisper—all this seems to me a confession of weakness, which can only persuade the rest of the world that we have indeed gone mad. If you had demanded in 1946 that the Communist party be outlawed, . . . your position would have been consistent. But to accept its existence when it was strong and now to outlaw it when it is weak seems to me an odd and futile position.

I should add that your amendment designed to make membership in the Communist Party a federal offense seemed to me to raise the most acute administrative problems. This amendment would surely have committed the Department of Justice to the immediate prosecution of all 25,000 of the current members of the Communist Party. I cannot feel that such a collective prosecution, with the spectacle of panic and repression it would present to the world, could have been justified for a moment by any threat which these 25,000 people brought to American security that could not have been handled better in some other way.

I am told that this was a smart political act. I don't believe this for a moment. It has manifestly not eliminated Communism or McCarthyism as an issue in the campaign. And it has destroyed one of the best Democratic talking-points—that is, that we have been an intelligent and responsible opposition. Our opposition record was excellent, until this bill came up. Thereafter, as some one said to me the next day, the Democrats started to behave like Republicans. Today no Democratic orator can boast of his party's record in Congress as constructive and responsible and keep a straight face. If we should continue behaving this way, why should the electorate feel that putting the Democrats in power is going to make material difference to the governing of the country?

I am glad to note that Wayne Morse[*] now concedes that the bill "has some legislative hodgepodge characteristics" and that "it is going to raise a good many administrative problems and serious questions of public policy." He adds, "If time had permitted, the best procedure to have followed would have been to send the entire bill . . . back to the Judiciary Committee"—with which I wholly agree, except that I do not understand why time did not permit. Wayne has announced his intention to prepare amendments to the bill for introduction in the next session. I honestly feel that you would strengthen your position now if you would say that you intend to join Morse in calling for a reconsideration and improvement of the bill at the start of the next session.

I am sorry to write at such length. I do want to make it clear that while I differ with you vigorously on this issue, I regard your re-election to the Senate as important as ever. I had no hesitation about signing the ADA letter asking for funds to help in sending you back. But I do not think that you should underestimate the doubts over your proposal, and even more over the manner of its enactment; and I hope you do not feel that those who differ with you in this matter are in some sense "soft" on Communism.

Anyway best of luck in the campaign![†]

Sincerely yours,
Arthur

---

[*] Wayne Morse (1900–1974). Law professor; maverick politician; elected senator from Oregon in 1945 as a Republican, became an independent in 1953, and a Democrat in 1955; one of only two senators (along with Alaska Democrat Ernest Gruening) to vote against the 1964 Gulf of Tonkin Resolution authorizing expansion of U.S. involvement in the Vietnam War; defeated for reelection in 1968.

[†] In the 1954 midterm election, the Republicans lost eighteen seats in the House, giving Democrats the majority, which they held until 1995. Republicans lost two seats in the Senate, giving the Democrats the majority, held until 1981. Humphrey was reelected by a wide margin.

To Adlai Stevenson

February 15, 1955

[Cambridge, Massachusetts]

Dear Adlai:

. . . As I have said before, I do not share the current Democratic pessimism about the party's prospects in '56. I think we have a reasonable chance of winning. . . .

I am really convinced that the one important doubt the American people have about you is whether you want to be President. (Don't say, "They are right!") The people regard this as the highest honor they have in their power to bestow; and they do not want to have to force it on people, or to coax them to accept it, or to see them indecisive and Hamletish in face of it. I think that if the image you present to the electorate in the spring and summer of 1956 is one of reluctance and hesitation, you may win the nomination by default but will lose the election. But I think that, if the image you present is one of clarity, vigor and decision, you will have an excellent chance of beating Eisenhower. . . .

I need not add that you—and nearly everybody else—know far more about politics than I do, and my views are to be judged accordingly. All I care about is having a good President in 1956 so that my children will have a better chance of living in a non-apocalyptic future. . . .

Yours ever,
Arthur

When Stevenson considered going on a fact-finding trip to South America, Arthur advised him not to include Venezuela on his itinerary and followed up with a letter to Adlai's associate, Bill Blair, detailing his reasons.

To William McCormick Blair, Jr.

February 15, 1955

[Cambridge, Massachusetts]

Dear Bill:

Before I forget it, I want to raise a warning flag concerning the question of Venezuela. The Governor seemed surprised when, in discussing the Latin American trip, I said that he should by all means stay away from Venezuela. I really think that this is terribly important. Venezuela at present is being ruled by a rather squalid dictator named Perez Jimenez.* This character overthrew a sound, progressive, anti-Communist regime based in good part on the trade unions. I do not see how the Governor could visit Venezuela without having some contact with the regime; and a picture of Stevenson shaking hands with Perez Jimenez would profoundly disappoint and disillusion the people in the hemisphere who most admire Stevenson and are most like him, from Munoz Marin† down. Perez stands for exactly the kind of thing we have to get away from in the hemisphere.‡ . . .

Yours ever,
Arthur

---

* Marcos Pérez Jiménez (1914–2001). President of Venezuela, 1952–58 (installed by coup, overthrown by coup); later charged with stealing $200 million, imprisoned for five years, and exiled to Spain.

† Luis Muñoz Marín (1898–1980). Puerto Rican poet, journalist, and politician; the first democratically elected governor of Puerto Rico, 1949–65; awarded the Presidential Medal of Freedom by JFK.

‡ The Latin American trip was delayed. Stevenson visited Venezuela in April 1960 on a six-week tour of twelve Latin American countries. He met with Venezuela's new president, Rómulo Betancourt, elected after Pérez Jiménez's ouster. Betancourt's daughter took Stevenson on a tour of the Caracas slums. "All Venezuelans evidently passionate Democrats and Stevenson fans!" he wrote in his diary.

To Jacob Fine*

May 9, 1955

[Cambridge, Massachusetts]

Dear Jack:

Thank you for sending me Mr. McWilliams's letter, which I herewith return. It strikes me as a characteristically disingenuous product. His statement that "*The Nation* never in its history indicated the slightest interest in or sympathy for Communism" is really beyond belief, unless one is to assume that Mr. McWilliams† never reads the magazine he edits.

I would not dream of writing for the *Nation* because the *Nation* has practically no connection with the kind of liberalism with which I am concerned. For me, liberalism implies clearcut and enthusiastic anti-totalitarianism, both anti-fascism and anti-Communism. I see no reason why a liberal should be any more apologetic about being one than about being the other. Yet the *Nation*, while admiring anti-fascism, deplores anti-Communism. Mr. McWilliams's attitude toward anti-Communist liberals was concisely indicated by his description of me as one "who speaks the language of McCarthy with a Harvard accent" (*New Statesman*,‡ Octo-

---

* Jacob Fine (1900–1980). Chief of surgery at Boston's Beth Israel Hospital, 1948–65; professor of surgery at Harvard Medical School.

† Carey McWilliams (1905–80). Lawyer; writer; left-wing political activist; editor of *The Nation* magazine, 1955–75. Fine had recently spent an evening with Schlesinger and Bernard De Voto and then written McWilliams that Schlesinger remarked that "he would not write for the *Nation* because he did not think its policy with respect to communism was straightforward and that it wavered between a sympathetic attitude and neutralist attitude most of the time, and was seldom sufficiently antagonistic." McWilliams sent Fine a list of articles published in 1953 "to show how utterly groundless is the contention you mention." But Schlesinger's complaints went back to the 1930s when *The Nation* tolerated Stalin's purges. "In spite of the trials, I believe Russia is dependable; that it wants peace, and will join in any joint effort to check Hitler and Mussolini. . . . Russia is still the strongest reason for hope," Freda Kirchwey, *The Nation*'s editor from 1933 to 1955, wrote in 1938, a year before the Hitler-Stalin pact. In his *New York Post* column of May 3, 1953, Schlesinger wrote that *The Nation* and McWilliams lived "in a dream world where Communists are the honest if crude agents of social revolution and Americans fight Communism because they fear social reform." (See the Ruth and David Freiman Archives at the Beth Israel Deaconess Medical Center.)

‡ *New Statesman*. British political and cultural magazine founded in 1913 by democratic socialists of the Fabian Society.

ber 27, 1951)—this at a time when the *New Leader** crowd regards people of my general views as dangerously soft on Communism!

So far as I know, the *Nation* still believes that American liberals and American Communists can and should work together in organizations. So far as I know, the *Nation* still regards attempts to identify and expose Communist influence in the liberal and labor community as McCarthyism. So long as this is the case, I cannot but regard the *Nation* as a morally sick magazine, still infected with the illusion that "somehow" there is a kinship between liberalism and Communism. I see absolutely nothing in common between liberalism and Communism, either as to means or as to ends; and I cannot but regard those who take the *Nation*'s position on these issues as the Typhoid Marys of the liberal community.

Sincerely yours,
Arthur

John F. Kennedy suffered from back problems beginning in 1938. He took steroids as a youth for colitis, which doctors partly blamed for thinning of his bones. He had an operation on his back in 1944 after his PT-109 ordeal. He mitigated pain through medications and a back brace. After a double spinal fusion operation on October 21, 1954, he fell into a coma and last rites were administered. He recovered and, after a second operation, returned to the Senate on crutches at the end of May 1955.

From John F. Kennedy

June 11, 1955

[Washington, D.C.]

Dear Arthur:

During my recuperation from the operation on my back, I have written a book on "political courage." Most of the book is devoted to the stories of eight Senators who risked or ended their careers by conscientiously speak-

---

* *The New Leader.* Liberal, anticommunist political and cultural magazine founded in New York City in 1924.

ing out for the principles in which they believed in opposition to the strong views of their constituents. Introductory and concluding chapters will attempt to point out the implications these stories have today. The manuscript has been accepted for publication by Harper's, who expects to publish it about the first of January next year.

Would you be so good as to review the manuscript within the next few weeks, and give me your frank criticisms, comments and suggestions? I would certainly be appreciative for whatever you could do to improve its historical accuracy, style and interest and general contribution; and if you feel that any or all of these chapters are inadequate, I would be most grateful if you would frankly tell me so.

Thanks very much for your consideration in this matter, and I hope I have the opportunity of seeing you in the not too distant future.

With every kind wish,
Sincerely yours,
John F. Kennedy

To John F. Kennedy

June 14, 1955

[Cambridge, Massachusetts]

Dear Jack:

I have been meaning to write and say how delighted we all are that you are back in Washington again. I am sorry that I had to miss the Jefferson-Jackson Day Dinner, but everyone says that you looked in fine shape.

I should be glad to take a look at your book. I am leaving for Wellfleet on Friday, June 17th; so you had better send it to me there. We will be there until the middle of July. Hope to see you before too long.

Yours ever,
Arthur

To Adlai Stevenson

June 15, 1955

[Cambridge, Massachusetts]

Dear Adlai:

. . . It seems to me that people might respond to some pointing up of the contrast between the increasing and staggering abundance in our private economics and the increasing dilapidation, neglect and impoverishment of our public efforts. The fact that the richest nation in the history of the world is unable to devote an adequate share of its resources to education, health, police protection, maintaining its national parks, keeping its streets clean; etc. is something which touches all Americans. It also provides a means of getting the problem of government outside of the government-centralization-versus-the-people framework into which the Republicans have successfully put it. . . .

I do feel that there is an issue lurking there, if we only could get it out.

Yours ever,
Arthur

From John F. Kennedy

June 23, 1955

[Washington, D.C.]

Dear Arthur:

I am most grateful for your willingness to read my manuscript on "political courage" which I am enclosing. Unfortunately, I have not yet completed the introductory and concluding chapters, which will attempt to provide some analysis of the meaning of political courage and its implications for today, and whatever conclusions can be drawn from the stories retold in the book.

As I indicated in my previous letter, I hope you will be ruthlessly frank in giving me your criticism, comments and suggestions, however major or however petty—not only on the historical accuracy of these chapters, but also on the general themes, style, interest and overall contribution. I am sincere in saying that if any or all of these chapters are inadequate, I would prefer to hear from you now. Feel free to make any comments and corrections you may desire in the margin of this mimeographed draft, of which I have several extra copies. Unfortunately, as is so often the case in these matters, the publisher's deadline looms more closely than I had realized; and thus I am anxious to receive your comments at your earliest convenience.

Thanks again for your gracious help on this project.

With every kind wish,
Sincerely,
John F. Kennedy

To Richard Sundt*

June 28, 1955

[Wellfleet, Massachusetts]

Dear Mr. Sundt:

I read your letter with interest. It would be easy enough to suggest a list of American radical authors—[Thomas] Paine, John Taylor of Carolina, the early [Orestes] Brownson, [Edward] Bellamy, [Henry] George, Jack London, Randolph Bourne, [Thorstein] Veblen, John Dewey, [Charles A.] Beard, etc.—but, when you ask for those who have influenced the development of one's own thinking, I find the problem much more difficult. I don't think any of those in the above list, except Beard,† ever had much impact on me.

Usable radicalism, in the sense of a radical tradition, implies, I think, two things: a willingness to tackle questions fearlessly and fundamentally, without regard to respectable opinion; and a spontaneity in response and expression, which has the effect of challenging and shaking up accepted attitudes and values. These qualities of radicalism, it seems to me, are far more alive and liberating than the sponsorship of any concrete social program. We do not particularly need today "radical" social and economic programs. My guess is that we can achieve great things for equality and

* Richard Sundt of San Francisco, California.
† Charles A. Beard (1874–1948). Progressive American historian; Columbia University, 1904–17; author of *An Economic Interpretation of the Constitution of the United States* (1913).

opportunity within the framework of a mixed economy and a welfare state—and that we can achieve more for people within this framework then by any form of social reorganization of which I have heard. Where we need radicalism today is in the moral and cultural areas of life; we need the revindication of the rights of spontaneity, of criticism, of dissent. What we need, above all, is a restoration of the sense that nothing is sacred so far as human inquiry and comment are concerned.

In this sense of the word radicalism—in the sense of an insistence on radical freedom of judgment—the American authors who have meant the most to me are these:

Emerson,[*] Thoreau[†] and Whitman:[‡] because all, in different ways, saw things freshly and fearlessly; because all loved America and erected standards for it and criticized it when it fell short of its promise; because all embodied the moral and cultural radicalism I think we need so desperately today.

William James: because he had the same qualities in a more urbane, skeptical, relaxed way; because he was a man of great sensitivity, intelligence and wit, never afraid to call the shots as he saw them.

Reinhold Niebuhr: because of living Americans he has, in my judgment, the most disinterested, penetrating and radical judgment on issues and life; because he has shown so profoundly the possibilities and relevance of Christian radicalism and Christian realism.

H. L. Mencken: a man whose specific positions on political and economic issues seem to me to have been largely terrible; but whose attitude toward America and life was immensely exhilarating and liberating—radical in precisely the sense of spontaneity, irreverence, nothing sacred, not caring a damn, saying anything which would rile people and make them reconsider what they had always assumed before, and saying it in a marvelously ordered and comic style.

---

[*] Ralph Waldo Emerson (1803–82). Poet; philosopher; essayist; lecturer; leader of the transcendental movement; preached self-reliance.

[†] Henry David Thoreau (1817–62). Writer; poet; philosopher; abolitionist; author of "Civil Disobedience" (1849) and *Walden, or Life in the Woods* (1854).

[‡] Walt Whitman (1819–92). Poet; essayist; journalist; author of *Leaves of Grass* (1855) and *Democratic Vistas* (1871).

Theodore Roosevelt,* [Woodrow] Wilson, Franklin Roosevelt,† Herbert Croly:‡ because they all show in different ways that people can be successful in politics, can make the compromises that democracy demands, and at the same time retain a large measure of freedom and integrity.

Among contemporaries, in addition to Niebuhr, people like the following have, it seems to me, radical qualities in different ways: Edmund Wilson, Harry Truman, Mary McCarthy, Al Capp,§ David Riesman, Elmer Davis, Thornton Wilder,¶ Ernest Hemingway,** Richard Rovere, James Wechsler, James Thurber,†† Bernard De Voto, Saul Steinberg,‡‡ Thomas Finletter. Recent radical books, I would say, were Davis's *But We Were Born Free*, Murray Kempton's§§ *Part of Our Time*, Jonathan Daniels's¶¶ *End of Innocence*, Riesman's *Lonely Crowd*.

I should be much interested in the general results of your inquiry.

Sincerely yours.
Arthur

---

* Theodore Roosevelt (1858–1919). Writer; naturalist; cowboy; reformer; Rough Rider; Republican governor of New York, 1899–1900; U.S. vice president, 1901; twenty-sixth U.S. president, 1901–9; candidate of the Progressive Party for president 1912.

† Franklin D. Roosevelt (1882–1945). Theodore Roosevelt's fifth cousin; assistant secretary of the navy, 1913–20; Democratic governor of New York, 1929–32; thirty-third U.S. president, 1933–45; created the New Deal; won World War II; suffered from polio.

‡ Herbert Croly (1869–1930). Exponent of progressivism; author of *The Promise of American Life* (1909), cofounder of *The New Republic* in 1914.

§ Al Capp (1909–79). Cartoonist and humorist; creator of *Li'l Abner*.

¶ Thornton Wilder (1897–1974). Novelist and playwright; author of the Pulitzer Prize–winning *Our Town* (1938).

** Ernest Hemingway (1899–1961). Author and journalist; author of *The Sun Also Rises* (1926), *A Farewell to Arms* (1929), and *The Old Man and the Sea* (1951); winner of the Nobel Prize in Literature 1954; committed suicide.

†† James Thurber (1894–1961). Author; cartoonist; longtime contributor to *The New Yorker*.

‡‡ Saul Steinberg (1914–99). Romanian-born American cartoonist and illustrator; best known for his work for *The New Yorker*, including almost ninety covers.

§§ Murray Kempton (1917–97). Liberal journalist; author; winner of the Pulitzer Prize and the National Book Award; wrote for the *New York Post*, *Newsday*, *The New Republic*, and *The New York Review of Books*.

¶¶ Jonathan W. Daniels (1902–81). Writer; novelist; editor of the Raleigh, North Carolina *News and Observer*; FDR's press secretary, 1943–45.

To John F. Kennedy

July 4, 1955

[Wellfleet, Massachusetts]

Dear Jack:

I have read your book with great interest and admiration. It seems to me, in the main, historically sound, skillfully written and a genuine contribution to political discussion. You deserve a lot of credit for having spent your months of convalescence in musing about the American past. I very much hope the results of your inquiry rub off on some of your colleagues!

I assume you will probably have an opening chapter defining political courage, and a final chapter of conclusions (in which I hope you will point out that political courage pays off politically more often than many politicians assume). On the chapters I have read, I have the following comments (I am writing this down at Wellfleet, where I am far removed from reference works, so I have assumed the factual accuracy of the narrative passages):

PROLOGUE TO CHS 3, 4 AND 5

Page 2, middle paragraph: I think you should mention the Mexican War here. The acquisition of territory as a result of this war was a major factor in accelerating the pace of the slavery controversy and in bursting the seams of compromise.

Page 4, line 17: suggest "believed" rather than "realized."

Ch 3 (Webster). I think this is a defensible chapter, but it is not particularly persuasive to me. In the first place, I think you assume too easily that Webster was right in his stand on the Compromise. For my money, Zachary Taylor,* a much underrated President, was right. The southern political drive to dominate the Union at any cost had to be stopped. Taylor, Seward and others saw the issue and resolved to hold the line. Webster dodged the issue, fuzzed it up with irrelevant rhetoric and recommended a course of appeasement of the South. If this was an act of political courage, so was Munich; indeed, you justify the Compromise by identically the arguments which Chamberlain fans invoke to justify Munich. In the second place,

---

*Zachary Taylor (1784–1850). A military leader serving forty years in the army; a Whig, he was the twelfth U.S. president, 1849–50.

even if Webster was wrong, he could still have been politically courageous by undertaking an unpopular course; but I do not think his course was particularly unpopular among his primary constituents—ie., the northern business community. Most northern businessmen were pro-slavery, and they all thought Webster was wonderful. The people who were indignant at him were mostly eggheads, liberals, etc., who never thought much of him anyway.

I think you are nearer right in the next chapter when you seem to approve Benton's opposition to the Compromise.

Page 2, lines 5–6: I question whether Webster was "undoubtedly the most talented parliamentary figure in our history." This phrase suggests skill as a parliamentarian, like Lyndon Johnson, and is not probably what you mean. You might be right if you said "the most impressive orator who ever sat in the Senate." I do not remember that Webster was particularly hot as a parliamentarian.

Page 4, next to last line: "repealing the Wilmot Proviso"?—was the Wilmot Proviso ever enacted?

Page 12, middle paragraph: what you say about the consequences of the Compromise is a defensible position; it is precisely the case made for Munich. But if statesmanship implies a capacity to see the real issues, then the architects of the Compromise were far from statesmen. Webster never saw either the political issue of southern domination of the Union or the moral issue of slavery.

Page 13, 4th line from bottom: Seward was a Whig, not a Free-Soiler (upper case). He was, of course, a free-soil Whig; but the Free Soil party was a separate party after 1848.

CH 4 (BENTON)

Page 1, line 14: "equally"?—I doubt whether any sarcasm, even Benton's, could be described as equal to bullets!

Page 8: "gentle" seems to be hardly the adjective for JQ Adams, especially in view of your own excellent characterization of him earlier.

CH 7 (LAMAR)

Page 6, line 11: "Stephens" (not "Stevens")

Pages 12–13: Lamar may well have displayed political courage in opposing free silver; but it is by no means clear that the sound money people were right on the economic issue, and the inflationists were wrong. Many modern economists (Alvin Hansen and Seymour Harris, for example) would contend that economic expansion is impossible without constant enlargement of the means of purchase; that the soft money forces have consequently advocated monetary policies which promoted economic expansion, while the hard money forces have advocated policies which would have held back economic expansion; and that the rate of economic expansion could be relied upon to take up the monetary slack, so that the inflation fear was pretty much a bugaboo (as shown by the general price stability in this period). I doubt whether you could find a modern economist who would regard the Bland Act, for example, as a bad thing.

As I said above, this does not disqualify the episode as an example of political courage. But I do not think that you should write about it in a way which suggests that Lamar was, of course, correct on this issue. The respectable position (which Lamar took) is not always the right position!

PROLOGUE TO CHS. 8, 9

Page 1, first para, last sentence: I question this. My guess would be (as your text later implies, cf. pp. 2–3) that the low point of senatorial prestige came in the 80s and 90s, with another low point in the 1920s. But for most of Norris's career and all of Taft's senatorial career, the political profession enjoyed much higher popular esteem than it had in the last quarter of the 19th century.

Page 4, last para: if you are going to couple Norris and Taft, I think you should mention the contrasts as well as the similarities. E.g., Norris's remarkable constructive achievements (TVA, Norris-LaGuardia Act, lame duck amendment, Nebraska's unicameral legislature, etc.) as contrasted with Taft's almost negative legislative career (unless one regards the Taft-Hartley Act as a great constructive achievement); or Norris's lack of personal ambition as contrasted with Taft's gnawing passion for the Presidency.

CH. 8 (NORRIS)

Page 15: in view of your characterization of Norris as an isolationist, it might be well to note that Norris changed his views in the late thirties and became a loyal and effective supporter of the Roosevelt foreign policy.

CH. 9 (TAFT)

I am not persuaded by this chapter at all, and it seems to me less defensible than the chapter on Webster. I wholly agree with your personal sketch of Taft (page 3). I knew him slightly, always enjoyed talking with him and agree with your phrase "a surprising and unusual personal charm." Also, I am by no means in disagreement with Taft's views on Nurnberg. I have never really tried to think the war crimes issue through; but there always seemed to me (in 1946 as well as now) much merit in Taft's argument (though I also can see merit in Bob Jackson's views). But, in my (doubtless biased) judgment, this chapter does not come off. For one thing, all your other examples of senatorial courage have been based on incidents which took place in the Senate. The Taft incident took place elsewhere. For another, I find it hard to recollect Taft's doing anything else which required political courage. His opposition to Truman's strike legislation in 1946 was a popular act. His positions on labor, OPA, etc., were highly popular with his constituency. He showed no courage at all in face of McCarthy.

If you want a post–World War II example of senatorial courage on the part of senators now dead, I would think that you could make a stronger case for Brian McMahon and his speech of 1950 calling for disarmament and increased aid to underdeveloped countries. His ideas are generally accepted now, but he thought he was taking his political life in his hands when he delivered that speech. Also, in view of the fact that Norris was a Republican, you might want to balance your 20th century fare by providing a Democrat.

Page 4, para 2, last sentence: this piece of rhetoric seems to me wildly exaggerated. As a point of fact, the Taft statement, whatever its merits, did not shine as a beacon light anywhere. If an American Senator speaking out his thoughts, however unpopular, on any subject, however sensitive, is what is wanted, why not Glen Taylor?

Page 7: "The speech exploded in the midst of the election campaign like an atomic bomb." I do not think the atomic bomb image should be used lightly; nor, in my memory, did the Taft Nurnberg statement have anything like this impact on the campaign—much less so, as I recall, than another Taft statement, the one exhorting people to eat less meat. I think you much exaggerate the political reactions to this whole episode, outside of the special case of New York

Page 12, final sentence: this seems to me exaggerated. Take the issue of civil liberties, for example. Taft spoke up for the defendants in the sedition trial in 1944 and for the Nazis; but I do not know another instance when he ever spoke up for civil freedom of anybody else. He regarded the security nonsense with entire complacency; urged McCarthy that, if one case didn't pan out, he should try another; and never displayed the solicitude for the personal rights of Democrats that he did of the Nazis and their American friends. I do not mean to imply that Taft was pro-Nazi. He was not. But he did feel (as he told me, and as he doubtless told you) that he thought the New Dealers had ridden high too long, and that they had a lot coming to them. Indeed, he thought that McCarthy was simply giving them their own medicine. This may not be a defensible position; but it is certainly not a principled position on individual freedom; nor did it display any great effort by Taft "to provide an atmosphere in America in which others could live in the same way."

CH 10—GRAB-BAG

I am not sure whether you ought not to consider leaving this chapter out. You can defend the selection of eight or ten figures for your story; but if you have a grab-bag chapter like this one, you imply fairly complete coverage and therefore invite sniping reviewers to complain over your omissions. For example, as one complaining reviewer, why omit the elder Bob La Follette?—surely a man of great courage. Or, among congressmen, Charles A Lindbergh, Sr.—a man who took a dreadful beating for his opposition to World War I—an experience which, I am sure, helps explain his son's position on World War II.

But even if you want to fill out the list of senators in this chapter, I think you are asking for trouble when you get into Presidents, Governors, etc. It is hard to argue, for example, that Cleveland's veto of the pension bills was a greater act of political courage than Jackson's veto of the United States Bank recharter. You mention John Adams in connection with the Boston Massacre. Perhaps his greatest act of political courage was his refusal to go to war with France as President in 1798–1800. As you remember, Adams wanted this carved on his tombstone.

I really do think that the W.H. Taft example is terribly far-fetched. Taft required far less courage to hold on to Ballinger than Truman did to hold on to Dean Acheson. Moreover, Taft was a notably timid President. He had less courage in his 375 pounds than T.R., Wilson, F.D.R. or Truman had in their respective little fingers. Taft's defense of Ballinger is minuscule compared, say, to Truman's decision on Korea or on the Berlin airlift, or to scores of decisions and policies taken by F.D.R. or Wilson. Also, why do you regard Glavis as an "overzealous" employee? Is it overzealous to try to prevent government coal lands from being disposed of in ways of doubtful legality for the private profit of a corporation? I wish we had a hell of a lot more of that overzealousness in Washington now! Ickes, of course, decided that Ballinger was right when he had his own fights in the 30s with Pinchot and Glavis; but most conservationists today still seem to think that Pinchot and Brandeis were right.

In general, this chapter seemed to me diffuse, weak and too much of a catch-all. I think the book would perhaps be stronger in its impact if you confined it to a few personalities about whom you could write at length.

I have put my doubts about the Webster and Taft chapters in strong language to save time, and because I know you would like these doubts to be expressed vigorously while there is still time; but obviously it is your book, and you cannot expect to please every reader! Again, let me say that I enjoyed reading the chapters; and that I think your real skill in characterization and in dramatic narrative should gain the book a large audience. It is a splendid achievement.

Sincerely,
Arthur S.

From John F. Kennedy

July 20, 1955

[Washington, D.C.]

Dear Arthur:

Many, many thanks for your very helpful comments and corrections. I have, to the extent possible, followed every one of your suggestions, and they were of considerable help in sharpening the manuscript. I am also grateful for your very kind comments about the book and my efforts in connection with it.

I have made changes in the Webster and Lamar chapters to make it clear that there is disagreement as to whether their position was necessarily the right one—a point which I am also making with respect to all chapters in my conclusion.

Although I am retaining the chapter on Senator Taft, I have attempted to eliminate some of the overstatement concerning his character and this particular issue. I share some of your concern about the final "grab-bag" chapter. I have rewritten it somewhat, eliminated some of the examples (including President Taft) and hope to talk further to the publishers about it.

I hope you will be pleased with the final product—and that we may have a chance to get together in the near future.

Again, my sincere thanks for your very real help.[*]

Sincerely,
John F. Kennedy

On September 24, 1955, after completing 27 holes of golf on a trip to Denver, President Eisenhower suffered a massive heart attack and was hospitalized for several weeks, during which time Vice President Nixon assumed executive duties.

Eisenhower would not take his first steps until October 25. The race for the White House suddenly looked wide open.

To William McCormick Blair, Jr.

October 4, 1955

[Cambridge, Massachusetts]

Dear Bill:

Now that 1956 begins to look serious I thought I had better write and set forth my situation over the next 12 months.

At present, I am engaged in completing the draft of the first volume of *The Age of Roosevelt*. This is due to be published in the fall of 1956, which means that a complete manuscript must be in Houghton Mifflin's hands by

* *Profiles in Courage* won the Pulitzer Prize for Biography in 1957.

early spring. Though I have written some 350,000 words, I still have a considerable distance to go. Accordingly I am having to subordinate everything else to bringing this to completion.

This does not mean that I am proposing to retire from political life. I should be more than glad to help on occasional speeches . . . ; as you know, speechwriting is a congenial diversion for me, and does not take too much time. Also, I have told Tom Finletter that I will help him in every way I can on the research side of things. But, until the manuscript is out of the way, my participation will have to be less total than I would like.

Once it is out of the way, I would be prepared (and happy!) to give all the time that is desired for the Stevenson campaign. I am due for sabbatical leave in 1956–57, so I will be free for full time labors from the convention (and before) to the election.

However,—and this is very important—*my availability must not impose on you or the Governor the feeling that I must therefore be used.* I think there are probably strong arguments for the Governor's assembling a new research and writing staff for the 1956 campaign. And there may well be cogent reasons for not using me. You know me well enough to know that I will cheerfully accept any decision as to where I can best make my contribution. So this letter of mine is not to be construed as an attempt to impose myself on the campaign! But—especially since the Governor appears to have raised the question about me with Ken [Galbraith] recently at Libertyville*—I thought it might help if I could let you know exactly what my availability is.

I am not writing the Governor about this because I don't want to bother him unnecessarily about it. But, if the question is on his mind at all, you might communicate the above to him.

Yours ever,
Arthur

---

* Libertyville, Illinois An affluent northern suburb of Chicago in Lake County on the Des Plaines River, where Stevenson built a house.

To Adlai Stevenson

October 10, 1955

[Cambridge, Massachusetts]

Dear Adlai:

I think the 1956 contest has gone into a new phase—a phase which in the long run will probably benefit both the party and your own candidacy, but which in the short run is going to create real problems. Here is the new situation as I see it (for what that is worth).

1. *Truman is out to get the nomination for Harriman.*[*] If I had any sense, I might have guessed this in Boston—partly because of HST's extraordinary disinclination to talk current politics with me (he kept switching the conversation back to his memoirs); and more significantly, because of the apparent shift in Paul Dever's[†] position. As I wrote you last week, Dever's people gave me to understand after your phone talk with him that there was a good chance of his coming out for you rather soon. But, after his talk with HST, Dever told the press that Massachusetts would have an unpledged or favorite son delegation next year. This suggests, I think, the Truman-Harriman strategy to tie up as many delegations as possible in unpledged or favorite son situations; to line up the bosses for Averell; and to hope that you and Estes [Kefauver] will kill each other off in the primaries.

2. *Why has Truman done this?* It seems to me fairly clear that HST shifted to Harriman as a result of Ike's illness. What has been his attitude toward you? As I gather it, his attitude has been like this: a) he thinks you look down on politicians as a class and on him as a politician; that you do not understand the role of the politician in American life; b) he is not sure whether you are enough of a liberal—a New-Fair Dealer; c) he is not sure whether you have enough relish for the kind of political slugging he admires; d) he thinks nevertheless that you would be the strongest Democratic candidate. Up till recently, the fourth consideration has been overriding. But, with Ike out of the picture, he probably feels that almost any Democrat would win. If so, he prefers Averell a) because he is closer

---

[*] W. Averell Harriman was elected governor of New York in 1954.
[†] Paul Dever (1903–58). Democratic governor of Massachusetts, 1949–53.

to Averell, who has courted him; b) because he thinks Averell is clearer on issues, a stronger liberal and New-Fair Dealer; c) because he does not think that Averell looks down on politicians; d) because he thinks that Averell will put on a slugging campaign. . . .

3. *Why the timing of the Harriman boom?* Partly accident, like everything else in politics (HST happened to come east last weekend to meet Margaret's* boat); but partly to interrupt the impetus of your candidacy before its momentum becomes irresistible. As people begin to digest the implications of the Albany weekend, and as HST begins to get the word around, there is likely to be a definite check to the Stevenson surge, especially among the pros, unless counteractive measures are undertaken.

4. *What can we do?* The developing situation threatens to put you in the position that Kefauver was in four years ago: the bosses and Truman against you; only voters are for you. But the bosses and Truman are less important than they were then, and you have far more of the voters than Estes had in 1952. I think you should play boldly and from strength.

a) Now is the time, in my judgment, to give a fast green light on the formation of Stevenson-for-President clubs. Let Bill [Blair] call 3 dozen people through the country; let them pass the word along; let everyone who has fifteen friends form a club; let a whole series of clubs bearing various names and designations be formed in the next weeks; and let each issue a press release. (As many as possible of these should be regular Democratic clubs.) The effect will be to furnish evidence of a popular demand that will underline the contrast between the popular support for you and the machine support for Averell (it will also cause many machine people to think twice before clambering on the Harriman bandwagon). Moreover, it will create a natural setting for your own announcement (which might well be advanced to early November or even perhaps—though this should be carefully considered—to before the New York dinner in October). In any case, it seems to me that now is the time to begin cashing in on your real strength—which is your strength with the people. . . .

*Margaret Truman (1924–2008). Harry S. Truman's only child; singer and writer; married Clifton Daniel, who was later managing editor of *The New York Times*, in 1956.

b) What you do yourself becomes especially important now. I can only make suggestions with regard to two conversations you are about to have—Dever and Lehman. In both cases, I wish you could bring yourself, however distasteful this might be, to say that you hope very much you can count on their support. Also in each case I think you should urge them to run for office in 1956.

Beyond this:

Dever: the points to be made, I believe, are (a) your popular strength—Gallup poll, letters, gubernatorial backing, etc.; and (b) your liberal position, especially on labor and social welfare issues. Dever will be impressed by the first and attracted by the second. He responds in a sentimental but real way to the notion of government helping the poor and disadvantaged to attain something nearer to equality of opportunity with the rich.

Lehman: I think you should tell him that you want to be President because you feel very strongly that the Eisenhower administration has degraded our nation in both domestic and foreign policy; that it has substituted misrepresentation for candor in dealing with the people; that it is terrible on public power (very important because of Lehman's fight with Averell over the Niagara deal), civil liberties, resources, education, health, housing, etc.; that the continuation of Dulles (whom Lehman hates) would be disastrous; etc. Add that you respect Averell, but that Averell will be too weak a candidate possibly to bring in a liberal enough Congress to achieve liberal objectives.

c) I think you should also move to establish contact with Kefauver when he returns so that there will be opportunity for a free exchange of views at any point. Paul Douglas* might be useful here. Personally I think that Kefauver should be put on the ticket as vice president; but he is not likely to be ready to settle for that at this stage. In any case, a real effort should be made to establish relations, if only not to let a Kefauver-Harriman axis arise by default.

5. *New York situation.* This is obviously crucial. What I have to say is based on a quick weekend and should be carefully checked, especially with Tom [Finletter] and Marietta. But I do think that an opportunity for stopping

---

* Paul Douglas (1892–1976). Professor of economics at the University of Chicago; liberal senator (D-Ill.), 1948–67.

Averell in his own backyard is shaping up. The *New York Post* today will have an editorial urging Liberals to enroll as Democrats so that, if necessary, they can vote for Stevenson delegates in the June primaries. (Dolly Schiff,* by the way, is inexplicably for you at the moment; it would be useful to keep her sweetened up; do at least call her and mention her registration campaign when you are in town; she plans to tee off on Averell next weekend.) . . .

6. In all this business, I hope you will follow your own instincts, which are better than those of any one else I have run into in politics. For my money, the so-called professional politicians are useful to have around for display purposes, but they live a lot of their life in dream worlds too. As Clemenceau[†] should have said, politics is too important to be left to the politicians. They do not always deliver what they promise or know what they are talking about, and they do not matter nearly so much as they think. . . .

7. I am not unhappy about these developments. I think that the ensuing struggle may help greatly to revise the national image of you—people may begin to see you as a happy warrior, not as a brooding Hamlet. But it is also important, of course, that the conflict not generate bitterness of a sort which would leave post-convention scars and diminish the value of the nomination. Restraint must be the line; and I trust that all three candidates will continue publicly to praise each other. The private Stevenson line on Harriman should be that he is just too weak a candidate. If De Sapio's[‡] boys start playing it dirty, I think that representations should be made directly to Averell through intermediaries for whom he has respect.

---

* Dorothy Schiff (1903–89). Owner and publisher of the *New York Post,* 1939–76; featured columnists Murray Kempton, Drew Pearson, Eleanor Roosevelt, Max Lerner, and Pete Hamill; sold the tabloid to Rupert Murdoch in 1976.

† Georges Clemenceau (1841–1929). Prime minister of France, 1906–9, 1917–20; "*La guerre! C'est une chose trop grave pour la confier a des militaires.*" ["War! It's too important to be left to the generals."]

‡ Carmine De Sapio (1908–2004). Democratic boss of New York City's Tammany Hall, 1949–61; supported Harriman for governor in 1954 over FDR, Jr.; supported Harriman for president in 1956; served as Harriman's secretary of state, 1955–59; served two years in federal prison for conspiracy and bribery, 1971–73.

Sorry to inflict so intolerably long and intrusive a letter on you; but you have endured these before, and thus invite their repetition.

Yours ever,
Arthur

P.S. I have just received a phone call from someone who spent yesterday afternoon with Mrs. Roosevelt. Mrs. R. thinks that Truman has behaved very badly and says that she is going to write him a letter telling him so. She is 100 per cent for you and feels that now is the time for you to come out fighting. She said: "He's got to make the people believe that he feels for these things—not that he's only for them intellectually." She also, according to my informant (Joe Rauh), was filled with sharp and sage reflections on De Sapio and the New York political situation. As you know, when she gets to New York politics all her sentimentality disappears. I think it would be an excellent idea for you to call her and ask her how she sees the situation.

Arthur first met the writer Mary McCarthy, with her husband Edmund Wilson, at a dinner party in Cambridge in the winter of 1940–41. Arthur was entranced by her beauty, wit, intellectual passion, eager eyes, and lustrous and penetrating smile; and he was full of indignation that she should be married to a man who, however interesting and distinguished, seemed infinitely old. In fact, Mary was then twenty-eight and Edmund forty-five.

To Mary McCarthy

November 1, 1955

[Cambridge, Massachusetts]

Dear Mary:

Bowden* gave me a copy of the novel† when I ran into him in New York, and I have now read it with pleasure and fascination. It seems to me a bril-

---

*Bowden Broadwater (1920–2005). Writer; teacher; Mary McCarthy's third husband, 1946–61.

† Mary McCarthy, *A Charmed Life* (New York: Harcourt Brace, 1955). Members of a writers-and-artists' colony cavort; the John Sinnott character is based on Broadwater,

liant and shattering performance, and it has left me considerably disturbed. The ending, though coming as a shock, is nonetheless absolutely right for the novel; it vindicates the whole sense of creeping apprehension which suffuses the book; but, in view of the relations between the novel and life, I found it really upsetting. The writing, of course, is superb, and the narrative seemed to me better paced than *The Groves*. But I was wholly unable to read it with detachment, and I have no idea what some one coming to it cold will think. I do think you were unfair to Edmund [Wilson], but I cannot make out whether this was because you were trying to obscure his identity or whether you really see him this way. The Jenckses* came off very well, and have nothing to complain about. (Bowden showed me Ruth's very sweet letter; and he tells me that Dwight† is mad because they were treated so much more lovingly than the Macdonalds were in *The Oasis*.) Marian thinks it is the best thing you have done. I can't tell; the counterpoint between life and literature is too baffling. All I know is that I could not put it down, and that I feel genuinely and considerably disquieted about it. . . .

Since returning, I have flung myself into a desperate attempt to finish the first vol[ume] of *The Age of R[oosevelt]* in time for publication next fall. I am now up to page 1189, and my volubility seems to know no end. But I rather like doing it, and find I resent interruptions, including politics. The European trip seemed to sever some continuity in my life, so that I have at the moment little zest for 1956. Doubtless this will return. In any case, I am currently sharply reducing my outside life and trying to concentrate on the book. (As you know, we are doing very well on the political side. I should think that AES would get the nomination without trouble. But I feel that I am in for a ghastly year, and I hope my enthusiasm will soon return.)

We have done little in Cambridge except work. Elizabeth Lowell‡ called up today. They have taken a 4 story house on Marlboro Street, to which we

---

and the Miles Murphy character is based on McCarthy's second husband, Edmund Wilson.

* Gardner Jencks (1907–89). Concert pianist and composer of twelve-tone music; and his wife, Ruth.

† Dwight Macdonald (1906–82). Writer; editor; film critic; Wellfleet neighbor of Schlesinger's.

‡ Elizabeth Hardwick (1916–2007). Literary critic; novelist; teacher; married to poet Robert Lowell, 1949–72.

are going Sat night for dinner with Lillian Hellman.* I reproached Liz for her puff for the incredible Fiedler† in the current PR. He seems to me so infinitely worse than Riesman that I could not see how she could do it. But apparently she met him in Rome and liked him. A convincing but still inadequate reason for praising him as a critic.

Life in Cambridge never changes, of course. The [Harry] Levins, [Perry] Millers, [Archibald] MacLeishes, etc., burble on forever. . . .

Look forward to seeing you back before too long.

Much love from us both,
Arthur

Eisenhower returned to the White House on November 11, 1955, and went almost immediately to his Gettysburg farm for further convalescence from his heart attack. On November 15, Stevenson announced that he was a candidate for the 1956 Democratic nomination and four days later gave a nationally televised speech attacking the Eisenhower administration as a government of special interests and big business, pursuing policies inimical to the ordinary man.

To Adlai Stevenson

November 25, 1955

[Cambridge, Massachusetts]

Dear Adlai:

I thought the speech Saturday night—especially the last fifteen minutes—was superb. It was also superbly delivered. And the Truman and Harriman comments could hardly have been better if you had written them yourself.

---

* Lillian Hellman (1905–84). Controversial playwright and screenwriter, author of *The Children's Hour* (1934), *The Little Foxes* (1939), and *Toys in the Attic* (1960); member of the Communist Party, 1938–40; refused to name names before HUAC in May 1952; companion of writer Dashiell Hammett.
† Leslie Fiedler (1917–2003). Professor; literary critic; argued a recurrent theme in American literature was an implied homoerotic relationship between men, using Huckleberry Finn and the escaped slave Jim as examples; author of *Love and Death in the American Novel* (1960).

I continue to think, though, that you will have to say something more on the civil rights issue. The attached column suggests the way that opinion is building up. As you know, Murray Kempton has been one of your warmest and most perceptive admirers. But he recently covered the Till case[*] in Mississippi and has been in a state of agitation—not unjustified—ever since.

I realize, of course, that there are problems in saying very much about civil rights in the pre-convention period. But I wonder whether it would not be safe and advisable to begin at least by taking a strong line in favor of law and order, of the Supreme Court and especially of the right of every American to vote as guaranteed by the Fifteenth Amendment. Why could you not call for the enforcement and, if necessary, the improvement of laws providing for federal protection of voting? This would be a slightly new angle on the situation; it would not raise the segregation issue; and it would show that you have been thinking about Negro problems and care about them. Also, it is an issue of great current importance in the Negro community, as shown by the Roy Wilkins[†] telegram. (In addition, the denial of American citizens the right to vote is, of course, shocking and outrageous, in itself, and you would want to speak out against it on the merits.)

Indeed, in a way the Wilkins line might really provide an opportunity. What might be considered is an exchange of letters between yourself and Wilkins—i.e. a sober, respectful letter from Wilkins (not hot and impassioned, like his wire), inquiring into your views on the voting problem; and a strong answer from you affirming your faith in law and the Constitution and your determination to assure constitutional rights to all Americans.

If you think there is anything in this idea, I would be glad to work out a possible exchange of letters along lines which I think might be acceptable to the NAACP. . . .

Yours ever,
Arthur

---

[*] Emmett Till, a fourteen-year-old black youth from Chicago, was beaten and shot to death while visiting relatives in Mississippi; two white men were tried and acquitted. Till was said to have "acted fresh" toward one of their wives.

[†] Roy Wilkins (1901–81). Journalist; editor of *Crisis*; executive director of the National Association for the Advancement of Colored People, 1955–77; criticized Stevenson's evident desire to keep civil rights issues out of the campaign.

To W. Averell Harriman

December 17, 1955

[Cambridge, Massachusetts]

Dear Averell:

I have been meaning for some time to write and say a word about the current political situation. As you know, I have been working during the past few years with Adlai in anticipation of the 1956 campaign. I think he made a fine candidate in 1952, and I believe that he would make a fine president. In view of all this, I am continuing my work with him.

I write you because, if it were not for these special circumstances, I would, of course, be working for you. I am sure you know how much our friendship with you and Marie has meant to Marian and me, and how devoted we are to you both. Beyond that, I feel that you are abundantly qualified for the presidency. I would not want you to think that my support of Stevenson diminishes my admiration and affection for you. I hope in general that on both sides emotions will not become too exacerbated in this pre-convention period. For my part I want to do everything I can to work—in this regard—for moderation!

Marian joins me in sending love to you both.

Yours ever,
Arthur

Arthur's unease over Stevenson's handling of the civil rights issue boiled over on the morning of February 8, 1956, when he read a report in The New York Times *that Adlai had backed "gradualism" in integration in a Los Angeles speech, irking his African American audience. Arthur immediately dashed off a punishing letter to Stevenson's closest campaign aide.*

To Willard Wirtz[*]

February 8, 1956

[Cambridge, Massachusetts]

Dear Bill:

As you know, I have been much concerned about the civil rights question in the campaign. Bill Lawrence's[†] story in the *Times* this morning on the Governor's remarks in Los Angeles does not allay my concern.[‡]

I wholly sympathize with the Governor's sense of responsibility about the issue. I know that the desegregation problem is infinitely complicated; that it will take all the patience and good will that we have; and that the gratuitous aggravation of feelings about an issue already so tense is unforgivable. I also respect the Governor's feeling that he should not indicate he will do anything now that he cannot deliver on as President (though here, I think, there is a traditional margin for "campaign oratory" which is fully understood by the electorate and which has been exploited by nearly every previous candidate for the Presidency, including A. Lincoln).

But I feel that the Governor could have made the identical points about integration without projecting—as at least the Lawrence story does—a pervading sense of coldness about the whole problem. In a context of genuine concern over the question of Negro rights and of law and order, the emphasis on gradualism and the rejection of force would take on quite a different aspect. I personally could not agree more on these points. But I wish he had made them *after* he had made a strong condemnation of interpositionism,[§]

---

[*] Willard Wirtz (1912–2010). Lawyer; professor of law at Northwestern University; Democratic Party activist; Stevenson speechwriter; secretary of labor, 1962–69.

[†] William H. Lawrence (1916–72). Journalist; *The New York Times*, 1941–61; ABC News, 1961–72.

[‡] Lawrence reported Stevenson saying, in regard to school desegregation, "We will have to proceed gradually. You do not upset the habits and traditions that are older than the Republic overnight."

[§] Interposition, a form of nullification (the unconstitutional theory that states can overrule federal actions), was the battle cry behind state resistance to *Brown v. Board of Education* (1954), the Supreme Court decision requiring integration of the public schools.

of the recent events at the University of Alabama,* of the failure of justice in the Till case, and so on. Nor do I see why anyone should feel that strong utterances on these questions constitute demagoguery. I would assume that all decent Americans feel this way.

When the Governor says that he opposes amendments to cut off federal funds from segregated schools, he is oversimplifying a more complicated issue. The serious amendment, as I understand it, does not for one moment propose to cut off federal funds from segregated schools. It would cut off federal funds only from schools which refuse to comply with the Supreme Court schedule. (See the attached discussion by Joe Rauh.) It is, in effect, not an anti-segregation rider but a law-and-order rider. Segregated schools which are held in compliance with the Supreme Court rulings would receive federal aid. Are we to take the position that schools which defy the Supreme Court should continue to receive federal aid? I don't know the answer to this question myself; but it is plainly a tough question—and a different question from the one to which the Governor addressed himself at Los Angeles (according to Lawrence). I am sure that thoughtful Negroes will feel that the Governor did not do justice to the issue. It is particularly unfortunate that southern leaders have been trying to fuzz up the issue in exactly the same way.

As for interpositionism, the Governor's statement that he did not "understand" what interpositionism was made him sound like Eisenhower. It is also, I may add, a hell of a commentary on his staff, which should long since have briefed him about it. And this admission of ignorance again displays an indifference to issues which concern millions of Americans more than anything else.

I am sorry to sound so waspish. It is all out of love. But I do think that this situation could be much improved by a change in moral and emotional attitudes and *without* any concessions in policy or any long-term irresponsibility. I call your attention to the speech† by Jack Kennedy, also reported on today's *Times*. I am sure that there is no substantive difference between

* A few days earlier, a mob had prevented the first black student (admitted by court order) from attending classes at the University of Alabama, Tuscaloosa. Stevenson made a statement on February 11, 1956, deploring the incident.

† Speaking at the New York Young Democratic Club on September 7, 1956, Kennedy called upon the Democratic Party to take a forthright stand in support of *Brown v. Board of Education* despite alienating Democrats in the South. The decision was "the law of the land" and the party must realize it "would cost us more elsewhere if we were to weasel on it."

Jack and the Governor on this issue. I also know that Jack is damn anxious to get southern support for the Vice-Presidency. Yet he gives an altogether different impression of his feelings on the subject. The important thing, I am sure—and this is true not just for Negroes but for labor and for the Israel question—is not what technical positions we take, but how effectively we communicate a deep and genuine sense of *concern*. If we can communicate the concern, then we can remain as responsible and uncommitted as we want when it comes to policy.

Yours ever,
A.S., jr.

To Elmer Gertz[*]

February 28, 1956

[Cambridge, Massachusetts]

Dear Mr. Gertz:

I am happy indeed to have the privilege of commenting on President Truman and his administration. There is no doubt in my mind that he will go down as one of the great American Presidents—as a man who faced the great decisions of his time with unfailing courage, intelligence and honor.

In the field of foreign affairs, he brought about a revolution in America's relations to the world—a revolution which, it is safe to say, will never be reversed. Such initiatives as the Truman Doctrine, the Marshall Plan, the North Atlantic Treaty Organization, Point Four, the support of the Berlin airlift and the intervention in Korea would have been inconceivable a decade earlier. Because he had the boldness and the imagination to carry these policies through, President Truman completed the process by which our nation at last assumed responsibilities in the world commensurate with our power. At the same time, he contributed perhaps more than any-

---

[*] Elmer Gertz (1906–2000). Chicago lawyer; law professor; writer; defender of civil liberties; represented writers Frank Harris and Henry Miller, Lee Harvey Oswald's assassin Jack Ruby, and child killer Nathan Leopold of Leopold and Loeb infamy. Gertz was a great admirer of President Truman, and as president of the Decalogue Society, a group of Illinois Jewish lawyers, presented Truman with the society's Award of Merit at a Chicago banquet in 1955.

one else to the development of the will and power in the free world necessary to check the further spread of Communism. When the history of our times is written, it will be seen, I think, that more than any other nation, it was the United States which rallied the west in the first years of Communist expansion after the end of the Second World War, and that, more than any other individual, it was Harry Truman who rallied the United States.

But I do not think that President Truman's record in domestic policy should be overlooked. The civil rights program of 1948[*] will go down as one of the great historical landmarks in the long labor by which Americans have sought to make the promises of the Declaration of Independence and the Constitution real for all our citizens. The series of measures summed up in the Fair Deal[†] represented a wise and essential consolidation and development of the economic and social reforms of the New Deal. While some of Mr. Truman's proposals, like the national health insurance program and the agricultural policy of income rather than price support, were too advanced for his time, I have no question in my mind that the nation will come round to them in due course. Above all, President Truman deserves the gratitude of his fellow citizens for the unquenchable courage he displayed in speaking the instincts of freedom in the American people against such unscrupulous demagogues as Senator McCarthy.

I do not believe that President Truman's administration was beyond criticism. I feel that he was slow in correcting evidences of maladministration and corruption in the lower levels of government. I regret some of his appointments to the federal courts and to the Departments of Justice and of the Treasury. I fear that the security system which he correctly instituted went too far in the direction of ignoring the rights of the individual. Yet I have no doubt that, in the verdict of history, the defects of the Truman record will sink into insignificance next to the great gains he helped achieve for good sense, freedom and courage, not just in our own land, but in the whole free world. And the world will not soon forget President Truman as an individual,

---

[*] Truman established the President's Committee on Civil Rights in 1946 and in February 1948 presented Congress with a comprehensive legislative civil rights program based on the committee's report. In July 1948 he integrated the armed forces by executive order.

[†] Truman pledged in January 1949 "to try to give every segment of our population a fair deal." This became the label for his domestic program, adapting the New Deal tradition to postwar prosperity.

the embodiment of American decency in our time, with the qualities so memorably described by another great man of this age, Winston Churchill, "his gay, precise, sparkling manner and obvious power of decision."

Sincerely yours,
Arthur

To Adlai Stevenson

May 2, 1956

[Cambridge, Massachusetts]

Dear Adlai:

I do not know whether this situation will arise; but here are a couple of quotations which might be of use if anyone thinks that it is *lese majeste* to criticize Eisenhower.*

In Louisville on October 18, 1916, Theodore Roosevelt, launching an attack upon President Wilson, said this: "At the outset of my speech I wish to point out that the doctrine, now often advanced, as to the impropriety of criticizing the President, without regard as to whether the criticism is or is not just, has no warrant either in history or on grounds of public morality." Continuing, Roosevelt declared Andrew Jackson in a message to the Senate on April 15, 1834, had put the case exactly as it should be put when he said: "The President is accountable at the bar of public opinion for every act of his Administration. Subject only to the restraints of truth and justice, the free people of the United States have the undoubted right, as individuals or collectively, orally or in writing, at such times and in such language and form as they may think proper, to discuss his official conduct and express and promulgate their opinions concerning it."

Yours ever,
Arthur

---

*With his health improved, President Eisenhower had announced in late February 1956 that he would run for reelection.

To Reinhold Niebuhr

May 9, 1956

[Cambridge, Massachusetts]

Dear Reinhold:

As you know, I have been working for some time on a multi-volume history to be entitled *The Age of Roosevelt*. The first volume is due to come out in the fall.[*] If you do not mind, I would like to dedicate this volume to you. The reasons for this are self-evident; and I can only add that friendship with you and Ursula has meant more for Marian and me than I can easily say, or than this inadequate measure can suggest.

Yours ever,
Arthur

To Adlai Stevenson

May 15, 1956

[Cambridge, Massachusetts]

Dear Adlai:

I understand that you and Estes have your joint interrogation on Monday. Having heard you both with Elmer Davis at the ADA convention last Sunday, I am taking my usual liberty of forwarding some suggestions.

1. *Don't* say that problems are intricate and complicated. Everyone knows that they are. Too much emphasis on this only sounds as if you were trying to avoid a clearcut answer, or as if you felt hopeless about solving the problem.

2. *Don't* profess ignorance on questions, or say that you don't know enough to give a definite answer. If you are running for the Presidency, people expect, not necessarily a detailed technical answer, but a clear and definite expression of the way you would propose to tackle the problem.

---

[*] Arthur M. Schlesinger, Jr., *The Crisis of the Old Order: 1919–1933* (Boston: Houghton Mifflin, 1957).

3. *Don't* hesitate to give a short answer. It is better to state bluntly the essence of your views with regard to a given policy than to surround it with reservations and complexities which have the effect of taking back or even smothering your main point. Sometimes you do this in the last part of your answers. Having taken a stand, you then seem to introduce a number of other factors which have the effect of diluting your own position and baffling your audience. My advice would be to *stop* after you have stated your main position.

4. *Do* not think that all this is in any sense a counsel of dishonesty. Politics, at its best, is an educational process. Any form of education involves the highlighting of certain points in order to pound home the main ideas. Every college lecturer in a sense oversimplifies; he must, if he is to educate. If he were to bring in all the precise qualifications, he would leave no impression except a kind of on-the-one-hand, on-the-other-hand vacillation. The great educators (and the statesmen) are the men whose oversimplifications correspond to correct principles.

In short, I think that you, like [Presidents] Lincoln, Wilson and the Roosevelts, should forget the refinements and concentrate on plain statements of what you think essentially is right.

Humbly and professorially yours,
Arthur

Senator Kennedy nominated Stevenson for the presidency at the Democratic National Convention in Chicago in August 1956, and Stevenson won on the first ballot. Violating tradition, he threw the choice of running mate to the convention. In an exciting contest between Kefauver and Kennedy, Kefauver scored a narrow victory. But Kennedy attracted national attention with his valiant effort.

To John F. Kennedy

August 21, 1956

[Cambridge, Massachusetts]

Dear Jack:

I was sorry to have missed you after the business on Friday afternoon. I wanted to say that, however the Vice Presidential contest came out, you clearly emerged as the man who gained most during the Convention. You hit the bull's eye on every one of your appearances; and your general demeanor and effectiveness made you in a single week a national political figure. You are bound to be in everyone's mind from now on in any future consideration of national candidates.

The campaign provides a further opportunity to consolidate this impression. I hope very much that you will be in a position to campaign all over the country. I know you will be greatly in demand; and there is no better way for you to get to know political leaders in all sections—and for them to get to know you—than by helping them in the campaign.

The headquarters will move to Washington by about Labor Day. I hope we can get together soon thereafter.

Sincerely yours,
Arthur

But President Eisenhower was not to be denied his second term. His personal popularity, replenished by his success in ending the Korean War, proved invincible, netting him 57.4 percent of the popular vote and 457 electoral votes to Stevenson's 42 percent of the popular vote and 73 electoral votes.

Eisenhower, in Arthur's opinion, perfectly suited the mood of the 1950s. Where his predecessors had roused the people, he soothed them; where they had defined issues sharply, he blurred them over; where they had called for effort and action, he counseled patience and hoped things would work themselves out. The American people were ready for a vacation from public responsibilities after the two preceding decades of crisis and government action. The nation needed an interval of repose in order to restore its physiological balance, and repose was what Eisenhower offered them.

But how much enforced lassitude could the nation take?

The Politics of Hope

1957–59

To John F. Kennedy

March 28, 1957

[Cambridge, Massachusetts]

Dear Jack:

I have your letter of March 8 concerning the nomination of five deceased senators for commemoration in the Capitol Reception Room under Senate Resolution 145.

After some thought, I would offer the following five names as those senators who, in my best judgment, deserve first consideration, with due regard to the claims of various parties, sections and interests. I list the names in chronological order (i.e., order of birth).

Henry Clay of Kentucky—a resourceful statesman as well as compelling orator and party leader, who left his imprint on our history in a series of compromises designed to hold the nation together in a period of tension and stress;

*Daniel Webster** of Massachusetts—the powerful spokesman for the industrial interests of the North as well as the leading champion of the nationalist interpretation of the Constitution;

---

* Daniel Webster (1782–1852). Lawyer; prominent conservative; skillful orator; first a Federalist, then a National Republican, then a Whig; representative (N.H.), 1813–17, (Mass.), 1823–27; senator (Mass.), 1027–11, 1845–50; secretary of state, 1841–43, 1850–52.

His participation in the 1956 Stevenson presidential campaign prepares
Schlesinger for 1960. Whom will he support? Who can win the presidency
and best carry out the liberal program?

*John C. Calhoun** of South Carolina—a penetrating political theorist and the ablest spokesman for the view of the Constitution which, in the end, divided the nation and brought about the Civil War;

George W. Norris[†] of Nebraska—a man of fierce integrity as well as a constructive statesman of a high order, who left his mark in the 20th Amendment, the Tennessee Valley Authority and the anti-injunction act;

Robert F. Wagner[‡] of New York—the first member of the Senate to understand fully the economic and social problems of industrial society and to propose action to bring about employment and social security.

I know that the members of your Special Committee must make the final decision. I would suggest, however, that these five names make a fairly balanced ticket. In terms of parties, there are two Whigs (Clay and Webster), one Republican (Norris), one Democrat (Wagner), and one independent who at various times was allied both with the Whigs and Democrats (Calhoun). In terms of sections, there is one southerner (Calhoun), one from the border states (Clay), one middle westerner (Norris), one from the middle Atlantic states (Wagner) and one New Englander (Webster). In terms of interests, there are two who were generally identified with the business community (Webster and Clay), one with the planting aristocracy (Calhoun), one with the independent farmer (Norris) and one with labor (Wagner).

I imagine that the first four names appear on most lists submitted to you. I would say in further support of the name of Robert F. Wagner that, as the only immigrant on the list, he would stand for the indispensable contribution foreign-born Americans have made to our life. He is also the only Catholic on the list. Some of your colleagues may remember Wagner

---

* John C. Calhoun (1782–1850). South Carolina planter; fiery orator and nationalist; representative, 1811–17; senator, 1832–43, 1845–50; U.S. vice president, 1825–32; supported states' rights; believed slavery was "a positive good"; resigned vice presidency after President Andrew Jackson opposed his efforts to nullify certain federal laws applying to his state.

† George W. Norris (1861–1944). Nebraska lawyer; progressive Republican representative, 1903–13; senator, 1913–43; supported FDR's New Deal, sponsored the Tennessee Valley Authority Act of 1933; served his final term as an independent.

‡ Robert F. Wagner (1877–1953). Prussian-born New York lawyer; senator (D-N.Y.), 1927–49; member of FDR's "brain trust", instrumental in passing the National Labor Relations Act and the Social Security Act in 1935.

only in his last days, when illness kept him from an active role in the Senate. But he should be recalled, of course, as he was in his prime. I would suggest that no Senator in the period from 1927 to 1940 saw more clearly the need for the control and humanization of our industrial order or worked more effectively to show that a free society could manage its economic destiny.[*]

Sincerely yours,
Arthur

With the Democrats in control of the Senate, Lyndon B. Johnson was the powerful Senate majority leader. Sensitive to liberal criticism of his leadership, Johnson suggested that Arthur drop by his office for a conversation when next in Washington, which Arthur did on a Saturday late in March. He found the tall Texan affable and expansive.

"[Johnson] began by saying he was a sick man (his heart attack had taken place in 1955) with no political future of his own. His main desire, he said, was to live. He had no interest at all in the presidential nomination," Schlesinger wrote in A Thousand Days *(1965).* *"He then poured out his stream-of-consciousness on the problems of leadership in the Senate. . . . He talked for an hour and a half without interruption. I had carefully thought out in advance the arguments to make when asked to justify my doubts about his leadership; but in the course of this picturesque and lavish discourse Johnson met in advance almost all the points I had in mind. . . . It was my first exposure to the Johnson treatment, and I found him a good deal more attractive, more subtle and more formidable than I expected. . . . I staggered away in a condition of exhaustion."*

A few weeks later, Johnson told Galbraith: "I had a good meeting with Schlesinger. I found him quite easy to get along with. The only trouble was that he talked too much."

---

[*]The Senate committee, of which JFK was chairman, selected Webster, Clay, Calhoun, La Follette, and Taft. Norris was vetoed by the two sitting senators from Nebraska, both conservative Republicans.

To Lyndon B. Johnson

April 3, 1957

[Cambridge, Massachusetts]

Dear Senator Johnson:

I greatly enjoyed our conversation the other day, and I much appreciate your suggestion that I send along any thoughts I might have.

It seems to me that one of the great dangers the Democrats face in the current season is the budget. There is obviously a great temptation to get cheap headlines in the Republican press by coming out strong for "economy" (as you suggested in connection with the rivers-and-harbors bill). But for Democrats to take this position is really madness. It will persuade nobody. It is contrary to the historic position of the modern Democratic party and to the public welfare; it makes neither political, moral nor economic sense.

It doesn't make political sense because the Democratic party will never win a national election as the party of retrenchment, economy and inadequate public services. It doesn't make moral sense because retrenchment is inexcusable at a time when our school children, our old folks, our sick people and many others are being manifestly neglected. It doesn't make economic sense because our nation, with a GNP of $400 billion, is wholly capable of dealing with a $70 billion budget.

I do not mean to imply that the Democratic party should not stand strongly against waste and extravagance in government. Of course it should. But it must surely not get in the position of demanding that vital public services be cut down in the name of "economy." The fact is that we are richer than we have ever been as a nation, and spending in the public sector has simply not kept pace with spending in the private sector. We are spending *less* of our GNP for welfare services than we were a few years ago. And our great historic position as the party which believes in the use of government to promote the general welfare will continue for a long time, I believe, to be the main source of our political strength.

I recognize that these general remarks are not new, and that they do not particularly meet the problems of day-to-day operation on the firing-line. I do have some concrete suggestions, however, about people who might be helpful in working out a position which might command the broadest possible support among Democratic senators.

On the general question of the size of the budget, its economic implications, the impact on the nation and the decay of governmental services, I am certain that J. K. Galbraith and Seymour Harris of the Harvard Economics Department would be glad to consult with you and other Democratic senators in working out a sound line on this matter. (It is spring vacation here this week, and both Galbraith and Harris are out of town; but I have no hesitation in committing their services!) I have had a certain amount of experience with economists in two presidential campaigns; and I think that Galbraith and Harris are the two most sensible, lucid, resourceful and easy-to-work-with that I know.

I suppose that in the current political mood the most vulnerable part of the budget is foreign aid. I was glad to hear you speak as you did on Saturday about foreign aid, because I think this will really be a major test of our responsibility as a party. I personally think that the present foreign aid program can and should be attacked, and that Democrats should demand a new foreign aid program. But a proper program, in my judgment, will address itself essentially to problems of economic growth and will involve a shift of funds in some areas from military to economic aid. I recognize that such a program would probably be less acceptable to some of our Democratic senators even than the present program. But I do think that our national interest calls for our moving in that direction, and that a persuasive case can be made for a new aid program along these lines. Two M.I.T. economists, Walt Rostow[*] and Max Millikan,[†] have done a lot of thinking about these problems. Both are eminently reasonable men with long government experience. Like Galbraith and Harris, they are fully aware of the political problems involved in any such program. I would think that, if you and other Democratic senators are planning any sort of fight for foreign aid, their counsel would be most useful. Walt Rostow tells me that he would be glad to come to Washington at any point to talk to you.

I can well imagine the problems you face with some Democratic senators on the budget and particularly on foreign aid. I do think, however, that,

---

[*] Walter W. Rostow (1916–2003). Economist; OSS; helped develop the Marshall Plan; taught economic history at MIT, 1950–61; State Department, 1961–66; national security adviser, 1966–69; Lyndon B. Johnson School of Public Affairs at the University of Texas, Austin, 1970–2003; hawkish; pro–Vietnam War.

[†] Max Millikan (1913–69). Conservative economist; founded Center for International Studies at MIT in 1951 with CIA funding.

under your leadership, the Senate Democrats could work out a broad position on both these issues which would command the support of the vast majority of Democratic senators. And it seems most important that leadership should be exerted on these matters soon. There is nothing less likely to inspire public confidence in our party than for one wing to denounce Eisenhower for the size of his budget while the other wing denounces him for doing so little to provide services for the people.

Sincerely yours,
Arthur

To Lyndon B. Johnson

17 June 1957

[Florence, Italy]

Dear Lyndon,

I left for Europe a few weeks after our talk in late March, so my knowledge of recent Washington developments is admittedly fragmentary. I do want to congratulate you on your foreign policy speech of June 8.[*] The complacency and folly of this administration's conduct of foreign affairs will become apparent to everyone in time, and the more effectively we can build up a record of responsibility and initiative in this field the better. Nor does a posture of responsibility in foreign affairs require any abstention from attacks on the President and the Secretary of State; Churchill in England in the late thirties did not go about pretending that he considered Chamberlain a great statesman. A few weeks in Europe make depressingly evident the extent to which we have lost the leadership of the free nations. There was a time, and not too long ago, when an American idea or initiative commanded automatic respect, if not always automatic agreement. Now the automatic reaction, whenever Mr Dulles opens his mouth, is one of suspicion and skepticism. This by itself doesn't mean, of course, that our policies might still not be wonderful; but who,

---

[*] Johnson called for an "open curtain" through which the United States could state its case for disarmament directly to the Russian people. He warned that "we now face the prospect of destroying ourselves not as the result of an armaments race but merely by indulging in the race."

in view of the record of the last four years, can blame anyone for being skeptical?

I must confess, though, to some dismay over the impression that the Democratic party is apparently making in its domestic policy. I deeply believe that we are heading into a dead-end street if we try to present ourselves as the party of economy and retrenchment, as the budget-cutting party.

In the first place, such a strategy would be *wrong*. A growing nation must expect to have a growing budget. The size of the Eisenhower budget is not at all out of line with our national and international responsibilities. Indeed, there is much more which our government ought to be doing, especially at home. Our country is getting into the ludicrous position of spending more and more on luxuries while the national plant, the basis of our wealth and prosperity—our schools, our welfare services, our housing, our medical care, our roads, our national domain—is running down.

And in the second place, such a strategy would be wholly unconvincing. If we try to identify ourselves with government retrenchment, who will ever take us seriously as a party again? And we won't pick up much political strength by such a tactic either. If the American people want a budget-cutting government, they will vote Republican. I can imagine the amount of pressure to which members of Congress have been subjected in recent weeks on the budget (and I can imagine too the temptation which some have felt to pick up easy applause from quarters which have been traditionally anti-Democratic). But the Chambers of Commerce are never going to go Democratic—and, if they do, then there will be need for a new party to stand for the things for which the Democratic party has stood. Andrew Jackson settled the states-rights issue in the Democratic party when he broke with Calhoun. The great tradition of the Democratic party is the tradition of affirmative government—the tradition of Jackson, Bryan,[*] Wilson and FDR—not the tradition which hates the national government, but the one which regards it as an indispensable means of promoting the national welfare. If Democrats reject this tradition, they reject any chance of national political success. And a frenzy for budget-cutting as an end in itself amounts certainly to a flat rejection of this tradition. Moreover, if Democrats assume

---

[*] William Jennings Bryan (1860–1925). Progressive populist; representative (D-Neb.), 1891–95; three-time Democratic nominee for president; secretary of state, 1913–15.

this stance, any subsequent Democratic appeal for better public and social services will seem thoroughly disingenuous and cynical.

Remarks from this distance can't be worth much. But, from this distance, it would certainly seem important for the Democrats in Congress to do something soon to remind the voters of the great tradition of our party—something which shows that we have not abandoned our determination to use affirmative government as a means of serving the people and enlarging their rights and opportunities. An obvious issue for this might be civil rights; but (for all too obvious reasons) we have let the administration seize the initiative on this, and it looks as if the party record on civil rights will only aggravate the impressions already created on the budget fight. But unless something is done to remind people what the Democratic party is really about, we run the risk of selling our birthright for a mess of agreeable telegrams from characters who have no intention ever of supporting a Democrat for president—while our own friends and supporters will have little incentive but to get fed up with all politicians and to sink into confusion and apathy.

Sincerely yours,
Arthur

PS. Also can't something be done to put over the point that the crooked labor leaders—the Becks,[*] Hutchesons,[†] etc.—are precisely the ones who have always been closest to the Republicans and most admired by them?—that this is exactly the kind of labor leadership which a business-dominated society desires and breeds?

Please don't bother to acknowledge this. I will be back in the U.S. after Labor Day.

On July 2, 1957, John F. Kennedy made a speech in the Senate criticizing American support of French colonialism in Algeria and calling for Algerian

---

[*] Dave Beck (1894–1993). President of the International Brotherhood of Teamsters, 1952–57; jailed for corruption in 1962.

[†] William Hutcheson (1874–1953). President of the United Brotherhood of Carpenters and Joiners of America, 1915–52; anti–New Deal; anti–intervention in Europe before World War II.

independence, a position repugnant to the foreign policy establishment—the Council on Foreign Relations, The New York Times, the Department of State, the Quai d'Orsay. Kennedy said: "No amount of mutual politeness, wishful thinking, nostalgia, or regret, should blind either France or the United States to the fact that, if France and the West at large are to have a continuing influence in North Africa . . . the essential first step is the independence of Algeria." Kennedy had criticized an ally and imperiled the unity of NATO, signs of his irresponsibility in foreign affairs. But in Europe the speech identified him as a fresh and independent voice of American foreign policy.

To John F. Kennedy

July 15, 1957

[Andermatt, Switzerland]

Dear Jack,

I hope you are not deterred by some of the unfriendly comment on your speech about Algeria. You are absolutely right in the long run; what you had to say badly needed saying; and the more frank discussion about Algeria, the better.

Unfortunately I have not seen the full text of the speech (I have been traveling in Europe since the middle of May with Marian and the children); but I hope that either then or on some other occasion you have acknowledged some of the complexities of the Algerian problem. One, of course, is the question of several million Frenchmen for whom Algeria is home and who have contributed greatly to the economic development of the country. As the French delight in saying, the British would not have got out of India so cheerfully if there had been a question of forty million Englishmen who had been assured by their government for years that India was a part of Britain and their own permanent home. The existence of the *colons* does not in the slightest qualify the principle you urged in your speech; but it does complicate the application of the principle. There are very hard human problems involved here (no matter how politically vicious the *colons* may be). The present French policy will, in the long run, only aggravate these human problems; but the problems nonetheless remain; and I do not see that the *colons* can be left to the mercy of exacerbated Algerian nationalism.

Another complexity is that it is an illusion to suppose that independence will benefit the ordinary Algerian. For him, an incompetent native oligarchy is not likely to constitute any great improvement over a French colonial administration. And there is little evidence that the Algerians have developed the political or administrative competence of even the Indians. But this again does not qualify your central point—the historical inevitability of Algerian independence—though it may qualify the illusions with which we watch the process.

I am going to be in Paris next week and hope to see Mollet* and Mendes-France† if they are in town. It would help if I had the full text of your speech; and I would be grateful if your office could send me a copy c/o American Express, Paris. I will let you know if I hear anything of interest.

Sincerely yours,
Arthur

To Marietta Tree

[August 1957]

[Blanes, Costa Brava, Spain]

Darling M.

I cannot say what a delight and a relief it was to see you in Paris.‡ We all had such a good time at Chantilly, and I cannot say too how refreshed I was by the all-too brief private glimpses. You seemed in very good post-African form, and I was only sad that it was all so short. I was particularly sorry that you could not have come along later that afternoon with [Adlai Stevenson]

---

* Guy Mollet (1905–75). French Socialist politician; prime minister, February 1956–June 1957; dispatched French troops to Algeria to conduct a campaign of counterterrorism that included torture (see Italian director Gillo Pontecorvo's 1966 film, *The Battle of Algiers*).
† Pierre Mendès-France (1907–82). French prime minister, 1954–55; withdrew France from Indochina after the fall of Dien Bien Phu in 1954; agreed to Tunisian independence.
‡ Marietta and Ronald Tree were part of the Stevenson entourage that had just arrived in Paris after an extensive tour of Africa.

and Servan-Schreiber.* I had not had a chance to read the newspaper that day and thus had not seen AES's Bonn statement about Algeria, in which he in effect defended the French government from Kennedy-like attack. I think that Aron, S-Schreiber, Kennedy, etc., are quite right, and that AES wholly underestimates the bitterness of the Algerian problem and the difficulties in the way of solving it, partly because he extrapolates too quickly from the evidently good French colonial record in West Africa, partly because he was overimpressed by tales Mollet told him in the spring about the French determination to push reform in Algeria. Anyway, S-S had seen it and tackled AES rather sharply about it. The discussion which followed was fascinating but fruitless and only succeeded in plunging both participants into deep gloom. I later talked to AES about it: it is exactly like talking to him about civil rights. What is most discouraging is the way he repeats the old cliches which have preceded every colonial drive for self-government: they are not prepared, there are no leaders, invitation to anarchy, etc. Precisely the same things were said about Tunis and Morocco, which seem to be surviving self-government. I don't think for a moment that independence will help the ordinary Arab in Algeria; he would probably do better under a chastened French rule. But the *inevitability* of Algerian independence is the massive central fact to which all policy must be adjusted, and this AES does not seem to recognize vividly enough. Also he knows far too little about Algeria to make public pronouncements about it. (So, it occurs to me, do I.)

You must be sure and meet S-S sometimes. He is a very brave and intelligent young man, filled with passion and at the same time cool and cocky. . . . We will dine with him when we stop by in Paris on the 19th to return our car.

The drive down here was very pleasant. We spent a night at Bourges and another at Rocamadour (a mistake—a dreadful, resorty town). We went to Lascaux to see the drawings in the caves—strikingly beautiful. Then we spent the third night at Albi, where they have very good Son et Lumiere around the Cathedral (otherwise, especially in its interior, strikingly ugly, and, as they

---

* Jean-Jacques Servan-Schreiber (1924–2006). Influential liberal French journalist and politician; founded *L'Express* in 1953. He ran the full text of Kennedy's speech in *L'Express* with Kennedy's photograph on the cover.

used to say about HH Richardson's[*] buildings, defensible only in a military sense). The Son et Lumiere dealt extensively with the Albigensian crusade. I immediately identified myself with the heretics, of course; but could not make out adequately whether the S & L took sides or simply deplored the whole affair. I should think, by the way, that S & L must be almost as responsible as Suez for the revival of nationalism in France. Every time I have seen it (twice), it has dwelt lovingly on the gloire and grandeur of other times.

We stopped the next day at Carcassonne and then went to Perpignan and on into Spain. I must say that my suppressed moral qualms flared up when a large billboard on the frontier proclaimed: "True Liberty is realizable only within Order—Francisco Franco."[†] But that has been the only sign of F and his works that I have seen (except for the stamp which will doubtless adorn this letter). We are, after all, in Catalonia which hates Franco most and resisted him longest.

I have mixed feelings about the Costa Brava. Some of the coast is strikingly beautiful, though as a whole it does not compare with the Amalfi drive. The swimming is good and the sun continuous; I am accumulating a formidable tan which will disappear rapidly in two weeks in England. But I have the general impression that it is all at once too primitive and too overrun. We are living with the Wintours[‡] in a ramshackle villa—an odd affair, with tall, narrow rooms, like boxes set on their side; stained glass windows; and a large number of terraces (and all too few bathrooms). It is not especially comfortable. It will be all right for a few days, but I do not have any wild passion to come back here again.

The Wintours are in good form. Charles is a cool, tough, intelligent man, wholly absorbed in the *Daily Express,* of which he is managing editor, and in the interior passions of the Beaverbrook[§] empire. He is shrewd and

* Henry Hobson Richardson (1838–86). Prominent American architect; designed Boston's Trinity Church in 1872 and Harvard's Sever and Austin Halls.

† Francisco Franco (1892–1975). Fascist dictator of Spain, 1938–75.

‡ Charles Wintour (1917–99). Influential British newspaperman; editor of the *London Evening Standard,* 1959–80; old Schlesinger friend from Cambridge University. Schlesinger introduced him to the woman who became his first wife, Eleanor ("Nonie") Baker, from Cambridge, Massachusetts; their daughter is Anna Wintour, *Vogue* editor-in-chief.

§ William Maxwell Aitken (1879–1964). Lord Beaverbrook; Canadian British newspaper baron, politician, and writer.

amusing on such subjects as Randolph,[*] Beaverbrook, Brit. politics, &c; but has an increasing tendency (which people with his sort of success so often have) of seeing everything in personal, manipulative, inside-dopester terms and of losing all interest in the substantive side of issues. Nonie is brittle, witty and highly intelligent. Their four children are charming, and they are charming with them, which is a most disarming trait.

I have done little here but lie on the beach. Last Saturday night we had a fiesta, in which the crowd performed the native Catalonian dance, the Sardana. This was rather fun, though it continued all through the night and rather deterred sleep. For the rest, I have read the new Evelyn Waugh[†] novel, which you must be sure and read. It is a meticulous account of his own nervous breakdown. One of its oddities is the fact the persecutors in his fantasies accused him of being all the things he is so down on in his own novels—an intellectual, a Jew, a pansy, a communist (not so odd, of course). Also, the implicit moral of the book is that anyone with sufficient fortitude can see the ordeal through himself; there is no need for truck with psychiatrists or the like. Somehow the final impact of the book is lighter than the human agony involved, as if Waugh were in the end trivializing the experience. But it is terribly entertaining and continually absorbing. I have also been reading Frank Harris's[‡] *My Life and Loves.* Have you ever read Hugh Kingsmill's life of Frank Harris?—a very funny, sardonic life of Harris, who lived an extraordinary life as a cow-puncher, a lawyer in Kansas, an editor in London, a Shakespearian critic, a great friend of [George Bernard] Shaw and [Oscar] Wilde (both of whom he wrote biographies of), and as one of the great liars of his time. Toward the end of his life he wrote his autobiography, an entertaining if highly unreliable account of his own exploits and of the great men he knew, all of whom (according to Harris) made the most extraordinary confessions to him, primarily of their love lives (thus Carlyle told Harris he was impotent, Ruskin explained what had gone wrong with his marriage, etc.). All this is interlarded with H's accounts of his own love

---

[*] Randolph Churchill (1911–68). Irascible son of Winston; writer; journalist; Conservative MP, 1940–45; first husband of Pamela Churchill Harriman, 1939–46; their union produced a son, Winston Churchill, a Conservative MP from 1970 to 1997.

[†] Evelyn Waugh (1903–66). Popular English novelist; author of *Decline and Fall* (1928), *Brideshead Revisited* (1945); and *The Ordeal of Gilbert Pinfold* (1957).

[‡] Frank Harris (1856–1931). Flamboyant British American author, editor, journalist, and publisher.

life—all sufficiently explicit to prevent the book from being introduced into England or the US. I had always meant to read it and picked up the four volumes in Paris. I am having great fun with it.

This has gone on long enough. Darling, do write when you have a moment. We will be here till August 13. . . . We will be [in London] till Sept 3, when we return to Boston via PanAm. I am sure you are having a gorgeous time in Venice. But I miss you here!

Much, much love,
Arthur

Felix Frankfurter, the Supreme Court justice, was an old family friend from the Schlesingers' first years in Cambridge when Arthur, Sr., was a new professor and Frankfurter taught at the Harvard Law School. Frankfurter was originally from Vienna and came to America at age twelve in 1894. He mixed progressive politics with an effervescent and affectionate personality; Arthur, Jr., felt a filial obligation to keep him informed of the latest tendencies of the American republic.

To Felix Frankfurter

November 26, 1957

[Cambridge, Massachusetts]

Dear Mr. Justice:

Nye Bevan was rightly disappointed by the quality of student questions both at Brandeis and Harvard; so was I, though I was less surprised than he and, in fact, warned him in advance to expect the worst. The same thing happened when Gaitskell* was here last year; the same thing always happens with speakers on public policy.

The sad fact of the matter, I believe, is that where questions of public policy are concerned, this is an uncommonly unoriginal, conventional-minded, sloganized and boring undergraduate generation. In the main, the

* Hugh Gaitskell (1906–63). Labour MP, 1945–63; leader of the Labour Party, 1955–63.

undergraduates are a collection of political young fogies—without conviction, curiosity, information or standards. Do not be deceived by the Law School products; they are the ablest and most interesting but, alas, not representative. The tutees and graduate students I have had who have been independent-minded on political subjects have gone either to Law School (like Vorenberg,[*] who later worked for you) or into journalism (like Bill Shannon[†] of the *New York Post* or Jim Reichley).[‡] But they are the great minority. The originality and creativity of this generation is substantially diverted from political concerns. It flows instead into a variety of fields, some useful, some not—analytical philosophy, mathematical economics, quantitative sociology, drama, music, homosexuality. Everything bears the mark of the political escapist—of the eunuch.

Why should this be? Whatever member of the faculty explained it to Bevan in terms of the fear of "the dossier" was evidently foolish. It is a far deeper malaise than this. These boys are not coerced into conformity; they desire it and seek it. Whyte[§] throws light on the problem in *The Organization Man;* so too do Riesman and Fromm.[¶] However, I do not accept their suggestion that a kind of inexorable sociological determinism is at work, condemning ourselves and society to greater and greater homogenization ("togetherness"). As a student of history, I note that American society has alternated between phases of political creativity and innovation and phases of political stagnation: our social progress has not been continuous, but by fits and starts. The age of Eisenhower is such a period of stagnation. But forces are gathering under the crust and will in time break through. And this is the best argument for this present generation—that their commitment to moral and artistic matters may in the end make up for the stupefying banality of their political reactions. I do not think we will have a

[*] James Vorenberg (1927–2000). Harvard Law School professor; Watergate associate special prosecutor, 1973–75; dean of the Harvard Law School, 1981–89.

[†] William V. Shannon (1927–88). Writer; journalist; *New York Post* Washington correspondent and columnist, 1951–64; *New York Times* editorial board; ambassador to Ireland, 1977–81.

[‡] Jim Reichley (b. 1929). Political journalist; author.

[§] William H. Whyte (1917–99). Journalist; author; urbanist; wrote *The Organization Man* (1956) after extensive interviews with CEOs of large corporations.

[¶] Erich Fromm (1900–1980). German American political psychologist, psychoanalyst, humanistic philosopher, and democratic socialist; author of *Escape from Freedom* (1941) and *The Art of Loving* (1956).

political revival until we have a moral revival—by which I mean, in Eisenhower terms, an *im*moral revival—a revival of skepticism, relativism, pragmatism, impiety, irreverence, satire and reason.

Ever sincerely yours,
Arthur

The economy had slipped into recession in August 1957, begetting the worst economic downturn since the Great Depression. Auto sales fell by 31 percent, and Detroit's unemployment rate reached 20 percent. In February 1958, President Eisenhower predicted the possible "beginning of the end of this recession" in March, creating political problems when the economy continued to falter.

To Lyndon B. Johnson

March 4, 1958

[Cambridge, Massachusetts]

Dear Lyndon:

It looks increasingly as if the President's optimism about March will not be borne out. This would suggest that the automatic recuperative forces within the economy are not sufficient to reverse the present downward tendencies, and that the government will have to take measures to stimulate the economy if things are not to get worse.

There is little disagreement about the next essential measure to be taken: the budget will have to be deliberately unbalanced. However, a critical disagreement may arise about *how* the budget should be unbalanced. I wonder whether it might not be useful to make an explicit issue between the Democratic party and the Administration on the question of the best way to unbalance the budget.

There are, of course, two possibilities: 1) the budget can be unbalanced by a tax cut; or 2) it can be unbalanced by spending programs.

The administration will doubtless favor the first. This means that the extra money pumped into the economy will be dissipated in consumer spending; it means longer cars, bigger fins and larger television sets

I believe that the Democratic party should favor the second. This means

that the extra money pumped into the economy will serve national purposes; it means more schools, hospitals, roads, water and resources projects, defense, foreign aid.

The program outlined in Bill White's[*] story in the *Times* of February
8th implies exactly this policy. What should be done now, I would suggest,
is to make public and definite the conviction of the Democratic leadership
that the budget, if it must be unbalanced, should be unbalanced in the interests of the nation as a whole, not in the interests of nonessential private
spending.

It may well be true, in addition, though this is less clear, that spending
programs will be more effective in stimulating the economy than a tax cut
would be. Though such programs are harder to organize, they are also
more lasting in their effect. Moreover, there is some reason to suppose that
we may be reaching a tapering-off of the period when economic growth
came through the expansion of hard consumers' goods. It may well be that
in the next stage of our economic growth, the steam will be generated by
the effort of the nation to make up the deficit in our public needs by the
maintenance and improvement of our national plant.

In any case, regardless of the economic argument, it would seem to me
clear that, at a time in the history of the world when we are losing ground
in our competition with the Communists the arguments are overwhelming
for using the money acquired through budgetary deficits to meet urgent
national needs rather than dispersing it generally and ineffectually for gad-
gets and gimmicks.

Sincerely yours,
Arthur

---

[*] William S. White (1906–94). Pulitzer Prize–winning journalist; Washington correspondent for *The New York Times,* 1945–58; nationally syndicated columnist, 1958–
73; LBJ protégé.

From Lyndon B. Johnson

March 6, 1958

[Washington, D.C.]

Dear Arthur:

Every once in a while when the skies are overcast, and it is difficult to determine an exact course, a mariner comes across a break in the clouds that reveals a very useful star which is ideal for navigators. Your letter was in that category.

I have not talked about the question of taxes, primarily because tax legislation is not only a basic function but is a prerogative of the House. However, I have had in the back of my mind, the thought, that the best way to handle growing unemployment is through investing in wealth-producing projects. I hope that this concept can become the focus of our concentration.

In our private correspondence, I like to be completely frank as to my own thinking because I believe that such a course stimulates reciprocal frankness on your part, and this is much more helpful to me than anything else.

I do not believe it would be possible to mobilize effective support by drawing a line between tax cuts and spending programs. I can easily foresee a situation where such a line would lead us into interminable arguments over what should be done that would dissipate our energies and prevent us from doing anything at all.

I do believe, however, that we can get a program rolling that will have momentum all by itself. Then it will become the focal point of action without the necessity of applying labels. I anticipate momentarily, the emergence of a broad-gauged housing program which will stimulate housing construction. I am optimistic about the possibility of early action on an effective and well-conceived public works program. I think we can soon look for a speedup under legislative mandate of a highway program. I am virtually certain that we can expand hospital construction under the Hill-Burton Act.* The important thing is to get the show on the road along lines that you have indicated. And once we have a solid record of achievement to point to, labels will take care of themselves.

You have clarified my own thinking. I agree with you that if we commit

---

*The Hill-Burton Act (1946) was designed to provide federal grants and loans to improve the nation's hospitals.

ourselves to meeting "urgent national needs" (and your list is virtually identical with mine), we will go a lot further toward meeting the economic problem and we will also be in a stronger position before the American people.

I thought you would like to see a copy of the speech that I made at the Truman Dinner.

Best regards.

Sincerely,
Lyndon

On March 3, 1958, The Saturday Evening Post *published an excerpt from Eleanor Roosevelt's new book,* On My Own: The Years Since the White House. *Mrs. Roosevelt wrote that she did not support Senator Kennedy for vice president at the 1956 Democratic National Convention because he "had avoided taking a position during the controversy over Senator Joseph McCarthy's methods of investigation." Kennedy, she noted, was in the hospital when the Senate censured McCarthy on December 2, 1954, and could not record his position. "But later, when he returned to the Senate, reporters asked him how he would have voted and he failed to express an opinion on McCarthyism." Mrs. Roosevelt was no fan of Joe Kennedy and suspected that his son was not really a liberal.*

To John F. Kennedy

March 11, 1958

[Cambridge, Massachusetts]

Dear Jack:

Mrs. Roosevelt's comments in the *Saturday Evening Post* raise a problem with which I would think you would want to deal before too long. It is obviously too late to retrace past steps and come out retroactively against McCarthy. But it would seem to me that you might well consider the advisability of making absolutely clear where you stand on civil freedom and due process by commenting on some current issue in this area. I would think that the Jenner bill[*] might afford an admirable opportunity to do exactly that. A strong statement at some point against the bill (if the Judiciary Committee has not killed the bill before this reaches you) with words expressing your faith in the Supreme Court as the guardian of American liberties might well be an appropriate and unforced way for you to clear up misunderstandings about your position in the civil liberties–due process field. I would not, by the way, underestimate the importance of the kind of misgiving expressed by Mrs. R. You will really have to meet it effectively before 1960.[†] . . .

Yours,
Arthur

To Lyndon B. Johnson

August 4, 1958

[Cambridge, Massachusetts]

Dear Lyndon:

I hope that you have under consideration the possibility of issuing a statement on the anniversary of Sputnik.[‡] Such a statement might set forth in blunt and dispassionate language the failure of the administration to take necessary action in these twelve crucial months. While the statement should lead with military matters, it would be a serious error to confine it to military technology alone. It should also, I believe, point out our lack of progress on the political and diplomatic front abroad as well as our stagnation in the

---

*William Ezra Jenner (1908–85). Lawyer; right-wing isolationist; senator (R-Ind.), 1944–45, 1947–59; proposed legislation limiting Supreme Court jurisdiction over civil liberties after a series of court decisions afforded "comforts to communists and criminals," as he put it. The bill failed to pass.

† Kennedy had expressed dislike of the McCarthy committee to Schlesinger but had shown no interest in saying so publicly. "Hell, half my voters in Massachusetts look on McCarthy as a hero," he said. His father liked McCarthy, a fellow Irishman, and invited him to Hyannis Port once or twice. JFK's silence on McCarthy contrasted with Stevenson's eloquent defense of civil liberties.

‡ On October 4, 1957, the Soviet Union launched *Sputnik 1*, the first artificial satellite to orbit the earth.

domestic economy and our inertia before such problems as the educational crisis. Such a statement coming on the Sputnik anniversary could be, I would think, an effective indictment of the collapse of national leadership.

Sincerely yours,
Arthur

To John Bartlow Martin[*]

August 15, 1958

[Cambridge, Massachusetts]

Dear John:

Let us suppose for a moment that we were interested in politics and that there was going to be an election in 1960. I would judge that the Republican nominee will be a man for whom our enthusiasm might be less than perfect. Yet it is evident that many people are sincerely convinced that the Vice-president has changed, that he is a new man, that he would never, never revert to the kind of behavior which marked his political career up to 1956. I find, for example, that someone as presumably discerning as Dick Rovere believes this. He says that he finds the "new Nixon" almost as repellent as the old, but has no doubt that there is a new Nixon and that Nixon would never again attack his critics as Communists and traitors.

I do not believe this for a moment (a belief strengthened by the report in the local press that he spent last weekend with Bill Bullitt[†] in the Berkshires). I believe Nixon to be a model of Riesman's "other-directed man," taking his coloration from the environment around him. In a McCarthy period, he becomes a more discreet McCarthyite. In a more liberal period, he assumes a warily liberal coloration. But none of his changes seem to me irreversible. If conditions made it profitable to do so, I have no question but

---

[*] John Bartlow Martin (1915–87). Author; journalist; Stevenson speechwriter; ambassador to the Dominican Republic, 1962–64.
[†] In 1954, Bullitt, a former Democrat, called for the United States to "reply to the next Communist aggression by dropping bombs on the Soviet Union."

that he would return to his mood of the Voorhis* and Douglas† campaigns—
or that he would do so with a certain enthusiasm, since I suspect that mood
expresses whatever there is of spontaneity in his character.

Nonetheless the idea of the "new Nixon" has taken hold. Plainly if the
Democrats have any sense, they must do something to combat it before
1960. A number of fairly wild ideas have been floating about as to how this
might be done. I myself doubt whether it can be done by Mad[ison] Avenue tricks. . . . Obviously there is no single solution to this problem; and
obviously, in the end, Nixon will have to destroy himself.

I do think, however, that there is one thing which can usefully be done.
That is for someone to write a biography of Nixon. This biography should
not be a polemical job or a hatchet job. It should be a serious and thoughtful attempt to penetrate the Nixon mystery and to explain the man; its
analysis should be fresh and detached enough to command the interest of
anyone, even of Republicans, puzzled by the Nixon phenomenon. It should
in particular serve two purposes: (1) it should put on the record everything
which Nixon has done in the past, so that when people say "Well, what did
he ever do or say that was so terrible?" the evidence can be quickly produced; and (2) it should supply a convincing theory (as, for example, the
other-directed thesis) to account for the changes in Nixon's performance
and in people's attitudes toward him without succumbing to the "new
Nixon" thesis.

I cannot imagine much more important in the domestic political field
today than this. It would be a gross failure if we got into 1960 without a
book of this sort being available.

It will not surprise you at this point for me to add that I think you
would be the best person to write such a book. There is, of course, one obvious objection—your past connection with Stevenson. But that connection is not widely known; and somehow you have been able to preserve
your repute and integrity as a writer from your contaminating political
associations (something I have wretchedly failed to do, as suggested by the
contrasting treatment you and I get from *Time*). Moreover, the character of
the book itself would, I think, suggest objectivity. You, damn it, sound ob-

* Jerry Voorhis (1901–84). Representative (D-Calif.), 1937–47; defeated for reelection
by Nixon, who suggested he was pro-communist.
† Helen Gahagan Douglas (1900–1980). Representative (D-Calif.), 1945–51; former
actress; defeated for Senate in 1950 by Nixon smearing her as a "Red."

jective even when you are being subjective, while I seem to sound subjective even when I am being objective.

You are a Harpers author; and Harper is bringing out a Nixon biography by Earl Mazo[*] of the *Herald Tribune*. The Mazo book will be wildly laudatory; but Harpers will no doubt be disinclined to publish two Nixon biographies. However, I have talked this situation over with Charles Bolte of Viking, and Bolte informs me that Viking would be glad to publish a Nixon biography of the sort I described above. I am sure that there would be no problem in getting enough money together to tide you over the period required for researching and writing.

John, do not dismiss this idea out of hand. I know you will agree as to the urgency of the matter. Let me know what you think.[†]

Yours ever,
Arthur

In August 1958, Communist Chinese forces began the artillery bombardment of Quemoy and Matsu, small islands in the Taiwan Straits captured by Chiang Kai-shek in his flight to the island of Formosa in 1949, where he established the Nationalist Chinese government. President Eisenhower on September 11, 1958, called the bombardment part of a plan "to liquidate all of the free world positions in the Western Pacific" and promised there would be "no Pacific Munich" concerning Quemoy and Matsu. On September 12, in Omaha, Kennedy made "a slashing attack" on Eisenhower's speech (according to The New York Times). *Kennedy predicted a terrible disaster if the United States became "bogged down" in a conflict with Communist China over the islands without the support of allies and world opinion.*

---

[*] Earl Mazo (1920–2007). Right-wing journalist; author of *Richard Nixon: A Political and Personal Portrait* (1959).

[†] In the end, Schlesinger wrote the book, entitled *Kennedy or Nixon: Does It Make Any Difference?*, published by Macmillan in September 1960.

To John F. Kennedy

September 15, 1958

[Cambridge, Massachusetts]

Dear Jack:

I was greatly pleased by the report in Saturday's *Times* of your Omaha speech, you are absolutely right, of course, in saying that Quemoy and Matsu are not essential to the defense of Formosa. You probably remember General Ridgway's[*] cogent discussion of the strategic value of these islands in his book of 1956 (*Soldier*, pp. 278–9).[†] The President's speech seems to me one of the most shameful applications of noble principles to irrelevant circumstances that I can remember. Indeed, it is hard to recall a time when bad diplomacy has exposed our country to a more unnecessary risk. I spoke a few days ago at the Air War College at Maxwell Field and found even there, ordinarily a hotbed of hotheads, great skepticism over what we were up to on the offshore islands.

I have been meaning ever since Congress adjourned to write and send you my warmest congratulations on your own record in the past session. The leadership you showed in the labor fight and in foreign policy fully justified Scotty Reston's excellent piece[‡] in the *Times*. Saltonstall's[§] answer to your speech on defense policy[¶] seemed excessively feeble; I would have

---

[*] Matthew Ridgway (1895–1993). U.S. Army general; assumed command of all UN forces in Korea after MacArthur's dismissal; chief of staff of the army, 1953–55. "To go to war for Quemoy or Matsu, to me would seem an unwarranted and tragic course to take."

[†] *Soldier: The Memoirs of Matthew B. Ridgway, as Told to Harold H. Martin* (New York: Harper, 1956).

[‡] "John Fitzgerald Kennedy, the Lochinvar of Back Bay, is riding off with quite a few honors at the end of his first term in the Senate," wrote Reston in an article entitled "Senator, His Eye on Presidency, Gains in Session and Is 'Swinging for Fences,'" *The New York Times*, August 18, 1958.

[§] Leverett Saltonstall (1892–1979). Republican governor of Massachusetts, 1939–45; senator, 1945–67.

[¶] On August 14, 1958, Kennedy delivered a major speech in the Senate criticizing the Eisenhower administration for allowing a missile gap with the Soviet Union. The launching of *Sputnik* stoked fears of Russian intercontinental ballistic missiles carrying hydrogen bombs aimed at America. Under the tutelage of Joe Alsop, Kennedy claimed that the United States was losing the satellite-missile race because of "complacent miscalculations, penny-pinching, budget cutbacks, increasingly confused

thought that the Pentagon could have handed him a better script than that. I am only sorry that you did not have a chance to take a more active part in the fight against the Supreme Court bills.* This is a good issue with which to overcome the misgivings of those who incline toward the view of you expressed by Mrs. Roosevelt in her new book.†

I am, however, a little depressed over recent tendencies in the Democratic party in the Northeast. I attach a piece from the current *New Republic* pointing to possible implications of the New York situation.‡ Sometime, by the way, I think it would be most useful for you to have a quiet talk with some of the New York liberal group. Perhaps after the election I could arrange an evening at Tom Finletter's. I also think it would be a good idea sometime for you to have a talk with Jimmy Wechsler and Dolly Schiff of the *New York Post*. . . .

I imagine you will be pretty busy in the fall; but, if you have a free moment, or if I can be of any help, do let me know.

Sincerely yours,
Arthur

Democratic prospects in the November 1958 midterm elections looked favorable, except for Harriman's reelection in New York. Joseph Alsop wrote in his October 17, 1958, column: "There is bad news for Governor Averell Harriman in the dingy two-family houses and the crowded apartment buildings of the Ninth Election District [of Queens]. . . . Harriman is in trouble in New York

---

management, and wasteful rivalries and jealousies. . . . We are facing a gap on which we are gambling America's security." The gap later turned out to be nonexistent.

* Schlesinger was referring to proposed bills, including the Jenner bill, to limit the jurisdiction of the Supreme Court in areas concerning the constitutional rights of citizens.

† Eleanor Roosevelt, *On My Own: The Years Since the White House* (New York: Harper, 1958).

‡ Arthur M. Schlesinger, Jr., "Death Wish of the Democrats," *The New Republic*, September 15, 1958. Schlesinger rued the choice of Frank Hogan over Thomas Finletter for the Democratic senatorial nomination in New York, and of Thomas Dodd in Connecticut over Chester Bowles and William Benton for the Democratic senatorial nomination. "It is a revolt of the low-level professional within the party organization against the New Deal and post–New Deal leadership of the Democratic Party. . . . The pros should never forget that, if the great natural resource of the Republican Party is money, the great natural resource of the Democratic Party is brains."

City at present." Arthur was concerned that the defeat of his old friend would hurt the cause of liberalism and create difficulties in 1960.

To W. Averell Harriman

October 20, 1958

[Cambridge, Massachusetts]

Dear Averell:

I do not know how seriously Joe Alsop's column and similar stories are to be taken. I am sure your record as Governor and your stature as a person will be decisive in the minds of the voters on election day. But I do have the impression that at the moment Rockefeller[*] is making considerable time with the independents and liberal voters on the De Sapio issue.[†]

I feel strongly that your reelection is essential for the cause of liberalism in the state and in the nation. I am not a New York voter, so there is all too little that I can do to help directly. But my recent *New Republic* article played a part in calling attention to the De Sapio problem;[‡] and if anyone can figure out a way that I can now make it clear that, regardless of what happened at Buffalo, I strongly believe that liberals and independents should support you. I would be more than glad to do so. In any case, I want you to know that I stand ready to help in any way I can. . . .

Marian joins me in sending best love.

Yours ever,
Arthur

[*] Nelson Rockefeller (1908–79). Businessman; liberal Republican; assistant secretary of state for American republic affairs, 1944–45; adviser to the U.S. delegation to the San Francisco UN conference; governor of New York, 1959–73; U.S. vice president, 1974–77.

[†] At the New York State Democratic convention in Buffalo in August 1958, Tammany boss Carmine De Sapio engineered the nomination of Manhattan district attorney Frank Hogan for the U.S. Senate over the liberals' choice, Thomas Finletter, making Harriman look supine before the machine.

[‡] Schlesinger wrote in the September 15, 1958, issue of *The New Republic:* "What [leadership can we expect] from Frank Hogan, a respectable district attorney who has hardly voiced a public thought on national issues in half a century and is now gravely presented by Carmine De Sapio to the voters of New York as a man worthy to sit in the seat of Wagner and Lehman?"

P.S. Can't anything be done to stop De Sapio from speaking? Every time he gets a headline, he identifies the Democratic party all the more with bossism and thereby plays into Rockefeller's hands.

To James Wechsler

October 27, 1958

[Cambridge, Massachusetts]

Dear Jimmy:

The more I watch the progress of the campaign the more I hope and trust that the [New York] Post will come out soon—and forcibly—for Averell.* It seems to me that Averell's record as Governor and his long career of service to the liberal cause entitle him to militant liberal support, however beguiling the Republican alternative. I have no doubt that Rockefeller is a man of decency and intelligence; but I do question whether his views on matters are profoundly held (the penchant for commissions always seems to me an ominous sign in an executive) or whether he has the will to impose his views on the Republican party. To reject Harriman for Rockefeller at this point would be to discard a man of proven ability for a man whose whole political meaning still remains speculative.

I have two further comments on 1960. So far as Rockefeller is concerned he will do almost as well if he gives Harriman a close run as he would if he were to beat Harriman. You will recall that Lehman beat Dewey in 1938, but that Dewey nevertheless did well enough to become the major contender for the Republican nomination in 1940 (until the Taft stalemate brought Willkie[†] into the picture). If Rockefeller runs well ahead of his ticket, he will be a major contender in 1960, win or lose.

---

* New York Post publisher Dorothy Schiff dragged her feet on the Harriman endorsement. She disliked De Sapio's hold on Harriman, wanted Finletter for the Senate nomination, and personally preferred Rockefeller.
† Wendell Willkie (1892–1944). Corporate lawyer; liberal internationalist; 1940 Republican nominee for president.

As for Harriman, his defeat in 1960 will deliver the Democratic delegation into the hands of De Sapio. This will remove the largest delegation in the convention from any effective role in the liberal coalition. If Averell is reelected, he will be able to control at least half the delegation. This may make a crucial difference in whether or not the Democrats nominate a liberal in 1960.[*]

Yours ever,
Arthur

To Eleanor Roosevelt

November 1, 1958

[Cambridge, Massachusetts]

Dear Mrs. Roosevelt:

I received a cable this morning from Nicolas Nabokov, the director of the Congress for Cultural Freedom, saying "We all feel that cable from Eleanor Roosevelt to Khrushchev[†] on behalf [of] Pasternak[‡] would have excellent effect." I agree—I do not know anyone who could speak more effectively the conscience of the free world on this occasion than yourself.

The Congress for Cultural Freedom, as you probably know, has among its sponsors Bertrand Russell,[§] Reinhold Niebuhr, Jacques Maritain[¶] and

---

[*] The *New York Post* endorsed Harriman on October 30, 1958, saying Rockefeller, despite liberal impulses, was unwilling to repudiate the right wing of his party.

[†] Nikita Khrushchev (1894–1971). Liberalizing first secretary of the Communist Party of the Soviet Union, 1953–64; ousted for mistakes over the Cuban missile crisis of 1962.

[‡] Boris Pasternak (1890–1960). Russian poet, novelist, and literary translator; author of *Dr. Zhivago*, which was banned in the USSR, smuggled out of Russia by Isaiah Berlin, and published to acclaim in the West in 1957. On winning the 1958 Nobel Prize for Literature, Pasternak was denounced in the Soviet press, threatened with arrest and exile, and finally compelled to decline the honor; he was rehabilitated in 1987.

[§] Bertrand Russell (1872–1970). British philosopher, mathematician, and social critic; winner of 1950 Nobel Prize for Literature; anti-imperialist; outspoken on nuclear disarmament.

[¶] Jacques Maritain (1882–1973). French Catholic philosopher; prolific author.

other leaders of western thought. Hugh Gaitskell, Ignazio Silone[*] and Raymond Aron are among those who have taken an active part in its proceedings; and, in this country, J. K. Galbraith, Sidney Hook[†] and myself. Nabokov is an old friend of mine, and I have implicit confidence in his judgment on these matters.

You might wish to say in such a cable that you are profoundly shocked at the way Pasternak was obliged to refuse the Nobel Prize; that the Soviet interpretation of his book is wholly erroneous; and that the world outside has read *Dr. Zhivago,* not as an expression of hostility on Pasternak's part toward his country but as an act of love and faith in Russia and the Russian people.

If you decide to send a cable, as I earnestly hope you will, I would be grateful if you could send me a copy so I could inform Nicolas Nabokov.[‡]

Ever sincerely yours,
Arthur

The 1958 midterm elections brought a Democratic landslide. The Republicans lost 48 seats in the House of Representatives and 13 in the Senate, increasing Democratic majorities to 282 to 153 in the House and 62 to 34 in the Senate. But Harriman lost the New York governorship to Nelson Rockefeller by more than half a million votes.[§]

Senator Kennedy ran hard in Massachusetts, hoping to win by the largest

---

[*] Ignazio Silone (1900–1978). Italian socialist politician and author; OSS.

[†] Sidney Hook (1902–89). American philosopher; youthful Marxist who became a pragmatic social democrat, then turned conservative, favoring the Vietnam War and Ronald Reagan.

[‡] Mrs. Roosevelt wrote in her November 3, 1958, My Day column: "To keep alive a fear of punishment for voicing one's honest opinion seems to be possible only in a very backward country with a very backward people. I hope the Soviet Union will rise above its past and that Mr. Khrushchev will show, by his treatment of the plea now voiced by a man who has brought honor to his country, that there is real advancement in the freedom for all intellectuals."

[§] In the waning days of the campaign, Harriman made an issue of Rockefeller's stint as a foreign policy adviser in the White House during the Suez Crisis, "when the first appeasement of President Nasser of Egypt took place." Then, on the eve of the election, *New York Post* publisher Schiff withdrew her paper's endorsement of Harriman, saying "his snide insinuation that Nelson Rockefeller is pro-Arab and anti-Israel" could not be condoned.

possible majority to boost his presidential prospects; he won by 875,000 votes, capturing 73 percent of the electorate.

To Marietta Tree

Monday, March 30 [1959]

[Topeka, Kansas]

Darling M.

I cannot resist writing to you from the heart of the Middle West. Why won't you come with me on one of these trips? You gently bred eastern girls ought to get to know America. I went out on Saturday to Independence [Missouri] for a meeting of the Board of Directors of the Truman Library. Old HST was himself, overflowing with charm and misinformation, and it was all jolly and pleasant. The Library itself looks like a mausoleum built for himself by some minor dignitary of Mussolini's Italy; I cannot imagine how, at a time when so many handsome buildings are being built, the Truman Foundation could have been so wrong. Remind me to repeat to you HST's diatribe on Picasso, Matisse and modern art in general.* We had only glancing political talk. It seems evident that his preferences are, in order, (1) [Stuart] Symington, (2) Johnson, (3), considerably behind, Humphrey. The two people he is against, I would judge, are Stevenson and Kennedy.

Then on to Topeka, where I am going through the papers of Alfred M Landon.† For a connoisseur of lost presidential campaigns like myself, reading the inner records of the 1936 campaign has an eerie and gloomy fascination. Landon himself is a charmer—a sort of minor-league Truman,

---

* In conversation with Schlesinger on March 29, 1959, Truman said: "I can't understand these modern fellows. I went to a chapel in Southern France decorated by—what's that fellow's name?—Matisse. I've never seen such a thing on my life. There was the Virgin with a couple of big tits spilling out over her dress. I walked through it and never said a thing. . . . Then one day I went to lunch with Picasso. A short, jolly man, bald, I liked him a lot. He had a picture of a goat, and there was the real goat wandering around the yard. I said to him, Do you mean to say that you took this beautiful goat and turned it into this monstrosity and can say to me that they look alike? He turned on his heel and walked away. The Boss [Truman's wife] was never so mad at me in her life."

† Alfred M. Landon (1887–1987). Oil man; governor of Kansas, 1933–37; Republican nominee for president, 1936; lost every state except Maine and Vermont.

grown very liberal in his old age. I have the impression that he much prefers HST to Ike. He has been extremely cordial to me—indeed, is giving me a dinner tomorrow night. He also has total recall and should be enormously helpful to *The Age of Roosevelt* if I only could get him off the oil business. And, since my tour of Midwestern ex-Presidents and candidates would not be complete without a stop in Chicago, I am going there on Saturday. Then to NY for two TV shows (*Great Challenge* and *Kaleidoscope*) on Sunday.

Marietta darling I hope that Monday the 13th is OK for you or I will never speak to you again. It is long since we have had a good, old-fashioned evening together and I need one *desperately*.

All dearest love,
A.

In his New Republic *article "Death Wish of the Democrats," Arthur had characterized Congressman William Green, Jr.,* * *the conservative Democratic Party boss of Philadelphia, as "the Know-Nothing revolt incarnate." Displeased, Green, in a message to his constituents, attacked Arthur as anti-Catholic, prompting Arthur to fire back.*

To William Green, Jr.

June 8, 1959

[Cambridge, Massachusetts]

Dear Congressman Green:

I have a copy of your recent letter to your constituents. I wish to say how profoundly I resent and reject the statement in your letter that I am anti-Catholic. Such a statement is a lie, as anyone who knows me knows. The first political campaign I remember was the campaign of 1928, when my father was an enthusiastic supporter of Al Smith and I got into fights at school on Smith's behalf. My first book, *Orestes A. Brownson,* was the biography of an early American convert to Catholicism and was a choice of the

---

* William Green, Jr. (1910–63). Conservative Democratic representative from Pennsylvania, 1945–47, 1949–63; Philadelphia party boss.

Catholic Book Club in 1939. In 1956 I supported Jack Kennedy for the vice-presidential nomination. I even took part in a debate with Paul Blanshard* in the *Atlantic Monthly* (January 1952) in which I urged and he opposed sending an ambassador to the Vatican.

Your statement is based on the fact that I dared criticize you as a politician. I do not see that a man's religious faith in any way exempts him from honest political comment. I shall continue to criticize politicians, Protestant or Catholic or of whatever faith or lack of it, on the basis of their performance. Religion is a private matter in a free society. It should operate neither as an obstacle to political advancement nor as a cloak behind which cowardly politicians can hide.

Sincerely yours.
Arthur

In May 1959, the British critic Kenneth Tynan[†] attended a panel discussion entitled "What Happened in the Thirties" with Arthur, Norman Mailer,[‡] Mary McCarthy, Norman Podhoretz,[§] and chair Lionel Trilling,[¶] sponsored by the Partisan Review *at Columbia University. Tynan's "Report from America: Looking Back in Apathy" appeared in the June 7, 1959,* Observer.

"The subsequent discussion resolved itself into a straight fight between Mr. Schlesinger and Mr. Mailer," Tynan wrote. "The latter insisted that the radical climate of the thirties unconsciously swayed the Roosevelt Administration to behave as it did. Mr. Schlesinger, bespectacled, shrill but inwardly secure, de-

---

* Paul Blanshard (1892–1980). Writer; editor; socialist; critic of Catholicism; author of *American Freedom and Catholic Power* (1949).

† Kenneth ("Ken") Tynan (1927–80). English theater critic and writer.

‡ Norman Mailer (1923–2007). Controversial novelist, journalist, playwright, filmmaker, and political activist; cofounder of *The Village Voice*; author of *The Naked and the Dead* (1948), *The Deer Park* (1955), *Harlot's Ghost* (1991), and the Pulitzer Prize winners *The Armies of the Night* (1968) and *The Executioner's Song* (1979); speaker at Schlesinger's New York City memorial service in 2007.

§ Norman Podhoretz (b. 1930). Writer; editor-in-chief, *Commentary* magazine, 1960–95; onetime liberal turned Reagan conservative.

¶ Lionel Trilling (1905–75). Writer; literary critic; Columbia professor; important figure in New York intellectual community; liberal anticommunist; author of *The Middle of the Journey* (1947); involved with *Partisan Review* magazine; married to essayist and critic Diana Trilling.

manded verification. What piece of legislation reflected left-wing influence? Which member of the Roosevelt brains-trust was a Leftist? Lacking facts, Mr. Mailer riposted by talking about the collective unconscious and how it would exert pressures that no historian could measure."

Arthur wrote Tynan a letter of appreciation.

To Kenneth Tynan

June 19, 1959

[Cambridge, Massachusetts]

Dear Ken:

I read with pleasure your all-too-accurate account of that dismal evening at Columbia [University]. Your strictures about myself were, alas, somewhat justified; I do not know why I allowed Mailer to irritate me so. I guess I have got awfully tired through the years of the megalomania of the New York radical intellectuals who feel that, if they had not made their dreary noises in the 30s, the New Dealers would not have had the intelligence or the will to do what they did. The facts of the matter were (a) that the New Dealers were more than adequately motivated to do all these things anyway, (b) that the New York radicals did not understand then—and apparently some do not understand till this day—what the New Deal was all about, and (c) that the New York radicals were demonstrably wrong on nearly every critical issue of public policy in the thirties. Their only political contribution, as I tried to say at Columbia, was in helping shape a climate of opinion in which Rooseveltian liberalism could be more effective. But they made no intellectual contribution to that liberalism, as is evident in boring detail in my volumes on the subject. As for the contribution of radicalism to literature, that is quite another matter, and I wish your question had received a more substantial answer.

I do wish you had made clear in the *Observer* piece that the symposium was about *radicalism* in the thirties. Neither Mary McCarthy nor I would regard the thirties as "a decade of stringent, doctrinaire dictatorship" outside the radical world—indeed, quite the contrary. For most of America, it was a decade of release and creation; it was narrow and confining only for the professional radicals and ideologists.

Some time we must talk about the question whether "socialism might have any relevance to America today." I am convinced that the sixties will be a decade of forward motion in the United States (I sent a memorandum of speculation along these lines to your New York address a short while ago), but I doubt whether socialism in any usual sense of the word will play much part in this political revival. It may well be that the moral and humane content of socialism has a better chance to be realized in a society which is not socialist (in the classical sense) in its economic structure. Culture and freedom both depend on diversification of ownership, and the arguments therefore for a mixed economy as against a socialist one seem to me very powerful.

Sincerely yours,
Arthur

From John F. Kennedy

June 29, 1959

[Washington, D.C.]

Dear Arthur:

Many thanks for your letter of recent date. I hope to spend sometime at the Cape this summer and perhaps I will see you at that time.

I saw Congressman William Green the other night and he informed me that he had been carrying on a correspondence with you and from this correspondence he learned that you were strongly anti-Catholic. I did not realize until at that time how versatile you were. In any case, I tried to get Billy Green with me as I feel that if I had his support it would be an effective answer to your statement "The trouble with Kennedy is that he has no politicians with him."

With every good wish.

Sincerely yours,
John F. Kennedy

To John F. Kennedy

July 3, 1959

[Cambridge, Massachusetts]

Dear Jack:

I was entertained by your note about Congressman Green. He thinks I am anti-Catholic because I am anti-him; and he apparently cannot conceive of any other reason why anyone should be against him. (He should talk to Joe Clark[*] or Dick Dilworth sometime.) . . .

Yours ever,
Arthur

Arthur feared that Kennedy's failure to condemn Joe McCarthy in the early 1950s was hurting him with liberals, a problem aggravated by the publication of Richard Rovere's new biography, Senator Joe McCarthy, *in June 1959.*

Kennedy agreed to review the book in the June 28, 1959, Washington Post. He admired the book but worried that Rovere was "overly optimistic in his estimate of how swiftly and fully the Nation has recovered its health" since McCarthy's decline and death. "Many who were directly affected—who lost jobs or friends or status—will neither forget nor forgive," wrote Kennedy. "And the indirect effects—in our educational system, our foreign service, our images abroad and scores of other areas—may well be with us for at least the duration of the 'Cold War.' " While condemning McCarthyism, Kennedy avoided personal reminiscence or denunciation of McCarthy.

Arthur was underwhelmed by the Kennedy effort.

*Joseph S. ("Joe") Clark. (1901–90). Lawyer; liberal Democratic mayor of Philadelphia, 1952–56; senator (D-Penn.), 1957–69; president, World Federalists, USA, 1969–71.

To John F. Kennedy

7 July 1959

[Cambridge, Massachusetts]

Dear Jack:

. . . All this raises, however, the larger question of what you can or should do about the McCarthy problem. The review of the Rovere book was OK so far as it went, but it didn't go far enough and, I fear, only raised in the minds of many the (alas, relevant) question: fine, but where the hell was he at the time all these dreadful things were going on? You are going to pay a serious price before you are through for having written a book called *Profiles in Courage;** people feel entitled to hold you to higher standards than they hold most other people. And, as you know better than I, the McCarthy thing is the great talking-point against you, the one thing which has caused most doubt about you (and which, indeed, is hard to defend). Pretty soon, someone will dig up the John Mallan piece which appeared in the *New Republic* in October 1952 and which represents you as pro-McCarthy, delighted with Nixon's victory over Helen Douglas and dubious as to why we were fighting in Korea.[†]

How does one handle all this? I certainly don't think there is much point in trying to answer every pin-prick. . . . A retrospective denunciation of McCarthy would be lacking in dignity. My instinct on the matter is that the best answer lies, not in explanations of the past, but in what you do now. The bill against the loyalty oath in the Defense Education Act was an admirable start. I think you should be alert to identify yourself whenever you appropriately can with contemporary civil liberties issues. What matters is how you stand now, not what you did (or, alas, didn't do) half a

---

* When Schlesinger first suggested to JFK that he would pay a heavy price for giving his book that title, JFK had replied drily: "Yes, but I didn't have a chapter in it on myself."

† John Mallan, a Harvard teaching fellow, wrote of a seminar that Congressman Kennedy had addressed in November 1950, claiming Kennedy had said he could see no reason why the United States was fighting in Korea, that he respected Joe McCarthy and thought McCarthy "may have something," that he supported the McCarran Internal Security Act, and that he was happy Nixon beat Helen Gahagan Douglas. The director of the seminar, Kennedy's former teacher Arthur Holcombe, wrote a letter to *The New Republic* saying Mallan's article was full of "false and misleading statements" and was a violation of classroom confidence.

dozen years ago. I think you should hit the civil liberties issue now when-ever you can, both in terms of affirming the general principle and in apply-ing the principle to any relevant concrete cases. I don't feel you gain a great deal by rehashing the past.

This feeling is based on the supposition that the current revival of inter-est in McCarthy is the result of the Rovere book. I know that, so far as you are concerned, the problem may go deeper than that. And I think you prob-ably ought to consider—and certainly have in reserve—a statement which would embody a franker examination of your own position in the McCar-thy years than you have thus far made publicly.

The risk in such a statement is obvious:

1) you revive the issue and identify yourself with it in an unsatisfactory way

2) you contrast yourself unfavorably with the image of statesmanship you drew so vividly in *Profiles*

3) some people will say: well, if Kennedy now admits that he was wrong over McCarthy, why should we suppose that he is right about anything today? isn't he just swaying with the prevailing winds?

On the other hand, *if* your opponents make this a persistent and critical issue for you, then #1 applies whether or not you issue a new statement.

As for #2, there will be an offsetting tendency to respect a man who admits error. Some editorials will praise any such statement as one requir-ing courage to make. Moreover, a lot of people who made the same error will identify with you and feel that, in speaking as you did, you spoke for them too. Also, if you put out such a statement soon enough, it will be ab-sorbed and forgotten by most people a year from now. The disadvantages of a statement may in the end be less than the disadvantages of trying to ride the thing out.

But what is crucial is what you could say in a statement. I tried my hand at writing something, was not satisfied with it, consulted with my good (and discreet) friend and neighbor Ed O'Connor,[*] worked with him on it;

---

[*] Edwin O'Connor (1918–68). Catholic novelist; author of *The Last Hurrah* (1956) and *The Edge of Sadness* (1961), which won the Pulitzer Prize; resident of Wellfleet and of Boston.

and we finally produced the attached draft. One trouble with it is that I don't think it is entirely candid. It might be a good idea, sometime when you have a moment, to set down as candid as possible an account of your feelings during the McCarthy period, and then see whether this could serve as the basis of anything. In the meantime, both Ed and I feel that it would be better to try and ride it all out than to attempt any full-dress explanation or apologia. (Unless, of course, there is some natural newspeg for it. The Rovere book provided such a newspeg; but I don't think the line implied in the review—that McCarthyism was terrible, but that you weren't involved and had no responsibility at the time—is a very satisfactory or convincing one.)

One other thought: the other night I heard Bill Benton* at a dinner party minimize the significance of your silence concerning McCarthy on the ground that practically everyone in Congress, except himself, Lehman and Monroney, walked away from the McCarthy fight. Bill probably inclines toward Hubert, but he is perfectly friendly to you; and conceivably he might at some point be induced to say or write something.

In the meantime, my inclination would be for you to continue your present course—make clear that you believe in civil freedom, defend it where it is under current attack, talk as little as possible about the McCarthy period, and, if forced into saying something, say that the nation as a whole—you among them—learned from the experience and what you learned accounts for your determination now to fight for the Bill of Rights.

Yours ever,
Arthur

DRAFT STATEMENT:

I have been repeatedly asked my position on Senator Joseph McCarthy.

Senator McCarthy is dead. He is a subject for the historian and not for current political comment. But these things must be said. In the early 1950s, many Americans, in Congress and out, failed to respond to a sustained se-

---

*William Benton (1900–1973) and Chester Bowles founded Benton and Bowles advertising agency in 1929 and invented the radio soap opera in the 1930s to promote their clients' products. Benton was publisher of the *Encyclopedia Britannica*, 1943–73; assistant secretary of state for foreign affairs, 1945–47; senator (D-Conn.), 1949–52. He introduced a resolution to expel Joe McCarthy from the Senate and was defeated for reelection.

ries of damaging and irresponsible assaults made in the Senate of the United States against innocent American citizens and against the very principle of liberty itself. It was an explosive and unhappy time. The Korean War had generated a nervous and unstable political climate. Many Americans in that atmosphere were so determined to do nothing that would give aid and comfort to the enemy that they kept silence over excesses committed at home and committed, moreover, in the name of patriotism.

They were wrong in keeping silent. And I was wrong in keeping silent. The few men in Congress who did speak up—men like Senator William Benton of Connecticut, Senator Millard Tydings* of Maryland, Senator Herbert Lehman of New York—deserve all credit. Whatever the motive, that was not a time for silence. We learn from our own mistakes and from the example of others. And, because we have learned, I know that the United States Senate will never again let itself be intimidated by demagoguery as it was in 1950–55. No man who learned the lessons of those dark days will permit the executive branch of government to be terrorized as it was at that time. For freedom of expression and conscience is our most precious heritage. To diminish it even slightly, except under the most positive threat to our national survival, is to diminish our nation and ourselves.

The policy of using slander, innuendos and unsubstantiated accusation to defame the patriotism of American citizens is likely to remain a permanent threat to a free democracy, particularly under conditions of cold war. Let no one mistake: I am deeply and unswervingly opposed to it.[†]

To Marietta Tree

July 17, 1959

[Wellfleet, Massachusetts]

Darling M.

I was so happy to get your wonderful letter. The yacht trip sounds as if it could not have been more fun. Bill Benton is really a nice man, and a

---

* Millard Tydings (1890–1961). Representative (D-Md.), 1923–27; senator, 1927–51; targeted by Joe McCarthy after calling McCarthy's claims of Communist penetration in government "a fraud and a hoax"; defeated for reelection.

† No such statement was issued; only the liberals seemed to care about McCarthyism.

generous one. I wish that we might have gone, but this summer was just too complicated (nothing to what it is going to be, however). . . . How entertaining to have run into Emmet Hughes![*] I am surprised that they let him back into Spain after his recent article on Franco in *Esquire* (very anti). He has written a vast new book (Emmet, that is, not Franco) called *America the Vincible*—very intelligent, very critical of the Eisenhower administration, especially of Dulles, but written in the most highly wrought rhetoric, eloquent for a moment but just too high-flown in the long run. Emmet's style shows the effects, I fear, of having written too many speeches (like ASjr). I gather that you ended up in the Ritz after all in Madrid, but am glad that you checked your mail at the other.

Life here goes on. The political pot is beginning to boil. Hubert has announced his candidacy or rather McCarthy[†] and Freeman[‡] have announced for him, and he has said that he would make his final decision in due course, thereby giving an unfortunate impression of coyness. Someone asked Gene during the press conference how Hubert's campaign was to be financed. Gene replied, "I might be mean and say that at least his father won't be paying for it." At least this shows disunity in the Irish-Catholic ranks.

The most interesting development, though, is Oregon. Charlie Porter[§] has just announced his intention of putting in Adlai's name. He told Joe Rauh that he would not do so unless he got a green light from Bill Blair (this is confidential), and presumably he has received the go-ahead. Apparently Porter met with Blair and AES in London in June. Does any of this make any sense to you or fit in with any talk you heard on the yacht? Jim Doyle[¶] is threatening to put in a Stevenson slate in Wisconsin. All this, of course, makes life so much harder for Hubert.

I spent a couple of days this week in Madison (talking to the American

* Emmet Hughes (1920–82). *Time-Life* journalist; speechwriter for President Eisenhower; liberal Republican.

† Eugene ("Gene") McCarthy (1916–2005). Quixotic liberal congressman (D-Minn.), 1949–59; senator 1959–71; challenged President Johnson in the 1968 Democratic Party primaries on an anti–Vietnam War platform, leading to LBJ's decision not to run again; poet.

‡ Orville Freeman (1918–2003). Liberal Democratic governor of Minnesota, 1955–61; secretary of agriculture, 1961–69.

§ Charles O. Porter (1919–2006). Lawyer; representative (D-Ore.), 1957–61.

¶ James E. Doyle (1915–87). Lawyer; liberal activist; federal judge in Wisconsin, 1965–87.

Public Relations Institute). I managed to get away one night for dinner at Jim Doyle's. Present were Gaylord Nelson[*] and his wife; Miles McMillin,[†] the dominating political reporter of the state (Madison *Capital-Times*), and his wife (Elsie Rockefeller[‡] of Greenwich, previously married to Bill Proxmire);[§] and Morris Rubin,[¶] editor of the *Progressive,* and his wife. It was an exceedingly gay and stimulating evening. I was quite taken by Nelson, who is young (our age), shrewd and liberal. We talked a good deal, of course, about the Wisconsin primaries. Nelson wants to avoid a contest; he is fearful that an all-out Kennedy-Humphrey fight would raise the Catholic-Lutheran antagonism and leave wounds in the Wisconsin Democratic party which it would take years to heal; also the Wisconsin Dems don't want to spend all that money on presidential primaries when they have a state contest coming up. However, he said that he had not been able to get both candidates to agree to stay out at the same time. Now the Humphrey people are firmly decided to go in; his only hope is to show the pros that he has popular strength.

All these Wisconsin people that evening were for AES. As I said a moment ago, Doyle is even considering putting together a Stevenson slate, partly as a means of deterring Hubert from coming in, partly in the hope that it might set off a great Stevenson groundswell. Nelson is for Stevenson (and expects a Stevenson-Kennedy ticket), though he says he thinks that Humphrey might make an even better president than Stevenson. All were friendly toward Kennedy but no more. But it looks as if the Nelson solution (a favorite-son delegation for Proxmire, with himself as chairman) will not work out. Jim Rowe[**] recently wrote me, "There is only one way I can see that Humphrey has a

---

[*] Gaylord Nelson (1916–2005). Democratic governor of Wisconsin, 1959–63; senator, 1963–81; a founder of Earth Day, 1970; counselor for the Wilderness Society.

[†] Miles McMillin (1913–82). Editor and publisher of the Madison, Wisconsin, *Capital Times.*

[‡] Elsie Rockefeller McMillin (1924–82). Great-grandniece of John D. Rockefeller; Miles McMillin shot her in the head in 1982, then killed himself. She later died of her wound.

[§] William Proxmire (1915–2005). Senator (D-Wis.), 1957–89; progressive iconoclast; created Golden Fleece Awards recognizing wasteful government spending; physical fitness enthusiast; filled unexpired term of the late Joe McCarthy.

[¶] Morris Rubin (1911–80). Editor and publisher of *The Progressive,* the liberal monthly magazine founded in 1909 by Robert La Follette, Sr., and based in Madison, Wisconsin.

[**] James Rowe, Jr. (1909–84). FDR White House aide; LBJ confidant; law partner of Thomas Corcoran; Democratic Party power broker.

chance to be nominated and that is the bloody and stern path of primaries because (1) it is the only way H can get national publicity with the national spotlight beating on him during the primary period and (2) the only way he can show the big pros—who may well have much more to say about the coming convention than in more than a generation—that H is a winner."

Jim has also altered his view of Hubert's strategy in rather an interesting way. He began thinking that H's liberal record was clear enough, and that he should put his emphasis on foreign affairs. Now he has come to believe that Hubert's only chance is to establish himself as so peculiarly and urgently the liberal candidate that liberal groups will have to support him, instead of saying that Humphrey *or* Stevenson *or* Kennedy would be OK. Hence H's NAACP speech. Jim writes, "Hubert must 'rally the troops' because, unless he does, the troops will not give him the early impetus he will need. I refer specifically to the liberals, whether ADA, Midwest variety, or Far West variety, and to labor. The trouble here is that the image is blurred. I find that these groups are today inclined to say that while they prefer Hubert they don't think he has too much of a chance and, besides, there is not too much difference between Humphrey, Kennedy and Symington on the liberal issues." He quotes a labor leader, "Humphrey must sharpen up the real differences between Kennedy, Symington and himself if he wants to get our people really working hard. You might as well face up to the fact you will never get the Southerners and you will never get the businessmen, unless you really start to look like a winner. At the same time you are not 'clipping your coupons' with the liberals and labor. You are carrying the burdens of both and getting the benefits of neither."

All this sounds sensible to me, and deepens my sense of guilt at not being actively out for Hubert. But it would be, I fear, a meaningless thing; it would not help Hubert in the slightest, and it would impair future usefulness for me.

However, enough of politics. We have been having a pleasant month. I play tennis with E J Kahn, jr., Arthur Kober* and Bill (*Two for the See-saw*) Gibson.† There are many parties and a generally agreeable atmosphere. We

---

* Arthur Kober (1900–1975). Press agent; playwright; screenwriter; humorist; married to Lillian Hellman, 1925–32.

† William Gibson (1914–2008). Novelist; playwright; wrote *Two for the Seesaw* (1958) and *The Miracle Worker* (1959).

have acquired a sailfish (from the Cuttings) and this has added to the general enjoyment of the pond.

When you get within the orbit of American books, be sure and read one called *The Manchurian Candidate* by Richard Condon.* It is an indescribable political fantasy derived from the McCarthy experience—very witty and sardonic and misanthropic and extravagant. I know you will find it most entertaining. I have also just received a massive novel *Advise and Consent* by Allen Drury,† a Washington newspaperman. It is apparently designed as *the* political novel of all time and looks interesting, though I have done no more than glance at the first page.

I will be fascinated to hear your views of the Middle East. My own travel plans continue vague, but apparently I am to go to the USSR around August 20, stay 2 weeks or so, and then spend a week each in Poland and Yugoslavia. I go out of a sense of conscience rather than great desire, but I suppose one must see what the future is going to be like. In the meantime, I miss you terribly and send, as ever, my dearest love.

All love,
Arthur

To Adlai Stevenson

September 12, 1959

[Belgrade, Yugoslavia]

Dear Adlai:

Just a line to say how grateful I am for your hospitality to my wandering family. They all apparently had a superb and memorable time.‡ It was sweet of you and Nancy to take them in and do so well for them.

I am completing my Iron Curtain tour here in Yugoslavia. I disliked the Soviet Union intensely, while acknowledging that movement there has

---

*Richard Condon (1915–96). Hollywood publicity man; popular political novelist; author of *The Manchurian Candidate* (1959) and *Prizzi's Honor* (1982).

†Allen Drury (1918–98). Washington journalist; novelist; author of the Pulitzer Prize–winning *Advise and Consent* (1959).

‡Marian Schlesinger and the four children stopped in Libertyville during the drive from Montana to Cambridge after a visit to a dude ranch and a tour of the West.

been in the right direction and really surprisingly fast in the last couple of years; but I greatly enjoyed Poland and think I will like Yugoslavia almost as much. I was in the USSR as a member of a writer's delegation (along with Ted Weeks,* Alfred Kazin and Paddy Chayefsky);[†] perhaps we had too many formal occasions; but I found the rigidity, incuriosity and complacency of so many Russians discouraging. It is quite different, as you know, here and in Warsaw.

I must tell you about one Warsaw experience. I encountered a Pole who prided himself on his mastery of American colloquial phrases. Your name came up, and the Pole said, "He is one of the leading headaches in America." I looked loyally indignant and said I didn't know exactly what he meant. He said, "You know—headache—an intellectual or scholar." It then occurred to me that he meant ache-head.

I will be back around the 23rd and will hope to see you soon thereafter.

Yours ever,
Arthur

To Marietta Tree

September 13, 1959

[Belgrade, Yugoslavia]

Darling M.

Your highly welcome letter arrived just as I was leaving Moscow for Poland. As you probably gathered from my earlier letter, I did not much like the USSR. The imperviousness, complacency, rigidity, intolerable abstractness of so many of the people we met all discouraged me a good deal. They are still possessed by the mysteries of a single truth and as long as this controls them, they are going to be lied to, as we were on a number of occasions. Still, to be fair, there can be no question that the USSR has made great progress since 1953. (So have you, the smart Communists would say. We had Stalin, you had McCarthy. Both countries are coming out of their

---

* Edward A. Weeks, Jr. (1898–1989). Writer; editor of *The Atlantic Monthly*, 1938–66.
† Sidney Aaron ("Paddy") Chayefsky (1923–81). Playwright; screenwriter; novelist; . won Academy Awards for writing *Marty* (1955) and *Network* (1976).

bad times. Now Khrushchev and Eisenhower exchange visits.) The night arrests have stopped; the secret police are under control; people feel an unprecedented sense of personal security. They talk with wonder and bitterness about the last days of the Stalin regime (though they are surprisingly non-bitter about the Old Man himself). They think more freely, they talk more freely. And old K. is obviously pushing this along in an indulgent, paternalistic way. Three years ago an American exhibition in Moscow, a Nixon visit to the USSR, a K. visit to the US—all would have been inconceivable. Now the street urchins clamor for red-white-and-blue USA buttons from the Fair, and everywhere there is sweetness and light. The movement within the USSR is certainly in the right direction, and the flow of consumer goods will push it farther and faster.

But there is still a hell of a long way to go—how long one begins to see when one visits Poland and Yugoslavia. The passage from Moscow to Warsaw is like a passage from a totalitarian country to a free country; the Iron Curtain obviously begins on Poland's eastern frontier, not in the middle of Germany. From the first moment, one feels in a western country again: here are English and American newspapers freely on sale (including *Life!*), pretty, slim-waisted girls, cocktail bars, shoe-shine boys and the whole apparatus of western culture. What is most fascinating is the conversation: everyone talks candidly, exuberantly, refreshingly. In the USSR, being a Communist controls every act and every idea: it means that you believe in "socialist realism," condemn abstract art and modern music, hate religion, detest Proust, etc. In Poland, Communism is a form of political and economic organization. No Polish writer has worried about "socialist realism" for years. An art show consisting exclusively of abstractions opened when I was there. Religion is unmolested so long as it stays out of politics; religious objects are everywhere for sale. Proust is being serialized in a leading Communist cultural weekly. It is all very queer. The Poles say that the ultimate logic of de-Stalinization is the de-totalitarianization of Communism, and that is what they claim to be about. I had never before thought anything in the form of liberal Communism would be possible. But this is what they seem to be attempting.

Gomulka,[*] in effect, has made two deals. He has made a deal with the

.*Wladyslaw Gomulka (1905–82). General secretary of the Polish United Workers' Party, 1943–48, 1956–70.

Russians by which he gives them control over Polish foreign policy in exchange for a free hand in domestic policy. And he has made a deal with the Polish people by which he gives them a measure of freedom in exchange for their acquiescence in Communist rule. Most Poles I talked with seemed to feel that Communist rule and subservience to Soviet foreign policy were the inescapable result of Poland's geographic situation, and that not much could be done about it. Accepting this, and accepting the economic structure of Communism, they are seeking to show that you can have all this and a large measure of intellectual and cultural freedom too.

The Poles have great charm. Warsaw is a pleasant and interesting city. It was mostly leveled during the war, but it has been rebuilt with great care; the old Town, for example, has been restored as closely as possible to what it was before the war, and it has great charm. I thoroughly enjoyed my week there. I went, by the way, to one of the student night clubs; I thought I was back at Harvard Square, except the girls were prettier, the men were better looking and better dressed, the paintings on the walls were more fashionably modern, and the music was snappier. It was great fun; I half expected to see Frankie* through the smoke. . . .

The Poles are great jokers. As one said to me, We have to be—after all, we have to produce jokes for the whole communist world. They tell the following one about Poland and Yugoslavia: in Yugoslavia, people can abuse the USSR to their heart's content but can't say a word of criticism of their own regime; in Poland, it's just the opposite. This seems substantially true. Yugoslavia, of course, is a less developed nation than Poland, and has less strong cultural traditions. Actually, it has gone farther than Poland in the direction of economic decentralization. But the conversation is less free and varied.

To Zagreb today (Monday); back here on Wednesday; to Paris, thank heaven, on Thursday; to London on Saturday; to the U.S. on Tuesday. I wish so much we could come for the weekend of the 25th. . . . But it will be my first weekend back, and I had better stay home. I note, however, that I am supposed to speak at a luncheon in NY on Sat, 10 Oct. Would you like us for that weekend? Your Canadian jaunt sounds marvelous.

---

* Frances FitzGerald (b. 1940). Journalist and author; winner of the Pulitzer Prize for *Fire in the Lake: The Vietnamese and the Americans in Vietnam* (1972); daughter of Marietta Tree.

I recommend Poland and Yugoslavia. Belgrade is an undistinguished city, but Dubrovnik, of course, is wonderful. And there are interesting things being tried in both countries. Also a high degree of pro-American feeling!

I look forward so much to seeing you and exchanging reminiscences! It has been months since we have talked—far too long when I miss you so much.

Dearest love A.

On November 15, 1959, after a blue-ribbon panel reviewing U.S. foreign aid policy recommended that the United States assist birth control programs in developing countries, an assembly of American bishops declared that American Catholics "will not support any public assistance, either at home or abroad, to promote artificial birth prevention, abortion, or sterilization, whether through direct aid or by means of international organizations."

Asked his position on the bishops' statement, John F. Kennedy told The New York Times: *"I think it would be a mistake for the U.S. government to attempt to advocate the limitation of the population of underdeveloped countries. . . . The U.S. government does not advocate birth control here in the United States. Nor have we ever advocated such a policy in Western Europe. Accordingly, I think it would be the greatest psychological mistake for us to appear to advocate the limitation of the black or brown or yellow peoples whose population is increasing no faster than in the United States. They must reach decisions on these matters based on their own experience and judgment."*

Arthur was chagrined by the whole discussion.

To John F. Kennedy

November 30, 1959

[Cambridge, Massachusetts]

Dear Jack:

I hope I am wrong; but everything I have heard this weekend confirms my feeling that your recent dialogue with the *New York Times* concerning birth control may turn out to be a very bad break.

I think you are absolutely right in your feeling that questions of public policy arising in connection with your religion are questions that can be legitimately put to you, and that the electorate is entitled to your answers to these questions. I do feel, though, that you are equally entitled to draw a distinction between private and public problems and that, in this particular case, you would have been justified in halting the interrogation at an earlier point.

The exchange was particularly unfortunate, of course, because many newspaper readers, being casual and careless, will feel that you were speaking out in response to—and, indeed, in obedience to—the recent statement by the Catholic bishops.

I am sure you will not underestimate the importance of the birth control problem. A lot of people are looking for a quasi-legitimate pretext for raising the Catholic issue. They want to prove that a Catholic can't take disinterested decisions on some significant problem of public policy. The bishops unfortunately handed them an issue. Every adult in the United States knows about birth control, and most of them care about it. Most Americans would be appalled by the thought of a society where birth control was illegal. From the viewpoint both of your own political future and of keeping religion out of this election, I think you should put this issue out of politics as quickly and efficiently as you can.

I sent Ted Sorensen* my earlier draft of the following statement:

> I believe that birth control is a question for individuals and for nations to decide according to their own most considered and earnest judgment.
>
> I myself disapprove of birth control.
>
> I recognize that many thoughtful and serious people, after conscientious consideration, have adopted a different position.
>
> Like many delicate questions of personal morality, this is surely a matter for private decision, not for public policy.
>
> This means that I am opposed to laws which would impose birth control on one group of people or deny it to another.
>
> If such laws were enacted by the Congress, any responsible official of government would, of course, be obliged to execute them to the best of his ability.

* Theodore C. Sorensen (1928–2010), Lawyer, author, JFK's speechwriter and White House special counsel; Democratic Party activist.

I hope very much you will consider something along these lines and then decline to say anything further about what you have declared to be a matter for the individual conscience, not for public policy. This would be a defensible and honorable position, in which you could preserve your own conscientious view without jeopardizing the traditional American separation between church and state. I deeply believe that the lid ought to be nailed back on this Pandora's box as fast as possible.

Yours sincerely,
Arthur

P.S. I don't suppose you want to begin your remarks on December 7th by saying: "As I look around me, I almost believe that, so far as potential presidential candidates are concerned, the Democratic party might well practice a little birth control."*

ASjr.

---

* The Democratic Advisory Council on December 7, 1959, held a $100-a-plate dinner at the Waldorf Astoria Hotel in honor of Eleanor Roosevelt to raise money for the Democratic Party. Among the 1,200 people at the dinner were potential presidential candidates Stevenson, Kennedy, Humphrey, Symington, Governor G. Mennen Williams of Michigan, Governor Pat Brown of California, and Governor Robert B. Meyner of New Jersey. Former president Truman presided. JFK cited an old Chinese proverb as best characterizing the Eisenhower administration: "There is a great deal of noise on the stairs but nobody comes into the room." Schlesinger's suggested witticism went unused.

The Tide Turns

1960

The beginning of a new political epoch is like the breaking of a dam. Problems that have collected in the years of indifference, values that have suffered neglect, energies that have been denied full release—all suddenly tumble as in a swirling flood. The chaos of the breakthrough offends those who like everything neatly ordered and controlled; but it is likely to be a creative confusion, bringing a ferment of ideas and innovations into the national life. So Arthur believed, forecasting a new mood in politics in the 1960s.

John F. Kennedy announced his candidacy for the presidency on January 2, 1960, in Washington and dined that evening with Arthur, Marian, and the Galbraiths at Locke-Ober restaurant in Boston, contemplating his uncertain future over a bowl of steaming lobster stew. Arthur noted that Kennedy conveyed an intangible feeling of depression. "I had the sense that he feels himself increasingly hemmed in as a result of a circumstance over which he has no control—his religion; and he inevitably tends toward gloom and irritation when he considers how this circumstance may deny him what he thinks his talents and efforts have earned."

The writer Gore Vidal* *had concocted a melodrama entitled* The Best Man *about clashing presidential candidates on the eve of balloting at a*

---

* Gore Vidal (1925–2012). Novelist; playwright; screenwriter; essayist; literary critic; left-wing political activist; author of *Burr* (1973) and *Lincoln* (1984); occasional actor; television personality; famous feudist with William F. Buckley and Norman Mailer. His mother married Hugh D. Auchincloss, Jr., who later became Jacqueline Kennedy's stepfather, creating a relationship of sorts with the Kennedys; his maternal grandfather was Senator Thomas Gore of Oklahoma.

Schlesinger welcomes Senator Kennedy to his Cambridge residence.
Copyright Bettmann/Corbis/AP Images

national convention. It featured characters based on Stevenson, Nixon, and Truman.

Vidal invited Arthur to the Boston premiere—before the play's opening in New York—and afterward they discussed the play over drinks at the Ritz. Arthur, theater critic manqué, was full of constructive suggestions.

To Gore Vidal

March 16, 1960

[Cambridge, Massachusetts]

Dear Gore:

The play will be a great success.[*] It is lively, sharp and arresting, and keeps the audience excited and absorbed. I don't know that I have a great deal to add to what was said last night; but I do think that Russell[†] suffers somewhat as a character next to Cantwell and Hockstader. Against their vividness and directness, he seems passive and at times a bit sententious. Of course, this is largely inherent in the sort of man he is supposed to be; but anything which would give the character a bit more punch and bite without violating the fundamental conception would help. I personally found the pacing on the carpet exaggerated and irritating; the Hamlet aspects of Russell are evident enough without rubbing it in this way.

The second act curtain didn't seem quite right—I think because the bulk of the act is about the Russell-Cantwell conflict, and the reversion of focus to Hockstader and his illness is something the audience is not quite prepared for.

As we said last night, the production rather fails to convey the atmosphere of a convention. There should be many more buttons, badges, newspapers, teletype sheets, reporters, delegates, clutter, noise, music, excitement. I don't mean to suggest an MGM production with hundreds of people

[*] *The Best Man* opened at the Morosco in New York City on March 31, 1960, and ran for 520 performances. A film adaptation was made in 1964.

[†] The main characters: the liberal candidate William Russell, thoughtful, intelligent, humorous; his rival, Joseph Cantwell, rigid, ruthless, a charlatan; and Art Hockstader, the former president, shrewd and conniving.

milling around; but a good deal more could be done, I would think, to *suggest* the convention atmosphere.

These are all minor quibbles. I have seen a lot of Boston openings, and you seem to me to be in astonishing good shape. Elliot Norton's[*] review, by the way, seemed to me much less perceptive than he usually is.

We look forward to seeing you Saturday night at 109 Irving Street, Cambridge, around 7:30. The Reinhold Niebuhrs and the Edmund Wilsons will be there and, I think, John Strachey[†] and possibly one or two others.

Yours,
Arthur

To Marietta Tree

March 16, 1960

[Cambridge, Massachusetts]

Darling M.

Tom [Finletter] and Gay came up yesterday for the night and we all went to the opening of *The Best Man*—dinner at Locke Ober's before with Ed O'Connor, and drinks afterward at the Ritz with Vidal, Stevens,[‡] Lee Tracy[§] and Melvyn Douglas.[¶] . . . It seemed to me a most entertaining political melodrama, sharp, lively and malicious. Lee Tracy is wonderful as Truman—the coarseness is exaggerated, but he convinces one that he really has been President; and Frank Lovejoy[**] does a remarkable job as Nixon.

---

[*] Elliot Norton (1903–2003). Longtime Boston theater critic; began with the *Boston Post* in 1934 and ended with the *Boston Herald* in 1982.

[†] John Strachey (1901–63). British Labour politician and writer.

[‡] Roger L. Stevens (1910–98). Real estate entrepreneur; major theatrical producer; founding chairman of the Kennedy Center for the Performing Arts and the National Endowment for the Arts.

[§] Lee Tracy (1898–1968). Played Art Hockstader on both stage and screen, receiving an Academy Award nomination for best supporting actor.

[¶] Melvyn Douglas (1901–81). Played William Russell on stage. Douglas was married to Helen Gahagan, the three-time congresswoman defeated by Nixon for the Senate in 1950 in California. Henry Fonda played Russell in the film.

[**] Frank Lovejoy (1912–62) played Joseph Cantwell on stage; Cliff Robertson played him in the movie.

Douglas does as well as he can, but the Stevenson role is rather passive and even at times sententious compared to the vividness and directness of the other two parts. The audience sat through the thing absorbed.

The play differs somewhat from the version you read in Barbados. Nixon, thank heavens, does *not* win the nomination. Stevenson withdraws, but he throws his support to a dark horse. A certain amount of the play has been cut; and some episodes, like Nixon's striking the man from Adak, did not play and were eliminated. The author's intention about the homosexual charge does not come through clearly. I thought that he was implying that the charge was true, but he told us later that the charge was false, but that Nixon feared exposure of his dirty part in framing and trapping his roommate. The only actual reference to Nixon (the line in which the Stevenson character is told that to clear himself from the insanity charge he will have to "pull a Nixon" and go on TV) was applauded, and evidently had been applauded the previous week in Wilmington. I don't think the play will have much political influence one way or the other. In a general way it confirms the impression of AES as too honorable a man to be President; but actually the characters have enough validity and life in their own right that most of the audience forgets that they were suggested by real people. You will enjoy seeing it when you get back. . . .

I had to interrupt this [letter] to give a lecture and have lunch (with Ed O'Connor and Barbara Ward). Barbara is just back from Washington where she saw Jack [Kennedy] and was much impressed by him. She tends to think that AES's only chance is as the liberal candidate; that therefore he has nothing to lose by coming out for Kennedy if K wins decisively in Wisconsin; and that, if he doesn't come out for K after Wisconsin, he may jeopardize his chances of getting K's support, if there is a stalemate, or of becoming K's Secretary of State later. I doubt the second, since I really can't believe that Jack would prefer Bowles; but I suppose that maybe he might. Is there any chance of Adlai's stopping off with you on his way back from LA?

Not much else has taken place here. We had an invasion of Soviet writers in retaliation for our literary visit to the USSR last summer. I gave a party for them Monday afternoon. They were all bleary-eyed after several weeks of intensive travel around the country. I scattered bottles of vodka around, but they all (quite rightly) preferred Bourbon. Exchanges were amiable but unedifying.

We have had a succession of pundits in transit. Two weeks ago, Walter

Lippmann; last week, Scotty Reston; next week, Joe [Alsop]. . . . I showed [Reston] the draft of my new memorandum*—the one intended as a follow-up to the one Mary Lasker† printed and circulated last summer. He was much excited about it and pinched a good deal of it for his Sunday column.‡ . . . However, the more discussion of the general problem the better. I won't burden the mails with a copy, but will bring one along, so you can read yourself to sleep with it after luncheon.

. . . All I can say is that I CANNOT WAIT FOR SUN AND RUM AND TENNIS AND LYING ON THE BEACH AND TALKING WITH YOU LATE IN THE EVENING (AND SEEING YOU MORNING NOON OR NIGHT).§ I am old and gray and tired and bored and demoralized and desperately in need of a new lease on life. Pam Berry¶ sent a wonderful gossipy letter—what fun you must all be having.

Anyway much love, and we will be with you as fast as possible.

Dearest Love,
A.

To Marietta Tree

March 22, 1960

[Cambridge, Massachusetts]

Darling M.

The weather remains cold, dark and horrid; and I cannot say with what eagerness I look forward to next week. I come back so late from Detroit that

---

* Re: the approaching liberal epoch, a time of affirmation, progressivism, forward movement, and the revival of the sense of the public interest.

† Mary Woodard Lasker (1900–1994). Health activist; political strategist; philanthropist; established the Albert and Mary Lasker Foundation with her millionaire advertising-executive husband to promote medical research in 1942; supported President Truman's abortive national health-care initiative; lifelong Democrat.

‡ Reston wrote in his March 13, 1960, column entitled "The Underlying Issue of the Campaign": "What do the Sixties require: more *consolidation*—a continuation of roughly the same foreign, defense, and domestic programs—or more *innovation* to meet the social, political, industrial and military revolutions of the day?"

§ The Trees had invited Arthur and Marian Schlesinger to Heron Bay in Barbados.

¶ Lady Pamela Berry (1914–82). Wife of Michael Berry, editor of *The Daily Telegraph*.

I won't be able to get away on the 29th; so we will arrive on the 30th on BWIA flight 395. I have never been more tired, dispirited and spent; and all I want is sun, tennis, rum and you. I fear I will contribute nothing, but I hope I can lie in some small corner and recover some traces of life.

It has been fairly busy here the last few days. John Strachey came to stay with us last Thursday and (rather to our horror) is still here, though it must be said that he is the greatest and pleasantest of guests. We had a big dinner Saturday night: the Niebuhrs (he was here to preach his last Harvard sermon), the Edmund Wilsons, Strachey and Gore Vidal. Gore was in a lively mood and dominated the evening, instructing Niebuhr in theology, Wilson in literary criticism and Strachey in economics and strategy. Next morning he called up and apologized for being tight. Also at the end of the evening, Barbara Ward and Borden Stevenson* came by after having seen *The Best Man*. Borden seemed very happy and satisfied about it. Gore, by the way, told of Ken Tynan's proposed first line for the review of *The Best Man*—"This is the finest play about Richard M Nixon since *Caligula*."

The next day I went to the Niebuhr sermon—very good and touching. In the afternoon we had a party for Strachey. Monday afternoon we went to a party given by Andrew Sinclair,† the young English novelist (*The Breaking of Bumbo*) and Mehta,‡ the blind Indian writer. This was filled with literary types and undergraduates (where was Frankie? has she abandoned the literary set?). Afterward another visitation from Lady J[ackson] [Barbara Ward], coming by after dinner at the Puseys.§ Today (Tuesday) George Kennan gave his first lecture on Soviet foreign policy—another party, etc., from which I have just returned. Tomorrow a luncheon for Joe Alsop—Strachey, Henry Kissinger,¶ Ed O'Connor, Tom Winship,** Archie

* Borden Stevenson (b. 1932). Adlai Stevenson's son; Harvard, class of 1955.

† Andrew Sinclair (b. 1935). British novelist, biographer, historian, and critic.

‡ Ved Mehta (b. 1934). Writer; born in British India; lost vision at age four; Harvard master's degree, 1961; staff of *The New Yorker*, 1961–94.

§ Nathan Pusey (1907–2001). Classical scholar; president of Lawrence College, 1944–53; president of Harvard 1953–71; wife Anne Woodward.

¶ Henry Kissinger (b. 1923). German-born American political scientist, writer, diplomat, and businessman; Harvard, class of 1950, PhD, 1954; taught at Harvard 1950–68; director of the Harvard International Seminar, 1951–71; author of *Nuclear Weapons and Foreign Policy* (1957); national security adviser, 1969–75; secretary of state, 1973–77; speaker at Schlesinger's New York City memorial service 2007

** Thomas Winship (1920–2002). Liberal editor of *The Boston Globe* 1965–84.

Cox[*] (a most attractive law school professor, probably an old friend of yours, who is now Kennedy's top brain truster) and David Riesman.

New Kennedy joke, by the way; attributed to Truman, when asked whether he was worried about papal intervention in American affairs: "It isn't the Holy Father I'm concerned about; it's the natural father."

I have been working on my Detroit speech[†] for Saturday.... I guess everybody will be at Detroit, and it sounds like the greatest fun. I wish so much that you were going to be there. At any rate, I hope to bring you the latest speculation.

There has been, as you probably know, a mild resurgence of Stevenson talk. The *Wall St[reet] Journal* had a piece about the Attwood[‡] office (what in the world is Attwood doing? He can't be writing speeches—he has never written a good speech in his life. He doesn't seem to be organizing research—at least he has approached none of the usual people. Barbara was told by AES to be prepared to work with Bill, but has heard nothing from him.) This was picked up and reprinted, and there has been a very mild flutter. My suspicion is that the Stevenson talk is being put out by the Johnson and Symington people in the hope of slowing down Kennedy by stopping the present drift to him of people who up to now have been 'waiting for Adlai.' But maybe there is more to it than that. Walter Lippmann, for example, believes that, as the convention draws near, everyone will recognize that AES is far better qualified than anyone else, and that consequently the thing will swing back to him; especially if he meanwhile returns from Latin America and gives some smashing speeches. This may be. You know how old political combinations dissolve under the stress of excitement; and it may well be that some very odd people will get behind Stevenson as the only way of stopping Kennedy, assuming that, once this is done, a switch can be made to Johnson or Symington.

---

[*] Archibald ("Archie") Cox (1912–2004). Longtime Harvard Law School professor; Democratic Party activist; U.S. solicitor general, 1961–65; first Watergate special prosecutor, 1973; fired by President Nixon for demanding secret White House tapes; later chairman of Common Cause.

[†] The Democrats of the Middle West held a conference in Detroit in late March at which Schlesinger made a speech entitled "New Frontiers of American Liberalism."

[‡] William Attwood (1919–89). Journalist; author; diplomat; ambassador to Guinea, 1961–63, and to Kenya, 1965–69; editor of *Newsday*, 1970–79. Attwood was hired by Agnes Meyer, wife of Eugene Meyer and mother of Katharine Graham, to work on issues and speeches to promote a Stevenson candidacy.

Anyway enough of this. I intend to bring you a fine new novel called *A Separate Peace** about Exeter. I think you will like it—it is very *wholesome*—no Manchurian Candidate–Ginger Man excesses—and done with the greatest economy and precision. It is ostensibly about life in a boy's school during the war, but is really about much more than this.

Please cable, by the way, if there is anything you would especially like us to bring (beside the New York papers).

I cannot really believe that I will be seeing you in a few days. And I cannot wait. In the meantime, dearest and fondest and most everlasting love.

All love,

A.

On April 21, 1960, JFK gave a speech to the American Society of Newspaper Editors entitled "The Religious Issue in American Politics." He charged the press with overplaying the religious issue. "I am not the Catholic candidate for President," he said. "I do not speak for the Catholic Church on issues of public policy—and no one in that Church speaks for me." In his column Scotty Reston called the speech "brave and eloquent," but found JFK's discounting of Catholic bloc voting disingenuous.

To John F. Kennedy

April 26, 1960

[Cambridge, Massachusetts]

Dear Jack:

I had a talk yesterday with Scotty and Sally Reston about the religious question, and it seems worthwhile to pass along one or two points which emerged.

I told Scotty that, while I thought the issues he raised against your ASNE speech were legitimate, the effect of his column was to give the Catholic-bloc

---

" John Knowles, *A Separate Peace* (New York: Macmillan, 1959). Action takes place at a fictional prep school modeled on Phillips Exeter Academy, which Knowles (and Schlesinger) attended.

issue an importance out of all proportion to its place in the speech and that, in doing this, he failed badly to do justice to what seemed to me in the main an exceptionally clear and courageous statement. We then talked about the general problem for a while. I think I now know what troubles the Restons, and others who, like them, are generally well disposed toward you but are still unsatisfied by your treatment of the religious problem. They are impressed by your own clear declaration of independence on the relevant issues; but they remain troubled, I think, by what they feel to be an implication in your discussion that bigotry is essentially a Protestant monopoly. They would respond to an attack by you on all bigots and on all those who vote their religion, whether Protestant or Catholic. Their apprehension springs particularly, I believe, from the problems of small communities where Catholic voting blocs have caused difficult problems for the public schools.

In your ASNE speech you took steps to correct any impression that you felt that an anti-Kennedy vote was automatically an anti-Catholic vote. Of course you don't believe that; and I think it is important to make this abundantly clear time and time again. I think that it would help to add to this a denunciation of religious bigotry in a way which would make it clear that you do not regard intolerance as an exclusively Protestant failing, that you recognize a tendency on the part of Catholics too to vote as a bloc, and that you condemn all tendencies to vote *for* as well as *against* candidates on religious grounds. ("I don't want a single Catholic to vote for me for the reason that I am a Catholic any more than I want a single Protestant to vote against me for that reason.")

You might also want to consider saying something sometime about Nixon's astonishing statement before the ASNE: "There is only one way that I can visualize religion being a legitimate issue in an American political campaign. That would be if one of the candidates for the Presidency had no religious belief." Apparently Nixon wants to impose a religious test for office-holding when none appears in the Constitution. The Constitution was, of course, designed to make America free for irreligion as well as for religion. I think it would take some wind out of the opposition's sails if you were the first candidate to make this point.

Yours ever,
Arthur

To John F. Kennedy

May 11, 1960

[Cambridge, Massachusetts]

Dear Jack:

Just a line to send warmest congratulations on your remarkable victory yesterday.*

I would hope that in the next few weeks the key northern liberals will come out for you, and I will do what I can to help bring this about.

The most important thing for you to do is to get a long rest between now and July. You will have none afterward, and it is more important to hit your peak in October than in May.

Again, congratulations to both of you.

Yours ever,
Arthur

To Adlai Stevenson

May 16, 1960

[Cambridge, Massachusetts]

Dear Adlai,

As I said in our phone conversation yesterday, I had a talk with Jack Kennedy on May 14. At that time, he described his position in these terms. He said that he needed perhaps 50–100 votes to win. He feels that if Nixon is to be beaten in November, the "atmosphere" in which the Democratic nomination is to be won will be terribly important. He considers it most important to the ultimate success of the party that he be nominated by the liberals rather than, say, by the south. If he can't get the liberal support necessary to put together a majority, he will have no choice but to go else-where to collect the necessary votes; but he would infinitely prefer to go to

---

* Kennedy defeated Humphrey in the West Virginia primary where the religious issue had threatened JFK's hard-fought campaign. He won 61 percent of the vote—proof that he could compete in a state with few Catholics.

Los Angeles* with the liberal vote united behind him; and he thinks he deserves this support, since he is the only liberal left in the running as an active candidate.

He regards you as the key to the picture and is very desirous of your support. I said that there were obvious difficulties in your asking an endorsement now—that anything you did would have to be consistent with your past positions and your political and personal style. He said quickly that he fully recognized this and fully understood why you would be reluctant to say anything which would give the appearance of jumping on a bandwagon or being otherwise out of character. He did not expect any immediate public statement. He would be satisfied if he felt that he could count on your assistance at some definite point before the convention. He was not trying to put on pressure of any sort and would disclaim any efforts by others to put on pressure supposedly on his behalf. But his objective in the next few weeks was, quite naturally, to assure his victory in Los Angeles; and he would like to think that he had earned the support of the liberals and particularly of you.

Kennedy's analysis of his situation seems to me wise and sound; it is also encouraging as a reflection of the spirit in which he is approaching the campaign. It seems to me that there is a strong argument for your giving him positive assurance of help before the convention. If Jack is nominated as the candidate of the liberals as well as of the eastern organizations, it will lay the best possible foundations for a vigorous and high-minded campaign in the fall, and it will draw the best possible contrast with Nixon. It will also give him a sense of indebtedness to the liberals. If, on the other hand, he is eventually nominated as the candidate of the eastern bosses and the southerners, with liberals left out or coming along at the last moment, it will hurt the party in the election; and it will saddle him as candidate and President with tacit obligations to the more hopeless elements in the party.

I think Jack is going to get the nomination one way or the other. I think it is most important for the sake of the election and for the sake of a future Democratic administration that his vital backing come from the liberal Democrats and that his vital sense of obligation be to them. The best way to assure these things would be for you to play a leading role in bringing his

* Los Angeles was the site of the Democratic National Convention, beginning on July 8, 1960.

nomination about, and for Minnesota, Michigan, Wisconsin and California to be in the forefront of his support in Los Angeles (rather than Charlie Buckley* and Governor Patterson).† In this way, a Kennedy candidacy and administration would seem the continuation of the Stevenson tradition in the party.

I understand that Walter Reuther has come to similar conclusions, and I imagine that after West Virginia many other Stevenson Democrats are thinking along these lines. I believe that Jack is entirely sincere in wishing to make the liberals the main base of his action in the campaign and thereafter, and I don't think liberals are likely to gain much by avoiding his overtures and forcing him to make his alliances in some other direction.

I am sorry to have gone on so long, and I am sure that there are many other considerations you will want to take into account before making your decision. But I do want to assure you that, in his conversation with me, Kennedy has shown a fine understanding of and respect for the problems of your position.

If West Virginia had come out differently, other courses could have been considered; but, as events have now developed, some such course as this seems to me the best hope of promoting and confirming the Stevensonian spirit and influence in the Democratic party.

Yours ever,
Arthur

To John F. Kennedy

May 22, 1960

[Cambridge, Massachusetts]

Dear Jack:

Are you by any chance to be in Hyannis Port on the weekend of June 4–5? Adlai Stevenson will be coming to dinner on the evening of the

---

* Charles Anthony Buckley (1890–1967). Boss of the Bronx Democratic Party; representative, 1935–65.
† John Malcolm Patterson (b. 1921). Democratic governor of Alabama, 1959–63.

5th and it would give us the greatest pleasure if you and Jackie* could join us.†

Stevenson says, by the way, that he felt his meeting with you was "entirely satisfactory" from his point of view.‡ He is impressed by your views on foreign policy and hopes you were impressed by his determination not to be a party—overtly or covertly—to *any* stop Kennedy movement. I think he hopes that you appreciate some of his difficulties and how easy it has been and would be to give some impetus to a movement for himself which would be largely at your expense.

Yours ever,
Arthur

To John F. Kennedy

June 6, 1960

[Cambridge, Massachusetts]

Confidential

Dear Jack:

Our mutual friend spent last night with us, and I discussed with him both then and this morning the possibility of an endorsement. He seems to feel that he has told so many people (especially present active candidates) that he would remain neutral that it would be a violation of his word to them if he were now to come out with an endorsement. When pressed, he said that he by no means precluded an eventual endorsement, and that he

---

* Jacqueline ("Jackie") Bouvier Kennedy Onassis (1929–94). Wife of JFK, 1953–63; wife of Aristotle Onassis, 1968–75; mother of Caroline and John F. Kennedy, Jr.; New York book editor; attended Vassar College, the University of Grenoble, and the Sorbonne, and graduated in 1950 from George Washington University; worked as an "inquiring photographer" for *The Washington Times-Herald,* 1951–53; as First Lady oversaw White House restoration.

† The Kennedys were unable to come to dinner on June 5.

‡ On May 20, 1960, JFK won the Oregon primary, defeating the favorite son, Senator Wayne Morse. JFK stopped in Chicago on May 21 to ask Stevenson for his support. Stevenson indicated that he did not want the nomination but was reluctant to endorse anyone, at least until the convention. He did not rule out the possibility of endorsing JFK.

would undoubtedly be inclined to endorse if it were necessary to save the party from making a conservative nomination.

He seems to have in his mind the feeling that, if he doesn't alienate the others by endorsing you, he can be more helpful in bringing everybody together after the convention; whereas if he should endorse you, then they would feel that his word is not to be trusted, and this would cause trouble later (especially in the relations between the new administration, if he were a part of it, and the Senate Majority Leader). Therefore he would like to stay out unless absolutely necessary to insure a liberal nomination.

My guess is that this is partly genuine, though there is of course a large element of rationalization in it. He could not help being impressed by the vast outpouring of mail and sentiment in his own favor since the summit.[§] It would be natural enough for him to feel that he is exercising considerable forbearance in not taking steps to consolidate and enlarge this great potential feeling; if he were to do this, it would obviously be primarily at your expense. I have no question but that he prefers you by a considerable margin among the present candidates. (He spoke in the highest possible terms of the clarity and courage of your foreign policy comments since the summit.) On the other hand, hope doubtless springs eternal.

All this raises another question. I have told Jock Saltonstall[¶] that I would sign a public letter for you. If I sign that letter, it will probably impair what usefulness I presently have as a bridge to our friend. (As you know, Bill B[lair] feels that he is no longer useful and has gone to Paris.) On the other hand, I do not seem to be very effective as a bridge; and in any case his decision will probably be settled by events rather than by arguments. So I am inclined to go ahead and sign the letter. If you think it would be more useful if I preserved a public neutrality a little longer, let me know.

Yours ever,
Arthur

---

§ On May 5, 1960, Khrushchev announced that a U-2 Air Force spy plane had been shot down over Soviet territory, setting off a chain of events that led to the cancellation of a U.S.-USSR summit conference scheduled for May 16 in Paris. In a speech on May 12, Stevenson castigated the Eisenhower administration: "Could it serve the purpose of peace and mutual trust to send intelligence missions over the heart of the Soviet Union on the very eve of the long-awaited summit conference?"

¶ John L. Saltonstall, Jr. (1916–2007). Liberal lawyer; member of the Boston City Council, 1968–72.

From Adlai Stevenson

June 7, 1960

[Libertyville, Illinois]

Dear Arthur and Marian:

It was a lovely evening! I felt guilty that I had imposed on you on such an important family feast day, but you made me content and comfortable and I enjoyed it very, very much—even Wiesner's* long "presentation." My only regret is that I can't recall what he was presenting.

I wish if any wandering Schlesingers were travelling this way during the summer they would take refuge in my prairie cabin. It would be a delight for me.

Arthur—I have been reflecting a little about our talk and find myself getting more provoked by the feeling I get from the Kennedy camp that I should do this or that to help if I expect any consideration later for myself. I have refrained from saying this until now, but I think I will at least say it to you before you leave for Europe, and say it no more to anyone!

I have always felt in a way responsible for Jack's recent political progress. After all, I had a lively regard for him as a classic example of the best in our new party leadership. For that reason, and also because of the importance of retrieving the Catholic defectors, I wanted him, as you know, to be my vice-presidential candidate in 1956, or at least I wanted him to have every chance of being the candidate. Hence, I asked him to nominate me, as you will recall, and thereafter, in view of Kefauver's withdrawal and endorsement of me, I threw the vice presidency open to the convention (Ed Plaut notwithstanding!), thinking that Kennedy's chances would be at least as good. As a result of the convention in 1956 he had a quickly earned national reputation and identification which he has exploited most effectively. Would it have been as easy to exploit it in this campaign year had I chosen to be a candidate or done anything to encourage my friends to promote a third candidacy? In short, I have felt that I launched him, in a sense, on the national scene and have conscientiously kept out of his way since not to impede or embarrass his progress, and have spoken about him in a flatter-

---

* Jerome Wiesner (1915–94). MIT professor of electrical engineering; JFK's science adviser; president of MIT, 1971–80.

ing way at every opportunity. With all this in mind, I have found the talk from his camp, albeit not from him, quite aggravating.

Do let me have any advice that comes to you before your departure and any inspiration that overtakes you in Europe. And have a good time too!

Affectionately and gratefully,
Adlai

Arthur was flabbergasted when he opened The New York Times *of June 8, 1960, and read that a "group of so-called eggheads closely associated with Adlai E. Stevenson in previous campaigns is planning a formal endorsement soon of Senator John F. Kennedy of Massachusetts." The leaders were listed as Schlesinger, Galbraith, Rauh, and the historian Henry Steel Commager.[*] Arthur felt like hell; he had not informed Stevenson of the pending endorsement.*

To Adlai Stevenson

June 8, 1960

[Cambridge, Massachusetts]

Dear Adlai:

I cannot say how terribly I feel. It never occurred to me when we talked on Sunday that the Kennedy letter was an imminent matter. It had been hanging fire for some time, and I had expected that it would hang fire until after I left for Berlin. To this moment, no statement exists. But the story got out, as I suppose was inevitable. Accordingly I issued the following statement:

I have always believed—and I continue to believe—that Adlai Stevenson is uniquely qualified among men of our age for the Presidency of the United States. However, he is not a candidate for the Democratic nomination.

[*] Henry Steele Commager (1902–98). American historian; Columbia University, 1936–56; Amherst College, 1956–72.

John. F. Kennedy is a man of first-class intelligence and strong liberal conviction. I believe that he has an extraordinary potential for creative statesmanship. Accordingly I am supporting him for the Democratic nomination.

This all arose because I told both Kennedy and Humphrey that I thought the one who survived the primary contests was entitled to liberal support. After West Virginia, John Saltonstall recalled this statement and asked whether I was now prepared to go along with Kennedy. I said I was. The fight in the party was clearly going to be between the old-timers (the Johnson-Symington-Truman syndicate) and the liberals, the new people—in effect, the Stevenson crowd. Kennedy, as a result of Hubert's withdrawal, had become the liberal candidate. I couldn't (and can't) be neutral in a fight against the Johnson-Symington-Truman domination of the party. (I know that Johnson has no use for Symington, but the backers of both are to a considerable degree interchangeable.)

I have long felt, as you know, that Kennedy would either get the nomination or name the nominee; that the best chance of advancing your influence would be on a pro-Kennedy rather than an anti-Kennedy basis; and that the party and nation would consequently be best served by a close Stevenson-Kennedy axis against the Old Guard. I know that others equally devoted to your interests feel differently. I had a long talk last night with John Sharon.* Though he insists that what he and Monroney are doing is not anti-Kennedy, obviously they are involved, whether they think so or not, in a stop-Kennedy movement. I do not think that the anti-Kennedy road is the way either to your nomination or to your usefulness in a future Democratic administration. They disagree, as is their right.

Because of these feelings, I have proposed that you consider coming out for Kennedy. I understand perfectly why you have felt precluded from doing so and have tried to explain your situation to Kennedy. I talked to him at some length this morning, at the end of which he said, "I think I understand for the first time that Adlai is helping me by doing nothing—that he could do me considerable harm by raising his finger."

---

* John Sharon (1927–80). Washington lawyer; George Ball's law associate; later law partner of Clark Clifford.

The blow-up of the Summit complicated everything. What seemed logical after West Virginia began to acquire new connotations after U-2. I wish to hell that I had not let myself be talked into putting out a formal statement yesterday. But I did, and have no one to blame but myself.

Yours ever,
Arthur

To John F. Kennedy

[June] 16, 1960

[Berlin, Germany]

Dear Jack:

I hope that you got my cable about Lippmann. He would like very much to see you. When I saw him on Tuesday, he had just been reading your foreign policy speech,* which he seemed to admire.

He is unfortunately spending the summer in Bar Harbor [Maine] and will not be back in Washington until the autumn. That is why breakfast Thursday seemed the best possibility for your getting together, if you were still planning to come to Cambridge for [Harvard's] Commencement.

Yours ever,
Arthur

To Marietta Tree

June 17, 1960

[Berlin, Germany]

Darling M.

I have been trying to write this letter for weeks; but everything has been happening, ranging from the collapse of the United States government to

---

* JFK gave a major foreign policy speech in the Senate on June 14, 1960, calling for more emphasis on economic development and less on military assistance in U.S. foreign aid, and suggesting that the next administration bring Communist China into the Geneva negotiations on banning nuclear testing.

Kathy's presentation at the local debutante cotillion and the end of the term at Harvard, and it has been hell.

I am sure you have been suitably informed on the important political events since you have been away. . . .

I can inform you authoritatively on an event which . . . has shaken and depressed me considerably and which you may not have heard about—the endorsement of Kennedy.

It all went back to the Wisconsin and W Va primaries. I took a position of neutrality, but had told both Kennedy and Humphrey in Detroit in March that I thought the winner of these primaries would be entitled to united liberal support. After West Virginia, Jock Saltonstall reminded me of this and asked whether I would sign a letter for Kennedy—a letter already signed by Commager, Walt Rostow and others and used in Wisconsin. I said that in principle I was ready to come out for Kennedy but objected to the text of the letter. So did Joe Rauh; Commager had never liked it; so further drafts were prepared, one by Rauh, another by Commager, a final one (or semi-final; so far as I know there is no final draft to this day) by Ken Galbraith. I stayed out of this but said I would sign an end-product which I approved.

Then the Summit exploded, and there followed the resurgence of interest in AES. The sudden outburst of Stevenson activity made me wonder whether I should sign the Saltonstall letter. But the drafting process was still going on; no one was pushing very hard; and I felt fairly certain that the whole thing would hang fire until I was safely off to Berlin. On June 5, AES came to Boston. He went on Mrs R[oosevelt]'s TV show at Brandeis, and then came to our house for dinner and the night. We talked privately a couple of times. He told me with all evident sincerity that he was not a candidate and that he did not wish to be President. He asked me whether I still thought he should come out for Kennedy; and I said that I thought he should, not now, but sometime before the convention (on the Blair theory which you have heard and I need not repeat). However, because nothing seemed imminent about the Saltonstall letter, I said nothing to him about it. My intention (cowardly in retrospect) was either to get off to Berlin without signing, or to tell AES well in advance that I intended to sign when something had been prepared for signature.

About 48 hours later the story leaked. This, I guess, was inevitable, and I should have been prepared for it. Saltonstall had been calling up people around the country asking them if they would go along with a pro-Kennedy statement to be signed by the Galbraith-Commager-Rauh-Schlesinger group. In a way, I suppose it was odd that the story had remained underground as long as it did. Anyway, it broke, and I was besieged by phone calls. I thought the honest thing to do was to issue a statement explaining my position; so I said that AES was best qualified, but that, since he wasn't a candidate, I was for K. (Ken, more astutely, refused to answer his phone and made no statement.)

By this time I felt absolutely sick. Marian was terribly opposed (she has since been signing draft-Stevenson ads), not on anti-Kennedy grounds but on the ground that loyalty to AES should have taken precedence over everything else. I rather agree with this view. If AES had been a declared candidate, I would have of course been for him. When I said this to Tom [Finletter], he said in effect that I was taking refuge in a technicality; that of course AES was a candidate, and that I damn well knew it. I was also impressed by the people, like Kenneth Davis,* who, when I explained why I had done it, said that, whether or not my argument was sound, I had no business as an intellectual in engaging in political calculations, that my job was to uphold standards and to settle for nothing than the best.

Let me interrupt this ghastly narrative to explain the political calculations. The great question dividing the friends of Stevenson is who would benefit from a stalemate in the convention. Mike Monroney, John Sharon, George Ball, Tom and others are convinced that a stalemate would nominate AES. Accordingly they are working for a stalemate, which means that in practice they are trying to stop Kennedy. The logic of this strategy is an alliance with Lyndon Johnson.

My belief—and the belief of Blair, Wirtz, Minow, John Bartlow Martin and most bystanders—is that a stalemate would nominate Johnson or Symington; in other words, that a strong Stevenson movement in the convention would defeat Kennedy without nominating Stevenson and thus deliver the party into the hands of the conservative wing. Rather than run this risk, it seems better to put Kennedy over as quickly as possible.

Anyway I was deluged with reproach, castigation, say-it-ain't-so-Joe letters, etc; none of which I would have minded except that I was overcome

---

* Kenneth S. Davis (1912–99). American historian and university professor; Stevenson speechwriter in 1956; author of biographies of Franklin Roosevelt, Dwight Eisenhower, and Charles Lindbergh.

with guilt and remorse over all this having taken place before I had a chance to talk it over with AES. I did penance by appearing the next night before the executive committee (about 50 people!) of the local Stevenson movement. I felt very badly: they were such devoted, earnest, selfless people; and, though they gave me a courteous hearing and I did persuade them, I think, that my action was not without logic, they so clearly felt that I had let them down.

Tom was mildly reproachful but later wrote me an affectionate letter. George Ball, who immediately perceived the advantages of a friend in the Kennedy camp, seemed rather pleased. Jim Doyle could not have been friendlier about it, while Bill Blair, who returned from Paris in the midst of it all, called and said he would have done the same thing if he had been free to do so. John Martin sent a letter of approval. Even Bill Attwood called and seemed rather favorable. But the bulk of correspondence was critical and unhappy.

I wrote to AES, at once. He replied in a day or so, perhaps a little coolly and casual but friendly enough. I think he must be somewhat hurt. I know I would have been if I were in his shoes. I still feel terrible about the whole business.[*]

But I am still convinced that the political analysis is sound—that AES has no chance as an undeclared candidate, and that activity on his behalf is likely to nominate Johnson. Both Scotty and Joe have written columns to this effect in the last few days. I should add that the first phone call at my office the day after the story broke was from a woman with a deep contralto voice who said, "Is Benedict Arnold there?" (It turned out to be your sister-in-law.)[†] Ken and I had a long session with Kennedy before leaving for Berlin. He was excellent on issues: seemed confident about the nomination; and wanted to talk most of the time about the campaign. His choice for VP, by the way, remains Hubert; and he said that Arthur Goldberg[‡] had told him that Hubert would accept it.

---

[*] Stevenson wrote Marian Schlesinger on June 13, 1960, saying, "I am distressed by all that has happened, and that I should be the cause of any embarrassment to Arthur whom I love as dearly as ever, as I am sure you both know. I think we will all survive the present distemper."

[†] Barbara Peabody (1922–2012). Wife of Marietta Tree's brother Endicott ("Chub") Peabody, a Massachusetts lawyer and politician.

[‡] Arthur Goldberg (1908–90). Lawyer; OSS; secretary of labor, 1961–62; U.S. Supreme Court justice, 1962–65; ambassador to the United Nations, 1965–68.

I am late for dinner—with Nicolas Nabokov, the von Hofmannsthals,[*] Mary McCarthy and [J. Robert] Oppenheimer! I wish you were going to be there. I miss you and can't wait to see you in Paris.

All love,
Arthur

John F. Kennedy was nominated as the Democratic presidential candidate on the first ballot in Los Angeles on July 11, 1960. Lyndon B. Johnson was selected as his running mate.

To Robert F. Kennedy

July 18, 1960

[Wellfleet, Massachusetts]

Dear Bob:

This could hardly be a more trivial point: but seeing Abe Ribicoff[†] on *Face the Nation* makes me wonder whether it would not be a good idea to encourage people appearing on Jack's behalf not to call him Jack. Calling him Jack emphasizes his youth and reinforces a central Republican argument against him.

The candidate should be referred to as "Senator Kennedy" or as "John Kennedy." People appearing on Nixon's behalf don't call him "Dick" all the time; and the contrast between "the Vice President" and "Jack"—particularly if our own people insist on drawing it—may do us a lot of harm in the long run.

Yours,
Arthur

PS. On the same principle people should stop calling you "Bobby."

---

[*] Raimundo von Hofmannsthal, son of Hugo, the Austrian novelist, poet, and librettist.
[†] Abraham Ribicoff (1910–98). Liberal representative (D-Conn.), 1949–53; governor of Connecticut, 1955–61; secretary of health, education, and welfare, 1961–62; senator, 1963–81.

Reinhold Niebuhr, like Mrs. Roosevelt, was no fan of the Kennedys. He had misgivings about the "thinness" of JFK's religion and about his personal morality. Arthur was unable to break free from the Los Angeles convention to visit the Niebuhrs in Santa Barbara, where they were spending the summer at the Center for the Study of Democratic Institutions. Back in Massachusetts, Arthur wrote them a letter expressing his mixed feelings about Kennedy's convention victory.

To Ursula and Reinhold Niebuhr

21 July 1960

[Wellfleet, Massachusetts]

Dear Ursula and Reinhold:

I wish so much that we could have come to see you in Santa Barbara, but the phone talk was a good deal better than nothing. As you probably gathered, I came away from the convention rather depressed. I never anticipated the emergence of a strong draft-Stevenson movement, and I was terribly torn when it appeared. If I had known it was coming, I would of course have stayed with Stevenson. But I believe the movement was a great error. It exposed Stevenson himself in his worst posture—the posture of indecision; and, for this and other reasons, may well have cost him the State Department. From what I saw of him in Los Angeles, I am sure that, if nominated, he would have been cruelly beaten in the election. It is a tragedy since he is by far the best and most intelligent man to appear in our public life this generation. He has a dimension that all these other fellows lack. But he lacks the will to command and the will to victory.

Kennedy has these qualities in abundance. He won the nomination and deserved it. He is a man of first-rate intelligence, authority and decision. Yet my liking for him and confidence in him declined in the course of the convention. I have come to agree with you about the Johnson nomination; I am willing to concede that it was not only politically sound but also conceivably a wise and brave move. But the dissimulation and deceit with which Kennedy brought Johnson out were depressing. I believe on the basis of L.A. that Jack has all the lesser qualities of F.D.R. Whether he has the greater qualities too one cannot say now, any more than one could say about F.D.R. in the autumn of 1932.

It seems to me inevitable that Kennedy should have beat out Stevenson. The Stevenson movement was too amateur and unserious to win; it was like a club of intelligent, civilized people, all of whom liked each other very much. There is no "we happy few" nonsense about the Kennedy movement. Nonetheless the fact remains that I was a member of the Stevenson club; and I fear that my enjoyment of national politics is now at an end. I do not think Kennedy will ask me to work for him during the campaign; and, after LA, I really don't care. Working in a Kennedy campaign would not be nearly so much fun as working in a Stevenson campaign. On the other hand, he will probably win, not an insignificant consideration.

I didn't mean to inflict all these thoughts on you (they are, of course, for you and Ursula alone).* . . .

Our best love to you both,
Arthur

To John Kenneth Galbraith[†]

August 3, 1960

[Cambridge, Massachusetts]

Dear Kenneth:

May I call your attention to the interview by Earl Mazo with Nixon in the *New York Herald Tribune* of July 29th. The headlines of the piece are "Nixon Tells of Humble Beginnings: Says He, Wife Prove The American Dream." Paragraph 18 of the piece reads as follows: " 'This year,' he pre-

---

* Niebuhr replied on July 23: "The Kennedy machine is more ruthless than the bosses and I dread the prominence which young Bob will have in the campaign and administration."

† The Galbraith family in 1951 had moved into a house on Francis Avenue in Cambridge separated by a brick wall from the Schlesinger residence. Ken and Arthur were old friends with a special relationship based on common interests: writing, politics, the Democratic Party, Harvard, the Kennedys, promoting the liberal agenda. They celebrated the same birthdate—October 15— although Galbraith was born in 1908, Schlesinger in 1917.

dicted, 'millions of Democrats will vote with us . . . not because they will desert their party, but because the Democratic party of Jefferson and Jackson has become the party of Schlesinger, Galbraith, Reuther and Bowles.' "

I call your attention to the order of names. It is perfectly evident that Goldwater,[*] no doubt in a fit of nervousness, left off the first name in the official list when he came to his peroration[†]. . . .

Yours ever,
Arthur

Mrs. Roosevelt remained wary and unconvinced by young Jack Kennedy despite his winning the nomination.

On August 14, 1960, Kennedy attended an observance in Hyde Park, New York, commemorating the 25th anniversary of the Social Security Act, and lunched alone with Mrs. Roosevelt at her Val-Kill cottage.

"A visit to Hyde Park is both a pilgrimage and a challenge," he said afterward. "I am grateful to you—Mrs. Roosevelt—for allowing me to be here today. For I come to Hyde Park not to instruct but to learn. And I think that we can all agree that Eleanor Roosevelt is a true teacher. Her very life teaches a love of truth and duty and courage. The wide world is her neighborhood. All its people are her daily concern. She is frank, she is outspoken, she is forthright—and I know she always will be."

Kennedy was persuasive. Mrs. Roosevelt agreed to serve as honorary cochair of the New York Committee for Kennedy.

---

*Barry Goldwater (1909–98). Senator (R-Ariz.), 1953–65, 1969–87; Republican presidential nominee, 1964; his family founded the Phoenix department store Goldwater's.

†When he withdrew his name from nomination at the Republican convention in Chicago in July 1960, Goldwater said the Democratic Party was no longer the party of Jefferson, Jackson, and Woodrow Wilson, but the party of "Bowles, Galbraith, and Walter Reuther," omitting "Schlesinger," to Arthur's apparent chagrin.

To John F. Kennedy

August 17, 1960

[Cambridge, Massachusetts]

Dear Jack:

I had dinner last night with Anna Roosevelt Halsted,* who reports that your talk with her mother on Sunday was a success. She put it much as follows: "Mother was afraid she would find a cold, opinionated young man, who wasn't interested in learning anything and was paying a routine call for political purposes. She was much impressed by his modesty and his willingness to listen and learn. She was also impressed by his candor and strength. She feels that his main problem will be to convey to people who feel themselves part of a neglected minority that he has a deep, personal concern for and identification with their problems."†

I am starting the Kennedy-Nixon pamphlet‡ today and would appreciate any thoughts of yours as to how the contrast should be developed (though I well recognize that more important matters are clamoring for your attention).

Yours ever,
Arthur

---

*Anna Roosevelt Halsted (1906–75). Writer; editor; daughter of Franklin and Eleanor Roosevelt.

†Mrs. Roosevelt wrote to Mary Lasker about the Val-Kill meeting with JFK: "I told him that he needed the Stevenson votes in New York and California and that he had to carry these two states or he would be in trouble because he probably could not hold the Solid South. . . . I liked him better than I ever had before because he seemed so little cocksure, and I think he has a mind that is open to new ideas."

‡Arthur Schlesinger, Jr., *Kennedy or Nixon: Does It Make Any Difference?* (New York: Macmillan, 1960).

To John F. Kennedy

August 26, 1960

[Cambridge, Massachusetts]

Dear Jack:

Things are getting off to a slow start; but it is still awfully early, and I know that you will not be unduly alarmed by expressions of Republican confidence emanating from a predominantly Republican press. However, a long conversation with Ken Galbraith after his return from the Middle West confirmed impressions of my own as to some of the reasons for the present lethargy in the campaign. Since the matters involved are remediable, I thought I might pass along my theory of it all to you.

The first point that I would make is that presidential elections are different from presidential primaries; and methods which may be brilliantly successful in winning primaries will not necessarily work as well in winning general elections. In particular, organization counts heavily in primaries. Organization counts much less in general elections. Carmine [De Sapio] is an asset in carrying the New York delegation but not in carrying the state. Bill Green could not have made Philadelphia a Democratic city in a million years. And so on. Organization has an important role to play, of course; but to suppose that organization per se will win New York or California is nonsense.

My second point is that the campaign thus far has failed to elicit the all-out support of the kind of people who have traditionally provided the spark in Democratic campaigns. These people are the liberals, the reformers, the intellectuals—in general, people who have entered politics, not because it is their livelihood, but because they care deeply about issues and principles. Those who think that everything can be solved by organization dismiss this group on the ground that it is numerically insignificant. This is a most naive reaction. The number directly involved may be small. But these are the kinetic people, and their participation or non-participation profoundly affects the atmosphere and drive of a Democratic campaign. In consequence, the number of voters indirectly influenced by the indifference or commitment of these people is very considerable.

It is because you were making progress in winning these people that your primary campaign began to develop considerable emotional momentum. You came to Los Angeles as a liberal candidate committed to a liberal theory of the campaign. For various reasons—many of them entirely persuasive—it seemed advisable to modify this theory. Putting Lyndon on the ticket had its advantages; it also exacted its price. It interrupted the emotional momentum of your drive. The kinetic people were set back and put off a bit. They are of course for Kennedy-Johnson over Nixon-Lodge, but they are not at the moment committed heart and soul to the Kennedy-Johnson campaign. As a result, the campaign thus far lacks much sense of crusading urgency.

And, because these people are not yet enthusiastically engaged, there results, as Ken points out, a sort of intellectual and emotional vacuum into which all sorts of other things rush. The recent revival of the religious issue is to be explained in great part by the existence of this vacuum. . . .

Setting up a religious desk in the headquarters will not solve the religious problem. The only way to do this is to *fill* the vacuum—to charge the campaign with intellectual and emotional content—to make people think of you in so many other ways that the question of your faith recedes into the background—and all this means to enlist the enthusiasm of the kinetic Democrats who alone can convert the campaign into a crusade. . . .

How to commit these people to the campaign? How to restore the mood that was developing just before Los Angeles? This is partly a job for yourself and partly for the campaign organization.

So far as you are concerned, I think you should exploit one of your strongest assets—i.e., that you are far more liberal than Nixon. There is no point, it seems to me, in playing this down and hope to catch some votes in Virginia at the price of losing New York. Herbert Lehman and Tom Finletter will bring you many more votes than Harry Byrd[*] and Howard Smith.[†] For that matter, Adlai Stevenson can bring you many more electoral votes than Lyndon Johnson seems likely to. I think you should take a strong liberal line from now on. . . .

Once the issue-minded Democrats catch fire, then the campaign will gather steam. Until they do, the Democratic campaign will have an air of

---

[*] Harry F. Byrd, Sr. (1887–1966). Owner of *The Winchester Star* and other newspapers in the Shenandoah Valley; farmer and politician; conservative Democratic governor of Virginia, 1926–30; senator, 1933–65; opposed racial desegregation of the public schools.

[†] Howard Smith (1883–1976). Lawyer; conservative representative (D-Va.), 1931–67; as chairman of the House Committee on Rules he kept civil rights legislation from coming up to vote on the House floor.

profound lethargy. The Republicans can disguise lethargy because they control the press. But the Democrats have no means of giving an impression of enthusiasm when it doesn't exist. To develop enthusiasm we have no choice but to give the enthusiasts something to believe in.

I apologize for the length of this document.

Yours ever,
Arthur

Arthur was quick to protest when Newsweek *ran an item suggesting strains in his relationship with JFK over the rejection of his draft of the acceptance speech.*

To John F. Kennedy

August 26, 1960

[Cambridge, Massachusetts]

Dear Jack:

I am sure that it is not necessary for me to say that the item in The Periscope of the current *Newsweek* is a thorough fabrication. The only pride I have in political authorship is my profound imperviousness to what is done (or not done) to anything I submit. The man who has to accept responsibility for the utterance must have it as he likes it; there is no other way.

I am sending the attached letter to *Newsweek* for publication.

Yours ever,
Arthur

To the Editors of *Newsweek*

August 26, 1960

[Cambridge, Massachusetts]

Gentlemen:

The item concerning me in The Periscope of August 29 is a fabrication. You state that relations between myself and Senator Kennedy have been "strained," that I was "hurt" because Kennedy "rejected" the draft of an acceptance speech. It is not true that relations between myself and Senator Kennedy have been "strained." It is not true that I was "hurt" at any use or non-use of counsel I have ever given to Senator Kennedy or to anyone else in politics. My theory of political consultation has always been that the advisor serves the principal and not himself. The man who must take public responsibility for the utterance has every right—indeed, every duty—to say what he himself wants to say. No one who does not unreservedly accept this should ever try to advise public persons.

What is as shocking as the story itself is the clear implication—conveyed by such phrases as Schlesinger "now admits" and "that's all patched up now, Schlesinger says"—that I was the source of this so-called information. I never said these things, and no one from *Newsweek* ever checked the story with me or discussed it in any other way. To invent statements of a defamatory sort and then to attribute them to the person defamed is enterprising but hardly responsible journalism.

Sincerely yours,
Arthur Schlesinger jr.

To John F. Kennedy

August 30, 1960

[Cambridge, Massachusetts]

Dear Jack:

When I heard that Nixon was going on the Jack Paar[*] show I hoped that this did not mean that you were going to appear too. When I read Scotty Reston's column[†] I felt all the more strongly that you should not. I came to my office this morning determined to write you to that effect. On arriving I found the attached letter from Jim Fleming of NBC.[‡] He is one of the best television producers in the business, and I think everything he says is absolutely true. Let Nixon have the monopoly on poor taste. In my judgment, it would be better to sacrifice a little exposure and retain the dignity of a Presidential candidate. I think you will gain much more by this in the long run.[§]

Yours ever,
Arthur

---

[*] Jack Paar (1918–2004). Radio and television comedian; host of *The Tonight Show,* 1957–62. After his nomination, Nixon appeared on *The Tonight Show* on August 25, 1960, for forty minutes.

[†] Reston wrote on August 27: "What other generation of Americans has ever had the opportunity of hearing the Vice President of the United States discuss the survival of the Republic with a night-shift comic?"

[‡] James Fleming (1915–96). Television producer; helped start the *Today* show at NBC in the early 1950s. He wrote Schlesinger: "Mr. Nixon made a most ill-advised (from his point of view) appearance on the Jack Paar program. . . . Essentially the mistake was one of his demeaning his person as a Presidential candidate vis a vis Mr. Paar. . . . Nixon got himself in a most subservient posture. . . . My suggestion is that Senator Kennedy resist any offer of equal time in the Paar program. . . . The important thing is that the Senator not allow himself to be caught in the posture. The aspirant for the Presidency cannot indulge in a public appearance at that level."

[§] JFK was a guest on *The Tonight Show* on June 16, 1960, before his nomination. He did not appear later as Democratic presidential nominee. Schlesinger was a guest on October 10, 1960.

To John F. Kennedy

August 30, 1960

[Cambridge, Massachusetts]

Dear Jack:

I sent you a letter the other day suggesting that one thing vitally needed to get the campaign off the ground was to activate the potential crusader in the Democratic party—the issue-minded people who would ordinarily by this time be covering their cars with Kennedy stickers, arguing with their friends, sending letters to the papers, manning local organizations, canvassing their neighborhoods and, in general, charging the campaign with emotion and zeal (and incidentally knocking down all efforts to insert the religious issue into the discussion). When I wrote you last week I assumed that the trouble with these people was apathy. After attending the meeting of the ADA National Board in Washington on Saturday, I am now convinced that the situation is more serious than I supposed.

I also apologize for the length of my last letter. This letter is even longer; and I am sorry for this, and I am sorry if the tone is unduly emphatic. But I am writing it this way because the situation seems to me urgent and because of my deep affection for you and because I think that you have it in you to be a great President and because I think it is essential for the country that you be elected. It may be that after this you won't want to hear anything from me for the rest of the campaign, which I would wholly understand. But I hope you will be able to spare ten minutes to read this.

The meeting of the ADA National Board was exceptionally well attended—nearly 60 people were there. The subject was the endorsement of a Presidential ticket. The meeting began with representatives of the various chapters reporting on the state of mind in their respective chapters. One after another rose and recited his piece. About half recommended on behalf of their chapters no endorsement at all; the other half recommended endorsement but with the utmost tepidity. The main discernible emotion on the part of these people was opposition to Nixon. Even the chapters which recommended endorsement said that the minority which opposed endorsement was far more definite about it than the majority which favored it. As someone put it, "We don't trust Kennedy and we don't like Johnson; but Nixon is so terrible that we have to endorse the Democrats."

Then the debate began. I must emphasize to you that every national leader of ADA urged an unqualified endorsement. Joe Clark came and argued strongly on your behalf. Julius Edelstein[*] read a splendid letter from Herbert Lehman. Joe Rauh, Bob Nathan,[†] Jim Loeb, Frank McCulloch,[‡] Marvin Rosenberg,[§] Gus Tyler,[¶] Sam Beer,[**] myself—all urged a strong endorsement. Because of Nixon, the group decided on endorsement. But the quality of their enthusiasm may be judged by the fact that the following paragraph about you was eliminated from the proposed statement by a vote of 23–17. "In the critical fields of human concern—foreign affairs, economic and social policy, civil rights—he has shown himself an aggressive champion of creative liberalism. He stands with deep conviction for national strength, for peace, for economic growth, for social welfare, for the guarantee to all our citizens of their constitutional rights. He has amply displayed the qualities of political skill and leadership essential in transforming platform pledges into national policy." The majority simply refused to believe these things about you. Eventually we moved for reconsideration, and Joe Rauh finally got some of the language restored, though in a much more subdued form. . . .

I was prepared for apathy on the part of grass-roots liberals. I was not prepared for the depth of hostility which evidently exists. . . .

I am putting these things sharply because time is racing by and because I want you to be President; so I hope you will forgive me![††]

Yours ever,
Arthur

---

[*] Julius Edelstein (1912–2005). Lawyer; New Dealer; executive assistant to Senator Lehman; executive assistant and close adviser to New York mayor Robert F. Wagner, Jr.; later senior vice chancellor, City University of New York.

[†] Robert R. Nathan (1908–2001). Economist; New Dealer.

[‡] Frank McCulloch (1905–96). Lawyer; top aide to liberal senator Paul Douglas (D-Ill.); chairman of the National Labor Relations Board under JFK and LBJ.

[§] Marvin Rosenberg (1907–87). Textile manufacturer; longtime Humphrey adviser and fund-raiser.

[¶] August ("Gus") Tyler (1911–2011). Labor activist, author, newspaper columnist; with the International Ladies' Garment Workers Union for more than forty years, ran the political and educational divisions.

[**] Samuel Beer (1911–2009). Liberal Democratic activist; journalist; FDR speechwriter; Harvard political scientist, 1946–82.

[††] JFK replied to Schlesinger in conversation: "I don't mind criticism at this point. I would rather have you tell me now than to wait until November."

P.S. I had lunch today with Henry Kissinger, who hardly qualifies as a bleeding heart. He said to me, "We need someone who will take a big jump—not just improve on existing trends but produce a new frame of mind, a new national atmosphere. If Kennedy debates with Nixon on who can best manage the status quo, he is lost. The issue is not one technical program or another. The issue is a new epoch. If we get a new epoch and a new spirit, the technical progress will take care of themselves."

To Robert F. Kennedy

September 4, 1960

[Cambridge, Massachusetts]

Dear Bob:

. . . I am sure that Jack has been successful with every audience to which he has spoken, but he has thus far been less successful in having a clearcut impact on the huge invisible audience trying to get an impression of what sort of man he is and what he stands for.

Lyndon has always felt that, because the Democrats could carry Congress, they could carry the Presidency in the same way—i.e., through the exploitation of an immense variety of local issues. I am sure there are people in your organization who think that you can win general elections the same way you can win primaries—again through local issues plus organization. They are wrong. Local issues are indispensable; organization is indispensable; but essentially you carry the Presidency by establishing a convincing and impressive *national* image, if I may use that horrid word.

Jack made an excellent start on the national image in the primaries and in the "New Frontier" speech. But the Johnson nomination—though there may have been offsetting arguments for it—harmed the "New Frontier" approach and made the Democratic ticket seem more old hat. Then the short session* came along, with its frustrations and general dreariness. Since then, at least as reported in the press, Jack seems to have been making predominantly local speeches. I don't object to local speeches in the right context, but at present the context doesn't exist. What is needed to

* Congress met for a short session in August 1960 after the national conventions.

give the campaign a lift is some *national* speeches at an early date, setting forth with some eloquence his vision of the campaign and the future of the country. This, among other things, is the way to activate the liberal-minded people.

What should his national speeches be about? There is only one big, all-absorbing issue. That is peace. The farmer cares about price supports, but he cares more about peace. The workingman cares about wages, but he cares even more about peace. Etc. Jack's line in this matter was fine during the spring (except for that one moment in Oregon). But I have regretted the extent to which he is not saying the things in foreign affairs he said in the spring. Instead he seems almost to be narrowing the gap between himself and Nixon.

Jack begins any discussion of foreign policy with a great advantage. Because he is a Catholic, no one can suggest very convincingly that he is soft on Communism. What he should stand for is quite simple, I should think: he should stand for (a) strength and (b) conciliation ("speak softly and carry a big stick") as against the administration's commitment to military weakness and diplomatic provocation. . . .

My point should not be misunderstood. These people are not pacifists or Wallace-ites. They have no illusions that a different line toward the Russians is going to work miracles. But they regard it as essential that the United States give the impression to the world of being determined to leave no stone unturned in the quest for peace. They fear that, if we don't, we hand the peace issue to the Communists and produce our own isolation. I have always argued that we should negotiate with the Communists at every opportunity if only to remind our allies what bastards they are. A sentence of Chip Bohlen's sticks in my mind: "We should prepare for the worst and work for the best." The Republicans have done neither. Jack has done well in emphasizing the first, but he has not yet done enough since the convention to affirm the urgent necessity of the second. That is what millions of people are waiting to hear. As Henry Kissinger said to me last week, "If all Senator Kennedy claims is that he can manage the status quo better than Nixon, he is not going to win."

One specific issue, of course, is disarmament, which he developed with great skill and effect in the primaries. I am sorry that two current issues have not been approached more affirmatively; Khrushchev at the UN; and

Castro.* I think Jack might well have gained more by saying that he would be glad to meet with Khrushchev, that he would welcome the opportunity to make the American position clear to him, that he would talk with anyone anywhere at any time if it served the interests of peace and the United States. Why say that he will do something only if Nixon does it? As for Castro, the point here is, not that revolution in Latin America is bad and should be contained, but that social desperation permits a revolution to be easily corrupted; and that different US policies would either have averted Castro or would have kept him in better channels or, if nothing could stop the Communization of Cuba, would have gained us support in the OAS for anti-Castro measures.

I am sorry for the length of this; but I feel certain on this matter, at least so far as the issue-minded constituency is concerned. In the end, they will come into the campaign when they see some viewpoint they want to fight for.

Yours,

Arthur

The president of New York's Union Theological Seminary, Henry Van Dusen,[†] wrote Stevenson that he was dismayed by reports that JFK was a philanderer and that, if grounded in fact, his "dubious morals" made him unfit for the presidency. Van Dusen claimed that Reinhold Niebuhr in casual conversation mentioned that "everyone" knew that JFK "had slept with anyone who was willing" and that Galbraith and Schlesinger had dismissed the matter as inconsequential. Van Dusen claimed that the rumors were widespread in Britain, where he was visiting. Stevenson replied, "I have some experience with rumors and have become a little cynical, I confess," but he sent Van Dusen's letter on to Arthur.

---

* Fidel Castro (b. 1926). Cuban Marxist revolutionary leader; overthrew dictator Fulgencio Batista in 1959; Cuban prime minister, 1959–76; president of Cuba, 1976–2008; First Secretary of the Communist Party of Cuba, 1961–2011.

† Henry P. Van Dusen (1897–1975). Doctor of divinity; president of Union Theological Seminary in New York City, 1945–63; editor of *The Spiritual Legacy of John Foster Dulles* (1960).

To Adlai Stevenson

September 4, 1960

[Cambridge, Massachusetts]

Dear Adlai:

I am returning the Van Dusen letter herewith. I must confess my extreme impatience with this sort of thing and couldn't sympathize more with your desire "to keep a mile away from such matters."

In the first place, even if such stories were true, I do not see how they bear essentially on Kennedy's capacity to be President, especially when one considers the alternative. You will remember that in the campaign of 1884 much was made of Grover Cleveland's illegitimate child, and the contrast was drawn with James G Blaine's spotless private life. Some people got so agitated about this issue that they completely lost sight of the public records of the two men. At that time, E. L. Godkin[*] of the *Nation*, trying to place the matters in some sort of perspective, wrote, "Chastity is a great virtue, but every man knows in his heart that it is not the greatest of virtues, that offences against it have often been consistent with ... the qualities which ennoble human nature and dignify human life and make human progress possible." Perhaps the best comment was made by someone who said that, in view of the respective public and private careers of the two men, "We should elect Mr Cleveland[†] to the public office he is so admirably qualified to fill and remand Mr Blaine[‡] to the private life which he is so eminently fitted to adorn."

In the second place, though I have no knowledge at all of the facts, my impression is that the stories in circulation are greatly exaggerated. One hears them in Northeast Harbor, in Fishers Island, in Easthampton and in all those circles where, in the past, vicious and lying stories have been told about Woodrow Wilson, Franklin Roosevelt, Harry Truman and you. My

[*] Edwin Lawrence Godkin (1831–1902). Irish-born American journalist and editor; founded *The Nation* magazine in 1865.

[†] Grover Cleveland (1837–1908). Lawyer; Democratic mayor of Buffalo, 1881–82; governor of New York 1883–85; twenty-second and twenty-fourth U.S. president, 1885–89, 1893–97.

[‡] James G. Blaine (1830–93). Newspaperman; representative (R-Maine), 1863–76; senator, 1876–81; secretary of state, 1881, 1889–92; Republican presidential nominee, 1884. Charges of political corruption dogged him.

own belief is that for some years after the war Kennedy, because of the trouble with his spine, believed that he had only a few years to live. I imagine that he meant to enjoy these years to the utmost. The turning-point in his life, I think, took place in the winter of 1955–1956 when he had the series of back operations which at first nearly killed him but from which at last he made a complete and definite recovery. So far as I can see, as soon as he knew that he had a full life to live, he decided to prepare himself for the Presidency. The stories about his private life seem to date from 1955 and before. I have heard no reliable account of any such incident in recent years.

In the third place, I question the purity of Dr Van Dusen's own motives. Have you seen his own nauseating new book—the one entitled, as I recall, *The Spiritual Legacy of John Foster Dulles*?

I think you should give Van Dusen hell for circulating rumors which are (a) out of date, (b) largely unsubstantiated and (c) even if true and contemporary—which they are not—would hardly seem crucial when the alternative is Richard M. Nixon.[*]

I shall send along tomorrow some thoughts about the Liberal Party. I am depressed about the way the campaign is going. I think that you are about the only hope for a Democratic victory.

Yours ever,
Arthur

---

[*] Schlesinger later asserted that he had never seen anything "untoward" while working in the White House, writing: "At no point in my experience did any preoccupation with women interfere with [JFK's] conduct of the public business (apart from Caroline crawling under the presidential desk)." Schlesinger also cited the journalist Ben Bradlee, who wrote in his 1995 memoir, *A Good Life*, "It is now accepted history that Kennedy jumped casually from bed to bed with a wide variety of women. It was not accepted history then. . . . [I was] unaware of this proclivity during his lifetime." (See the foreword to the 2002 edition of *A Thousand Days*, published by Mariner Books).

To Robert F. Kennedy

September 8, 1960

[Cambridge, Massachusetts]

Dear Bob:

One factor feeding the resurgence of the religious issue is the fear that Jack's victory would mean that your co-religionists would take over the Democratic party and convert it into a Demo-Christian party. This fear is both illogical and self-pitying, but it exists.

I don't suppose you have had time to follow the Massachusetts gubernatorial primary; but the situation has changed here quite a lot in recent weeks, largely as a result of Chub Peabody's* indefatigable campaigning. Some polls now show him in the lead, and it is generally agreed that he has a good chance of winning.

Nothing would help more to allay some of the fears I mentioned above than to have Peabody emerge as the Democratic candidate for governor in Jack's home state. If he should win the Democratic primary next Tuesday, therefore, you might want to consider how this can be best turned to national purposes. A strong and well-publicized telegram from Jack would certainly be in order. Photographs of Jack congratulating Chub or you congratulating Chub might be even better—or anything which would put across for the whole country the fact that Kennedy's own state has nominated a Protestant.

Of course, after all this, he will probably run behind, and John F. Kennedy will win! But local indications are that Peabody stands a good enough chance for some consideration in Washington as to how this can be best capitalized nationally.

Yours,
Arthur

---

* Endicott ("Chub") Peabody (1920–97). Lawyer; brother of Marietta Peabody Tree; grandson of the Reverend Endicott Peabody, founder of Groton School; Democratic governor of Massachusetts, 1963–65.

To J. Leonard Reinsch[*]

September 12, 1960

[Cambridge, Massachusetts]

Dear Mr. Reinsch:

I understand that the name of James Fleming has been mentioned as one of the possible moderators for the big debate. This is just to say that Fleming is an old friend of mine, and I know that he can be counted on for a fair, effective and sympathetic job.

While I am writing, I would like to raise another point. I gather that the decision has been made to confine nationwide TV to a minimum. I don't think there is any magic in nationwide TV per se; but I do feel that there are distinct disadvantages in excessive reliance on statewide or regional TV; and I wonder if these have been fully taken into account. The central disadvantage is that concentration on a regional and state audience leads almost inevitably to concentration on regional and state themes. But a presidential campaign can never be won just by the exploitation of local issues. You can win primaries that way, but never the finals. A successful presidential campaign requires the establishment of a *national* image, and that can only be done by the projection of *national* themes.

The current feeling (cf. the recent Reston columns) that the campaign lacks coherence and pattern is due in great part to the fact that speeches have given the impression of preferring local to national themes. I am not even sure that this is true, but it is hard to tell, since, with the exception of the Detroit speech (full text carried in the *Times*) the speeches have not been available except in snippets either on TV or in the newspapers. . . . Something has to be done to put the campaign in national focus. Once this is done, *then* regional and local issues fall easily into their proper place.

Nationwide TV can be useful in establishing not only the image of the candidate but the image of the party. In this connection, I wonder whether you are familiar with the "magazine" format which the British Labour Party employed with considerable success in the last general election. The magazine format is, as the name suggests, a political variety show which enables

[*] J. Leonard Reinsch (1908–91). Radio broadcaster; White House radio adviser, 1945–57; TV-radio director for the 1960 Democratic presidential campaign; later president of the Cox Broadcasting Company.

a single half-hour program to press a number of issues and present a number of political personalities. There is no better way to give the impression of the strength of a party and the range of its concern. It is easy to conceive of a program on foreign policy, for example, which would present dramatically various aspects of the problem, bring on, say, Stevenson, Bowles, Harriman, Fulbright,* Symington, in brief statements, showing the resources of experience available to a new Democratic administration, and build finally to a strong plea by Kennedy for strength and peace. A similar wrap-up could be done on the main domestic issues. If necessary, even a religious program could be put over, with say, exposure of the K[nights] of C[olumbus's] fake anti-bigotry statements† or conversations by Reinhold Niebuhr and other churchmen and a final statement by the candidate.

In any case, I enclose a sample Labour Party telecast for your consideration.

Sincerely yours,
Arthur

P.S. How about putting some of the speeches on nationwide radio? It is not very expensive, and a lot of people still own them.

Arthur's book Kennedy or Nixon: Does It Make Any Difference? *was published in September and became an immediate bestseller. Arthur concluded that "under Nixon the country would sink into mediocrity and cant and payola and boredom," while the election of Kennedy would represent "the splendor of our ideals."*

---

* J. William Fulbright (1905–95). Representative (D-Ark.) 1943–45; senator, 1945–74; chairman of the Senate Committee on Foreign Relations, 1959–74; opposed Bay of Pigs invasion; leader in anti–Vietnam War effort.

† The Knights of Columbus is a fraternal order of Roman Catholic men, one million strong at the time, of which JFK was a member. In circulation in cities and towns mostly in the South was a fake version of the oath of the Knights of Columbus, including this sentence: "I do further promise and declare that I will, when opportunity presents, wage relentless war, secretly and openly, against all heretics, Protestants, and Masons, as I am directed to do, to extirpate them from the face of the whole earth."

To Jacqueline Kennedy

[Handwritten]

Thursday [September 22, 1960]

[Cambridge, Massachusetts]

Dear Jackie:

I have just returned from a few days in California to find your marvelous letter about the book. I have not received any letter from any one for years which pleased me half so much. I am glad that you liked the book and think it might help, and I am glad that you bothered to write.

I went west the morning after the Liberal Party dinner.* I think we are perhaps still slightly behind in California, but Jack's trip there was a great success, and things are moving visibly in a Democratic direction. Everywhere I went I found great enthusiasm for him. I would begin to feel reasonably optimistic except for the Eisenhower performance before the UN.† For one thing, I think that Nixon's ugliness is going to boomerang before too long.

Marian told me what a good time she had with you on the flight to Boston.‡ *Don't* worry about the press—your great strength is being yourself—you are irresistible anyway, and one decisive advantage that you and Jack have

* At a dinner on September 14, 1960, JFK formally accepted the New York Liberal Party's nomination for president. Both JFK and Stevenson asked Schlesinger to contribute to their speeches for the event, which he did, keeping his activities secret, especially from the two principals. Reinhold Niebuhr introduced JFK, giving him a ringing endorsement. Stevenson commended JFK as one "who represents the highest ideals of the Democratic Party and of the Liberal Party." JFK said: "Clear-sighted, tough-minded, warm-hearted liberalism is our best hope in the world today. For the liberal society is a free society—and it is at the same time, a strong society."

† President Eisenhower spoke to the UN General Assembly on September 22, 1960, praising the United Nations as "the forum of all peoples and the structure about which they can center their joint endeavors to create a better future for our world." He called for all nations to join in settling the world's problems by negotiation and cooperation in the United Nations. Khrushchev listened in stony silence, but later called the speech "conciliatory" and hinted he would be receptive to an invitation to meet the president despite May's summit debacle, Harrison Salisbury reported in *The New York Times*.

‡ The day after the Liberal Party dinner, the two women flew from New York City to Boston on a commercial flight. Jackie Kennedy, seven months pregnant, continued by car to Hyannis Port.

over Dick-and-Pat is that you two are not putting on an act. There will always be people trying to trip you up, but that is routine in politics (and in life).

Hope to see you soon—

Ever affectionately,
Arthur

To Robert F. Kennedy

September 23, 1960

[Cambridge, Massachusetts]

Dear Bob:

Jim Doyle and I have returned from our trip to the coast. . . . Jim will write you separately; but I think I am correct in saying that we both felt that the problem of the Stevenson Democrats and of the liberal Democrats in general is, in the main, well on its way to solution. We visited strong Stevenson areas, and nearly everywhere the Stevenson people were actively at work. We encountered no hostility to Jack and very little resistance; on the contrary, most people seemed eager to hear good things about him. Whatever emotions were in the few weeks after the convention, most liberal Democrats in California seem now to be actively involved in the campaign (where they are permitted to be). I attribute this to three things, in addition to the healing effect of time: (1) Jack's speeches;* (2) Adlai's speeches; and (3) Nixon's speeches. . . .

Sincerely yours,
Arthur

The 1960 campaign saw an innovation in American politics—a series of television debates in which the two candidates responded to questions put by

---

* JFK's speech on September 12, 1960, before the Greater Houston Ministerial Association was deemed especially effective: "I am not the Catholic candidate for President. I am the Democratic candidate for President who also happens to be a Catholic. I do not speak for my Church on public matters—and the Church does not speak for me."

newspaper reporters. Kennedy's poise and command in these confrontations countered the Republican argument that he was too young and inexperienced for the presidency.* The campaign itself revolved around the question of America's condition as a nation. Kennedy contended that the United States was falling behind both in the world competition with Communism and in meeting its own goals of economic growth and social progress. The process of decline could be reversed only by a "supreme national effort," under strong presidential leadership, to "get the country moving again."

On election eve, Arthur, Marian, and the children attended the final rally held at the Boston Garden, standing amid a raucous and ecstatic crowd of twenty thousand supporters shouting their hearts out. "This race is a contest between the comfortable and the concerned, between those who believe that we should rest and lie at anchor and drift, and between those who want to move this country forward in the 1960s," said Kennedy. "I ask you to join us tomorrow, and most of all, I ask you to join us in all the tomorrows yet to come."

Kennedy's margin was slim—only 119,057 out of 68.3 million votes cast†— but decisive. If the hallmark of the 1950s was the belief in the sanctity of private interests, the hallmark of the 1960s would be the revival of a sense of the public interest.

The tide had turned.‡

---

* There were four debates. Schlesinger considered the first debate, on September 26, 1960, in Chicago, the turning point of the campaign. "Nixon's key issue—Kennedy's supposed youth and inexperience—had been eliminated from the campaign in one stroke," Schlesinger wrote in *A Thousand Days*.

† JFK won in the electoral college 303 to 219, with 15 votes going to Senator Harry F. Byrd of Virginia.

‡ On November 9, 1960, Galbraith and Schlesinger sent a joint telegram to JFK, saying: "With your highly developed sense of history, [we] trust you will note that you are the first presidential candidate since Truman to survive our support"—no doubt a Galbraithian effusion.

To John F. Kennedy

14 November 1960

[Cambridge, Massachusetts]

Dear Mr. President:

I saw Mrs. Roosevelt yesterday, and she expressed herself with absolutely unprecedented enthusiasm about you. She described your determination to tell the people the truth during the campaign as "heroic." She was particularly impressed with the way you visibly grew in strength and confidence. She said, "I don't think anyone in our politics since Franklin has had the same vital relationship with crowds. Franklin would sometimes begin a campaign weary and apathetic. But in the course of campaigning he would draw strength and vitality from his audiences and would end in better shape than he started. I feel that Senator Kennedy is much the same—that his intelligence and courage elicit emotions from his crowds which flow back to him and sustain and strengthen him."

She was eloquently and unaffectedly enthusiastic.

Yours ever,
Arthur

The Schlesingers drove down to Hyannis Port on Friday, November 11, 1960, for luncheon with the president-elect and his wife.

Jackie said, "I cast only one vote—for Jack. It is a rare thing to be able to vote for one's husband for President of the United States, and I didn't want to dilute it by voting for anyone else." JFK attributed his slim margin to the prevailing sense of prosperity and peace and to anti-Catholic sentiment.

To John F. Kennedy

14 November 1960

[Cambridge, Massachusetts]

Dear Mr. President:

Marian and I could not have had a better time at luncheon on Friday. You were infinitely kind to have thought of us at such a busy moment; and I am deeply grateful, as a friend and as an historian.

Now about the State Department: you have very likely made your decision; but, if not, some of the following considerations may be of interest.

Three theories of the Secretary of State occur to me:

You could choose someone who does not necessarily have detailed views on foreign affairs but commands the confidence of the country and, more particularly, would automatically bring you 30 votes in the Senate for moves which might otherwise be unpopular or unacceptable. This is the Cordell Hull[*] solution. It has something to commend it, especially when, as in FDR's case and your own, the President will be in essential respects his own Secretary of State.

However, the man who would best meet this theory has already been elected to the Vice Presidency. I can't think of anyone else in the Senate who would exert influence comparable to Lyndon's.

You could choose someone who has had experience in foreign affairs but who appears primarily as a neutral or nonpartisan or technical figure rather than as a political figure. This is the Lord Home[†] solution. Of the various people in this category, the most appealing is David Bruce. I have known Bruce since the days I worked for him in OSS in London in 1944; his wife is a very old and close friend. He is a man of splendid qualities and abilities. He is an excellent negotiator and an effective administrator; and he surrounds himself with first-class men. But his cast of mind is somewhat conventional; his orientation is almost completely European; and I am not sure how much energy and initiative he would bring to the prose-

[*] Cordell Hull (1871–1955). Lawyer; representative (D-Tenn.), 1907–21, 1923–31; senator, 1931–33; FDR's secretary of state, 1933–44; co-initiator of the United Nations.

[†] Alec Douglas-Home (1903–95). Conservative Party politician, foreign secretary, 1960–63, 1970–74; UK prime minister, 1963–64.

cution of foreign policy. He would make a perfect Undersecretary. He would also make a perfect Ambassador to Rome (and this, I think, is a post he would very much like). He would make an able but unimaginative Secretary of State.

Another possibility in this category is Dean Rusk.[*] Rusk is a man of ability, drive and intelligence. But he is essentially the perfect chief-of-staff. I am not sure whether he would have the inner confidence and security to make a fully effective Secretary. But I hope very much that his very considerable talents can be utilized somewhere.

Then there is Eugene Black.[†] He has done a fine job at the Bank and has earned considerable respect in the underdeveloped countries. He is an older man, however; his health is uncertain; and I don't think he would strike many people as precisely a New Frontier figure.

Then, I suppose, there is Paul Nitze.[‡] For a long time he was under the intellectual domination of Dean Acheson. In recent months he has to some degree moved away from that; but he still remains Acheson's candidate for the job. He is a clever, resourceful and ambitious man with drive and a certain imagination. He is also opinionated and perhaps a little rigid. I don't think he is a man for a top job.

There is also, I suppose even more reluctantly, Douglas Dillon.[§] Dillon, of course, shines by comparison with his colleagues in the Eisenhower administration. His designation would emphasize the continuity in our foreign policy. But, in view of your justified criticism of the Eisenhower conduct of foreign affairs, I wonder whether continuity is exactly the thing that needs to be emphasized. Moreover, I think it would understandably

---

[*] Dean Rusk (1909–94). Teacher; lawyer; diplomat; State Department, 1945–52; president of the Rockefeller Foundation, 1952–61; secretary of state, 1961–69.

[†] Eugene R. Black, Sr. (1898–1992). President of the World Bank, 1949–63; chairman of the Brookings Institute, 1962–68.

[‡] Paul Nitze (1907–2004). Investment banker; vice chairman of the U.S. Strategic Bombing Survey, 1944–46; director of policy planning in the State Department, 1950–53; secretary of the navy, 1963–67; deputy secretary of defense, 1967–69; member of the U.S. delegation to the Strategic Arms Limitation Talks, 1969–73; assistant secretary of defense for international affairs, 1973–76; advised President Reagan on arms issues.

[§] C. Douglas Dillon (1909–2003). Investment banker with Dillon, Read and Co.; ambassador to France, 1953–57; undersecretary of state, 1957–61; secretary of the Treasury, 1961–65; a Republican moderate.

disappoint many who worked for you in the campaign if you were to appoint a supporter of Nixon to a top cabinet job. Of course, the Establishment press is trying to persuade you to do just this. I don't know why it is that "statesmanship" requires Democratic Presidents to appoint Republicans to high office but never requires Republican Presidents to appoint Democrats.

You could choose someone who has had experience in foreign affairs and who also is identified as a political figure. There are three obvious men in this category—Fulbright, Bowles and Stevenson.

I am sure that you know Fulbright far better than I. He is a man of sharp intelligence, imagination and somewhat unpredictable courage. It is too bad that he signed the Southern Manifesto[*] and filed an *amicus* brief[†] on behalf of Faubus;[‡] but, assuming that these things expressed political caution rather than personal conviction, he could overcome them by subsequent words and deeds. In the Senate he has shown an occasional inability to sustain his fights and to follow through to conclusions. Nor am I sure how much weight he would carry among his colleagues on the Hill.

Chet Bowles is a man of unlimited decency, intelligence and knowledge. He is an excellent administrator and has an exceptionally inventive and resourceful approach to policy. He believes that all questions can be solved; and, though this sometimes generates a kind of Eagle Scout optimism, it is also a source of buoyancy and ideas. He is not so hopelessly sentimental as Joe Alsop thinks and has a firm appreciation, for example, of the role of military strength. He would be an extremely loyal Secretary. Next to Stevenson, he would mean most abroad. Though he has opponents at home, they are mostly among enemies of the administration; and he has, of course, many enthusiastic supporters. My main doubt would be whether you would

---

[*] The Southern Manifesto of March 1956, signed by nineteen southern senators and eighty-two southern representatives, pledged the signers to exert "all lawful means" to reverse the Supreme Court's 1954 *Brown v. Board of Education* decision ordering school desegregation. The Southern Manifesto charged the Supreme Court with "clear abuse of judicial power." Refusing to sign the manifesto were Senators Al Gore, Sr., Estes Kefauver, and Lyndon B. Johnson.

[†] In August 1958, Fulbright filed a brief with the Supreme Court, *Amicus curiae, Aaron v. Cooper,* urging a delay in desegregation; the brief was rejected.

[‡] Orval Faubus (1910–94). Democratic governor of Arkansas, 1955–67; defied federal court order to desegregate Little Rock's Central High School in 1957; became a symbol of southern resistance.

not begin to find his tempo and flow a little wearisome. I have the impression that you would prefer something harder, sharper, more trenchant.

This leaves Stevenson. I am not a detached witness here; but I do think I have a realistic knowledge of his strength and weakness. I would rate him top of the list so far as both intellectual ability and international reputation are concerned. He has good friends and general respect in the Senate and a fanatical following in the country. He worked hard in the campaign and must surely be credited with producing part of the margin in California. His tempo of mind is close to your own. Unlike Bowles, he has a sense of tragedy.

The real question here is compatibility. I have always regretted the fact that you and Stevenson never had a chance to get to know each other in more relaxed circumstances. Knowing you both, I am pretty sure that genuine rapport would have developed. For obvious reasons, these past months have been a difficult time for Stevenson, and at times he has shown the strain. But this is all past. The question now is: are there unbridgeable gaps between you in policy or in personal relations?

As for policy, I doubt very much (despite Joe Alsop) whether there are serious gaps. I don't know what he said to you about Berlin; but I have seen no evidence in him of any basic softness on Germany. He has always been a strong advocate of the need for military strength. Moreover, as changes have to be made in US policy, other countries would take them more on faith from Stevenson than from any other possible Secretary of State.

As for personal compatibility, I can't say. I do feel strongly that Stevenson as Secretary of State would serve you with the utmost loyalty.

I think an ideal slate would be Stevenson as Secretary, Rusk as Undersecretary, Chip Bohlen as Counsellor, Bowles as Ambassador to the United Nations. Fulbright as chairman of the Foreign Relations Committee. Bruce in Rome.

You spoke on Friday of the NATO assignment. I think that Finletter would be great for that, though I would very much hope you still have him under consideration for the Defense Department. I admire your magnanimity in seeking to make use of Acheson, but I wonder whether, with all his superb abilities, he is not too consumed in vanity and bitterness to have gone past the point of usability. I had a few moments' talk with him about you in Washington early in October and started to tell you about it at Hyannis Port and then decided that I shouldn't since I hate to make mischief about people behind their backs. But his remarks to me at that time lead me to urge you to consider the matter very carefully before you confide any important responsibility to him.

This is a presumptuous letter, and I will trespass on your patience only a moment longer. Before you make up your mind, you might well want to have a frank talk with Allen Dulles[*] and Dick Bissell of CIA. And you also might well want to have a session with Stevenson and Bowles to find out what they really think about things and to make sure that an all-Choate[†] ticket will be best for the country (as I think it would be).

Forgive me for going on at this length.

Yours ever,
Arthur

From Groucho Marx[‡]

December 5, 1960

[Beverly Hills, California]

Dear Mr. Schlesinger:

I rarely read a book[§] that requires six hundred pages to tell its story. This is because I am not as young as I used to be. (I know very few people who are.)

My only criticism of your book is its length. It was much too short.

Reading it was a wonderful experience, and if your royalties increase you can attribute it partly to my enthusiasm. I am eagerly awaiting your next one, so get going, Junior.

Sincerely,
Groucho Marx

[*] Allen Welsh Dulles (1893–1969). Lawyer; diplomat; younger brother of John Foster Dulles; partner at Sullivan and Cromwell; OSS; director of Central Intelligence, 1953–61; dismissed over the failure of the 1961 Bay of Pigs invasion of Cuba; member of the Warren Commission investigating JFK's assassination.

[†] The Choate School, a private preparatory school founded in 1896 in Wallingford, Connecticut, graduated Stevenson in 1918, Bowles in 1919, and JFK in 1935.

[‡] Groucho Marx (1890–1977). Comedian and film star; one of the Marx brothers.

[§] Arthur Schlesinger, Jr., *The Politics of Upheaval, 1935–1936*, vol. 3 of *The Age of Roosevelt* (Boston: Houghton Mifflin, 1960); dedicated to J. K. Galbraith and Seymour Harris.

On May 5, 1961, along with Vice President Johnson, U.S. Navy admiral Arleigh
Burke, and President Kennedy and Mrs. Kennedy, Schlesinger watches television
coverage of the liftoff of *Freedom 7* carrying Commander Alan B. Shepard, Jr.,
into space three weeks after the Soviet Union launched the first man into space.
Cecil Stoughton, White House/John F. Kennedy Presidential Library and Museum, Boston

A Thousand Days

1961–65

To Marietta Tree

January 1, 1961

[Cambridge, Massachusetts]

Darling M.

I hope that the sun shone and the sea glittered at Heron Bay. It is safe to say that you are missing (have missed) nothing of consequence in the USA, except a certain amount of gray and dirty winter weather.

You will have noted all the public appointments. On balance, not bad, I think, except for an undue capitulation to the Establishment in the foreign and defense field. I had thought that JFK, having operated outside the Council on Foreign Relations* orbit (and indeed having defied it in the past), would be more independent of it once in office. But I suppose a dreadful sense of his own relative inexperience must occasionally afflict him; and in such moments he doubtless turns to those names which the *New York Times* identifies to him as the foreign policy elders of our society. Too many of his appointments seem designed to win applause in the respectable press. Thus I regret the instinctive preference for Lovett,[†]

---

*A nonpartisan foreign policy think tank founded in 1921 and headquartered in New York; members include both Republicans and Democrats.

† Robert A. Lovett (1895–1986). Republican official, partner at Brown Brothers Harriman investment bank; assistant secretary of war for air affairs, 1941–45; undersecretary of state, 1947–49; secretary of defense, 1951–53; member of establishment "wise men" who advised leaders of both major U.S. political parties.

McCloy,* Dillon, over, say, Averell [Harriman] and Tom [Finletter] and George Ball. The latter 3 are no doubt deemed controversial. Why? Because they are Democrats and actively worked for the Kennedy-Johnson ticket. I could well understand why young NY lawyers, hesitating before deciding to join the Lex Club,† might well conclude that they will have a better chance for preferment under a Democratic administration if they remain Republicans or neutralists.

I really feel that the only hope for new departures is to bring in outsiders; I look for more constructive action from Mennen Williams,‡ for example, than I do from Dean Rusk. Jack has placed foreign and defense policy too much in the hands of insiders. Still, the situation is not too bad. Averell has got his roving job, and Tom will get NATO, and maybe some of the others will come to life. It is the attitude more than the consequences (thus far) which troubles me.

As for myself, Ken [Galbraith] went down to Palm Beach and brought back word that I was to be appointed to the Gordon Gray§ job at the White House. A few days later (to the accompaniment of by-play which I will describe when I see you), the job went to Mac Bundy. This is all right: he is a more logical appointment as well as one who will give greater pleasure to the *NY Times*. At this point I was offered an assistant secretaryship of State in charge of cultural relations, which I promptly turned down. This brought a new message from JFK saying that he didn't mean the State Dept idea too seriously, that he is still thinking of me in terms of the White House, and that he wants to talk about it when he comes to Cambridge on January 9. So we shall see. My general view is that I will be

---

* John J. McCloy (1895–1989). Lawyer and banker; assistant secretary of war in the FDR administration; president of the World Bank, 1947–49; U.S. high commissioner for Germany; served on the Warren Commission investigating the JFK assassination; member of establishment "wise men" who advised leaders of both major U.S. political parties.

† Lexington Club. A liberal Democratic political club in Manhattan.

‡ Gerhard Mennen ("Soapy") Williams (1911–88). Democratic governor of Michigan, 1949–61; assistant secretary of state for African affairs, 1961–66; ambassador to the Philippines, 1968–69.

§ Gordon Gray (1909–82). Lawyer and businessman; secretary of the army in the Truman administration; national security adviser in the Eisenhower administration.

prepared to suspend the *A[ge] of R[oosevelt]* for a reasonable White House job but not for some dull spot in State.[*]

I see I have thus far neglected my first purpose in writing this letter—that is, to thank you for those splendid and beautiful braces, of which I am very proud, and also for the marvelous pitcher. How in your busy life do you find time for Christmas presents chosen with such obvious thought and care? It is because you are so well-organized and wonderful.

Anyway I have missed talking to you this last fortnight and hope you will be back by the time you receive this letter.

Happy New Year and dearest love, as always, A.

On January 9, 1961, the president-elect came to Cambridge to address the Massachusetts Legislature and attend a meeting of the Harvard Board of Overseers. After luncheon, he set up headquarters in the Schlesinger house on Irving Street and received a stream of visitors—McGeorge Bundy, MIT president Jerome Wiesner, and others who would serve in his administration. At one point, Kennedy turned to Arthur and asked him whether he was ready to work at the White House. Arthur replied: "I am not sure what I would be doing as Special Assistant, but, if you think I can help, I would like very much to come." Kennedy said: "Well, I am not sure what I would be doing as President either, but I am sure there will be enough at the White House to keep us both busy."

Arthur was assigned an office in the East Wing. His portfolio would include speechwriting, Latin American and European affairs, cultural matters, and liaison work with the liberal community.

---

[*] In December 1960, Robert F. Kennedy suggested to Schlesinger the possibility of his working in the White House as a special assistant, acting as a sort of roving reporter and troubleshooter. Schlesinger liked the idea, and Robert F. Kennedy said he would bring it up with the president-elect.

To Mike Mansfield*

February 4, 1961

[Washington, D.C.]

Dear Senator Mansfield:

I note in the *Congressional Record* of February 2 allusions to remarks attributed to me concerning the "welfare state."† I fear that those allusions were based on a misunderstanding of the definition I attached to this phrase— a phrase not of my own liking, by the way, but imposed on me by the debate topic to which Mr. Buckley‡ and I were asked to address ourselves.

Two quotations sum up my definition of the "welfare state":

The scheme of society for which we stand is the establishment and maintenance of a basic standard of life and labor below which a man or woman, however old or weak, shall not be allowed to fall. The food they receive, the prices they have to pay for basic necessities, the homes they live in, their employment must be the first care of the state, and must have priority over all other peacetime needs.

I believe that the American people feel that our production is so great that we can afford to put a floor under the necessities of life—food, education, medical care, housing—so that every family may have available a minimum decent living.

The conception of a "floor under the necessities of life" seemed to me the heart of the matter. I should add that the first quotation is from Win-

---

* Michael ("Mike") Mansfield (1903–2001). Academic; liberal representative (D-Mont.), 1943–53; senator, 1953–77; Senate majority leader, 1961–77; ambassador to Japan, 1977–88.

† Schlesinger asserted that the welfare state was the best defense against Communism in a debate on "Freedom and the Welfare State" with William F. Buckley, Jr., at the Newton College of the Sacred Heart on January 30, 1960. Senator Strom Thurmond (R-S.C.) challenged Schlesinger on the Senate floor on February 2, saying that "not only is the welfare state no defense against Communism, but there is a serious question as to whether, in practical effect, the welfare state is even an alternative to Communism."

‡ William F. Buckley, Jr. (1925–2008). Florid conservative author and columnist; founder and editor of *National Review*, 1955–90; host of PBS's *Firing Line* 1966–99; longtime adversary/friend of Schlesinger.

ston Churchill and the second from Robert A. Taft. I can hardly believe that those who denounced me really regard Churchill and Taft as "state socialists." My own strong conviction is that the goals set forth in these quotations can be fully achieved under our present economic system.

I should add that I took part in this debate *before* I assumed my present duties.

Sincerely yours,
Arthur Schlesinger, jr.

To Isaiah Berlin

February 11, 1961

[Washington, D.C.]

Dear Isaiah:

Everybody is back in Washington—I even lunched with Prich[ard]* at the Hay-Adams last Sunday—except you; and you are greatly missed. You were missed at a succession of parties for Susan Mary.† You were particularly missed at the White House last Thursday night when the President gave a party for Mrs. Longworth. The other guests were the Vice President and Lady Bird, Sam Rayburn‡ and his sister, the Fulbrights, the Arthur Krocks,§ and me, which will give you an idea of the baffling composition of the New Frontier.

I am uncertainly established in an office in the East Wing formerly occupied by James F. Byrnes.⁋ I am almost immediately off to Latin America in order, I take it, to symbolize the transition from the Old Frontier to the New. I will be back around the first of March and hope to write again.

---

* Edward F. Prichard, Jr. (1915–84). Lawyer; prominent New Dealer in the FDR administration; jailed for 1948 ballot stuffing in his home state, Kentucky; remained influential in liberal circles behind the scenes.

† Susan Mary Alsop (1918–2004). Author; Washington society hostess; married to diplomat William Patten and later to columnist Joseph Alsop.

‡ Sam Rayburn (1882–1961). Representative (D-Texas), 1913–61; longest serving Speaker of the House in history, 1940–61.

§ Arthur Krock (1882–1974). Influential *New York Times* columnist and reporter; nicknamed "Dean of Washington newsmen."

⁋ James F. Byrnes (1882–1972). Representative (D-S.C.), 1911–25; senator, 1931–41; governor, 1951–55; U.S. Supreme Court justice, 1941–42; secretary of state, 1945–47.

We have a house in Georgetown, and Marian and the children are coming down almost any of these days.

Nicolas was with us this week, bringing us word of you and of culture. I took him for a drink with Mrs. [Jacqueline] Kennedy.

I wish you would come over this spring before the bloom goes off the rose. Our love to Aline.[*]

Yours ever,
Arthur Schlesinger, Jr.

To Eleanor Roosevelt

March 4, 1961

[Washington, D.C.]

Dear Mrs. Roosevelt:

I have just returned from Latin America[†] to find your most welcome letter. I hesitated a long time before accepting President Kennedy's invitation to come to Washington, because I regard myself as essentially a scholar and writer, and hated the thought of interrupting my work on *The Age of Roosevelt;* but in the end, I reflected that no American historian has ever been privileged to watch the unfolding of public policy from this particular vantage point, and I concluded that I could not decline. I know this experience will very much enrich my historical understanding.

The best news of all is that you have agreed to rejoin the Delegation to the U.N.![‡]

Sincerely yours,
Arthur

---

[*] Aline Berlin (b. 1915). Lady Berlin, formerly Aline Elisabeth Yvonne; wife of Sir Isaiah Berlin; daughter of a French baron, onetime lady golf champion of France.

[†] Schlesinger accompanied George McGovern on a Food for Peace mission to Brazil, Argentina, Bolivia, Peru, and Venezuela.

[‡] Eleanor Roosevelt had served as a U.S. representative to the UN Commission on Human Rights, 1945–46 and 1948–53. She was instrumental in drafting the United Nations' 1948 Universal Declaration of Human Rights. She was a member of the UN delegation during the Kennedy administration, 1961–62.

To Arthur and Elizabeth Schlesinger

Saturday afternoon [mid-June, 1961]

[Washington, D.C.]

Dear Mother and Dad:

This has been another exceptionally busy week. As part of my effort to disengage slightly from Latin America, I am becoming an expert on Italy and hence was the White House staff man on the Fanfani* conversations. This meant that I sat in on the talks between Fanfani and the President—less interesting than it sounded, because Fanfani had very little on his mind and is not a deeply fascinating man.

The President is obviously in continuing pain over his back and moves about with great care.† It seems pretty clearly to be a case of bad strain and nothing more serious than that; but it has reduced his mobility, both physical and emotional. He is taking the weekend off and, with rest and treatment, we hope he will be OK in a few days.

We finally have an Asst Secretary of State for Latin American Affairs. Bob Woodward,‡ who as you know is taking the job, always seemed to me the best of the Foreign Service possibilities. I am sorry that we could not get a non-pro, because even the best pros have a built-in conventionality of thought and action which gets in the way of decision and effective policy. You probably have noticed the long *NY Times* campaign against Berle,§ Goodwin,¶ and myself. This has evidently proceeded from State Dept sources, and no doubt they are irritated over there over White House intervention in Latin American policy. But all we have been doing is filling the

---

* Amintore Fanfani (1908–99). Career Italian politician; leader of the Christian Democratic Party; served five terms as prime minister.

† In mid-May 1961, during a visit to Canada, JFK took part in a tree-planting ceremony and severely wrenched his back while shoveling dirt.

‡ Robert F. Woodward (1908–2001). Career foreign service officer; specialist in Latin American affairs; assistant secretary of state for inter-American affairs, 1961–62; ambassador to Costa Rica (1954–58), to Uruguay (1958–61), to Chile (1961), and to Spain (1962–65).

§ Adolf Berle, Jr. (1895–1971). Lawyer; educator; author; diplomat; member of FDR's "brain trust"; professor at Columbia Law School, 1927–64; specialist on corporations and Latin American affairs.

¶ Richard Goodwin (b. 1931). Writer, adviser, and speechwriter for Presidents Kennedy and Johnson; married to American historian Doris Kearns Goodwin.

vacuum created by their own lack of energy. This is a pretty important area; and very little would have happened there, especially in the economic field, if it had not been for White House planning and pressure. Nor is it true that anyone has turned down the job because of fear of not having a free hand. Berle turned it down himself because he had held it once before; Linc Gordon[*] because he preferred to be Ambassador to Brazil; Clark Kerr[†] because he could not get leave; Ellsworth Bunker[‡] because of poor health; and now Carl Spaeth.[§] Spaeth's reasons are not altogether clear to me, but he is an old personal friend of both Berle and myself and he has made it clear locally that he did not decline the job because of fear of the White House. I find it interesting as an historian to note how this mythology, as soon as it was perpetrated by Kenworthy[¶] of the *Times*, was adopted by other papers, repeated, imbedded in everyone's minds—and eventually, no doubt, to be taken by some conscientious graduate student as an accurate description of the situation.

Last night we all went to the Grahams in Virginia (all meaning Kathy and Stephen as well as Marian and me) for Lally Graham's[**] coming out party. It was a great affair given in a pavilion on the Mellon estate. (I wondered a little what Paul Mellon,[††] who is of course Andrew's[‡‡] son, thought of

[*] Lincoln Gordon (1913–2009). Academic; diplomat; ambassador to Brazil, 1961–66; assistant secretary of state for inter-American affairs, 1966–68; president of Johns Hopkins University, 1967–71.

[†] Clark Kerr (1911–2003). Academic administrator; educational policy maker; first chancellor of the University of California, Berkeley; later president of California university system.

[‡] Ellsworth F. Bunker (1894–1984). Lawyer; American businessman; diplomat; served in five different ambassadorial posts, most notably in South Vietnam, 1967–73; known for hawkish views.

[§] Carl Spaeth (1908–91). State Department, 1940–46, including term as assistant secretary of state for American republics affairs; dean of Stanford Law School, 1946–62.

[¶] E. W. Kenworthy (1909–93). Longtime Washington *New York Times* reporter covering, among other beats, the White House and the State Department.

[**] Lally Graham Weymouth (b. 1943). Daughter of Katharine and Philip Graham; special diplomatic correspondent of *Newsweek*; senior associate editor of *The Washington Post*.

[††] Paul Mellon (1907–99). American philanthropist; art collector; racehorse owner; friend of Kennedy family, son of Andrew Mellon.

[‡‡] Andrew Mellon (1855–1937). Republican banker; industrialist; philanthropist; art collector; secretary of the Treasury, 1921–32; one of the wealthiest men in the United States.

having the authors of *The Affluent Society* and *The Crisis of the Old Order* drinking his champagne and walking in his garden.) The children had a fine time and so did we. Tonight we go to a dinner dance at Bobby Kennedy's, which should be fun too.

What are your plans now? We couldn't have enjoyed your visit more and look forward to your coming again.

Much love, Arthur

To Orville E. Dryfoos[*]

July 5, 1961

[Washington, D.C.]

Personal

Dear Orvil:

Just a line to say how much I enjoyed lunching with the *Times* on Friday. I do feel that we got to a fairly basic issue in judging how a government is doing; that is, the question as to whether one wants an orderly government or a creative government. There may be an occupational difference here between newspapermen and historians: historians reach their verdict, not in terms of orderliness of procedure, but in terms of creativity of result. A government can be orderly when it deals with recurring situations according to well-established procedures; such governments are not likely to overflow with innovation. Creative government will always be "out of channels"; it will always present aspects of "confusion" and "meddling"; it will always discomfit officials whose routine is being disturbed or whose security is being threatened. But all this is inseparable from the process by which new ideas and new institutions enable government to meet new challenges. Orderly governments are very rarely creative; and creative governments are almost never orderly.

In the thirties, the *Times* acted as if orderly government were more important than creative government. Hence it missed a lot of what we would all acknowledge now as the great achievements of the New Deal; the *Times*

---

[*] Orville Dryfoos (1912–63). Publisher of *The New York Times*, 1961–63; married to Marian Sulzberger, daughter of former publisher Arthur Hays Sulzberger.

editorials of this period make very irrelevant reading today. I expect that the Kennedy Administration will continue to the end to be one of ferment and concern—and I hope that the *Times* won't be so busy recording trivia in the sideshows that it misses the main events!

Sincerely yours,
Arthur Schlesinger, jr.
Special Assistant to the President

To Isaiah Berlin

September 9, 1961

[Washington, D.C.]

Dear Isaiah:

. . . My own life continues full and animated, though I must confess that I feel more gloomy about international developments than I have felt since the summer of 1939.[*] Khrushchev's remarks to Drew Pearson,[†] of his great admiration for John Foster Dulles, seemed to me revealing. I think we are seeing the most massive and hazardous exercise in brinkmanship since the days of Hitler. Fortunately K and H differ in other respects.

What are your plans?
Our love to Aline.

Yours ever,
Arthur

---

[*] In less than six months, the disastrous Bay of Pigs invasion of Cuba had taken place; President Kennedy had had a confrontational summit with Soviet premier Nikita Khrushchev in Vienna; East Germany had erected the Berlin Wall; and the Russians had resumed nuclear testing in the atmosphere.

[†] Drew Pearson (1897–1969). Author of the syndicated muckraking newspaper column Washington-Merry-Go-Round, with sixty million readers.

From W. Averell Harriman

October 24, 1961

[Geneva, Switzerland]

Dear Arthur:

I am enclosing a translation of a couple of paragraphs in Khrushchev's speech to the Party Congress, in which he refers to my comments on the word "capitalism." Since the White House reads all publications, I thought you might have seen it and my cartoon in *Pravda,* and would want an explanation. This is not the first time that he has referred to my speeches on this subject, and this convinces me that it is rather a sore point with him.

For several years and in a number of speeches, I have suggested we were making a mistake to let Khrushchev get away with labeling the differences between us as a struggle between two economic systems, "socialism" vs. "capitalism," when in fact it is between two political ideologies— dictatorship and freedom. I have used the usual range of expressions: totalitarianism, the all-powerful state as opposed to human rights, individual dignity, the worth of the individual, etc. etc. I have at times quoted from a delightful book written by a French Dominican monk, who as a friend of the United States, wrote about our faults in an amusing manner. In one chapter he advises us to recognize that "capitalism" to people in most underdeveloped parts of the world, is synonymous with colonialism and exploitation, and that even we Americans, with all of our Madison Avenue prowess, cannot rehabilitate this discredited word. Therefore, he contends, we ought to bury it, particularly as Western economic systems are today a far cry from the capitalism taught by Marx. He doesn't offer any substitute word, but leaves that to us. I have never attempted, as some have, to find a word to describe our economic system. I have simply insisted that we should challenge Mr. Kh[rushchev] on his contention that the world struggle was over economic systems, but rather human values.

I'm sure I don't have to belabor this with you, but I find it is odd how many people have fallen into the trap of using Khrushchev's terminology. The fact that Khrushchev has attacked me again in this speech shows that he is sensitive on the point and wants to see us stuck with this discredited word. In all seriousness, I feel this is an important subject, as there is no doubt the word "socialism has a favorable connotation in most underdeveloped countries, and "capitalism" is distrusted. We will never win the ideological conflict under its banner.

More of this when I see you. In the meantime, warm regards.

Sincerely,
W. Averell Harriman

To Jacqueline Kennedy

[Handwritten]

December 22 1961

[The White House]

Dear Jackie:[*]

Just a line to wish you the best of Christmas. It is such a shame that the holiday is shadowed by the Ambassador [Joseph Kennedy]'s[†] sickness, but we have all been cheered here by reports of his improvement.[‡]

This must have been an exhausting year for you both, but one of which you both are entitled to be proud. You are obviously becoming the administration's secret weapon—I hope you don't find it too appalling.

I thought you might be amused by the attached report of a confidential interview with Milovan Djilas,[§] the Yugoslav revolutionary who broke with

---

[*] After spending an evening with John F. and Jacqueline Kennedy in Hyannis Port in July 1959, Schlesinger concluded that Jackie Kennedy concealed tremendous awareness, an all-seeing eye, and a ruthless judgment "underneath a veil of lovely inconsequence," as he wrote in *A Thousand Days*. During the campaign Mrs. Kennedy feared that she was a political liability and that people considered her a snob from Newport with bouffant hair, French clothes, and a hatred of politics. Schlesinger thought she was a remarkable young woman and sought to reassure her and encourage her as First Lady. In fact, after Kennedy's election, her negatives quickly turned into positives.

[†] Joseph P. Kennedy Sr. (1888–1969), wealthy American businessman, served as first head of SEC, 1934–35, U.S. ambassador to Great Britain 1938–40; resigned over appeasement views toward Hitler; father of President John F. Kennedy.

[‡] Ambassador Joseph Kennedy, while playing golf, suffered an intracranial thrombosis, paralyzing his left side and impeding his ability to speak.

[§] Milovan Djilas (1911–95). Yugoslav Communist politician and theorist who fell out with the Communist Party; wrote the acclaimed book *The New Class: An Analysis of the Communist System* (1957), contending Communism had created a class society.

Tito a few years ago, wrote a book called *The New Class* criticizing the Communist elite and was rewarded by imprisonment.

I am in negotiation with Ken [Galbraith] about India—your letter spurred me on.*

> Marian joins me in sending you both holiday greetings and much love,
> Arthur

To John Oakes†

May 21, 1962

[Washington, D.C.]

Personal

Dear John:

The *Times* editorial today on "Politics and Medical Care" was excellent so far as its comment on the substance of the medicare proposal‡ was concerned; but I am a little surprised at your objections to the idea of an Administration campaign on behalf of the proposal. For months, the *Times* has been demanding that the President carry his program to the people. Actually he has been doing so in a variety of ways—but apparently never dramatically enough to please the *Times*. Then yesterday he spoke at a great rally in support of a bill approved by the *Times*. His speech went to 32 other rallies and to millions of homes through the country. It was all a superb exercise in public education and in mobilizing support for the Administration program—exactly the sort of thing the *Times* has been demanding. And how did the *Times* react? By references to "hippodrome tactics."

---

* Kennedy appointed John Kenneth Galbraith to be U.S. ambassador to India (1961–63). Galbraith used his personal relationship with JFK to bypass the State Department and send dispatches from New Delhi directly to JFK commenting on economic, political, and diplomatic matters, and cautioning against a Vietnam misadventure.

† John Oakes (1913–2001). Journalist; influential progressive editor of the *New York Times* editorial page, 1961–76; nephew of *New York Times* publisher Adolph Ochs.

‡ In the 1960 campaign, JFK endorsed the Medicare proposal to provide health care to the elderly.

I was also a little surprised by the remark that the AMA[*] is "at a manifest disadvantage in the competition for mass support." If you would take a look at press reaction to the King-Anderson bill[†] (with a few honorable exceptions, like the *Times*), I hardly think that you would regard the AMA as an underprivileged and voiceless underdog.

I continue to feel a certain unreality in the *Times*'s conception of the process of leadership in a democracy. The *Times* constantly calls for leadership—but, when it comes, the *Times* too often rejects it as impassioned or partisan or vulgar or something. If the tone and manner of *Times* editorials were sufficient to do the job of public education, then the *Times* would not have to call so insistently for more potent methods!

Yours sincerely,
Arthur Schlesinger, Jr.
Special Assistant to the President

To Hugh Scott[‡]

June 2, 1962

[Washington, D.C.]

Dear Senator Scott:

I notice that you inserted in the *Congressional Record* of May 21 a column by Henry J. Taylor[§] alleging that I am a socialist and an enemy of patriotism and religion. I need hardly say that these allegations are nonsense, as I am confident you will agree if you will examine the evidence.

Taylor's allegations are based on an article I wrote for the *Partisan Re-*

---

* The American Medical Association (founded 1847), the largest association of physicians in the United States; fierce, conservative opponent of government-sponsored medical insurance programs.

† The King-Anderson Bill of 1962, a precursor to the 1965 Medicare legislation.

‡ Hugh Scott (1900–1994). Moderate Republican congressman and senator from Pennsylvania who served almost continuously from 1941 to 1977; Senate minority leader, 1969–77.

§ Henry J. Taylor (1903–84). Right-wing journalist; author; ambassador to Switzerland, 1957–61; columnist for United Feature Syndicate, 1961–81.

view[*] in 1947. I was asked, as a scholar, to contribute to a symposium on "The Future of Socialism" and did so, but as an analyst, not as an advocate. The fact that I, as an historian, participated in a symposium on the future of socialism no more makes me a socialist than participation in a symposium on "The Future of the Steel Industry" would make me Roger Blough.[†] My personal views of socialism had already been made amply clear in the concluding pages of a book called *The Age of Jackson*, published in 1945; as my views of communism were made amply clear in an article I wrote for *Life* on July 29, 1946, called "The U. S. Communist Party"—one of the first exposures and condemnations of the activities of the American Communist Party to appear in a magazine of national circulation.

If you will read the quotations in the Taylor column, you will see that they are either purely descriptive (e.g., saying that, if socialism is to preserve democracy, it must be brought about gradually and not through revolution) or else have been wrenched ruthlessly from context. For example, he charges me with using the phrase "the capitalist ruling class." Yet the full quotation (which Taylor proceeds to give) shows that I was using that phrase, not as an expression of my own thought, but as a paraphrase of a familiar Marxist argument ("The classical argument against gradualism was that the capitalist ruling class . . . ").

Even more offensive is Taylor's attempt to suggest that I am, or was in 1947, opposed to patriotism and religion. His allusions are, in fact, to my ironic restatement of *Marxist* views on patriotism and religion—a restatement made for the exact purpose of showing how ridiculous the Marxist interpretation of these matters is. Taylor, in short, ascribes to me views that I ascribed to the Marxists for the purpose of deriding them. This fact was entirely evident to a person unknown to me who wrote a letter to the *Washington Daily News* on May 10 commenting on Taylor's distortions of my views. I attach a copy of this letter and ask you to read it.

I might add that I am not a Marxist, nor have I ever been a Marxist, as any examination of my all too copious writings over the last twenty years

---

* *Partisan Review* (1934–2003) was an American political and literary quarterly with a liberal anticommunist viewpoint.

† Roger Blough (1904–85). Chairman and CEO of U.S. Steel Corporation, 1955–69; clashed in 1962 with President Kennedy over Blough's violation of his promise not to raise steel prices; Blough ultimately backed down.

will show. Even with regard to the 1947 article on which Taylor exclusively rests his case, I would ask you to read a few representative quotations from this article, and then say whether or not they justify Taylor's description of my views.

On the question of capitalism vs. socialism:

After all, which system has more successfully dehumanized the worker, fettered the working class and extinguished personal and political liberty? . . . The socialist state is thus worse than the capitalist state because it is more inclusive in its coverage and more unlimited in its power.

On the ownership of property:

The more varieties of ownership the better: liberty gets more fresh air and sunlight through the interstices of a diversified society than through the close-knit grip of collectivism.

On revolution:

A revolutionary elite always has the wistful conviction, based on experience, that it is easier to dispose of opposition by firing squads than by arguments.

On the Soviet Union—"the radical expansionists in the Politburo":

The mystique of the working class has faded somewhat since the First World War. In its place has arisen a new mystique, more radiant and palpable, and exercising the same fascinations of power and guilt: the mystique of the USSR. Each success of the Soviet Union has conferred new delights on those possessed of the need for prostration and frightened of the responsibilities of decision. In a world which makes very little sense, these emotions are natural enough. But surrender to them destroys the capacity for clear intellectual leadership which ought to be the liberal's function in the world. In an exact sense, Soviet Russia has become the opiate of the intellectuals. . . .

Communism gives Russian expansionism its warhead. On a prearranged signal, the Russian drive can explode internally in every country on the globe. Russian national objectives are limited; Communist international objectives are not.... The problem is to prevent the Soviet Union from breaking out of the reservation during its period of messianic intoxication.... Reduced to its fundamentals, the American problem is to arrange the equilibrium of forces in the world so that, at every given moment of decision, the Soviet general staff will decide against aggressions that might provoke a general war on the ground that they present too great a military risk.

On fellow-travelling liberals:

For the most chivalrous reasons they cannot believe that ugly facts underlie fair words: however they look at it, for example, the USSR keeps coming through as a kind of enlarged Brook Farm community. Nothing in their system has prepared them for Stalin.... The official liberal runs interference for the Communist with a system of intellectual evasion and subterfuge that results directly from a desperate attempt to square a superficial and optimistic creed with a bitter century.... Worship of the proletariat becomes a perfect fulfillment for the frustrations of the intellectual.

I have no doubt that you and I differ on all sorts of issues. I am perfectly prepared to be denounced for things in which I believe. But I am getting increasingly tired of being attacked for beliefs I do not have and have never had. My record of anticommunism and anti-Marxism is documented in books and articles over a period of twenty years. Feel free to condemn me as a Democrat or as a liberal or as a New Frontiersman; but please stop condemning me for positions which I do not take and which I have demonstrably never taken.*

Sincerely yours,
Arthur Schlesinger, jr.
Special Assistant to the President

---

* A few days later Schlesinger received a handwritten note that read: "In connection with your letter to Senator Scott on whether you're a communist or something, you looked like a subversive with Marilyn Monroe in New York and Mark De Wolfe Howe likes you, so don't expect any support from over here. Teddy's brother." It was signed by Robert F. Kennedy, the attorney general.

To Arthur Schlesinger, Sr.

12 August 1962

[Washington, D.C.]

Dear Dad:

Here is a postscript to my recent letter. Last Monday I took Frank Freidel[*] to lunch at the White House. I stopped in a minute to introduce him to the President. The matter of your article[†] again came up. JFK again expressed his surprise over [Woodrow] Wilson's high rating, and also over Theodore Roosevelt's. In discussing Wilson, JFK argued that his Mexican policy[‡] was a disaster for which we still have not been forgiven; that he had messed up the League fight;[§] and that, though he was right to bring us into the war, he did so for the wrong reasons. On the subject of unrestricted submarine warfare, JFK said, he thought the Germans had good reason to object. As for TR, JFK said that he talked a lot but didn't do very much. He could not see why TR rated above Polk[¶] or Truman.

What is most interesting is that his criterion is obviously that of concrete achievement rather than political education. People who educate the nation, without achieving all their goals, like Wilson and TR, evidently seem to him to rate under people with a record of practical accomplishment, like Polk and Truman, even if they do little to transform the intellectual climate of the nation. It is also interesting that, contrary to

---

[*] Frank Freidel (1917–93). Professor of American history at Harvard, 1955–81; University of Washington, 1981–86; biographer of Franklin Roosevelt.

[†] Arthur Schlesinger, Sr., "Our Presidents: A Rating by 75 Historians," *The New York Times Magazine,* July 29, 1962. The top-rated presidents were Lincoln, Washington, FDR, Jefferson, Jackson, and Theodore Roosevelt. The lowest rated were Warren G. Harding, Ulysses S. Grant, James Buchanan, and Calvin Coolidge.

[‡] During the Wilson administration, the United States intervened several times in the ongoing Mexican Revolution with damaging results.

[§] President Wilson failed to convince the U.S. Senate in 1919 to ratify the League of Nations covenant that he had personally championed during the peace talks at Versailles that ended World War I.

[¶] James K. Polk (1795–1849). Representative (D-Tenn.), 1825–39; Speaker of the House, 1835–39; governor of Tennessee, 1839–41; eleventh U.S. president, 1845–49; remembered for defeating Mexico in a controversial war, 1846–48, that led to a vast expansion of U.S. territory.

present fashions, he is skeptical about TR and Wilson but admiring of FDR. . . .

Much love, Arthur

To G. P. Putnam's Sons[*]

February 5, 1963

[Washington, D.C.]

Dear Sir:

I note that your advertisement for a new book by William F. Buckley, Jr. quotes me as saying: "He has a facility for rhetoric which I envy, as well as a wit which I seek clumsily and vainly to emulate."

So far as I can remember, I have never made such a statement in my life. Will you kindly let me have immediately the source of this statement or else discontinue its use.

Sincerely yours,
Arthur Schlesinger, jr.

To Thomas Wallace[†]

February 12, 1963

[Washington, D.C.]

Dear Mr. Wallace:

Thank you for your letter of February 8. I have no memory of having made the remark your advertisement ascribes to me at the Newton Convent of the Sacred Heart (or elsewhere). I have never seen, cleared or, up to this point, heard of any transcript of the Newton debate. If I made any

---

[*] Prominent publishing house founded in 1838; responsible for many bestselling authors; now part of Penguin.
[†] Thomas Wallace (b. 1933). Trade book editor at G. P. Putnam's Sons; later, editor with Holt, Rinehart and Winston and with Norton; literary agent

remark along these lines, it was obviously in a spirit of ironic derision and not as a sober judgment.

Let me say for the record that the supposed quotation does not express my opinion of Mr. Buckley. I have amply expressed my opinion in reviews of his books and in other writings, and it is very different from that attributed to me in the quotation you are using. I am sure that you could not have been aware of the source of this supposed quotation; and I know that a reputable house like Putnam's would not knowingly employ a quotation which misrepresents the views of the person to whom the quotation is ascribed. I trust therefore that you will cease to use this quotation in your future promotion of Mr. Buckley's book.

Sincerely yours,
Arthur Schlesinger, jr.

To John Kenneth Galbraith

March 1, 1963

[Barbados]

Dear Kenneth:

Marian and I are down here at Marietta's for a few days of recuperation. Barry and Mary Bingham[*] and Clayton [Fritchey][†] are also here. We wish you were along in spite of your notorious hatred of the seashore.

Everything seemed OK in Washington when I left. We seem to be moving along rather placidly in a somewhat lower gear than I would like. The President is held down by the lack of imagination of his advisers as well as by the obstructionism of Congress; and, though he recognizes and quite often resents the situation, he also in the end accepts it.

I wonder how you will find Cambridge in the fall. I do not think I could ever again return to a full-time teaching schedule as envisaged by the History Department; and, though I feel increasingly a desire to resume my

---

[*] Mary Bingham (1905–95). Married to Barry Bingham, proprietor of a Kentucky media empire, including the Louisville *Courier Journal*.

[†] Clayton Fritchey (1904–2001). Journalist; syndicated columnist; public information officer in the Truman, Kennedy, and Johnson administrations; press secretary to UN envoy Adlai Stevenson, 1961–65.

own work, it will have to be done in circumstances where I can concentrate on that and not on ministering to a collection of graduate students or tutees. Life is too short, and I have too many things I want to write.

I see that the Pres. has jettisoned tax reform. I have sent you a memo I gave [Walter] Heller* on economic policy before departing.

Will you return before the guillotine falls?

Yours ever,
Arthur

From William F. Buckley, Jr., to AMS's Lawyers

April 3, 1963

[New York, New York]

Gentlemen:

Mr. Walter Minton of Putnam's advised me several weeks ago that on behalf of your client, Mr. Arthur Schlesinger Jr., you were demanding that we desist from using Mr. Schlesinger's words in connection with my new book, *Rumbles Left and Right*,† or you would sue for invasion of privacy. I note from the issue of the *New York Post* dated March 30, that Mr. Schlesinger advised a reporter that it was not his intention to bring suit. Am I then to proceed on the understanding that Mr. Schlesinger has adjourned his objections to my continuing to use his quotation? Or rather, that he has abandoned any idea of seeking to restrain me from doing so by appealing to the courts? If I do not hear from you by April 9, I shall assume that the *Post* correctly reported his new attitude.

Yours faithfully,
Wm. F. Buckley, Jr.

---

*Walter Heller (1915–87). Liberal Democrat; longtime professor of economics at University of Minnesota; chairman of President Kennedy's Council of Economic Advisers, 1961–64.

† *Rumbles Left and Right* (1963) is a collection of diverse essays assailing liberal icons such as Norman Mailer, praising Republicans such as Senator Barry Goldwater, and recounting various sailing trips.

P.S. While you are at it; would you be so kind as to ask Mr. Schlesinger to okay the translation of his quotation into French: *"Monsieur Buckley a une facilite de rhetorique que j'envie de meme qu'un bel esprit que je tache maladroitement d'imiter et sans success."*

To the Editor of *Publishers Weekly*

April 13, 1963

[Washington, D.C.]

Dear Sir:

The publishing house of G. P. Putnam's Sons placed an advertisement in the February 12 issue of the *National Review* which read, with appropriate typographical flourishes, as follows: "Watch for a new book by W. F. Buckley, Jr. . . . Here's what the critics say." There followed quotations from a number of critics, including a quotation ascribed to me expressing uncontrollable admiration for Mr. Buckley's rhetoric and wit.

Having never seen—or indeed heard of—Mr. Buckley's-book, I was naturally startled to find myself listed among its critics. And, having no great admiration for either Mr. Buckley's rhetoric or his wit, I was equally startled to find myself listed among his fans. On application to Putnam's, I learned that the quotation ascribed to me came from the transcript of a debate between Mr. Buckley and myself—a debate which took place in January 1961, some two years before the new book was announced. It is further evident from an examination of the transcript that the remark was entirely ironic in nature—that, in fact, it reeked with sarcasm—and therefore that Putnam's use of it in promoting Mr. Buckley's book was invalid not only because it had no application to the book but also because its meaning was opposite to that implied in the advertisement.

When I pointed these things out to Putnam's early in February, Mr. Peter Israel, the editor-in-chief, finally wrote me (on February 26), "I am going to see to it personally that no further use of the quotation is made in our publicity or advertising for Mr. Buckley's book." He declined, however, to do anything about the use of the quotation on the jacket on the ground that "since the jacket has already been printed there is literally nothing I can do about its use at this point." He did not explain how Putnam's happened to put the quotation on the jacket without authorization in the first place or why, after I communicated with Putnam's on February 8, nothing was done to stop the use on the jacket. I thereupon directed my lawyers to take up with Putnam's the question of the jacket or, alternatively, the possibility of working out with Putnam's a statement which would make clear that the quotation attributed to me was used without authentication or authorization and did not express my view of Mr. Buckley or his book.

The discussion with Putnam's was recently interrupted by Mr. Buckley, who seized the occasion to put out a release stating (a) that I had announced my intention of suing him and (b) that I was trying to keep not only his book but his magazine from being published. Both claims were false.

My desire remains a simple one—that is, not to be cited as among the enthusiastic "critics" of a book which, to this day, I have never seen, nor to have my sardonic statements in a debate presented to the book-buyer as solemn and rhapsodic praise. I might add that, speaking as an author, I would even think there might be a matter of publisher's ethics involved here—though it must be stated that Putnam's, while it has agreed under pressure to stop the use of the quotation, has continued to act as if the unauthorized application of a questionable and ambiguous quotation to a book unread by the supposed critic is in accordance with the highest traditions of the publishing profession.

Sincerely yours,
Arthur Schlesinger, jr.

From William F. Buckley, Jr., to the Editor of *Publishers Weekly*

April 19, 1963

[New York, New York]

Dear Sir:

Mr. Arthur Schlesinger Jr. wrote you in the last issue to register a series of complaints centering upon the appearance on the dust-jacket of my new book, *Rumbles Left and Right*, of a quotation from Mr. Schlesinger, to wit, "He has a facility for rhetoric which I envy, as well as a wit which I seek clumsily and vainly to emulate."

(1) Says Mr. Schlesinger: The statement was made "some two years before the new book was announced," about a book "which to this day I have never seen." Say I: Estimates of an author's generic skills are not self-lapsing, like souffles. The author must do something concrete to change the critic's mind about him. If I have done any such thing, Mr. Schlesinger has yet to remark it; and if I have done such a thing in my new book, Mr. Schlesinger is unaware of it, having said repeatedly that he has yet to read it.

(2) Says Mr. Schlesinger: When I made the statement about Mr. Buckley in the first instance, it "reeked with sarcasm." Say I: As a matter of fact, it did not—and the vast audience who heard it clearly interpreted it as sincerely intended, perhaps because it took for granted Mr. Schlesinger's general sincerity. If he intended it sarcastically, then it must be said that his powers of sarcasm are becoming as dull as his wit, which by now everyone surveying his recent behavior knows is approaching the dimensions of a Depressed Area, worthy of federal intervention. But I should not want my word for it to be automatically accepted, and would risk a thousand copies of *Rumbles* against a thousand copies of *The Politics of Hope,* to be sent to college libraries, that an impartial jury reading the transcript, and listening to the tape-recording, would rule that Mr. Schlesinger's sentence was not rendered with obvious sarcasm.

And a couple of supplementary observations of my own:

(3) Mr. Schlesinger is perfectly free to change his mind. Indeed, I wish he would change his mind about things much much more often than he does. But he is not free, having changed it, or having been caught up in an act of hypocrisy, to go rampaging about making a nuisance of himself, getting lawyers to harass us, and planting the suggestion that either I or Putnam's behave unconventionally or unethically. Under the circumstances,

(4) Putnam's has decided to bring out the next printing of *Rumbles,* which has already gone to press, without replacing the original jacket copy, and I shall continue to circulate Mr. Schlesinger's quotation until I have from him a letter (a) admitting he said it without sarcasm, (b) acknowledging I had every right to use it, and (c) requesting me to do him the

personal favor of removing it. So long as he tries to get me to drop it under the pressures of Messrs. Greenbaum, Wolff and Ernst,* I'll go to the electric chair first, and instruct my heirs to put on my tombstone,

Wm. F. "Envy His Rhetoric" Buckley, Jr.

In November 1963, President Kennedy was widely perceived as having consolidated his standing in the country. His approval rating among the American people was 59 percent, according to Gallup. He had faced down the Soviet Union in Berlin and in the Cuban missile crisis, passed the test-ban treaty, and begun to embrace the civil rights movement. Under his stewardship, the U.S. economy had recorded the longest sustained expansion since World War II. Kennedy now foresaw a spirited campaign against Barry Goldwater and re-election.

But that was not to be.

A few minutes after 1:30 p.m. on November 22, 1963, Arthur was sipping cocktails before luncheon with Katharine Graham,† Ken Galbraith, and the editors of Newsweek *at their Manhattan offices when a man entered in his shirtsleeves and said, a little tentatively, "I think that you should know that the President has been shot in the back of the head in Texas." Arthur momentarily thought this was some sort of ghastly office joke. Then they all huddled desperately around the nearest television.*

Soon Arthur, Ken, and Katharine were on a plane bound for Washington. Bitterness, shame, anguish, disbelief, and emptiness mingled furiously in Arthur's mind. It was the saddest journey of his life. He reached the White House at about 4:30 p.m., three hours after the shots were fired. At 6, he went out to Andrews Field where the plane arrived from Texas carrying Kennedy's body. He returned to the White House and then went home to his family.

---

* A New York City law firm founded in 1915.

† Katharine Meyer Graham (1917–2001). Publisher of her family's newspaper *The Washington Post*, 1963–79; married Philip Graham. Her memoir, *Personal History*, won a Pulitzer Prize in 1998.

To Jacqueline Kennedy

[Handwritten]

[November 22, 1963]

[Washington, D.C.]
Friday evening

Dearest Jackie:

Nothing I can say can mitigate the shame and horror of this day. Your husband was the most brilliant, able and inspiring member of my generation. He was the one man to whom this country could confide its destiny with confidence and hope. He animated everything—he led with passion and gaiety and wit. To have known him and worked with and for him is the most fulfilling experience I have ever had or could imagine.

Dearest Jackie, the love and grief of a nation may do something to suggest the feeling of terrible vacancy and despair we all feel. Marian and my weeping children join me in sending you our profoundest love and sympathy. I know that you will let me know when I can do anything to help.

With abiding love,
Arthur*

---

* Schlesinger returned to the White House later that night. Around four in the morning of November 23, 1963, the casket containing the president's body was brought from the Bethesda Naval Hospital and placed on a stand in the East Room. Robert F. Kennedy asked Schlesinger to look at the bier and give his opinion as to whether to keep it open or shut. Schlesinger viewed the uncovered head and found it looking too waxen and made up—not really like the man he knew so well. He (and others) recommended that the casket be closed, which it was.

To Rómulo Betancourt[*]

December 17, 1963

[Washington, D.C.]

Dear Mr. President:

No letter I have received about our recent tragedy has moved me more than yours. These have been hard days here—the hardest I have ever known—and things do not seem to grow easier. President Johnson has taken charge in splendid fashion; but the sense of personal and public loss remains, and will never disappear.

As you know, President Kennedy had the greatest respect and affection for you. He followed your courageous fight for Venezuelan democracy with high admiration and hoped that the example of Venezuela would strengthen democratic forces throughout the hemisphere. More than once during this autumn, he expressed concern over your own personal safety and hoped you were taking prudent precautions during the election campaign.

My own plans are uncertain. President Johnson has asked me to stay on for the period of transition, and I shall, of course, do everything I can to help. I look forward very much to returning to my own work and shall therefore plan to move on at some appropriate time.

We all look forward to your visit to the United States next spring.

Ever sincerely yours,
Arthur

* Rómulo Betancourt (1908–81). "The Father of Venezuelan democracy"; president of Venezuela, 1945–48, 1959–64; survived assassination attempt by Rafael Trujillo, the dictator of the Dominican Republic.

To Charles Wintour

December 18, 1963

[Washington, D.C.]

Dear Charles:

I need not say how grateful I was for your letter. These have been hard days—the worst I have ever had—and they do not get easier. I have lived a relatively protected life, and, with the exception of Benny DeVoto, no one to whom I have really been close has ever died. To lose so great a President and so beloved a friend—and in such a senseless way—is difficult. My depression does not seem to lift.

My own plans remain uncertain. President Johnson has asked me to stay, and I told him that I would stick around during the transition period. However my intention is to fade away fairly soon and return to my own work, though I have not yet decided when or where.

My love to Nonie.

Yours ever,
Arthur

To Jacqueline Kennedy

[Handwritten]

January 6, 1964

[Washington, D.C.]

Dearest Jackie:

I cannot say how deeply I was touched by your note in the beautiful copy of the *Inaugural Addresses*.[*] These last three years have been the most

---

[*] *Inaugural Addresses of the Presidents of the United States from George Washington 1789 to John F. Kennedy 1961*, inscribed by Jacqueline Kennedy: "For Arthur Schlesinger jr.— / The President was going to give you this for Christmas—Please accept it now from me—With my deepest appreciation for your devotion to Jack—and all our shining memories of him / Jackie / December 1963." The book was one of eighty-five bound copies in special binding of maroon leather with the presidential seal, gilt edges, and a red silk place marker ribbon. "A.S." was stamped in gilt on the front.

exciting and fulfilling of my life—less because of the experience of working in the White House, fascinating as it was, than because of the inexhaustible delight of working in close association with the President. He gave all of us the greatest experience of our lives, and I shall always prize the book and your inscription.

In your note a few weeks ago, you mentioned a possibility which has been much in my mind—that is, of doing a book on the President. I have thought a good deal about this in the last few weeks; and I have come to the conclusion that I want to write such a book, a rather personal book about the President, how he operated, a portrait of the man at work, showing him in certain crises and turning-points of the administration, and trying to explain the mystery of how one man, with so little time for great accomplishment, could transform the temper of America and the image of America in the world.

The book I have in mind would not be a systematic or comprehensive history of the administration. That will have to be done later and by some one who was not personally involved. It would rather be an account of the way John F. Kennedy ran the Presidency, an attempt to define the achievement and impact of these years, and also an attempt to set forth the legacy of the President for those who come after. As I read the nonsense in the press these days, it seems to me important that some of these points be made clearly and strongly, and in the very near future. I feel also that I owe it to myself, and to the historical profession, to do something like this when memories are still fresh and vivid.

I would not of course wish to undertake such a work unless you and Bobby thought it a good idea. In the next few days, I will try to write a more ordered memorandum setting forth my conception of the book and some of the problems involved. I will send the memo over to you and Bobby, and then you might perhaps let me know what you think.

I will hope to see you tomorrow night. (I began this letter on Monday but finished it on Tuesday.)

Love,
Arthur

To Arthur and Elizabeth Schlesinger

January 8, 1964

[Washington, D.C.]

Dear Mother and Dad:

Forgive my delay in writing, but I have been surprisingly busy, both on the Kennedy Library and on the State of the Union address, to which I made negligible contributions.

First let me express belated thanks for the Christmas presents. I loved the ties, and the flask is something I have long needed. (It will no doubt come in very handy in 1964.)

Next, I am sure you have been mystified by the succession of stories in the papers about my plans. Let me warn you not to believe anything until you hear it from me! My plans remain as uncertain as ever. I hope to get away for a few days in a couple of weeks and reach a final decision then. In any case, I plan to leave at times and places of my own choosing. I am inclining more and more to the idea of writing a book about the Kennedy Administration, though I understand that Ted Sorensen has this in mind too. He was more deeply involved in a wider range of public policy than I; but I still think I might have something to contribute.

As for Goldman,* he has been to see LBJ a few times and apparently they strike it off well. In order to facilitate my own disengagement, I suggested to Bill Moyers† that, when I go, they might want to get Goldman in to take my place. I hardly know Goldman. He is not much of an historian; but I understand that he is a liberal, and I do not think he would do any harm. Moyers insists that there is no intention of taking him on in the near future and no connection in any case between his position and mine. I think that Goldman is under the impression that he has been asked, but that is denied to me here. As I say, I am rather in favor of the Goldman idea since, when I go, his availability would enable me to leave with less argument.

My views on the book are still tentative. I have discussed it in a prelimi-

---

* Eric Goldman (1916–89). American historian; taught at Princeton University, 1942–85; special adviser to President Johnson, 1963–66.

† Bill Moyers (b. 1934). American journalist; special assistant and press secretary to President Johnson, 1963–67; publisher of *Newsday,* 1967–70; producer and host of TV news journal programs at CBS and PBS.

nary way with Bobby and have sent a note to Jackie about it (I am going to Jackie's for dinner tonight and will perhaps get her provisional reaction). I intend to set out my thoughts in an ordered way in a few days, try to consider whether the Sorensen book presents an obstacle, and then discuss the project more seriously with Jackie and Bobby.

I note that Galbraith and [Seymour] Harris are waging a campaign in the [*Harvard*] *Crimson* to make it possible for me to return to Harvard! My view on that is that I do not want to exclude this as an eventual possibility, but that I want to spend at least a couple of years, and perhaps more, on my own work. The Stanford Center has invited me to go there for a year; but Stanford seems awfully far away.

In short, everything remains uncertain, which is why I look forward to an opportunity to go away and collect my thoughts.

I trust that all goes well in Cambridge. I will write at more length in a few days.

Much love,
Arthur

From Henry Kissinger

February 14, 1964

[Cambridge, Massachusetts]

Dear Arthur:

Somewhat belatedly I want you to know with what regret I learned of your decision to leave the White House. Your decision is perfectly understandable, of course, and I have no doubt that you will make a major contribution to our society no matter where you are.

However, I want to tell you that your presence in the White House seemed to me always a guarantee that humane values would receive their proper hearing. Though my path and that of the Kennedy Administration diverged,* I never questioned the validity of these concerns. Nor will I ever

---

* Kissinger served as a part-time foreign policy adviser in the White House in 1961–62 but was shunted aside and undermined by McGeorge Bundy, the national security adviser. Kissinger believed that Bundy as dean of faculty at Harvard ensured that he was not offered a tenured position in the government department. "[Bundy] tended

forget the exhilaration of those early months. The hope they held out was in no small part represented by people like you.

I hope we can stay in close touch.

With affectionate regards.

Sincerely yours,
Henry A. Kissinger

To Mary McCarthy

February 29, 1964

[Washington, D.C.]

Dear Mary:

I was delighted to receive your note. . . .

As you probably know, I am leaving the White House in order to write a book on President Kennedy. This will be personal and informal and not in any sense an organized account of the Administration. I don't know whether I can pull it off or not, and I confess certain worries in the dark of night; but I am deeply persuaded that I have no choice but to try. We will stay on in Washington at least till the end of the year. I am establishing myself in a small office strategically located next to La Salle du Bois. The address is 1180 18th Street, N.W., Washington, D.C. 20036.

Will you be in Paris at the end of April or early in May? I have been invited—I am sure much to Dwight [Macdonald]'s indignation—to be a judge at the Cannes Film Festival;* and this seemed to me too zany a proposition to be resisted. Perhaps you could be lured down to Cannes yourself for the spectacle. In any case, I will hope to see you somewhere. . . .

Marian joins me in sending love to you both.

Ever affectionately,
Arthur

---

to treat me with the combination of politeness and subconscious condescension that upper-class Bostonians reserve for people of, by New England standards, exotic backgrounds and excessively intense personal style," Kissinger wrote in his memoirs.

* Schlesinger wrote movie reviews for *Show* magazine; Macdonald, for *Esquire*. At the film festival, Schlesinger became friends with director Fritz Lang and actor Charles Boyer, who were also judges.

To John Sherman Cooper[*]

May 14, 1964

[Cannes, France]

Dear John:

I have been in France and Italy for the last three weeks and have been struck by the depth of the conviction on every side that the facts about the President's murder are being deliberately withheld. Very few people seem to accept the notion that [Lee Harvey] Oswald[†] and [Jack] Ruby[‡] were each acting on their own. Nearly everyone appears convinced that there must have been an organized effort of some sort in the background. And many people fear that our government has reasons of its own to suppress the full truth. The other night, for example, the novelist Sybille Bedford[§] (who covered the Ruby trial for *Life*) asked me why the proceedings of the Warren Commission were secret, pointing out that comparable British tribunals always conducted their work in public except when national security was involved. A number of people both in Italy and in France have cited to me a statement attributed to the Chief Justice[¶] to the effect that the full story cannot be told for a hundred years. All this leads people to believe that our security agencies are somehow implicated. They can see no other reason for the secrecy of the proceedings or for the Chief Justice's alleged statement.

I have done my best to cope with these questions; but in the end all one can do is to ask people to wait for the report of the Warren Commission and to remind them that the chief law officer of the United States is the man who has the largest stake of anyone in the world in uncovering the full

* John Sherman Cooper (1901–91). Liberal Republican senator from Kentucky, 1946–49, 1952–55, 1956–73; ambassador to India, 1955–56, and to East Germany, 1974–76; friend of President Kennedy; served on the Warren Commission.

† Lee Harvey Oswald (1939–63). Former U.S. Marine; brief defector to Soviet Union; assassinated President Kennedy on November 22, 1963 (according to four governmental investigations); murdered by Jack Ruby.

‡ Jack Ruby (1911–67). Nightclub operator in Dallas, Texas; killed Lee Harvey Oswald two days after President Kennedy's assassination.

§ Sybille Bedford (1911–2006). German-born English writer of eleven books, including novels, travel books, and legal works.

¶ Earl Warren (1891–1974). Liberal Republican three-term governor of California; chief justice of United States, 1953–69; chaired the Warren Commission.

truth about his brother's murder. I am writing you now to express the hope that, when the report is prepared, it will deal effectively and decisively with the gaps and anomalies in the evidence and with the questions and doubts in the minds of European observers. . . . There is a good summary of prevalent doubts in a piece by a Leo Sauvage* in the March or April *Commentary*.† If the report does not answer such questions in an explicit and convincing way, I very much fear that serious damage will be done to the confidence abroad in the integrity of our government.

Please don't bother to acknowledge. I expect to be back in Washington soon. Love to Lorraine.

Yours ever,
Arthur

The Senate passed the Civil Rights Bill 73–27 on June 19, 1964, and President Johnson signed it into law on July 2. The act outlawed discrimination in all public accommodations and in employment, housing, publicly owned facilities, and federally aided programs; the attorney general was empowered to initiate suits to end discrimination and to speed school desegregation. Vice President Humphrey called it "the greatest piece of social legislation of our generation."

* Leo Sauvage (1913–88). New York correspondent for *Le Figaro;* later chief drama critic for *The New Leader;* wrote about his doubts concerning Oswald's guilt in March 1964 *Commentary* article.
† *Commentary* magazine. Founded in 1945 by the American Jewish Committee; neo-conservative in outlook.

To Hubert H. Humphrey, Jr.

June 22, 1964

[Washington, D.C.]

Dear Hubert:

I hasten to send my warmest congratulations on the civil rights success. The nation stands deeply in your debt. . . .

Yours ever,
Arthur

To Lyndon B. Johnson

July 2, 1964

[Washington, D.C.]

Dear Mr. President:

Now that the Civil Rights Act is a reality, I hasten to send you my most respectful congratulations and thanks for your great leadership in the fight. The Civil Rights Act of 1964 will go down in history as one of the turning-points in the long struggle for equal rights for all Americans. You have more than fulfilled the expectations *and* hopes of your supporters and have demonstrated superbly your commitment to the cause of decency and justice.

Ever sincerely yours,
Arthur Schlesinger, jr.

To Jacqueline Kennedy

July 10, 1964

[Washington. D.C.]

Dear Jackie:

I left Wellfleet [Massachusetts] after the weekend; and your sweet letter was forwarded to me down here. I shall be back, however, from the 15th to the 20th (except for the 17th) and again from the 25th to the 31st, at which point we, like you, evacuate the Cape for the summer. We would love to come over at any time that would be convenient for you. Marian or I will call when I get back.

I have begun to write the book. It is the hardest thing I have ever tried to do, and I despair of doing justice to the subject. But I guess that if enough of us do our best the future historian will be able to get the idea, like Matterhorn painted from a number of angles. . . .

You are everlastingly right to decide to leave Washington, though it will be a great sadness for those of us who remain. But life in Georgetown must have been unendurable for so many reasons. Bobby tells me that you have an apartment near the Museum. That sounds ideal.

. . . I continue to keep my fingers crossed about [RFK and] the Vice Presidency. The White House could not be more sphynxlike.

I look forward to seeing you very soon.

Much love,
Arthur

To Henry Kissinger

July 22, 1964

[Washington, D.C.]

Dear Henry:

. . . I am sorry not to have answered your invitation to speak before the Seminar.* As you can imagine, this has been an extremely busy summer; and in view of the book and the convention I fear that I will not be able to make it this year. I am sorry, because I have always enjoyed my meetings with the Seminar.

Sincerely yours,
Arthur

---

* Kissinger founded the Harvard International Seminar and was its director from 1952 to 1969. The summertime program drew young and rising foreign leaders and thinkers to Harvard to network and discuss international affairs. Schlesinger spoke at the seminar in August 1962 and in previous years.

P.S. I shall be interested sometime in your impressions of [the Republican Convention in] San Francisco.

From Henry Kissinger

July 29, 1964

[Cambridge, Massachusetts]

Dear Arthur:

Thank you for your letter of July 22nd.

We shall miss you at the Seminar. Having let me down two years in a row, I will be particularly insistent next year.

San Francisco was a depressing and indeed outraging experience. It has cured me of ever trying to dabble again on the fringes of Republican politics.[*]

Warm regards.

Sincerely yours,
Henry A. Kissinger

To Jacqueline Kennedy

[July 29, 1964]

[Wellfleet, Massachusetts]

Dearest Jackie:

I couldn't be sorrier to have missed the party last night; but for some reason I had not realized that it was your birthday. I asked Bobby last week whether I need come to New York for the trustees' meeting in view of the fact that this was my last week on the Cape, and he said no but did not remind me what day it was. So I herewith send my belated

---

[*] Kissinger supported Nelson Rockefeller, the liberal Republican New York governor, for the 1964 Republican presidential nomination, but the delegates at San Francisco's Cow Palace chose Arizona's senator Barry Goldwater, "Mr. Conservative." The delegates heaped scorn and verbal abuse on Rockefeller when he stood up to speak against extremist organizations like the John Birch Society. Republican Party chairman William E. Miller, a Congressman from upstate New York, was selected as the vice-presidential nominee.

birthday greetings—and wish so much I had been there to submit them in person.

You probably know much more than I about the Vice-Presidency; but I will bring you up to date as to what I know. After my talk with Kenny [O'Donnell]* and Larry [O'Brien]† last week and their fear that LBJ's thoughts were turning toward Eugene McCarthy, I began to feel an urgent need for a united front between the RFK and Humphrey forces, so that the choice should be either one or the other. I spoke to Joe Rauh, who is for Hubert first but very definitely for Bobby second; he strongly agreed and encouraged me to call Walter Reuther in the hope that Walter could bring about a united front and lay the situation before Johnson. I then called Bobby who insists that he is entirely out of the picture but prefers Hubert to Eugene and saw no harm in my calling Reuther. When I spoke to Walter, he grasped the situation at once and said emphatically that it must be either Hubert or Bobby. He then sent Jack Conway‡ to talk to Kenny, who confirmed the general picture and made it clear that he and Larry have Hubert as their second choice.

Walter called me today to say that he is going to New York tonight and have breakfast with Dave Dubinsky and Alex Rose tomorrow. He is also going to raise the matter at the AFL-CIO executive committee meeting next Monday in Chicago. His hope is to be able to present a united labor position in support of either Hubert or Bobby, and no one else. This means that, if LBJ is really persuaded, as he professes to be, that he must have a Catholic on the ticket, RFK may be back in the picture. Anyway let us keep our fingers crossed.

I will be back in Washington on Monday. If you would like some bulletins while you are abroad, send me an address, and I will do my best.

I know you will have a pleasant and relaxed time along the Dalmatian

---

*Kenneth ("Kenny") O'Donnell (1924–77). Special assistant and appointments secretary to President Kennedy, 1961–63; aide to President Johnson, 1963–65; former Harvard roommate of Robert F. Kennedy.

†Lawrence ("Larry") O'Brien (1917–90). Democratic political strategist; director of 1960 Kennedy presidential campaign; postmaster general in the Johnson administration; Democratic Party national chairman, 1968–72; commissioner of the National Basketball Association, 1975–84.

‡Jack Conway (1918–98). Longtime United Auto Workers official, 1946–61; worked in the Kennedy and Johnson administrations, helping to launch Head Start, the Job Corps program, and the War on Poverty.

coast, especially with David and Sissy* along. And hurry back, because we all miss you very much.

Love, Arthur

[Handwritten]

P.S. Bobby has just called to tell me about his talk with LBJ,† so I guess it is all over. I wish to hell there was something that could still be done.

On August 22, 1964, two days before the Democratic National Convention in Atlantic City, Robert F. Kennedy announced his candidacy for the Democratic senatorial nomination in New York. But many New York liberals, seeing the move as a power grab by a madly ambitious, arrogant, opportunistic, and dangerous young man, had to be persuaded to support him. That was Arthur's job.

When he read an editorial in The New York Times *denouncing "The Kennedy Blitzkrieg," he took up his pen.*

To the Editor of *The New York Times*

August 29, 1964

[Washington, D.C.]

Sir:

The *Times* has commented with surprising vehemence on the decision of the Attorney General to enter the senatorial contest in New York. I hope that it will not be regarded as further carpet-bagging if a Massachusetts voter offers an opinion on Mr. Kennedy's record.

1. Obviously carpet-bagging is not the gravamen of the objection to Mr. Kennedy, since the *Times* has expressed its readiness to endorse Gover-

---

* David Ormsby-Gore (1918–85). Conservative MP, 1950–61; British ambassador to the United States, 1961–65; friend of President Kennedy; married to Sylvia ("Sissy") Ormsby-Gore; known as Lord Harlech.

† Johnson informed Robert F. Kennedy that he had decided against him for the vice presidential slot and later issued a cover story saying he had ruled out all of his cabinet officers for the post.

nor Stevenson as Senator from New York. Nor, I am sure, would the *Times* presume to add on its own to the qualifications laid down by the Federal and New York Constitutions—qualifications which Mr. Kennedy obviously fulfills.

2. The real question then is whether Robert Kennedy would be a good Senator. The *Times* seems to feel that Kennedy is unqualified for the Senate— too young, too inexperienced, too ambitious, too hungry for power and position. I doubt whether those who have observed Kennedy in Washington would accept this verdict. I believe that the general feeling here is that he has been the best Attorney General this country has had for a generation—the best since Francis Biddle twenty years ago. He has made the Department of Justice one of the best departments of the government, extraordinarily high both in talent and morale; he has handled the civil rights issue with notable intelligence, judgment and courage; and, in addition, he has dealt effectively with a number of problems of concern to the citizens of New York—juvenile delinquency, immigration, economic concentration, organized crime, defense of the indigent.

3. Beyond this, Mr. Kennedy has played a larger role in the United States Government than any Attorney General in the history of the country. Every student of the crisis of October 1962 knows the vital contribution he made in killing the proposal that the United States take out the Soviet missile bases in Cuba by a sneak air attack. He has been a powerful advocate of the policy of multiplying our contacts with the third world and with the nations behind the Iron Curtain. No American has been more effective in persuading the students, intellectuals and labor leaders of the world that the United States is their friend, not their enemy.

His record of accomplishment is formidable. He has shown himself in the most difficult situations a man of strong and consistent character, liberalism, imagination and idealism. He would not only represent the state of New York with fidelity and power, but he would express for all Americans the ideals of strength and magnanimity which were the essence of his brother's New Frontier.

Sincerely yours,
Arthur Schlesinger, jr.

Stepping up to the rostrum at the Democratic National Convention in Atlantic City to introduce a film about President Kennedy, Robert F. Kennedy received a tremendous ovation from the delegates that continued for twenty-two minutes, no doubt filling President Johnson with untold rage and fear that the presidential nomination might be snatched from his hands and that he might be kicked unceremoniously out of the White House.

Kennedy appeared slight, almost frail, standing on the dais in the packed convention hall with a wistful half smile on his face, shyly raising his hand again and again, trying to still the uproar and speak his piece.*

To Robert F. Kennedy

August 31, 1964

[Washington, D.C.]

Dear Bob:

Your speech Thursday night was perfect (except for sending Jefferson and Madison on their botanizing expedition in 1800—they actually went in 1791)† and the ovation was far and away the most moving and most authentic moment at the convention. As I pointed out later that night on ABC (to a listening audience composed mostly of my relatives), the delegates had been feeling frustrated all week, and now they were giving voice to their true emotions, as shown by the fact that the organ stopped after a minute or two but the ovation went on and on.

I had a pretty good talk with Arthur ("Punch") Sulzberger‡ and John Oakes on Thursday morning. Sulzberger is amiable and fairly open-minded; Oakes is going to be the harder one to win over. The essence of Sulzberger's problem, and a good part, though not all, of Oakes's, is the question of the

---

* RFK thanked the delegates for their support of President Kennedy and lavishly praised the utility of a great political party.

† RFK said, "[President Kennedy] used to take great pride in telling of the trip that Thomas Jefferson and James Madison made up the Hudson River in 1800 on a botanical expedition searching for butterflies; that they ended up down in New York City and that they formed the Democratic Party."

‡ Arthur Ochs Sulzberger (1926–2012). Publisher of *The New York Times*, 1963–92; renowned for publishing *The Pentagon Papers* on secret U.S. strategy during the Vietnam War.

bosses. They feel that the *Times* has been fighting Buckley, etc., for years, that these men have blocked the emergence of a healthy Democratic Party, that they have consistently preferred hacks to good candidates, and that they have been a corrupting and demoralizing influence in the state. The *Times* people now fear that your appearance in the State will give the bosses a new lease on life and will set back the people who have been working for a decent Democratic Party. They will need strong reassurance on this point before there is any possibility of their endorsing you.

On Wednesday, they will probably begin by asking you some of your foreign policy views (opening up the Iron Curtain, what can we do with the uncommitted countries, etc.); but they will get to the bosses soon, and this will be the critical part of the conversation. I think they are more or less satisfied (Sulzberger more, Oakes less) about your ability and ideas; they are just afraid that your influence within the state will be exercised on behalf of the people the good Democrats have been resisting for years.

As I am sure everyone has been telling you, you will be encountering this reaction on every side. Jack Bingham[*] says that his people in the Bronx are very disaffected, and that one of his chief fund-raisers told him that she would not raise any money for him in the campaign just because he went to your reception in Atlantic City. Bingham is personally well disposed, and I would urge you to have a meeting with him as soon as possible. He has never been an all-out Reform Democrat, and his notions as to what might be done should therefore be detached. Adlai Stevenson is prepared to be friendly, and I think it would be an excellent move for you to go and see him and ask his advice. Marietta Tree is all for you and will be helpful. Jimmy Wechsler is, of course, a good friend, and the *Post* should be OK if Mrs. Schiff can be kept sweet. I hope too you can have a meeting soon with Ruth Field[†] and her group.

I discovered when I got back from Atlantic City that my letter to the *Times* had been held up because it was too long. I have accordingly written a shorter version which, I trust, will be published this week.

---

[*] Jonathan Brewster ("Jack") Bingham (1914–86). Democratic reformer; UN diplomat; New York representative, 1965–83.

[†] Ruth Field (1908–94). Liberal activist; wife of Chicago newspaper publisher and philanthropist Marshall Field III, owner of the *Chicago Sun-Times* and other newspapers and retail stores.

Let me know what I can do to help. I would be glad, for example, to talk privately (or publicly) to reform and liberal groups if it seemed a good idea.

Yours ever,
Arthur Schlesinger, jr.

President Johnson selected Hubert H. Humphrey, Jr., as his vice presidential running mate for the 1964 election.

To Hubert H. Humphrey, Jr.

August 31, 1964

[Washington, D.C.]

Dear Hubert:

I need not say with what joy the Schlesingers welcomed the end of the long suspense. It was a perfect denouement—and no choice could have been more popular nor more merited. . . .

Yours ever,
Arthur Schlesinger, jr.

To Hubert H. Humphrey, Jr.

September 4, 1964

[Washington, D.C.]

Dear Hubert:

As you know, President Segni* of Italy is gravely sick. Reports from Rome suggest that he will probably die in the next week or ten days. If this should happen, I wonder whether it would not be a good idea if you were to go to Rome as the representative of the American Government at the funeral.

---

* Antonio Segni (1891–1972). Lawyer; Italian Christian Democratic politician; twice Italian prime minister; president of the Italian Republic, 1962 64.

Quite apart from its favorable effect on the Italian vote in the United States, this would give you an excellent opportunity for contact with the top Italian political leaders. Your appearance in Italy would also be an effective expression of continued American support for the progressive political experiment of the Center Left.

Yours ever,
Arthur

To Jacqueline Kennedy

Saturday, September 5

[Washington, D.C.]

Dearest Jackie:

I was so sorry to miss you in Atlantic City. I spent the whole afternoon of the reception in the Kennedy Library exhibit, taping some material for ABC (which, like most of the things I did at the convention, was never used). Everyone said how wonderful the reception was. The best moment in the convention, of course, was that extraordinary ovation that night when Bobby introduced the film. As you probably noticed, they cut the organ off after the first minute or so, but it went on and on and on. The delegates were finally having a chance to express their real feelings.

There have been a round of parties for RFK this week—Tuesday in New York at Pavillon [Restaurant] after the convention; then the Dillons on Wednesday night; and a marvelous Dept of Justice party Thursday night, with a splendid collection of *My Fair Lady* parodies ("All I want is a state somewhere," and "I expect to get elected in November . . . but get me to New York in time"). I think it is going to be a tough campaign in New York; I fear there will be a lot of people who will vote for Keating[*] because they think he is a double underdog (as against both Goldwater and Bobby), or because they want to help the anti-Goldwater Republicans, or because they resent carpetbaggers or bosses. But I have no doubt that Bobby will be a

---

[*] Kenneth Keating (1900–1975). Moderate representative (R-N.Y.), 1947–59, and senator (1959–65); ambassador to India, 1969–72, and to Israel, 1973–75.

great candidate; and the more people see him, the less they will pay attention to the Gore Vidal stereotypes about him. He is in great spirits.

He saw Dolly Schiff last Friday. Jimmy Wechsler, who was present (and who has been writing excellent things about the campaign), called me afterwards and said that he had been through a great number of these confrontations between Dolly and candidates, and that the only person who had ever done better than Bobby was his brother.

What are your plans? When do you come to New York? I would love to see you at some point. I may be going to Cambridge in the next week or two to put Andy in Andover and Chrissie in Radcliffe, see Teddy [Kennedy], etc., and I could drive down to Newport for lunch or something if you were still to be there. I have written about 35,000 words on the book but am not very satisfied with it. It is by far the hardest thing I have ever attempted.

Much love,
Arthur

To Reinhold Niebuhr

September 21, 1964

[Washington, D.C.]

Dear Reinhold,

I was so sorry that we could not see you here for the Medal of Freedom ceremony. I did have a nice chat with Christopher,[*] and he cheered me by saying that things are progressing with you.

I hope to see you before long for a number of reasons—among them, to talk about Robert Kennedy, about whom I hear you have reservations. I have seen a great deal of him in the last four years and have very high admiration for him and confidence in him. I think you will find this to be the case with nearly all people who have seen much of him at close range—Dick Neustadt,[†] for example. Next to his brother, he was the person who more

---

[*] Christopher Niebuhr, Reinhold Niebuhr's son, accepted the Presidential Medal of Freedom on behalf of his father, who was absent because of illness.

[†] Richard ("Dick") Neustadt (1919–2003). American political scientist; taught at Columbia University, 1954–64, and at Harvard University, 1965–89, occasional adviser

than anyone else was regarded by the younger New Frontiersmen as their leader and rallying point during the Kennedy years—and this was true in foreign policy and in many domestic questions beyond the immediate concern of the Department. He will make an excellent Senator, far better than Keating; and I do not think anyone should have any apologies about being for him. It is odd to hear people in New York saying almost exactly the same things about Bobby now that they were saying about his brother in 1959–60. . . .

Yours ever,
Arthur

To the Editors of *The New Republic*

September 29, 1964

[Washington, D.C.]

Sirs:

May I comment on some of the points in the letters on the Kennedy-Keating campaign reprinted in your issue of October 3?

One of the writers describes Senator Keating as "a genuine liberal, with an excellent record." Senator Keating is an amiable gentleman; but a glance at his congressional career shows that, when he had a conservative constituency as a member of the House of Representatives, he voted with the conservative Republicans, and, now that he has a liberal constituency, he votes with Senator Javits.* Even in his "liberal" phase, Senator Keating is identified with no national issue, except Cuba; and recently, as in his astonishing charge that Mr. Kennedy made a deal with Nazis in disposing of General Aniline,† he has shown disturbing tendencies to revert to the Keating of the House.

---

to Presidents Truman, Kennedy, Johnson, and Clinton; author of a landmark book on the U.S. presidency, *Presidential Power*.

* Jacob Javits (1904–86). Liberal representative (R-N.Y.), 1947–54, and senator, 1957–81.

† Keating accused Kennedy of allowing, as attorney general, the sale of General Aniline, a German chemical company seized at the end of World War II, for the benefit of its former Nazis owners.

Some of your writers seem to regard his refusal to endorse Barry Goldwater as an act of transcendent moral heroism. But surely, if Senator Keating had endorsed Goldwater, he would be politically dead in a state like New York. His silence about Goldwater is only the most minimal injunction of self-preservation. One remembers the liberal Republicans of past years who courageously rejected their party when it nominated men like William Howard Taft[*] and Herbert Hoover,[†] both far more reasonable men than Goldwater, and then wonders at seeing liberals today faint with excitement over the moral triumph of *silence* in the face of the most reactionary candidate for President nominated by either major party in this century.

Few of your writers seem much impressed by the residence point, and rightly so. The Constitution was written in a day when the States of the Union were far more remote from each other than they are today; yet all it stipulated was that a Senator shall, "when elected be an Inhabitant of that State in which he shall be chosen." It would be odd for a generation living in the age of television and jet aircraft to add residential restrictions which the Founders did not deem necessary.

But most of the objections seem in the end to come to the character of Robert Kennedy. He is attacked as one whose "ruthless ambition . . . knows no bounds," "basically anti-libertarian," a McCarthyite, etc. I must testify in the strongest possible language that this stereotype bears no resemblance at all to the Robert Kennedy whom the liberals of the Kennedy Administration found their strong and faithful ally (and, on many occasions, leader) in the policy debates of 1961–63 both in domestic and foreign affairs. It is incomprehensible to me how any liberal can possibly prefer Senator Keating's Jingoism on Cuba to Mr. Kennedy's record in the Cuban missile crisis (when he blocked the proposal for a sneak air attack against the missile bases) and to his powerful support for the Alliance for Progress—or Senator Keating's stubborn commitment to the cold war to Mr. Kennedy's tireless efforts to strengthen relations with uncommitted nations and to break down the Iron Curtain.

[*] William Howard Taft (1857–1930). Lawyer; Ohio Republican; governor-general of the Philippines, 1900–1904; secretary of war, 1904–8; twenty-seventh U.S. president, 1909–13; chief justice of the United States, 1921–30.

[†] Herbert Hoover (1874–1964) Iowa Republican; mining engineer; secretary of commerce under Presidents Harding and Coolidge, thirty first U.S. president, 1929–33, blamed for the Great Depression of the 1930s.

I despair of persuading those who have hopelessly committed themselves to the devil theory of Robert Kennedy. I can only remind them that many of them were saying exactly the same things about his brother in 1959–60. Events, I believe, convinced them once that they were wrong, and I am sure that events will convince them again; but how many times do we all have to go through this experience?

Sincerely yours,
Arthur Schlesinger, Jr.

Arthur reviewed Reminiscences *by General Douglas MacArthur in the September 27, 1964, New York Herald Tribune Book Week: "It is a defensive, self-congratulatory work, devoid of doubt or magnanimity. Its basic thesis is the infallibility of the author and the wickedness of those who dared disagree with him [including FDR, Truman and General George C. Marshall]. . . . MacArthur was in his way a great man, but this is a sad book. . . . [It] reminds us that the nation has been best served by military leaders who have seen themselves not as saviors, prophets and martyrs, but as men assigned to hard and bitter tasks in the service of the republic."*

The review was entitled "The Supreme Cavalier."

To R. Sargent Shriver[*]

October 20, 1964

[Washington, D.C.]

Dear Sarge:

I very much appreciate your letter about the MacArthur review. Two days later I took Jackie to luncheon at the Colony. As we came in, a lady said "Hello, Mrs. Kennedy." Jackie said, "Hello," and then said "May I introduce

---

[*] R. Sargent ("Sarge") Shriver (1915–2011). Lawyer; first director of the Peace Corps, 1961–66; ran LBJ's War on Poverty; ambassador to France, 1968–70; vice presidential nominee in George McGovern's 1972 presidential campaign; married to President Kennedy's sister Eunice.

Mr. Schlesinger, Mrs. MacArthur."* Jackie may not have read the review, but Mrs. MacArthur obviously had.

I hope all goes well on the poverty front.

Yours ever,
Arthur Schlesinger, Jr.

The Johnson-Humphrey ticket swept the Goldwater-Miller ticket, winning 61.1 percent of the popular vote and carrying all but six states. The victors added 37 northern Democrats to the House of Representative—enough to assure a working progressive majority for the first time since 1938. Under President Johnson's leadership, the new Congress produced the most impressive record of domestic legislation since the early New Deal, including the creation of Medicare and Medicaid, enactment of the Voting Rights Act of 1965, increasing federal aid to education, establishment of public broadcasting, the formation of Head Start and Volunteers in Service to America (VISTA), liberalized immigration laws, and the creation of the Department of Housing and Urban Development and the Department of Transportation.

Robert F. Kennedy won the race for senator of New York, helped greatly by Johnson's enormous victory. Johnson carried the state by 2.5 million votes, Kennedy by 720,000. Kennedy vowed to work with Johnson, but the strains between the two men from past years did not easily go away.

---

* Jean MacArthur (1898–2000). Married General MacArthur, eighteen years her senior, in 1937; she was his second wife. They had one child and remained together until his death in 1964.

To Jacqueline Kennedy

April 2, 1965

[Washington, D.C.]

Dearest Jackie:

Attached you will find the first twelve chapters of my manuscript. I thought it might be better to give you a batch now than confront you with the whole lot in the summer. I am also sending this batch to Bobby.

I will well understand it if you do not feel like reading this. If you do read any, I would be most grateful if you could correct errors, mark any passages which you think might cause trouble or give the wrong impression or betray confidences which should not be betrayed or seem too personal or too trivial or too self-serving or of doubtful taste. Don't hesitate to scribble on the manuscript. And I would particularly appreciate it if there are times when you can throw additional light on the events I am writing about. If you do not feel like going through the whole thing, I would particularly like your reaction to chapter four.

I also attach a sheet showing where I am going from here.

My intention in writing the book is to serve the interests of history and the memory of the President. It has turned out to be much longer than I expected, but it became evident to me as I wrote that the only way to display his full stature is to show him in action in considerable detail—in adversity and in triumph. This book is by far the hardest thing I have ever tried, and I realize every day with sinking heart how wretchedly I have fallen short of what I would like to do and of what the occasion deserves. My hope is that it will convey something at least of the extraordinary quality and character of the man and of the purposes, problems and achievements of the administration.

Please do not spare my feelings in your criticisms, for I will be everlastingly grateful for your help in making the book a faithful account of the greatest man I shall ever know.

Much love,
Arthur

President Johnson appointed Richard Helms as the new deputy director of the Central Intelligence Agency.*

To Richard Helms

April 14, 1965

[Washington, D.C.]

Dear Dick:

Just a note of warmest congratulations on your promotion. My only regret is that they didn't escalate one step further.[†]

Yours ever,
Arthur

To the Children

26 April 1965

[Beverly Hills, California]

Dearest children:

The first week of the tour is over, and I am just finishing a weekend of semi-retirement at a luxury hotel and feel a little restored. I began in Denver last Monday. On Tuesday I went on to Salt Lake City—an evening notable only because a pillar of the radical right named W Cleon Skousen,[‡] who had just written a tract exposing my nefarious activities, was in the audience. However, he listened silently and silently went away. Governor

---

[*] Richard ("Dick") Helms (1913–2002). Director of Central Intelligence, 1966–73; ambassador to Iran, 1973–77; convicted of lying to Congress, claiming no CIA involvement in the 1973 coup in Chile.

[†] Helms replied to Schlesinger's letter six days later, saying, "As I take this new job, it is good indeed to know that I have the good wishes of friends like you." Schlesinger regarded Helms as the most honorable of the CIA crowd.

[‡] W. Cleon Skousen (1913–2006). Author of far-right books; John Birch sympathizer; claimed Dwight D. Eisenhower was a Communist agent; opposed federal income tax, unions, minimum wage, and national parks.

Calvin Rampton* of Utah was also in the audience, and I had lunch with him the next day. He is a liberal Democrat and was most pleasant. On Wednesday I went on to Fresno in California. Here I was picketed by a fine group of American patriots calling themselves Alert Americans of Clovis (a town nearby). They carried signs saying that "Schilesinger" was anti-business, anti-labor (!) and pro-communist, also an "enternal threat"—whether they meant an internal, external or eternal threat I do not know. Four of them were dressed as undertakers and carried a coffin marked: "Here lies the U.S. Constitution." My talk in Fresno, like my later talk in Sacramento, was sponsored by the McClatchy papers (the McClatchys have a chain of liberal papers through the inland valley).

On Thursday I proceeded to San Diego. In the afternoon I hired a car and drove over to La Jolla to see the [Seymour] Harrises. Seymour was needless to say away, but I had a nice talk with Ruth and, though the day was overcast and a little chill, a swim in the Pacific. The Harrises have a house on the beach rented from an Arizona rancher (and pal of B Goldwater's). After my San Diego talk, I went on to Phoenix where I spoke Friday. Here a party was given for me in the afternoon by the Arizona Democratic Council before my talk at Arizona State in the evening. Then Saturday on to Sacramento. Here I had dinner with Grace Kennan McClatchy (George Kennan's daughter and a former student of mine, now married to C K McClatchy,[†] the heir of the empire) before the lecture. No pickets. The next morning Governor Brown[‡] entertained me for breakfast with some of his people. I must say that he is one of the most likable and decent men in politics.

Then on to Los Angeles and the Beverly Hilton, where I promptly collapsed beside the swimming pool. After a while I had a call (courtesy of George Stevens jr.)[§] from a producer named Alan Pakula[¶] (*To Kill a Mock-*

---

* Calvin Rampton (1913–2007). Popular Democratic governor of Utah, 1965–77.

† Carlos K. McClatchy (1927–89). Liberal media owner; chairman of the McClatchy chain of newspapers.

‡ Pat Brown (1905–96). Progressive Democratic governor of California 1959–67; lost to Ronald Reagan in 1966; father of California governor Jerry Brown.

§ George Stevens, Jr. (b. 1932). Award-winning film and TV writer; playwright; founder of the American Film Institute; producer of the annual Kennedy Center Honors; son of famed director George Stevens; motion picture division head, United States Information Agency, 1962–64.

¶ Alan Pakula (1928–98). Director of conspiracy thriller films; movies include *Klute*, *The Parallax View*, *All The President's Men*, and *Sophie's Choice*.

ingbird) so I went over to their house and collapsed beside their swimming pool. He is married to an actress named Hope Lange,[*] who is mildly pretty and very pleasant. After the swim, I spent 20 minutes in Pakula's sauna at 180 degrees. Then I returned to the hotel and worked. This morning I lecture at UCLA and this evening in San Jose.

I have been giving 3 lectures—one on foreign policy, one on domestic policy and one on the future of the Presidency. There is great but rather unfocussed apprehension about Vietnam, vague confidence in LBJ but not much warmth about him. In Utah and Arizona I was assured that the radical right had reached its zenith and was nothing like the menace it was 2 or 3 years ago; but in California Tom Braden[†] (with whom I talked over the phone) and others say that it is continuing to grow. Polls are said to show that Ronald Reagan,[‡] the right-wing ex-film star, could beat Pat Brown!

Tomorrow I go to San Francisco and then east; though I note that my Wednesday lecture is in the middle of what I take to be the flood region in Illinois, so it may be cancelled and I might have a free day in SF, which would be great. I expect to be back in Washington next Sunday or Monday. I hope that I will find a great pile of letters awaiting me.

MUCH LOVE,
Daddy

---

[*] Hope Lange (1933–2003). Film, stage, and television actress; her 1963 marriage to Pakula ended in divorce in 1971.

[†] Thomas ("Tom") Braden (1917–2009). American journalist; CIA official, 1950–54; owner of *Blade-Tribune* newspaper in Oceanside, California; syndicated columnist and TV commentator; author of *Eight Is Enough*, later an ABC show.

[‡] Ronald Reagan (1911–2004). Actor; president of the Screen Actors Guild; Democrat who voted four times for Franklin D. Roosevelt, turned Republican; governor of California, 1967–75; fortieth U.S. president, 1981–89.

To Walter Lippmann

May 6, 1965

[Washington, D.C.]

Dear Walter:

The passage from Tocqueville* is to be found in his chapter "Why American Writers and Orators Often Use an Inflated Style." It reads as follows:

> In democratic communities, each citizen is habitually engaged in the contemplation of a very puny object, namely himself. If he ever raises his looks higher, he perceives only the immense force of society at large, or the still more imposing aspect of mankind. His ideas are all either extremely minute and clear, or extremely general and vague: what lies between is a void. When he has been drawn out of his own sphere, therefore, he always expects that some amazing object will be offered to his attention; and it is on these terms alone that he consents to tear himself for a moment from the petty, complicated cares which form the charm and the excitement of his life.
>
> This appears to me sufficiently to explain why men in democracies, whose concerns are in general so paltry, call upon their poets for conceptions so vast and descriptions so unlimited.
>
> The authors, on their part, do not fail to obey a propensity of which they themselves partake; they perpetually inflate their imaginations, and, expending then beyond all bounds, they not infrequently abandon the great in order to reach the gigantic. By these means, they hope to attract the observation of the multitude, and to fix it easily upon themselves: nor are their hopes disappointed; for, as the multitude seeks for nothing in poetry but objects of vast dimensions, it has neither the time to measure with accuracy the proportions of all the objects set before it, nor a taste sufficiently correct to perceive at once in what respect they

---

*Alexis de Tocqueville (1805–59). French political thinker and historian; author of the classic 1835 study of the American political system *Democracy in America*.

are out of proportion. The author and the public at once vitiate one another.

I greatly enjoyed our luncheon today.

Yours ever,
Arthur

On April 28, 1965, President Johnson, claiming an imminent Communist takeover, dispatched American troops to the Dominican Republic to put down an uprising by rebel forces backing former president Juan Bosch* against a military regime.

To the Children

May 9, 1965

[Washington, D.C.]

Dearest Children:

I forget where I stopped last time in the saga of my participation in the Dominican crisis. Was it Sunday afternoon a week ago? I think so, because I do not think I had seen President Betancourt. Betancourt, as you all know (I trust), is one of the very great men of the Americas. He is the only man in the history of Venezuela to serve out his constitutional term as president; he is a strong progressive democrat and a strong anticommunist; and he & JFK much admired each other. His term expired a few months ago, and he happened by coincidence to be in Washington last weekend. I thought LBJ should see him. In my presence Mac Bundy called Johnson and suggested this, but Johnson didn't want to see Betancourt. Then I urged Bundy or Goodwin or Moyers to see Betancourt, but they were always too busy or unwilling to act where Johnson wouldn't. So on Monday I decided that I would see Betancourt myself.

---

* Juan Bosch (1909–2001). Dominican literary figure; politician; democratically elected president of the Dominican Republic in 1963; ousted same year in a military coup.

Up to the time I had seen Betancourt I accepted the LBJ thesis that the revolution was about to be taken over by the communists. This thesis emerged, so far as I can tell, out of a combination of Tom Mann's[*] instinctive anti-liberal views and fragments of misinformation sent along in good faith, I guess, by the CIA. On the other hand, Bundy, Moyers & Goodwin all agreed that we had made a bad mistake in acting without consultation with the OAS.[†] No one was quite clear how this happened except, again, Tom Mann didn't think the OAS very important. Now Betancourt said that on the basis of his information from trusted people (Venezuelans) in Santo Domingo, he was sure that the communists had *not* taken over the revolution and that there had been no significant defection of the original revolutionary leaders.

By the time I left him and called Dick, Johnson was about to record his speech. Dick said, "Oh my God; this undermines the whole thesis of the speech." So it did; but it was too late. Dick insisted that LBJ see Betancourt the next morning, but I fear that the effect of the visit wore off quickly. The fact is that the communists have *not* captured the revolution; and, if we had had any sense, we should have accommodated ourselves to this and let the OAS work out a provisional regime based on Colonel Caamano[‡] and the non-communists among the revolutionaries. Instead, it looks today as if we were putting our own counter-revolutionary junta into the picture, and this will only compound the errors of last week.

I cannot help feeling that Johnson, who must feel terribly frustrated over Vietnam, seized upon the Dominican crisis to show how tough, vigorous, effective, &c, he can be and to shove Vietnam off the front pages. In the short run, I imagine that his Dominican policy is popular. But my guess is that in the longer run, when it becomes increasingly evident how badly he

[*] Thomas ("Tom") Mann (1912–99). Conservative U.S. diplomat specializing in Latin America; served in the State Department, 1942–66; assistant secretary of state for inter-American affairs, 1960–61; ambassador to El Salvador, 1955–57, and Mexico, 1961–63.

[†] Organization of American States. Founded in 1948; a regional assemblage of Northern and Southern hemisphere countries formed to safeguard democracy and national sovereignty throughout the Americas.

[‡] Colonel Francisco Caamaño (1932–73). Dominican soldier and politician who backed democratically elected president Juan Bosch against a military coup in 1963; served briefly as Dominican president in 1965; killed leading an insurgency against the government of Joaquín Balaguer.

misjudged and overreacted (sending in 20,000 Marines to the DR is ludicrous), it will damage people's faith in his reaction to subsequent crisis.

Then Johnson seized this moment to demand a vote of confidence from the Congress in the guise of an appeal for $700 million for the war in Vietnam. The White House thought this was a very cunning stratagem, but it aroused great resentment on the Hill. There has been mounting concern about Vietnam; there was great doubt about the Dominican Republic; but it is almost impossible to vote against an appropriation for troops engaged in combat abroad, so the Congress had to choose between expressing its reservations about the LBJ policy or voting for the appropriations. The matter was made the more irritating because the request for the $700 million was a fake; the Defense Department already has all the funds it needs for the Vietnam fighting.

I talked to Bobby Kennedy about this several times on Tuesday and Wednesday. He has found himself increasingly unhappy about our Vietnam policy, where he thinks we have construed as a military problem what is primarily a political and diplomatic problem and where he has recommended to Johnson a pause in the bombing and more vigorous efforts at negotiation; and he was outraged by the Dominican affair. But he has been reluctant to speak out lest it lead to an impression that the Kennedys were breaking with the administration. Nonetheless, by Thursday morning, when Burke Marshall[*] and I went over to see him, he had about decided to vote against the resolution. Both Burke and I thought that he had to vote for the resolution, but that he should place his own interpretation on what he was approving. I accordingly wrote a speech outlining his differences and Bobby gave it early Thursday afternoon. Though the language was low-keyed and tactful, the import of the speech was unmistakable. But to our astonishment no one paid much attention to it. Neither the *Times* nor the *Herald Tribune* the next morning mentioned the fact that the junior senator from NY had spoken out about the Johnson foreign policy—all the more inexcusable in the case of the *Times* because it had been expressing editorial concern over some of the very points Bobby raised in his speech. Fortunately the *Post* and the *World Telegram* had better news sense and

[*] Burke Marshall (1922–2003). Lawyer; assistant attorney general heading the Civil Rights Division in the Kennedy administration; one of the authors of the Civil Rights Act of 1964.

played up the speech. This led the *Times* the next day to run an interview with Bobby in which he made some of his points about the Dominican Republic—but nowhere in the interview did the *Times* mention the fact that he had already said these things the day before in a speech on the floor of the Senate which the *Times* had not bothered to report.

A bulletin from Stephen in Paris (which I will circulate as soon as it is copied) reports his deep indignation about our Dominican policy; it went, I gather, to the point of sending a letter to the international edition of the *Times*. (The *Times*, by the way, has still not mentioned Bobby's remarks in its editorial page; John Oakes's hatred of Bobby, which I have tried in vain to understand and deflect in the past, is apparently consuming and unshakable.) I agree with Stephen's reaction, I think, with one possible exception: suppose this had been, in fact, a communist revolution or one which the communists had, in fact, taken over? If anything like this were to happen, I would not hesitate to send in the Marines. The Cuban missile crisis justifies us, I would think, in taking such action in the interests of our own national safety. The problem is that just because the opponents of a revolution, or the CIA, say it is communist does not make it so.

Per the rest of the week I have been working away. On Tuesday I lectured in Pennsylvania; then went on to NY and lunched with Jackie who gave me her comments on the first 400 pages of the book, generally favorable & very helpful. (The book, by the way, has been taken by the Book of the Month Club, which finally matched the Literary Guild offer and has given me freedom to publish whenever ready.) On Wednesday night we had a dinner party: Bradlees,[*] Evanses,[†] Goodwins, Franklin Roosevelts. . . . On Thursday I went to NY to celebrate the 50th birthday of my old friend and college classmate Teddy White.[‡] It was a very pleasant small party—the

---

[*] Benjamin ("Ben") Bradlee (b. 1921). *Newsweek* Washington bureau chief, early 1960s; executive editor of *The Washington Post*, 1968–91; renowned for publishing *The Pentagon Papers*; oversaw *Post* coverage of 1973 Watergate scandal; friend of President Kennedy.

[†] Rowland ("Rowlie") Evans, Jr. (1921–2001). Political journalist; author; cowriter (with Robert Novak) of influential syndicated column Inside Report; TV commentator; friend of President Kennedy.

[‡] Theodore White (1915–86). Political journalist; author; correspondent for *Time* magazine; won a Pulitzer Prize for *The Making of the President, 1960;* wrote subsequent volumes on the elections of 1964, 1968, and 1972; Harvard classmate of Schlesinger.

Luces,[*] John Herseys,[†] etc. I lunched on Thursday with Walter Lippmann who is now seriously worried about LBJ's stability—all his compulsive grabbing at TV cameras, spending long hours of self-justification with the press, etc. I was worried myself after watching his TV performance on the Dominican Republic a week ago, but I ascribed this to my anti-LBJ prejudices; but Lippmann has been very pro-LBJ up to now. Yesterday I went out to Bobby [Kennedy]'s for lunch, played tennis, had a *sauna*, and discussed the first 500 pages of the mss. In effect, both Bobby & Jackie now approve the use of the things they have told me at one time or another over the years. . . .

Love to all, Daddy

To Richard Goodwin and Bill Moyers

May 10, 1965

[Washington, D.C.]

Dear Dick and Bill:

I am increasingly concerned about our policy in the Dominican Republic. I had thought we could get out of our original difficulties if we would only observe the neutrality we profess and let the OAS come up with a provisional government including non-communist leaders of the revolution. But if we are really determined now to back a Tony Imbert[‡] junta against the Caamano group, we are, I am sure, heading for serious trouble. Imbert is a political primitive; he will not be able to lead the Dominican Republic along democratic lines; and everyone will assume that we are doing this because we are absolutely determined to destroy the rebel forces and establish a right-wing government under our own control. Certainly

---

[*] Henry Luce (1898–1967). Powerful conservative media figure; founder of magazine empire including *Time, Life, Fortune, Sports Illustrated,* and other publications; married to Republican congresswoman Clare Booth Luce.

[†] John Hersey (1914–93). Writer; authored *New Yorker* pieces on JFK's PT-109 collision and on the 1945 Hiroshima bombing; won a Pulitzer Prize for his novel *A Bell for Adano;* taught writing at Yale University.

[‡] Antonio Imbert Barrera (b. 1920). Official in regime of Dominican dictator Rafael Trujillo, 1930–61; helped plot Trujillo's 1961 assassination, part of a military junta running the Dominican Republic in the mid-1960s.

the setting-up of Imbert and our opposition to hearing both sides at the OAS hardly square with our professions of neutrality. Do we really want to make the non-communists in the revolution despair of us and conclude that they have no alternative, if they are constantly being treated as communists, but to become communists? That is a very likely effect of the Imbert policy.

And all this has a wider implication than the future of the Dominican Republic. What is at stake is the administration's capacity to estimate the character and urgency of a crisis. I do not think anyone should be deceived by the superficial comment and applause (largely from Republicans) about "another TR," "at last we have someone who will stand up against the commies," etc. Any President at a moment of apparent crisis will get national support. But, if it turns out that the crisis was in fact less desperate than represented, the longer-run effects on the administration's credibility are likely to be harmful. I am afraid that the administration will be held vulnerable on three counts: for having prejudged the nature of the revolution, for having unnecessarily ignored the OAS and for having sent far too many troops into the Dominican Republic.

All this will add up in the minds of many at home and abroad as a large and jittery over-reaction to a situation. This has already given rise to grave doubts about our judgment and leadership among anti-communist progressive governments in such countries as Venezuela, Chile and Peru. And its impact will go far beyond Latin America. If people feel we have miscalculated this situation, they will be less inclined to accept both our present judgment of Vietnam and our reaction to future crises. My son Stephen who, as you know, is in England this year, writes that people who had been willing enough to go along with us on Vietnam are now, as a result of what they regard as a trigger-happy, communist-obsessed, self-serving and unilateral policy in the Dominican Republic, beginning to doubt our judgment in Southeast Asia.

It would, of course, be going too far to say that this miscalculation might become an equivalent of the Bay of Pigs; but it might well be bad enough, it seems to me, to justify a comparable program of reappraisal within the government. Why, when we talked week end before last, did we all believe that there had been a significant defection of the original leaders of the revolution? that many of these leaders had taken refuge in foreign embassies in flight from their own revolution? that Caamano had personally machine-gunned a number of his opponents? that the 58 or 54 or 53 communists ("I hold in my hand ...") were running the revolution? Can it really be true, as Dan Kurzman* wrote in Sunday's *Washington Post*, that the CIA list of subversive figures given posts in the revolutionary government included a conservative who had been a supreme court justice for 26 years (Alfredo Conde Pausa), a conservative naval officer who holds no official position (Luis Homero Lajara Burgos), and a fifteen year old kid (Alejandro Lajara)? Obviously all this suggests a gross intelligence failure and must raise serious questions about the reliability of our informants in Santo Domingo. Are we still relying on these same sources when we make decisions in favor of Tony Imbert today?

In addition: why have members of the American occupying forces told Dominicans that Bosch was a communist? (I sent Dick a clipping from the [Washington] *Star* reporting one incident.) Why have we captured and interrogated rebels on behalf of the military crowd and, according to some reports, turned over rebel prisoners to the "government" people? Why have we taken one side in the conflict instead of trying to restore constitutional processes on an impartial basis? ... Either because our pose of neutrality is a phony or because our system of command and control is inadequate. Nor do I see great virtue in goading the rebels into anti-American action and then denouncing them for it.

I do think that the White House, not for punitive reasons but to avoid a future misjudgment of this magnitude, ought to conduct a serious inquiry into the political and intelligence failures—i.e., as, for example, the fact that no one thought it worthwhile to cut in the OAS before we sent in the Marines, though this could have been done without delaying the landings one minute; or the fact that in the next 72 hours we were so crassly misinformed about what was going on.

I have a feeling, in addition, that there is a larger and more significant issue in all this: that is, our relationship to the Soviet Union itself. In the period from the Cuban missile crisis to the recent intensification of the Vietnam crisis, there had been marked progress toward a stabilization of

---

* Dan Kurzman (1922–2010). Journalist; foreign correspondent for *The Washington Post*; authored seventeen books primarily on military history.

relations between ourselves and the Russians. We were beginning to discover a real, if limited, community of interests; and we were achieving *de facto* agreements in a number of areas—in our determination to avoid head-on collisions, to stop the testing of nuclear weapons in the atmosphere, to stop the spread of nuclear weapons to nations which did not have them, even, perhaps, for a time, to block Chinese expansion in Southeast Asia. Now two things have happened: (1) there is a new Soviet leadership, relatively inexperienced and unsure of itself and therefore uncertain in its response to our actions; and (2) there is an apparently mounting tendency on our part to see critical problems as primarily military problems and to tackle them by primarily military means. My impression is that the Soviet Union had been clinging pretty well to the *detente* line, despite the real difficulties our policy in Vietnam created for them; but that it is now acting almost as if it were beginning to doubt the judgment of the leadership in Washington. I fear, in short, that we may be inviting a reversion of Soviet-American relations to the mood of 1961–62; and this, of course, would be not only a grave setback to hopes of world peace but also to hopes of doing very much about the Great Society. I may very well be off base, but I can't escape the feeling that, unless we do something, we will be moving into a period of considerable, and perhaps unnecessary, conflict with the Soviet Union.

Forgive the length of this letter.

Yours ever,
Arthur Schlesinger, jr.

To Adlai Stevenson

May 10, 1965

[Washington, D.C.]

Dear Adlai:

I am considerably disturbed over our present course in the Dominican Republic and its possible implications. Bill Moyers asked me to come back from a lecture tour on May 1 and help out at the White House, as I was of course glad to do; but, when it seemed to me that we were making some doubtful judgments, I receded from the situation, hoping, however, that the OAS and the pressure of events would put us back on the right course. I fear now that we are heading into even worse trouble, and that justifiable doubts over our Dominican policy will weaken acceptance in our own country and through the world of the things we must do in Vietnam. I have accordingly sent the attached letter to Bill Moyers and Dick Goodwin, and am sending you a copy for your personal information.*

Yours ever,
Arthur

Adlai Stevenson, walking in the sunlight with Marietta Tree along Grosvenor Square near the U.S. Embassy in London on July 14, 1965, suffered a massive heart attack and died. He was sixty-five years old. "Keep your head high," he said to Marietta. Then, "I am going to faint." His head hit the pavement with a heavy thud.

In October, Arthur's father died of heart failure at age seventy-seven in Cambridge, Massachusetts.

Arthur's book about the Kennedy administration, feverishly written over fifteen months, A Thousand Days: John F. Kennedy in the White House, was due in bookstores in December. Jackie received an early copy and wrote Arthur on November 23, "It takes wings—and when you read it—Jack is alive again."

---

* Schlesinger sent a similar letter to Secretary of Defense Robert McNamara. OAS peacekeeping forces were eventually dispatched, but U.S. troops remained in the Dominican Republic until September 1966.

From Hubert H. Humphrey, Jr.

December 2, 1965

[Washington, D.C.]

Dear Arthur:

I've just finished reading William Shannon's article[*] in *The New York Times Magazine* of November 21. It appears to me that, after reading what you had to say about me in this article, a cease-fire ought to be in order.[†]

I have tried to indicate to you that my remarks concerning your comments on Rusk were too sharp and unnecessarily critical. I wish you had not said what you did about the Secretary but, even more, I regret what I had to say about you and your comment. I hope you will accept my apology.

May I also add that I needed to make no attempt to ingratiate myself with the President. After all, it was the President who asked the Convention to nominate me.

Now furthermore, Arthur, there is a great deal of difference between being a Senator critical of a policy or an officer of the government, particularly when you are in the opposition party and not at all privy to the most intimate details of the Administration's deliberations and policies. In other words, my criticism of Dulles was the criticism of but one Senator and a junior member at that—and the criticism of a Senator that was in the opposition and seldom, if ever, consulted by the Administration. In your instance the situation was considerably different. You were a part of the Administration, an intimate of the President's, a close working associate of the Secretary.

I only say these things so that the record may be somewhat balanced and not to be argumentative. I know that I may have offended you, and for

---

[*] William V. Shannon, "Controversial Historian of the Age of Kennedy," *The New York Times Magazine*, November 21, 1965.

[†] After an excerpt from *A Thousand Days* was published in *Life* magazine, Humphrey publicly chastised Schlesinger for writing that Kennedy had decided to replace Rusk as secretary of state after the 1964 election. "I think it has been harmful. I think it has been mischievous. I don't think it has helped the country," said the vice president on August 16, 1965, on the *CBS Morning News*. "[Schlesinger] sees Humphrey's criticism as a vulgar attempt to ingratiate himself with President Johnson," wrote William V. Shannon in *The New York Times*.

this I am sincerely regretful. I admire you a great deal, and I am proud of the fact that we have worked side by side for many important causes. I see no need of continuing the acrimonious comment. It is of no benefit to either of us and, frankly, the book should be closed on it. I'm ready to do so.

Sincerely,
Hubert H. Humphrey

To Hubert H. Humphrey, Jr.

December 7, 1965

[Washington, D.C.]

Dear Mr. Vice President:

I appreciate more than I can say your letter of December 2. I should note, first, that my conversation with Bill Shannon[*] took place in October, long before I received the very kind letter you sent me at the time of my father's death. I regretted the sharpness of my own comments when I saw it in print, and all the more so after the thoughtfulness of your letter.

We will probably continue to disagree about the propriety of my remarks; but I continue to think that the historian must take his stand with Jefferson: "There is not a truth existing which I fear, or would wish unknown to the whole world." However, I am all for a cease-fire, and my admiration and affection for you remain undiminished. This book is closed!

Yours ever,
Arthur Schlesinger, jr.

---

[*] Shannon also wrote Humphrey on December 7, 1965, saying: "I have known Arthur fairly well for the past eighteen years and I can honestly tell you that I have never heard him—except in our September interview—speak of you in anything but the highest and warmest terms. Indeed, it was my impression that he was so upset in August and early September because he was so surprised that you should be critical of him."

To McGeorge Bundy

[Handwritten]

December 10, 1965

[Washington, D.C.]

Dear Mac:

I read the news of your resignation with the greatest regret. You served two Presidents with the greatest brilliance and devotion, and the nation will be very much the loser by your departure. I do not envy you your next assignment,* but if anyone can do that job and preserve his human qualities it is you.

In any case, I have enjoyed and cherished our friendship through the last quarter century and trust that we will both be situated where we can sustain it in the future.

My love to Mary.

Yours ever,
Arthur

Arthur appeared on the cover of Time *magazine on December 17, 1965, dubbed "The Combative Chronicler."* Time *called* A Thousand Days *"by all odds the best of the 90-or-so Kennedy books that have appeared in the two years since Dallas . . . a virtuoso demonstration of the skills that helped make Schlesinger a Pulitzer prize winner at 28."*

His friend Charles Wintour sent him a telegram calling the Time *portrait "far more glamorous than* Newsweek," *which had the actress Julie Christie on its cover.*

---

* Bundy was the new president of the Ford Foundation, serving from 1966 to 1979.

To Charles Wintour

December 17, 1965

[Washington, D.C.]

Dear Charles:

Personally I prefer Julie Christie. I thought *Time* was much better on the book than on the author—though I must say the description of the author fully lived up to the sulky and petulant figure on the cover.

Merry Christmas to all the Wintours.

Yours ever,
Arthur

Reviewing A Thousand Days *in the December 28, 1965,* New York Times Sunday Book Review, *historian James MacGregor Burns called the book "a remarkable feat of scholarship and writing, set in the widest historical and intellectual frame.... A great President has found—perhaps he deliberately chose—a great historian." The book was a bestseller and won the Pulitzer Prize and National Book Award.*

But the sadness lingered.

In January 1967, Schlesinger accompanies Jacqueline Kennedy to a New York preview of the film *Marat/Sade,* based on the Peter Weiss play *The Persecution and Assassination of Jean-Paul Marat as Performed by the Inmates of the Asylum of Charenton Under the Direction of the Marquis de Sade.*

A Crisis of Confidence

1966–68

To Sammy Davis, Jr.[*]

February 4, 1966

[Washington, D.C.]

Dear Sammy:

I have been meaning to write and thank you for your generous reference as recently reported in Martha MacGregor's column[†] in the *New York Post*.

I am flattered to be associated with Sandburg[‡]—and I need hardly say that I would seize every opportunity to stand in line for you!

Sincerely yours,
Arthur

---

[*] Sammy Davis, Jr. (1925–90). Singer; television and film actor; member of Frank Sinatra's "Rat Pack"; Kennedy family friend.

[†] "There are only two authors I'd stand in line for—Arthur Schlesinger and that man who wrote about Lincoln—Sandburg," said Davis, autographing copies of his new book, *Yes I Can*, at Brentano's, Martha MacGregor reported in the January 23, 1966, *New York Post*.

[‡] Carl Sandburg (1878–1967). Prolific writer, poet, journalist, author of a multivolume biography of Abraham Lincoln.

To the Children

February 21, 1966

[Phoenix, Arizona]

Dearest Children:

I have given 14 speeches in the last 14 days and feel that way. When I was younger, I used to like lecture tours; but I am getting old, and three weeks is too long. A different audience every evening, a different sponsor, a different bed every night, except they are all the same and merge indistinguishably in retrospect as well as prospect. I can hardly remember where I was yesterday and where I am supposed to be tomorrow. I began in the east—Providence and Springfield—then to the midwest (Ohio, Illinois, Minnesota, Wisconsin, Kansas)—then to the south (Louisiana, Texas, Arizona). The audiences have been cordial and responsive. I regret to report that there have been no pickets: I fear I am getting respectable. There is great concern about Vietnam, but no particular crystallization of view, at least among the young; my older audiences seem much more inclined to believe that whatever the President wants must be right. There is no question that Fulbright's hearings[*] have helped a great deal in legitimatizing dissent. I thought RFK's statement[†] excellent. I spent one night at Adlai Stevenson's old house in Libertyville; John Bartlow Martin is living there now (and working on the biography). It was sad to be in that nice house so filled with pleasant memories. I saw something of Adlai jr in Chicago. He is an attractive and intelligent young man and will probably run for State Treasurer. I was in Chicago twice and saw Newt Minow the second time; he is thriving in the practice of law. Saul Bellow, Dick Wade,[‡] [and]

[*] Nationally televised hearings on the Vietnam War in February 1966, held by the Senate Foreign Relations Committee under the chairmanship of Senator J. William Fulbright of Arkansas, helped shift public opinion against the war. Witnesses included Dean Rusk, General Maxwell Taylor, and foreign policy expert George Kennan. Fulbright challenged administration assumptions, arguing that American vital interests were not involved and that the conflict could be a "trigger for world war." President Johnson came to hate Fulbright, whom he privately mocked as "Senator Halfbright."

[†] Robert F. Kennedy released a statement on February 19, 1966, saying: "A negotiated settlement means that each side must concede matters that are important to preserve positions that are essential." He believed the price of settlement was bringing the National Liberation Front into the political process—an unacceptable condition to the Johnson administration.

[‡] Richard ("Dick") Wade (1921–2008). Urban historian; taught at the University of

Ben Heineman* were all out of town. I don't think I have seen anyone else of particular interest, except Peter Duchin† with whom I rode on the plane from New Orleans to Dallas. In San Antonio I had lunch with Prof. Merle Curti‡ of Wisconsin, an eminent historian and former student of Grandpa's. . . .

Civil rights note: when I spoke at a black tie dinner attended by the leading citizens of El Paso, I noticed that some had brought transistor radios; it turned out that the group could not wait to learn the results of the Texas Western basketball game that night. Later I was told that the Texas Western basketball first team consists entirely of Negroes though the college is overwhelmingly white. But this has evidently not interfered in the slightest with local pride.

Along the way a letter from Jackie caught up with me, or rather a note scribbled along the margin of an article about me in the Italian weekly *Oggi*. She wrote: "Dearest Arthur: Please try to get through this in Italian—it is really very moving and says things about you that would make you so happy—and make me so proud that you wrote the book. 4 people I sat next to in Rome were reading it—and as I sat next to 6 people while I was there I hope that is the ratio for Italy. Everywhere it is advertised in bookstores—in Switzerland too—I think you will be a Plutarch or Thucydides when as many years separate us from now, as they are behind us. All love, Jackie. P.S. There is such a nostalgia for JFK in Europe—their memory of him is the only thing that keeps them liking America now—so they fall back on your book to understand what now seems the mystery of those days. I know that from reading as people are too kind to ever mention JFK to me."

. . . Only one more week, and I can return to Princeton§ and my own work. I can hardly wait. I hope all goes well with everybody, and that at

---

Chicago, 1963–71, and the City University of New York, 1971–93; adviser to Senators Robert F. Kennedy and George McGovern.

* Benjamin Heineman (1914–2012). Lawyer; president of Chicago and North Western Railway, 1956–72; supporter of Adlai Stevenson; adviser in the Kennedy and Johnson administrations; influential figure in Chicago Democratic politics.

† Peter Duchin (b. 1937). American pianist and band leader; son of musician and band leader Eddy Duchin; raised by W. Averell and Marie Harriman.

‡ Merle Curti (1897–1997). American historian at the University of Wisconsin; helped to establish peace and conflict studies; winner of the 1944 Pulitzer Prize for History for his book *The Growth in American Thought*.

§ Schlesinger spent 1966 in Princeton, New Jersey, at the Institute for Advanced Study as a visiting fellow.

some point I will get word from someone. It would be an exciting day in my life. In the meantime,

All love,
Daddy

To J. William Fulbright

March 10, 1966

[Princeton, New Jersey]

Dear Bill:

The tactical problems in the Senate, it would seem, are (a) how to keep the debate going and (b) how to put some ceiling on the war without placing the Senate in the vulnerable position of interfering in the details of military operations and superseding the constitutional authority of the Commander-in-Chief. It is essential, I think, for the Senate not to get itself in the position of the Committee on the Conduct of the War during the Civil War.*

I wonder whether a resolution along the following lines might not have useful restraining effect without tying the hands of the executive in ways which could be properly criticized. I don't know the parliamentary language but the substance might be something like this:

It is the sense of the Senate that (a) no United States troops should be placed in North Vietnam and (b) no United States planes should strike large population centers or bomb along the Chinese border without a formal declaration of war by the Congress.

I can only add that you and your colleagues have put the nation greatly in your debt these last weeks.

Yours ever,
Arthur Schlesinger, jr.

---

* The Joint Committee on the Conduct of the War (1861–65) investigated military strategy, contracts, treatment of soldiers, and trade with the enemy. The committee was accused of conducting "witch hunts" related to battle defeats, second-guessing war efforts, and meddling in army affairs. It ended up discredited.

To Oscar Sachs*

March 10, 1966

[Princeton, New Jersey]

Dear Dr. Sachs:

I regret that I cannot accept your invitation to take part in the conference on May 8. While I am deeply concerned about the direction of events
in Vietnam, I must frankly say that the methods employed by your
committee—as, for example, the so-called Read-In for Peace—do not seem
helpful. I do not think it very useful to combat one form of irrationality by
whipping up another. Did the Read-In for Peace[†] contribute a single
thought toward the resolution of the Vietnam conflict? This problem requires hard and careful analysis; not displays of emotion, however virtuous.

I am distressed most of all by the tendency on the part of some intellectuals to abandon their distinctive weapon—i.e., consecutive reason—in
times of crisis. This is not only unworthy; it is also ineffectual. I have no
doubt that the thoughtful speeches of senators like Fulbright, McGovern,
Robert Kennedy, Church[‡] and others have done far more to make people
think a second time about the war in Vietnam than all the mass demonstrations put together. I should add that the senatorial concern derived from
their analysis of the way our policy was moving and, if anything, was slowed
up in its expression by hysterical protest outside.

The dilemmas here are serious and acute. They are not to be solved by
rhetoric. A Read-In for Peace in Vietnam is no answer to Secretary Rusk. I
don't happen to agree with Secretary Rusk, but I believe he is entitled to a

---

* Dr. Oscar Sachs (1919–86). South African–born psychiatrist; director of psychiatric
staff at Mt. Sinai Hospital; chairman of the New York–based Committee of the Professions to End the War in Vietnam.

† Participants in the February 20, 1966, "Read-In for Peace in Vietnam," held in Manhattan's Town Hall before 1,500 people, included Norman Mailer, Jules Feiffer, Robert Lowell, Alfred Kazin, Lillian Hellman, William Styron, Susan Sontag, Stanley
Kauffmann, and other literary and cultural figures.

‡ Frank Church (1924–84). Liberal senator (D-Idaho), 1957–81; anti–Vietnam War
leader; chaired 1975 Church Committee investigating abuses in the FBI and CIA and
other U.S. intelligence agencies.

response at least as carefully reasoned as his own argument. If intellectuals of all people reject reason and attempt demagoguery, why should they expect the rest of our volatile society to hold back?

Sincerely yours,
Arthur Schlesinger, jr.

P.S. In addition, I cannot understand how the eminent writers who appeared on February 20 could ever have rallied to an appeal so uncouth as that of bearing witness to "the viability of the American conscience."

To McGeorge Bundy

March 11, 1966

[Princeton, New Jersey]

Dear Mac:

I gather that you were recently asked on the *Today* show to comment on an alleged statement of mine to the effect that the historian could not believe the press. What I actually said was as follows (in *Foreign Affairs,* April, 1963):

> . . . involvement not only makes the historian understand a good deal more about the trauma of choice; it also teaches him to distrust a good deal of the evidence on which the historian's reconstruction of that choice is likely to rest.
>
> Nothing in my own recent experience has been more chastening than the attempt to penetrate into the process of decision. I shudder a little when I think how confidently I have analyzed decisions in the ages of Jackson and Roosevelt, traced influences, assigned motives, evaluated roles, allocated responsibilities and, in short, transformed a dishevelled and murky evolution into a tidy and ordered transaction. The sad fact is that, in many cases, the basic evidence for the historian's reconstruction of the really hard cases does not exist—and the evidence that does exist is often incomplete, misleading or erroneous.
>
> Memoranda pro and con cannot necessarily be relied on for an adequate description of the dynamics of decision—or sometimes even for an

adequate definition of the genuine issues. Diaries are ex parte evidence, designed, consciously or not, to dignify the diarist, and to dish his opponents. Memory is all too often hopelessly treacherous. As for newspaper or magazine accounts, they are sometimes worse than useless when they purport to give the inside history of decisions; their relation to reality is often considerably less than the shadows in Plato's cave. I have too often seen the most conscientious reporters attribute to government officials views the exact opposite of which the officials are advocating within the government to make it possible for me to take the testimony of journalism in such matters seriously again.

As you can see my point was the general defectiveness of all forms of evidence. The press, with typical paranoia, has taken the passage as an exclusive attack on itself. This is another one of those bum raps which I will probably never escape, but I continue to make feeble efforts to set the record straight.

How do you find life in the private sector?

Yours ever,
Arthur

To Philip Potter*

March 23, 1966

[Princeton, New Jersey]

Dear Phil:

My feeling about Vietnam is that it is a damned complicated and difficult issue and consequently one on which men of good will, equal in patriotism and liberalism, can reach opposite conclusions. If this is so, then surely the obligation on both sides is to understand this and to refrain from attacks on the motives of those on the other side of the debate.

My own position is very much that of senators like Robert Kennedy, George McGovern and J. W. Fulbright (if I understand their position correctly): a conviction that Vietnam is ultimately a political rather than a military problem; doubt about further escalation of the war; skepticism that the benefits of bombing North Vietnam outweigh the disadvantages and risks; support for a holding strategy in South Vietnam; belief that, if we mean business about negotiation, we must accept Viet Cong participation as an independent body in the peace talks and cannot exclude a Viet Cong role in the future political life of South Vietnam, conditioned on their willingness to lay down their arms, open up their territory and abide by the results of free elections.

I take it that the Vice President disagrees with some or all of these points. But, given the complexity of the issues, I do not think that there is a fixed or unanimous liberal "position" on Vietnam or that the Vice President's views have resulted in his "excommunication" by the liberal community. What has given more distress, I think, is the tone of some of the Vice President's statements—i.e., the suggestion in his speech in Minneapolis last Saturday that liberals who do not share his own enthusiasm for the war in Vietnam are motivated by a lack of concern for the freedom of non-white peoples.

I hope you will send me a copy of your piece when you complete your survey.

Sincerely yours,
Arthur Schlesinger, jr.

---

*Philip Potter (1908–88). Longtime journalist with the Baltimore *Sun*; foreign correspondent; chief of Washington bureau; editor, 1941–74.

To Louise A. Bern[*]

March 31, 1966

[Princeton, New Jersey]

Dear Louise:

I am glad, but a little appalled, to know that I have been chosen as your topic for a term paper. . . .

I guess that my "major theme" in writing has been to explore the area where ideas intersect public actions—in other words, to use intellectual history as a perspective on political history. The primary literary task of the historian, in my judgment, is to join analysis and narration in a consistent text. As for influences shaping my decision to become a professional historian, I imagine that the fact that my father was a professional historian was most decisive of all. Growing up in an historical household, I have been fascinated by history all my life.

Probably you have come upon two articles I wrote about history in 1963—"The Historian and History" (*Foreign Affairs*) and "The Historian as Artist" (*Atlantic Monthly*).

Good luck on your paper.

Sincerely yours,
Arthur Schlesinger, jr.

From Hubert H. Humphrey, Jr.

April 1, 1966

[Washington, D.C.]

Dear Art:

Art, I am scheduled to speak to the National ADA Convention. If ever I needed the advice and counsel of a friend, I would welcome it now. I know how busy you are and, indeed, I have very little right to ask for your help. I would, however, greatly appreciate your suggestions as to what I might say

* Louise A. Bern of Portage, Pennsylvania

to ADA that would be constructive and worthy of that audience. I am afraid that too many of us have indulged in a degree of emotionalism pertaining to our differences. I stand guilty of this on some occasions.

You know how deeply I feel the necessity of our people in government becoming more knowledgeable about Asia and to develop a much more responsible and constructive Asian policy. I happen to believe that the tragic struggle in Vietnam has forced us to a realization of the inadequacy of our policies relating to Asia and compels us to search for new answers. I have thought that I might develop this theme for the ADA message. I would welcome your thoughts and, indeed, any comments that you would feel free to make.

Now as to RFK and HHH, many times I've said and I sincerely believe that it is indeed foolish to try to contemplate what will happen in 1972. Surely the untimely and tragic death of President Kennedy should remind us of the uncertainty of life. I know there is no way that we can escape the comments of the columnists or the frenzied activity of friends. I can assure you that I want to work with Bob—not against him. I'm sure there are more things upon which we agree than disagree. You've said all of this much better than I.

My thanks again and best wishes.

Sincerely,
Hubert H. Humphrey

To Hubert H. Humphrey, Jr.

April 11, 1966

[Princeton, New Jersey]

Dear Mr. Vice President:

I very much appreciate your letter; and I have thought a good deal about the question of the ADA speech. I have come to the reluctant conclusion, however, that I differ so basically from the administration's interpretation of the Asian situation that I could not in all conscience submit any remarks in explanation of our present policies.

The administration view, at least as set forth so lucidly by the Secretary of State in the Senate hearings, would appear to be that the conflict in Vietnam is a clearcut case of aggression, organized in Hanoi and governed ulti-mately by Peking; that the Viet Cong are therefore the spearhead of a Chinese program of expansion; and that Asian communism is a homoge-neous and coordinated system of aggression. I am frank to say that all this seems nonsense to me, and that in my judgment any policy founded on such assumptions is doomed. Obviously you cannot—even if you should wish—dissent from the policy of your own administration; so it might be better to avoid all this in your ADA talk.

You might want, however, to consider making some of the following points:

(1) The questions of Vietnam in particular and Asia in general are exceed-ingly complicated and difficult. All liberals are united on the broad objectives—a negotiated settlement in Vietnam, a stable and progres-sive order in East Asia, an improvement in mass living standards for the peasants and workers and a steady movement toward functioning democracy—but it is not so easy to decide on the best way of achieving these objectives. Men of good will, equal in patriotism and in liberal-ism, can—and do—after conscientious reflection and analysis end up on opposite sides of these issues. What is essential is for each side to respect the honesty of the other—not to denounce the one side as ap-peasers or the other side as warmongers. All of us may have sinned a little on this in the past, and all must be scrupulous to avoid such error in the future. The essential thing is to preserve mutual confidence in each other's good will and integrity and not to transform disagreement over tactics into heresy hunts. Our duty as liberals is to rational and responsible dialogue. Anyone who yields to emotionalism and dema-goguery only lowers the level of discourse and assists the forces of ir-rationality.

(2) As for Asia, the country is paying the price today for two decades of blindness to Asian realities. That blindness was bipartisan: none of us can afford to be self-righteous about the past. In 1943–45 FDR repeat-edly proposed that Indochina be not restored to the French and be placed instead under a UN trusteeship and prepared for independence. If he had lived long enough to carry out this policy, we would probably be spared much trouble and agony today. But after his death we chose

another course. We have consistently underestimated the power of nationalism in Asia, the need for generous and bold democratic support for nationalist movements, the need to help Asians in their quest for political independence and economic modernization. We have consistently construed Asia too much in terms of western ideas, models, structures and issues. We have not known enough about Asia, nor have we tried to understand the problems of Asia in Asian terms. (But, Hubert, this is the argument I find hard to carry much farther, because it leads, in my view, to the irresistible conclusion that the premises on which our current Asian policy is apparently based are dead wrong.)

You see my problem. I do not see how it is possible to argue for a rational Asian policy within the framework of the rather rigid conspiratorial theory of Asian developments set forth by the Secretary of State. I hope you can do better! Anyway, please forgive me for not being able to be more helpful, best of luck on the night, and I trust that our liberals will act like adults.[*]

Yours ever,
Arthur Schlesinger, Jr.

To Wayne Morse

May 20, 1966

[Princeton, New Jersey]

Dear Wayne:

As I said at Newark, I hesitate to engage in a debate on constitutional matters with a former Law School dean; but, as an historian, I am not persuaded by the argument that the American presence in South Vietnam is illegal and unconstitutional.

---

[*] Speaking at the ADA annual convention in Washington, Vice President Humphrey defended the Vietnam War, saying, "Saigon is as close to this ballroom tonight as London was in 1940." He received a standing ovation. Yet the membership earlier had debated and passed an antiwar resolution deploring "the continuing intensification by the United States of the Vietnam military conflict." The resolution stated that the United States had "only a marginal interest in Vietnam, or at most a self-created interest," and called on President Johnson to "promote achievement of negotiations among all parties to the conflict."

For better or worse, American Presidents have committed our armed forces overseas without congressional declarations of war since John Adams first sent our Navy into an undeclared war with France in 1798. Thomas Jefferson in his First Annual Message, writing about Tripoli's requisitions on American commerce, simply informed Congress, "The style of the demand admitted but one answer. I sent a small squadron of frigates into the Mediterranean." (Actually the "small squadron" was two-thirds of the American Navy.) In 1836 John Quincy Adams wrote, "However startled we may be at the idea that the Executive Chief Magistrate has the power of involving the nation in war, even without consulting Congress, an experience of fifty years has proved that in numberless cases he has and must have exercised that power." In the century after 1812 there were at least forty-eight separate occasions of the use of our armed forces abroad without formal declarations of war. Our involvement in the Korean War in 1950 has been, I suppose, the most spectacular example of war through presidential decision without congressional sanction.

The historical precedent for legality of our involvement in Vietnam thus seems to me overwhelming. This does *not* mean that I accept the administration arguments that we are "obligated" to do the things we are doing in Vietnam; and I consider your demolition of the Secretary of State's invocation of the SEATO treaty brilliant, conclusive and a great public service.* But I do not think for the reasons outlined above that the argument that our presence in Vietnam is illegal and unconstitutional [as far as U.S. law] can be sustained. If I am wrong, I am willing to be convinced!

With warm personal regards,
Sincerely yours,
Arthur

---

*"We are using SEATO not as a collective commitment among interested and affected parties, but as an American hunting license to do what we choose to do in Vietnam," said Morse at the University of Notre Dame on March 30, 1966. He pointed out that SEATO (Southeast Asia Treaty Organization) created no obligation on the part of the United States, contrary to the administration's claims, since it required unanimous agreement, which the United States never got.

To W. Averell Harriman

May 27, 1966

[Princeton, New Jersey]

Dear Averell:

I am more pleased than I can say that my *alma mater* is coming through this year; it honors itself a good deal more than it honors you. I understand, of course, that this is top secret and will say nothing to anyone.[*]

As for your remarks: I wonder whether this might not be an appropriate time to talk about the absolute importance of idealism in our foreign policy. I know that this is a theme close to your heart and . . . this is a kind of speech which would both help the President and also restrain those who think that firepower is the only thing that matters.

You might make the point that America's world influence is in direct proportion to the extent to which our country embodies ideals which stir the people of the world—and not just to our military strength. For example: the early days of the republic, when we were a nation of 4 million souls on the periphery of world power; Wilson; FDR; JFK. Our greatest instrument today in world affairs is not our nuclear arsenal but the conception of the Great Society. Our real and lasting power rests, not in our capacity to terrorize or intimidate other nations, but in our capacity to understand the inarticulate yearnings of plain people and hold out the hope that we can work with them in fulfilling their hopes for a better life for themselves and their children. Military force, of course, has an indispensable role in the affairs of a great nation; but it is a subordinate role. What matters is our ability to identify ourselves with the future in a time of incessant and increasing change—and this depends in part on what we do ourselves in our national community and in part on the spirit we carry to foreign countries.

I wish I could send you a couple of pages; but unfortunately I am leaving for London tonight and then on to Peru. I will not be back in Princeton

---

[*] Harvard University awarded W. Averell Harriman an honorary doctor of laws degree in June 1966: "Quick and generous to serve the public good, he has bountifully expended his high talents in his country's cause."

until June 8. If you want to send anything to me here, I will be glad to take a look at it then.

Love to Marie. I hope to see you both soon.

Yours ever,
Arthur

To William Weston[*]

August 15, 1966

[New York, New York]

Dear Major Weston:

Thank you for your letter, which I read with much interest though without total agreement.

On the question at which point in dissent one would cry, "Hold Enough," it would seem to me that the line is to be drawn when the words create a clear and present danger of bringing about overt acts in violation of law. In the case of civil rights, I would certainly not equate a demonstration demanding obedience to the law of the land with a demonstration inciting resistance to that law. Nor do I think it is right for people who have callously condemned their Negro fellow citizens to exclusion and oppression now to be self-righteous when the Negroes belatedly seek the rights due them as American citizens. I would very much doubt, for example, that, if you were a Negro yourself, you would passively acquiesce in the denial of rights pledged to you by the constitution. The exercise of putting oneself in the other fellow's shoes is always useful.

I have much sympathy with your account of the "great mass of the population" which lies between the intellectual and the anti-intellectual classes. Nor do I assert for one moment the infallibility of the intellectuals, whatever they are. But I do agree with Justice Holmes that "the best test of truth

* William Weston of Santa Rosa, California.

is the power of the thought to get itself accepted in the competition of the market," and I think that this is the standard to which we all must repair.

Sincerely yours,
Arthur Schlesinger, Jr.

To Clayton Fritchey

September 14, 1966

[New York, New York]

Dear Clayton:

Your African columns have been first class; but I was particularly struck by your piece of September 5 from Tanzania arguing the merits of a one-party system in a developing country. I have long believed that, given the limited amount of political and administrative talent in such countries, a two-party system threatened an unnecessary waste and diversion of political energy. As a Latin American buff, I cannot refrain from pointing out that Tanzania has adopted a system which has worked so well in Mexico, where, as you know, basic political conflicts are thought out within the P.R.I.[*] The congress party in India is another example. Nor should it be forgotten that George Washington himself was opposed to a party system and obviously had in mind for the United States something resembling the Tanzanian theory far more than our present system.

In another week I shall be established at the City University of New York.[†] ...

Yours ever,
Arthur

[*] The Institutional Revolutionary Party.

[†] In 1966, Schlesinger was appointed to the Albert Schweitzer Chair in the Humanities at CUNY. He spent the next thirty years teaching at the university's Graduate Center.

From Allen Welsh Dulles

October 4, 1966

[Washington, D.C.]

Dear Arthur:

Under separate cover I am sending you an inscribed copy of my book, *The Secret Surrender,** which will be coming out on October 10th. As one of Bill Donovan's[†] earliest and staunchest recruits no man knows better than you the problems and difficulties of secret operations. If the OSS had not been in existence when the secret surrender operation was started we never would have been able to accomplish it.

Faithfully yours,
Allen W. Dulles

To Allen Welsh Dulles

October 10, 1966

[New York, New York]

Dear Allen:

Just a line to say how delighted I am to have a copy of *The Secret Surrender* with your generous inscription.

I was so irritated by the wild Alperovitz[‡] review in the *New York Review of Books* that I sent them a letter[§] which I hope will be published in due

---

* *The Secret Surrender* is Allen Welsh Dulles's account of his clandestine deal with the head of Nazi SS troops in northern Italy to arrange their surrender in 1945, an effort that Washington ultimately turned down.

† William ("Bill") Donovan (1883–1959). Lawyer; Republican politician; World War I Medal of Honor winner; World War II OSS director.

‡ Gar Alperovitz (b. 1936). Author; political economist and historian at the University of Maryland; revisionist historian of the Cold War.

§ Schlesinger's letter to the *New York Review of Books* appeared on October 20, 1966. It stated:

> Surely the time has come to blow the whistle before the current outburst of revisionism regarding the origin of the cold war goes much further. In your issue of September 8, Mr. Gar Alperovitz, in effect, blames the Soviet decision to turn against the west on poor old Allen Dulles and his part in arranging the

course. I am glad to know that in more sensible journals the book has received the serious treatment to which it is entitled.

I hope all goes well with you.

Yours ever,
Arthur

From Allen Welsh Dulles

October 12, 1966

[New York, New York]

Dear Arthur:

I sincerely appreciated your kind note of October 10th. I, too, was somewhat irritated at the Alperovitz review in the *New York Review of Books*. In fact, it was not a review of the book, but it was the author's view of me. As far as I know, I never have met the man, and I have been able to find out very little about him. However, having become somewhat philosophical, as well as somewhat hardened to criticism, I am not losing any sleep over this particular attack, vicious though it is. I hope that sometime in some way your own views, which I gather you have expressed in your letter, will also see the light of day. From the tactics the *New York Review* has followed I would rather doubt that they would publish it. Having published their attack a month before the release date of the book and its availability in the book stores, it does not seem that they employ the ordinary and usual techniques of reputable reviewers.

I was not too happy at the *Washington Post*'s choice of David Wise[*] as their reviewer for the Sunday, October 9th, issue of Book Week. I have the

------

surrender of the German armies in Italy. By his handling of the affair, Mr. Alperovitz concludes, "Dulles helped set in motion the events that we know as the Cold War." . . . [Stalin and his associates] regarded the United States as the enemy, not because of anything Allen Dulles did, but because the United States was, by definition, a menace to Soviet security. Nothing the United States could have done in 1945 would have dispelled Stalin's mistrust—short of the conversion of the United States into a Stalinist despotism.

[*] David Wise (b. 1930). Author; longtime reporter for the *New York Herald Tribune*; renowned for his books about espionage and intelligence agencies; cowrote the controversial book *The Invisible Government* (1964), exposing CIA operations.

feeling that if you gave a copy of the Sermon on the Mount to David, he would find it an argument that the CIA required further supervision. Accordingly, it has not been difficult for him to twist and turn my book into another argument in support of *The Invisible Government* thesis.

I hope that you will give me a call when you are next in Washington. I should like very much to see you.

Sincerely,
Allen W. Dulles

To Johnny Carson*

February 4, 1967

[New York, New York]

Dear Johnny:

Just a line to thank you for your generous remarks about *The Bitter Heritage*† on Monday night. I have never enjoyed an interview more, and I am glad to report that the evening has been reflected in the sales.

Sincerely yours,
Arthur

To Joseph Alsop

February 8, 1967

[New York, New York]

Dear Joe:

I was baffled by the tone of your column ["Schlesinger's Silly Book," 1/16/67], and I am even more baffled by your insistence on returning to

---

* Johnny Carson (1925–2005). Important American television figure; hosted *The Tonight Show Starring Johnny Carson*, 1962–92; known for inviting progressive writers and intellectuals onto his TV show.

† Arthur M. Schlesinger, Jr., *The Bitter Heritage: Vietnam and American Democracy, 1941–1966* (Boston: Houghton Mifflin, 1967). A critique of U.S. involvement in Vietnam prescribing a political rather than military solution to the conflict.

the attack in your recent letter to the *Washington Post*. Your attempt to identify my position on Vietnam with Hans Morgenthau's[*] is, as you must know, grotesque.

Personally I think the Vietnam question sufficiently complicated that men of conscience and intelligence can agree to disagree; it seems to me hardly so open and shut as to destroy a friendship of more than twenty years. If you wish to challenge the propositions I have advanced, you are of course entirely within your right to do so; but, so far as I can see you have not discussed any of them, except for the contention that the independent states of Asia are not behind American policy in Vietnam. If they are behind American policy, they are damn far behind, as can be easily seen by counting the number of troops they have sent to our assistance. Even Lee Kuan Yew[†] has not been an advocate of the widening of the war or of the extension of the bombing of the north.

Your outrage appears to stem from my audacity in daring to write about Vietnam without having visited it in recent years. As an historian, I often write about things I have not seen; I didn't visit the White House in Jackson's time either, any more than you were around in the days of the ancient Greeks. In any case, this whole argument springs from an elementary logical fallacy: that is, the failure to understand that the origin and the value of a proposition are entirely independent matters. An ignorant man can utter an intelligent remark, just as a knowledgeable man can be extremely silly. The propositions in *The Bitter Heritage* may be right or wrong, but this cannot be proved by citing the author's experience of East Asia. (For that matter, John Fairbank[‡] has written an approving letter about the book as well as Edwin Reischauer.)[§] The propositions have to be discussed on their

---

[*] Hans Morgenthau (1904–80). Political scientist; early anti-Vietnam figure; professor of international relations at the University of Chicago and the New York–based New School for Social Research; famous for his "realist" philosophy embodied in his 1948 book *Politics Among Nations,* which argued a country's national interest dictates its foreign policy.

[†] Lee Kuan Yew (b. 1923). Authoritarian prime minister of Singapore, 1959–90; outspoken critic of the West; transformed a small nation into economic powerhouse.

[‡] John Fairbank (1907–91). Historian of China; professor at Harvard, 1936–77; established the Center for East Asian Research, later renamed the Fairbank Center; married to Wilma Cannon, sister of Arthur's first wife.

[§] Edwin Reischauer (1910–90). Leading scholar on Japan and East Asia; taught at Harvard for forty years, retiring in 1981; ambassador to Japan, 1961–66.

own merits. Just as I am prepared to stand by Fairbank and Reischauer against Alsop on the question of history, so I am prepared to stand by Ridgway and Gavin* against Alsop on the question of strategy. Do you think we are all fools? Can you not admit the possibility that the problem is complex and that honorable men might differ?

I suppose that, in a way, I should be grateful to you. Your column produced an agreeable and astonishing outpouring of sympathy from many of our common friends. Nor, so far as I can see, has your column affected any subsequent opinion of the book—not even *Time*'s. I remain puzzled by the sharp personal edge—the ridiculous statement, for example, that President Kennedy excluded me from Vietnam discussions. I have never claimed to have had any part in these discussions, nor did he ever exclude me, since I was working on European and Latin American affairs and the question never arose. He did, however, chat with me about Vietnam on numerous occasions. As for Stevenson, I did not mention him in my book, and I cannot figure out how he came into your column, except as the expression of an obsession.

At any rate, I am sorry, because I have regarded you for years with admiration and affection, and I have greatly valued our friendship. I am entirely ready, if I take positions, to be attacked about them. But, when the attack goes not to the positions but to the person, I can only assume that other factors than intellectual disagreement are controlling. Too bad, but I guess we will both survive.

Yours,
Arthur

---

* Lieutenant General James M. Gavin (1907–90). Career officer in the U.S. Army, 1924–58; youngest major general to command a division in World War II; pushed for integration of the armed forces; president and chairman of the board of consulting firm Arthur D. Little, 1960–77; took leave to serve as JFK's ambassador to France, 1961–62.

To Joseph Rauh, Jr.

March 7, 1967

[New York, New York]

Dear Joe:

As you know, I have carefully refrained from any critical remarks about the Vice President (except during the few weeks when he launched a personal campaign against me). As I travel around the country delivering lectures, I am constantly asked, "What has happened to Hubert?" I have always defended him in strong and clear terms as one of the greatest resources of our nation. I have always explained the constitutional position of the Vice President and the absolute necessity of the Vice President's supporting the presidential policy.

However, I have never really understood why Hubert could not be the kind of Vice President that Lyndon Johnson was, and that practically all Vice Presidents in our history have been—i.e., correct, self-effacing and silent. I have just happened to read his article in *Diplomat* as read into the *Congressional Record* by that sterling liberal Bob Byrd[*] of West Virginia (March 3, 1967, pp. S 3094–5). I have rarely read a more disingenuous, unfeeling and phony argument. If this represents the Vice President's considered assessment of the Vietnam war and of the opposition to widening that war, I feel discharged from the policy of restraint. Joe, I know you love Hubert, but please read that piece, consider the position of the country and tell me that you still want this man to be President. I know that 67 per cent of the electorate, or whatever it is, are supposed to agree with him; but is that an argument for supporting a vulgar and disastrous course? What is wrong with keeping his mouth closed?

Remember that John C. Calhoun resigned as Vice President of the United States when he could no longer agree with the policy of the administration with which he was associated.

Yours ever,
Arthur

---

[*] Robert Byrd (1917–2010). Representative (D-W.V.), 1953–59; longest serving senator in U.S. history (1959–2010); Senate majority leader, 1977–80, 1987–88; onetime conservative foe of civil rights legislation and advocate of Vietnam War; later promoter of desegregation and opponent of 2003 Iraq invasion.

To Robert F. Kennedy

May 15, 1967

[New York, New York]

Dear Bob:

I have not seen the full text of your welfare speech, but it looks great from the newspaper excerpts.* I hope you continue to press this issue. It is sound on its merits, and I am sure it is also sound politically, since a lot of people, from the far right to the far left, are dissatisfied with the present system.

However, this is primarily a letter about Vietnam. My impression is that events are moving toward a climax faster than could have been supposed in March. The primary reason for this is the simple fact that the bombing people are running out of targets. I understand that there is one remaining major possibility of escalation—the docks and harbor of Haiphong, which would, of course, carry with it the risk of sinking Russian ships. Beyond that the only untouched targets left in North Vietnam involve the civilian population in one way or another (bombing the irrigation dikes or the center of cities); and I am told that the JCS has declined to recommend promiscuous assaults of this sort.

Since we are running out of new targets, and since there is no indication that pounding the present targets is going to be any more successful in the next year than it has been in the last two years, it is evident that aerial escalation is at the end of its string. This may well confront the President with the choice between escalation on the ground—i.e., an invasion of North Vietnam—or negotiation. There are vague indications that we may be preparing for an invasion. Rusk keeps talking about those three or four North Vietnamese regular divisions just above the DMZ.† Joe Alsop had a column saying that these divisions are poised for the invasion of the south—a natural line for the Pentagon to take if we are seeking a pretext to invade the north ourselves. Jim Gavin says that the aerial activity over this territory might well be pre-invasion reconnaissance.

---

* Robert F. Kennedy described the current welfare system and other assistance to the poor as a "system of handouts, a second-rate set of social services, which damages and demeans its recipients," according to a report in *The New York Times* entitled "Kennedy Assails Welfare System." Kennedy said he wanted to replace the system with renewed job creation, family support, and a welfare safety net.

† Demilitarized zone.

Now it is possible (as Rowlie [Evans] believes, or says he believes) that the President is at last convinced of the bankruptcy of escalation and will therefore reject the next military proposals. On the other hand, there are reasons to think that he may be driven to invasion. (1) He has so locked himself into bombing that he cannot call it off now without opening himself to the Republican citation against him of his own claims that American soldiers are dying because of hand grenades brought into South Vietnam during the last pause, etc. And he cannot begin negotiation without calling off the bombing. (2) Psychologically he is a bully who has made his way in life by leaning on people, and he recently has been extending the bully's approach to Hanoi. He may simply feel that his failure has been in not knocking North Vietnam around enough. (3) He would probably count on the invasion generating a great surge of chauvinism, which would silence his critics, unite the country and perhaps carry him through 1968. I imagine he thinks that, the larger the conflict, the more families involved and therefore the more support for the war. (On this point, he might be right in the short run, but would surely be wrong in the long run. The larger the Korean War became and the longer it lasted, the more *un*popular it became.)

I realize that it isn't all this open and shut—that Johnson may decide just to keep on bombing the same old targets, or that he may try to work a simultaneous announcement of the cessation of bombing and the agreement to negotiate. But the bankruptcy of the bombing policy—now evident even to Evans and Novak*—may well lure him on into invasion.

At the same time, another policy is evidently bankrupt—that is, the substantial Americanization of the war and particularly the so-called pacification policy. Putting pacification in the hands of our military will not save it, because the assignment is inherently impossible. Americans will never in a hundred years be able to bring democracy to the countryside of South Vietnam. We do not know the traditions, we do not know the customs, we can't even speak the language. It is, so far as we are concerned, an alien, mysterious and impenetrable culture. Even the French, who get along better with natives than we do, failed in a comparable policy in Algeria. And it is not our sort of thing anyway. We wouldn't be able to do it in Latin

---

* Robert Novak (1931–2009). TV commentator; cowriter (with Rowland Evans, Jr.) of syndicated column Inside Report, 1963–2008; known as "the Prince of Darkness" for his gloomy demeanor and conservative politics.

America, despite the common moral and cultural heritage, we can't even do it in Mississippi and Alabama.

My impression is that a good many people through the country are beginning to have second thoughts about both escalation and pacification. The Evans-Novak column is one symptom. On May 5 the Cleveland *Plain Dealer*, previously a hawk paper, came out against further escalation. A number of stories have appeared in various newspapers describing the failure of the pacification program.

I wonder whether we are not approaching a crucial time. LBJ is pondering whether or not to invade North Vietnam. Skepticism about both escalation and pacification is appearing in the most improbable places. The Westmoreland visit[*] backfired badly against the administration, and the McGovern[†] speech had an astonishing response (long excerpts were carried in papers all over the country[‡]).

Perhaps the moment is approaching for some one—i.e., you—to give a statesmanlike speech, without recrimination or rancor, saying in effect:

(a) The problem of the proper policy in Vietnam has been exceedingly complex and difficult from the start. Honorable men could easily come to opposite conclusions, and no one could be absolutely sure whether his own position was right or wrong.

(b) After conscientious consideration, the administration, for reasons which seemed persuasive to many at the time, embarked on the course of military escalation in the north and Americanization of the war and pacification in the south.

---

[*] General William Westmoreland (1914–2005). Commander of U.S. forces in Vietnam, 1964–68; on a visit to the United States in April 1967, charged critics of the war encouraged the enemy to believe "he can win politically that which he cannot accomplish militarily"; promised Congress that "we will prevail"; U.S. Army chief of staff, 1968–72.

[†] George McGovern (1922–2012). Representative (D-S.D.), 1957–61; first director of Food for Peace program, 1961–62; senator, 1963–81; Democratic presidential nominee, 1972; U.S. ambassador to the UN Food and Agriculture Agencies, 1998–2001.

[‡] On April 25, 1967, a day after U.S. planes bombed air bases in North Vietnam, McGovern stood up in the Senate and blasted administration policy as "madness which sooner or later will envelop my son and American youth by the millions for years to come." His remarks were seconded by senators Robert F. Kennedy, William Fullbright, and Frank Church.

(c) These policies have had a fair try. It is now evident that they are not working. No one could have been certain of this in advance; we are blaming no one. We are only asking for a candid recognition of our present dilemma and a candid discussion of where we go from here.

(d) Persistence in the course of escalation can only lead to an invasion of North Vietnam. Such a decision would be a disaster. It would increase Soviet aid, probably bring Chinese "volunteers" into the war, further estrange America from the rest of the world and rush mankind toward the Third World War. Persistence in the course of pacification along present lines would only embroil Americana more deeply in the Vietnam quagmire.

(e) There is no dishonor in acknowledging that a policy has not produced the desired results. As FDR used to say, if we try one policy and it fails, admit it frankly, and try another. . . . This is a fateful question. It involves the lives of Americans and the peace of the world. Let us as a nation say that policies, adopted perhaps for good reason, have simply not worked. Let us, as a nation, take a fresh look.

(f) As one man's contribution to this fresh look, the case now seems more convincing than ever for the policy of slowing down the war and seeking negotiation. This is the way to save lives, to restore this conflict to its proper proportion, to revive the world's confidence in the soberness and sanity of American power and American purpose, etc., etc.

It is possible that a speech somewhat along these lines, even if delivered by you (joke), could have a powerful effect at a most critical time.

Yours ever,
Arthur

To Joseph Schwab[*]

May 16, 1967

[New York, New York]

Dear Mr. Schwab:

Thank you for your note. . . . As for American support of the socialist and Christian trade unions of Western Europe during the Marshall Plan years, I do regard this as wise and appropriate. I see the obvious disadvantages of this course; but, on balance, I think it would have been far worse for us to stand virtuously aside and watch very decent people lose a battle which had great significance for us as well as for them. As Michael Walzer[†] (of the New Left) puts it in the current *Dissent*, "If the danger of a Communist take-over of India were really very great, and if the results of such a take-over were certain to be a totalitarian regime, surely a secret U.S. subsidy to an anti-Communist union—assuming there were no better way of giving assistance—would be perfectly justified." Do you really disagree with this? Would you really have objected to CIA secretly helping anti-Nazi unions in Europe before the war?

As for *The Bitter Heritage,* I would suggest that you read the book (now available in paperback) and not a *Ramparts*[‡] review. In my experience *Ramparts* is about as reliable as *Confidential*.

Sincerely yours,
Arthur Schlesinger, Jr.

---

[*] Joseph Schwab of New York, New York. Critic of CIA aid to European trade unions during the Cold War.

[†] Michael Walzer (b. 1935). American political philosopher; coeditor of *Dissent* magazine; professor at Harvard, 1966–80; fellow, Princeton's Institute for Advanced Study, 1980–present; promoter of "just war" thesis, recognizing the importance of ethics in wartime.

[‡] *Ramparts* magazine (1962–75). A self-styled radical publication on the left; Schlesinger critic Noam Chomsky reviewed *Bitter Heritage* in its April 1967 edition.

To Anne Remiche[*]

June 7, 1967

[New York, New York]

Dear Mlle. Remiche:

I very much appreciate your letter and the invitation to come to Belgium in December. Unfortunately, since I am very much in disagreement with my government's Vietnam policy, I feel that I should confine my attacks on that policy to the United States. It seems to me inappropriate to go abroad to criticize one's government when one has ample facilities to do it at home. I also regret to say that my French, while adequate for ordering dinners, would not sustain me through a lecture.

Sincerely yours,
Arthur Schlesinger, Jr.

To Robert F. Kennedy

July 8, 1967

[Paris, France]

Dear Bob:

I am just back from a week in the Soviet Union. I had not been there since 1959 and was surprised at the absence of much in the way of physical improvement or change (though they are beginning to build glass skyscrapers in the Madison Avenue model). It remains on the whole a seedy, dilapidated society and conveys no impression of great dynamism, energy or forward movement. I did seem to detect, however, a certain relaxation in ideological tension. People did not seem so hopelessly insistent on defending every detail of Soviet policy; and some even have developed a capacity for irony which enables them to signal appreciation of a point without having explicitly to endorse it. This means that one can come closer to having genuine conversations. I had almost none 8 years ago and had a few this time.

I had talk with Kornienko[†] (who used to be counselor in their Washington

---

[*] Anne Remiche of Brussels, Belgium. Anti–Vietnam War activist.
[†] Georgy Kornienko (1925–2006). Soviet diplomat.

Embassy and is now head of the American department at the Ministry of Foreign Affairs), Yuri Zhukov* of *Pravda* and assorted professors; also with our old friend Voznesensky.[†] Most of the official talk was predictable. They are very tough on the question of Israel. Zhukov told me that, while up to now the USSR has recognized Israel's right to exist, this was not necessarily a permanent policy and that, if the Israelis did not withdraw their troops, it might change; also that the USSR would have intervened directly in the Middle East if the Israeli forces had proceeded to Damascus.[‡] They all seemed far from reality on the Middle East; I hope that the UN votes may have a salutary effect.

I had not realized until this trip the inordinate pride the Russians are taking in the celebration of the 50th anniversary of the Revolution. They regard this as a sacred occasion and are even said to be suspending some of their own internal quarrels until it is over. A number of people spoke to me about a story which apparently appeared in *Pravda* in mid-June claiming that the USIA[§] had sent out instructions around the world for a campaign to denigrate the 50th anniversary. They expressed great resentment about this. Obviously the existence of the 50th anniversary should not stop the US from doing anything it can in a serious way to expose the illusions of communism; but I do doubt whether a campaign of pin-pricks, designed to discredit the 50th anniversary, would serve a useful purpose. Tommy [Thompson][¶] strongly agrees and has said this to Washington. There are times for magnanimity in relations between nations; and this anniversary would seem an occasion in which we would help ourselves more by being generous than by sniping.

In this connection they all believe that the publication of Svetlana's[**]

---

*Yuri Zhukov (1908–91). Soviet journalist and *Pravda* columnist; served on the *Pravda* editorial board, 1946–87; speechwriter for Nikita Khrushchev.

†Andrei Voznesensky (1933–2010). Acclaimed Russian poet and writer; one of the leaders of the 1960s literary thaw in the USSR; gave poetry recitals to sold-out stadiums in Russia and abroad.

‡In the Six-Day War of early June, Israeli forces captured the Gaza Strip, the Sinai Peninsula, the West Bank, East Jerusalem, and the Golan Heights.

§United States Information Agency.

¶Llewellyn ("Tommy") Thompson (1904–72). Ambassador to Austria, 1955–57; ambassador to the Soviet Union, 1957–62, 1967–69; key adviser to President Kennedy during the 1962 Cuban missile crisis.

**Svetlana Alliluyeva (1926–2011). Joseph Stalin's daughter by his second wife; defected to the United States in 1967, denounced the Soviet regime, and published memoir, *Twenty Letters to a Friend;* later, after marriage, changed her name to Lana Peters.

book in October is intended as the climax of the carefully orchestrated official American campaign. I tried to explain the difficulty of controlling American publishers, especially Harper & Row, but to little avail. I do plan to write Cass Canfield[*] and say that I think it would make a genuine difference if publication could be postponed till 1968 or even till December 67, after the celebrations.

Kornienko, Zhukov and Voznesensky all spoke to me about the possibility of your coming to the Soviet Union. Their motives obviously differed. Voznesensky, I imagine, thinks that a visit by you might strengthen the position of writers like himself who are fighting for greater freedom of expression and foreign travel. I suppose that Kornienko and Zhukov hope that you might say or do something which could be represented as opposition to the LBJ policy in Vietnam. Tommy [Thompson] thinks it would be a mistake for you to come as long as the Vietnam war is going on, since you would too often be placed in the position of having to defend or denounce American policy. On balance I think Tommy is right. I think there is no great point in your going anywhere unless you can be relatively candid; this is your style and one of your greatest strengths. Candor about Vietnam in the Soviet Union would be, I think, wholly unprofitable. . . .

I left the USSR with great relief and travelled to Paris with Vivi Crespi,[†] who had been staying with the Thompsons. De Gaulle, as you know, is taking a real beating here as a result of his [anti-Israeli] position on the Middle East. Chip [Bohlen] tells me that this has been totally his personal policy and that a good deal of the time he has not even bothered to inform the Quai d'Orsay what he plans to say. Some people have the impression that, for the first time, he is showing his age, and that he is now on the run politically. The Middle East business has also isolated the Communists once again on the left, since they are de Gaulle's only enthusiastic supporters on this issue, while the Socialists, etc, are strongly pro-Israel. I go on to London tomorrow for a few

---

[*] Cass Canfield (1897–1986). President, board chairman, and executive committee chairman of Harper and Brothers publishers, 1931–67; Harper senior editor, 1967–86.

[†] Countess Vivian "Vivi" Stokes Crespi (b. 1927). International socialite; grew up in Newport with Jacqueline Kennedy; at eighteen married Henry Stillman Taylor, son of the president of Standard Oil; later married Count Marco Fabio Crespi.

days; then on July 13 or 14 I will join the Sam Spiegel[*] yacht. I will be back in NY about July 22. Love to Ethel—I hope all goes well with everybody.

Yours ever,
Arthur

To William Styron

July 27, 1967

[New York, New York]

Dear Bill:

It is a marvelous book.[†] I attach a copy of a review[‡] I have written for *Vogue*. I would wish that I had had more space (and a different audience).

I would be curious to know sometime why you decided not to use the episode described in the *Confessions* when, apparently in 1825, Nat ran away from an overseer "and after remaining in the woods thirty days, I returned, to the astonishment of the Negroes on the plantation, who thought I had made my escape to some other part of the country, as my father had done before. . . . And the Negroes found fault, and murmured against me, saying that if they had my sense they would not serve any master in the world." This seemed to me to yield an interesting insight both into Nat and the general slave mood.

Love to Rose. I hope to see you both at some point this summer.

Yours ever,
Arthur

* Sam Spiegel (1901–85). Acclaimed Austrian-born film producer of such movies as *Lawrence of Arabia* and *On the Waterfront;* winner of three Academy Awards; invited Schlesinger for summer cruises on his yacht, *Malahne,* in the Mediterranean Sea.
† William ("Bill") Styron, *Confessions of Nat Turner* (New York: Random House, 1967). Fictional "first-person" narrative of slave revolt in Virginia in 1831 as "written" by Nat Turner, who, according to an account in an 1831 book, actually existed and led such an uprising. Styron's book won the 1968 Pulitzer Prize for Fiction.
‡ Schlesinger called the novel "a superb and responsible exercise of the artistic imagination . . . the finest American novel in many years," in *Vogue* magazine, October 1967.

To Robert F. Kennedy

August 22, 1967

[New York, New York]

Dear Bob:

Our Vietnam policy seems to me to be getting increasingly risky and crazy. This business of hovering around communist frontiers always leads to trouble. The Russian insistence on dominating their own borderlands was one of the major causes of the Cold War; the Chinese reaction to our crossing of the 38th parallel led to their intervention in Korea. We cannot fool around with this forever and hope to get away with it. As General Shoup* said to me a few weeks ago, "If you keep poking your finger in a fellow's eye, he is bound to react, no matter if he is having a fight with his wife."

. . . It would be even better if you would call George Kennan and ask him to chat with you over the phone about the problem of Russian and Chinese sensitivity to violations of their frontiers. Enough might come out of this to warrant another set speech. I have never in my lifetime felt that such madness had seized the American government.

Yours ever,
Arthur

To James MacGregor Burns†

September 3, 1967

[New York, New York]

Dear Jim:

I am a little troubled by the statement attributed to you in a recent *Newsweek*—that FDR, Truman, Eisenhower or Kennedy would be doing

---

* General David Shoup (1904–83). Career U.S. Marine Corps officer; awarded Medal of Honor in World War II; twenty-second commandant of the marine corps, 1960–63; critic of the Vietnam War.

† James MacGregor ("Jim") Burns (b. 1918). American history professor at Williams College; failed Democratic candidate for Congress in 1951; won 1971 Pulitzer Prize for *Roosevelt: Soldier of Freedom, 1940–45*.

exactly what Johnson is doing today in Vietnam. My guess, for what it is worth, is that none of them, except possibly Truman, would have carried out anything like the Johnson policy (and even Truman sharply opposed the advocates of escalation, while Johnson has steadily given ground to them). I don't believe for a moment, for example, that Kennedy would have permitted the situation to develop to the present point, nor do most of those who worked with him (including his brothers, O'Donnell, Sorensen, Goodwin, etc.). However, I have never said anything like this in public.

In any case, this is less important than the point that these are all guesses. No one can possibly predict what a President who is dead would be doing about issues which have evolved since his death; it is hard enough to predict what living Presidents are going to do about them. It is also rather presumptuous to claim to know what dead men would have done if they were still alive. A couple of years ago Dick Neustadt wrote somewhere to the effect that, if Kennedy were alive, be would have done such-and-such. I wrote him to say that, as charter members of the President Watchers' Club, we ought to obey a basic rule: *no one can possibly know what a dead President would be saying or doing if he were still alive*, and therefore all invocations of dead Presidents in connection with new situations should be avoided. You too are a charter member of this illustrious, nonexistent organization, and I make the same plea to you!

Let me know some time when you are in New York. I am sending you under separate cover a description of a project I have dimly in mind for a conference to take a fresh look at the thesis of the strong Presidency in the light of the Vietnam War and to consider whether it is possible to strengthen the role of Congress without inviting congressional government. I would much appreciate your reactions.

Yours ever,
Arthur

To John Kenneth Galbraith

September 26, 1967

[New York, New York]

Dear Ken:

... I am coming to believe that it would be useful and illuminating if someone would enter the New Hampshire Democratic primary against LBJ not as a serious presidential candidate but in order to give the Democratic voters of New Hampshire a chance to vote on the war. [James] Gavin would be ideal if he could be steered to the Democratic primary. Otherwise how about yourself? I think that such a candidacy would enlist a lot of enthusiastic support, that it might have unexpected appeal, and that, if it worked, it might even begin to discourage LBJ about running again. Think this over, and let us talk after I return from London. ...

Yours ever,
Arthur

To Hubert H. Humphrey, Jr.

October 25, 1967

[New York, New York]

Dear Mr. Vice President:

I am very grateful indeed for your birthday greeting. I had done my best to keep the occasion a secret this year, of all years; but your kind words will cheer me as I begin the melancholy descent into the second half-century.

My daughter Kathy was thrilled the other day to receive a letter from you regarding her service in VISTA. However, as your office could not have known, she was subsequently married and is now living in Beckley, West Virginia, where her husband* is director of the community action program. I hope your office would not consider it too large an imposition to retype

---

*Gibbs Kinderman (b. 1943). Married to Katharine Bancroft Schlesinger, 1966–72; social activist in West Virginia; director of three noncommercial radio stations in West Virginia and Virginia; Harvard classmate of Katharine's twin brother, Stephen Schlesinger.

the letter to Mrs. Gibbs Kinderman, East Beckley, West Virginia, and begin it "Dear Kathy."

I hope all goes well with you in these troubled days. It is more important than ever not to permit disagreement over issues to strain the ties of personal affection and sympathy.

Yours ever,
Arthur Schlesinger, Jr.

To Robert F. Kennedy

November 3, 1967

[New York, New York]

Dear Bob:

Here are some reflections on 1968 before I go off to Venezuela for a week (back on November 12).

[Eugene] McCarthy has definitely decided to go [for the Democratic presidential nomination]—unless you decide to go. If you don't and he does, what do you say and do?

It would be a fatal error, in my judgment, to say anything which would be construed as your backing Johnson against McCarthy. To do so would be to convince a lot of people, especially the young, that you prefer politics to principle. (I might repeat—as I guess I have said ad nauseam—that it seems to me a great mistake for any Kennedy to say anything about Johnson beyond "I expect to vote for the candidate of the Democratic party, and I expect that President Johnson will be that candidate." Saying Johnson is a great President doesn't impress anyone; it only disillusions the Kennedy people without persuading the Johnson people.)

To get back to McCarthy: if it would be fatal to back Johnson, it would not seem to make great sense to back McCarthy. If you are going to do that, you might as well run yourself. Nor does it seem to me that, if McCarthy's issue is Vietnam, you can be neutral and try to stay out of it without casting doubt on the sincerity of your own critique of the Vietnam policy. Possibly the line to take would be something like this: "Vietnam is the most important issue we face, and I congratulate Senator McCarthy for opening up a debate on this subject within our party and giving Democrats a chance to express themselves on this vital question." I doubt, however, whether you could get away with this position for very long.

The prospect of a McCarthy candidacy raises, of course, the further question: what would the effect be on an RFK candidacy in 1968? This can be argued in two ways:

1) *it would help you*—by opening up the situation; by getting the administration mad at someone else; by permitting you, if circumstances become propitious, to enter, not as a ruthlessly ambitious politician out for yourself, but in an effort to meet a genuine difficulty and need within the party. In this view, McCarthy would in effect, run interference for a Kennedy candidacy.

2) *it would hurt you*—because McCarthy, by being courageous enough to take on Johnson on Vietnam and challenge his renomination, will become the hero of countless Democrats across the country disturbed about the war. Many of these Democrats, nearly all of whom would rather be for you, would in the course of the fight become committed to McCarthy, emotionally or otherwise. If you were to enter at some later point, there might well be serious resentment on the ground that you were a Johnny-come-lately trying to cash in after brave Eugene McCarthy had done the real fighting. In other words, McCarthy might tie up enough in the way both of emotion and even of delegates to make another anti-LBJ candidacy impossible.

Until recently I have argued against the idea of your trying anything in '68. My main ground has been that, while you might conceivably get the nomination (I think Johnson is as vulnerable as Truman was in '48, and Truman probably could have been beaten then in the Democratic convention if his opponents had had a plausible candidate), the fight would shatter the party, render the Democratic nomination worthless and encourage the Republicans to nominate the man they will only nominate (I believe) if they think any Republican can win: i.e., Nixon. In other words, I have feared that your candidacy would result in making Nixon President.

I am now having second thoughts about this argument. I think the country is feeling increasingly that the escalation policy has had a full and fair trial, that it just hasn't worked, that Johnson is not going to come up with anything new or different and that we must therefore have a new President.* I think that events are moving faster than one could have supposed three months ago, and that the situation may be highly fluid indeed in another three months. I think that you could beat LBJ in the primaries and that you have unexpected reserves of strength in the non-primary states. And, if all this should lead the Republicans to nominate Nixon, so much the better. He is the one Republican candidate who would reunite even a divided and embittered Democratic party. I am sure he would be the easiest Republican for you, or any Democratic candidate, to beat.

All this is speculative. I have not had time to do the arithmetic, and, it is, of course, imperative that the arithmetic be done. Perhaps it has been. The only point of this letter is to urge you to take a fresh look at the situation.

One other point: if you were to decide to go, careful thought would have to be given to the way in which this came about. Obviously it would have to be done in a way which would not reinforce the theory of ruthless ambition or the theory that you are indulging a personal feud against the President. Ideally you ought to be asked to run by a group of leading Democrats. In this connection, I tentatively wonder whether you should not have a talk with McCarthy. I know well that he has not been high on the Kennedys through the years; also that he is a somewhat indolent and frivolous man. On the other hand, he evidently cares deeply about the Vietnam mess. He has told a number of people privately that he hopes you will run (e.g., Jimmy Wechsler last spring). He seemed to be saying the same thing publicly at Berkeley the other day. In other words, it is still probable that he might be willing to stand aside and support you, since you would so obviously be the stronger candidate. Is it possible that he and McGovern might help organize a draft-Kennedy group? Even if it does not seem wise to talk the situation over with Gene [McCarthy], you might want to consider such a talk with George [McGovern], and he might serve as a kind of intermediary with Gene.

---

* Mass demonstrations against the Vietnam War were becoming more frequent. Three hundred thousand people turned out in New York City to protest the war in April 1967. In October, 100,000 people rallied at the Lincoln Memorial, and many of them marched on the Pentagon. Violence erupted when demonstrators clashed with soldiers and U.S. marshals protecting the Pentagon. Among the 647 protesters arrested was Norman Mailer, who documented his experience in his award-winning book *The Armies of the Night: History as a Novel, the Novel as History* (1968).

I am sorry for the length of this letter, but the situation is perplexing and time is passing awfully fast.

Yours ever,
Arthur

To Walt W. Rostow

November 15, 1967

[New York, New York]

Dear Walt:

I am troubled by the suggestion in the attached piece from the [*Boston*] *Globe* [by James Doyle] that "he [i.e. you] finds Schlesinger and Galbraith fostering the sour criticisms of their former colleague perhaps more than any others."

If it is "sour criticism" to register disagreement with the view that the continuous widening of the war over the last thirty-two months has served the national interest, I suppose I must plead guilty. But I have scrupulously refrained from personal criticism of my former colleagues; and in your case, because we have been friends for so long a time and because I have total confidence in your integrity of motive, I have on many occasions defended you from the personal attacks of others.

None of this is important, except that I would hope that private relations could survive disagreement even on so weighty a public issue as the war in Vietnam. All of us, those in the government as well as those in opposition, must fight off symptoms of paranoia!

Yours ever,
Arthur

To James T. Farrell[*]

November 16, 1967

[New York, New York]

Dear Jim:

I am grateful for your long letter of a few weeks back, even though I guess I disagree with some of it. I agree that the cold war is far from over; but surely you must agree that it has taken a somewhat different form? Is it anti-anti-communist to suggest that there is no longer such a thing as a unified, coordinated, disciplined world communist movement, controlled and directed by Moscow? Those days are plainly gone, probably forever. This surely means that a communist take-over no longer represents an automatic extension of the national power of Russia, or of China. One can no longer assume that every communist party or government will be the obedient instrumentality of Russian or Chinese expansionism. The age of Stalin is gone, we face a new situation, and we have to adjust our policy to the reality of a poly centrist communism. Communism is as terrible as ever, but it presents a different sort of problem. . . .

Best,
Arthur

To Michael Collins Todd[†]

November 16, 1967

[New York, New York]

Dear Mr. Todd:

. . . I would define "history" as an effort to achieve a truthful reconstruction of the past and an "historian" as one who undertakes that effort. The ideal historian, it seems to me, should unite narrative and analysis in a homogeneous text. I really have no favorite historian; nor do I have any idea what my eventual place might be in American scholarship.

---

[*] James T. ("Jim") Farrell (1904–79), American novelist, famous for his Studs Lonigan trilogy; regular correspondent of Schlesinger's.
[†] Michael Collins Todd. Unknown correspondent.

I do not think that active participation in public affairs need damage the technical capacities of an historian, though it no doubt places weapons in the hands of his critics. In my own case, I have no doubt that such experience as I have had in nonacademic affairs has increased my understanding of certain historical problems. "The Captain of Hampshire Grenadiers," as Gibbon[*] put it, "was not useless to the historian of the Roman Empire." As for the murder of President Kennedy, it has reinforced my feeling about the inscrutability of history—that is, the role of contingency and fortuity and hence the difficulty of accepting conspiratorial interpretations or of using history for prediction. . . .

The most interesting and fruitful development in the writing of history since 1945 seems to me the rise of intellectual history. The "consensus" history favored in the 1950s seemed to me to have some value in emphasizing the underlying unity of the American political experience, but it often went too far in minimizing the role of conflict as the engine of change in American life. . . .

Sincerely yours,
Arthur Schlesinger, Jr.

From Walt W. Rostow

November 17, 1967

[Washington, D.C.]

Dear Arthur:

Just for the record: What Doyle[†] said was wholly, I repeat, wholly his own deduction. The question of criticism of our Vietnam policy never came up. In fact, it did not enter my mind in the course of the interview.

I would not for one moment resent personally a position taken by you, Ken, or anyone else on a public matter. And I am conscious of the way you

---

[*] Edward Gibbon (1737–94). British historian; author of *The History of the Decline and Fall of the Roman Empire* (1776–89); served under his father in the Hampshire Grenadiers during the Seven Years War; MP.

[†] James S. Doyle (b. 1935). Washington bureau chief, *The Boston Globe,* 1965–70; assistant to Watergate prosecutors, 1973–75; *Newsweek* chief political correspondent, 1976–83; later senior adviser to Business Leaders for Sensible Priorities.

have, as you properly say, "scrupulously refrained from personal criticism" of former colleagues.

Although Ken has a somewhat different style in these matters, I am conscious—as he reminded me by a generous act the other day—of the underlying warmth that survives after so many years of a major difference of view.

So, let me assure you, without the slightest ambiguity, that what Doyle wrote was Doyle's. I gave him no occasion to make the deductions he did about my frame of mind; and, in fact, they are not in any way accurate.

I am grateful to you for writing and permitting me to make this clear. Now tell me: Are you back on FDR? If not, what are your plans? All the best.

Yours,
Walt

On November 29, 1967, President Johnson leaked the news to the media that he was appointing Robert McNamara as head of the World Bank. This was done without McNamara's prior knowledge, following McNamara's public expressions of doubt concerning the bombing of North Vietnam to a Senate committee.

To Robert McNamara*

[Handwritten]

November 30, 1967

[New York, New York]

Dear Bob:

I need hardly say with what concern I have been following the events of the last few days. You have been one of the greatest public servants in American history, and your departure from the government is an incalcu-

* Robert McNamara (1916–2009). Business executive, one of the "whiz kids" who rebuilt Ford Motors; Secretary of Defense 1961–68; head of World Bank 1968–81, blamed for Vietnam War, later confessing it was a "mistake."

lable loss to this nation. When the history of these years is written, you will emerge as a crucial figure in ways in which the public is as yet only dimly aware. For myself personally, the opportunity to know you and work with you has been one of the most happy and satisfying things that has ever happened to me.

I am sorry for a number of reasons that you have decided to go to the Bank, important as that job is. But that decision has been taken, I know after the most thoughtful considerations, so I am all for it and wish you all success. I hope, though, that you won't be removed for too long a time from the field of national policy to which you have made—and will, I am sure, make in the future—such brilliant considerations. . . .

My best love to Margee.* I hope to see you both before too long.

Yours ever,
Arthur

Eugene McCarthy announced on November 30 that he would challenge President Johnson for the Democratic nomination and enter the party's primaries, beginning in March in New Hampshire. Robert Kennedy called a "council of war" in New York City on Sunday, December 10, with six of his closest advisers to decide whether to run for the presidency. Arthur was the strongest proponent for the run and for challenging McCarthy in the primaries. The meeting ended inconclusively.

To Robert F. Kennedy

December 13, 1967

[New York, New York]

Dear Bob:

Now that the meeting last Sunday cleared up all your problems, I will append a few subsequent thoughts.

---

* Margaret McNamara (1915–81). Wife of Robert McNamara, married in 1940, founded "Reading Is Fundamental," a nonprofit children's literacy organization, the largest in the United States.

(1) In general, should you not follow the Rockefeller strategy? That is, make every contingency preparation from briefing on issues to bracing of delegates. Also from time to time make non-candidate's speeches. Perhaps you should consider in particular a high-level speech dealing with the national malaise, the need for a revival of purpose, the urgent problems of national community—a speech which would locate Vietnam as a central source of our trouble but would not make it the exclusive issue of 1968. Such a speech should provide a definitive diagnosis of our problems and suggest, without saying so, the mood and measures for the campaign. It should be a speech which would be reprinted in full text across the country. Why not get Dick to do a draft just in case?

(2) Also, if there is some outrageous new development, like the invasion of North Vietnam or the bombing of Cambodia, I wonder whether this would not so alter the situation that your candidacy might seem entirely logical and necessary. It might even be useful to have someone ... imagine that something terrible has already happened and prepare a statement. The statement might say, in effect, that this is all impossible; the nation and the world cannot endure this kind of leadership and policy; that it is false to our own best traditions; and that, win or lose, you are determined to fight to restore the Democratic party and the country to its traditions of rationality, responsibility and idealism.

Even should you lose the fight for the nomination (which I do not think you will) you will be vindicated in the end if Johnson is hopeless as we think he is. . . .

Yours ever,
Arthur

To Joseph Shunskis*

December 27, 1967

[New York, New York]

Dear Mr. Shunskis:

I regret that you found my remarks about Dr. Graham[†] and Dr. Peale[‡] offensive.[§] My objection to their form of religiosity is that, in the words of Bishop Sherrill,[¶] it "seems to place the emphasis on using God for our own purposes of success, of health, of freedom from burdens and strains. [But] the heart of true religion has to do with offering ourselves to God." True religion in my judgment would urge the church to reestablish transcendent norms and reaffirm the distinctive Christian message rather than to use faith to sanction the official values of contemporary society. The object of faith, as I understand it, is to induce not contentment but contrition, not complacency but repentance. This is surely what distinguishes Dr. Graham and Dr. Peale from someone like Jonathan Edwards.[**]

Sincerely yours,
Arthur Schlesinger, Jr.

On March 12, 1968, Senator McCarthy scored a moral victory over President Johnson by winning 42 percent of the vote in the Democratic presidential primary in New Hampshire, the first electoral challenge to Johnson's renomination. On March 16, Robert F. Kennedy announced that he was running for president.

* Joseph Shunskis of East Lansdowne, Pennsylvania.
† Billy Graham, Jr. (b. 1918). Influential Christian evangelical leader; spiritual adviser to Presidents Eisenhower, Johnson, Nixon, Ford, Carter, Reagan, Bush, and Clinton; preached via TV and radio and in crusades to more than 2.2 billion people.
‡ Dr. Norman Vincent Peale (1898–1993). Conservative Protestant minister; author of bestselling 1952 book *The Power of Positive Thinking;* reputation stained by public opposition to Kennedy's election over his Catholic faith.
§ Schlesinger called Graham and Peale "religious vulgarians."
¶ Bishop Henry Knox Sherrill (1890–1980). Progressive Episcopal religious leader; supported birth control and racial justice; showed compassion on divorce.
** Jonathan Edwards (1703–58). Christian preacher and dogmatic theologian; sought moral awakenings through revivalist crusades in Colonial times.

In a spirit of conciliation, Arthur kept his commitment to speak at a McCarthy fund-raising breakfast the next day, explaining that he supported McCarthy against LBJ in the next two primaries (Wisconsin and Ohio) in which RFK's name was not on the ballot.

To Eugene McCarthy

March 20, 1968

[New York, New York]

Dear Gene:

Last Sunday, March 17, I spoke at a fund-raising breakfast for the McCarthy for President group in Cleveland. I explained that, while I was for Robert Kennedy, I none the less felt that you deserved backing and support, and that I was happy to have this opportunity to speak on your behalf. We raised, I understand, about $8000 for you. I was accordingly surprised later in the day to read in the *Chicago Sun-Times* your attack on me as a "parasite" who had defected from your campaign.

I imagine that you were laboring under considerable emotional strain, but I remain perplexed as to how I could have defected from a campaign of which I was never a member. As you well know, we have talked to each other only once in the last six months. While I strongly advocated your endorsement by the ADA, I am, as you also well know, a close friend and longtime associate of Robert Kennedy's; I have been urging him to run for a long time; and naturally I backed him when he announced.

I am sorry you felt compelled to issue a declaration of war against me. Now that you have got this out of your system, I would hope we can all turn to the larger cause—that is, stopping the renomination of Lyndon Johnson.

Sincerely yours,
Arthur Schlesinger, jr.

On Sunday, March 31, 1968, President Lyndon B. Johnson announced that he would not run for reelection. Later that evening, Arthur attended a gathering at RFK's New York City apartment near the United Nations. The mood was one of astonishment, a certain perplexity, and a general under-

stated but incredulous feeling that RFK could be the next president of the United States.

Why did LBJ get out? Arthur guessed political cowardice: The president's polls showed that he would be humiliatingly defeated in the next primary (Wisconsin) and he decided to abandon the race while it could appear to be his own decision. "He is a bully who likes to flex his muscles and beat up inferiors but avoids trouble with his peers," Arthur wrote in his journal.

To Robert F. Kennedy

[Handwritten]

April 3 [1968]

[New York, New York]

Dear Bob:

Here are some hasty thoughts which I am asking John Martin to give to you.

1. The post-Johnson situation obviously requires a new approach. For the moment, the case against military escalation in Vietnam has been won. For the moment, LBJ is out. The choice is now between you and McCarthy (and possibly Humphrey). Some who were ready to support you as the only realistic means of stopping Johnson will now draw back. The choice will become much more a question of personalities as between you and McCarthy.

2. Indiana is a peculiar state—it is in certain respects a Johnson state. Also the Indiana primary comes at a crucial moment in the campaign. You have made the national point about momentum, razzle-dazzle, etc. Now I think is the time to slow down—to establish yourself as a responsible leader well aware of the gravity and complexities of the problems we face. John Glenn[*] would be helpful in Indiana, but not Andy Williams.[†]

---

[*] John Glenn, Jr. (b. 1921). Marine combat aviator; astronaut; first American to orbit Earth; senator (D-Ohio), 1974–99; friend of the Kennedy family.
[†] Andy Williams (1927–2012). American singer; won eighteen gold-certified albums; emceed seven Grammy telecasts; hosted *The Andy Williams Show,* 1962–71; sang at

3. This is all part of a larger question about the tempo of the campaign. I think that from a national as well as an Indiana viewpoint you need a couple of careful, sober speeches. One might be about the limits of American power and the consequent need for the establishment of priorities in American foreign policy. Another might be about the mission of reconciliation at home—between races, generations, labor-management, etc.

4. You have already created an impressive and exciting blitzkrieg effect. But this pace cannot be sustained from now until November. Would it be possible that, after this trip and before the Indiana campaign gets into a state of frenzy, you could take a few days off? This would enable you (a) to get caught up on sleep, (b) to reduce the whirling dervish impression, (c) to work out in your own mind the strategy for this new phase in the campaign.

Since I gather that Indiana may not be the ideal state for a slambang, razzle-dazzle effort, I would think that a short bombing pause might be helpful there too.

I am for other reasons exhausted myself and plan to go to Hobe Sound (with the Harrimans) April 11–16. Thereafter I will be ready for speaking, travelling or anything else in Indiana, California or wherever else I can be helpful.

In the meantime, our thought and hopes are with you.

Yours ever,
Arthur

The next day, April 4, 1968, the Reverend Martin Luther King, Jr., was assassinated in Memphis, Tennessee. King had preached against the Vietnam War*

Robert F. Kennedy's funeral; later turned conservative, condemning President Obama for "following Marxist thought."

* Martin Luther King, Jr. (1929–68). Baptist minister; civil rights leader; preached nonviolence; led the 1955 Montgomery, Alabama, bus boycott; cofounded the Southern Christian Leadership Conference in 1957; helped organize the 1963 March on Washington, where he delivered his "I Have a Dream" speech, awarded the Nobel Peace Prize in 1964; announced his opposition to the Vietnam War in early 1967.

in Manhattan's Riverside Church in early 1967, calling the United States gov-
ernment "the greatest purveyor of violence in the world today." He had said, "A
nation that continues year after year to spend more money on military defense
than on programs of social uplift is approaching spiritual death. . . . If Ameri-
ca's soul becomes totally poisoned, part of the autopsy must read 'Vietnam.' "

After King's assassination, riots exploded in more than one hundred cities
across the United States. More than a thousand buildings were burned down
and twelve people were killed in five days of mayhem in Washington, D.C. The
disorders ultimately resulted in 43 deaths, 3,500 injuries, and 27,000 arrests
around the nation—as if the war in Vietnam had spread to the streets and
neighborhoods of America.

To the Editor of *The Washington Post*

May 21, 1968

[New York, New York]

Sir:

In the *Post* of May 12, Joseph Alsop has a public tantrum in which he first berates me for "putting on a borrowed Field Marshal's hat" and then berates the press in general for having "misled" the American public about the war in Vietnam. I have no wish to escalate an argument with an old friend; but, since Joe is evidently determined to turn a disagreement into a vendetta, I can only suggest that no newspaperman has misled the American public more assiduously than Mr. Alsop, especially when he puts on *his* borrowed Field Marshal's hat.

The most cursory research makes the point. Let us consider Mr. Alsop on Vietnam through the years: February 1964, "In Communist North Vietnam, to begin with, the situation is close to desperate"; September 1965, "The whole pattern of the war has been utterly changed. . . . At last there is light at the end of the tunnel"; October 1965, "Final defeat is beginning to be expected, even in the ranks of Vietcong hard-core units"; February 1966, "The enemy's backbone of regulars can even be broken this year. And when and if that happens, this war will be effectively won"; April 1966, "The Vietnamese and American forces are now imposing a rate of loss on the Vietcong which the enemy cannot indefinitely withstand"; October 1966,

"Within six, eight, ten or twelve months—before the end of 1967 at any rate—the chances are good that the Vietnamese war will look successful"; October 1967, "by any rational test, General William C. Westmoreland at last has the other side over a barrel." What a test! What a barrel!

I forbear to continue. We all remember Mr. Alsop's demonstration that the Tet offensive was a brilliant American victory. As for Khe Sanh,[*] I would suggest (a) that the recent probes by the 304th North Vietnamese division around Khe Sanh indicate the possibility that the business is not so finished and done with as Mr. Alsop assures us it is; (b) that it is still not clear whether the temporary North Vietnamese withdrawal from Khe Sanh was just a military response to American firepower or also a political response to President Johnson's speech of March 31; (c) that in any case, since Mr. Alsop evidently remains dedicated to the search-and-destroy strategy of which Khe Sanh was such a notable monument, I would propose that he read and meditate the call for "a complete switch of strategy" in the April *Foreign Affairs* by Sir Robert Thompson[†] who organized the successful campaign against the Malayan guerrillas and headed the British Advisory Mission in Saigon in 1961–65. Beyond all this, of course, lies Mr. Alsop's ultimate delusion: that it is possible in the second half of the 20th century for armed white men to determine the destiny of a country on the mainland of Asia.

Sincerely yours,
Arthur Schlesinger, Jr.

On June 6, 1968, following his victory in the California Democratic presidential primary, Robert F. Kennedy was assassinated in Los Angeles by a Jordanian immigrant, Sirhan Sirhan.

[*] The battle of Khe Sanh (January–July 1968): U.S. Marines held this isolated South Vietnam outpost for seven months against repeated Vietcong attacks following General Westmoreland's battle plan, but the outpost was abandoned in July on grounds that it no longer served any strategic purpose.

[†] Sir Robert Thompson (1916–92). British military officer and counterinsurgency expert; helped defeat Communist guerillas in Malaya in the 1950s, but his advice on Vietnam to stop bombing villages in favor of training police, instructing troops to act within the law, and helping peasants with agriculture was disregarded; author of April 1968 *Foreign Affairs* article entitled "Squaring the Error," critiquing U.S. Vietnamese policies.

Arthur was in Chicago for a conference on Vietnam sponsored by the Adlai Stevenson Institute. He watched the returns with Frances FitzGerald, Dick Wade, and Saul Bellow at Bellow's apartment. Back at his hotel, he heard the terrible news. It was all too much.

"I loved Bobby. I cannot bear the thought that he too is gone," Arthur wrote in his journal on June 9, 1968. "What kind of a President would he have made? I think very likely a greater one than JFK. He was more radical than JFK, he understood better the problems of the excluded groups: and he would have been coming along in a time more propitious for radical action. He would . . . have restored the idealism of America."

A few days later, in a commencement address at City University of New York, Arthur proclaimed: "[W]e have permitted murder to become a major technique of domestic politics."*

An editorial in The Washington Post *criticized Arthur for damning both Humphrey and McCarthy for their lack of presidential qualities, provoking a truculent response.*

To Philip Geyelin†

June 17, 1968

[New York, New York]

Dear Phil:

I have just now seen the editorial in the *Post* of June 11, and I must confess a certain puzzlement about it.

In the first place, it gives a false account of what I said on *Face the Nation.*‡ According to your editorial, Schlesinger spoke "with the same dogmatic certainty about the future that he uses to describe the past, as though there were as much certitude about one as about the other." That is simply

---

* Schlesinger elaborated on this theme in a chapter of his book *The Crisis of Confidence: Ideas, Power, and Violence in America* (1969), entitled "Violence as an American Way of Life."

† Philip ("Phil") Geyelin (1923–2004). Reporter for *The Wall Street Journal* for two decades; editor of *The Washington Post* editorial page, 1968–79; helped turn *The Washington Post* against the Vietnam War.

‡ CBS's Sunday morning political interview show since 1954.

a lie. The passage which offended you so much reads as follows (I quote from the transcript; but it was all in the *Post* the day before): "The President of the United States, ideally, ought to be a man of strength and he ought to be a man of generosity, and one doubts whether the Vice President has the first or that Senator McCarthy has the second." Can not the *Post* editorial writers distinguish between the expression of a doubt and the promulgation of a certitude? between a question and a prophecy?

The implied doctrine of the *Post* editorial, I gather, is that one is not allowed to express even doubts about Humphrey and McCarthy. Since we are old friends, let me tell you why I expressed these particular doubts. In my last conversation with the Vice President about Vietnam, he repeatedly and reverentially cited General Wheeler* and General Westmoreland as if they were final authority. This led me to doubt whether he would have the strength to stand up against the Joint Chiefs of Staff if he were to become President. Is this in your view an impermissible doubt?

As for McCarthy, the *Post* did not even quote accurately what I said. I did *not* say that he "would not be a compassionate president." I have no idea whether he would be a compassionate president or not. I said that he lacked generosity; and, if your people do not know the difference between compassion and generosity, I suggest that they consult a dictionary. The reason I said that I doubted his generosity was because of the mean-spirited campaign he conducted in Oregon and California and because of his general addiction to sarcasm and self-pity. I might add that Dick Harwood† of the *Post,* who was on the panel, said to me afterward that he wholly shared my doubt about McCarthy's generosity. In fact, Dick said that after covering McCarthy for some time he had concluded that he was one of the most arrogant, selfish and ungenerous men he had ever encountered.

I realize that I am a favorite target of editorial writers, though I am surprised that the *Post* should join in the pack. I am also surprised that to do so the *Post* should (a) falsify what I said, (b) imply a general doctrine that it is forbidden to express doubts about the strength or generosity of presiden-

---

* General Earle Wheeler (1908–75). Career military officer; U.S. Army chief of staff, 1962–64; chairman of the Joint Chiefs of Staff, 1964–70; argued for U.S. troop increases in Vietnam, which President Johnson rejected in 1968; presided over U.S. withdrawal under President Nixon's "Vietnamization" policy.

† Richard (Dick) Harwood (1925–2001). Combat marine, journalist and editor at *The Washington Post,* 1966–92; twice served as *Post* ombudsman.

tial candidates (or at least forbidden to me), and (c) regard this as a matter of such high moment and priority that you picked it as one of the top issues of June 11, 1968, for your heavy-handed censure.

Because the editorial is so stupid and the whole business so trivial, I am not writing this as a letter for publication. Because the attack seemed so gratuitous and required such a falsification of what I actually said, I am interested in what the hell was on your mind.[*]

Sincerely yours,
Arthur Schlesinger, Jr.

To David Ginsburg[†]

July 9, 1968

[New York, New York]

Dear David:

I read your plea for HHH with interest and sympathy; and you may be sure that I have thought very hard about the general problem. May I make a couple of comments?

I think that Hubert is making a disastrous error if he continues to pursue the nomination along his present road—i.e., by backroom manipulation of delegates and without serious discussion of issues. He has avoided public confrontation in the primaries; now he is avoiding public confrontation in debates (which, happily for Hubert, McCarthy is only requesting in his usual languid and dopey way). You know the Democratic party as well as I do; and you realize, I am sure, that if Hubert gets the nomination by a base on balls, without daring to take on anyone in a primary or a debate, he will face a bitter party; and the bitterness will be greatest among the

---

[*] Geyelin replied on June 18, 1968, that he had not written the editorial but had he done so, "I would have said somewhat the same thing about your statement as you said about the editorial." Additionally he admonished Arthur for being "a little stupid" for not supporting either Democrat in order to block Nixon.

[†] David Ginsburg (1912–2010). Washington lawyer influential in Democratic politics; one of the founders of Americans for Democratic Action; appointed by President Johnson as executive director of the 1968 Kerner Commission investigating civil disorders that found white racism and de facto segregation was responsible for black unrest.

issue-oriented activists, whose support is essential for a Democratic victory.

I can imagine why Hubert is dodging confrontations. Some sagacious fool has said to him, "Just sit tight, stay out of trouble and sew up the nomination. Don't worry about the liberals. Nixon will reunite the Democratic party; he will bring the liberals back. *After all, they have no place to go.* I can only say that many Democrats have already reached the conviction—and I am not so sure that I am not among them—that, if we are to have a stupid and reactionary foreign policy, it should be carried out by a Republican administration, not by a Democratic administration. To make it specific: if we were going to follow a course of military escalation in Vietnam, it would, in retrospect, have been much wiser to elect Goldwater than Johnson in 1964; for the simple reason that, if President Goldwater had pursued the exact policy actually pursued by LBJ, the revolt against that policy would have taken place much earlier and saved this country a lot of trouble and lives. If we are going to continue to pursue "idiot" policies in Southeast Asia, I would much rather that they be pursued by a Nixon administration than by a Humphrey administration; and, after all, Hubert himself has assured us (*U.S. News and World Report,* May 27), "If Nixon and Humphrey should be the candidates in the general election, I don't think our views of the war would be too far apart." If this is so, then give me Nixon—on the simple ground that, with the Democratic party in the opposition, we could stop his idiocy quicker.

I suppose some one will tell me that Hubert didn't "mean" this. Everyone in politics, I know, says things they don't mean at one time or another. What I cannot escape, though, is the feeling that Hubert really believes in this ghastly war—really believed, as he said in his incredible speech at Doylestown, Pennsylvania, October 15 last, that "the aggression of North Vietnam is but the most current and immediate action of . . . militant, aggressive Asian communism, with its headquarters in Peking, China"; really believed, as he said on that CBS conversation in April 1966, that the US is "going to be in Asia for a long, long time" and that the goal of our policy must be to realize "the dream of the Great Society in the great area of Asia, not just here at home." The tragedy of the war is precisely this: that it represents such a catastrophic misapplication of honorable ideas—the idea of the containment of aggression and the idea of a global New Deal—the ideas which dominated the decade of the forties and which shaped, I fear forever, the mind of HHH. When I see Hubert talking about a Marshall Plan for the cities to audiences composed of people who were five years old in 1948 and have never heard of the Marshall Plan, I weep over his own failure of imagination and sympathy; and I grieve that this great and vivid time should have produced a condition of arrested intellectual growth for so many bright people. We went wrong on Vietnam because we imposed the truths of the forties—containment of a unitary communism; of social reform—on a world which has radically and fundamentally changed.

Johnson, Humphrey, Nixon—they are all children of the forties. Rockefeller too, though he has better advisers on foreign policy and, unlike some of the others, *listens to them*; also, being unable to read a sentence [of a prepared text], he is not seduced by his own rhetoric. Moreover, my last conversation with Hubert on the war at . . . Joe Rauh's came to a dead end because he kept quoting General Westmoreland and General Wheeler to us as if they constituted the final authority to which we must all bow down.* I frankly do not see Hubert overruling the JCS as Kennedy did (after the Bay of Pigs), as Rockefeller would and as Gene McCarthy easily would. Possibly one trouble is that it is hard for someone who never had military service to recognize what a collection of clowns generals are.

This letter has become longer than I intended; but it may explain why a Kennedy Democrat who regards McCarthy with contempt cannot support Hubert and is wholly unimpressed by your Nixon-will-get-you-if-you-don't-watch-out argument. This is *not* an effective means of blackmailing people into supporting a candidate who genially says he doesn't disagree too much with Nixon on Vietnam.

Your turn!

Yours ever,
Arthur Schlesinger, Jr.

---

* On April 17, 1967, Rauh invited Humphrey to dinner to hear the views on the Vietnam War of longtime liberal friends, including Schlesinger, Galbraith, Clayton Fritchey, and James Wechsler. "An impassioned Humphrey gave us a defense of the war, at once voluble and pathetic. He talked as if the whole thing were a Chinese Communist plot," Schlesinger wrote in *Robert Kennedy and His Times* (1978). "Not once in his long discourse did he express any dismay over the human wreckage wrought by the American policy. . . . This trailing off of humanity [was] accompanied by an obvious delight in hobnobbing with statesmen—many mentions of the Pope, de Gaulle, Radhakrishnan, etc., etc."

P.S. One other thing: if you have any influence with Hubert, *please* get him to stop referring to himself in the third person. This is vulgar and offensive; and it makes one wonder about the psychology of a man who thinks that way (how often do you refer to yourself as Ginsburg?). Also the only other men in public life in our time who have done this are Joe McCarthy and Nixon.

To Marcus Cunliffe*

July 9, 1968

[New York, New York]

Dear Marcus:

Forgive my delay in writing this letter; but it is hard to describe the sadness which has overtaken this country, and me especially, in the last few weeks.

You ask about my relationship to my father. God knows how to answer such a question; but I think it was a very good relationship. I have no doubt that the intellectual framework within which I operate as an historian was essentially derived from him, though my historical interests have moved in somewhat different directions (e.g., intellectual rather than social history; also I have a good deal more of a polemical temperament than he had). One of his great qualities as a father was a deep and undeviating respect for the identity and purpose of his sons. This meant that even when I did things which I am sure disappointed him (e.g., not returning to Harvard after the White House), I always felt that I had his basic understanding and support.

Why did I adopt his middle name? I guess because I wanted at that point to be Arthur Schlesinger Jr. In retrospect, I sometimes wish I had stuck to "Bancroft"† since I do feel a sort of intellectual and political kinship with old George.

---

* Marcus Cunliffe (1922–90). British scholar celebrated for his work in American studies; author of books on the early postrevolutionary period in the United States; taught in England and the United States.

† George Bancroft (1800–1891). American historian famous for his monumental multivolume *History of the United States, from the Discovery of the American Conti-nent;* Democratic politician; secretary of the navy, 1845–46; Schlesinger was his third cousin, five times removed, according to genealogist Tim DeWerff.

How much did I consciously shape my own career on his? I suppose that my upbringing inclined me—no doubt conditioned me—toward becoming an historian. Also my father, in a quiet way, had always been something of a political activist; and no doubt this legitimated my own excursions into politics. However (and this may well have been an inheritance—and one I prize—from my mother), I was always less detached and judicious than my father, more eager for commitment and combat. I think this from time to time disconcerted him, but, as I noted earlier, he always backed me in everything, no matter how misguided he may privately have thought my activities to be.

Was I aware of his essay in *New Viewpoints* on Jacksonian America when I wrote *The Age of Jackson*? I do not think that I was consciously aware of it at the time, and I remember reading it some years later and being surprised at the extent to which I was developing insights he had already set forth. However, I have no doubt that he had communicated to me the substance of these insights in the incessant (and fascinating) conversations we held through the years on all manner of historical topics.

Did I in my teens accept/draw a good deal from his general views on politics, liberal issues, etc.? I am sure that I did; and I am sure that his skepticism about extreme views played an important role in keeping me out of political nonsense in my youth. I was, for example, always an anti-communist, even in the thirties; not that my father was a crusading anti-communist, as I became for a season in the forties and fifties, but that his faith in reasoned democracy and his dislike of absolutisms inoculated me at an early point against apocalyptic politics.

Did I ever take a course of his? Not formally—i.e., not for credit (he rightly thought this a poor idea)—but I audited his famous course on American social and intellectual history.

Were other Harvard historians of particular importance for me as an undergraduate? Yes: I gained from Sam Morison[*] a tremendous sense of the role of *style* both in writing history and in being an historian. I gained from Fred Merk[†] a tremendous sense of what meticulous, scrupulous,

---

[*] Samuel Eliot Morison (1887–1976). American historian at Harvard, 1925–55; winner of Pulitzer Prizes for biographies of Christopher Columbus and John Paul Jones; rear admiral, U.S. Naval Reserve, 1942–51.

[†] Frederick Merk (1887–1977). American historian at Harvard, 1916–57; friend of Arthur Schlesinger, Sr.

passionate scholarship was all about. Perry Miller was my tutor in my second and fourth years; he helped develop my interest in intellectual history and taught me highly useful techniques of clarity, astringency and indictment. Bernard De Voto, from whom I took a course in English composition and who later became a very close friend, helped redress my eastern/urban orientation, taught me about the west (particularly in a trip we took together along the Santa Fe trail in the summer of 1940, preparatory to his writing *The Age of Decision*), made me understand the complexity of the frontier and the importance of things like conservation and also encouraged my instinct toward polemics and participation. I must also mention F. O. Matthicsscn,[*] my tutor in my junior year. Though we were later separated by sharp political differences (for a time after the war he stopped speaking to me because of my anti-communism), he was a superb teacher, and I learned a great deal from him, especially about modern poetry (which I began reading with him and have read ever since) and, more generally, about the relationships between literature and society.

What about Niebuhr? I met him, I think, before I read much of him. I saw something of him when ADA was founded in the winter of 1946–47. I was greatly impressed and charmed by him, and I then began reading his books. I suppose that *The Nature and Destiny of Man*[†] had more influence on me (and my attitudes toward history) than any other single book. Niebuhr's rendition of the Christian interpretation of human nature, his sense of the frailty of human striving along with the duty none the less to strive, his sense of the tension between history and the absolute—all these things gave form to my own gropings about human nature and history and showed me how skepticism about man, far from leading to a rejection of democracy, established democracy on its firmest possible intellectual basis. *The Children of Light and the Children of Darkness* was also vital in this connection. Niebuhr also articulated and confirmed my sense that irony was the best human and historical stance—an irony which does not sever the nerve of action. The line leads straight from Niebuhr to the Kennedys. Also,

---

[*] F. O. Matthiessen (1902–50). Harvard professor, renowned for his critical studies of nineteenth-century American writers; closeted gay man who was attacked for his left wing views; committed suicide.

[†] Reinhold Niebuhr, *The Nature and Destiny of Man: A Christian Interpretation* (New York: Charles Scribner's Sons, 1941–43), based on lectures given in 1939.

through the years, Niebuhr more than anyone else I have known has served as the model of a really great man.

The Society of Fellows?[*] This was primarily of importance in giving me an opportunity to avoid the Ph.D. mill and work uninterruptedly on *The Age of Jackson*. Also, in seeing L. J. Henderson[†] and A. Lawrence Lowell[‡] Monday after Monday for two years, I had my first sustained exposure to a formidable conservatism; and I learned a great deal from this. I would say that they powerfully reinforced the anti-utopianism I inherited from my father, and that Niebuhr provided the means of accepting the Henderson-Lowell anti-liberal critique and incorporating it into a darker and wiser liberal philosophy.

Peterhouse? A most fascinating year—partly the eeriness of being in England during that twilight year between Munich and the war; partly the intellectual excitement of getting to know I. A. Richards,[§] Postan[¶] and Ernest Barker;[**] partly the immersion in another, slightly discrepant, culture; partly, I suppose, a stimulus to the worldliness which has entertained me ever since but which has somewhat removed me from my profession. . . .

Yours ever,
Arthur

---

[*] The Society of Fellows (established 1933) is an exclusive organization providing three-year fellowships to scholars at early stages in their careers to pursue studies in any department at Harvard free of formal requirements.

[†] L. J. Henderson (1878–1942). Medical doctor; Harvard professor of chemistry; founder of Society of Fellows; later pioneered work in sociology.

[‡] A. Lawrence Lowell (1856–1943). President of Harvard, 1909–33; legal scholar; progressive educator with illiberal views toward minorities, especially blacks and Jews.

[§] I. A. Richards (1893–1979). Influential English literary critic; father of "New Criticism" movement; poet.

[¶] Sir Michael Postan (1899–1981). Professor of economic history at Cambridge focusing on medieval Europe.

[**] Sir Ernest Barker (1874–1960). British political scientist at Cambridge University.

From Hubert H. Humphrey, Jr.

July 13, 1968

[Washington, D.C.]

Dear Arthur:

Our mutual friend David Ginsburg shared with me your letter to him of July 9.

John Kennedy got nominated exactly the way I am trying to get nominated, namely by the delegates. He surely didn't get the nomination because he was in the primaries. Nor did I get any particular praise from the press or some of my liberal friends because I entered the primaries.

John Kennedy and his organization did not hesitate to work with the political leaders of New York, New Jersey, Ohio, Michigan, Illinois and, indeed, the South. So let's quit kidding each other. The convention system is doing fairly well for American public life. It has given us Presidents like Andrew Jackson, Abe Lincoln, Grover Cleveland, Theodore Roosevelt, Woodrow Wilson, FDR, Truman, Eisenhower, Kennedy and Johnson. Also, you may recall your devoted work for Adlai Stevenson. Well, Adlai didn't get nominated because he won in some primaries. In fact, he lost in some in 1956. But both you and I supported him at the Convention, and he was a great man.

One final point on this primary situation: You know that I could not enter those primaries. I had two or three days' time to enter about three of them, but with no chance to really get organized for such a kind of a campaign that a primary requires. How foolish it would have been of me to try to contest in a primary when my forces were not ready. I will add, however, that in the California poll I was running nip and tuck with Bob Kennedy. But since my name was not on the ballot and we never launched any write-in anyplace, it is grossly unfair and irresponsible to talk about my being defeated in the primaries on the one hand, as some people do, and then to criticize me for not being in the primaries. You can't have it both ways.

I notice, however, you are not the only one to have changed your stripes on this primary situation. The *New York Times* called the state primaries in the spring of 1960 "ridiculous, wasteful and unrepresentative." They editorialized repeatedly in opposition to the primaries. Now they are all for them insofar as I am concerned. I am criticized day after day for not having entered the primaries. McCarthy is lauded for being such a courageous man. But why is it that Mr. Nixon isn't praised for entering the primaries and Mr. Rockefeller condemned because he didn't? He had much more freedom of action than I did. After all, I couldn't be entering any primaries or doing anything for my own political situation until after March 31. Mr. Rockefeller could have been a candidate as early as Nixon. Now you are a fair-minded man, Arthur, so just ponder these thoughts.

Paragraph three of your letter is so fallacious that I can't believe it came from you. I am not sitting tight, taking this nomination for granted, refusing to go out and speak. I have traveled all over this country during my three and a half years as Vice President. I have been in each of the 50 states and in over 600 of the cities and towns and, since declaring my candidacy, I have been on the go almost constantly. I have addressed myself to more issues in one month than your candidate has in the last year. I have discussed East-West relations, a global system of economic and technical assistance, delivered a major speech on the peace-keeping operations of the United Nations and the development of regional organizations, a major speech on my concept of the Presidency, a speech outlining my policy on education, another speech outlining my program for urban America. And, only recently, a review of what I believe will be the foreign policy priorities of the next 20 years.

I have not taken the liberals for granted, nor anyone else. But I will stack up my record of liberalism against anyone's. And you know as well as I that it is a good, solid, constructive record. And, frankly, I resent your snide comments about it.

My ideas about policies in Southeast Asia are not idiotic. I will be back to you with a much more detailed description of U.S.-Asian policy.

Now, let me say a word to you about urban affairs. When did you get to be an expert in this field? I have been a mayor of a great city. I outlined 20 years ago what many in these cities are trying to do now. I have served for almost four years as the President's liaison officer with the mayors and other officers of local government. I have had over 50 seminars, some of them lasting as long as two days, with the mayors, county commissioners, city managers. These seminars, as you know, have included Cabinet officers, technicians, and experts who have sat for several hours and answered the questions of our local government officers. These have been closed sessions so that we could do some work. I have held 12 regional meetings across this country. I attended every major conference of the U.S. Conference of Mayors, National League of Cities, City Managers Association, National Association of County Officials. My knowledge of urban problems did not come from technical discussions. It comes from practical experience as a mayor, continuous up-to-date contact with the mayors who are on the scene. My knowledge of urban problems also comes from a continuing study of urban problems with some of our top urban experts.

I am sorry if I offended you with the title "Marshall Plan." It may be out of date for you, but most people like our mayors today remember the Marshall Plan. This isn't a "kiddie" government. A mayor of a city who is 35 years of age has a pretty good recollection of the Marshall Plan for Europe. He might even have read about it. At least that caption attracted the attention of the press. It put in capsule form the outlines of a program that can be effective. I must say in all candor, Arthur, that all of your reference to my addiction to the past is the by-product of your being a professor of history. You write history, and I help make it. And, my, how much easier it is to have hindsight than foresight. But it is downright insulting from a man of your intelligence to have you accuse me of being all wrapped up in the 1930s and 1940s. My biggest problem in public life has been that I have been too far ahead of the times. I have never been a tag-along. I have been a leader, and you know it. So, in the parlance of the street, knock it off.

My final point is to comment on a very unfair and rude statement of yours: "Possibly one trouble is that it is hard for someone who never had military service to recognize what a collection of clowns generals are." Well now, General Schlesinger, when did you get to be such an expert on military matters? I don't claim to be a militarist. And, if my memory is correct, neither Rockefeller nor McCarthy had military service—at least battlefield service. Gene McCarthy was in the civilian branch during World War II. I was an instructor for the Army Air Corps. Your comment in that letter to David is just about the same sort of thing that FDR, Jr., spewed out in West Virginia. He came and apologized. It might help your soul if you did the same.

Don't overrate yourself, Arthur. No one's trying to blackmail you or anyone else into coming over to support my candidacy. On the basis of your earlier and more mature liberal convictions, you ought to be supporting me but undoubtedly something has happened in your life that has made you angry and bitter. These are two qualities that destroy a healthy sense of liberalism.

Sincerely,
Hubert H. Humphrey

To William Styron

July 16, 1968

[New York, New York]

Dear Bill:

I thank you for sending me a copy of that sad little book.[*] They so desperately miss the point of everything you were trying to do. And, in attacking you for supposedly creating your own Nat Turner, they ignore the fact that very little is known historically about Nat Turner, that he must therefore by definition be semi-mythic and that their Nat Turner is therefore just as much an imagined figure as yours. Clarke[†] writes in the introduction, "Why did [Styron] ignore the fact that Nat Turner had a wife whom he dearly loved?" But Turner's marriage is not, of course, a "fact" in any sense acceptable to historians; all the references to Nat Turner's wife, so far as I know, come thirty years after his execution. So too the Aptheker[‡] idea of a long series of slave revolts is pure mythology.

I know how disturbing this kind of assault can be, especially when mounted by legitimately distraught men, but I hope very much it will not get you down. The vulgarity of prose and argument in this book insures

---

[*] John Henrik Clark, ed., *William Styron's Nat Turner: Ten Black Writers Respond* (Boston: Beacon Press, 1968).

[†] John Henrik Clarke (1915–98). Historian; helped establish the field of African American studies; taught at Hunter College and Cornell University.

[‡] Herbert Aptheker (1915–2003). American Marxist historian; author of more than fifty books, many dealing with African American history; blacklisted in academia in the 1950s for his membership in the Communist Party.

that it will defeat its own purpose. Its interest in the long run is mainly clinical, and it will not diminish your own superb achievement.

Love to Rose.

Yours ever,
Arthur

To the Editor of *The New York Times*

July 18, 1968

[New York, New York]

Sir:

In his column of July 18, Mr. Wicker[*] asks why more of the supporters of Robert Kennedy have not come out for Eugene McCarthy. His answer is that the real objection of the Kennedy people to McCarthy is "McCarthy's lack of political orthodoxy." This answer seems to me nonsense, and I hope you will permit one who could not care less about preserving "past practices and attitudes," to suggest why.

I favored Robert Kennedy for the Presidency because he seemed to me the only candidate capable of dealing with the two supreme issues which will face our next President: the resolution of the war in Vietnam and the reconciliation of the races at home. The logic of Robert Kennedy's position on foreign policy would unquestionably lead to the support of Senator McCarthy. Equally, it seems to me, the logic of Robert Kennedy's position on domestic policy would lead to the support of Vice President Humphrey; for, on racial justice, urban problems and poverty, the Humphrey record is vastly better than the McCarthy record. Indeed, until Senator McCarthy became a candidate for President, though he had been in Congress during twenty years of urban crisis and black revolution, he displayed only the most nominal interest in this range of problems. I do not doubt that the primaries have educated him to some extent; but to this day he is not a convincing candidate to the excluded groups nor to many of those who

_____

* Tom Wicker (1926–2011). Journalist; novelist; liberal *New York Times* columnist, 1966–92; author of *A Time to Die* (1975) on the 1971 Attica, New York, prison revolt

honor Robert Kennedy's commitment to these groups—not because of any alleged "unorthodoxy" but simply because he conveys no intensity of concern about the victims and casualties of our society and no persuasive determination to see that justice is done them.

Senator McCarthy's conception of the Presidency is vitally related to the problem of racial justice, for strong presidential leadership will be essential if the peaceful struggle for racial justice is to succeed. Yet Senator McCarthy said at Milwaukee (March 23) that the next President "should understand that this country does not so much need leadership" and at Cleveland (June 18), according to the UPI lead:

> Senator Eugene J. McCarthy said today the powers of the Presidency should be decentralized.
>
> He said one of his campaign objectives was to offer a new concept of the office of President. . . .
>
> McCarthy said he would offer an alternative to "the sort of presidential power which extends itself in a personal way into every institution of government."

He even went on to raise the question: "Has the integrity of Congress, of the Cabinet and *of the military* been impinged upon by undue extensions of the executive power?"

This approach to the Presidency no doubt has its merits. But certainly no supporter of Senator McCarthy can claim that he intends to be a President in the tradition of Wilson, Roosevelt and Kennedy. Indeed, he proposes to cut back the powers of the Presidency at precisely the time when only a strong President will be able to hold the nation together in dealing with our most urgent and difficult national problems. A progressive Buchanan or a liberal Eisenhower is hardly what the nation presently requires.

I have no quarrel with former associates in the Kennedy movement who may choose to go to George McGovern (who would have my vote were I a delegate to the Democratic convention) or to McCarthy or to Rockefeller or even to Humphrey (though this last requires a massive and perhaps inconceivable act of faith with regard to foreign policy). I know they do what they do after conscientious consideration. I do quarrel with self-righteous newspaper stories suggesting the *only* moral course for Kennedy supporters is to back McCarthy.

Sincerely yours,
Arthur Schlesinger, Jr.

To Hubert H. Humphrey, Jr.

July 24, 1968

[New York, New York]

Dear Mr. Vice President:

I don't know whether I should thank you for your recent letter; but I am certainly complimented that you took the trouble to write at such length and with such candor.

Let me say at once that I obviously made a mistake when I told David Ginsburg he could show you my letter to him. That letter had been written in some haste; when he asked me whether he could pass it along, I did not have a copy in front of me. If I had taken another look, I would have recognized that the points I was trying to make deserved a more measured context. I am particularly sorry that you should have read my remark about military service as a reprise of FDR, Jr.'s West Virginia crack of 1960.[*] That was, of course, not my intention. I was making, I thought, the rather obvious point that one utility of military service is the skepticism it induces about the infallibility of officers. I had no intention of reviving Roosevelt's discredited charges; and, if you read my statement in this way, I regret it very much and am happy to withdraw it.

I would also claim one point of personal privilege: that is, your reference on the second page, line 12, to "your candidate." This at first perplexed me, since your remark could not possibly apply to Robert Kennedy, who is the only candidate I have had this year. I finally concluded that you must have been misled by a *Washington Post* story suggesting that I had come out

---

[*] Stumping for Senator John F. Kennedy in the West Virginia Democratic presidential primary, Franklin Roosevelt, Jr., attacked Humphrey for failing to serve in the armed forces in World War II. In fact, Humphrey had twice tried to enlist but was rejected on medical grounds.

for Nelson Rockefeller. This story was wrong; the correct sense of my California remarks is conveyed in the story which appeared in the *New York Times*. . . . I have come out for no one since Senator Kennedy's murder, and I have no intention of doing so.

You will also note in the *Times* story that I said then—as I have said on every occasion my opinion has been asked—that your record is excellent on domestic affairs. Of course you would be far better on racial justice, urban problems and poverty than McCarthy. I have said this repeatedly; and the passage in your letter defending your record on these matters is therefore unnecessary. You do not need to convince me that you know about urban problems!

What troubled me most about your reply, though, was your last paragraph. Here you seem to say that you are unable to envisage any principled reason for liberal opposition to your candidacy; it can only be, in my case, as you wrote, that "something has happened in your life that has made you angry and bitter." You go on to say that these two qualities destroy a healthy sense of liberalism. I admire your continuing fidelity to the idea of the politics of happiness. But I am compelled to say that there seem to me sound *public* reasons for a certain anger and bitterness today. In particular, if you do not understand and will not recognize that some of your old friends might oppose your candidacy on grounds of principle—because they sharply dissent from the position you have taken on Vietnam—then you have lost your own sense of reality and are in deep trouble. The almost complete opposition of ADA to you is to the point. You kid yourself dangerously if you attribute all such opposition to discreditable personal motives.

The part of your letter dealing with Asian policy seems to me—and I am emulating your own spirit of candor—hectoring and evasive. After all, you did say in Pennsylvania only a short while ago that "the aggression of North Vietnam is but the most current and immediate action of . . . militant, aggressive Asian communism, with its headquarters in Peking, China." You must have believed that when you said it. Do you regard it as impermissible that old friends might differ with this proposition and raise questions about it? It is the same with your 1966 statement that the United States is "going to be in Asia for a long, long time" and that the goal of our policy must be to realize "the dream of the Great Society in the great area of Asia, not just here at home." Am I forbidden to say that this seems to me a fantastic policy—and one which departs seriously from the standard laid down in what I would regard as the wisest remark made this decade about American foreign policy (and one, I believe, written by JFK himself):

> We must face the fact that the United States is neither omnipotent nor omniscient—that we are only 6 per cent of the world's population—that we cannot impose our will upon the other 94 per cent of mankind—that we cannot right every wrong and reverse each adversity—and that therefore there cannot be an American solution to every world problem.
>   (President Kennedy, November, 1961)

You may not wish to comment on these questions. But you must understand that it is questions like these—and *not* your record on urban affairs, and *not* some embittering personal experience—which make many of your old friends feel doubtful about your presidential candidacy.

I must add that I still remember with dismay the reverence with which you kept quoting Generals Wheeler and Westmoreland at Joe Rauh's. You write, "Well now, General Schlesinger, when did you get to be such an expert on military matters?" All I can say is that—and I shudder to repeat the banality—war is too important to be left to generals. Lincoln was better *on military matters* than his generals were in the Civil War. Lloyd George was better *on military matters* than his generals were in the First World War (as Winston Churchill amply demonstrated in *The World Crisis*). Your remark to me implies that being an "expert on military matters" is like being an expert on nuclear physics—and that the mere layman must of course bow to this expertise. I hope we never have a man as President of the United States who believes this. I served for three years in the White House, and I well remember that President Kennedy followed the advice of the Joint Chiefs of Staff only once on a major issue. That was the Bay of Pigs—and he never made that mistake again. He rejected the advice of the JCS on Laos, on the Berlin crisis of 1961, on the Cuban missile crisis, on the test ban treaty. But, judging by what you said at Joe Rauh's and what you write in your letter, you seem to take these military characters seriously, as if they knew something the rest of us didn't. Is it forbidden to disagree with you on this point?

I don't see much purpose in getting into an argument about primaries. I simply have no idea what you are talking about when you accuse me of having "changed your stripes on this primary situation." So far as I recall, I have always believed it a good idea for presidential candidates to enter primaries. And I must, of course, register my dissent from your statement that Kennedy "surely didn't get the nomination because he was in the primaries." He could not conceivably have got the nomination if he had not entered the primaries. I salute your call for platform hearings in which Democrats can express their views; and I only hope that you will apply this principle to yourself, and tell the country your views on military escalation in Vietnam, the ABM,* the Greek dictatorship, the Dominican intervention, Cuba and other tough issues of the day.

I can imagine something of your problems these days, and can well understand why my letter infuriated you, and am genuinely sorry for it. Now that you have discharged your fury on me, I hope that you will recognize that there are serious problems involved, quite apart from the infelicity or impertinence of my statement of them, and that your resolution of these problems, perhaps even your election as President, requires a somewhat different approach from that taken in your letter.

I hope you will not consider *this* letter *lese-majeste*. Please believe that my affection for you is undiminished and that my concern, like yours, is for the good of our country.

Ever sincerely yours,
Arthur Schlesinger, Jr.

The 1968 Democratic National Convention was held in Chicago from August 26 to 29. Outside the convention hall, thousands of antiwar protesters clashed with Chicago police and National Guardsmen, who used tear gas and beat protesters, bystanders, and reporters alike. Inside, Senator Ribicoff nominated McGovern for president and denounced the violence, saying that "with George McGovern we wouldn't have Gestapo tactics on the streets of Chicago."

Humphrey won the nomination on the first ballot, and Senator Edmund Muskie† of Maine was selected as the vice presidential nominee.

---

* Anti–ballistic missile system.
† Edmund Muskie (1914–96). Lawyer; Democratic governor of Maine, 1955–59; senator, 1959–80; 1968 Democratic vice presidential nominee; secretary of state, 1980–81.

To W. Averell Harriman[*]

August 29, 1968

[Hong Kong]

Dear Averell:

I should have written long since to thank you and Marie for that most delightful dinner (Servan-Schreiber, by the way, came away very impressed); but I thought I would wait so that I could send you a report on the convention. I had not intended to go. But when George McGovern entered the competition I told him I would stop in Chicago on my way to the Far East and do anything I could to help.

It was a dismal convention—far the saddest I have ever attended. The delegates acted like a collection of condemned men. They knew they were going to nominate Hubert. But they regarded him as a loser; they did not think McCarthy competent to be President (especially after his fatuous statement on Czechoslovakia);[†] and they did not know McGovern well enough. In their frustration they indulged in the fantasy of drafting Teddy [Kennedy],[‡] but this of course remained a fantasy.

George did very well, considering his hopelessly late start. He made a strong impression at the convention, stole the show when he appeared with Humphrey and McCarthy before the California delegation and won some helpful senatorial endorsements (Tydings, Joe Clark, Ribicoff). But the result was preordained, and I left the stricken city with great relief. Hong Kong is as beautiful as ever, and Chrissie & I will have a great time here.

I am sure that Hubert is in great trouble. He has wobbled all over the place on Vietnam and inspired confidence in no one. I think you should go back and explain to him what the problems are. I still think your plan might

[*] Harriman served as chief U.S. negotiator at the Paris peace talks on Vietnam, 1968–69.

[†] McCarthy told reporters that the Soviet invasion of Czechoslovakia in August 1968 was "not a major world crisis" and that a meeting of President Johnson's National Security Council at midnight was uncalled for.

[‡] Edward M. ("Ted") Kennedy (1932–2009). Dominant liberal voice in the U.S. Senate (D Mass.), 1962–2009, younger brother of John and Robert Kennedy. Speaker at Schlesinger's Manhattan memorial service in 2007.

be the only thing which could save him. It could provide him the excuse for taking a new line.

Much love to Marie. I hope you are well, and that I will see you both before too long.

Yours ever,
Arthur

To Reinhold Niebuhr

September 8, 1968

[Tokyo, Japan]

Dear Reinhold:

In case this Prague despatch never reached the U.S., I send it along. I congratulate you on your transmutation into a Czech poet! [see below]

I am over here as a guest of Japanese TV with my younger daughter Christina. In a few more days she will go on to India (she graduated from Radcliffe in June) and I, gloomily, back to New York. What a sad year this has been! The murder of Robert Kennedy terminated my interest in the campaign, and perhaps in American politics for some time to come. Hubert seems to me a burnt-out case, emasculated and destroyed by L.B.J. and unlikely ever to become a man again; McCarthy an ungenerous, self-pitying man who has no concern for the other America and no belief in the Presidency. When George McGovern became a candidate, I rallied round; as you may remember, George is a very close friend of mine, and he seemed to me better qualified to be President than the other two. But of course his candidacy was never realistic.

What do we do now? I have always supposed that anyone would be better than Nixon. But, if Hubert and Nixon have pretty much the same Vietnam policy, might it not be better to have Nixon on the ground that it will be easier to block further escalation if the Democratic party is opposing a Republican President than it would be if half the Democratic party feels it must go along out of loyalty to a Democratic President? Certainly Goldwater, had he been elected in '64 and pursued the identical policy pursued by L.B.J., could never have got so far with it because the entire Democratic party would have been mobilized against it.

I hope you had a tranquil and productive summer. I will be back in another ten days or so and will give you a ring. Love to Ursula.

Yours ever,
Arthur

Note: Clipping from *Japan Times*—8 Sept. '68

Poem Advises Czechs on Life

PRAGUE (Kyodo-Reuter)—A poem recited on Prague television and printed in the trade union newspaper *Prace* Friday morning appears to set the guideline for a Czechoslovak living under occupation. It goes:

Calm, so I can accept things which I cannot change.
    Courage, to change things which can be changed.
    Wisdom, that I can tell these two apart.*

On November 6, 1968, Nixon narrowly defeated Humphrey for the presidency. Nixon received 31.8 million votes, Humphrey 31.3 million votes, and Governor George Wallace† of Alabama, running as an independent, 9.9 million votes.

Arthur believed that Humphrey would have won the election if he had broken with President Johnson and come out against the Vietnam War.

---

*Reinhold Niebuhr is credited with writing the Serenity Prayer: "God, grant me the serenity to accept the things I cannot change; courage to change the things I can; and wisdom to know the difference."

†George C. Wallace, Jr. (1919–98). Democratic governor of Alabama, 1963–67, 1971–79, 1983–87; paralyzed from the waist down after an assailant shot him five times in May 1972 while Wallace was campaigning for president in Maryland. Wallace was a staunch segregationist who renounced his views later in life.

Schlesinger relaxes with his stepson Peter Allan and the economist
John Kenneth Galbraith at the Galbraith farmhouse in Newfane, Vermont.
Burt Glinn/Magnum Photos

The Imperial Presidency

1969–76

To Clayton Fritchey

January 29, 1969

[New York, New York]

Dear Clayton:

I am glad you wrote that excellent column on whether the United States is a republic or a democracy. People like Kilpatrick[*] think that the distinction in the minds of the founding fathers between "democracy" and "republic" had something to do with majority rule. They are, as you point out, crazy. Cf. The Fourteenth Federalist: "The true distinction between these forms . . . is, that in a democracy the people meet and exercises the government in person; in a republic, they assemble and administer by their representatives and agents. A democracy, consequently, will be confined to a small spot. A republic may be extended over a large region." The founding fathers saw no difference between a republic and a democracy on the question of majority rule. Hamilton[†] in the Twenty-Second Federalist speaks of "the fundamental maxim of republican government, which requires that the sense of the majority should prevail."

---

[*] James J. Kilpatrick (1920–2010). Longtime editor of the conservative *Richmond (Va.) News Leader;* syndicated right-wing columnist of A Conservative View, 1964–93; fierce opponent of desegregation, arguing that federal policies violated states' rights; ultimately accepted civil rights legislation.

[†] Alexander Hamilton (1755–1804). Lawyer; soldier; political philosopher; coauthor of *The Federalist Papers;* argued for a strong centralized national government; founded the Federalist Party; first U.S. secretary of the Treasury; killed in a duel by Aaron Burr.

I send along these points in case you want to return to the subject.

Yours ever,
Arthur

To Odile Cail[*]

June 16, 1969

[New York, New York]

Dear Miss Cail:

I agree with much of the analysis of Maoism contained in your paper "Thoughts on the Chinese Cultural Revolution."[†] I have no doubt that Mao[‡] is fanatically determined to avoid the degeneration that he thinks had overtaken the Russian Revolution, and that he hopes to assure the permanence of the Chinese Revolution by creating the new revolutionary man. I would, however, have given more emphasis than you do to certain aspects of this effort (and here I touch on some of your other points):

—*The hopelessly utopian character of Mao's effort:* He is the third man this century to try and remake human nature. Hitler in the thirties and Stalin in the forties were both supposed at the time to have achieved totalitarian societies and to have produced new revolutionary men. In retrospect, we can see how far they fell short of these goals in spite of the immense cruelty of their regimes. I doubt whether Mao has been, or will be, very much more successful.

—*the great social and technical costs for China:* I am not sure what you mean by "the ambitions of Chinese nationalists," but, if these ambitions include the transformation of China into a great modern state and power, then the

---

* Odile Cail (1937–94). Wife of a French diplomat stationed in China; wrote a 1972 guidebook to Peking.

† Cultural Revolution (1966–76). Internal Chinese "revolution" initiated by Mao Tse-tung to retake power from regime pragmatists, with the claimed goal of eliminating capitalism; sent thousands to the countryside for "reeducation."

‡ Mao Tse-tung (1893–1976). Communist Party chairman; historic unifier of People's Republic of China beginning in 1949; caused the deaths of 40–70 million people in campaigns such as the Great Leap Forward and the Cultural Revolution; raised literacy rates, women's status, health care, housing standards, and life expectancy.

Cultural Revolution, with its mania against specialization in society, would hardly be compatible with this ambition. China apparently has maintained technical progress only in the few sectors, like nuclear weapons development, which have been protected from the Cultural Revolution. In general, the attack on education and intellectuals can only hold back the development of China as a modern state.

—*the inevitable creation of new forms of class rule:* Someone must run a country; it is the most elementary of illusions to suppose that a populous nation can run itself, as if by spontaneous combustion. Mao's war against the institutions which he feared were corrupting the revolution evidently created a vacuum of authority that he has attempted to fill by his own personality cult. Your paper seemed to me to miss the horrid significance of his demand that his nation regard him as infallible; indeed, Mao's insistence on national sycophancy seems to have surpassed even that of Hitler and Stalin. He has not ended class rule in China. Whether or not this was his intention, he has tried to establish a fantastic personal dictatorship based on himself and those around him who will continue to tell him how marvelous he is.

—*the extent of the failure of the Cultural Revolution:* This effort was bound to fail in all its aspects. Mao cannot remake human nature; he cannot forever stifle those who wish to make China a powerful modern state; he cannot forever persuade people that he is infallible and that their only role in life is blindly to follow his every command. My impression is that the Army, which may well be the refuge of the modernizers, has begun to establish control, province by province, in collaboration with elements in the CCP,[*] and that Mao will increasingly serve as a facade for military rule. Such actions as the decision to resume normal diplomatic relations with the outside world suggest that the period of religious mania is coming to an end.

Can Maoism be tried outside China? Obviously it can be tried "from the top" in any country where a communist dictator wants to try it. Maoism "from the bottom" will remain in most countries, developed or underdeveloped, a species of infantile leftism, capable of arousing passions for a while but deficient in staying power. Maoism will always be defeated by the fact that it is not set up to cope with the problems of a high-technology

* Chinese Communist Party

society. Therefore its influence on societies committed to technological progress will only be metaphorical. The student rebels who invoke Mao are invoking a symbol, not a policy. In China they would be sent to work in the rice fields and perhaps would be less enthusiastic about Maoism.

As for your questions about humanism, I see no relationship at all between Mao and humanism. Humanism, as I understand it, means the fulfillment, not the manipulation and obliteration, of the human personality. Humanism involves tolerance, not bigotry, repression and fanaticism.

I shall be interested in the results of your inquiry, and I hope you will send me a copy of your book on publication. . . .

Sincerely yours,
Arthur Schlesinger, jr.

To Arnold Gingrich[*]

August 5, 1969

[New York, New York]

Dear Mr. Gingrich:

I have your letter of July 9—addressed to Arthur "Schlessinger"—asking me to give you, apparently for nothing, my notion of what our greatest challenge will be in the 1970s. This is the most recent in a series of requests from your magazine that I make some unpaid contribution to your columns. Let me candidly say that I can think of many better objects for literary philanthropy than *Esquire*. I do not think your magazine is any good; and I am astonished, in any case, that you should expect me to give things to a magazine which, so far as I can recall, has not mentioned me for years without misrepresentation or insult.

Please stop sending me these idiotic requests.

Sincerely yours,
Arthur Schlesinger, jr.

---

[*] Arnold Gingrich (1903–76). Cofounder and editor of *Esquire* magazine, 1933–45; later *Esquire* publisher; published Ernest Hemingway, John Steinbeck, John Dos Passos, Norman Mailer; launched the "New Journalism."

To Jeff M. Eliot*

August 7, 1969

[New York, New York]

Dear Mr. Eliot:

I have recently returned from a European trip to find your thoughtful letter of some weeks back. You state very perceptibly the dilemma in which sensitive people find themselves in an era when the individual finds his life increasingly defined for him by the domination of structures. Of course this is not a new situation. As Emerson put it more than a century ago, "Society is a joint-stock company in which the members agree, for the better securing of his bread to each shareholder, to surrender the liberty and culture of the eater." But today the sense of individuality is heightened and democratized at just the time when a high-technology society encourages the reign of structures; and probably more people than ever before are torn by the contradictions of life.

How does one survive? I am an historian, and I suppose that the historical perspective makes it easier to endure the anguish of the present. Certainly one finds great consolation from reading great thinkers who have wrestled with this dilemma. I find, for example, William James, Reinhold Niebuhr, Emerson and Pascal† particularly helpful. The trick, I believe, is to understand the intractability of life but not to permit this to sever the nerve of action.

Sincerely yours,
Arthur Schlesinger, jr.

Senator George McGovern in March 1969 became the first senator to criticize President Nixon's Vietnam policy, and he was a featured speaker in October before one hundred thousand demonstrators in Boston at the Moratorium to End the War in Vietnam. "Let's stop saving face and begin saving lives," he said. He also spoke at the antiwar demonstration in November in Washington,

---

* Jeff M. Eliot of Los Angeles, California.
† Blaise Pascal (1623–62). French mathematician; physicist; inventor; philosopher; father of probability theory; famous for his ruminations on life entitled *Pensées*.

D.C., which drew an estimated five hundred thousand people. Yet he represented the socially conservative state of South Dakota.

To George McGovern

October 6, 1969

[New York, New York]

Dear George:

You have been doing a great and necessary job in pressing the Vietnam issues; but I wonder whether at some point you ought not to take action to protect your right flank. I notice a certain tendency in the press to identify you with the most extreme get-out-at-any-cost position. This could be harmful.

What is most important, I think, is to make it clear that the advocacy of disengagement from Vietnam does *not* imply any indifference to the fate of young Americans who, through no choice of their own, are in Vietnam and exposed every day to the risks of death. There are two ways in particular, it seems to me, in which you could indicate your human concern for our troops without at all compromising your view that we should get out as soon as possible.

One is the question of prisoners-of-war. Would it not be possible to make a speech calling attention to the urgent need for renewed efforts to procure the release of Americans now in North Vietnam prison camps? Abba Schwartz[*] was working on this problem during the Johnson administration and has, I believe, kept in touch with it since. Averell Harriman has also had considerable interest in the problem.

The other is the question of the protection of American forces during the period of withdrawal. If the whole situation should collapse, we might face another Dunkirk; and we ought to do a lot of advance planning to prevent the cutting-off or slaughter of American troops in the course of retreat. It might be worthwhile to talk to someone like Townsend Hoopes[†]

[*] Abba Schwartz (1916–89). Lawyer; former UN official; assistant secretary of state for security and consular affairs, 1962–66; advocated immigration reform.

[†] Townsend ("Tim") Hoopes (1922–2004). Writer; historian; Department of Defense, 1948–53, 1964–69; undersecretary of the air force, 1967–69; president of the Association of American Publishers, 1973–86.

or Paul Warnke* and see whether it would be useful to say anything publicly about this problem. I don't know Warnke, but I hear good things about him. Tim Hoopes is an old friend of mine and would be inclined I think, to be cordial and cooperative. You must by all means get hold of his new book *The Limits of Intervention;* it is a remarkable account, very well written, of the debate within the Pentagon leading up to LBJ's March 31 [1968] speech. Hoopes is still living in Washington. . . .

I hope to see you sometime.

Yours ever,
Arthur

To Dean Acheson

October 16, 1969

[New York, New York]

Dear Dean:

I have read *Present at the Creation*† with the greatest admiration and delight. It is a distinguished contribution to the history of our times—but few historians, alas, can write with such fascination and wit.

Yours ever,
Arthur

---

*Paul Warnke (1920–2001). Diplomat; assistant secretary of defense for international security affairs, 1967–69; director of the Arms Control and Disarmament Agency in the Carter administration.

†Dean Acheson, *Present at the Creation: My Years at the State Department* (New York: Norton, 1969).

From Dean Acheson

October 21, 1969

[Washington, D.C]

Dear Arthur:

How kind and thoughtful of you to write me such a lovely note about the book. I shall cherish it.

If I ever come to believe that the book is as good as my friends tell me it is, I shall be insufferable, but then there are some who think I am already.

With warm greetings and many thanks.

Sincerely yours,
Dean

To W. Averell Harriman

January 5, 1970

[New York, New York]

Dear Averell:

Some thoughts on Vietnam:

So far as I can see, the administration has been trying to ride two horses on Vietnam, and the two horses have been going in different directions. Nixon began by giving the lead rein to the negotiation horse. However, if he had been in dead earnest about negotiation, he would have slowed down the fighting, begun to cut loose from the Saigon regime, taken measures to protect the potential leaders of a coalition government and responded promptly and imaginatively to the Ho Chi Minh[*] letter and to other signals from Hanoi. The administration did none of these things; and, in the meantime, it has begun to ride off in another direction on its second horse, which is Vietnamization.[†]

---

[*] Ho Chi Minh (1890–1969). Communist revolutionary leader of Vietnam; prime minister, 1945–55; president, 1945–69.

[†] Vietnamization: Nixon's policy of de-Americanizing the war by expanding, equipping, and training South Vietnamese forces and assigning them to an increasing combat role, at the same time steadily reducing the number of U.S. combat troops.

Vietnamization requires an incompatible set of actions: the prosecution of the fighting; the strengthening of the Saigon government; acquiescence in Thieu's* repression of opposition; rejection of signals from Hanoi. More and more, it seems to me, the administration has shifted from the negotiation horse to the Vietnamization horse; and now it has practically abandoned negotiation.

The reason for this shift is quite clearly the new wave of military optimism. Nixon is evidently convinced that the Viet Cong are at last in a bad way, that the North Vietnamese have been beaten, that ARVN† is beginning to fight, that pacification is becoming a success and that, so far as the military balance is concerned, time is on our side. The more we strengthen the Saigon regime, he calculates, the more the military balance will be in our favor, the better terms we can demand in Paris, and the greater his political success will be in the United States. In the meantime, by judicious reduction of American forces, combined with the suggestion that his plan will work only if dissent is silenced, and with the rallying of the right through Agnew,‡ he hopes to keep domestic public opinion under control. Obviously the negotiation idea is designed to bring the war to an end; the Vietnamization plan is designed to keep the war going, though with much reduced American participation.

Each course involves a gamble and consequently a risk. Negotiation involves the gamble that the other side does not wish to negotiate on any terms except unconditional surrender. Vietnamization involves the gamble that the South Vietnamese Army will prove no more effective in the future than it has been in the past.

Of these two risks, there is strong reason to believe that the first is the lesser one. There is much evidence that the other side *does* wish a negotiated settlement. It is to their interest to have an evacuation of American bases and withdrawal of American troops. It is to their interest to have a formal end to the war. On the other hand, there is little evidence that our

---

* President Nguyen Van Thieu (1923–2001). Authoritarian president of South Vietnam, 1965–75; fled the collapse of the South Vietnamese government in 1975 and resettled in the United States.

† Army of the Republic of Vietnam (South Vietnam).

‡ Spiro Agnew (1918–96). Republican governor of Maryland, 1967–69; U.S. vice president, 1969–73; resigned in disgrace for accepting bribes while in office in Maryland

Vietnamese have a greater will to fight than they have had in the last half dozen years or, indeed, that the Thieu regime could survive the very marked reduction of American troops. In any case, the Vietnamization course, because it would keep the war going rather than bring it to an end, would hold out the constant possibility of American re-involvement.

For all those reasons, the course of negotiation would seem to make much more sense than the course of Vietnamization—and the administration is kidding the people when it pretends that we can ride both horses equally fast at the same time.

This seems to me the situation as the electorate ought to begin to understand it. The question of timing, as you said over the phone, is all-important when one considers which elements of the situation should be presented when. If you could give the UPI[*] a crisp, persuasive argument as to why you think the other side will negotiate, it might be helpful. I hope your DAC[†] group will go into the whole picture and present as sober and *tough* a statement as possible. No Humphrey-type "statesmanship," I trust. The politics of Vietnam lie, I am sure, in being right in the long-run, not in being popular in the short-run. This is also best for the country.

Yours ever,
Arthur

Over the years, meeting in crowded auditoriums across the nation, Arthur sparred with William F. Buckley, Jr., over the meanings of liberalism and conservatism, deepening a relationship forged in mutual ideological antipathy and disdain.

---

*United Press International.
† Democratic Advisory Council (established 1953). A body of the Democratic Party consisting of activists, strategists, and intellectuals advising on policy and assisting on fund-raising.

From William F. Buckley, Jr.

January 15, 1970

[New York, New York]

Dear Arthur:

I am sorry the Cambridge debate didn't work out, but as you know, the causes of the cancellation were not of my doing.

I hope that Mr. Steibel* inaccurately reported the ensuing conversation with you concerning a proposed appearance on *Firing Line*. He told me that you declined to appear on the program because you do not want to "help" my program, and you do not want to increase my influence, although to be sure you hope that the program survives. It seems to me that the latter desire is by definition vitiated by the initial commitment. If all the liberals who have appeared on *Firing Line* reasoned similarly, it would necessarily follow that the program would cease to exist—or is it your position that other liberals *should* appear on the program, but that *you* should not? And I should have thought that it would follow from your general convictions that a public exchange with me would diminish, rather than increase, my influence. And anyway, the general public aside, shouldn't you search out opportunities to expose yourself to my rhetoric and my wit? How else will you fulfill your lifelong dream of emulating them?

Yours cordially,
Wm. F. Buckley, Jr.

To William F. Buckley, Jr.

January 20, 1970

[New York, New York]

Dear Bill:

Can it be that you are getting a little tetchy in your declining years? Nothing would give me greater pleasure than debating you on neutral ground; you are quite right in detecting my feeling that such public ex-

* Warren Steibel (1925–2002). Longtime *Firing Line* producer, 1966–99.

changes would diminish rather than increase your influence. But is it really *lese majeste* to suggest that I am under no obligation to promote your program? As for others, let them make their own decision. Don't tell me that you have stopped believing in freedom of individual choice!

You remind me of my other favorite correspondent, Noam Chomsky.*

Best regards,
Arthur

Arthur had slammed Noam Chomsky's new book, American Power and the New Mandarins, *in a March 23, 1969, review in the* Chicago Tribune. *"Somewhere in the book Chomsky writes with his usual sententiousness, 'It is the responsibility of intellectuals to speak the truth and to expose lies.' He must be putting us on. . . . One can only conclude that Chomsky's idea of the responsibility of an intellectual is to foreswear reasoned analysis, indulge in moralistic declamation, fabricate evidence when necessary and shout always at the top of one's voice."*

Thus was precipitated an ongoing correspondence of mutual recrimination in letters to the editors of Commentary *and the BBC magazine* The Listener. *Chomsky charged Arthur with "fabrications and errors with respect to Cuba, Vietnam, American policy, my writings, and other matters," and with being an apologist for American imperialism. Arthur responded, "He begins as a preacher to the world and ends as an intellectual crook."*

To the Editor of *The Listener*

January 20, 1970

[New York, New York]

Sir:

Try as hard as I can, I fear I cannot match Professor Chomsky in self-righteousness, long-windedness or mendacity. Rather than protract

---

*Noam Chomsky (b. 1928). Left-wing activist; professor of linguistics at MIT for more than fifty years; prolific author, strident critic of U.S. foreign policy; longtime antagonist of Schlesinger.

what your readers cannot but regard as a boring and mystifying correspondence, I would beg interested bystanders to look at the documents and make their own judgment as between Professor Chomsky and myself. In particular, let them read the text of President Truman's speech (in his *Public Papers* for 1947, pages 167–172) and decide whether that speech proves (as Professor Chomsky claims in *American Power and the New Mandarins,* pages 318–319) that the United States for twenty years had planned to use "its awesome resources of violence and devastation to impose its passionately held ideology and its approved form of social organization on large areas of the world." And let them read my book *The Bitter Heritage* and see whether any sane person can describe the position taken in that book as "a shade to the hawkish side of the Pentagon."

Certainly Joseph Alsop, who denounced *The Bitter Heritage* in a furious and unbridled way, did not think so. When Professor Chomsky talks about "the Alsop-Schlesinger ideology" in his letter to the *Listener* (as when he talked about "the Rusk-Schlesinger concept" in *American Power,* page 306), he creates alliances that would astound Messrs. Alsop and Rusk as much as they do me. Does not Professor Chomsky understand that the foundation of political analysis lies in the capacity to make distinctions? Someone who is unable to see the difference between a supporter and an opponent of the Vietnam war ought to shut up shop as a political seer and return to the linguistic factory.

As for the Bay of Pigs, Professor Chomsky denies that I said anything at the time about such clandestine undertakings as incompatible with a democratic society. Wrong again. Let him read the italicized quotation from one of my anti–Bay of Pigs memoranda to President Kennedy quoted on page 254 of *A Thousand Days.*

Sincerely yours,
Arthur Schlesinger, Jr.

After Robert F. Kennedy's death, Arthur embraced Senator McGovern as the new liberal hope. He began meeting with McGovern regularly, contributing ideas for policy and offering strategic advice. In March 1970, McGovern asked him for help on a speech he was making on April 18 to the Western States Democratic Conference.

To George McGovern

April 13, 1970

[New York, New York]

Dear George:

I will hope some time in the next few days (I am swamped in the midst of the spring lecture season) to take a fresh look at the speech and make some specific suggestions.

In the meantime, here are two points you might want to consider:

1. On November 6, 1968, Nixon said that "bring us together" would be the keynote of his administration. A distracted and divided America warmed to these words and prayed that this indeed would be the essence of his purpose. Let us now, eighteen months later, consider how well he has succeeded in terms of the objective he set himself. Instead of trying to bring the nation together, he has evidently decided to slough off all those whom he considers minorities—the young, the blacks, the poor, the opponents of the war—in favor of what he calls the Great Silent Majority. He has unleashed the Vice President to stimulate and promote the task of polarizing the country. In so doing, the administration has intensified the divisions that are already tearing the country apart—between white and black, between middle class and poor, between hawks and doves and now (after Carswell)* between north and south. But the words "bring us together" still represent the national necessity. What we need now is a genuine politics of reconciliation founded, not on an elevation of one group at the expense of the rest of our people, but on a determination to give all Americans a sense that this is their country and that they have a voice in the great national decisions. To do this, we must return to our earliest traditions. The Constitution begins, "We the people of the United States," not "We the Great Silent Majority." Nixon and Agnew have not improved on the Declaration of Independence; and, as we approach the 200th anniversary of July 4, 1776, let us honor the principles of the Declaration by acting on them.

---

* George Harrold Carswell (1919–92). Federal judge, 1958–69; nominated in 1970 by President Nixon to the U.S. Supreme Court; rejected by the Senate for controversial decisions on civil rights and women's rights, and substandard performance on the bench.

2. As for Nixon's policy in Vietnam, he told us that he was going to wind up American participation in that war. Instead, by pursuing the mirage of Vietnamization, he has only lengthened and now widened the war. What began as a war in Vietnam is becoming a war also in Laos and Cambodia. It is more urgent than ever that we follow the only course which can bring about an honorable disengagement from Vietnam—that is, the resumption of negotiations in Paris. . . .

I will be in touch again as soon as the pressure relaxes.

Yours ever,
Arthur

In March 1969, the United States secretly began a bombing campaign in Cambodia, a neutral country, designed to eliminate Vietcong sanctuaries. In late April 1970, U.S. forces invaded the ancient Buddhist kingdom.

Henry Kissinger, Arthur's old friend, was serving as President Nixon's national security adviser, overseeing the destruction of Cambodia.

To Henry Kissinger

May 7, 1970

[New York, New York]

Dear Henry:

I have forborne from writing because of my confidence in your own intelligence and purpose and because of my full awareness of the difficulty of judging complex internal situations from the outside. But you have said to me more than once that, if the time should come when your own situation begins to seem indefensible, you would appreciate it if your friends were to let you know. In all candor I think that time has come. I honestly cannot imagine what circumstances could justify the Cambodian adventure. As you well know, this scheme has been kicking around Washington for years. Even President Johnson had the sense to reject it when the Joint Chiefs hawked it to him some time back; and I do not see that the situation has changed all that radically so that it becomes a brilliant stroke now.

The speech in which President Nixon explained the adventure was intellectually contemptible.* The notion that the United States would have been acting like "a pitiful, helpless giant" if we had not decided to burn down a lot of Cambodian villages is really extraordinary. If the President does not know his Shakespeare, I am sure you do: "O! it is excellent / To have a giant's strength; but it is tyrannous / To use it like a giant."† I *know* that you cannot accept the basic thesis of the speech that, if we do not fight to the end in a part of the world where we have no vital interests, our adversaries will assume that we won't fight in parts of the world where we do have vital interests. According to this thesis, once the Russians had withdrawn their missiles from Cuba, where they had no vital interests, we could have attacked them with impunity in Eastern Europe, where they have vital interests. Can President Nixon really believe this?

I have said nothing about the impact on our own country of this weird and wild policy. Did the administration really not anticipate the reaction? Did it really suppose it could get away with widening the war? It is hard to overstate the combination of fury and impotence sweeping over the young and, worse than that, the accompanying profound disillusion with the democratic process. We are all prisoners of our experience. The experience of our own generation, which had the luck of FDR, Truman and JFK, convinced us that the democratic process was an effective way of changing things. From the viewpoint of the young today, who were born way after FDR and Truman and can barely remember Kennedy, the democratic process, as they have seen it in action, is a sham and a phony.

In 1964 they backed Johnson against Goldwater—only to have Johnson adopt Goldwater's policy of military escalation after the election. They flocked behind McCarthy and Robert Kennedy in 1968, only to see a second Kennedy murdered, McCarthy and McGovern defeated in Chicago, the police rioting against the protesters. Still, the administration which had escalated the war was beaten, and a new administration, pledged to end the war, was in office. Now, fifteen months later, the new administration has widened the war, strengthened the American commitment to the Saigon regime and practically abandoned negotiations in Paris. It is little wonder

---

* Nixon justified the invasion of Cambodia as a strategy to win the Vietnam War in his speech of April 30, 1970.
† William Shakespeare, *Measure for Measure,* act 2, scene 2.

that the young are a little skeptical about the efficacy of the democratic process. What do we tell them now? To wait until 1972, by which time God knows how many Americans, and Vietnamese, now alive, will be dead?

Does the President not know how his policies are tearing this country apart and eroding faith in democratic methods of effecting change? You surely must know this; and, as an old and admiring friend, I hope you will consider in the most serious way whether the time has not come for you to dissociate yourself from an administration that, on the record of the last few weeks, will surely go down as one of the most confused and irrational administrations in the history of our country. Let history not record that Walter Hickel* was the only man in the crowd with a trace of moral courage.†

Yours ever,
Arthur

To Francis Burr‡

June 1, 1970

[New York, New York]

Dear Mr. Burr:

This is in response to your letter regarding the Corporation's search for a new Harvard president.

Let me offer a few thoughts; I hope their expression will not seem too blunt.

---

* Walter Hickel (1919–2010). Alaskan construction magnate; Republican governor of Alaska, 1966–69, 1990–94; secretary of the interior, 1969–70; fired in 1970 for criticizing Nixon's Vietnam policies.

† Schlesinger lunched with Kissinger on May 21, 1970, at the Metropolitan Club in Washington. "I have been thinking a lot about resignation," said Kissinger (according to Schlesinger's journal), but there were reasons why he could not resign immediately. It would be "dishonorable" for him to get out so soon after the Cambodian controversy. More important, he was engaged in something that he could not talk about but that only he could pursue and carry through and, if it worked, would justify his staying (the opening to Mao's China). About Nixon, Kissinger said, "He is a shy man, and he needs compassion."

‡ Francis Burr (1915–2004). Lawyer; longtime chairman of the Harvard Corporation; instrumental in the selection of Harvard Law School dean Derek Bok as Harvard University president in 1971.

1. The next president should have the intellectual respect of the faculty. Presidents Lowell and Conant had such respect; President Pusey, alas, did not, and this accounted for part of his troubles. Harvard has deteriorated as a university in recent years. Twenty-five years ago, it was far and away the best university in the country; now, in all manner of specific fields (such as my own), it is surpassed by one or several universities. It needs first-class intellectual leadership if it is to recover its past greatness. All this implies, I think, that the new president should be an academician, or at least someone who has proved himself in intellectual activity, whether in the library or the laboratory.

2. The next president should have the desire and capacity to keep in close touch with the students. I don't mean someone who will woo and appease the young, but someone who can convey the fact that he understands and sympathizes with their urgencies and frustrations; only such a man is in a position to check their excesses. My impression is that Kingman Brewster[*] and Bob Goheen[†] have both met this standard fairly well.

3. The next president should have demonstrated an instinct for public policy in the nation and the world so that he can on occasion speak out on matters of public moment beyond the university. In this regard I would mention Presidents Lowell and Conant again as models—not necessarily the views they expressed, but their willingness to express views. This criterion would argue for the appointment of someone with a measure of experience in government.

4. I would further suggest that the next president be appointed for a term—say ten years. The increased pace of social change and the multiplying pressures of educational leadership will drain most people by a decade; indeed, most university presidents in modern times have made their notable contribution in the first ten years. Also the stipulation of a ten-year term would widen the field of choice. Once we get over the notion that the candidate must be president for twenty or thirty years, then

---

[*] Kingman Brewster, Jr. (1919–88). Lawyer; law professor at Harvard, 1953–60; president of Yale University, 1963–77; outspoken critic of the Vietnam War; civil rights activist; ambassador to Great Britain, 1977–81.

[†] Robert Goheen (1919–2008). Taught classes at Princeton, 1939–57; president of Princeton, 1957–72; ambassador to India, 1977–80.

we can consider, for example, people in their late fifties who might well have ten good years of energy and leadership ahead of them.

5. You ask for "the names of specific individuals to whom consideration might be given." I recognize that I am not adding to your existing list when I say that, if something is done to limit the presidential term, Archie Cox would seem to me an excellent candidate despite his age. I say this without being altogether certain, however, whether he may have to some degree compromised himself by the mediatorial activities he has undertaken on behalf of the university.

Among younger candidates, I would strongly recommend Carl Kaysen[*] of the Institute for Advanced Study. I first met Kaysen in the Second World War and have worked closely with him in the years since both in academic life and in government. In my judgment, his brilliance and originality of mind, his capacity (demonstrated at the Institute) to exert leadership in the natural as well as the social sciences, his administrative control and drive, his rare mixture of intellectual toughness and humane concern—this combination of qualities is very much what Harvard needs if it is going to hit the comeback trail.

Sincerely yours,
Arthur

Dr. David Rothstein, a psychiatrist specializing in the study of assassins, invited Arthur to participate on a panel at an American Psychiatric Association meeting to discuss the "presidential assassination syndrome," identifying potential assassins as inadequate, isolated loners.

---

[*] Carl Kaysen (1920–2010). Economics professor at Harvard; deputy national security adviser in the Kennedy administration; headed Princeton's Institute for Advanced Study, 1966–76; MIT professor, 1976–2010.

To David Rothstein *

September 15, 1970

[New York, New York]

Dear Dr. Rothstein:

I appreciate your note, and I read the attached material with much interest. One of the problems involved, I suppose, is a natural difference of emphasis between the psychiatrist and the historian. The psychiatrist tends to believe that, if things happen to people, it is very often because, in some unconscious manner, they want these things to happen to them. Carried very far, this would lead to the proposition that Presidents who are killed became President in order to be killed. The historian, on the other hand, would tend to suppose that anyone becoming President in the United States must accept the risk of assassination as something inseparable from his office, and, if he is "assassination-prone," it is because of the nature of his office, not because of the repressed yearnings of his unconscious. This is really the situation suggested on page 12 of "The Assassin and the Assassinated"—that the behavior of Presidents "might indicate that the leader has come to terms with and accepts his own mortality."

I find much of value in the psychiatric approach to historical problems; but there is also what appears to be an almost inescapable tendency toward reductionism—i.e., toward the minimization of the objective, public problems a political leader must face and toward an exaggeration of the extent to which his public decisions represent the acting out of private fantasy. . . .

Sincerely yours,
Arthur Schlesinger, jr.

---

* Dr. David Rothstein (b. 1935). Staff psychiatrist at the U.S. Medical Center for Federal Prisoners in Springfield, Missouri, in mid-1960s; Chicago-based psychiatrist.

To Daniel Patrick Moynihan[*]

November 17, 1970

[New York, New York]

Dear Pat:

I have just got round to reading the President's bold statement denouncing pornography; and I note that he concludes with a quotation he ascribes to Tocqueville: "America is great because she is good—and, if America ceases to be good, America will cease to be great."

This doesn't sound like Tocqueville to me, whether on America or anything else. Are you fellows spending your time dreaming up Tocqueville quotations? Or if you, as the custodian of philosophical philosophy in the White House can tell me where one can find such a sentiment in Tocqueville, I will gladly send you my apologies![†]

Best regards,
Arthur

To Katharine Graham

December 10, 1970

[New York, New York]

Dear Kay:

I read the *Newsweek* take-out "In Search of a Foreign Policy" [December 14, 1970] with much interest; but I think its drift is mistaken, so I am writing this letter in the hope that you might want to reconsider before committing the magazine irrevocably to this foreign policy line.

The argument, I take it, is summarized in the conclusion—"the retrenchment implied by the Nixon doctrine[‡] may be a dangerous invitation

---

[*] Daniel Patrick ("Pat") Moynihan (1927–2003). Sociologist; Harvard professor; Democratic policy maker; assistant secretary of labor in Kennedy and Johnson administrations; counselor to President Nixon for urban affairs, 1969–70; called for "benign neglect" on black problems; ambassador to India, 1973–75; senator (D-N.Y.), 1977–2001.

[†] The so-called Tocqueville quotation was indeed a fake.

[‡] President Nixon enunciated the Nixon doctrine on July 25, 1969, at a press confer-

to the Soviet Union to test America's mettle." I don't want to get into the question whether Nixon really believes in the Nixon doctrine, which I doubt, or whether he is propagating it in an intelligent way, which he obviously isn't. I want to address myself to the *Newsweek* thesis that the contraction of our overseas military commitments will cause, as they say at the Pentagon, a loss in our credibility and thereby tempt the Soviet Union to new aggressions.

This argument seems to me in error—by about 180 degrees. Let us apply it to Vietnam. The *Newsweek* piece implicitly endorses the Nixon thesis about Vietnam. You will recall his deathless words:

> If we fail to meet this challenge, all other nations will be on notice that despite its overwhelming power the United States, when a real crisis comes, will be found wanting.
>
> And, again: if we don't make a stand in Vietnam, there will be a collapse of confidence in American leadership not only in Asia but throughout the world . . . . Our defeat and humiliation in South Vietnam without question would promote recklessness in the councils of those great powers who have not yet abandoned their goals of world conquest.

My guess is that Nixon—and *Newsweek*—are dead wrong in the implication that withdrawal from places where we do not have direct and vital interests would reduce our general credibility and embolden the USSR to new attacks. On the contrary, I would suggest that withdrawal of military commitment from Vietnam (and from other places beyond the range of our vital interest) would have precisely the opposite effects, that it would *increase* our credibility in those parts of the world where we have direct and essential interests.

After all, Vietnam has already done more than anything to wreck our military and political credibility. Our failure, with overwhelming superiority in numbers, airpower and artillery, to lick the badly outnumbered Viet

---

ence on the island of Guam, providing intellectual heft to his Vietnamization plan. Nixon assured his Asian allies that the United States would keep all its treaty commitments and provide protection in the case of nuclear threat, but in relationship to military defense he said that the United States "has a right to expect that this problem will be increasingly handled by, and the responsibility for it taken by, the Asian nations themselves" (supplied generously with U.S. military and economic aid).

Cong is hardly a striking testimonial to our military power and skill. And, if the only way we have to protect a country is to obliterate it, this does not do much for our credibility either: what other country would ever wish to be protected in the way we have protected South Vietnam? Moreover, the whole Vietnam adventure has long since reduced our political credibility, since very few people outside the United States can understand why in the world we think that the communization of Vietnam would be such a mortal threat to our security, and it is surely this—and not the thought that we might adjust our commitments to our capabilities—that has produced the worldwide erosion of confidence in American judgment and leadership.

Just as going into Vietnam (and comparable places) has produced the crisis of our military and political credibility, so getting out of Vietnam (and comparable places) would, I believe, help restore, and not further diminish, that credibility. Withdrawal would not abolish our military power or dissolve our nuclear arsenal. What it would do is to liberate that considerable proportion of our Army, Navy, Air Force defense funds and public attention that are currently bogged down in Vietnam. So long as we stick to the doctrine of keeping only enough armed force in being to fight one-and-a-half wars, the liquidation of the Vietnam fiasco would appear the only way by which we can regain tactical military credibility in other parts of the world. It is hard to suppose, for example, that Moscow or Cairo can take very seriously the prospect of serious American intervention in the Middle East so long as we remain deeply involved in Vietnam. As for our political credibility, the probability is that the world, seeing America at last come to its senses, would have after withdrawal greater, not less, confidence in American leadership.

The basic fallacy in the *Newsweek* thesis is that there is no alternative between global interventionism, on the one hand, and isolationism, on the other—that, if the United States declines to fight to the end in a part of the world where its vital interests are not involved, other nations, both our allies and our enemies, will conclude that we will not fight at all where our vital interests are involved. As soon as you think about it, I am sure you will see the error here. By this argument, once Russia withdrew its missiles from Cuba, where Russian vital interests were not involved, then the United States could have moved against Russia with impunity in Eastern Europe, where Russian vital interests are involved. *Newsweek* obviously never believed any such nonsense with regard to the Soviet Union. Why should

Newsweek now suppose that the rest of the world will believe it with regard to the United States? The fact that we leave places where we have no national reason for being in the first instance is hardly likely to persuade anyone that we will therefore abandon places where our national security is directly engaged.

In short, selective disengagement, far from constituting, as *Newsweek* thinks, an incitement to the Soviet Union to undertake new adventures, will be (if properly done) the only way by which the United States can recover the political and military credibility necessary to deter the Soviet Union from such adventurism.

Sorry to write at such length; but I really think some basic issues are involved. I hope to see you very soon.

Much love,
Arthur

To Joseph S. Clark[*]

January 5, 1971

[New York, New York]

Dear Joe:

Forgive my delay in answering your recent letter; but I have recently moved to a new place, and that plus Christmas has rendered me *hors de combat*. In assessing JFK and Vietnam, it is important to remember that Vietnam was really a marginal issue during most of his presidency. While he did increase considerably the number of American military personnel in South Vietnam, there were still many fewer troops there than, for example, in South Korea or in West Germany. Moreover, they were there not organized in American combat units but as advisors attached to units of the South Vietnamese army and government. The total number of Americans killed in Vietnam during the Kennedy presidency was 69. President Johnson hardly mentioned Vietnam in his first State of the Union message in January 1964; and in his second message a year later Vietnam received only

---

[*] Clark, the former senator from Pennsylvania, was now president of the World Federalists, USA.

brief mention towards the end of the message. As you note in your letter, serious escalation began with Johnson's 1965 decision to send American bombers to North Vietnam and American combat units to South Vietnam.

It would be presumptuous for anyone to claim to know what JFK would have done had he lived. I always had the most distinct impression, however, that his visit to Vietnam in the French days had left him with the definite conviction that it was impossible to enlarge the western presence very much without arousing all the power of nationalism against the white invader. I would find it hard to believe that he would have pursued the Johnson course; and I am sure that he would have been far more open to possibilities of negotiation. He thought, and often said, that we were "overcommitted" in Southeast Asia. I think it can be claimed with justification that RFK's speeches in 1965–68 represent the truest continuation of the JFK attitude toward Vietnam. As JFK showed at the time of the Bay of Pigs, he was quite prepared to cut losses and never felt that he had to prove his manhood by irrational bellicosity.

JFK's basic attitude toward foreign policy was best expressed, I think, in his speech at the University of Washington in November 1961 when he said:

> We must face the fact, that the United States is neither omnipotent nor omniscient—that we are only 6 per cent of the world's population—that we cannot impose our will upon the other 94 per cent of mankind—that we cannot right every wrong or reverse each adversity—and that therefore there cannot be an American solution to every world problem.

Let me know some time when you are in New York.

Yours ever,
Arthur

To Richard Schickel*

March 11, 1971

[New York, New York]

Dear Dick:

Not having read the Trumbo† book,‡ I have no idea what views Trumbo attributes to me about congressional committees; but I would certainly not, on general principles, advise you to accept him as an authority on what I think.§ For the record, I was, of course, a persistent public critic of the House Un-American Activities Committee, the McCarthy Committee and all the rest; indeed, I was attacked by McCarthy in a nationwide broadcast in 1952. As for testifying before committees, the proper course seemed to me, then and now, a matter of conscience. If, after rigorous search of conscience, one decided to cooperate, OK. I did not (and do not) feel inclined to make lofty moral judgments in either case. I must confess that I never felt there was transcendent moral heroism involved in taking the 5th Amendment rather than owning up to one's political view; but there was never any doubt about the legal right to do so.

What troubles me most in your letter is the implication that Stalinism was somehow "a matter of taste" (to borrow the phrase Molotov used about

---

* Richard Schickel (b. 1933). Author of books on American film; longtime movie critic for *Time* magazine.

† Dalton Trumbo (1905–76). Screenwriter; member of the Communist Party, 1943–48; one of the "Hollywood Ten" blacklisted for refusing to testify before HUAC; imprisoned for eleven months for contempt of Congress; won two Oscars under pseudonyms; openly resumed screenwriting career in 1960; wrote the novel *Johnny Got His Gun* (1939) and films including *Gun Crazy, Roman Holiday,* and *Spartacus.*

‡ *Additional Dialogue: Letters of Dalton Trumbo, 1942–1962,* ed. Helen Manfull (New York: M. Evans, 1970).

§ In *Additional Dialogue,* Trumbo published a letter to the editor of the *Saturday Review of Literature* written in 1949 attacking Schlesinger. Schlesinger had called Trumbo a fellow-traveling, ex-proletarian Hollywood hack in the July 16, 1948, edition of the magazine. Trumbo responded: "Wherever inquisitorial courts have been set up, Mr. Schlesinger and his breed have appeared in eager herds to proclaim: 'I do not wish to imply approval of your questions, but I am not now nor have I ever been a dissenter. I am not now nor have I ever been a trade unionist. I am not now nor have I ever been a Jew. Prosecute those who answer differently. O master, silence them, send them to jail, make soap of them if you wish. But not of me, for I have answered every question you chose to ask, fully, frankly, freely—and on my belly.'"

Nazism after the Stalin-Hitler pact). Stalinism involved the defense of exceedingly cruel and squalid realities. My regret about what happened to Trumbo was always tempered by the thought of what he would have done to liberals and democrats if he had ever been in any position of power. You have seen *The Confession,*[*] so I won't labor this point; but that, to members of my generation, is what Trumbo stood for. . . .

Sincerely yours,
Arthur Schlesinger, Jr.

To Reinhold Niebuhr

March 15, 1971

[New York, New York]

Dear Reinhold:

I think you should know that Jim Loeb, as toastmaster at the ADA Roosevelt Day dinner on March 11, surpassed himself in the grace and eloquence of his opening remarks. He reminisced for a moment about the beginning of ADA and concluded with a superb tribute to you. The audience was deeply stirred and moved.

It was a good dinner. Jack Gilligan,[†] the new governor of Ohio, gave a most thoughtful and interesting speech.

Life staggers on here in New York. We were all greatly saddened (as I know you and Ursula were) by Adolf Berle's death. There was a good memorial service, bringing out everyone from Lionel Trilling to Jim Farley.

In spite of my desire to retire from politics, I find myself somewhat involved in George McGovern's presidential campaign. I worked closely with McGovern when he ran the Food for Peace program for President Kennedy in 1961–62 and have seen a good deal of him in the years since. He grows steadily; he is right on nearly every issue; and, the more impact he has, the more likely the Democratic party is to end up with a reasonably liberal

---

[*] *The Confession,* or *L'aveu,* directed by Costa-Garvas, is about oppression by a Communist regime during the Stalinist period.
[†] John J. ("Jack") Gilligan (b. 1921). Democratic governor of Ohio, 1971–75; administrator of the U.S. Agency for International Development, 1977–79, father of President Obama's secretary of health and human services, Kathleen Sebelius.

candidate and program, even if it may not be McGovern himself. (Also, McGovern is the only American historian in the running!) I don't know how you feel about 1972, and would fully understand it if you prefer to wait before making up your mind; but we are forming a national committee for McGovern (under the chairmanship of John Douglas,* Paul's very able son), and nothing would please us more than if you cared to join it.

Love to Ursula.

Yours ever,
Arthur

A young PhD candidate named Rodney M. Sievers† wrote Arthur in the spring of 1971, asking him to answer a series of questions about Adlai Stevenson for his doctoral dissertation at the University of Virginia. Years later, Sievers published his dissertation as a book, The Last Puritan? Adlai Stevenson in American Politics.

To Rodney M. Sievers

May 19, 1971

[New York, New York]

Dear Mr. Sievers:

I will do my best to answer your questions about Governor Stevenson. As you probably know, John Bartlow Martin is writing a biography of Stevenson based on his papers. It should be finished soon; and it will doubtless throw light on some of your problems.

1. Stevenson was, I think, conservative by instincts and rather liberal by intelligence and conscience. The 50s were not a propitious time for the declaration of new and original ideas in social policy; but it must be re-

---

* John Douglas (1921–2010). Head of Justice Department's Civil Division, 1963–66; partner at Covington and Burling; human rights activist; son of Democratic senator Paul Douglas (D-Ill.).

† Rodney M. Sievers (b. 1943). Author of *The Last Puritan? Adlai Stevenson in American Politics* (1983).

membered that Stevenson was the first politician to raise the issue, as he did in the 1956 campaign, of the "quality of life" in America. He was neither so liberal nor so free in his thought about social questions as, say, the Kennedys. But as JFK used to say, when people criticized Stevenson's indecision to him, one never knew what Stevenson might have been like had he been elected President instead of having been twice defeated. Had Stevenson achieved the presidency, I think he would have been less conservative than his own instincts might have preferred.

2. I always felt that Stevenson's protestations of dislike for campaigning were partly a put-on. He enjoyed politics, he enjoyed campaigns and he thought that Eisenhower had been a mediocre president. In addition, it must be remembered that Eisenhower's sickness in 1955 made the question of his reelection seem less certain when Stevenson decided to go for the nomination.

3. Stevenson's instincts, as suggested above, were somewhat conservative; and, as a state governor, he had a certain mistrust of Washington. On the other hand, he recognized intellectually that the national government was the only institution that could do certain things that society badly needed to have done. I always felt that, like other governors translated to the White House, he would have acquired a different view of the proper distribution of power between state capitols and Washington.

4. My strong impression is that Stevenson's thoughts on Vietnam were very much in flux at the time of his death. He had more or less gone along with Vietnam policy until the Dominican intervention. He regarded this as a mistake; and his dissent there made him begin to wonder whether the Johnson administration had any better idea of what it was doing in Southeast Asia. I know that a letter was released after his death declaring support for the Vietnam policy on the ground that it was necessary to stop the expansion of China; but he did not personally write that letter, and I don't know how much he really believed it. He had already been active in seeking out openings for negotiation, and I have no doubt that he would have continued that course.

5. Stevenson, as you suggest, had a mixed view of the human condition; and that certainly was one reason for his fascination with Lincoln. He was an exceptionally gay and witty man, but the gaiety and wit sprang from a

certain vein of melancholy. I always felt that the childhood tragedy—which he never mentioned but probably could never forget—accounted in part for his occasional moments of somberness.

6. Stevenson was, in a sense, an incomplete man—because, as Kennedy commented, one never knows what he might have been like had he become President. He did not have the clear, purposeful views of the Kennedys—nor of FDR either—about the challenge and excitement of the future. He was rather a decent, old-fashioned American of unusual style and intelligence and a certain personal ambition who wanted to affect history and humanize his country. I believe he would have risen greatly to the opportunity of the presidency and might have struck out on new courses; but defeat, in a way, ended his life, and in his later years one often had the sense that he was only going through the motions.

I hope this may be of some help.

Sincerely yours,
Arthur Schlesinger, Jr.

Arthur's friend and mentor Reinhold Niebuhr, the Christian realist who infused moral purpose with a sense of political realism, died on June 1, 1971, after a long illness. He had taught Arthur that wisdom comes with the humble recognition of the limits of our knowledge and our power. "The righteous know they are not righteous," he had preached. But humility must temper, not sever, the nerve of action.

Arthur attended Niebuhr's funeral in Stockbridge, Massachusetts, and later reported the events to his English friend Isaiah Berlin.

To Isaiah Berlin

June 21, 1971

[New York, New York]

Dear Isaiah:

Just a line to say that I have passed your note along to Ursula. Joe Rauh and I drove up to Stockbridge for the funeral (and returned with the Trillings in the back seat). It was a lovely, clear, sunny day, and the service was held in the church of which Jonathan Edwards had been pastor two centuries and a half before. Of course, Reinhold's death was in a sense a deliverance, since he had had a very bad winter. Ursula seems OK and is planning, I think, to go to England for a time.

We are bound shortly for Aspen, where we will see the Nabakovs and, I fear, ... Mortimer Adler;* then, about July 20, to Washington through Labor Day. Alas, we will not get to Europe this summer unless some television corporation comes through with a dramatic offer.

I have just received a four-page letter from Joe Alsop demanding to know why I support George McGovern and saying, "If we lose the game of Russian roulette, it will pretty surely mean the end of our own kind of society, and indeed, the end of freedom just about everywhere." Life was easier in that tranquil time when Joe stopped speaking to me!

Alexandra† joins me in sending love to you both.

Yours ever,
Arthur

---

*Mortimer Adler (1902–2001). American philosopher and educator; sought classical-based education; encouraged the publication of fifty-four "Great Books" of the Western world; served on the board of Encyclopaedia Britannica; wrote about religious experiences; established the Institute for Philosophical Research.

†Alexandra Emmet Allan (b. 1936). Schlesinger's second wife; daughter of William Temple Emmet, a stockbroker and descendent of Thomas Addis Emmet, the Irish-American lawyer and brother of the Irish patriot Robert Emmet. Her mother was Mrs. Alston Boyd, better known as Lily Cushing, a painter and daughter of Howard Gardiner Cushing (1869–1916), the celebrated portraitist who lived in Newport, Rhode Island. A graduate of the Shipley School and Radcliffe College, Alexandra married Schlesinger on July 9, 1971, following his divorce from his first wife, Marian, in 1970. Alexandra's first marriage to Donald Allan ended in divorce; Alexandra and Donald's son, Peter Allan, was born in 1963.

To Joseph Alsop

July 19, 1971

[New York, New York]

Dear Joe:

This is a belated answer to your letter of some weeks back. Why do I believe that the defense budget can be cut, and why do I back George McGovern?

I believe the defense budget can be cut because nearly all the officials I know who have dealt with the budget in their time—former Secretaries of Defense, of the Army, of the Navy, of the Air Force—believe that it can be cut. Per a detailed exposition of possible cuts, you might want to take a look at the analysis by Robert Anthony,* who was Comptroller and Assistant Secretary of Defense 1965–68, in the National Urban Coalition's *Counterbudget* . . . or at Morton Halperin's[†] testimony of June 10, 1971, before the Defense Subcommittee of the House Appropriations Committee. I don't think that, on the track record, there is much future in letting the service chiefs determine unilaterally the defense requirements of the United States. Obviously they will ask for all the traffic can bear, but this does not prove they are right.

As for McGovern, I think he has earned his right to have views on defense matters. As you know, he was a real enough hero as a bomber pilot in the Second World War.[‡] I don't put too much stock in pre-presidential declarations. Any man elected President in 1972 will revise his pre-inaugural utterances if he can be convinced that he was wrong. So I am not worried about what McGovern would do if elected. He is an intelligent and realistic man.

---

* Robert Anthony (1916–2006). Professor at Harvard Business School for more than forty years; innovator in the field of management accounting.

† Morton Halperin (b. 1938). Foreign policy analyst; head of the American Civil Liberties Union Washington office; deputy assistant secretary of defense in the Johnson administration; wiretapped by the FBI while serving on Henry Kissinger's National Security Council staff; head of policy planning in the State Department, 1998–2001; father of notable political TV writer and analyst Mark Halperin.

‡ McGovern volunteered for the U.S. Army Air Forces, becoming a B-24 Liberator pilot and flying some thirty-five missions over German-occupied Europe; he was awarded a Distinguished Flying Cross for making a hazardous emergency landing of his damaged plane and saving his crew.

I fear this won't persuade you!—but I hope it will do until we meet, which I trust will be shortly. Alexandra has not yet quite recovered from double pneumonia, so our social life will be restricted for a little while; but we shall count on seeing you very soon. She joins me in sending love.[*]

Yours ever,
Arthur

To George J. Buscaglia[†]

October 27, 1971

[New York, New York]

Dear Mr. Buscaglia:

Thank you for the letter and your birthday greetings.

Your point that the moral case for the Vietnam war was altered by changes in the nature of the war is, of course, quite right; and I was wrong in suggesting a contradiction between earlier moral justifications and current moral condemnations. As for the question of war crimes, I do not think that the charge of waging aggressive war can be profitably raised. Few of those who wish to place Johnson on the dock on this ground were equally zealous to prosecute the North Koreans for invading South Korea or the Russians for invading Hungary and Czechoslovakia or the Indians for invading Goa. That particular charge has, I think, fallen since Nuremberg through disuse. As for atrocities and torture, these should, in my judgment, be pursued up through the chain of command as far as they reasonably can. . . .

Sincerely yours,
Arthur

---

[*] Alsop was a great friend and admirer of Alexandra's mother, Lily Cushing, and knew Alexandra as an infant.

[†] George J. Buscaglia. Longtime letter writer to Schlesinger; regularly sent news clippings of articles about Schlesinger and other items of interest; worked in the sales department of *The Buffalo News* in Buffalo, New York.

In his November 11, 1971, New York Times column, entitled "The Rehnquist Dilemma," Tom Wicker argued that rejecting William Rehnquist* for a seat on the Supreme Court solely because of his conservative political views would be "dangerous business" that would politicize courts, punish individuals for their ideas, and lead to Republican retaliation.

Arthur could not disagree more.

To Tom Wicker

November 12, 1971

[New York, New York]

Dear Tom:

I am sure you thought about the problem carefully before you wrote the column of November 11 on the dangers of politicizing the Supreme Court; but, speaking as an historian, I must register a strong dissent. The argument that the Senate should pay no attention to the political philosophy of prospective justices has no warrant in history and very little, so far as I can see, in logic. The Court is of course and inevitably an instrument of politics and policy. As Tocqueville wrote long ago, "Scarcely any political question arises in the United States that is not resolved, sooner or later, into a judicial question." It would be totally unrealistic to ignore this fact, and, indeed, the Senate never has. You can't depoliticize the Court at this late date by pretending that political philosophy is irrelevant. There is very little more relevant than political philosophy (I *don't* mean party affiliation)—particularly when, as in the case of Rehnquist, the man may be there for the next thirty years. . . .

I only bother to write, of course, because I admire your column 90 per cent of the time and therefore am unhappy about what seem to be lapses!

Best regards,
Arthur Schlessinger, Jr.

---

*William Rehnquist (1924–2005). Conservative Republican lawyer; U.S. Supreme Court associate justice, 1972–86; chief justice of the United States, 1986–2005; dissented in the Roe vs. Wade decision that legalized abortion; favored prayer in schools, the death penalty, and states' rights.

At its national convention in Miami Beach in July 1972, the Democratic Party nominated Senator McGovern for president and Senator Thomas Eagleton* of Missouri for vice president. But after the convention, when it was reported that Eagleton had undergone electroshock therapy for depression, he was forced to withdraw, and R. Sargent Shriver of Maryland replaced him as vice presidential nominee.

McGovern's statement that he backed Eagleton "1,000 percent" a few days before accepting his resignation dogged McGovern for the rest of the campaign.

To Marietta Tree

August 17, 1972

[New York, New York]

Darling M.:

It was great to hear from you. We have had rather a ragged summer. It began auspiciously enough with the baby[†] (whom we have named after those two eminent revolutionaries, Robert Emmet[‡] and Robert Kennedy) and with the Miami Beach convention, which was great fun. But on our return from Florida the baby developed an obstruction in his stomach which required an operation. As soon as he recovered from that—he is fine now—my mother came down from Cambridge to inspect her new grandson, and then she suffered a heart attack. She seems OK now too, though she is still in the hospital at Southampton (we were at East Hampton) and anything like this is disturbing at the age of 86.

This is all apart from the Eagleton imbroglio, which has badly interrupted the momentum of the campaign and done much general damage. I do not despair, however. . . . I am particularly confident that, if nothing else, Nixon's personal entrance into the campaign will begin to reverse the tide. In any case, I am sure things will be much closer than they appear at

---

* Thomas Eagleton (1929–2007). Liberal senator (D-Mo.), 1968–87.

† Robert Emmet Kennedy Schlesinger was born on June 27, 1972. "Odd how this is by far the most exciting human experience," Arthur noted in his journal.

‡ Robert Emmet (1778–1803). Irish patriot and orator from a wealthy Protestant family; led revolt against British rule in 1803; captured, tried and executed; his older brother Thomas Addis Emmet immigrated to the United States and served as the New York State attorney general and was Alexandra Schlesinger's forefather.

present. After all, with all McGovern's troubles, the party is in a much better situation than it was after Chicago four years ago, and Humphrey only lost by 400,000 votes.

I don't know whom George might have in mind for Secretary of State, but I would not be surprised if Frank Church would not receive the most serious consideration.

We are off to Aspen on Sunday for a fortnight of serious thinking. . . . Back after Labor Day—and I hope to see you soon thereafter.

Much love,
Arthur

At the height of the 1972 presidential campaign, Israel's ambassador to the United States, Yitzhak Rabin,* lavishly praised the Nixon administration's support for Israel, telling one interviewer: "While we appreciate support in the form of words from one camp, we prefer support in the form of deeds that we are getting from the other camp."

To Nicolas Nabokov

October 16, 1972

[New York, New York]

Dear Nicolas:

. . . When you see Isaiah [Berlin] and [Teddy] Kollek,† I hope you will communicate to them in the most severe possible terms that leading Democrats are irritated beyond description by the gross and impertinent Israeli intervention in the presidential election. If Kollek says that we shouldn't worry because Rabin will be recalled in November, tell him that to expect

---

* Yitzhak Rabin (1922–95). Israeli military strategist; Labor Party politician; ambassador to the United States, 1968–73; prime minister, 1974–77 and 1992–95; assassinated by right-wing extremist opposed to the 1993 Oslo agreement giving formal Israeli recognition to the Palestine Liberation Organization (PLO).

† Theodore ("Teddy") Kollek (1911–2007). Mayor of Jerusalem, 1965–1993; bridge builder between Arabs and Jews; preached racial and religious tolerance while in office.

us to be satisfied by the recall of Rabin after the election is in itself an expression of contempt for our intelligence. So long as Rabin remains here and continues his pro-Nixon line, we can only assume that he is executing the instructions of his government. I ran into him the other night at Lally Weymouth's. He looks like the air force general played by Sterling Hayden[*] in *Dr. Strangelove*[†] and was absolutely unrepentant in his praise of the Vietnam War, his admiration for Nixon and his hatred of American intellectuals, especially Ken [Galbraith] on whose "stupidity" he made a hysterical attack.

As you may remember, I accepted an invitation to go to Israel this winter and deliver a lecture; but I am reaching the point where I think I will cancel it. It is shortsighted on the part of the Israeli to permit Rabin to pursue this course; it is absurd for them to suppose that a Democratic administration will be less solicitous about the safety of Israel than a Republican administration; and it is shocking that they should feel entitled to intervene this way in internal American politics.

So pass the word along—and give Isaiah my love. See you soon.

Yours ever,
Arthur

Nixon trounced McGovern, winning more than 60 percent of the popular vote and capturing every state but Massachusetts. The Republicans characterized McGovern as the candidate of "acid [LSD], amnesty [for draft evaders], and abortion," a heady brew, spooking Middle America.

McGovern telephoned Arthur the day after the election, saying: "Nixon is really a diabolical son-of-a-bitch. He knows all the ways to divide the country—and to profit from division. . . . He has been using code words to hit the racial nerve all through the campaign—'welfare,' 'crime,' 'quotas,' and so

---

[*] Sterling Hayden (1916–86). Well-known movie actor in Westerns and films noir; briefly member of the Communist Party; cooperated with HUAC; acclaimed for playing crazed general Jack D. Ripper in *Dr. Strangelove.*
[†] *Dr. Strangelove or: How I Learned to Stop Worrying and Love the Bomb,* directed by Stanley Kubrick; a 1964 black comedy about a deranged U.S. general who orders a nuclear attack on the USSR, forcing the United States and Russian presidents to try to recall or shoot down the U.S. planes to prevent a nuclear holocaust.

on. . . . I wonder what would have happened if [George] Wallace* *had been able to run on his own. I think we would have won."*

To Everett M. Sims[†]

December 15, 1972

[New York, New York]

Dear Mr. Sims:

Thank you for your recent letter. I trust that with the Third Edition *The National Experience*[‡] will begin to hit the road back.

I recently received a copy of a Harcourt, Brace book, the second edition of *Twentieth-Century America: Recent Interpretations,* edited by B. J. Bernstein[§] and A. J. Matusow.[¶] The book was sent to me because it contains a piece of mine on "Origins of the Cold War" and, in the introductory note to the piece, I find, along with much tendentious argument, the following sentences: "Staying with the Johnson administration for six months after Kennedy's death Schlesinger at first ardently defended the administration's policy in Vietnam. Not until late in 1966 did he publicly dissent from the continued escalation of the war."

In case there should be a third edition, I would like to make the following points. I resigned from my White House job the day after President Kennedy's death. At his successor's urgent request, I agreed to stay on for the transition. I resigned again on January 25, 1964, and the resignation was accepted with alacrity.

As for the statement that I "ardently defended" the Johnson administra-

---

* McGovern was suggesting that the Democrats would have won the presidency if Wallace had run on a third-party ticket in 1972 as he had in 1968.

† Everett M. Sims. Director, College Department, Harcourt Brace Jovanovich publishers.

‡ John M. Blum, Bruce Catton, Edmund S. Morgan, Arthur M. Schlesinger, Jr., Kenneth M. Stampp, and C. Vann Woodward, *The National Experience: A History of the United States* (New York: Harcourt, Brace and World, 1963), an American history textbook.

§ Barton J. Bernstein (b. 1936). Professor of American history at Stanford; revisionist historian of the Cold War; blamed the United States for initiating it.

¶ Allen J. Matusow (b. 1937). History professor at Rice University.

tion's policy in Vietnam (checking back to the first Bernstein-Matusow edition, I see that "ardently" was added in the second edition; escalation!) until "late in 1966," this conveys a quite mistaken impression of my attitude and activities. During most of 1964 and 1965 I was writing *A Thousand Days*. On May 15, 1965, I did participate in a teach-in in Washington. I replaced Mac Bundy, at his personal request, but made it clear to him and to the audience that I was not speaking for the administration. The text of my remarks is to be found in *Teach Ins: U.S.A.*, Louis Menashe,[*] pp. 165–171. I began by criticizing the State Department White Paper on Vietnam. I then challenged both the policies of "precipitate withdrawal" and of further escalation. In spite of the Bernstein-Matusow assertion that I did not publicly dissent from the continued escalation of the war until late in 1966, I said the following in May 1965:

> The second possible policy is enlargement of the war. I hope I need spend no time here explaining why this seems to me the tragically mistaken course. I will save that lecture for the Air War College. Air power alone cannot win this war. Widening the war with the idea of somehow "winning" it would mean the extensive commitment of American ground forces—perhaps, as Hanson Baldwin[†] has said, 1 million troops. It would require our forces to fight in terrain much more difficult than Korea, with much more vulnerable lines of communication and supply. It would very possibly provoke the entry of Communist China, with its inexhaustible reserves of ground forces. It would force the Soviet Union to declare itself within the Communist empire and give major assistance to Hanoi. It might even temporarily revive relations between Moscow and Peking. And behind all this would be the possibility that, as the warfare inevitably intensified in intensity, one side or the other might be tempted to nuclear war. For all these reasons, it seems to me the course of enlargement must be rejected.

I then defended the policy of negotiation, which I said I took to be the administration policy, while at the same time dissenting from methods

---

[*] Louis Menashe. History professor, the Polytechnic Institute of New York University.
[†] Hanson Baldwin (1903–91). Military editor of *The New York Times* for forty years; won a Pulitzer Prize in 1943 for his coverage of World War II.

taken by the administration to induce negotiation. I opposed the bombing of North Vietnam but did (I regret to say) favor "a limited increase in our ground-force commitment in South Vietnam" as a means of moving Hanoi toward negotiation. Insofar as I defended the Johnson administration, it was on the theory, stimulated by LBJ's Johns Hopkins speech of April 7, that "the administration has negotiation at the forefront of its policy in Vietnam." I was abysmally mistaken in this; but it is obvious that my remarks did not constitute an "ardent" defense of "continued escalation of the war."

In addition, I attacked the escalation policy repeatedly in public lectures in the winter of 1965–66; and I published articles against escalation in *Look* (August 9, 1966); *New York Times Magazine* (September 18, 1966); and the *Saturday Evening Post* (August 13, 1966).

One does not expect accuracy or fairness from New Left historians; but I would like to correct this record.

Sincerely yours,
Arthur Schlesinger, jr.

To the Editor of *The American Historical Review*

[February 1973]

[New York, New York]

To the Editor:

. . . In the hope of reducing gratuitous confusion, I would make a proposal for terminological precision.

This proposal first arose in my mind when I participated in a session on the American election of 1948 at the 1971 AHA[*] convention. Younger historians in the discussion gave considerable, and unsympathetic, attention to the anticommunism of Americans for Democratic Action and other liberals in that period. It was readily apparent that "communism" and "anti-communism" meant something very different for historians born after 1940 from what these terms had meant to liberals who were active in the 1940s.

---

[*] American Historical Association.

When younger historians hear the word "communism," the image that flashes into their minds is that of the Vietcong, or of the Chinese Communists, or of Castro and Che Guevara.* They think in terms of a fragmented and polycentrist communist world in which communism has its vivid meaning as a spearhead of popular-nationalist efforts to reclaim political and economic independence. When they hear the word "anticommunism" the image is one of counterrevolutionary intervention in the interests of foreign holders of political and economic power.

It is obviously a temptation to transport these contemporary images back a quarter of a century and suppose that this was what "communism" and "anticommunism" meant then. But this is not at all what anticommunist liberalism had in mind when they condemned communism in 1948. Communism had a clear and specific meaning for them: it meant Stalinism. My terminological plea is simply that historians writing about America in the 1940s replace the words "communism" and "anticommunism" by the more precise words "Stalinism" and "anti-Stalinism." (If the historians who have rather righteously condemned the "anticommunism" of the forties were to have used instead the word "anti-Stalinism," their writings might perhaps have lost some of their piquant flavor of moral superiority.) . . .

It may be that the younger scholars think that anti-Stalinism is reprehensible, too. But in the interests of historical clarity, they should at least acknowledge that it is a different thing from the latter-day, messianic anticommunism they tend to read back into the forties. If we could agree to call Stalinism Stalinism and anti-Stalinism anti-Stalinism, we would at least know what we are talking about.

Arthur Schlesinger Jr.

---

* Che Guevara (1928–67). Medical doctor; Argentine Marxist revolutionary; guerilla leader during Cuban Revolution; top official in Castro regime; author of *The Motorcycle Diaries* (1993), which was made into a film in 2004; killed in Bolivia leading a Communist insurgency

To Jason Epstein*

April 30, 1973

[New York, New York]

Dear Jason:

I found Gore [Vidal's] novel† most engaging and enjoyable. The historical atmosphere is well rendered; I have only a few minor suggestions.

I think the best thing ever said about [Aaron] Burr‡ was said by Jackson—"Burr is as far from a fool as I ever saw, and yet he is as easily fooled as any man I ever knew" (Marquis James, 117)—and Gore's portrait of himself as Burr catches a good deal, though, out of understandable partiality, not quite all of this. The Burr's-eye portraits of Washington, Jefferson and Hamilton are all eminently plausible as coming from Burr (and have some further plausibility, especially in the case of Jefferson, on their own merits).

Gore succeeds most artfully in weaving in random characters and incidents of the time—so much so that I began to wonder what it all reminded me of, and I finally remembered: G. A. Henty,§ the favorite reading of my boyhood, whose heroes were always at the right spot with the right people at the right time. I do think, though, that he missed a couple of tricks. Philip Nolan—the man without a country—was exiled because of his participation in the Burr conspiracy, and it might have been amusing to have borrowed him from Edward Everett Hale¶ and introduced him into the

* Jason Epstein (b. 1928). Influential New York publishing figure; longtime editorial director of Random House; helped introduce paperbacks into book industry; cofounder of the fortnightly *New York Review of Books*.

† Gore Vidal, *Burr: A Novel* (New York: Random House, 1973). Fictional biography of roguish American politician Aaron Burr.

‡ Aaron Burr (1756–1836). Lawyer and politician; senator from New York, 1791–97; U.S. vice president, 1801–5; killed Alexander Hamilton in a duel in 1804; arrested for treason in 1807 for trying to set up an empire in the Southwest; later acquitted of charges.

§ G. A. Henty (1832–1902). Prolific English novelist; author of 122 books; wrote historical adventure stories about young boys living in troubled times.

¶ Edward Everett Hale (1822–1909). American author of some sixty books and short stories, most famously the story "The Man Without a Country" about Philip Nolan, who was tried for treason as part of the Aaron Burr conspiracy, renounced the United States, and was condemned to live on shipboard the rest of his life, but reembraced his country just prior to his death.

narrative. And I think Gore should certainly have brought in John Van Buren,[*] who, by the book's genealogy, would have been Burr's grandson and had, much more than his father, the charm, imperiousness and recklessness of the old adventurer. Maybe Lannie, I mean Charlie Schuyler,[†] could come back to the United States in a sequel and help the Van Burens in the 1848 campaign (at which time Gore might also want to explore the idea, which I believe to have been technically possible, that both Lincoln and Jefferson Davis[‡] were illegitimate sons of John C. Calhoun).

I should add that much as I admire the historical reconstruction and much as I enjoyed the book, I do not want to be quoted on it. It would be unseemly after all the things Gore has written about my dearest friends (as well as about me).[§] . . .

Best regards,
Arthur

On October 12, 1973, President Nixon nominated Gerald Ford[¶] as vice president under the terms of the Twenty-Fifth Amendment, replacing Spiro Agnew, who had resigned over corruption charges.

Arthur did not think that Ford was presidential material and advised George McGovern to think hard before voting on the appointment.

[*] John Van Buren (1810–66). American lawyer and politician; New York State attorney general (1845–47); son of President Martin Van Buren; antislavery activist.

[†] Charles Schuyler. The hero "narrator" of Vidal's novel; an apprentice in Burr's law firm who gets caught up in Burr's complicated schemes and faces an agonizing dilemma over his loyalty to Burr.

[‡] Jefferson Davis (1808–89). Senator (D-Miss.), 1847–51, 1857–61; president of the Confederacy, 1861–65; imprisoned in 1865 for two years by the Union; stripped of his eligibility to run for office; later urged reconciliation between the North and the South.

[§] Schlesinger escorted a drunken Vidal out of a White House dinner dance in November 1961 at the request of several members of the Kennedy family. Vidal held that incident against Schlesinger (and Robert F. Kennedy). See Vidal's "The Holy Family," in *Esquire*, April 1967, on his antipathy toward the Kennedys.

[¶] Gerald Ford (1913–2006). Conservative representative (R-Mich.), 1949–73; served eight years as House Republican minority leader; thirty-eighth U.S. president 1974–77; pardoned Richard Nixon; pursued détente with the Soviet Union.

To George McGovern

October 15, 1973

[New York, New York]

Dear George:

. . . Congress has been going on for years about its desire to reclaim its role in the constitutional order. Now, offered a patently unqualified man for the Vice Presidency, it apparently cannot wait to confirm him for no other reason than that he has been one of their own for a quarter of a century. The fact that Gerald Ford is a man of unchallenged mediocrity, that he has been an unswerving hawk in foreign policy and a total reactionary in domestic policy, that he is remembered only for practicing cheap deceits in connection with campaign contributions and for trying to impeach Bill Douglas, that no Republican convention has ever considered him of presidential caliber and that he was nominated by Nixon for Vice President for the reason that he would not be acceptable to any rational American as President—if Congress ignores all this, ignores in addition all its own fine words about improving the system of vice presidential choice and sweeps Ford through just because he is one of the boys, then it will be hard to take very seriously all those splendid protestations about the congressional desire to play a serious and responsible role in the American system.

Remember, for heaven's sake, that you are not confirming a minor cabinet official—even there Gerald Ford would very likely be over his head—but a Vice President, and you may very well be giving Nixon his strongest argument against his own impeachment.[*]

Best regards,
Arthur

On June 17, 1972, during the presidential campaign, a break-in took place at the Democratic National Committee headquarters in the Watergate office complex in Washington, and five men were arrested. The FBI connected cash found on the burglars to a slush fund used by the Committee for the Re-Election

---

[*] Ford was confirmed by both branches of Congress and took office on December 6, 1973.

*of the President (CREEP). As evidence mounted against the president's staff, Nixon began firing his closest aides. In May 1973, Attorney General Elliot Richardson** appointed a special prosecutor, Archibald Cox, to investigate the burglary. During the Senate Watergate hearings in June, it was revealed that a secret audiotaping system existed in the Oval Office and the Cabinet Room. Cox immediately subpoenaed the tapes—which could reveal a cover-up orchestrated by the president—but Nixon refused to release them, citing executive privilege.*

On October 20, 1973, Nixon demanded the resignations of Richardson and his deputy for refusing an order to fire Cox and inveigled Solicitor General Robert Bork† to fire him in what became known as "the Saturday Night Massacre."

Within days, Arthur had composed a letter to the chairman of the House Judiciary Committee, Peter Rodino, who would manage any impeachment hearings, alerting him to historical precedents.

To Peter W. Rodino‡

October 26, 1973

[New York, New York]

Dear Congressman Rodino:

One point that you and members of your committee may want to consider making to your colleagues and to the press is that, whatever merit in certain circumstances a presidential claim of executive privilege may have, that claim is automatically and totally dissolved when the House undertakes an inquiry with a view to the exercise of its constitutional power of impeachment. This means, among other things, that, if the White House continues to withhold information necessary to the exposure of lawless be-

---

* Elliot Richardson (1920–99). Lawyer; Massachusetts Republican politician; secretary of health, education, and welfare, 1970–73; secretary of defense, 1973; attorney general, 1973; secretary of commerce, 1976–77.

† Robert Bork (1927–2012). Lawyer; legal scholar; solicitor general, 1973–77; judge for the U.S. Court of Appeals for the District of Columbia Circuit, 1982–88; his 1987 nomination to the Supreme Court by President Reagan was rejected by the Senate.

‡ Peter Rodino (1909–2005). Liberal representative (D-N.J.), 1949–89; chairman of the House Judiciary Committee; oversaw impeachment hearings leading to Nixon's resignation in 1974.

havior, it may leave the Congress no alternative but to use the impeachment process to open up the files of the executive branch.

I would suggest that the following passage from James K. Polk's message to Congress of April 20, 1846, be emblazoned in large letters in your hearing room:

> It may be alleged that the power of impeachment belongs to the House of Representatives, and that, with a view to the exercise of this power, that House has the right to investigate the conduct of all public officers under the Government. This is cheerfully admitted. In such a case the safety of the Republic would be the supreme law, and the power of the House in the pursuit of this object would penetrate into the most secret recesses of the Executive Departments. It could command the attendance of any and every agent of the Government, and compel them to produce all papers, public or private, official or unofficial, and to testify on oath to all facts within their knowledge.

Sincerely yours,
Arthur Schlesinger, jr.

W. Averell Harriman was to be the guest of honor at a major Democratic Party dinner at the Sheraton Park Hotel in Washington in May 1973 and asked Arthur for some ideas for his speech. Franklin Roosevelt, Jr., Margaret Truman Daniel, Jackie Kennedy Onassis, and Lynda Bird Johnson Robb would be there, along with 750 prominent Democrats and their spouses. Averell would be accompanied by his glamorous new wife, Pamela Churchill Harriman,* whom he married after the death of Marie in 1970.

Arthur had a longstanding previous engagement and would miss the star-studded fest, but he gamely offered up some useful remarks to his old friend, now eighty-two and still very sharp.

---

* Pamela Churchill Harriman (1920–97). English-born socialite; Democratic Party activist; U.S. ambassador to France, 1993–97; married to Winston Churchill's son, Randolph, 1939–46; married to Broadway producer Leland Hayward, 1960–71; married to W. Averell Harriman, 1971 to his death in 1986.

To W. Averell Harriman

April 30, 1974

[New York, New York]

Dear Averell:

It sounds like an historic evening on May 15, and I wish to hell we could come. Unfortunately the annual dinner of the Arthur and Elizabeth Schlesinger Library at Radcliffe—the library on the history of women in America established in honor of my father and mother—takes place in Cambridge on the 15th; and (especially since this may be the last year my mother, who is 88 and in frail health, may be able to come) we must go there. I do look forward to seeing you and Pam in Kansas City on May 11.

As for your remarks at the dinner, you generally know better than anyone else what it might be appropriate to say. I was glad to note that the *New York Post* picked up your use of the FDR quote about "moral leadership" in its report of the Four Freedoms dinner. But it occurs to me that you might want to use your four Presidents to illustrate a general theme. It would be hard, with LBJ, to use the theme of moral leadership. But I wonder whether a good theme, especially in view of our present leader, might not be that of presidential willingness to take responsibility.

[Draft remarks] Andrew Jackson once said that the President must be "accountable at the bar of public opinion for every act of his Administration." This sense of accountability is the essence of democracy. The Presidents whose families grace our dinner tonight were men diverse in background, temperament and style. But they had two great things in common: they were devoted to liberal ideals, and they took responsibility for the actions of their administrations. Nothing will carry us more quickly from a constitutional Presidency into a personal autocracy than the idea that the man we elect President can dodge responsibility for the things his administration does.

I (WAH) well remember FDR's press conference when he set up the Advisory Defense Council in December 1940. "The Constitution," FDR said, "states one man is responsible. Now that man can delegate, surely, but in the delegation he does not delegate away any part of the responsibility from the ultimate responsibility that rests on him." Later he was asked, "Mr.

President, just to what extent can you divest yourself of responsibility?" He answered, "I can't, under the Constitution."

It was in this same spirit that President Truman kept that little sign on his desk that said: "The buck stops here." It was in this same spirit that President Kennedy after the Bay of Pigs fiasco told his press conference, "I'm the responsible officer of the Government." Lest anyone miss the point, JFK had Pierre Salinger[*] put out a press statement a couple of days later saying: "President Kennedy has stated from the beginning that as President he bears sole responsibility. . . . He has stated it on all occasions and he restates it now. . . . The President is strongly opposed to anyone within or without the administration attempting to shift the responsibility." (Get Jack Valenti[†] to give you a comparable statement from LBJ.)

These Presidents accepted responsibility because they were strong, mature and honorable men and because they understood that accountability is the heart of free government. They would have been chagrined and appalled by the spectacle of one of their successors dishonoring the White House by making a presidential career of buck-passing and the rejection of his personal and constitutional responsibility—a President who blames everyone but himself for the acts of his closest advisers, from the making out of his income tax to the burglary at Watergate. The sign on Mr. Nixon's desk must read: "The buck *never* stops here." What this nation needs is a return to honorable leadership in the White House—a return to the spirit of FDR, HST, JFK, LBJ—a return to the idea of the President of the United States not as a man trying to sneak away from the obligations he has assumed but as a man who understands and acts on the principle that leadership in a free state requires decency, candor and the courage to accept responsibility.

You might also want to quote FDR's advice on speechmaking: "Be sincere; be brief; be seated."

---

* Pierre Salinger (1925–2004). Journalist; TV commentator; White House press secretary for Presidents Kennedy and Johnson; ABC correspondent in Europe, 1976–90.
† Jack Valenti (1921–2007). Special assistant to President Johnson, 1963–66; president of the Motion Picture Association of America, 1966–2004.

I hope this may be of some slight help; but long experience persuades me that your instincts on these occasions are much better than mine!

Alexandra joins in love to you both.

Yours ever,
Arthur

In May 1974, impeachment hearings began before the House Judiciary Committee, chaired by Congressman Rodino. On August 8, the Supreme Court voted 8–0 to reject President Nixon's claim of executive privilege. Nixon resigned from office the next day to avoid impeachment and was replaced by his vice president, Gerald Ford.

President Ford in September 1974 appointed George H. W. Bush* to be the first chief of the United States Liaison Office to the People's Republic of China. A former Republican congressman from Texas who had served as ambassador to the United Nations, Bush was a friend of Arthur's. His father was the late Prescott Bush, who represented Connecticut in the Senate; George's sister, Nancy Ellis,† was a resident of Concord, Massachusetts, and a social friend.

* George H. W. Bush (b. 1924). Representative (R-Texas), 1967–71; ambassador to the United Nations, 1971–73; ambassador to China, 1974–75; director of Central Intelligence, 1976–77; U.S. vice president, 1981–89; forty-first U.S. president, 1989–93; ordered invasion of Panama and later Kuwait in the first Gulf War; father of President George W. Bush.

† Nancy Ellis (b. 1926). Longtime liberal Democrat who joined the Republican Party when her brother George H. W. Bush ran for president.

To George H. W. Bush

September 9, 1974

[New York, New York]

Dear George:

Warmest congratulations! I can't imagine a more challenging job. I had my 16th birthday in Peking 41 years ago; and, if it is still as enthralling a city as it was then, you are in for a fascinating time.

Best regards,
Arthur

P.S. At some point you should get together with my onetime in-laws (and still dear friends) John Fairbank and his wife, Wilma. Between them they can give you and Barbara the best possible briefing.

Joseph Alsop announced in early fall 1974 that he was giving up his syndicated column. His final column appeared on December 30, 1974, four months before the fall of Saigon.

To Joseph Alsop

October 1, 1974

[New York, New York]

Dear Joe:

I read the news of your decision with great regret. It cannot be said that I have totally agreed with every word you have written in the last decade; but your column has been part of one's life all the same, and I feel that an epoch is coming to an end. I know, though, that you have contemplated this for a long time and that you have other fields to cultivate and other books to write.

We are sorry to learn too that you have sold the house, in which all of us have had such delightful times and of which we will forever have happy memories. What are your plans now? Alexandra will be calling you in due course (as soon as she can get organized) to invite you to a dinner for Jean[*] and Steve Smith,[†] who have just moved to 62nd Street and are thus once again in our neighborhood. In the meantime, love from us both.

Yours ever,
Arthur

On June 11, 1974, Secretary of State Kissinger held a press conference in Salzburg, Austria, in which he threatened to resign over charges that he had initiated a wiretapping program that intercepted calls of seventeen government officials and journalists. Kissinger insisted the program was used only to stop national security leaks. He demanded that his name be cleared.

From Henry Kissinger

Not for Publication

October 20, 1974

[Washington, D.C.]

Dear Arthur:

I have just read in Sunday's *Washington Post* excerpts from an article written by you for the *NEA Journal* entitled, "The (Expletive Deleted) Language of Politics." It is a brilliant article.

Nevertheless, I am compelled to register the strongest possible objection to the reference to me contained therein. To be specific, you say "Watching Henry Kissinger babbling about his honor at his famous Salzburg press conference, one was irresistibly reminded of another of Emerson's nonchalant observations: 'The louder he talked of his honor, the faster we counted our spoons.'" That statement is made in the context of a contention by you that " . . . words, divorced from objects, became instruments

---

* Jean Kennedy Smith (b. 1928). Sister of President Kennedy; ambassador to Ireland, 1993–98; played a key role in Northern Ireland peace process; philanthropist; married Steve Smith in 1956.

† Steve Smith (1927–90). Oversaw Kennedy family investments; campaign manager for 1968 Robert F. Kennedy and 1979–80 Edward Kennedy presidential races; shrewd behind-the-scenes operative.

less of communication than of deception. Unscrupulous orators stood abstractions on their head and transmuted them into their opposites. . . . "

I find your statement, coming as it does from someone I had considered to be a long-time friend, unfair in the extreme. My honor is important to me, and I make no apology for having made that fact clear. It has been important to me throughout the past six, sometimes difficult, years. It is a personal thing, not lightly to be referred to by me and certainly not lightly to be challenged by others.

I will not debate whether I have achieved anything of merit since I entered the Government. That is a judgment I am content to leave to history. But I do believe I have conducted myself honorably, and that I have kept in close touch with the liberal community and my liberal friends. I have, I believe, sought their advice and counsel frequently and with good will. Nor have I indulged in public attacks against them. Thus, I find it increasingly difficult to accept or countenance the growing wave of what I can only describe as McCarthyism of the left. I find it particularly difficult to accept in good grace from someone so clearly and so nobly identified with the fight against the McCarthyism of another era.

Sincerely,
Henry Kissinger

To Henry Kissinger

November 5, 1974

[New York, New York]

Personal

Dear Henry:

I regret that my reference caused you distress. On reflection, I should not have written "babbling"; "going on" would have been sufficient. For the rest, I must confess that I still stand with Emerson.

We have known each other for a long time. I think you will agree that I have displayed my friendship and admiration for you on more than one occasion over the years. So I will write with the candor that an old friendship deserves. I have some sense of the pressures you have been under and refrained for a long time from any form of criticism. I did not, for example, join in the rush to judgment of some of our former Harvard colleagues in 1970. Watergate made such abstinence more difficult. I thought your plea early on for compassion for Haldeman[*] and Ehrlichman[†] was most distasteful, especially in the cause of an administration that had never shown any compassion for anyone. At Salzburg you brought up your honor and in effect demanded from Congress an unconditional vote of confidence if you were to stay in office. The outsider can only feel that it is a remarkably flexible and tenuous conception of honor which permitted you to serve, and on occasion to defend, a crooked President and lawless administration for so many years. I do not quarrel with your decision to stay with Nixon; I can see strong reasons for it; but I don't think it was a decision that would have led a prudent man thereafter to make a big deal of his honor. Nor, as a matter of simple manners, did I much like your Salzburg outburst. Would Dean Acheson, whom we have both admired, ever have made a statement of that sort? Honor was for him a deeply private concern. Though his honor was impugned a good deal more mercilessly than yours has ever been, he never went public on it.

What I felt in your Salzburg remarks—and feel even more, I must frankly say, in your letter—is that you seem almost to have come to suppose that any criticism of you is indefensible. I hope fervently that this is not the case. You have enjoyed the most consistently favorable, not to say enraptured, press of any maker of American foreign policy in this century. I don't think anyone has been more generally exempt from criticism. It is hardly seemly, when criticism at last begins, for you to start talking about "the growing wave of McCarthyism of the left." Don't you think it is possible for informed, disinterested and responsible people to have legitimate disagreements with some of your policies—or even to doubt that a man who put up with Nixon for five years is well advised to make thereafter a great public issue of his honor?

Anyway I am sorry that it has come to this. I wanted to write to you at

---

[*] H. R. ("Bob") Haldeman (1926–93). J. Walter Thompson executive for twenty years; White House chief of staff to President Nixon, 1969–73; imprisoned for eighteen months in Watergate scandal for perjury and conspiracy.

[†] John Ehrlichman (1925–99). Lawyer; counsel and assistant for domestic affairs to President Nixon; jailed for eighteen months in Watergate scandal for obstruction of justice and perjury.

the time of your marriage. Nancy* is a lovely girl of high intelligence and dignity, and we both wish you years of endless happiness.

The above is what is primarily on my mind. Your time is taken up with pressing matters, and the rest of this letter can wait for a moment of leisure. But, since communication has been reopened after several years, I might as well take opportunity of the situation to address myself to a couple of other points.

My first is minor but, I fear, symptomatic. The other day I read an AP despatch from New Delhi (printed in the *New York Post* on October 29) reporting you as having said that the United States at last had abandoned its Cold War opposition to neutral states. You are quoted as calling this a "new American view" and saying that it should have been adopted long since. You are further quoted as saying that "support of national independence and of the diversity that goes with it has become a central theme of American foreign policy." This seems to me a quite extraordinary distortion of history—and especially unseemly in the city where Ken Galbraith and Chester Bowles had spent years making the same point. You surely must know that this view was not some bold and original innovation of the present administration but had been put forward strongly and consistently by the Kennedy administration a considerable time ago. Take a look, for example, at JFK's speech at Berkeley on March 23, 1962, and you will find the isms point, practically in the words you adopted a dozen years later: "The revolution of national independence is a fundamental fact of our era. . . . Diversity and independence, far from being opposed to the American conception of world order, represent the very essence of our view of the future of the world," and so on. What is the point of making the claim you reportedly made in New Delhi, apart from the imminence of an election in the United States? Does not honor enjoin a decent respect for history? The New Delhi matter is, alas, symptomatic of a general view of things, which suggests that detente was a courageous invention of Richard M. Nixon—as if Kennedy's American University speech, for example, or Johnson's bridge-building effort had never taken place.

One further point, on which I perhaps owe you an explanation. On

---

* Nancy Kissinger (b. 1934). Longtime aide to New York governor Nelson Rockefeller; philanthropist; second wife of Henry Kissinger.

September 18 last I gave a lecture at Long Beach, California—a rather prosaic disquisition on the Presidency. In the question period someone asked me whether I thought President Ford should appoint a cabinet of his own. I said that there had been two models in recent times: Truman, who had replaced most of Roosevelt's cabinet, and Johnson, who had kept most of Kennedy's cabinet; and that I thought Truman was right in wanting his own men in the cabinet. I was asked whether I would include the Secretary of State in this proposition. I said that I did not think the world would come to an end if there were a new Secretary of State. This began as a rather technical question at the end of a long evening; but I should not have been surprised at the headline in the *Los Angeles Times* the next morning: SCHLESINGER URGES FIRING OF KISSINGER. The wire services picked up the *Times* story, and I guess it appeared across the country. While I stand by my general proposition, I am sorry that an impression was created that I was trying to incite some sort of campaign against you. If President Ford should reconstitute his cabinet, as I think on the whole he should, you would be, in my view, at the end of the list for replacement.

You may nevertheless be interested in knowing why I think the world would not come to an end if you ceased being Secretary of State. Though I cannot feel, despite the "close touch" you believe you have kept with the "liberal community," you really care all that much what your liberal friends think, I might as well take this occasion to set down at least what I think. I think you have been effective with the Russians and the Chinese. I also think you have done an extraordinary job in the Middle East. Whether or not the arrangements eventually hold, you have moved the situation much farther than anyone could have expected. I also think you have performed nobly, against disagreeable opposition within our own government, in the area of nuclear arms control.

On the other hand, I cannot but feel that you are a good deal more patient and tolerant with adversaries than with friends and more concerned with political and military issues—the issues that mainly concern our adversaries—than with the economic, commercial and monetary issues that preoccupy our friends. I do believe that our international economic policy has been a shambles, that our United Nations policy has been a disgrace, that our Latin American policy has been a disaster and that our European policy has been amazingly insensitive and ineffectual.

Beyond all this, I cannot but feel that our foreign policy in recent years has removed the United States from what historically has been the source of our greatest impact on mankind. We have most influenced the world as a nation of ideals, conveying a sense of hope and a faith in democracy—as in the times of Wilson, of FDR, of Kennedy. It may well be said that such hope was often delusory and that it often concealed a tough sense of American self-interest. Yet it also sustained such values as democracy and freedom in hard times and helped move the planet marginally toward a larger justice. In any case the United States surely has mattered most when it has made a difference to the thinking not just of foreign offices but of people. The conception of world affairs as a chess game played by foreign secretaries contains an instinctive preference for authoritarian states, where governments can be relied on to deliver their people, as against democracies, where people might always turn on their governments.

The Nixon administration thus aligned the United States with the colonels in Greece, with the generals in Brazil and Chile (though not in Peru, where the generals lacked suitable reverence for American business), with the dying dictatorship in Portugal as well as with the despots in Moscow and Peking. I feel that this policy has gone far to sever the bonds that once existed between the United States and the democratic aspirations of ordinary people around the world. If we are in trouble now with successor regimes in Greece and Portugal, for example, it is the predictable and predestined result of a policy that ran counter to the oldest and best American impulses. No doubt we will in due course reap the harvest of this pro-authoritarian policy in Brazil, Chile and elsewhere. I would like to think that this point had been made to you by those in the liberal community with whom you have been in such close touch.

Forgive the bluntness with which I express myself. My affection for you is too deeply rooted to disappear; with age one understands that disagreements over policy and even over manners are part of life and should not destroy personal relationships. In recent years even Dean Rusk and I have become friends again. You, as an old and valued friend, are entitled to a candid dissent. I hope you do not continue to feel that I am, as your letter asserts, a McCarthy of the left because I express that dissent publicly.

Sincerely yours,
Arthur

To Jo-Ann E. Molnar[*]

January 27, 1975

[New York, New York]

Dear Ms. Molnar:

Thank you for your letter. My hope is that Watergate will have a chastening effect on all the elements in our political order and will help keep the presidency within constitutional bounds for a long time to come. Or at least this will be the case if the American people carry forward the work of secularizing the presidency. Let us never forget, as Lord Acton said, that "there is no worse heresy than that the office sanctifies the holder of it."

Best of luck on your paper.

Sincerely yours,
Arthur

While continuing his teaching at the City University of New York, Arthur began working on a biography of Robert F. Kennedy. Granted unrestricted access to RFK's personal papers by Ethel Kennedy[†] and the Kennedy family, Arthur drew on diaries, letters, aide-mémoire, and oral histories, and carried out his own personal interviews. The book would become a sort of sequel to A Thousand Days, *though the earlier book was a personal memoir and this one a biography.*

To Daniel Patrick Moynihan

May 2, 1975

[New York, New York]

Dear Pat:

. . . Before we lunch on RFK, I wish you would think about the following question. One great puzzle for me is how a father as powerful, demand-

* Jo-Ann E. Molnar of Garfield, New Jersey.
† Ethel Kennedy (b. 1928), Widow of Robert F. Kennedy; mother of eleven children; human rights activist.

ing and determined as Joe Kennedy not only failed to crush and destroy his children but succeeded in giving them a strength and independence of their own. My question is: is there a difference between Irish Catholic and Protestant families that explains why Kennedy apparently helped his children while Churchill and Roosevelt, two incomparably greater men, pretty well ruined theirs?

Yours ever,
Arthur

Arthur believed that the Central Intelligence Agency as constituted was a danger to American democracy. He shared his thoughts on reforming U.S. intelligence operations with former CIA director John McCone,* under whose administration outdated and illegal operations had continued without his knowledge.

To John McCone

January 7, 1976

[New York, New York]

Dear John:

Thank you for your letter, and also for the copy of your remarks before the Business Council. I shall look forward to your testimony before the Church committee and hope your office will put me down for a copy of that.

Your proposal that there should be periodic review of all covert operations seems to me eminently sensible and might have spared us a lot of trouble had it been enforced a dozen years ago—if, that is, one can assume that CIA officials will tell everything they are doing even to their own Director. One of the most disconcerting elements in the Church committee's *Assassination* report is that Bissell and Helms withheld from you any infor-

*John McCone (1902–91). Republican politician; businessman; chairman of U.S. Atomic Energy Commission, 1958–60; director of Central Intelligence, 1961–65; adviser to President Kennedy during the Cuban missile crisis.

mation about the Castro assassination project. It seems quite unreasonable to suppose that, if they would not tell you, they would tell Robert Kennedy and the President. And pledge them not to mention it to you? It is disconcerting also that Bissell and Edwards made their initial contact with the mob without telling Allen Dulles anything about it.

Still, it seems to me absolutely essential to preserve a strong and imaginative intelligence service, including a covert action capability. The problem is to reassure Congress and the press that there is a way to prevent a repetition of the excesses of the past.

Best regards,
Arthur

In late 1975, Arizona congressman Morris Udall* announced that he was seeking the Democratic presidential nomination. As a longtime progressive legislator, he was immediately the leading liberal candidate in the race, and Arthur became one of his major backers. But Udall, a tall (six foot five), Lincolnesque figure with a self-deprecating wit, would lose to Jimmy Carter† in the primaries.

To Morris Udall

March 18, 1976

[New York, New York]

Dear Mo:

I am sorry I can't make the meeting on Friday (I have to lecture in Illinois), but I am asking Dick Wade to hand you this letter.

I wonder whether it would not be sound politically as well as morally to make more of an issue of foreign policy? [Scoop] Jackson stands for a sys-

---

*Morris ("Mo") Udall (1922–98). Progressive representative (D-Ariz.), 1961–91; leading liberal candidate for Democratic presidential nomination in 1976.

† James Earl ("Jimmy") Carter, Jr. (b. 1924). U.S. Naval officer; peanut farmer; centrist Democratic governor of Georgia, 1971–75; thirty-ninth U.S. president, 1977–81; negotiated Panama Canal Treaty and Camp David Accords; reelection derailed in 1980 by Iranian hostage crisis; later founder of the Carter Center dealing with human rights; winner of 2002 Nobel Peace Prize.

tematic revival of the Cold War, and Carter seems to be moving in that direction. It would not be true to say that the Cold War is over; but I am sure that a lot of people in this country see no alternative to the effort to develop areas of agreement with the Soviet Union and are alarmed by the present recoil from detente.

You might well say that detente has been oversold. Detente does not, as the Republicans have told us, represent a broad solution of the question between ourselves and the Soviet Union. The Russians understand it to mean specific and limited agreements, and we must understand it the same way. But specific and limited agreements are essential to moving the world toward peace. It would be fatal to turn our back on this effort. We must stand for detente without illusions.

Nor is it correct to say that detente has made the United States a second-class power. This is sheer demagoguery. In fact, those who say it don't believe it themselves because in the next breath they cry that we should start throwing our weight around and tell other people they had better shape up or else. We are still militarily the most powerful nation in the world. (Paul Warnke or other people in Washington can get you the figures on this.) And the greatest danger that faces the world is a spiraling arms race, piling overkill on overkill, a race that can only end in nuclear war. That is why the policy of saber-rattling is so dangerous and the policy of arms control so essential. A hard line in Washington will produce a hard line in Moscow. Jackson would generate his Soviet mirror image. The result would only be to increase tensions and to set the world back perhaps fatally in the battle for peace.

I think that, if you could identify yourself as the candidate who stands realistically for the persisting search for peace, you would find much support. The Cranston Resolution* points the direction. The fact that Jackson decided to become a co-sponsor shows that he feels his own vulnerability in this area. This is the issue that might above all differentiate you from Jackson and Carter.

I would, if I may, add a point on domestic policy. There are two great economic concerns: jobs and prices. We Democrats tend to concentrate on

---

* The Cranston Resolution, introduced by Senator Alan Cranston (D-Calif.) in 1976, would have required the president to obtain approval from Congress before initiating any first use of nuclear weapons.

jobs. That is natural and right, but it should not exclude equal concentration on prices. Inflation hurts the poor and the pensioners more than it hurts the rich. It was always wrong to let the Republicans make inflation their issue. You are prepared for this, because you are the only one of the candidates who has spoken about the need for standby controls in sectors of the economy where market forces do not determine prices. Perhaps you could make more of this and say at every opportunity that not only jobs for all who wish to work but stable prices are the two essential goals of economic policy. Here is an FDR quote: "Let me be frank in saying that the United States seeks the kind of a dollar which a generation hence will have the same purchasing and debt-paying power as the dollar value we hope to attain in the near future" (1933). That should continue to be the Democratic party's objective.

Best regards,
Arthur

To Ursula Niebuhr

May 24, 1976

[New York, New York]

Dear Ursula:

. . . I think that the recent primaries show a clear unease about Carter, but he has already accumulated the major share of delegates and will be hard to stop. I am of two minds about him. He has, I believe, intelligence of a high order; he is obviously a gifted politician; he would come to office unencumbered, owing nothing to Strauss,[*] Meany[†] and the other obsolescent panjandrums of the party; and, most important of all, he is the only candidate to ring any kind of bell in the black community. Racial justice seems to me our most important issue; and I value anyone—especially a

---

[*] Robert Strauss (b. 1918). Lawyer; influential conservative Texas Democrat; chairman of the Democratic National Committee, 1972–77; U.S. trade representative, 1977–79; ambassador to Russia, 1991–93.

[†] George Meany (1894–1980). Powerful leader of the AFL-CIO, 1955–79, representing some fifteen million union members; advocated neoconservative foreign policy; favored the Vietnam War and distrusted the USSR; antagonistic toward the liberal wing of the Democratic Party.

southern governor—who can command a measure of confidence among low-income blacks as well as low-income whites. I am not too greatly concerned about his present position on issues; I think his intelligence will carry him to sensible solutions, even despite his regressive anti-government prejudices. On the other hand, he seems to me a humorless, ungenerous, cold-eyed, crafty, rigid, sanctimonious and possibly vindictive man. I guess, even with that, I would prefer the risk of Carter to the dreary certitude of Humphrey; but cannot doubt the risk. Udall would be the best, but I don't suppose that he or Church have much chance. Brown[*] seems to me a Carter with a sense of humor. I think Ted Kennedy would make the best president, but I would shudder at the ugliness and danger of the campaign. . . .

Let us know when you are making more than a hit-and-run visit to our noble if decaying city.

Love,
Arthur

On May 2, 1976, Arthur wrote a piece for The Washington Star, *warning voters to steer clear of Reagan and Carter as politicians too sure of God's purposes. In fact, Arthur argued, the "Founding Fathers were determined to keep religion out of politics."*

To Charles Fahy[†]

May 25, 1976

[New York, New York]

Dear Judge Fahy:

I very much appreciate your thoughtful letter. When I wrote that the Founding Fathers "were determined to keep religion out of politics," I did

---

[*] Edmund Gerald "Jerry" Brown (b. 1938). Democratic governor of California, 1975–83, 2011–present; son of Governor Pat Brown of California; longtime quixotic candidate for president.
[†] Charles Fahy (1892–1979). Lawyer; New Dealer; solicitor general, 1941–45; judge of the U.S. Court of Appeals for the District of Columbia, 1949–79; helped desegregate the U.S. military.

not, of course, mean to imply that they regarded politics as divorced from morality, or that most of them did not feel that morality was most reliably based on religion faith. What I meant was that they did not care for personal religious avowal as a form of political appeal or sanction. Not only did they leave God out of the Constitution, but Washington, as the Convention's presiding officer, permitted no religious invocations and, when Franklin moved that the Convention pray for divine guidance, his motion was defeated.

As for the Declaration of Independence, the formulation there—"the Laws of Nature and of Nature's God"—seems to me significant and rather deistic than Christian in its emphasis. As Carl Becker[*] put it in his chapter on the philosophy of the Declaration, the 18th century had "deified Nature and denatured God" (*The Declaration of Independence*, 51). Theirs was essentially natural rather than supernatural religion. . . . [Note] the Treaty with Tripoli, negotiated during the Washington administration, signed on June 7, 1797; Article XI of that treaty states "the Government of the United States of America is not in any sense founded on the Christian Religion."

I would not disagree that religion was "an important element in the birth of the United States and in her political life." But I do not think that the Founding Fathers wished to make religion an active factor in politics. Perhaps I overreacted to Reagan and Carter; but I guess I was exasperated by Carter's invocation of Reinhold Niebuhr for applications of religion to politics that Niebuhr would have abhorred. I knew and loved Niebuhr. He was one of the great intellectual influences on my life (and my reading of his views is confirmed by a letter from his widow applauding the column). I think Carter should run on his own merits, which are considerable, and not on a claim to a special relationship with the Almighty. Politics and morality are inseparable; but public religiosity is by no means a guarantee of moral character. Think of Nixon!

Lest I appear to sail under false colors, I should comment on your last paragraph. I do have, I hope, "reverence for the Almighty" in the sense that I believe man should be humble before mysteries in life beyond the human capacity to understand, and I value the idea of an Almighty as a symbol of these mysteries. I also have found greater wisdom and instruction in the Christian analysis of human nature and of history than anywhere else. And

---

[*] Carl Becker (1873–1945). American historian at Cornell University; wrote primarily about the founding era of the United States and on the Enlightenment.

I believe with Chesterton[*] that the trouble when people stop believing in God is not that they thereafter believe nothing but that they thereafter believe anything. Yet the tepid Unitarianism in which I was reared has long since dwindled away and left me personally in a state that can perhaps be best described as Christian agnosticism. . . .

Ever sincerely yours,
Arthur

To John Warner[†]

July 28, 1976

[New York, New York]

Dear John:

I am writing to comment on *America at the Movies.*[‡] . . .

As historical consultant for the film, I must at once declare an interest. But this experience also enables me to testify that those who made the film were highly sensitive from the start to the importance of portraying the diversities of American life. They were also, however, confronted by the dismal fact that the American film has been characteristically stereotyped, condescending and very often mean-spirited in its representation of blacks, women, Indians and other groups.

The purpose of *America at the Movies,* as we understood it, was to offer a faithful picture of the way fiction films have rendered the American experience—not a faithful picture of that experience per se. As the commentary clearly says, it is an exercise in dream, not in history. . . . The AFI-ARBA[§] contract say[s] that the film was to be an "expression of the

---

[*] G. K. Chesterton (1874–1936). English writer of philosophy, poetry, plays, journalism, biography, art criticism, and fiction; author of Father Brown detective series.

[†] John Warner (b. 1927). Secretary of the navy, 1972–74; moderate senator (R-Va.), 1979–2009; briefly married to film star Elizabeth Taylor; appointed by President Ford to direct the American Revolution Bicentennial Administration, 1974–76.

[‡] *America at the Movies.* A 1976 documentary produced by the American Film Institute (AFI) that compiled scenes from eighty-three U.S. films in five different segments: "The Land," "The Cities," "The Families," "The Wars," and "The Spirit"; narrated by Charlton Heston.

[§] American Film Institute-American Revolution Bicentennial Administration.

American experience and spirit, *as captured and revealed by seventy-five years of American motion pictures.*"

For most of these seventy-five years movies have, alas, been sexist and racist. So have the American people, most of them. After earnest discussion, the makers of the film decided that they would be false to their obligation if they tried to show American movies as different from what they were. We did decide to suppress, as much as possible, vicious stereotypes and to seek out positive moments when they could be found. But we would have been dishonest if we had put together a film that portrayed Hollywood movies over the last seventy-five years as pro-black, pro-Women's Liberation, pro-Indian, and so on. One really cannot quarrel with history.

A final point: I particularly regret the attack on the motives and integrity of the fine artists who wrote and played in the touching and disturbing scenes from *Claudine* and *Raisin in the Sun*. It makes as much sense to regard these scenes as anti-black as it would to regard *An American Tragedy*, for example, as anti-white.

Sincerely yours,
Arthur Schlesinger, Jr.

From Lillian Hellman

[Handwritten]

[no date]

[New York, New York]

Dear Arthur—

It was, of course, no surprise that you would agree with Kramer,[*] nor would I have cared.

---

[*] Hilton Kramer (1928–2012). Chief arts editor and arts critic for *The New York Times*, 1965–82; cofounded the neoconservative publication *The New Criterion* in 1982; became a columnist for the conservative *New York Post* in 1990s, often criticizing *The New York Times* for liberal bias. Kramer wrote a controversial essay in the October 3, 1976, *New York Times* entitled "The Blacklist and the Cold War," attacking Lillian Hellman's political views and her defense of the Hollywood Ten.

But in my cricket book you don't sit next to people at dinner in apparent friendship and not tell them that you have publicly embraced their attacker.*

My regrets,
Lillian

To Lillian Hellman

[Handwritten]

20 October 1976

[New York, New York]

Dear Lillian:

Honestly!—I have supposed through the years (a) that our friendship assumed the exclusions of the political disagreements of another age and (b) that politics is such an inferior part of life that the more important things survive political disagreement.

You have always known how I felt, and feel, about Stalinism. No doubt we still differ as to whether one had to choose *either* Stalinism *or* McCarthyism, or whether it was not only possible but necessary to take one's stand against both.

I have never felt it necessary to interrupt a friendship I value to go into disagreements which we both know exist. As for the other night, I had forgotten my note to Kramer and did not suppose it was going to appear in the *Times*—though I have no objection to their having printed it. Though you may now hate me, I will continue to regard you with unrelenting affection and admiration for your charm, wit, inexorable human dignity and the passion that has produced so much including, I suppose, your letter to me. Forgive me if I hurt you. I did not intend to do so—but I cannot repeal my convictions any more than you can. And I would hope that, in the future as in the past, we will continue to be friends in that more essential 80 per cent of life.

Arthur

---

*"I wish Hilton Kramer's article could be made required reading for everyone born after 1940," Schlesinger wrote in a letter to *The New York Times* praising Hilton Kramer's piece.

From Lillian Hellman

[Handwritten]

[no date]

[New York, New York]

Dear Arthur—

That's the nicest note I ever had. I have no serenity. I'm just tired; of me and most others.

In the end, on Election Day, Arthur could not bring himself to vote for a man who believed that Adam and Eve once existed and that Eve was literally made out of Adam's rib. He left the presidential space blank.

Jimmy Carter and Minnesota senator Walter Mondale* narrowly defeated President Gerald Ford and Senator Robert Dole† of Kansas in the 1976 presidential election.

---

*Walter ("Fritz") Mondale (b. 1928). Liberal senator (D-Minn.), 1964–76; opposed the Vietnam War; U.S. vice president, 1977–81; Democratic presidential candidate, 1984; ambassador to Japan, 1993–96.

† Robert ("Bob") Dole (b. 1923). Representative (R-Kans.), 1961–69; senator, 1969–96; Senate majority leader, 1985–87, 1995–96; Senate minority leader, 1987–95; Republican vice presidential nominee, 1976; presidential nominee, 1996.

Except for the fact that Ronald Reagan is president, Schlesinger enjoys the 1980s. He holds his professorship at City University of New York, writes a column for *The Wall Street Journal,* appears on television news and documentary programs, travels around the world making speeches, and at the end of the day relishes a stiff drink and a good party.

The Conservative Reaction

1977–92

To Henry Kissinger

January 17, 1977

[New York, New York]

Dear Henry:

Jack Plumb* tells me that he has invited you to present the Samuel Eliot Morison Award next September to the best work published in 1976 by an American author about American history. This is the first year of what we hope will be the most celebrated award in the field; and I want to add my own strong personal hope that you will consider doing this. I can't imagine a better way to get the Morison Award off to a distinguished start. After all, when everything is considered, you remain (I believe) an historian at heart. So do think about it seriously.

While I am writing, let me add a few words of my own. I have had periods of disagreement with your conduct of foreign affairs during these last years—sometimes acute disagreement, as over what seemed to me the undue protraction of the Indochina War. But I do want to thank you for the way you have steadily illuminated and elevated the discussion of foreign policy, for your indomitable skills as a negotiator, for your (general) good

---

* Sir John Harold ("Jack") Plumb (1911–2001). Influential British historian at Cambridge University; author of more than thirty books, primarily on eighteenth-century British history; acclaimed for lecturing in all but three states in the United States.

humor under criticism and for the creative directions in which you have pointed policy in the last years—in SALT,[*] in the Middle East, in Africa, [and] in Latin America. Historians will have to reckon with your proconsulship for the rest of our lives.

We look forward to seeing you and Nancy at Brooke Astor's.[†]

Yours ever,
Arthur Schlesinger, Jr.

To Al Capp

February 23, 1977

[New York, New York]

Dear Al:

I had a nice talk with your sister the other day, and she told me that you have been falling victim, like the rest of us, to the various infirmities of age and high living. I just want to take this occasion to note that I have always regretted the way our paths have diverged in recent years[‡] and to say that I have not forgotten the happy times in the 1950s when we tried to crack television together and [*Li'l*] *Abner* was a musical and Eisenhower was hitting golf balls and you were bringing a new and unlikely spirit to Brattle

---

[*] Strategic Arms Limitation Talks, between the United States and the Soviet Union.

[†] Roberta Brooke Astor (1902–2007). Progressive-minded American philanthropist; New York socialite; married three times; her third marriage was to Vincent Astor, 1953–59. After his death she ran the Astor Foundation; her only child (from her first marriage) was later convicted of grand larceny for stealing from her bank accounts while she was ailing.

[‡] A supporter of Adlai Stevenson in the 1950s, Capp, a contrarian, turned conservative in the 1960s, supporting the Vietnam War and Richard Nixon. His cartoon strips mocked antiwar protesters and legislators such as Ted Kennedy. In 1968, there were reports that Capp had made indecent advances to four female students on a college tour. In 1972, he pleaded guilty to propositioning a married women in a Wisconsin hotel room. Hundreds of newspapers subsequently dropped his comic strip. Capp had moved to Cambridge in the 1950s and lived on Brattle Street. He died two years after receiving Schlesinger's letter.

Street. I trust that you will be restored to full health and vigor as speedily as possible. My affections to Kathy.

Best regards,
Arthur

To Bill Moyers

[July 5, 1977]

[New York, New York]

Dear Bill:[*]

No one can question the power of television to inform, to educate, to persuade—and to mislead. As an historian, I have therefore watched the recent outpouring of quasi-historical essays on the tiny screen with mixed feelings. Little is more effective than a responsible television rendition of history; little more mischievous then an irresponsible rendition.

One must distinguish, I suppose, between dramatizations and documentaries. When actors impersonate historical figures, the viewers know (I trust) that they are not really seeing Truman fire MacArthur but some re-enacted version hereof. This is not history but historical fiction. Yet even a television drama, like a good historical novel, ought to pay a decent respect to the facts. If it is true, for example, that the scene in a recent show depicting Joe McCarthy in his hospital ward raving like a lunatic was made up, that is surely inexcusable.

Documentaries raise sharper issues of responsibility. They show us real people in a newsclip or interview and purport to tell us what actually happened. A documentary represents itself not as fiction but as history. It demands to be judged therefore at the least by the standards of good popular history.

Your show on June 10, *The CIA's Secret Army,* was a highly effective

---

[*] Schlesinger's letter to Bill Moyers was published in *The Wall Street Journal* on July 5, 1977, replying to charges made in Moyers's June 10, 1977, CBS News television program *The CIA's Secret Army,* alleging that the Kennedy brothers had intended to kill Castro.

piece of television. Haynes Johnson[*] of *The Washington Post* called it "the most powerful, disturbing television news special I've ever seen." It left powerful and disturbing impressions in the minds of the audience. "The broadcast was notable," said *The Nation* admiringly, "for the strong conclusions forced upon the viewer." Among the conclusions forced on *The Nation* were that John Kennedy was "determined to bring [Castro] down by whatever dreadful means, including the use of gangsters and every refinement of the assassin's art" and that the missile crisis was "the result of Kennedy's own bungled attempts . . . to eliminate Fidel Castro."

Such allegedly hard-headed newspapermen as Jimmy Breslin[†] ("this story about Kennedy trying to have Castro assassinated") and Miles McMillin ("a shocking and almost unbelievable story of the assassination conspiracy on the part of the Kennedys") came away with the same impressions. None of these commentators appeared to know any more about these incidents than you care to tell them in your show. Haynes Johnson, who once wrote an excellent book on the Bay of Pigs, did know more and criticized your show as "singularly one-dimensional" and as "bad history." Most of your viewers, though, shared the ignorance of Messrs. Breslin and McMillin, not the knowledge of Mr. Johnson. They relied on you for a balanced presentation of facts.

I write this with some reluctance because I am sufficiently known as a friend of the Kennedys and run the risk of having anything I say discounted for that reason. I might perhaps add that I regard the secret war against Cuba as a blot on the Kennedy administration and eminently worth exposure and condemnation. But the available facts refute your portrait of the Kennedys as, in Haynes Johnson's words, "the villains of the piece . . . the agents of deceit" and, of course, the instigators of assassinations.

Take, for example, the assassination question. You concede that the CIA set out to murder Castro well before Kennedy took office, that it hired the Mafia for this purpose in the Eisenhower administration. But you do not

---

[*] Haynes Johnson (b. 1931). Journalist; TV commentator; *Washington Post* reporter/columnist, 1969–94; journalism professor at the University of Maryland, 1998–present.

[†] Jimmy Breslin (b. 1930). Novelist; Pulitzer Prize–winning New York City journalist/columnist; worked at four New York newspapers over six decades; involved in the murder investigation of the infamous Son of Sam; sought the presidency of the New York City Council with Norman Mailer, who was running for mayor, in 1977, urging the city's secession from New York State.

say, as a fair-minded historian would, that not a scintilla of hard evidence has ever emerged to show that Kennedy, or Eisenhower for that matter, authorized, or even knew about, the CIA murder plots.

You try to deal with this problem by putting Richard Bissell of the CIA before the camera to talk about a presumed presidential wish that such abhorrent operations be deniable. But why did you not also interview, for example, Thomas Parrott,* the CIA officer who served as secretary of the Special Group? Mr. Parrott told the Church Committee that Allan Dulles's practice as head of the CIA was to insist on specific orders rather than "tacit approval." Mr. Parrott said he found Mr. Bissell's theory of the circumlocutious approach "hard to believe." Mr. Bissell himself characterized his own theory when he testified before the Church Committee as no more than "my guess." This is pretty casual evidence on which to make the most damning innuendo about Presidents.

You say, correctly, that the CIA briefed Robert Kennedy about the Mafia plot in 1962. You do not say that the reason they briefed him was, not to rejoice with him in their exploits, but to get him to call off the prosecution of Robert Maheu,† a CIA associate, in a wiretapping case. Kennedy, you say, "may have thought the plot had been discontinued. Still, his response was instructive." *May* have thought? The man who did the briefing testified unequivocally that he *told* Kennedy "the activity had been terminated." As for Kennedy's response the briefer said, "If you have seen Mr. Kennedy's eyes get steely and his jaw set and his voice get low and precise, you get a definite feeling of unhappiness."

Your program implies that the celebrated Operation Mongoose had as one of its objectives the assassination of Castro. In fact (this is all in the Church Committee report), its objectives were intelligence and sabotage, never the assassination of Castro. You say that Mongoose "aimed for the overthrow of Castro by October 1962." In fact, that target date was no more than a proposal. It was never approved as a Mongoose objective. You introduce balefully a reference to "sensitive work" in a 1962 memorandum by

---

* Thomas Parrott (1915–2007). U.S. Army colonel; twenty-four-year career with the CIA; assistant director for national intelligence programs; handled CIA relations with the White House during the Cuban missile crisis.

† Robert Maheu (1917–2008). American businessman and lawyer; FBI official, 1941–47; assistant to secretive industrialist Howard Hughes (whom he never met) 1955–70; helped the CIA enlist Mafia operatives to kill Castro.

General Lansdale,[*] the man in nominal charge of Mongoose, without quoting General Lansdale's statement to the Church Committee that this phrase did not refer to assassination and that he "never took up assassination with either the Attorney General or the President."

You imply that the assassination attempts all came to an end with Kennedy's death; there were, you say, "no new assassination plots." Yet, having read the Church Committee report, you must be well aware that the CIA kept trying to kill Castro till the summer of 1965. Lyndon Johnson apparently knew as little [about] what the CIA was up to as his predecessor had known.

Quite apart from one's judgment of the character of the Kennedys, there are strong circumstantial reasons to conclude that they knew nothing about CIA's continuing assassination activity. John McCone, the CIA director, did not know about it. His subordinates deliberately kept him in the dark. Would these subordinates have told the Kennedys—and then told them not to tell Mr. McCone, their intimate friend?

There is the problem too of the Bay of Pigs prisoners, whom the Kennedys were determined to bring out of Cuba. Nothing would have doomed these prisoners more surely than an assassination attempt on Castro. And there is the fact, which you inexplicably omit, that the Kennedys in the autumn of 1963 were actually exploring the normalization of American relations with Castro at the same time that the CIA was still trying to kill him. You could have put our friend William Attwood of *Newsday* on the screen to tell that story. As an American ambassador at the UN, he was the official conducting the explorations.

Your history is slipshod and polemical. Do you really believe, as you seemed to say, that, if Kennedy had not cancelled an air strike, the Bay of Pigs would have succeeded? That 1,500 men on the beachhead would have defeated Castro's 200,000 men? As for the idea that the secret war caused the missile crisis, you surely know that, though Castro wanted Soviet arms, he did not want nuclear missiles. Khrushchev wanted them in Cuba for his own reasons. "When Castro and I talked about the problem," Khrushchev said in his memoirs, "we argued and argued. Our argument was very heated.

---

[*] Edward Lansdale (1908–87). U.S. Air Force major general; worked for the OSS and CIA; stationed in Saigon, 1954–57 and 1965–68, as a military adviser; handled special operations for the Defense Department, 1957–63.

But, in the end, Fidel agreed with me." The nuclear missiles were installed—and the missile crisis resulted—because Khrushchev wished to alter the world's balance of power, not because Castro wished protection against Kennedy.

The implicit message of your program is really the exculpation of the CIA. You present an obedient, compliant agency thrust into excess by the bludgeonings of the Kennedys. Yet repeated investigations, internal and external, have shown that the CIA operatives had plenty of initiative of their own. They started planning the Castro assassination and approached the Mafia before they even informed Mr. Dulles, not to mention anyone higher, and as we have seen, they never informed Mr. McCone they were continuing the work.

As early as 1956, David Bruce and Robert Lovett reported to the President's Board of Consultants on Foreign Intelligence Activities, "No one, other than those in the CIA immediately concerned with their day to day operation, has any detailed knowledge of what is going on." The Board itself the next year described the CIA's covert action branch as "operating for the most part on an autonomous and free-wheeling basis." In the last month of the Eisenhower administration, it called for "a total reassessment of our covert action policies." The CIA was a rogue elephant from way back. I am sorry to see you fall for its latest disinformation campaign.

The flagrant one-sidedness of your show is difficult to understand. In your two hours you screened 16 interviews, of which 13 were self-serving talks with former CIA people and their Cuban spooks—nearly all presented as if these were honorable witnesses whose word was gospel. (The other three were Castro, Somoza[*] and Senator Morgan.)[†] I am astonished that in the interests of historical responsibility you did not find time to interview others knowledgeable about those events and give the show at least a pretense of balance—William Attwood, for example, or Richard Goodwin or General Lansdale or McGeorge Bundy or Theodore Sorensen.

Long ago Edward R. Murrow[‡] had a famous documentary report on Joe

---

[*] Anastasio ("Tachito") Somoza Debayle (1925–80). President of Nicaragua, 1967–72, 1974–79; longtime head of the Nicaraguan National Guard; overthrown by the Sandinistas in 1979; assassinated in Paraguay.

[†] Robert Morgan (b. 1925). Conservative senator (D-N.C.), 1975–81.

[‡] Edward R. Murrow (1908–65). CBS broadcast journalist, 1937–61; famous for his radio bulletins from London during World War II; hosted TV news shows, including

McCarthy. It was brilliantly done, but it deeply worried the late Gilbert Seldes, who remains to this day the most thoughtful commentator television has ever had. Mr. Seldes detested Senator McCarthy as much as Mr. Murrow did, but he saw dangers in doing what Mr. Murrow had done— employing the resources of television to create "an integrated one-sided picture of McCarthy." Edward R. Murrow's *See It Now* series, Mr. Seldes said, had up to that point given its audience confidence that each show "will have a specific gravity, that it will be important, and, above all, that it will be what it claims to be"—an objective report. *See It Now* had rightly earned public trust because it resembled "the summing-up of a judge who marshals the evidence but does not prejudice the jury." The McCarthy report, Mr. Seldes felt, abused that trust. "Except in this single instance," Mr. Seldes said, the Murrow series "never was the summing-up of a hanging judge."

You, like Ed Murrow, have rightly earned the trust of your audience. This shabby, tendentious polemic abuses that trust. It was the summing-up of a hanging judge. I hope that in the end people will be able to say of you, as Gilbert Seldes said of Edward R. Murrow, "except in this single instance."

Best regards,
Arthur Schlesinger Jr

To Martin Davis[*]

July 29, 1977

[New York, New York]

Dear Martin:

Your grandmother tells me that you and she have been having a discussion of the decision to drop the atomic bomb on Japan. I agree with you that it was a most tragic decision. However, it is not at all clear that the Japanese were on the verge of surrender at the time the bomb was dropped. Even after Hiroshima, the Japanese military vetoed the desire of the civilian

---

a 1954 report exposing Senator Joseph McCarthy's reckless anticommunist crusade; head of the United States Information Agency, 1961–64.
* Martin Davis of Long Island City, New York.

government to accept the Potsdam declaration. As you will remember, two days after Hiroshima, the Red Army invaded Manchuria and, on the third day, with no word from Tokyo, the American Air Command dropped the second bomb on Nagasaki. In Tokyo, the military *still* objected to unconditional surrender. It required the personal intervention of the Emperor to overcome their opposition. This was fortunate because we had used up our stockpile of bombs. All this suggests, I fear, that the war would have gone on for several months, with considerable loss of American and Japanese life (not to mention the lives of thousands of English, Dutch and French soldiers in Japanese prisoner-of-war camps through South Asia—like *The Bridge on the River Kwai*)[*] had the tragic decision not been taken. I don't know how you weigh one form of killing against another, but, as one who was in the United States Army in 1945, I still remember my infinite relief when the war came to an and.

These are difficult questions, on which reasonable men differ. In any event, I am delighted to know of your interest in history. Keep it up.

Sincerely yours,
Arthur

To Peter B. Meyer[†]

June 28, 1978

[New York, New York]

Dear Mr. Meyer:

Please forgive my long delay in responding to your letter of some time back. I have been seeing a book of my own through the press,[‡] and this has been an exceptionally busy spring. Also I don't think I have any particular thoughts about Carter beyond those I have printed on occasion in the *Wall Street Journal*. His preoccupations—government reorganization; winning

---

[*] *The Bridge on the River Kwai*, a 1957 British film directed by David Lean; based on a novel about British prisoners of war in Thailand forced by the Japanese to construct a bridge to enable the Japanese to invade Burma.

[†] Peter B. Meyer of New York, New York.

[‡] Arthur Schlesinger, Jr., *Robert Kennedy and His Times* (Boston: Houghton Mifflin, 1978), winner of the National Book Award.

business confidence—seem to me those of a Republican rather than a Democrat; I discern little evidence of great concern on his part for traditional Democratic issues—the poor, the minorities, the cities, racial justice, civil liberties. Under his mask of rigid control, I imagine that he is a rather insecure fellow. The fact that his staff consists mostly of much younger people suggests that he feels threatened by his equals in age and experience. However, I have met Carter only once, and all this is speculation.

Sincerely yours,
Arthur Schlesinger, Jr.

To Patsy Mink*

July 11, 1978

[New York, New York]

Dear Patsy:

I couldn't be more delighted to know that you have agreed to become the new President of ADA.

For what it is worth, I do not think that Carter is, or is likely to become, either a liberal or even a Democrat; and I hope that ADA will take this position as soon and as forcefully as possible. Otherwise he is likely to win renomination through sheer default.

Best of luck.

Sincerely yours,
Arthur Schlesinger, Jr.

* Patsy Mink (1927–2002). Liberal representative (D-Hawaii), 1965–77, 1990–2002; known for her work to increase federal education aid; assistant secretary of state for oceans, international environment, and scientific affairs, 1976–80; national president of ADA, 1978–81.

To Jean Marie Hamilton[*]

November 20, 1978

[New York, New York]

Dear Ms. Hamilton:

I hope my absence from New York has not made this response too late; but of course I am for the Equal Rights Amendment, and my reason is that I think the time is long overdue for this republic to make a constitutional affirmation of the equality of all American citizens regardless of sex. The alleged malign consequences of the ERA are all, in my judgment, entirely fictitious. As an historian, I must add that this nation, like all nations, would be better off today if through its history it had drawn systematically on the intelligence, imagination and commitment of American women. Our wisest foreign observer, Alexis de Tocqueville, wrote long ago in *Democracy in America*, "If I were asked, now that I am drawing to the close of this work, in which I have spoken of so many important things done by the Americans, to what the singular prosperity and growing strength of that people ought mainly to be attributed, I should reply: To the superiority of their women."

Sincerely yours,
Arthur Schlesinger, Jr.

To Dean Rotbart[†]

November 30, 1978

[New York, New York]

Dear Mr. Rotbart:

Who knows? but if history is still being written five hundred years from now, I would guess that the 20th century will be remembered, if remembered particularly at all, as above all the century in which man began the exploration of space.

As for the impact of the moon shot in America, I imagine it is not un-

[*] Jean Marie Hamilton, of St. Paul, Minnesota. Editor, NWA *Passages*.
[†] Dean Rotbart of Evanston, Illinois.

like the impact of Christopher Columbus on Spain in the 1490s. It takes time to recognize and absorb changes of phase. As for me, I regard the landing of men on the moon as the most exciting event of my lifetime.

As for John Kennedy, I think he had a sense that man had lived through history by exploring the furthest frontiers, and that to refuse the challenge of space would do something seriously damaging to man's self-conception and hence to the future of humanity.

Best of luck on your thesis.

Sincerely yours,
Arthur Schlesinger, Jr.

To Eugene D. Genovese[*]

November 30, 1978

[New York, New York]

Dear Gene:

. . . As for the question of the relationship between private property and freedom, I hope your lecture turns up, because I would very much like to see someone explain how the means of political opposition and of free expression can survive the abolition of private property. In this context freedom seems to me to require two conditions: economic resources relatively safe from the state, and a system of justice relatively independent of the state. The socialization of the means of production and distribution would, I think, destroy both these conditions. Nor do syndicalist fantasies of decentralization, workers' control, etc. seem to me to provide any realistic answer to the power drive of the modern communist state.

I hope I need not add that recognition of the vital role of private property in establishing the conditions of freedom does not imply that private property should control society. I believe, as I have always believed, that freedom requires constant, determined and unrelenting opposition to the

---

[*] Eugene ("Gene") D. Genovese (1930–2012). Historian of the American South and slavery, known for his Marxist orientation; called for a Vietcong victory in the Vietnam War; by 1988 had shifted rightward politically and converted to Catholicism.

pretensions of property. It does not, however, require—and I doubt whether it can survive—its abolition. . . .

Best regards,
Arthur

To John Norbutt[*]

January 26, 1979

[New York, New York]

Dear Mr. Norbutt:

. . . I suppose that what makes a literary work endure is its capacity to interpret human experience, often at several levels simultaneously. We continue to read authors who illuminate our own lives, relationships and problems, who make us understand ourselves and our motives better. We read them all the more avidly if their style conveys the writer's discipline, originality and integrity. As Thoreau said, "Every sentence is the result of a long probation. The author's character is read from title-page to end. Of this he never corrects the proofs."

As for a writer's life, I can imagine no other. It is sometimes lonely, and the working day never comes to an end, but you are accountable only to yourself, which is a relief in this age of organization.

May I add a word of heartfelt thanks to you for your work in Bedford-Stuyvesant. By dealing with young people before their lives have crystallized into a mold, you have the opportunity really to make a difference. Beat of luck to you.

Sincerely yours,
Arthur Schlesinger, Jr.

---

[*] John Norbutt. African American social worker who helped rehabilitated drug addicts in Bedford-Stuyvesant, New York; Norbutt wrote Schlesinger that he had his recruits start reading one of Schlesinger's works and that he was "amazed at the hearty reception displayed by the kids."

To John A. Davenport[*]

March 2, 1979

[New York, New York]

Dear John:

... I find the question of southern Africa deeply depressing and see nothing but disaster there. I do not see how white rule can survive and have the greatest doubts that black rule will bring stability or democracy. The State Department view, I take it, is really that the Patriotic Front,[†] or some faction thereof, is bound to win in the end and that, if the Front regards us as its enemy, the Soviet Union will have scored a great victory. In other words, the policy derives, I think, from some form of anti-Soviet machiavellianism. It also pleases a domestic constituency; nor indeed can it be said that the governments of South Africa and Rhodesia have provided models of racial statesmanship.

My own uninformed feeling is that we should stay out as much as we can. I would let England and France take the initiative in Africa. They have more experience and more interests there than we have. I think *we* expend too much concern on Africa and too little on Latin America. Nor do I think the Soviet Union is going to establish any kind of permanent presence in Africa. African leaders are skilled at playing off superpowers against each other for their own advantage. Nationalism remains the most potent political emotion of the age. Involvement leads to complicity, and I see no great advantage in accepting responsibility for a course of events that we cannot control and that looks to be heading straight for catastrophe.

Best as always,
Arthur Schlesinger, Jr.

[*] John A. Davenport of Middletown, New Jersey.
[†] A political group fighting for majority rule in Rhodesia (now Zimbabwe).

To Roger Stavis[*]

May 14, 1979

[New York, New York]

Dear Mr. Stavis:

...It has always seemed to me that there are three basic lessons to be learned from history. One is that everything changes, and therefore anyone who wants blindly to hold fast to things as they are is sure to be wrong. The second is that no one is infallible, and therefore anyone who explicitly or tacitly claims infallibility should be regarded with mistrust and aversion. The third is that choice and decision in human existence are inescapable and therefore the refusal to choose is itself a form of choice. History suggests that the real trick of human existence is, recognizing the limits of human wisdom, to act nonetheless.

Good luck on your future career.

Sincerely yours,
Arthur Schlesinger, Jr.

To Elizabeth Carpenter[†]

September 17, 1979

[New York, New York]

Dear Liz:

I am delighted to know you are doing a book on presidential humor (or lack thereof). It is alas true that some very fine Presidents have been humorless—Washington, for example, and Jefferson. Those, however, were more stately times. I would be unhappy about modern Presidents who lacked humor. But there are many varieties of humor; and for Presidents a crucial distinction, I think, is between those who make jokes exclusively at the expense of others and those who occasionally turn their wit on them-

---

[*] Roger Stavis of Bayside, New York.
[†] Elizabeth ("Liz") Carpenter (1920–2010). Writer; journalist; author; humorist; speechwriter; feminist; aide to Vice President Johnson, 1961–69; press secretary to Lady Bird Johnson, 1963–69; public relations executive.

selves. Another crucial distinction is between those who originate their jokes and those who procure them from gagmen. Spontaneous, self-mocking humor is the best possible evidence that a political leader retains the capacity to see himself with a modicum of objectivity, and the best protection against that fatal process of withdrawal and self-isolation so well described by our friend George Reedy.*

Affectionately,
Arthur

Arthur and his old friend John Kenneth Galbraith rarely disagreed on political endorsements. But in the 1980 presidential campaign, Arthur supported the independent candidacy of the former liberal Republican congressman from Illinois, John Anderson,† while Galbraith stayed with Jimmy Carter.

To John Kenneth Galbraith

October 30, 1980

[New York, New York]

Dear Ken:

I too regret the divergence. But I really don't understand why you are so agitated about Reagan. It is not like you. On this issue your old friend Gene McCarthy's relaxed view . . . seems to me about right. When old Ron was at the height of his vigor, he served two terms as governor of California and, so far as I know, did nothing very much except to flow with the tide. He is an accommodator, not an ideologue. As President tottering around in his seventies, he would be, I would guess, in the do-nothing Eisenhower model.

As for the "people around him," I would much rather have Kissinger

---

* George Reedy (1917–99). Aide to Senator Lyndon B. Johnson, 1951–61; White House press secretary, 1964–65; dean of Journalism School, Marquette University, 1972–76; professor, 1976–96.

† John Anderson (b. 1922). Representative (R-Ill.), 1961–81; moved from conservative to liberal wing of the party as an anti–Vietnam War activist; ran as an independent during the 1980 presidential race, gaining almost 6.6 percent of vote.

dominating our foreign policy than Zbig [Brzezinski],* whom you are voting to extend for four more machine-gun-waving years. Greenspan† and George Shultz‡ are no more reactionary and considerably brighter than Miller§ and Charlie Schultze.⁵ After all, it was Carter who appointed Paul Volcker** and a majority of the Federal Reserve Board he now so piously denounces. The people I know around Reagan (George Bush, Bill Casey,†† Caspar Weinberger)‡‡ are conservatives but not loonies. They survive comparison with Hamilton Jordan§§ and Bob Strauss. I am sorry to see people like you fall for the Carter cartoon of Reagan as the Great Satan.

In any event, there will be a Democratic Congress to contain Reagan's

* Zbigniew ("Zbig") Brzezinski (b. 1928). Polish American academic, Harvard, 1951–59; Columbia, 1959–66; member of the State Department Policy Planning Council, 1966–68; President Carter's national security adviser, 1977–81; professor at Johns Hopkins University; endorsed George H. W. Bush in 1988 and Obama in 2008.

† Alan Greenspan (b. 1926). Conservative Republican; chairman of the Federal Reserve, 1987–2006; acolyte of free market enthusiast and writer Ayn Rand; blamed for easy money policies leading to the Great Recession; *Time* magazine listed him third among those responsible for the 2007–8 U.S. economic collapse.

‡ George Shultz (b. 1920). Moderate Republican; MIT economics professor, 1948–57; University of Chicago business school dean, 1962–69; secretary of labor, 1969–70; secretary of the Treasury, 1972–74; head of the Bechtel Corporation, 1974–82; secretary of state, 1982–89.

§ G. William Miller (1925–2006). Democratic businessman; executive of Textron, Inc., 1957–74; chairman of the Federal Reserve, 1978–79; secretary of the Treasury, 1979–81.

⁵ Charles Schultze (b. 1924). Centrist American economist; author; director of the Bureau of the Budget, 1965–67; chairman of the Council of Economic Advisers, 1977–81; Brookings Institution fellow, 1968–present.

** Paul Volcker (b. 1927). Democratic investment banker; undersecretary of the Treasury, 1969–74; chairman of the Federal Reserve, 1979–87, helping end high inflation; chairman of President Obama's Economic Recovery Advisory Board, 2009–11, where he promulgated the "Volcker rule" barring speculative trading by retail banks with federally insured deposits.

†† William ("Bill") Casey (1913–87). Republican lawyer; Schlesinger's superior in the OSS, 1944–45; chairman of the Security and Exchange Commission, 1971–73; director of Central Intelligence, 1981–87.

‡‡ Caspar Weinberger (1917–2006). California Republican politician and businessman; chairman of the Federal Trade Commission, 1969–70; budget director, 1972–73; secretary of health, education, and welfare, 1973–75; secretary of defense, 1981–89; presided over Reagan's military build-up; later an executive of *Forbes Magazine;* Harvard classmate of Schlesinger.

§§ Hamilton Jordan (1944–2008). Democratic Georgia politician; influential chief of staff to President Carter, 1977–81.

excesses; and, once liberated from the need to defend Carter's policies and hypocrisies, the Democratic party can become itself again. Four more years of complicity with this crypto-Republican and incompetent Democratic president will discredit our party, I fear, for a long time to come.

But I was particularly sorry to see you join in the ADA statement blackguarding John Anderson. I can understand why those who accept the devil theory of Reagan might give a reluctant vote to Carter. But why is it necessary to indulge in a totally unfair attack on Anderson? To indict him on his "20-year Congressional record" is like indicting Hugo Black[*] according to a formula that gives equal weight to his membership in the Ku Klux Klan in 1925 and his fight for the Holding Companies Act in 1935. People change; and John Anderson has moved steadily to the left at a time that the country has been moving steadily to the right. He deserves something better than the cheap ADA attack.

After all, the major distinguishing liberal issue, as you and I have agreed for years, is belief in affirmative government as an instrument of the general welfare. Carter has rejected that belief in the most explicit language. His presidential campaign in 1976 was based on a demagoguery about the "horrible" federal bureaucracy. In 1978 he delivered his famous tirade against the New Deal tradition in his state of the union message: "Government cannot solve our problems. It can't set our goals. It cannot define our vision. Government cannot eliminate poverty or provide a bountiful economy, or reduce inflation, or save cities, or cure illiteracy, or provide energy." Can you imagine FDR uttering these words? or Truman? or JFK? or LBJ? or J. K. Galbraith?

In 1977, long before he became a presidential candidate, John Anderson said of Carter: "He campaigned against Big Government and he has planted the seeds of doubt in the minds of the American people on the ability of government to solve problems. It may be almost something that comes back to haunt him." And this is the man that the ADA statement now says is less of a liberal than Jimmy Carter? Have you compared Anderson's anti-inflation program with Carter's? And Anderson, unlike Carter, is anti-limited nuclear war, anti-MX, anti-Brzezinski. He's keeping these issues alive. Why go out of your way to blackguard him?

I might add that Shull[†] put out this statement in spite of the fact that the

---

[*] Hugo Black (1886–1971). Staunch New Dealer; senator (D-Ala.), 1927–37; U.S. Supreme Court justice, 1937–71; civil libertarian.

[†] Leon Shull (1914–2007). Plainspoken, independent-minded national director of Americans for Democratic Action, 1964–84.

ADA national board, in the meeting that voted to endorse Carter, also voted *against* an anti-Anderson statement in the endorsement resolution. This kind of servility to the White House has brought me to the verge of resignation from our old organization. I would not have dreamed of resigning over the endorsement decision itself; but the crookedness the national office has shown since is discouraging. My secretary called Shull's office a week ago to request a copy of the anti-Anderson statement you signed, and I still have not received it. Joe Rauh eventually got hold of a copy and sent it along.

I am sorry to write at such length, and do so to explain my own position and to regret your joining the attack on Anderson. You will note that Ted Kennedy, despite much White House pressure that he attack Anderson, has honorably refused to do so.

I love you all the same—and our paths will not diverge for long.

Yours ever,
Arthur

Ronald Reagan won a landslide victory over Jimmy Carter, garnering almost 50.7 percent of the popular vote to 41.0 percent for Carter, with nearly 6.6 percent going to independent John Anderson. Arthur was dismayed by the people Carter dragged down with him, including Senators George McGovern, John Culver, Birch Bayh, Gaylord Nelson, and Frank Church, and Representative John Brademas. The Republicans captured the Senate for the first time since 1952.

To Daniel Patrick Moynihan

January 6, 1981

[New York, New York]

Dear Pat:

Thank you for sending a copy of your excellent lecture on "The University and the State."* I share your feeling that *one* of our subjects must be the defense of society against the political state; but, in our zeal, we must surely not forget *another* of our subjects, which is the defense of society against

* Lecture at Columbia University, September 30, 1980.

politically unaccountable private concentrations of wealth and power, such as our great corporations, trade unions and crime rings. . . .

Best regards,
Arthur

To George Kennan

March 9, 1981

[New York, New York]

Dear George:

I appreciate your note more than I can say. I am afraid I guessed wrong about the Reagan crowd: they turn out to be far more doctrinaire than I expected. It is a regime of *terribles simplificateurs*. We can survive their simplifications at home, but abroad it is another matter. As JFK used to say, "Domestic policy can only defeat us. Foreign policy can kill us." Reagan and Haig* obviously see the entire planet, and all recent history, through the lens of the Cold War; and heaven knows into what awful straits their combination of ignorance and arrogance may lead us. Keep up your contributions to the Op Ed page. I think (hope) that the audience for counsels of reason will soon rapidly expand.

Yours ever,
Arthur

President Reagan on June 5, 1981, presented a gold medal to Ethel Kennedy honoring her husband's service to his country. "[Robert F. Kennedy] roused the comfortable," said Reagan. "He exposed the corrupt, remembered the forgotten, inspired his countrymen, and renewed and enriched the American conscience."

---

* General Alexander Haig, Jr. (1924–2010), deputy national security advisor under Henry Kissinger, 1970–73; White House chief of staff for President Nixon 1973–74; supreme allied commander Europe 1974–79; U.S. secretary of state during Reagan administration 1981–82.

To Anthony Dolan[*]

September 25, 1981

[New York, New York]

Dear Mr. Dolan:

You were kind to send along a copy of President Reagan's felicitous remarks about Robert Kennedy. I was extremely sorry that I had to miss the occasion. Those who attended were most appreciative of the President's graciousness and concern.

I imagine you are having a fascinating time, and I would very much like to get together at some point and exchange notes about the speechwriting process. I don't go to Washington often these days (do I even qualify for a visa?), but, if anything brings you to New York, let me know.[†]

Sincerely yours,
Arthur

To George H. W. Bush

June 21, 1982

[New York, New York]

Dear George:

I don't know whether you happened to see a piece in the *Wall Street Journal* of June 9 in which I took the liberty of suggesting that, in order to repair our crumbling position in Latin America, the President might be well advised to send you on a tour of South American capitals, so that the Latin leaders might have a chance to discuss at length their problems and concerns.

Subsequently someone wrote a letter to the *Journal* pointing out what had happened when Eisenhower sent his Vice President to Latin America in

---

[*] Anthony Dolan (b. 1948). Pulitzer Prize–winning journalist; chief speechwriter to President Reagan 1981–89.

[†] Dolan replied on December 9, 1981: "Do let me know if you are down this way—I think I can arrange the visa you mentioned. I must say though that the thought of having you to lunch in the White House Mess is an intriguing one. I would just love to see the look on the faces of some of my colleagues."

1958 at a time of comparable resentment against the United States.* There may well be a point here; but one way to meet it, I would think, might be for you (should you go on such a mission) to take Jeane Kirkpatrick† with you. The Falklands troubles have left her identified as a strong friend of Latin America, and her presence would greatly reduce the possibility of the demonstrations that greeted Nixon.

All this assumes that the *Journal* piece was not the kiss of death for what Latin American friends assure me would really be a most useful initiative on the part of the administration.

Yours ever,
Arthur

From John Kenneth Galbraith

December 6, 1982

[Cambridge, Massachusetts]

Dear Arthur:

You have probably been asked by *Esquire* to do a piece on the people who in their lifetime have made a difference. They have asked me to write—briefly—on Eleanor Roosevelt. What should I stress? I need some beginning (and energizing) ideas.

It was a pleasure to see you the other day and, in a quiet way, to reflect on what you do for my reputation and how you enlarge my sanity.

Yours faithfully,
Ken

---

* In May 1958, Vice President Nixon's car was attacked by an angry crowd and almost overturned in Caracas, Venezuela, during a goodwill tour of Latin American nations.
† Jeane Kirkpatrick (1926–2006). Neoconservative Democrat turned Republican; ambassador to the United Nations, 1981–85; sought U.S. support for anticommunist dictatorships on theory they would eventually become democracies; professor at Georgetown University, 1967–81, 1985–2006.

To John Kenneth Galbraith

[no date]

[New York, New York]

Dear Ken:

I too am joining the *Esquire* team; my assignment is Reinhold Niebuhr. The best way to prime the pump for Mrs. R. would be immersion in Joe Lash's* excellent book *Eleanor and Franklin,* with a brief glance at the foreword by (I sound like Bill Buckley) your honorable servant.

A chaotic childhood gave Mrs R a low sense of self-worth. She hungered all her life for affection. She endured shocks in marriage. But she triumphed over all this by her immense capacity for self-discipline. The thing that always struck me about her is that underneath the Lady Bountiful aspect she was a very tough old bird, who used artlessness as the cloak under which she moved in a sometimes steely way toward her objective. She was a political realist, who played a most useful role for FDR as envoy to and placater of minorities (youth, blacks, radicals, women, etc). I think that, despite Lucy Mercer,† she and FDR worked out an effective partnership. He valued her highly and was prepared to put up with what other observers saw as her deficient sense of priority when it came to harassing him about one or another problem. One must never forget (and I guess she never let him forget) that she was a genuinely *good* woman.

But you know all this. We are sorry that you can't come down for the Jenkins‡ dinner, but I gather you will be seeing them on the weekend. Have a good and productive time in Gstaad; stay off the slopes, and keep in

---

* Joseph Lash (1909–87). Socialist student radical; Democratic political activist; friend of Eleanor Roosevelt; *New York Post* reporter, 1950–66; won 1972 Pulitzer Prize for *Eleanor and Franklin,* the first volume of a two-book biography of the First Lady.

† Lucy Mercer (1891–1948). Personal secretary to Eleanor Roosevelt, 1914–18; carried on a secret affair with FDR for most of his life; she was with him the day he died.

‡ Roy Jenkins (1920–2003). Historian; British politician; author of biographies of William Gladstone and Winston Churchill; Labour MP, 1948–77, 1982–87; chancellor of the exchequer, 1967–70; broke with the Labour Party over its opposition to joining the European Common Market; European Commission president, 1977–81; helped found the short-lived Social Democratic Party; Chancellor of Oxford University, 1987–2003; friend of Schlesinger.

touch. I greatly appreciate your concluding lines. The feeling is more than reciprocal.

Yrs ever,
Arthur

To Ray Jenkins*

December 20, 1982

[New York, New York]

Dear Mr. Jenkins:

Your loyalty to Mr. Carter does you credit, and I am sorry if my words gave offense. You do me an injustice, however, if you think my assessment of the Carter administration has anything to do with Senator Kennedy.

My concern from the start was with Carter's systematic attack on the great creative contribution of the modern Democratic party—the idea of affirmative government. His demagoguery in 1976 against the horrible, swollen, etc., federal bureaucracy pandered—or so it seemed to me—[to] the most vulgar American prejudices, and I could not bring myself to vote for him. For the first and only time in my life, I did not vote for President at all.

The Carter administration verified these forebodings. You will recall the gratuitous attack on affirmative government in the 1978 state of the union message ("Government cannot solve our problems. It can't set our goals. It cannot define our vision. Government cannot eliminate poverty, or provide a bountiful economy, or reduce inflation, or save our cities," etc.). These were not words ever likely to have been uttered by Franklin Roosevelt, or Harry Truman, or John Kennedy, or Lyndon Johnson. A President has an obligation, it seems to me, to educate and enlighten the people, not to pander to prejudice.

I may be wrong in my conviction that we cannot solve our problems without affirmative national government, but it is that conviction, right or wrong, that accounts for my belief that Carter was not a real Democrat and that, human rights and Camp David apart, the Carter years were wasted

---

* Ray Jenkins (b. 1930). Special assistant to President Carter; White House press officer, 1979–81.

years. Had Ford been reelected, we would have got Salt II as well as Panama Canal treaties; and, though the appointments to regulatory commissions would have been worse, the basic economic policy of combatting inflation through recession would have been the same.

In short, my concern about Carter has nothing to do with Senator Kennedy, except in the sense that Kennedy does stand for the Roosevelt-Truman-Kennedy-Johnson philosophy that, in my view, Carter has done his best to discredit.

Let me know some time when you are in New York, and we can chat about these matters further.

Sincerely yours,
Arthur Schlesinger, Jr.

To William Safire*

January 18, 1983

[New York, New York]

Dear Bill:

I have long been interested in the word "egghead"—I suppose because I was one of those to whom the word was first applied. I believe that the first mention of John Alsop's sense of the word (which Stewart Alsop had told me about when I asked him about his 1952 column) came in my piece in the March-April 1953 *Partisan Review* entitled "The Highbrow in American Politics."

The other night I saw on television a film that had given me much enjoyment when it came out half a century ago—*Hallelujah, I'm a Bum* [1933]. Lewis Milestone directed; Al Jolson, Frank Morgan and Madge Evans were the leading players; and the screenplay was by S. N. Behrman and Ben Hecht. To my surprise one character in the film, an amiable left-wing agitator with a large, smooth, oval head, played by Harry Langdon, is called "egghead." Whether John Alsop saw *Hallelujah, I'm a Bum,* and the word lingered

---

*William ("Bill") Safire (1929–2009). Public relations official; author; journalist; TV commentator; lexicographer; speechwriter for President Nixon, 1969–73; *New York Times* columnist, 1973–2005. See *Safire's Political Dictionary.*

thereafter in his unconscious to be revived twenty years later by Adlai Stevenson, I do not know. I am sending John a copy of this letter to see whether there is anything in this. In any event, I offer this item for your next edition.

Sincerely yours,
Arthur

To Mary Haws*

March 2, 1983

[New York, New York]

Dear Ms. Haws:

... In answer to your questions, I suppose I became an historian more through nurture than conscious decision. My father was an historian; I grew up surrounded by historical books and talk; and it never really occurred to me to be anything else. My father was a considerable influence on me, as were other members of the Harvard faculty at the time, especially Perry Miller and Samuel Eliot Morison. In later years I have learned a good deal from British scholars, notably Isaiah Berlin, D. W. Brogan,[†] Herbert Butterfield[‡] and A. J. P. Taylor.[§] I have always felt that the historian cannot but benefit from exposure to practical affairs and practical decisions, and I have no doubt that my years in government were of great benefit to me as an historian. One remembers Gibbon[¶] on his military service: "The captain

---

* Mary Haws of Malibu, California.

† Denis Brogan (1900–1974). British political scientist who specialized in American history; professor at Cambridge University, 1939–68; friend of Schlesinger.

‡ Sir Herbert Butterfield (1900–1979). British historian at Cambridge University, 1928–79; focused on eighteenth-century constitutional history, as well as Christianity's influence on history.

§ A. J. P. Taylor (1906–90). Controversial leftist British historian of nineteenth- and twentieth-century European diplomacy; taught at Oxford University, 1938–76; Labour Party member; journalist; notable TV lecturer; author of *The Origins of the Second World War* (1961), which argued that Hitler was a "normal" European leader and the war was an "accident."

¶ Edward Gibbon (1737–94). British historian; author of *The History of the Decline and Fall of the Roman Empire* (1776–89); MP.

of the Hampshire grenadiers . . . has not been useless to the historian of the Roman empire."

I am told that students today are not much interested in history. If this is true, it is a cause for regret. The study of history seems to me not only a fascinating intellectual enterprise but a necessary background for wise public decisions and for a civilized personal life. I am glad that you are an exception to what is alleged as the general rule.

Best of luck on your paper.

Sincerely yours,
Arthur Schlesinger, jr.

Knowing that W. Averell Harriman was due to meet with Soviet leader Yuri Andropov in early June 1983, Arthur sent Averell a letter advising him on what he might say to Andropov—and what he might expect from him.

To W. Averell Harriman

May 13, 1983

[New York, New York]

Dear Averell:

Brian Urquhart,[*] as you know, is the number two man at the United Nations; and he accompanied the Secretary-General[†] at his recent talk with Andropov.[‡] This meeting took place at Andropov's initiative and suggests, in Urquhart's view, both Andropov's frustration over the virtual

[*] Sir Brian Urquhart (b. 1919). Soldier; author; advised five UN secretary generals 1946–86; undersecretary-general of the United Nations, 1971–85; in 1944 warned against failed airborne attack on Dutch bridges that inspired the 1977 movie *A Bridge Too Far;* biographer of Ralph Bunche and Dag Hammarskjöld.

[†] Javier Pérez de Cuéllar (b. 1920). Peruvian diplomat who served as UN secretary-general, 1982–91.

[‡] Yuri Andropov (1914–84). Longtime Communist Party official; Soviet ambassador to Hungary, 1954–56, during the Hungarian uprising; head of the KGB, 1967–82; supported the Soviet war in Afghanistan, 1979–88; general secretary of the Communist Party, 1982–84.

breakdown in communications with the Reagan administration and his desire to open up as many channels as possible with the West.

Urquhart found Andropov frailer in person than photographs had suggested. His hands tremble a good deal, and Urquhart wonders whether he might not have Parkinson's disease. Apparently he likes to limit his talks to an hour and a half; after that time, secretaries came in to try to bring the meeting to an end, but the talk went on for another thirty or forty minutes. Whatever his physical infirmities, Andropov was plainly in detailed intellectual command of the topics under review. He appeared direct, lucid, candid, businesslike and tough. Gromyko* and Alexandrov, Andropov's chef de cabinet, were present at the meeting. The Secretary-General and Urquhart found Gromyko, by the way, more relaxed, affable, self-confident and free-spoken than ever before.

Andropov himself brought up Afghanistan and gave the impression that the Soviet Union was incurring serious costs (in casualties, resources and world disfavor) and would like to get out—on certain conditions. He would, the UN people thought, even be willing to dump the present Kabul regime—if the west would stop supporting the insurgency and would permit Pakistan to develop better relations with the Soviet Union. Andropov laid great stress on the Soviet insistence on protecting frontiers. The insurgents apparently operate in northern Afghanistan, near the border, and are thus a particular irritant. Andropov seemed convinced that the United States does not want a settlement and prefers to keep the war going.

Andropov also brought up the Iraq-Iran war. His fear apparently is that, if it continues, it might lead to an American intervention in the Gulf to save the oil. He did not seem to suggest that the U.S. is trying to keep that war going but apparently thinks that the superpowers can do more to bring the fighting to an end.

His main concern, however, was arms control. He is depressed by the Reagan attitude and referred several times to Reagan's Orlando ("evil empire") speech, saying that such unrestrained abuse did not help the cause of peace. (Urquhart commented to me that Andropov did not appear to note

---

*Andrei Gromyko (1909–89). Soviet ambassador to the United States, 1943–45; foreign minister, 1957–85; supported ascension of Mikhail Gorbachev in 1985.

the irony of this complaint in view of the years of unrestrained abuse the Soviet Union has lavished on the United States.)

Urquhart had the impression that Andropov is well aware that the Soviet Union is in trouble at home, in Eastern Europe and with world opinion but is very sensitive to Soviet dignity as a superpower and wants to be taken seriously and treated with respect in world affairs. However, he does not want a summit meeting or anything that might help Reagan's reelection. Andropov also said, "We have our economic problems, but our economy is not so weak as the Americans think."

You will come to the meeting with the prestige both of a world statesman and of someone who the Russians know has always dealt fairly and candidly with them. It might well be that you might want to begin by asking Andropov how he sees the future; how he visualizes the evolution of relations between the Soviet Union and a pluralist world made up of nations with very different economic systems and political creeds. What will this world be like for our grandchildren?

It might be possible to observe that both superpowers have problems and to inquire how the democratic world can help the Soviet Union in the quest for modernization and peace.

You might also want to point out that, given the present political atmosphere in the United States, American opinion needs some reassurance on the question of the verification of agreements. To what extent, for example, might the Soviet Union be willing to permit on-site inspection in cases of recorded explosions that might or might not be earthquakes? (On the other hand, verification, given the means of detection, is something of a phony issue, and you might not want to get into that.) . . .

However, there is no point in trying to teach your grandfather how to suck eggs, so I will refrain from further advice. You know infinitely more than I do about the Soviet Union and about talking with world leaders.[*]

---

[*] Harriman met with Andropov in his office at the Central Committee headquarters for eighty minutes on June 2, 1983. They agreed that both nations should pursue peaceful coexistence and work to end the arms race. "The General Secretary said, and authorized me to say, that it is the most sincere and fervent desire of the Soviet Government to have normal relations with the United States and to develop them in the best tradition of our relations in the past," said Harriman, who had first visited Russia in 1899.

We will be abroad from May 23 to June 10. Will you be in your New York retreat when we get back? I will be eager to hear what happened. Best of luck—you may be saving the world.

Alexandra joins in love to you both.

Yours ever,
Arthur

To John Thomson[*]

July 12, 1983

[New York, New York]

Dear John:

... The problem of reconciling steadiness in foreign policy with democracy—i.e., the polity in which free elections enable one party to displace another in control of the government—has tormented commentators from Tocqueville to Kennan. Some states mitigate discontinuity by giving special power to the permanent bureaucracy; but this solution has its disadvantages too, for no active foreign policy can stick in a democracy unless the people understand and support it. The long-run answer, it seems to me, lies in the continuity of national interest—and in a clear and compelling projection to the electorate of the nature of a nation's vital interests. But I don't see how we can prevent short-run fluctuations and still keep a genuinely democratic polity. . . .

Best regards,
Arthur Schlesinger, Jr.

President Reagan in 1983 established a National Bipartisan Commission on Central America to help resolve conflicts and alleviate economic hardships in the region. He appointed Henry Kissinger to chair the group.

---

[*] Sir John Thomson (b. 1927). UK ambassador to the United Nations, 1982–87.

To Henry Kissinger

July 25, 1983

[New York, New York]

Dear Henry:

I am sure you are flooded with advice these days, and I have no wish to add to your burdens. But a couple of points do occur to me.

First, you must recognize that, seen from the outside, this Central American commission seems to be in a different class from the earlier Reagan commissions. The social security commission was set up to resolve a genuine perplexity. Its membership covered a wide range of views, from Alan Greenspan to Claude Pepper.* The Scowcroft commission† was set up less to resolve a genuine perplexity than to win acceptance for a projected course of action; but, since the action was still projected, the Scowcroft commission had a certain freedom of decision, though not nearly so much as the social security commission.

Your commission appears to be set up not to resolve a perplexity but to ratify policy already decided upon and already in place. This impression may not be an accurate representation of your charter. But it would appear to be verified every day by the administration's evident determination to commit the country to a military course long before the commission completes its work. It is verified too by the composition of the commission, which, so far as the public knows, contains no active critics of the administration's policy—no moral equivalents of Claude Pepper.

My second point is that, since the commission does not offer such prospect of internal debates, you should make a systematic effort to expose the members to adversary testimony. If you make your judgments only on the basis of information provided by the government itself, no one will take you seriously. It would serve the interests not only of your recommendations but of the reputation of the commission to make sure its members listen to the views of those who think the whole project of solving the

* Claude Pepper (1900–1989). New Dealer; liberal senator (D-Fla.), 1936–51; representative, 1963–89; turned conservative in his last years, supporting Contras against Sandinistas in Nicaragua and expressing anti-Castro views.

† The President's Commission on Strategic Forces, chaired by air force lieutenant general Brent Scowcroft, President Ford's national security adviser, was empaneled in January 1983 and addressed the future of America's intercontinental ballistic missiles.

problems of Central America by means of unilateral U.S. military intervention is a lot of nonsense. (I should add that, though I am extremely skeptical about the course for reasons suggested in the attached column, I am not nominating myself as a witness. There are many people available who have followed the situation in much closer detail than I have.)

Good luck! I wish your group would adopt this Niebuhr quote as an epigraph for your report: "Escape from our ironic situation obviously demands that we moderate our conceptions of the ability of men and nations to discern the future; and of the power of even great nations to bring a tortuous historical process to, what seems to them, a logical and proper conclusion."*

Best regards,
Arthur

To the Editor of *The Wall Street Journal*

13 December 1983

[New York, New York]

Sir:

It is pathetic to see the United States Ambassador to the Organization of American States adopt (in his letter of 8 December) the identical arguments in defense of the invasion and military occupation of Grenada[†] that the Soviet Union used to justify its invasion and military occupation of Hungary in 1956.

The Soviet Union acted, the Kremlin claimed in 1956, in response to a request from the "legitimate" government of Hungary and "in accordance with the terms of the Warsaw treaty." In the same style, Ambassador Mid-

---

* In a January 17, 1984, *New York Times* op-ed piece entitled "Failings of the Kissinger Report," Schlesinger branded the report "seriously deficient in its sense of political reality."

† On October 25, 1983, President Reagan ordered U.S. troops to invade the Caribbean island of Grenada following a military coup during which the nation's leftist leader, Maurice Bishop, who had seized power four years earlier by coup, was assassinated. The United States said it acted to protect the lives of American medical students. Washington reinstated the governor-general until 1984 when elections were held.

dendorf* tells us the United States acted in 1983 in response to a request from the "authoritative representative of the Government of Grenada" and pursuant to the terms of the Organization of Eastern Caribbean States [OECS] treaty.

Ambassador Middendorf's reliance on a "confidential direct appeal made by the Governor General of Grenada" is ridiculous. Mrs. Thatcher† is perhaps a higher authority than Ambassador Middendorf on the legal powers of the Queen's officials. She has rejected the argument that the Governor General's appeal legitimized the American invasion and has pronounced the invasion illegal.

As for Ambassador Middendorf's invocation of the OECS treaty, if such an argument has any validity the Soviet Union had a much better case in 1956. For the Soviet Union is at least a member of the Warsaw Treaty organization, while the United States is not a member of the OECS and therefore not bound by its decisions. Moreover, the OECS mutual defense treaty provides for military action only by unanimous request of all OECS parties. As we all know, the OECS request was far from unanimous.

In appropriating these tattered Soviet arguments, Ambassador Middendorf competently exposes the feebleness of the legal rationalization offered by the Reagan administration for an action that, whatever its other merits or demerits, has no visible justification in international law. Margaret Thatcher was everlastingly right, alas, when she said: "If you are going to pronounce a new law that, wherever communism reigns against the will of the people, even though it has happened internally there, the United States shall enter, then we are going to have really terrible wars in the world."

Sincerely yours,
Arthur Schlesinger, jr.

---

* J. William Middendorf (b. 1924). Republican investment banker; Goldwater supporter; ambassador to the Netherlands, 1969–73; secretary of the navy, 1974–77; ambassador to the Organization of American States, 1981–85.

† Margaret Thatcher (1925–2013). British prime minister, 1979–90; longest serving and only female prime minister in the twentieth century; fiercely conservative; favored deregulation, state privatization, reduction in union power, and minimal integration with the European community.

To Charles Wyzanski, Jr.[*]

14 December 1983

[New York, New York]

Dear Charlie:

My delay in thanking you cannot conceal the immense pleasure your letter about the JFK piece[†] has given me. Your words are characteristically generous, and they supply needed encouragement as I plow ahead on volume iv of the FDR series.

I appreciate your point about the cyclical rhythm.[‡] I have always been troubled by the contradiction between the determinism of the cycle and my own belief in the reality of historical choice (at least in the sense defined by Tocqueville in the last paragraph of the second volume of *Democracy in America*).[§] Still there are evident alternations between fatigue and recuperation, withdrawal and return; as Emerson said, "A good deal of our politics is physiological." . . .

I wish we met more often, because there is so much in the world to discuss—not least my classmate Caspar Weinberger's steady progress toward blowing up the world. If you ever come to New York and are free for luncheon or dinner, please let me know. And again thank you for a most heartening letter.

Yours ever,
Arthur

---

[*] Charles ("Charlie") Wyzanski, Jr. (1906–86). New Dealer; U.S. federal judge, 1941–86.

[†] Arthur Schlesinger, Jr., "What the Thousand Days Wrought," *The New Republic*, November 21, 1983, on the twentieth anniversary of President Kennedy's assassination.

[‡] The cyclical theory of U.S. history, as propounded by both Schlesinger and his father, is that American history swings between progressive periods and conservative periods about every thirty years or so.

[§] Tocqueville: "The nations of our day cannot prevent conditions of equality from spreading in their midst. But it depends upon themselves whether equality is to lead to servitude or freedom, knowledge or barbarism, prosperity or wretchedness."

To A. M. Rosenthal[*]

12 April 1984

[New York, New York]

Dear Abe:

The *Times* is *the* newspaper of record. Is it not therefore obligated to run full and accurate texts of documents? If Barry Goldwater writes Bill Casey that he is "pissed off," or if Nixon recalls telling Eisenhower to "shit or get off the pot," should the *Times* really edit or expurgate their remarks, however offensive the words may be? Historians depend on the *Times*, and the *Times* must not let history down.

Best regards,
Arthur Schlesinger, Jr.

On May 7, 1984, the Public Broadcasting Service presented an American Playhouse *drama entitled "Concealed Enemies" recounting the accusations by Whittaker Chambers that Alger Hiss was a Communist spy during his service in the Roosevelt administration.*

To Charles Wyzanski, Jr.

17 May 1984

[New York, New York]

Dear Charles:

The Hiss-Chambers T.V. series is really quite good. At least the first two installments are; I have videotaped the last two but have not yet seen them. The atmosphere is carefully done, and the characterizations are

---

[*] A. M. Rosenthal (1922–2006). *New York Times* journalist/editor, 1943–99; managing editor and executive editor, 1969–88; columnist, 1987–99; conservative columnist for the New York *Daily News*, 1999–2004.

properly enigmatic. Having been told by Jerry Frank[*] and Pat Jackson[†] about Alger's close friendship with Lee Pressman[‡] and John Abt[§] in AAA,[¶] I had always supposed (as Jerry and Pat did) that he was guilty at least of perjury.

A few years ago, when Nixon lived over our back fence,[**] I began one day by looking out our bedroom window to see Nixon walking up and down his garden. When I returned some hours later after my weekly seminar, the first person I encountered in entering the house, where a party was in progress, was Alger Hiss. He was there because a girl named Sally Belfrage,[††] a great friend of Alexandra, had come over from London to promote her new book, and we were giving a party for her. She had put Alger on the list of those to be invited. I had told Alexandra to go ahead and ask him but said he would not dream of coming; I had long been on the record as one who believed in his guilt. When I saw him, I decided that, if he were willing to come to my house, the least I could do was to be friendly; so I went over at once, and we had an amiable though inconsequential conversation. It seemed appropriate to begin the day by seeing Nixon and to end it by seeing Hiss.

Why does Hiss, if guilty, continue to insist on his innocence? I have long

---

[*] Jerome ("Jerry") Frank (1889–1957). Lawyer; general counsel of the Agricultural Adjustment Administration, 1933–35; chairman of the Securities and Exchange Commission, 1939–41; judge of the U.S. Court of Appeals for the Second Circuit, 1941–57.

[†] Gardner ("Pat") Jackson (1896–1965). Journalist; defender of Sacco and Vanzetti (two suspected anarchists eventually executed for murder on questionable evidence in a 1920 Massachusetts robbery); joined FDR's Agricultural Adjustment Administration in 1933; later a liberal anticommunist labor reporter for *PM*.

[‡] Lee Pressman (1906–69). Labor attorney; Communist Party member, 1934–35; worked in the FDR administration, 1933–35; general counsel to the CIO, 1936–48; accused of spying for the USSR in 1948; named names at a HUAC hearing in 1950.

[§] John Abt (1904–91). American lawyer and politician; worked in the FDR administration and in Congress, 1933–38; later longtime chief counsel to CPUSA.

[¶] Agricultural Adjustment Administration.

[**] In October 1979, Nixon moved to an East 65th Street brownstone that overlooked the back of Schlesinger's brownstone on East 64th Street. On learning of Nixon's arrival, Schlesinger told the press, "There goes the neighborhood."

[††] Sally Belfrage (1936–94). American-born British-based nonfiction writer; left the United States when her parents were deported because of their Communist affiliations; wrote about Northern Ireland and the U.S. civil rights movement.

thought that Robert Penn Warren's[*] novel of 1950 *World Enough and Time* helps explain the psychological puzzle. It is a novel about a man who commits a murder; then some years later is accused of the murder in contrived circumstances that *so* outrage him that, with all sincerity, he asserts and fights for his own innocence. Then there is the further consideration, to which you allude: that, if he were ever to admit anything, he would be exposed as a man who betrayed his friends—including you . . . —by permitting them to go bail for him.

I have had to put aside my work on volume iv [of *Roosevelt*] for a few months in order to write a small book on American politics,[†] drawn from papers I have written in recent years. I have to do this because I need the money. As soon as this is out of the way, it will be back to FDR. . . .

Yours ever,
Arthur

To Gore Vidal

16 August 1984

[New York, New York]

Dear Gore:

I have finally had a chance to read your *Lincoln,* and I hasten to congratulate you on a truly fine historical novel. (Better than Henty.) The characterizations are superb; the dialogue is immensely persuasive, the atmosphere splendidly evoked. Even my skeptical eye caught very few slips. I am not so sure as you are that Lincoln believed in colonization of ex-slaves to the end. I doubt that Lincoln read Clausewitz[‡] in 1862; *On War* was not translated into English until 1873. It was Emerson, not Machiavelli, who said, "When you strike at a king, you must kill him." . . . And, as you know

---

[*] Robert Penn Warren (1905–89). Southern novelist, poet, and literary critic; defended southern segregation as a young man, later embraced integration; won a 1947 Pulitzer Prize for *All the King's Men;* won Pulitzers for poetry in 1958 and 1979.

[†] Arthur Schlesinger, Jr., *The Cycles of American History* (Boston: Houghton Mifflin, 1986).

[‡] Carl von Clausewitz (1780–1831). Prussian soldier; military theorist stressing moral and political aspects of war; famous for his book *On War* published after his death.

(and show elsewhere), we had no ambassadors then, only ministers; so the allusion to an "ambassadorship" (201) is askew. But these are trivial flaws in a really notable achievement.

Best regards,
Arthur

Democrats nominated former vice president Walter Mondale as their presidential candidate at their San Francisco convention in July 1984. Arthur had originally supported Senator Gary Hart[*] of Colorado, but quickly embraced Mondale as a fellow liberal.

To Walter Mondale

21 September 1984

[New York, New York]

Dear Fritz:

When I was young and hopeful (and presumptuous), I thought nothing of writing letters of advice to Adlai, Jack, Hubert, Bobby and so on; but, now that I am old and disenchanted, I ordinarily don't bother.

However, I am moved to write now—partly because the nation and the world cannot afford four more years of Reaganism and partly because I fear that your campaign, as presently conceived, will do [to] the Democratic party in the United States what John Turner[†] recently did to the Liberal party in Canada.

Turner's great mistake was to move the Liberal party to the right. The theory was that this would impress and convert conservative voters. The result, as we all know, was catastrophe for the whole party.

The reason why the Turner strategy failed is that, if the voters want conservative government, they will choose the real thing every time, not an imitation. And, while it fails to win over conservatives, the rightward move-

---

* Gary Hart (b. 1936). Lawyer; writer; teacher; Democratic Party activist; ran McGovern's 1972 campaign; senator (D-Colo.), 1975–87.

† John Turner (b. 1929). Canadian lawyer and politician; Liberal Party prime minister for seventy-nine days in 1984; leader of opposition, 1984–90.

ment of a liberal party turns off the activists whose crusading zeal alone can get the poor and the minorities to the polls (and who have been the source of every Democratic presidential triumph this century). When you defend Grenada and talk about quarantining Nicaragua, you don't impress the conservatives, but you do discourage people who might otherwise be working day and night for you. As Joe Rauh has insisted for so long, the "intensity factor" is indispensable for Democratic success. Your campaign has thus far extinguished the intensity factor.

The emphasis on the deficit seems to me folly. The Republicans have used the deficit as an issue for fifty years—literally—and they have gotten nowhere with it. Voters are profoundly unimpressed by the deficit specter. They have heard too many boys cry wolf for too many generations. The only people who worry about the deficit are businessmen most of whom have always voted Republican and will doubtless do so again. And if by any chance you should succeed in establishing the deficit as an issue, I fear that this will only help the Republican party; for the Republicans, since they have been wailing about deficits longer, are still probably perceived as the party that cares most—an impression reinforced by their phony balanced-budget amendment.

I think you should ignore the Ben Wattenbergs[*] of the world and go all out on issues that will activate your core support—fairness, racial justice, honesty in government, women's rights and, above all, peace in Central America and negotiations with the Soviet Union.

And you should not hesitate to portray Reagan as all-things-to-all-men, concealing consistent regressive purpose under a mask of geniality and jokes. Continue spelling out, in the most stark terms, what Reagan's reelection would be a mandate for. It would be a mandate to pursue with redoubled zeal the policies of his first term. At home it would be a mandate to continue cutting taxes for the rich and social programs for the poor; a mandate to press the assault on food stamps, on aid to the cities, on health care, on our natural resources; a mandate to accelerate the retreat from equal opportunity and civil rights; a mandate to keep women out of the Constitution; a mandate to deny higher education to the sons and daugh-

[*] Ben Wattenberg (b. 1933). American conservative author and TV commentator; worked in both Democratic and Republican administrations; hosted numerous PBS television shows; fellow at the right-wing American Enterprise Institute.

ters of the poor; a mandate to weaken government when it serves the general welfare and to strengthen government when it interferes with people's private lives and choices; a mandate to relax our national provisions for the protection of the environment and for occupational health and safety; a mandate for higher prices and higher interest rates; a mandate to permit the continuing deterioration of our roads, bridges, harbors, mass transit, dams, sewage systems, parks. And in foreign affairs a mandate to press on with the nuclear arms race, to militarize outer space, to intervene militarily in Central America, to have ever more grandiose and wasteful military budgets, to estrange our allies and isolate ourselves in the world.

I wish you all good fortune in turning this around. The John Turner strategy having failed so dismally in Canada, why adopt it here? It is the road to disaster.

Best regards,
Arthur Schlesinger, Jr.

The incumbent president thrashed Mondale, who won only his home state of Minnesota and Washington, D.C. Reagan won 59 percent of the popular vote to Mondale's 41 percent.

Arthur visited Cuba in May 1985 at the invitation of former U.S. ambassador to El Salvador Robert White, a critic of Reagan's Latin American policies. They met with Fidel Castro, who in a fascinating four-hour conversation peppered with facts, allegations, jokes, statistics, insights, metaphors, and sarcasm, all punctuated by vivid gestures and facial expressions, "inexplicably" reminded Arthur of Joseph Alsop. Arthur also met with Rafael Hernández, editor of a Cuban quarterly social science journal, Temas, *and a sometimes independent thinker in Cuba.*

To Rafael Hernández

3 June 1985

[New York, New York]

Dear Dr. Hernandez:

I am most grateful for the excellent cigars, one of which I am smoking at this moment, and I am exceedingly sorry that we could not get together for a chat. But, as you will understand, our group was intensively scheduled, and things got out of my control.

In answer to your questions:

1. The Bay of Pigs left President Kennedy with deep skepticism about the Joint Chiefs of Staff and the CIA. Thereafter he had no hesitation about rejecting JCS advice (as over Laos, Vietnam, the Berlin crisis of 1961, the missile crisis, the test ban treaty, etc.). He reorganized his system of making foreign policy decisions and, in particular, brought Robert Kennedy into the foreign affairs picture. RFK had had nothing to do with the Bay of Pigs but played a key role during the missile crisis.

2. With regard to CIA, Kennedy got rid of Dulles and Bissell as soon as he decently could and brought in John McCone in order to get the Agency under control. McCone was a man of conservative views but honest, and he did his best to carry out the President's wishes. I do not think that the CIA was a major factor in any of Kennedy's important foreign policy decisions after the Bay of Pigs.

3. The Soviet action in persuading Cuba to accept nuclear weapons was both a political and a military threat to the United States. Khruschev's purpose, as he wrote in his memoirs, was to equalize the balance of power. The missiles would have increased by half Soviet first-strike capacity against U.S. targets. The political consequences of successful Soviet emplacement of nuclear missiles in Cuba would have been perhaps even more destabilizing; for it would have proven the Soviet ability to act with impunity in the very heart of the U.S. zone of vital interest. The object of the quarantine was to force the removal of the missiles both for military and for political reasons.

4. Since the Soviet Union was attempting to introduce the missiles, it was obviously necessary to negotiate with the Soviet Union regarding their withdrawal. Cuba seemed to us a pawn in a Soviet maneuver. This was eventually demonstrated when the Soviet Union made its decision to withdraw the missiles without consultation with Cuba. If the Soviet Union did not negotiate with Fidel Castro on this point, there seems no reason for the United States to have done so.

5. It is my understanding that the Kennedy-Khrushchev agreement never went into formal effect. That agreement called for UN verification of the dismantlement and removal of the missiles, in exchange for which the United States would give a pledge not to invade Cuba. Since Cuba rejected UN inspection, the agreement was never completed. In practice, aerial reconnaissance took the place of UN inspection, and the United States refrained from invasion, which it had never intended in any case (except in connection with the removal of the missiles). Since Cuba prevented the US-USSR agreement from going into formal effect, I do not see that this agreement can serve as a basis for further steps in negotiation.

6. As you will see in chapter 23 of *Robert Kennedy and His Times,* the determination in the autumn of 1963 to explore the possibility of normalization of relations between the United States and Cuba was favored by President Kennedy, Robert Kennedy, McGeorge Bundy, Averell Harriman and Adlai Stevenson. It was opposed by elements in the State Department, but they were not in the position to reverse the President's decision.

7. The Bay of Pigs was followed by the Operation Mongoose program of sabotage and harassment. This was one of the worst errors of the Kennedy administration, and after the missile crisis the program was terminated. In the spring of 1963 the administration moved to stop raids against Cuba from the United States. The CIA undoubtedly continued to finance Cuban exiles. It also continued its assassination plots against Fidel Castro. These plots began in the Eisenhower administration and continued well into the Johnson administration. For reasons set forth in chapters 21 and 23 of *Robert Kennedy and His Times,* I do not believe that any of the three Presidents authorized or were aware of these plots. In the

case of Kennedy, the CIA people involved testified before the Church Committee that they had not informed John McCone of the plots. This means that, if they ever informed Kennedy, they would have had to tell him not to mention the plots to McCone, which would have been a most improbable bureaucratic situation.

As for "the most influential characters in U.S. Cuban policy," it must be remembered that, except for the Bay of Pigs and the missile crisis, Cuba was not a major concern for U.S. policy-makers in these years. Robert Kennedy was a key figure, both in the Operation Mongoose period and in the later search for accommodation. Richard Goodwin played a role, as did McGeorge Bundy and various middle-level people at State. The main responsibility for Cuban policy rested, I would judge, at the White House.

I hope these comments may be of some help.

Sincerely yours,
Arthur Schlesinger, Jr.

To John Huston*

24 June 1985

[New York, New York]

Dear John:

Marietta [Tree] showed me your letters about the nuclear arms race. I couldn't agree more about the urgency of the problem. I fear that my classmate Caspar Weinberger really believes that nuclear weapons are usable and nuclear wars winnable. If he proceeds on this assumption, it will be inadequate consolation to know that the human race was extinguished by a fellow member of the Harvard class of 1938.

The trouble with Star Wars is that there is no such thing as an impermeable shield. If we continue in that direction, the Russians are bound to re-

---

*John Huston (1906–87). American film director, screenwriter, and actor; onetime companion of Marietta Tree; nominated fourteen times for Academy Awards, winning twice; his notable movies include *The Maltese Falcon* and *The Treasure of the Sierra Madre*; his father was actor Walter Huston and his daughter is actress Anjelica Huston.

spond by building more ICBMs[*] in order to overwhelm the shield and more Cruise and submarine-launched missiles in order to go under the shield. We would do the same thing in their place. Star Wars, in short, guarantees an immediate and terrifying intensification of the arms race. So long as we insist on Star Wars, there seems no chance of serious movement toward arms control.

The proposal of unrestricted power of inspection is more promising, though it encounters the rooted Russian (pre-Soviet as well as post) fear of external intrusion into their society. I wish that someone would revive Eisenhower's 1955 Open Skies plan, by which the superpowers would exchange blueprints of military establishments and permit mutual photographic overflights. Such a system of continuous reciprocal monitoring would reduce fears of surprise attack. The Russians turned down Open Skies then as an American espionage scheme. Perhaps they would think better of it now. In the meantime, the proposal of a joint American-Soviet crisis center, where each side could monitor the other side's radar screens and to which war rumors would go for resolution, would do much to reduce the chances of accidental war.

Also a comprehensive nuclear test ban is long overdue. If Kennedy had been able to get a comprehensive ban in 1963 (he wanted it, but the Joint Chiefs killed the idea), the world would be a much safer place today.

The real horror will begin when some terrorist group manages to get hold of a nuclear weapon. Perhaps you should make a movie about this.

Let me conclude these rambling remarks by saying how very much I enjoyed *Prizzi's Honor*.[†] I guess film directors should be added to orchestra conductors and (I hope) historians in the small list of those professions in which adepts do not seem to lose their touch with age.

Yours ever,
Arthur

---

[*] Intercontinental ballistic missiles.
[†] *Prizzi's Honor*. Black comedy directed by John Huston about mob hit men, released in 1985; it starred Jack Nicholson, Anjelica Huston, and Kathleen Turner.

To Jimmy Breslin

July 10, 1985

[New York, New York]

Dear Jimmy:

Ordinarily you are infallible, but you nodded in your July Fourth column. You have President Kennedy reading James Bond in 1960 and hiring the mob to kill Castro. It is true enough, as you say, that the CIA in 1960 installed Giancana[*] and Roselli[†] in a Miami Beach hotel and conspired with them to murder Castro. But Kennedy had nothing to do with this. Kennedy was not President till 20 January 1961. The Eisenhower CIA brought in the mob. (I do not think, however, that either Eisenhower or Kennedy ever authorized the assassination attempts. If you will read Stansfield Turner's[‡] *Secrecy and Democracy*,[§] you will see how hard it is even for the CIA director to find out what the agency is up to.) The Kennedy administration pursued Giancana, and eventually he was sent to prison. You will find all this in chapter 21 of that notable work *Robert Kennedy and His Times.*

Best,
Arthur

---

[*] Sam Giancana (1908–75). Sicilian American mobster; contracted by CIA in 1960 to murder Fidel Castro; later killed in mysterious circumstances, reportedly by fellow Mafia thugs.

[†] John Roselli (1905–76). Influential Chicago mob figure; fixer in Hollywood circles; racketeer in Las Vegas; recruited by CIA to kill Fidel Castro in 1960; shot to death by unknown gunmen.

[‡] Stansfield Turner (b. 1923). Admiral; U.S. Naval officer, 1947–78; president of the Naval War College, 1972–74; director of Central Intelligence, 1977–81; opposed second Iraq War and criticized the George W. Bush administration for advocating torture; research scholar at University of Maryland.

[§] Stansfield Turner, *Secrecy and Democracy: The CIA in Transition* (Boston: Houghton Mifflin, 1985), reviewed past CIA abuses, discussed difficulties of running the intelligence agency, and recommended changes.

To Jack Warren[*]

17 January 1986

[New York, New York]

Dear Mr. Warren:

I share your sense of urgency about the need to stop nuclear war. However, I doubt that world government is the practical possibility. Government must be an expression of community. Our world today is too deeply divided on fundamental questions for world government to be feasible—or so it seems to me.

Sincerely yours,
Arthur Schlesinger, Jr.

To Jimmy Breslin

7 April 1986

[New York, New York]

Dear Jimmy:

Every once in a while the Pulitzer prizes make some sense, and the boys outdid themselves this year with Breslin and Feiffer.[†] Alexandra joins in sending warmest congratulations. We are glad you've joined the establishment.

Yours ever,
Arthur

[*] Jack Warren of West Los Angeles, California.

[†] Jules Feiffer (b. 1929). Progressive syndicated cartoonist; screenwriter; playwright; featured in *The Village Voice* for forty-two years; won the 1986 Pulitzer Prize for Editorial Cartooning; known for his play/movie, *Carnal Knowledge*.

To John F. Kurey*

18 June 1986

[New York, New York]

Dear Mr. Kurey:

I am greatly encouraged by the recent revival of interest in the classics. Western civilization had its vital origins in Greece and Rome, and no one can hope to be truly civilized without due appreciation of what the Greeks gave us in philosophy, drama and sculpture and the Romans in literature and law.

This is something the men who led the American republic in its earliest years well understood. "To live without having a Cicero and a Tacitus at hand," wrote John Quincy Adams, "seems to me as if it was a privation of one of my limbs." Thomas Jefferson thought Tacitus "the first writer of the world without a single exception." "The Roman Republic," Alexander Hamilton wrote in the 34th Federalist paper, "attained to the utmost height of human greatness."

One has the impression that the United States had more great men in 1786 with a population of 3.5 million than it does in 1986 with a population nearly one hundred times as large. Perhaps the decline in study and knowledge of the classics is one of the reasons why. So I send my best wishes to the National Junior Classical League on the occasion of its fiftieth anniversary. Nil desperandum; carpe diem.

Sincerely yours,
Arthur

* John F. Kurey of Brookfield, Wisconsin.

To Mary McCarthy

2 July 1986

[New York, New York]

Dear Mary:

. . . As for Lillian [Hellman], she was a character in her way, and I rather enjoyed seeing her when I first came to New York in the 1960s. But she excommunicated me in the 1970s for writing a letter to the *Times* praising a piece written by Hilton Kramer about the *Scoundrel Time* approach to the 1940s. She sent a savage, handwritten letter and cut me for a long time thereafter. Once when we were visiting Kay Graham on the Vineyard, Kay was disinvited from one of Lillian's dinners when she proposed bringing me along. Of course I made no secret, when your case arose, of my total agreement with your characterization of her truth-telling capacities.[*] I am glad to have known Lillian, but the relation was bound to end. My only regret was that I ever went into print in praise of Hilton Kramer. I did not know then who he was and what he stood for. I do now.[†]

Love,
Arthur

[*] Hellman sued McCarthy for defamation in 1979 after McCarthy had said on TV that "every word [Hellman] writes is a lie, including 'and' and 'the.' " Hellman died in 1984 and her executors dropped the suit.
[†] From his perch at *The New Criterion,* the monthly journal of culture and ideas that he cofounded in 1982 and edited, Kramer became known as a neoconservative cultural warrior, attacking the Kennedys and Schlesinger when he was not writing acutely about art and literature.

To Jefferson Morley[*]

4 August 1986

[New York, New York]

Dear Mr. Morley:

I read your piece in the August *New Republic* with interest. But I don't think I have ever argued that there is a single role or responsibility for intellectuals. Temperaments, as William James used to say, determine philosophies; and the intellectual, like everyone else, must follow his (her) temperamental bent. "Some intellectuals will participate in the world of power, some will criticize, some will denounce, some will cultivate their own gardens, some will, at one time or another, do all these things. A spectrum of opinion and action among intellectuals is indispensable if reason is to civilize power" (*The Crisis of Confidence*, 93–94). In my own life I followed the bent of my own temperament; but that does not mean that I think that every intellectual ought to do as I have done.

Sincerely yours,
Arthur Schlesinger, Jr.

To Walter Kerr[†]

29 September 1986

[New York, New York]

Dear Walter:

As one of the few people around New York who saw the original London production of *Me and My Girl*, I read your Sunday piece with special interest. I remembered thinking the show old-fashioned then; and, if anyone had told me in 1938 that it would be the hit of New York in 1986, I would have been incredulous. But I must say that I enjoyed the current production immensely.

---

[*] Jefferson Morley (b. 1958). Journalist; blogger; author; staff writer at Salon.com; worked at *The New Republic, The Nation,* and *The Washington Post.*
[†] Walter Kerr (1913–96). Broadway theater critic; writer; playwright; lyricist; director; theater reviewer for the *New York Herald Tribune,* 1951–66, and *The New York Times,* 1966–83; won the 1978 Pulitzer Prize for Criticism.

On returning home, I checked the journal I have kept intermittently through the years and discovered that I had seen *Me and My Girl* on 19 September 1938—almost precisely 48 years before I saw it again. You are right in surmising that a lot of Robert Lindsay's[*] business and acrobatics are derived from Lupino Lane,[†] though Lindsay's performance is much less broad (but then I saw Lane after 400 performances). My comment as of 1938: "Feeling too excited [I had just arrived in London] to go to bed but too sleepy to be kept awake by anything less than a bright and snappy musical show, I visited in the evening the reigning musical success *Me and My Girl*. The Victoria Palace was crowded—and this was a *Monday* night—with SRO[‡] signs about, so for two shillings I stood behind the dress circle. But the show was vile. Under sensible direction Lupino Lane might be very funny, and the score was quite nice; but the production, performances and lines were incredibly antique and crude. The audience roared with laughter, while I stood behind them, gaping in amazement. When I think what a New York producer might have done with the Lambeth Walk—and compare it with the way the English did it . . ." Anyway it is a better show now than then by a good deal, or else I have mellowed dangerously through the long years.

Best regards,
Arthur

To James E. Wood[§]

22 October 1986

[New York, New York]

Dear Mr. Wood:

I doubt that either of us is going to convince the other of anything; but let me try to answer your question. I believe that the Soviet Union is help-

---

[*] Robert Lindsay (b. 1949). English actor in theater, TV, and film; left-wing critic of Prime Minister Tony Blair's administration over Iraq invasion and other issues.

[†] Lupino Lane (1892–1959). English actor in film, theater, and television; theater manager; renowned for his role in *Me and My Girl*.

[‡] Standing room only.

[§] James E. Wood of Raleigh, North Carolina.

ing the Sandinistas partly out of a sense of revolutionary solidarity and partly out of the desire to cause trouble for the United States on a low-cost, low-risk basis. I doubt that the Soviet Union has any delusions about its capacity to take over Central America and Mexico when the great Red Army cannot defeat a group of ragged Afghan tribesmen in a country on the Soviet border.

If I cannot persuade you that communism is a burned-out ideology, at least let me express my admiration for your eloquence and fervor at the age of 85.

Sincerely yours,
Arthur Schlesinger, Jr.

To Robert McNamara

28 October 1986

[New York, New York]

Dear Bob:

Bill Buckley and I are having a contention about the number of nuclear warheads in existence today. I said 50,000 and cite the piece you and Hans Bethe[*] wrote for the *Atlantic* in July 1985. He says 25,000 and cites the attached warhead count from a recent issue of *Time*. Is the difference that the *Time* count is of warheads deployed and does not include warheads stockpiled? Can you throw any further light on the matter?[†]

Yours ever,
Arthur

---

[*] Hans Bethe (1906–2005). German American nuclear physicist; 1967 Nobel Prize winner in physics; worked at Los Alamos during World War II on atomic bomb; professor at Cornell, 1935–2005; notable campaigner for the end of the nuclear arms race.

[†] McNamara's handwritten reply of November 5, 1986, scrawled on the top of the Schlesinger letter: "As usual, Buckley is wrong and you are right. The total of 50,000 is correct. . . . The *Time* figures exclude substantial numbers of tactical weapons and stockpiled warheads. Best wishes, Bob."

To William F. Buckley, Jr.

19 November 1986

[New York, New York]

Dear Bill:

Bob McNamara tells me that the *Time* figures (on the number of nuclear weapons) exclude substantial numbers of tactical weapons and stockpiled warheads. The attached table from Bob's new book adds up to 50,698 (including the 10,000 warheads stockpiled but not deployed). Since this figure does not include British, French, Israeli, Pakistani, South African, etc., warheads, the actual number is even larger.

Have I won an argument?

Best regards,
Arthur

From William F. Buckley, Jr.

[23 November 1986]

[New York, New York]

Dear Arthur:

I can only think that, as a conscientious historian, you should go over there and count them. If you agree, I will give you the Verification Chair at the university of your choice.... Hope your book is doing well. Not *too* well; well will do.

Cordially,
Wm. F. Buckley Jr.

To Nancy Amestoy[*]

10 September 1987

[New York, New York]

Dear Ms. Amestoy:

. . . True religion, as I understand it, should lead to a sense of human frailty before the awful mystery of eternity. It should lead to an understanding that, as Lincoln said, "The Almighty has His own purposes." Lincoln added privately, "Men are not flattered by being shown that there has been a difference of purpose between the Almighty and them. To deny it, however, in this case, is to deny that there is a God governing the world."

I am bound to distrust those who have the arrogance to claim that they know the Almighty's purposes. As Mr. Dooley[†] put it, a fanatic is one who "does what he thinks th' Lord wud do if He only knew th' facts in th' case."

Sincerely yours,
Arthur Schlesinger, Jr.

On the twentieth anniversary of Robert F. Kennedy's assassination on June 6, 1988, a special mass was held in his memory at the Arlington National Cemetery in Virginia where he was buried near his brother John.

---

[*] Nancy Amestoy of Stone Mountain, Georgia.

[†] A fictional Irish immigrant living in Chicago, Mr. Dooley expounded on the political and social issues of the day from his stool in a neighborhood pub; his "commentary" appeared in Chicago newspapers and national syndication. Mr. Dooley was the creation of Finley Peter Dunne (1867–1936), an American humorist and author. Dunne's articles were collected in several books, including *Mr. Dooley on Peace and War* (1898).

To Ethel Kennedy

13 June 1988

[New York, New York]

Dear Ethel:

We could not have been sorrier to miss the Mass for Bobby; but it was my 50th reunion at Harvard and I had long since been committed to appear on a panel in Cambridge that evening (and to take a group of my classmates to visit the Kennedy Library the first thing the next morning—an experience they found deeply moving, even if most of them are Republicans). I have heard on every side how beautiful the Mass was, and it broke my heart not to be able to attend.

But I am writing especially to tell you about another panel held at the Kennedy School on Wednesday the 8th on Robert Kennedy and his Vision of Public Service. Though Michael* was delayed in arrival by Eastern Airline snafus, he rose splendidly to the occasion and gave a very touching and perceptive talk about his father—as Bobby, Jr.,† also did at an RFK memorial meeting in New York last month.

You should be very proud of your children—and they should be very proud of you.

Love,
Arthur

* Michael Kennedy (1958–97). The sixth of eleven children of Robert F. Kennedy and Ethel Kennedy; lawyer; killed in a skiing accident in Aspen, Colorado.

† Robert F. Kennedy, Jr. (b. 1954). Third child of eleven; lawyer; writer; environmental activist; nationally syndicated radio host.

To Ernest Daniels*

1 August 1988

[New York, New York]

Dear Mr. Daniels:

... Of course, democracy is a most unsatisfactory form of government. The argument for it, as Churchill famously pointed out, is that it is less unsatisfactory than all the other forms. Despite the ignorance and infirmities of a mass electorate, the democratic form contains more possibilities of intelligent self-correction than any other form—or so it seems to me. But I have never supposed democracy to be a self-executing process. "Perhaps no form of government," as Bryce[†] said, "needs great leaders so much as democracy." You may be interested in some of the reflections in "Democracy and Leadership," the last chapter in *The Cycles of American History*.

I doubt, by the way, that those whom you call the "plebeians" really constitute "democracy's ruling class." Power in the American democracy resides elsewhere.

Sincerely yours,
Arthur Schlesinger, Jr.

To Joseph Alsop

18 August 1988

Vineyard Haven, Mass.

Dear Joe:

A call from Alexandra after her talk with you prompts this letter. I need hardly say how much I grieve over this latest turn of fate.[‡] You and I first met over forty years ago, in the winter of '45–'46. Stewart and I had met in

---

* Ernest Daniels of Brooklyn, New York.

† James Bryce (1838–1922). 1st Viscount Bryce; British academic; historian; taught at Oxford, 1870–93; Liberal MP, 1880–1907; wrote a landmark book on U.S. society, *The American Commonwealth* (1888); ambassador to the United States, 1907–13.

‡ Alsop was diagnosed with lung cancer. He died the following year.

France during the war, and one day we ran into each other on the streets in Washington, and he invited me to one of your wonderful stag dinners of that era. It was a heady evening—Felix, Jimmy Byrnes, Dean, Averell, Chip, George, heaven knows who else; and, a young historian back from the wars, I felt transported to some higher realm of intellect and power.

You have been the most generous, stimulating, joyous, exasperating of friends ever since. I know that you have not always approved of my views on one or another matter. But, whether in agreement or disagreement, you have been a source of boundless delight, exhilaration, happiness for Alexandra and me, and for all your friends. (And I cannot resist the conviction that you are in an important sense a liberal-AL at heart, on the vital matters—civil liberties and equal opportunity and racial justice. Your interventions in these fields have provided some of your noblest moments.)

I will phone when we get your number; but, since it is sometimes easier to write things than to say them, I want to tell you now that you have been a beloved friend through the long years and that our love and prayers are with you forever. We will hope to come and see you before too long.

Love from us both,
Arthur

To Jonathan H. Mann[*]

12 September 1988

[New York, New York]

Dear Mr. Mann:

Thank you for your nice letter, and of course I am happy to inscribe your copy of *Robert Kennedy and His Times*.

Objectivity is the historian's ideal, but total objectivity is an impossible dream. Every scholar is the prisoner of his own experience; no one can shed his deepest prepossessions, values, prejudices. The biographer may conceive a special attachment to his subject (or in some cases a special dislike), and the wise biographer tries to be conscious of bias and not permit it to

* Jonathan H. Mann of Brooklyn, New York.

control judgment. As you have perhaps noted, I deal with some of these questions on page xiii of *Robert Kennedy*.

Sincerely yours,
Arthur Schlesinger, Jr.

To Daniel Beaudoin[*]

27 September 1988

[New York, New York]

Dear Mr. Beaudoin:

You ask my favorite time period of history. I guess I believe with the 19th century German historian Henke[†] that "every epoch is immediate to God," and, as a mere mortal, I would hesitate to prefer one to another. But I have concentrated my own historical work on the United States in the 19th and 20th centuries. I suppose that my particular interest lies in the convergence of intellectual and political history and in the impact of ideas on public policy.

"The duty of an American historian"? To tell the truth about the past as best he (she) can—and let the chips fall where they may. . . .

Sincerely yours,
Arthur Schlesinger, Jr.

In the November 24, 1988, issue of The Times Literary Supplement, *in his review of Don DeLillo's[‡] novel* Libra, *Christopher Hitchens[§] wrote that President Kennedy "approached the mafia in order to discuss 'hitting' Castro." Ar-*

---

[*] Daniel Beaudoin of Troy, Michigan.

[†] Ernst Ludwig Theodor Henke (1804–72). German historian; taught at Jena and Marburg universities.

[‡] Don DeLillo (b. 1936). American novelist, playwright, and essayist.

[§] Christopher Hitchens (1949–2011). English-born American author and journalist; contributor to *The Nation*, 1981–2002, and *Vanity Fair*, 1992–2011; TV commentator; held socialist views as a youth, later turning neoconservative; favored the 2003 invasion of Iraq, wrote bestseller on atheism, *God Is Not Great: How Religion Poisons Everything* (2007); harbored longtime disapproval of Schlesinger.

thur replied to Hitchens in the January 26 issue, pointing out that the Eisenhower administration had initiated the Mafia plot. Hitchens riposted with further charges of Kennedy family complicity in murderous activities—charges that Arthur went to some effort to refute.

To the Editor of *The Times Literary Supplement*

3 February 1989

[New York, New York]

Sir:

I wish that Christopher Hitchens's polemical verve were matched by his historical knowledge. My letter was written to refute his flat assertion that John F. Kennedy "approached the Mafia in order to discuss 'hitting' Castro." Mr. Hitchens now demurely admits that the "CIA's first approach to the Mafia took place during the Eisenhower presidency." The retraction is evasive. "First approach?" By the end of September 1960, weeks before the election and months before Kennedy's inauguration, the CIA had already recruited and briefed the two gangsters, Giancana and Roselli, and installed them in the Kenilworth Hotel in Miami. Some first approach.

Let me deal seriatim with Mr. Hitchens's numbered points.

1) Mr. Hitchens claims that in the 1960 campaign Kennedy attacked "Eisenhower's failure to 'remove' Fidel Castro." Kennedy did indeed attack the Eisenhower administration for failing to prevent Castro from coming to power, and he did pledge support to "non-Batista democratic anti-Castro forces." But I challenge Mr. Hitchens to produce a Kennedy attack on "Eisenhower's failure to 'remove' Fidel Castro." The quotation marks around "remove" imply that Kennedy used the word. I cannot find that he did, and, unless Mr. Hitchens can produce evidence to the contrary, his statement must go down as another fabrication. (Actually the word is ambiguous in any case; there is a wide difference between removal from power and removal from life.)

2) Mr. Hitchens writes, "CIA Director Richard Helms only revived 'Operation Mongoose' as an assassination scheme *after* a meeting with Attorney General Robert Kennedy." This sentence reveals Mr. Hitchens's hopeless

ignorance of the matters about which he writes with such a show of certitude. Richard Helms did not become CIA Director for another five
years. Operation Mongoose was established, not "revived," in November
1961. It was not "an assassination scheme." It was a scheme of intelligence
collection, propaganda and sabotage with the ultimate objective of stimulating the overthrow of Castro through internal revolt. For details of
Mongoose, see the Church Committee report of 1976 "Alleged Assassination Plots Involving Foreign Leaders," especially pages 154–157. The CIA
assassination effort meanwhile continued on another track; it was not
part of the Mongoose program. As for Mr. Helms's meeting with Robert
Kennedy, "Helms testified that he had never told Attorney General Kennedy about any assassination activity" ("Assassination Plots," 151).

3) Mr. Hitchens writes that Robert Kennedy was told by Lawrence Houston,[*]
the CIA general counsel, in May 1962 of the CIA recruitment of mobsters in an effort to kill Castro. This is correct. But what Mr. Hitchens
slyly omits is that, as Mr. Houston testified before the Church Committee, "it was his 'understanding that the assassination plan aimed at Castro had been terminated completely,' and that Kennedy was told 'the
activity had been terminated as of that time'" (132). In other words,
Robert Kennedy was told that the assassination effort was over and done
with when in fact the CIA kept it going for several more years.

4) Mr. Hitchens says that the Attorney General had already been informed
of the CIA-Mafia connection a year earlier in a memorandum from
J. Edgar Hoover on May 22, 1961. "There is no record of either Kennedy's
ever trying to cancel any such anti-Castro operation." The implication is
clear that Hoover told Robert Kennedy about the assassination plots in
May 1961. Wrong again. The Hoover memorandum, which followed a
CIA briefing of the FBI, says *nothing* about assassination plots—for the
ample reason that, as the Church Committee reported, the CIA briefing
"did not reveal the specific objective of the Giancana operation to the
FBI" (127). The Hoover memorandum referred in very general terms to
the CIA's use in "clandestine efforts against the Castro government" of
"hoodlum elements" with "sources and contacts in Cuba."

---

* Lawrence Houston (1913–95). Lawyer; OSS operative in World War II; helped draft
legislation setting up the CIA in 1947; CIA general counsel, 1947–73.

5) Mr. Hitchens quotes President Johnson as saying that President Kennedy had been trying to kill Castro and quotes Garry Wills[*] as saying that "Johnson was in the best position to know—how and whether a President directs the CIA 'unofficially.' " Of course this generalization also convicts both Eisenhower, in whose administration the assassination plots started, and Johnson himself, since the plots continued well into his own administration.

But is Mr. Hitchens really so naive as to believe that intelligence services do not strike out on their own? that intelligence operatives do not come to believe that they know the requirements of national security better than transient elected officials? that the CIA never lifted a finger except at presidential instruction? Come on. Of course that is the CIA story; but who would dream that Christopher Hitchens would swallow such obvious disinformation? Let him study the record of MI-5, or of French intelligence, or of Mossad, or, for that matter, of the KGB. The CIA is no different. Hitchens must be kidding.

In the case in point, all witnesses before the Church committee agreed that John McCone, who was appointed by Kennedy to clean up the CIA after the Bay of Pigs, was never informed of the plots. If a CIA official had informed the Kennedys, he would have had to stipulate that they must not mention the plotting to McCone. Given John Kennedy's reliance on McCone to bring the CIA under control and Robert Kennedy's close personal friendship with McCone, it strains credulity to suppose that either would have accepted such a stipulation from some subordinate spook.

Mr. Hitchens would be well advised in the future to do a modicum of homework before galloping into print.

Sincerely yours,
Arthur Schlesinger, jr.

---

*Garry Wills (b. 1934). Author of almost forty books; journalist; historian; devout Catholic; began as theater critic at William F. Buckley's *National Review*; by 1960s espoused liberal political views; *New York Review of Books* contributor, 1973–present; professor at Johns Hopkins University, 1962–80, and at Northwestern University, 1980–present.

To Jack Hyde[*]

19 July 1989

[New York, New York]

Dear Mr. Hyde:

When I grew up in the 1930s, the men I most admired wore bow ties. Franklin Roosevelt wore bow ties. Winston Churchill wore bow ties. Harry Truman and Humphrey Bogart[†] wore bow ties. I naturally followed their example.

In later life I became ever more appreciative of the advantages of bow ties. Most signally, it is impossible—or at least it requires extreme agility—ever to spill anything on a bow tie. Four-in-hand ties, after a bout with the cleaner, are never the same. For sloppy eaters bow ties are a godsend.

Bow tie wearers? In addition to those you mention, I think of the pianist Vladimir Horowitz,[‡] the lawyers Archibald Cox and Joe Rauh, the correspondents Joe Alsop and Drew Middleton, the writer August Heckscher,[§] the former Surgeon General C. Everett Koop,[¶] the TV commentator Gene Shalit;[**] on occasion, if not on the air, John Chancellor.[††] Walter Lippmann and Jimmy Wechsler used to wear them. What do such men have in common? Fastidiousness, nonconformity, high intelligence, a sense of style.

---

[*] Jack Hyde, Fashion Institute of Technology, New York, New York.

[†] Humphrey Bogart (1899–1957). Iconic American film actor and liberal Democrat; featured in *The Petrified Forest, The Maltese Falcon,* and *Casablanca;* his fourth wife, Lauren Bacall, was a close Schlesinger friend.

[‡] Vladimir Horowitz (1903–89). Renowned Russian-born American classical pianist and composer; settled in the United States in 1928; recorded for RCA and Columbia Records; won numerous Grammy Awards.

[§] August Heckscher (1914–97). Author; civic administrator; editorial writer at *New York Herald Tribune,* 1952–56; arts consultant to the Kennedy administration, 1961–63; New York City Park Commissioner, 1967–72; opened parks to outdoor concerts, antiwar demonstrations, and marathon running.

[¶] C. Everett Koop (b. 1916). Pediatric surgeon; surgeon-general, 1982–89; opposed cigarette smoking, alerted nation to AIDS epidemic, and refused to condemn abortion.

[**] Gene Shalit (b. 1926). Author; arts critic; NBC radio essayist, 1970–82; longtime film and book critic for NBC *Today* show, 1973–2010; known for his outsized mustache and colorful bow ties.

[††] John Chancellor (1927–96). American journalist; head of Voice of America, 1965–67; anchor of *NBC Nightly News,* 1970–82.

Of course one must tie one's own bow tie so long as one is physically able.

Best of luck on your inquiry.

Sincerely yours,
Arthur Schlesinger, Jr.

To Samuel Kaplan[*]

4 January 1990

[New York, New York]

Dear Mr. Kaplan:

Our invasion of Panama[†] seemed to me to break three vital rules: that the United States should never, except in cases of extreme emergency, take unilateral military action in the hemisphere; that superpowers should never, except in cases of extreme emergency, launch sneak attacks on small countries; and that an American President should never, except in cases of extreme emergency, go to war without the consent and authorization of Congress. Since Noriega,[‡] odious and detestable as he is, certainly did not present any clear and present danger to the national security of the United States, these rules, in my view, should have prevailed.

In the longer run, we have a greater interest in the establishment of a world of law than in the overthrow of noxious dictators. Or so it seems to me. Best of luck with your peace group.

Sincerely yours,
Arthur

---

[*] Samuel Kaplan of Chapel Hill, North Carolina.

[†] The invasion of Panama took place in December 1989 to "protect" the lives of American servicemen and to arrest the nation's dictator, Manuel Noriega, for complicity in drug smuggling into the United States.

[‡] Manuel Noriega (b. 1934). Politican and military officer; Panamanian dictator, 1983–89; toppled by U.S. invasion and imprisoned for drug trafficking, 1989–2010; currently in Panamanian prison as of 2011.

To Jon Winokur[*]

11 January 1990

[New York, New York]

Dear Mr. Winokur:

Our dog Polo is our third Cavalier King Charles Spaniel. When my wife and I were married in 1971, we felt the family deserved a dog; and her son Peter, then six years old, after poring over a book of dog pictures, decided we must have a King Charles Spaniel. It took a little trouble to find one, but we finally succeeded. Peter named him Sinbad, and we all adored him. Then one day, running in Central Park without a leash, Sinbad dashed into a roadway, and a taxi killed him.

To alleviate the grief we then acquired Molly of the same breed. Peter and our new son Robert, then about five, thought that Molly as a lady should have progeny; so we mated her with Blenheim, Lauren Bacall's[†] beloved King Charles Spaniel. After several unproductive weekends together at a hospitable kennel, Molly finally became pregnant. In the summer of 1980 she gave birth to two small puppies. Robert promptly named them Marco and Polo. Since Blenheim was the father, Lauren Bacall had the choice of the litter, and she took Marco. Polo, now nearly ten years old, is not so frisky as he was, but he still brightens our lives every day.

Sincerely yours,
Arthur Schlesinger, Jr.

P.S. If you want to make a contribution, Polo's favorite charity is the Schlesinger Library on the History of Women in America, Radcliffe College, Cambridge, Massachusetts 02138.

---

[*] Jon Winokur of Pacific Palisades, California.

[†] Lauren ("Betty") Bacall (b. 1924). American actress in film, TV, and theater; married to actor Humphrey Bogart, 1945–57; later married to actor Jason Robards, Jr., 1961–69; liberal Democrat; gave eulogy for Schlesinger at his memorial service in London.

To Shawn Nunnally[*]

12 January 1990

[New York, New York]

Dear Shawn:

I regret to say that I am one of the world's worst drawers, but I send the result with best wishes to you for the New Year.

Sincerely yours,
Arthur Schlesinger, jr.

To Daniel Patrick Moynihan

19 March 1990

[New York, New York]

Dear Pat:

Since you know about everything, you undoubtedly know about holography, which is, in effect, three-dimensional photography. Some time you should visit the Museum of Holography at 11 Mercer Street in Soho. The holographic effects are quite stunning. I attach a brochure.

The Museum is assembling an exhibit of photographs of New York notables. They already have done Paul Moore[†] in episcopal vestments, Gloria

---

[*] Shawn Nunnally of Marion, North Carolina.

[†] Paul Moore, Jr. (1919–2003). Marine veteran of World War II; joined Episcopal ministry in 1949; New York City Episcopal bishop, 1972–89; social activist in the civil rights and antiwar movements; married twice with nine children; his daughter Honor Moore revealed her father's bisexuality in 2008 *New Yorker* piece.

Steinem,* me and others. The exhibit would hardly be complete without you, and, since Ana Maria Nicholson, the portrait holographer, lacks confidence in her ability to get an invitation through to you, I volunteered to serve as advance man.

The actual process of being holographed, or hologrammed, is brief, painless and interesting. The results are really quite breathtaking. I do hope you might consider letting them do your portrait, and you should hear soon from Ms. Nicholson ... about the possibility of setting up an appointment. (Obviously the $1,500 charge does not apply to this exhibit.)

Best,
Arthur Schlesinger, Jr.

To George H. W. Bush[†]

30 April 1990

[New York, New York]

Dear Mr. President:

I would like to take the liberty of calling your attention to a forthcoming anniversary—one that recent events around the planet endow with special significance. January 6, 1991, will be the fiftieth anniversary of the address to Congress in which President Roosevelt set forth his vision of the world of the Four Freedoms.[‡] This was a distinctively American vision,

---

* Gloria Steinem (b. 1934). American feminist, journalist, and political activist; cofounder of *Ms.* magazine; leader in Equal Rights Amendment crusade; adviser to Democratic candidates on women's issues.

† On November 8, 1988, Republican vice president George H. W. Bush defeated Massachusetts Democratic governor Michael Dukakis in the race for the presidency, winning 53.4 percent of the popular vote against 45.6 percent for Dukakis.

‡ The Four Freedoms as articulated by FDR in his 1941 State of the Union address:

In the future days, which we seek to make secure, we look forward to a world founded upon four essential human freedoms. The first is freedom of speech and expression—everywhere in the world. The second is freedom of every person to worship God in his own way—everywhere in the world. The third is freedom from want—which, translated into world terms, means economic understandings which will secure to every nation a healthy peacetime life for its inhabitants—everywhere in the world. The fourth is freedom from fear—which, translated into world terms, means a world-wide reduction of

hailed by our citizens of all parties and creeds, and it has never been more relevant than it is today.

Now that dramatic changes in Eastern Europe, within the Soviet Union itself and in other parts of the world bring that vision within sight if not quite within reach, it would seem an appropriate time to recall and celebrate the Four Freedoms. I don't know what form such a celebration might take—perhaps a joint session of Congress in which you and other speakers might renew the national commitment to the Four Freedoms. But I do hope something can be done to commemorate the fiftieth anniversary of that historic day.

I will only add that the Franklin and Eleanor Roosevelt Institute, of which I am a co-chairman and Ambassador vanden Heuvel[*] is president, stands ready to help in any way; and Bill Emerson[†] and the Roosevelt Library at Hyde Park will of course be glad to do anything they can.

Sincerely yours,
Arthur Schlesinger, Jr.

P.S. Another subject: I think you and Jim Baker[‡] have been handling the Lithuanian problem just right.[§]

---

armaments to such a point and in such a thorough fashion that no nation will be in a position to commit an act of physical aggression against any neighbor—anywhere in the world. That is no vision of a distant millennium. It is a definite basis for a kind of world attainable in our own time and generation. That kind of world is the very antithesis of the so-called new order of tyranny which the dictators seek to create with the crash of a bomb.

[*]William vanden Heuvel (b. 1930). Lawyer; diplomat; businessman; Democratic Party activist; special assistant to Attorney General Robert F. Kennedy; ambassador to the United Nations in Geneva, 1977–79; deputy ambassador to the United Nations, 1979–81; founder and chairman emeritus of the Franklin and Eleanor Roosevelt Institute; father of Katrina vanden Heuvel, editor of *The Nation;* Schlesinger family lawyer.

[†]William Emerson (1923–97). Military historian; director of the Franklin Roosevelt Presidential Library at Hyde Park, New York, 1974–1991.

[‡]James ("Jim") Baker (b. 1930). Lawyer; Republican moderate; undersecretary of commerce in the Ford administration, 1975; managed Ford's unsuccessful 1976 presidential campaign; chief of staff to President Reagan, 1981–85; managed Reagan's 1984 reelection campaign; secretary of the Treasury, 1985–88; secretary of state, 1989–92, overseeing the fall of the Berlin Wall and the first Gulf War.

[§]Lithuania had declared its independence from the Soviet Union on March 11, 1990, prompting Soviet economic countermeasures. While supporting Lithuanian inde-

To John O'Keefe[*]

13 December 1990

[New York, New York]

Dear John:

Do you remember that during (I believe) the Christmas holiday of 1931 you invited me out to your house for a meal? Rosemary Kennedy[†] was spending—was it the winter?—with your parents and sisters. Rosemary was the first Kennedy I ever met.

I thought of this a couple of weeks ago when Jean Kennedy Smith asked Alexandra and me out to Bridgehampton for the weekend after Thanksgiving. Jean and her husband Stephen Smith, who died this summer, have been our closest friends. It turned out that Rosemary Kennedy was in Bridgehampton for the weekend—the first time I had seen her for nearly sixty years. I felt as if a circle had been closed.

As you know, the Ambassador succumbed to the prevailing medical advice of the day, and a lobotomy was performed on Rosemary during the war. I asked Jean whether Rosemary would remember her stay with the O'Keefes, and Jean feared that she wouldn't. I could faintly see in this tragic old woman the features of the young girl I recall from so many years back.

How are you, John, and your family? What about Mary and Frances? Drop a line some time, and do let me know if anything brings you to this wicked city.

Merry Christmas, and warmest regards across the long years,
Arthur

---

pendence, President Bush was eager to not damage improving relations with the Soviet Union and acted with restraint, calling for peaceful negotiations. His critics on the right called his failure to act agressively "another Munich."

[*] John Aloysius O'Keefe (1916–2000). Schlesinger's roommate at Phillips Exeter, of Swampscott, Massachusetts; his father was a doctor and his mother went to high school with Rose Fitzgerald Kennedy. O'Keefe became an astrophysicist and worked at NASA, 1958–95, where he is credited with the discovery that the earth is pear-shaped.

[†] Rosemary Kennedy (1918–2005). Third child of Joseph and Rosemary Kennedy; sister of President Kennedy; underwent a prefrontal lobotomy at age twenty-three for behavioral issues; spent life at a special school in Jefferson, Wisconsin.

To George H. W. Bush

1 February 1991

[New York, New York]

Dear Mr. President:

I want to thank you for your readiness to come to the Four Freedoms anniversary and for the fine and felicitous words you spoke on that occasion. It was one of those rare ceremonies that gave pleasure to all involved.

As you probably know, I have had reservations about our course in the Gulf; but, now that we are at war, I fervently hope that it can be brought to a quick and victorious conclusion and that the brave young Americans out there will be home as soon as possible.

Best regards,
Arthur

To Osha Gray Davidson[*]

22 March 1991

[New York, New York]

Dear Mr. Davidson:

In belated response to your letter of some weeks back, I suppose that what Americans should have learned from My Lai[†] is that Augustine[‡] and

---

[*] Osha Gray Davidson (b.1954). Journalist; *Rolling Stone* magazine contributor; author of nonfiction books on the environment and human rights, including *Under Fire* and *The Best of Enemies*.

[†] The My Lai massacre occurred in South Vietnam on March 16, 1968, when American soldiers killed 347 to 504 civilians, mostly women and children. Twenty-six U.S. soldiers were charged, but only one, Second Lieutenant William Calley, was prosecuted. He served three and a half years under house arrest.

[‡] Augustine of Hippo, or St. Augustine (354–430). Bishop; priest; Latin philosopher; theologian from Roman Africa; influenced the Catholic Church on salvation, original sin, freedom of will, just war, and divine grace; best known for *Confessions*, about his early life.

Calvin* (and Hawthorne† and Niebuhr) were right about the depths of iniquity in the human heart. As William James said about America, "Angelic impulses and predatory lusts divide our hearts exactly as they divide the hearts of other countries." . . .

Sincerely yours,
Arthur Schlesinger, Jr.

People magazine on May 27, 1991, reported that Jean Kennedy Smith had "endured infidelity and anger" from her husband for years and was estranged from him before he died from cancer. This false report about his very good friends enraged Arthur.

To the Editor of *People* Magazine

25 May 1991

[New York, New York]

To the Editor:

I don't know from what sewer *People* dredges up its weekly budget of misinformation; but the magazine really surpasses itself in its comment in the 17 May issue on the marriage of Stephen Smith and Jean Kennedy.

For the last twenty years we saw more of Steve and Jean Smith than we did of any other couple. We dined with them, went to the theater and the movies with them, played tennis with them, spent weekends with them, took holidays with them in America and in Europe. *People*'s picture of the Smith marriage could hardly be more false. The idea that the couple "started living apart, and before long . . . were completely estranged" is fantasy. So too is the notion, as any New Yorker can tell you, that Jean Smith ever "stopped venturing out into the world." So too is *People*'s account of the

---

* John Calvin (1509–64). French theologian; broke with the Catholic Church in the 1530s; helped to spur Protestant Reformation; expounded on spiritual thinking, sin, and damnation.

† Nathaniel Hawthorne (1804–64). American novelist; Democratic political activist; wrote Puritan-inspired moral allegories such as *The Scarlet Letter*, authored biography of President Franklin Pierce.

Smith children "ensconced in elite prep schools"; three out of four Smith children were at home till they went off to college, and a fourth spent only two years away at prep school.

The Smith family is a cohesive and devoted family, and Steve and Jean Smith had a lively and joyous marriage, mutually loving and mutually reinforcing. *People* should be ashamed of itself, if your magazine retains any capacity for shame.

Alexandra Emmet Schlesinger

and

Arthur Schlesinger, jr.

To John Boehner[*]

19 July 1991

[New York, New York]

Dear Congressman Boehner:

I note your "quotations" from Abraham Lincoln in the *Record* of 11 July. You have fallen for a famous and transparent Lincoln forgery. Of course Lincoln never said the things you attribute to him. They are quotations from an "Industrial Decalogue: Ten Don'ts" published in 1916 by a lecturer on industrial relations named William J. H. Boetcker.[†]

In 1942 the Committee for Constitutional Government put out a leaflet entitled "Lincoln on Limitations." On one side was a genuine Lincoln quotation; on the other was Boetcker's Industrial Decalogue. This leaflet evidently led some people to attribute Boetcker's deep thoughts to Lincoln.[‡]

This fake has been exposed again and again in the last half century. I am sorry to see a member of the U.S. Congress give this obvious and well-known

---

[*] John Boehner (b. 1949). Conservative representative (R-Ohio), 1991–present; House majority leader, 2006–7; House minority leader, 2007–11; Speaker of the House, 2011–present; strident opponent of the Obama administration.

[†] William J. H. Boetcker (1873–1962). Conservative Presbyterian religious leader and public speaker.

[‡] "You cannot bring about prosperity by discouraging thrift. You cannot strengthen the weak by weakening the strong. You cannot help little men by tearing down big men. You cannot help the wage earner by pulling down the wage payer. You cannot further brotherhood of man by encouraging class hatred." And so on.

forgery new currency. Seriously, Congressman, do you really think those quotations sound like Abraham Lincoln? Come on!

Sincerely yours,
Arthur Schlesinger, jr.

To Tim Drake[*]

29 July 1991

[New York, New York]

Dear Mr. Drake:

I suppose the lesson that all of us should take away from Watergate is all too familiar: that power corrupts. As the Supreme Court said in *ex parte Milligan*: the republic has "no right to expect that it will always have wise and humane rulers, sincerely attached to the principles of the Constitution. Wicked men, ambitious of power, with hatred of liberty and contempt of law, may fill the place once occupied by Washington and Lincoln."[†]

As for teaching Watergate, there is no better place to begin than to read the articles of impeachment to your class, reminding your students that Nixon resigned in order to escape being found guilty on those charges. Remind them also what Barry Goldwater wrote in his 1988 autobiography about Nixon: "He was the most dishonest individual I ever met in my life. President Nixon lied to his wife, his family, his friends, long-time colleagues in the U.S. Congress, lifetime members of his own political party, the American people and the world."

Sincerely yours,
Arthur Schlesinger, Jr.

---

*Tim Drake of Eagan, Minnesota.

† *Ex parte Milligan* (1866). A U.S. Supreme Court decision ruling that the application of military tribunals to citizens when civilian courts are still operating is unconstitutional.

To Linda Delgado[*]

15 August 1991

[New York, New York]

Dear Linda:

... Of course history should be taught from a diversity of perspectives: I am all in favor of having kids see the arrival of Columbus from the viewpoint of those who met him as well from the viewpoint of those who sent him. The more we learn about others the better.

But I don't think that public schools should strive to perpetuate a sense of ethnic differences or that ethnicity is the defining experience for most Americans or that the role of history is to make people feel good about their ancestors. We have always been a multicultural society, and are now more so than ever, but we should not press multiculturalism in opposition to a sense of national identity.

By the way, I got a friendly letter about *Disuniting*[†] from Henry Louis Gates.[‡] ... See you in the fall.

Sincerely yours,
Arthur Schlesinger, jr.

---

[*] Linda Delgado, board of directors, National Association for Ethnic Studies.

[†] Arthur Schlesinger, Jr., *The Disuniting of America: Reflections on a Multicultural Society* (New York: W. W. Norton, 1992.) First published 1991 by Whittle Direct Books. "I suppose outrage over the way the cult of ethnicity leads to flagrant abuse of history is why I am involved. Or it may be simply the folly of old age," said Schlesinger at the time.

[‡] Henry Louis Gates, Jr. (b. 1950). Scholar; educator; writer; editor; literary critic; professor at Harvard, 1991–present; director of the W. E. B. Du Bois Institute for African and African American Research.

To the Editors of *The Reader's Companion**

6 September 1991

[New York, New York]

Dear Messrs. Bratman and Lewis:

I am happy to attach a list of books I think Americans should read to achieve "cultural literacy" about our own nation.

Emerson's *Essays*
Abraham Lincoln, *Speeches and Writings* (Library of America)
Alexis de Tocqueville, *Democracy in America*
James Bryce, *The American Commonwealth*
Reinhold Niebuhr, *The Irony of American History*
Edmund Wilson, ed., *The Shock of Recognition*
Gunnar Myrdal, *An American Dilemma*
Herbert Croly, *The Promise of American Life*
William James, *Pragmatism*
Henry Adams, *The Education of Henry Adams*
H. L. Mencken, *The American Language*

Sincerely yours,
Arthur Schlesinger, jr.

To Isaiah and Aline Berlin

10 September 1991

[New York, New York]

Dear Isaiah and Aline:

I have been meaning to write to you about Marietta [Tree]'s last days.†
As you know, she kept her illness a secret from her friends and even from

---

* Fred Bratman and Scott Lewis, *The Reader's Companion: A Book Lover's Guide to the Most Important Books in Every Field of Knowledge, as Chosen by the Experts* (New York: Hyperion, 1994).

† Marietta Tree died at New York Hospital of cancer on August 15, 1991. "She once said that her ideal was to be a combination of Carole Lombard and Eleanor Roosevelt. She realized that ideal," Schlesinger wrote in an appreciation.

her brothers; only Frankie [Fitzgerald, her daughter] knew. But there was obviously something wrong. She was losing weight in the spring, and, though she was more beautiful than ever, there was a fragility about her beauty and a vulnerability about her temperament that were somewhat troubling. But she maintained her gaiety, her curiosity about life, her circle of activities.

We saw her quite regularly in the spring and early summer. Her cover story was that she was having a bad reaction to antibiotics. But, after dinner with her one night, I came back terribly worried and called Frankie, who said finally that it was indeed serious. Marietta was obviously determined to play out the hand on her own terms and not to be a burden or a worry for her friends.

We went to Northeast Harbor for the funeral—the old austere Anglican ceremony in a rustic church. There will be a memorial service in New York on Friday 4 October. Frankie has been wonderful throughout. I still really can't believe that it has all happened. Marietta was such a close and dear friend for over forty years that her death leaves a terrible void.

. . . Joe [Alsop]'s memoir will be out in February. The title: *I've Seen the Best of It*. I read the unedited manuscript last year—very good up until about 1950, but thereafter, with Joe's energy and memory flagging, very sketchy and opinionated. My impression is that the published version is an improvement.

We miss you and hope we will meet somewhere before too long. Can you believe the latest installments in the great Soviet serial? Thank heavens for CNN. If only Nicholas [Nabokov] and Chip [Bohlen] were around to provide commentary!

Alexandra joins in sending love to you both,
Arthur

To Robert F. Lambertson[*]

11 September 1991

[New York, New York]

Dear Mr. Lambertson:

I am not unsympathetic to your paper on the pledge of allegiance, but I doubt that much can be done about it at this point. It has always amused me that the pledge was written by Francis Bellamy,[†] a Christian socialist and a nephew of Edward Bellamy[‡] (*Looking Backward*)—and that superpatriots today are demanding that this socialist document be mandatory for all children! "Under God" was added in 1954, and Bellamy's granddaughter, Barbara Bellamy Wright, said recently, "My grandfather would have objected strongly to this change."

You will find sustenance in Justice Jackson's[§] opinion for the Court in West *Virginia [State Board] of Education v Barnette* (319 US 624).[¶]

Sincerely yours,
Arthur Schlesinger, jr.

---

[*] Robert F. Lambertson of Auburn, California.

[†] Francis Bellamy (1886–1973). American author and editor; Baptist minister and Christian socialist; wrote "The Pledge of Allegiance" in 1892 to promote the efforts of the magazine *Youth's Companion* to distribute American flags to schools and sell subscriptions.

[‡] Edward Bellamy (1850–98). Socialist; wrote a bestselling utopian novel, *Looking Backward* (1888), about an Eden-like paradise in the year 2000 where there were no conflicts and the state owned all industry.

[§] Robert Jackson (1892–1954). Liberal Democrat; attorney general, 1940–41; U.S. Supreme Court justice, 1941–54; chief U.S. prosecutor at the Nuremberg trials in 1946.

[¶] *West Virginia State Board of Education v. Barnette* (1943) overturned a public regulation making it mandatory to salute the flag and imposing penalties of expulsion and prosecution on students failing to comply.

To Joseph Califano[*]

16 January 1992

[New York, New York]

Dear Joe:

Robert Blakey[†] was right, and you, I regret to say, were quite wrong in the discussion on ABC this morning about Robert Kennedy and the attempted assassination of Castro. Robert Kennedy had nothing to do with the assassination plots, nor did the Church Committee ever find otherwise.

RFK's involvement was with Operation Mongoose—a CIA propaganda, intelligence collection and sabotage program designed to keep Castro off balance with the hope it might lead in time to an internal uprising in Cuba. Mongoose was a stupid and ineffectual operation; but it was *not* the CIA assassination effort. This was conducted on a separate track. RFK had nothing to do with it. Dick Helms testified before the Church Committee that he had "never told Attorney General Kennedy about any assassination activity" (Church Committee, "Alleged Assassination Plots Involving Foreign Leaders," 151). Larry Houston, the CIA general counsel, did tell RFK in May 1962 of the CIA recruitment of mobsters in an effort to kill Castro; he recalled before the Church Committee that RFK was "upset" by this, and he assured RFK that "the assassination plan aimed at Castro had been terminated completely (page 132), though in fact it continued well into the Johnson administration.

The assassination plots began, as you will recall, in the Eisenhower administration. The CIA hired Sam Giancana and other mobsters to do the job and installed them in the Kenilworth Hotel in Miami in the fall of 1960—months before JFK became President. The plots continued through the Kennedy administration and well into the Johnson administration. There is no evidence that any of three presidents authorized or knew of the

---

[*] Joseph Califano, Jr. (b. 1931). Author; lawyer; served in the Kennedy and Johnson administrations, 1961–69; special assistant to President Johnson, 1965; secretary of health, education, and welfare, 1977–79; founded the National Center on Addiction and Substance Abuse in 1992 at Columbia University.

[†] G. Robert Blakey (b. 1936). Lawyer; U.S. Department of Justice, 1961–64; law professor at Notre Dame, 1964–69, 2010–present; chief counsel to the House Select Committee on Assassinations, 1977–79.

CIA effort to murder Castro. For a full account of all these matters, *please* take a look at *Robert Kennedy and his times,* pages 477–498.

Best regards,
Arthur Schlesinger, Jr.

To Shimshon Arad*

22 January 1992

[New York, New York]

Dear Shimshon:

Sorry to be so late in answering your questions; but I have been out of the country. Here goes:

1. George Bush's presidency is like Winston Churchill's celebrated pudding: it lacks a theme. Mr. Bush is a decent, civilized and rather cautious man (except around election time, when he will say and do almost anything to win). His main interest lies in foreign policy. Here, with the astute assistance of Secretary of State Baker, he has done pretty well in responding to immediate challenges; less well in follow-up. He seems to be deficient in what he himself calls "the vision thing." His conception of a New World Order lacks flesh and bones and appears in retrospect to be mostly rhetoric. In domestic affairs, Mr. Bush seems bored, baffled and bewildered. And, with the Cold War over, domestic issues will dominate the election.

2. Both the Democratic and Republican parties are "special interests" parties. If the Democratic party pays particular attention to labor, women, minorities, intellectuals, the poor, etc, the Republican party pays particular attention to speculators, developers, bankers, arms manufacturers, automobile tycoons, etc. In the greedy 1980s, the Republican "special interests" man-

* Shimshon Arad (b. 1923). Israeli diplomat and author; served in the Jewish brigade fighting Hitler in World War II; Israeli consul in New York City; later aide to Israeli mission to the United Nations and the Israeli ambassador to the United States; Israeli ambassador to Mexico and the Netherlands, director of the American Department in the Israeli Foreign Office; luncheon companion of Schlesinger at the Century Club for some thirty years.

aged to appear "mainstream." In the hard-pressed 1990s, the Democrats may very well appear the "mainstream" party. Reflect on the currant uproar in the United States over the indefensibly high salaries business leaders pay themselves while they discharge workers and close down factories.

3. American politics has a cyclical pattern. The Reaganite 1980s were a re-play of the Eisenhower 1950s, as the conservatives 1950s were a replay of the Harding-Coolidge-Hoover 1920s. Similarly at 30 year intervals the country moves into a reform phase of the cycle:

   Theodore Roosevelt ushering in the Progressive Era in 1901; Franklin Roosevelt and the New Deal in 1933; John Kennedy and the New Frontier in 1961. If the rhythm holds, the 1990s should see the republic re-enter the progressive mode. There are many signs that the tide is beginning to turn. Of course 1992 is still early, and an incumbent President enjoys obvious advantages; but at this writing the Democrats would seem to have a fair chance of winning in November.

4. A Democratic President would, I believe, put flesh and bones on the New World Order (which, after all, is a Democratic idea, formulated by Woodrow Wilson and developed by Franklin Roosevelt). It would do this by strengthening and using international institutions. It would also favor the consolidation of regional organizations like the European Community and the Organization of American States. Despite campaign oratory, I believe that a Democratic administration would support the party's historic commitment to a freely trading world—but it would expect reciprocity from Europe and Japan. Despite campaign oratory, it would, I think, follow the general Bush-Baker line in the Middle East. It probably would not rush unilaterally into wars, as the Bush administration did in Panama and the Gulf, preferring instead to build UN or other multilateral forces and regarding unilateral military action as a last resort. However, it would maintain American defenses and have no problem about reacting if vital interests of the United States should be threatened. The alternative to unilateral interventionism is not traditional isolationism but responsible internationalism.

   I hope this is sufficient!

Best regards,
Arthur

To Philip Gramm[*]

26 February 1992

[New York, New York]

Dear Senator Gramm:

I am touched by your letter of 20 February in which you kindly say that you are "holding open a Roundtable membership" for me. For five thousand bucks per annum, you promise me "a host of special benefits" denied ordinary American citizens, including "private briefings," "hospitality suites," "passes to lavish Galas and dinners" and even a discourse by Dan Quayle[†] on world trade. Such rare treats!

It gives me great comfort to know that the Roundtable computer is as incompetent as the rest of the Republican administration.

Sincerely yours,
Arthur Schlesinger, Jr.

From Philip Gramm

March 13, 1992

[Washington, D.C.]

Dear Dr. Schlesinger:

Thank you for your thoughtful letter. Please be assured that no mistake was made in inviting you to support the Republican Party. We believe in redemption.

Yours respectfully,
Phil Gramm
United States Senator

---

[*] Philip Gramm (b. 1942). Conservative economist; taught at Texas A&M, 1967–78; representative (D-Texas), 1979–83; converted to the Republican Party, serving in Congress, 1983–85, and Senate, 1985–2002; closely identified with the push for federal deregulation in the 1990s, leading to the Great Recession.

[†] Dan Quayle (b. 1947). Lawyer; conservative representative (R-Ind.), 1977–81; senator, 1981–89; U.S. vice president, 1989–93; earned a reputation as a lightweight political figure; related to the Pulliam family newspaper publishing empire in the Midwest.

To George Kennan

19 March 1992

[New York, New York]

Dear George:

Forgive my delay in thanking you for your thoughtful letter about the *Disuniting* book; but I have been away from the city. I don't disagree with you at all about the limits on our capacity to absorb newcomers; indeed, I originally had a passage in the book arguing the need to reconsider our immigration policy, but finally I dropped it lest it distract attention from the main thesis.

Historically the two great agencies of assimilation have been the public school and the workplace. With the flight of the mass production industries to the Third World, the public school becomes all the more crucial, and I fear that today our public schools, at least in the great cities, are weaker reeds than ever before. The current effort through curriculum revision to convert the public schools into agencies for the preservation of ethnic identities seems to me more troubling than "political correctness" in the universities.

I do think that since the blacks are here and since we brought them here, we owe them special effort to give them a break and bring them into the mainstream. There is no gainsaying the racism in our history, our institutions and very likely our souls. Only in the last generation have we faced up to this, and we still have a long way to go. I have favored affirmative action as a transitional device, and it may be that its time is coming to an end. The emergence of debate about affirmative action and other matters within the black community is, I think, heartening.

I very much agree that the melting pot goes too far if it boils us into bland homogeneity. It remains a vital part of America for people to cherish their own cultures, traditions, observances, rituals, creeds, customs. It is these strands of particularity that lend richness, texture and variety to our society. But the preservation of such strands, it seems to me, is the task of the individual, the family, the church, [and] the subculture. The public school has a different task—which is to emphasize what brings children together as Americans. . . .

Take care of yourself, and affections to Annaliese.

Yours ever,
Arthur

To Amitai Etzioni*

11 May 1992

[New York, New York]

Dear Professor Etzioni:

Thank you for your cheering letter about *Disuniting,* and also for sending *The Responsive Community,*† which I have been reading with much interest.

I find myself sympathetic with much, perhaps most, of your program. But there is, alas, something about the word "community" that turns me off. Perhaps it is a defect of my generation, but the word "community" brings to mind Spoon River, Gopher Prairie, Winesburg, Ed Howe's *Story of a Country Town.* "Community" connotes (in my mind) the smug, conformist, stifling majority; individual liberation requires a revolt against the community.

Nor do I find the thought of "community" any more attractive in the political than in the social realm. The great illusion of Jeffersonian democracy was that the local government is more responsive to the people than are levels of government more remote from them. I think that history refutes that proposition. Most of the time, local government is responsive to the most powerful local interests. I accept the principle of subsidiarity up to a point, but in the end the way the locally powerless have found to vindicate their rights has generally been through appeal to the national authority.

It is the national government, not the community, that has been the great protector of the powerless. As Madison saw from the start, national authority was essential to counter the aggressions of local majorities against minority rights and individual liberties. I just don't believe that (to quote from the *US News* story) "it is best to handle problems at the government level closest to citizens." Had strict communitarianism prevailed, we should still have slavery.

---

* Amitai Etzioni (b. 1929). German Israeli American sociologist; professor at Columbia University, 1958–78; White House senior adviser, 1979–80; George Washington University, 1980–present; celebrated for seeking communitarian solutions to excessive individualism.

† *The Responsive Community: Rights and Responsibilities,* the quarterly journal of the Communitarian Network, edited by Etzioni, 1990–2004.

Anyway, for better or worse, the word "communitarianism" sends a chill down my spine. At the same time, I respect much that you and your group are doing—as in the coupling of rights with responsibilities and your emphasis on civic participation and on the cohesive family. Some time when you are planning to come to New York, let me know. And perhaps we can discuss these matters over a leisurely lunch.

Sincerely yours,
Arthur

To Dokun Shonekan[*]

12 May 1992

[New York, New York]

Dear Ms. Shonekan:

. . . Apart from what most scholars, some black as well as white, regard as egregious exaggerations, I have a more general concern about Afrocentrism.

As a historian, I am bound to regard black Americans, who have been here for five or six generations, as part of American culture, not of African culture, just as German Americans or Italian Americans or Russian Americans, even though they have been here for much shorter periods, seem to me to be part of the American and not of German or Italian or Russian culture. All of us may cherish particular traditions, but surely we are all part of a common culture.

Indeed, as Orlando Patterson[†] observed of black Americans the other day, "Not since ancient Rome conquered and then surrendered to the culture of its Greek slaves and freedmen has the culture of a dominant world civilization been so enormously influenced by so small a minority of people." The notion that black Americans are in some mysterious way more closely connected to African culture would appear artificial and fictitious—the "invention of tradition."

* Dokun Shonekan of New York, New York.
† Orlando Patterson (b. 1940). Jamaican-born American sociologist at Harvard University; special adviser to Michael Manley, prime minister of Jamaica, 1972–79; author of notable books on race.

I think also that we are passing from an age of the warfare of ideologies into an age of the warfare of ethnicities. Ethnicity is tearing apart country after country around the world. The United States is the only multi-ethnic country that has (precariously) held together for a couple of centuries. It has held together because it produced an American nationality that absorbs the diverse cultures brought to these shores and an American creed that, as Myrdal pointed out, holds out the hope of equality even for those most cruelly excluded.

That is why the effort to celebrate, promote and perpetuate separate ethnic and racial communities does not seem to me what the country needs at this point in history. Not that the Afrocentrists started it: Michael Novak's[*] *Rise of the Unmeltable Ethnics* illustrates an earlier brand of ethnocentric attacks on an American identity. Let us not make Yugoslavia or Lebanon our model. Let us stick with Mahatma Gandhi:[†] "We must cease to be exclusive Hindus or Muslims or Sikhs, Parsis, Christians, or Jews. Whilst we may staunchly adhere to our respective faiths, we must be Indians first and Indians last."

Sincerely yours,
Arthur Schlesinger, Jr.

In June 1992, Bill Clinton,[‡] governor of Arkansas, was on the verge of capturing the Democratic Party presidential nomination. Arthur was a supporter, having known him over the years and admired his intelligence and progressive views.

---

[*] Michael Novak (b. 1933). Conservative American Catholic philosopher; author; senior fellow at the American Enterprise Institute, 1978–present; onetime Democrat anti–Vietnam War activist; later pro–free market ideologue with Republican sympathies.

[†] Mohandas Gandhi (1869–1948). Lawyer; political activist; employed nonviolent civil disobedience to win India's independence from British rule; assassinated.

[‡] Bill Clinton (b. 1946). Democratic governor of Arkansas, 1979–81, 1983–92; forty second U.S. president, 1993 2001; spoke at Schlesinger's Manhattan memorial service in 2007.

To Bill Clinton

2 June 1992

[New York, New York]

Dear Bill:

I am off to Europe today (before the California primary) for a couple of weeks; but, before I go, I thought I might offer some comments from afar—in case you need any more free advice.

For the time being, I doubt that there is much you can do in face of the Perot[*] high except to go on as the only candidate talking about serious issues. *Don't* go into the confessional mode. Let others talk about your hard life, etc., but you mustn't begin to sound Nixonesque. In the longer run, concentration on what you think about the American future will, I believe, start to pay off.

In mid-July you are bound to regain the national spotlight. The convention will make you the focus of public attention. Newspapermen like you, and my impression is that some at least feel a little guilty about the role of the press first in tearing you down and then in ignoring the substantive side of your campaign. I believe they are looking for an opportunity to redress the balance.

The convention and your acceptance speech will provide that opportunity. That speech will probably be the most important speech you will give in the entire campaign. It is a speech that must look toward the future and set the agenda for the campaign. Bush is a man of a now discredited past. Perot is the Wizard of Oz. (I hope that Toto will pull back the curtain well before November.) You are the man of vision with the professional skills to

---

[*] Ross Perot (b. 1930). Conservative Texas businessman; founded Electronic Data Systems in 1962 and sold it to General Motors for $2.4 billion in 1984; independent populist candidate for the U.S. presidency in 1992, gaining 18.9 percent of vote; candidate in 1996, earning 8 percent of vote; favored gun control and cutting Social Security; against first Gulf War in 1991 and the outsourcing of American jobs.

define the tasks of national renovation and to get the country moving again.[*]

Anyway best of luck.

Best regards,
Arthur

From William F. Buckley, Jr.

July 22 [19]92

[Stamford, Connecticut]

Dear Arthur:

I told you that if we were in New York the following day (Tuesday of Convention Week) Pat and I would happily come by to visit you during your open house. Well, we didn't stay in town, returning to the country and receiving our inspiration second hand. (I did spot you on the screen was it—Thursday? The distraction was a relief, I remember.) I did want to thank you and Alexandra for your proffered hospitality even if I couldn't take advantage of. It was especially reassuring that you thought that even if Ken [Galbraith] wasn't there, you would find someone who would consent to talk to me.

With cordial regards,
Wm. F. Buckley Jr.

[*] On July 15, 1992, Clinton accepted the Democratic Party presidential nomination at the party's convention in New York City. Senator Al Gore, Jr., was nominated for vice president.

To Robert Gorham Davis*

27 July 1992

[New York, New York]

Dear Bob:

Of course I am in basic agreement with you on the question of a literal interpretation of original sin (and I thank you by the way for your generous professional characterization of me in the letter to the *Times* ["perhaps our best American historian"]). I meant "original sin" metaphorically—as shorthand for human frailty, self-pride and self-deception.† Do not fear: I have not gone religious in my old age. In a sentence the *Times* cut from the Niebuhr column for space reasons, I made it clear that I am still enlisted in what Morton White‡ called Atheists for Niebuhr (agnostics in my case).

The influence of religion seems to me wholly pernicious when it leads people to believe they have access to absolute truth. As Mr. Dooley used to put it, a fanatic "does what he thinks th' Lord wud do if He only knew th' facts in th' case." Religious absolutism is today the cause of most of the killing that is taking place around the world. But then absolutists forget that they are not exempt from original sin. The claim to be doing what the Lord would do is the supreme example of self-pride and self-deception.

Most politicians invoke religion in an honorific or propitiatory gesture, hoping to reassure those who care. Few, including such religious show-offs as Jimmy Carter, use religion as a basis for decision. Maybe Clarence Thomas,§ who attends a church where they speak in tongues, does.

---

*Robert Gorham ("Bob") Davis (1908–98). Professor of English at Columbia University, 1957–76; literary critic; commentator on religious—especially Judeo-Christian—issues.

†"[Niebuhr] persuaded me and many of my contemporaries that original sin provides a far stronger foundation for freedom and self-government than illusions about human perfectibility," wrote Schlesinger in a June 22, 1992, *New York Times* op-ed piece commemorating the centennial of Niebuhr's birth.

‡Morton White (b. 1917). American philosopher and historian of ideas; taught at Harvard University, 1948–70; fellow at Princeton's Institute for Advanced Study, 1970–87; coedited *Paths of American Thought* (1963) with Schlesinger.

§Clarence Thomas (b. 1948). Conservative Republican; chairman of the Equal Employment Opportunity Commission, 1982–90; U.S. Supreme Court justice, 1991–present; at confirmation hearings he was accused of sexual harassment by onetime aide Anita Hill.

I note that last Sunday's *Times* ("The Week in Review," page 5) cites a Gallup poll of November 1991 reporting that 47% of the respondents are creationists as against 40% theistic evolutionists and 9% agnostic evolutionists. Can this really be the case? If so, I would be really worried about our future.

I trust all goes well with the Davises. Affections to Hope.

Yours ever,
Arthur

To George Kennan

28 September 1992

[New York, New York]

Dear George:

I thank you for sending a copy of that superb letter to Les Gelb.[*] The *Times* should run the letter as an Op Ed piece. Your point that the undue militarization of our policy delayed rather than hastened the Soviet collapse deserves more attention than it has received.

I trust that the election will be OK, but I am worried. The present situation reminds me of 1960. Kennedy had a good lead in October. But the Republicans kept hammering away on the risk of confiding the country to a forty-three-year-old senator without executive experience as against a vice president who had been in the midst of great affairs for eight years. In the last week one felt a swing to Nixon, as if voters had suddenly become frightened of the adventure of Kennedy. Had the campaign gone on a week longer, I think Nixon would have won.

This time the Republicans will continue going on about the risk of Clinton, a young governor of a poor, rural, southern state, a draft-dodger and philanderer to boot, as against a president with a dozen years' experience in dealing with the nation and the world; Bush may not be an inspir-

[*] Les Gelb (b. 1937). Foreign policy analyst; taught at Wesleyan College, 1964–67; director of policy planning and arms control at the Department of Defense, 1967–69; helped write *The Pentagon Papers;* diplomatic correspondent at *The New York Times,* 1973–77; assistant secretary of state, 1977–79; editor and columnist at *The New York Times,* 1981–93; president of the Council on Foreign Relations, 1993–2012; supported the 2003 invasion of Iraq.

ing leader, but we know what we are getting; better than the risk of an unknown, etc. I would not underrate the power of this appeal.

I have known Clinton for a decade or so and have a high regard for his intelligence, his resilience and his priorities. I think he will (would) make a good president. But I fear that he is a vulnerable candidate. Anyway let us pray.

Yours ever,
Arthur

On November 3, 1992, Democratic candidate Bill Clinton defeated President George H. W. Bush and the independent candidate, Texas businessman Ross Perot, to win the U.S. presidency. Clinton received 43 percent of the vote, Bush 37.4 percent, and Perot 19 percent. Senator Al Gore, Jr. of Tennessee was elected vice president.*

Arthur happily saw Clinton's election as a sign of the changing rhythms of the country's political history, the cycle now swinging back toward liberalism and activism after a period of conservatism and retrenchment.

To Bill Clinton

5 November 1992

[New York, New York]

Dear Bill, Dear Mr. President-elect:

I send warmest congratulations on the election. If you run the country as well as you ran the campaign, we can look forward to the future with the greatest confidence. And, as a holder of an Oxford degree (unearned), I am especially delighted to have an Oxford man as president!

"Westward, look, the land is bright."

Ever yours,
Arthur

---

* Albert ("Al") Gore, Jr. (b. 1948). Representative (D-Tenn.), 1977–85; senator, 1985–93; U.S. vice president, 1993–2001; lost the 2000 presidential election despite winning the popular vote; won the Nobel Peace Prize in 2007 for his work on climate change.

In the fall of 1992, Congress enacted the Cuban Democracy Act sponsored by New Jersey Democratic senator Robert Torricelli. * *The legislation prohibited foreign-based subsidiaries of U.S. companies from trading with Cuba, banned travel to Cuba by U.S. citizens, and outlawed sending family remittances to Cuba. Arthur feared that the newly elected Clinton administration might succumb to the Cuban lobby and vigorously implement the Torricelli bill.*

To Warren Christopher[†]

26 November 1992

[New York, New York]

Dear Warren:

I am writing out of concern that overreaction to the UN vote on the Cuban embargo may dig us in deeper into the Torricelli hole.

I have been marginally involved in Cuban matters for a long time. I made my first visit to Havana over forty years ago, wrote the Cuban White Paper in 1961 in preparation for the Bay of Pigs operation (which, however, I opposed) and have visited Cuba several times in recent years. During my last trip in January (with Bob McNamara, Wayne Smith,[‡] Bob Pastor[§] and others), I spent time not only with Castro but with Elizardo Sanchez,[¶] a

---

* Robert Torricelli (b. 1951). Liberal representative (D-N.J.), 1983–97; senator, 1997–2003; resigned over fund-raising controversy; fervent supporter of anti-Castro Cuban community in home state.

† Warren Christopher (1925–2011). California liberal Democrat; lawyer; diplomat; deputy attorney general, 1967–69; deputy secretary of state, 1977–81; secretary of state, 1993–97.

‡ Wayne Smith (b. 1932). Career diplomat, 1957–82; chief of mission, U.S. Interests Section, in Havana, Cuba, 1979–82; resigned from government over Reagan administration policies; fellow at the Center for International Policy in Washington, D.C., 1992–present; adjunct professor at Johns Hopkins University, 1985–present.

§ Robert ("Bob") Pastor (b. 1947). National security adviser on Latin America, 1977–81; Emory University professor of international relations, 1985–2002; fellow at the Carter Center, 1985–present; American University vice president for international affairs, 2002–7; professor of international relations and director of Center for North American Studies at American University, 2007–present.

¶ Elizardo Sánchez (b. 1944). Notable Cuban human rights campaigner; founder of Cuban Human Rights and National Reconciliation Commission, 1987; former political prisoner.

leading dissident who has spent eight and a half of the last ten years in Castro's prisons.

I perfectly understand the domestic political considerations that led to the endorsement of the Torricelli approach. But the approach is wrong and is condemned not only by the 59–3 vote in the UN General Assembly but, more to the point, by the anti-Castro dissidents in Cuba itself—the people on the firing line in the anti-Castro fight.

The Torricelli approach is wrong because, as Elizardo Sanchez and eleven other leading dissidents said in a message sent to Congress on 24 September last opposing the bill, "The embargo has and will only serve as a pretext for the maintenance of a virtual state of siege in our country." The embargo provides Castro with an all-purpose alibi. It gives him an excuse for cruel and ruthless repression within Cuba. And it makes it easy for him to blame the Cuban mess on the United States. The Cubans are proud people, and nationalism is Fidel's last and best card.

And the Torricelli approach is wrong because of the signal it sends to Cuba: that the US plans to replace Castro by Jorge Mas Canosa[*] of the Cuban American National Foundation (where the Torricelli approach originated). Mas Canosa is bad news: just ask David Lawrence,[†] the publisher of the *Miami Herald;* or look at the Americas Watch report last August "Dangerous Dialogue: Attacks on Freedom of Expression in Miami's Cuban Exile Community"; or talk to Cuban exiles like Ramon Cernuda,[‡] Miami representative of the Havana-based Coordinated Organizations of Human Rights in Cuba, or Ernesto Betancourt,[§] the first director of Radio Marti.

---

[*] Jorge Mas Canosa (1939–97). Right-wing head of Cuban American National Foundation; participated in Bay of Pigs invasion of Cuba in 1961; leader among fiercely anti-Castro Cubans in Florida; champion of U.S. embargo on Cuba; opposed any diplomatic relations with Havana.

[†] David Lawrence, Jr. (b. 1942). Publisher of the *Detroit Free Press,* 1985–89; publisher of *The Miami Herald,* 1989–99, when newspaper won five Pulitzer Prizes; later organizer of various programs for children.

[‡] Ramón Cernuda (b. 1947). Family fled Cuba in 1960 to United States; publisher of the *Enciclopedia de Cuba* and other works; critic of U.S. sanctions on Cuba.

[§] Ernesto Betancourt (1927–2011). Former ally of Castro who went into U.S. exile in 1960; director of budget and finance at the Organization of American States, 1960–75; director of Radio Marti, 1985–90; consultant to the World Bank, the International Money Fund, and the Inter-American Development Bank.

Betancourt has written that the CANF is "dominated by former collaborators of the hated Batista dictatorship" and that Washington's support of Mas and the CANF leads dissidents within Cuba to see "Castro's removal as more threatening to their interests than his staying in power. They fear that the US intends to impose on Cuba the advocates of revenge and restoration of the past. . . . Cuba needs another *maximo* leader like a hole in the head." Dread of the return of the rightwing Miami exiles is a major source of Castro's strength. "If the alternative to Castro is a return to the past," says Ramon Cernuda, "many Cubans will continue to support the government even during hard economic times." Even Elliott Abrams[*] recently said, "Some distancing [from the CANF] is now needed to avoid verifying Castro's propaganda that Cuban-American millionaires and Washington are in collusion."

In an ideal world we should be moving in the opposite direction: toward a relaxation of the embargo in exchange for relaxation of Castro's repressive policies. In a way, the embargo actually protects Castro. Nothing would subvert his revolution more quickly than flooding Cuba with US tourists and US consumer goods.

But of course we don't live in an ideal world, and reform of our Cuban policy will no doubt have to wait. In the meantime, however, let us not bind ourselves any closer to a policy that is opposed by the brave men and women who fight Castro not from luxurious villas in Miami but at tremendous personal risk inside Cuba itself, and is also opposed by most of our friends in Latin America and around the world.

All the best,
Arthur

---

[*] Elliott Abrams (b. 1948). Lawyer; Republican conservative policy analyst; chief of staff for Senator Moynihan, 1977–79; assistant secretary of state for human rights, 1981–85; assistant secretary of state for inter-American affairs, 1985–89; convicted of two misdemeanors in 1991 for unlawfully withholding information from Congress related to the Iran-Contra affair; pardoned by President George H. W. Bush; national security council director for Near East and North African affairs, 2002–5; deputy national security adviser for global democracy strategy, 2005–9.

On April 12, 1995, President Clinton and Schlesinger meet in Warm Springs, Georgia, to celebrate the life and accomplishments of President Franklin Roosevelt, who died there fifty years earlier of a cerebral hemorrhage at age sixty-three.

The Precariousness of Life

1993–2006

With his latest book, The Disuniting of America: Reflections on a Multicul-tural Society, *written in fifteen days in February 1991, Arthur seemed to touch a raw nerve and enjoyed renewed interest in his work and ideas. He had the odd experience of being praised by conservatives and Republicans. At a lun-cheon in May 1994, Prime Minister Margaret Thatcher told him how much she admired his book (although she referred to it as* "The Dismantling of the American Dream"). *George Will, Newt Gingrich, and Lynne Cheney were fans. However, when Cheney met Arthur and held forth on the great threat of multiculturalism, he replied that monoculturalism was even a greater threat, especially as propounded by born-again zealots and imposed on small-town school and library boards.*

To Toby Roth[*]

18 August 1993

[New York, New York]

Dear Congressman Roth:

I thank you for your generous words about *The Disuniting of America* and also for your kind invitation to come to the hearing on 24 August.[†] I

---

[*] Toby Roth (b. 1938). Representative (R-Wis.), 1979–97.

[†] As chairman of the Congressional English Language Task Force, Roth had invited Schlesinger to take part in a special hearing to discuss the merits of making English the official language of the United States.

regret to say that this will not be possible, and I must add that, though I sympathize with the concerns that lie behind HR 739[*] and though I emphatically agree that a common language is an essential bond of national cohesion, I am against the attempt to make English the official language.

I am against it because it implies that English is somehow in danger. HR 739's proposed declaration really expresses a considerable lack of faith in the future of the language. But is the English language really beleaguered and on the way out? I would suggest rather that English has never been more triumphant. Four million people spoke it in Shakespeare's day. Now a billion people speak it everywhere in the world. English will (ironically) be the *lingua franca* of the 21st century.

Nothing can stop it. Immigrants to the United States have tended to keep to their native language, but their children want to learn English and join the mainstream—and the polls show that this is as true of Latino and Asian kids today as it was for children of European immigrants in years past. I am all in favor of intensified campaigns and accelerated programs to teach new immigrants English. I am also in favor of re-examination of the present bilingual machinery so that it will serve to facilitate the transition to the English-speaking community and not as a means of institutionalizing linguistic separatism.

But the effort to make English the "official language" seems to me both unnecessary for a language so triumphantly on the march and an additional source of racial tension and resentment. Let nature takes its course, and the English language will be OK.

Sincerely yours,
Arthur Schlesinger, jr.

---

[*] Roth's bill, HR 739, the Declaration of Official Language Act of 1993, would have made English the official language of the United States, repealed the multilingual ballot provisions of the Voting Rights Act and Bilingual Education Act, and established an English language proficiency standard for citizenship applicants. The bill was not passed.

To Jean Kennedy Smith[*]

30 August 1993

[New York, New York]

Dearest Jean:

... The summer seems endless—and endlessly hot. Every day is sticky, humid and airless, and the temperature rarely falls below 90. You are lucky to be in cool, if rainy, Ireland. We spent a weekend with the Galbraiths [at their farm in Newfane, Vermont], and the brisk Vermont weather (45 degrees at night) was a wonderful refreshment.

You are missed terribly, but you *have* missed very little. Last week the Bernstein family celebrated Lennie's[†] 75th with a gala evening at Alice Tully Hall. Adolph[‡] and Betty[§] were billed to perform, but Adolph has been so frail lately that there was much concern as to whether he could, or should, go on. Of course, he insisted on going, and he was *superb*—sitting down, but his voice clear and on key and his gestures and even expressions (they did "Carried Away") were perfect. He is the most gallant of old troupers. Betty B[acall] was m.c. part of the time, dividing the job with Jamie Bernstein,[¶] and it was a joyous evening.

What else? It looks as if Giuliani[**] will be our next mayor, unless he makes some major mistakes between now and the election (which is of

---

[*] Smith had been appointed ambassador to Ireland and was living in Dublin.

[†] Leonard Bernstein (1918–90). Composer; conductor; author; lecturer; pianist; music director of the New York Philharmonic Orchestra, 1959–69; wrote music for *West Side Story, Candide, On the Town,* and *Wonderful Town.*

[‡] Adolph Green (1914–2002). Lyricist; playwright; screenwriter; collaborated with Betty Comden on *On the Town, Singin' in the Rain, The Band Wagon, Wonderful Town, Bells Are Ringing, Applause, On the Twentieth Century, The Will Rogers Follies;* married to actress Phyllis Newman.

[§] Betty Comden (1917–2006). Lyricist and screenwriting partner of Adolph Green; they formed a musical comedy troupe in 1938 with Judy Holliday and Leonard Bernstein that played at the Village Vanguard; success on Broadway and in Hollywood followed.

[¶] Jamie Bernstein (b.1952). Narrator, writer, and broadcaster; daughter of Leonard Bernstein.

[**] Rudy Giuliani (b. 1944). Republican lawyer; businessman; U.S. attorney for the Southern District of New York, 1983–89; mayor of New York City 1994–2001.

course entirely possible). I shall vote for Dinkins.[*] There has been a series of parties for departing ambassadors—Holbrooke[†] to Germany, Gardner[‡] to Spain. Bill Clinton has wowed the folks on the Vineyard. Hillary joined Bill Styron on one of his walks. The Peter Jennings[§] and the Andy Steins[¶] have broken up. Everyone else appears to be sticking together. This week I resume teaching—my last term, thank God.

No need to answer—I just wanted to bring you up to date!

Love from all Schlesingers,
Arthur

To Neil Jumonville[**]

30 November 1993

[New York, New York]

Dear Professor Jumonville:

Forgive my delay in answering your letter, but I have been much away from the city in recent weeks.

You of course have my permission to quote from any of my letters to Henry Commager. I sometimes shudder a bit when I read what I wrote

---

[*] David Dinkins (b. 1927). Democratic lawyer; Manhattan borough president, 1986–89; mayor of New York City, 1990–93.

[†] Richard Holbrooke (1941–2010). Diplomat; author; Democratic Party activist; investment banker; assistant secretary of state, 1977–81, 1994–96; ambassador to Germany, 1993–94, and to the United Nations, 1999–2001; special representative for Afghanistan and Pakistan, 2009–10.

[‡] Richard N. Gardner (b. 1927). Lawyer; diplomat; professor at Columbia Law School; ambassador to Italy 1977–81, and to Spain, 1993–97.

[§] Peter Jennings (1938–2005). Canadian American journalist; ABC's *World News Tonight*, anchor 1977–2005; his third marriage, to author Kati Marton, ended in 1993; Marton married Richard Holbrooke in 1995.

[¶] Andrew ("Andy") Stein (b. 1945). Democratic Manhattan borough president, 1977–85; New York City Council president, 1986–94; his second marriage, to Lynn Forester, ended in 1993; Forester married Sir Evelyn Robert de Rothschild in 2000.

[**] Neil Jumonville. American historian; Florida State University; author of *Henry Steele Commager: Midcentury Liberalism and the History of the Present* (1999).

privately in years past, but it is all part of the record, and as a historian I can hardly claim immunity that historians routinely deny to the dead! . . .

Sincerely yours,
Arthur Schlesinger, Jr.

To Alan Singer[*]

3 December 1993

[New York, New York]

Dear Professor Singer:

. . . I generally agree with your version of the multicultural approach; my unhappiness begins where multiculturalism seeks to promote and perpetuate separate ethnic and racial communities in the United States. I really don't think the nation would be better off today if in the nineteenth century it had obeyed contemporary multicultural extremists and encouraged German-Americans to retain their language, their social practices, their political ideals; and the Italian-Americans the same; and the Swedish-Americans the same; and so on down the line, each group huddled in its own linguistic and ethnic enclaves. Surely the cultivation of ancestral culture is hardly a better idea now.

I am sorry you think that I am fighting to maintain the status quo. My view (see page 19 of the Norton edition of *Disuniting*) is that racism is the American problem; Afrocentrism and similar aberrations are an understandable response.

Sincerely yours,
Arthur

* Alan Singer. Professor of curriculum and teaching, Hofstra University

To James B. Lockett[*]

12 February 1994

[New York, New York]

Dear Dr. Lockett:

You ask how I feel about criticism of the discussion of the Afrocentric curriculum in *The Disuniting of America*. I accept criticism philosophically and sometimes learn from it; but in this case I have read nothing to cause me to change my view that the "self-esteem" argument has no known empirical basis (as Henry Louis Gates, Jr., has pointed out) and that the Afrocentric curriculum disables students for entry into the modern world and into the American mainstream. I do not think that my doubts exceed what black scholars like Skip Gates and Cornel West[†] have said about the Afrocentric curriculum.

In general, my feeling is that racism is the problem, and that the Afrocentric curriculum is an understandable but ill-judged and counterproductive response.

Sincerely yours,
Arthur Schlesinger, Jr.

To Bill Clinton

22 March 1994

[New York, New York]

Dear Mr. President:

It is with diffidence that I send this letter. But your administration, with all its high purpose and abundant hope, is in serious trouble. Unless this stupid Whitewater problem[‡] can be put in perspective quickly, the press

---

[*] James B. Lockett. Professor of history at Stillman College, Tuscaloosa, Alabama.

[†] Cornel West (b. 1953). Controversial African American philosopher; author; civil rights activist; professor at New York's Union Theological Seminary.

[‡] The Whitewater affair concerned a failed investment in an Arkansas land-development scheme made by Bill and Hillary Clinton in the 1970s and 1980s. Official investigations led to fifteen convictions. The Clintons were never charged, although Republicans exploited the affair mercilessly.

hunt, the grand jury proceedings, the special prosecutor, etc, will create running sores for a long time to come. As a historian with experience in an earlier White House, I venture to offer some observations.

The urgent thing now is to take further action to rebuild confidence in the White House. The appointment of Lloyd Cutler[*] is an excellent first step, but I gather that Lloyd can only stay for six months. For the longer haul, you must look for persons who combine experience in government and loyalty to the purposes of your administration with sufficient stature and seniority to tell you the hard things that old friends and younger staffers may be reluctant to tell you. They should serve you as Sam Rosenman served FDR and Clark Clifford served Truman—with fidelity, candor and good judgment.

Recommendations are not terribly helpful without names. I urge you to consider my old Kennedy associate Ted Sorensen. He knows the executive branch, he knows the Hill, he knows the press and in his recent years as an international lawyer he has come to know the corporate community and the world. He is of course highly intelligent, and he is also well-organized, clear-headed, judicious, discreet, and excellent company.

I know there is the feeling that anyone who worked in government thirty years ago must be an antiquity today; but Ted was a very young fellow when he worked for JFK and LBJ. He is a decade younger than Lloyd Cutler and a few years younger than your Secretary of State.

I am sure there may be others around of similar qualifications. If you had had people like Sorensen by your side, a lot of the present trouble would have been avoided. I am confident that, if the right steps are taken to restore confidence, Whitewater too will pass and that you will have the chance to fulfill the rich promise of your administration. I am also sure that you will learn valuable lessons from this ordeal, as JFK learned so much from the Bay of Pigs.

My very best wishes to you and to Hillary in these difficult times.

With warmest regards,
Arthur

---

[*] Lloyd Cutler (1917–2005), Democratic lawyer; cofounded Wilmer, Cutler, and Pickering in Washington in 1962; President Carter's White House counsel.

Robert McNamara had asked Schlesinger to read a draft of his forthcoming book, In Retrospect: The Tragedy and Lessons of Vietnam *(1995). In it, the former defense secretary said that the Vietnam War was "wrong, terribly wrong"—which created controversy after the book's publication. But Arthur thought the book was an important contribution to history.*

To Robert McNamara

31 March 1994

[New York, New York]

Dear Bob:

I have read your Vietnam chapters with the greatest interest and admiration. I think the tone is exactly right—honest, forthright, candid. You admit misjudgments and do not try to shift blame. No doubt there will be complaints from true believers who still feel that the USG* was right on Vietnam and the American people let them down; but there is not much you can do about them.† Your obligation is to the historical record as best you see it, and I think these chapters fulfill that obligation admirably. . . .

Yours ever,
Arthur

To Isaiah and Aline Berlin

9 August 1994

[New York, New York]

Dear Isaiah and Aline:

We have had a disaster—a fire in our house. 171 East 64th Street now looks like something left over from the London air raids of 1940. Fortunately no lives or vital papers or books were lost, but otherwise the house is a mess. We are presently around the corner at the Barbizon Hotel; reoccu-

---

* U.S. government.
† The head of the American Legion demanded McNamara be tried for treason.

pation of the house is not expected much before Thanksgiving.* Accordingly we will have to cancel the visit to London to which we were looking forward so much.

In the meantime, our love to both of you.
Arthur

Under the leadership of Republican Newt Gingrich[†] of Georgia, the Republicans gtained control of both the House and the Senate in the November midterm elections. Clinton was reeling. On January 5, 1995, Arthur received a fax from the White House asking him to contribute ideas to Clinton's upcoming State of the Union Address. Arthur feared that his letter of "sagacious counsel," bluntly stated, might finish any Clintonian connection.

To Bill Clinton

6 January 1995

[New York, New York]

Dear Mr President:

A prime purpose of this year's State of the Union, I would think, would be to restore Bill Clinton's credibility as a President and as a man.

This purpose has, I guess, one aspect in Washington and a different aspect outside Washington. Washington seems to be dominated these days by the supposed onset of the Age of Gingrich; this overshadows everything else and generates pressures to come to terms with the conquering hero. But Gingrich is not a hero to most of the country. Polls show him to be a rather unpopular figure nationwide. Nor is his interpretation of the election results infallible.

The administration has seemed to accept the Republican view that the

---

* The townhouse was never reoccupied; the Schlesingers moved into an apartment at 455 East 51st Street overlooking the East River.
† Newt Gingrich (b. 1943). Right-wing writer, historian, and politician; representative (R-Ga.), 1979–99; Speaker of the House, 1995–98; masterminded the election of Republican House majority in 1994; named *Time* magazine's "Man of the Year" in 1995; ousted from speakership in 1998 by his fellow party members.

election was a repudiation of activist government. Other interpretations are possible. As Lord Salisbury* said after a British general election, "The Great Oracle speaks, but no one is quite sure what the Great Oracle said." There is no doubt that the middle class is angry, but, as a historian, I am fairly sure that "big government" is more the scapegoat than the cause. People are mad at big government because big government has not solved their problems; and these are problems generated not by government but by something much deeper—by the massive structural shift from an industrial economy to an economy based on the microchip.

I wish that you would seize the opportunity to put our present situation in historical context. We are living through the most fundamental structural change since the Industrial Revolution; and, like the Industrial Revolution, it brings dislocation, apprehension and foreboding in its wake. People are frightened of the future, and understandably so. The new age calls for new knowledge and new skills; it may well bring about more disemployment than employment; the transition will be a time of uncertainty and instability.

The middle class is especially frightened. They regarded personal economic insecurity with equanimity so long as it was confined to blue collar workers; but now they see their own jobs "downsized" out of existence. As Felix Rohatyn† put it recently, "Hundreds of thousands of people have been laid off by companies going through restructurings, while technology and competition have kept average incomes from rising. . . . What occurred was a huge transfer of wealth from lower skilled middle-class American workers to the owners of capital assets and to a new technological aristocracy." No wonder there is panic in the suburbs.

They were mad at Bush in 1992 and beat him. They were mad at you in 1994. They will still be mad in 1996—very likely at both major parties. Gingrichery will not solve their problems. They will eventually recognize that the anti-government crusade is self-defeating. For most of the problems that bedevil the nation—the decay in education, in infrastructure, in health care, in law and order, in race relations, in urban living, in environ-

---

*The 3rd Marquess of Salisbury, also known as Lord Robert Cecil and Viscount Cranborne (1830–1903). Conservative politician; prime minister, 1885–86, 1886–92, 1895–1902.

† Felix Rohatyn (b. 1928). Austrian American investment banker; managing director of Lazard Frères; longtime adviser to the Democratic Party; ambassador to France, 1997–2000.

mental protection—call for an increase, not a reduction, in public action. The uncontrolled market will not protect living standards during a time of anguishing transition.

If I may speak frankly, your December speech[*] was, in my view, a great mistake. Its appeasing tone may have seemed required by the Washington atmosphere, but it didn't help in the rest of the country. The speech, as read by friend and foe alike, hoisted a white flag—and did so before a crowd that won't be satisfied by anything short of unconditional surrender. And too much of what the administration has said and done since the election sends a message to the country that everything the Republicans have been saying is right and everything the Democrats have been doing is wrong.

But the administration cannot succeed by trying to out-Republican the Republicans. This will not only destroy credibility; it won't even work politically. Voters will always prefer the real thing to a Democratic imitation. Look what happened to McCurdy[†] and Cooper.[‡] More than that, capitulation to Gingrichery pulls the rug out from under the legislators who have been the strongest supporters of the administration's agenda. Some liberal congressmen are so fed up by what they regard as betrayal of the cause that they are thinking of retiring. The State of the Union address should be designed to strengthen the administration's base rather than to curry favor with the Gingrich crowd.

Don't worry too much about polls. Polls do not report fixed and irrevocable positions. They only report what people think they think in a thoughtless moment—and they therefore provide leaders with clues as to what might be done to change minds. If polls prove anything, they prove the volatility of opinion—the readiness with which people do change their minds. In short, polls define the challenge to leadership.

I am not arguing for a Trumanesque attack on the Republican program. It is not yet time for that. It is quite appropriate to express a desire for cooperation and to welcome some of the procedural reforms (not the uncon-

---

[*] Addressing the nation from the Oval Office on December 15, 1994, President Clinton offered tax breaks for the middle class and reduced government spending, including privatization of government operations; it was seen as a sop to the right.

[†] David McCurdy (b. 1950). Lawyer; representative (D-Okla.), 1981–95; lost 1994 Senate race to conservative Republican James Inhofe.

[‡] James Cooper (b. 1954). Lawyer; representative (D-Tenn.), 1983–95, 2003–present; lost 1994 race for Al Gore, Jr.'s former Senate seat to actor Fred Thompson.

stitutional supermajority idea, however). But this may be your last big chance to define yourself and your administration—to stake out a position, draw lines in the sand and stick by them. Tell the people what you really feel about the direction of our national life.

You need not defend old policies, agencies, etc. The challenges of the 1990s are very different from the challenges of the 1930s or 1960s. But the spirit with which Roosevelt, Truman, Kennedy met those challenges abides—and you could say that you propose to apply that spirit to the challenges of the 21st century. After all, those are three pretty popular and admired Presidents.

Here are some possible themes:

—we must recognize the deep-running and irreversible structural changes that are giving rise to the present frustration, fear and anger; and we must act to cushion the transition to a new age.

—we must outgrow the illusion that we can solve our problems by turning them over to the marketplace and thinking they will solve themselves.

—we must also outgrow the illusion that power taken away from government falls to the people; much of it goes rather to corporations not accountable (as government is) to the people. You can confound the Republicans by quoting Theodore Roosevelt on this. Ask who will benefit from the Gingrich program: it won't be the average middle-class or working-class family.

—tax reduction is not cost-free. It has its consequences: reduction in governmental services; and increase in governmental deficits.

—we must clean up our politics and limit the role of private money and lobbies in the political process.

—the technological revolution calls on us all to reason and work together to meet the unprecedented challenges of the transition. If we do this, we can enter with confidence into a new epoch of unparalleled abundance, opportunity and hope. Finish on a ringing note of optimism.

Anyway, best of luck!

Always sincerely yours,
Arthur

To Richard D. Lamm[*]

9 February 1995

[New York, New York]

Dear Dick:

... I am, of course, deeply concerned about "political correctness" as a threat to the First Amendment. But I believe the PC of the right is more of a general menace than the PC of the left. Leftwing PC is an intolerable nuisance, but it is pretty much confined to colleges and universities where students are mature enough to take care of themselves. But rightwing PC is a weapon with which smalltown zealots across the country intimidate school boards and library boards and teachers and students and do their best to ban Darwin, Marx, secular humanism, sex, etc. Rightwing PC gets the kids before they are old enough to take care of themselves. Remember Mr. Dooley's definition of a fanatic: someone who "does what he thinks th' Lord wud do if He only knew th' facts in th' case." These people are the real menace to the Bill of Rights. ...

All the best,
Arthur

To Al Gore, Jr.

24 February 1995

[New York, New York]

Dear Mr Vice President:

I am writing to say how sorry I am that I was obliged to miss the last two dinners in your recent series on race.[†] Alexandra and I found the first dinner most interesting; but we were out of the country when the second was held, and my hope of attending the third was frustrated when I fell behind

---

[*] Richard D. ("Dick") Lamm (b. 1935). Lawyer; college professor; Democratic governor of Colorado, 1975–87.

[†] Vice President Gore gave a series of three dinners to discuss race relations. Guests included John Hope Franklin, William Julius Wilson, Henry Louis Gates, Jr., Jesse Jackson, John Lewis, Stanley Crouch, Lani Guinier, Shelby Steele, Richard Goodwin, and Marty Peretz.

schedule in the preparation of a lecture I had to deliver in New York the next night.

I want to congratulate you on taking the trouble to organize these dinners. We had at Robert Kennedy's initiative a somewhat similar but less organized series in the Kennedy years. RFK's idea in the Hickory Hill seminars was to expose high government officials to issues and ideas not normally in their administrative jurisdiction; and the interchange between officials and outsiders was stimulating and fruitful for both sides. You might want to consider including more top administration people in the dinners so that they might have a chance to hear and challenge what is on the minds of outside experts.

Anyway best of luck for your future evening—and again thank you for asking us to the recent series.

All the best (and to Tipper),[*]
Arthur

To Bill Clinton

17 April 1995

[New York, New York]

Dear Mr President:

I heard the Warm Springs ceremony again last night on C-Span, and I want to say how very well your remarks caught the spirit of FDR.[†]

Of course a vital part of FDR's success in governing was his readiness to take on the opposition, and I was much heartened by the tone of your radio

---

[*] Mary Elizabeth ("Tipper") Gore (b. 1948). Author; photographer; estranged wife of former vice president Al Gore, Jr.

[†] "[President Roosevelt] showed us how to be a nation in a time of great stress," said Clinton in Warm Springs, Georgia, on April 13, 1995, at a ceremony celebrating FDR's life and works half a century after his death at a nearby spa where he sought relief from the effects of polio. "He taught us again and again that our government could be an instrument of democratic destiny, that it could help our children do better. He taught us that patriotism was really about pulling together, working together, and bringing out the best in each other. . . . I wish he were just sort of on our shoulder to deride those who are cynical, those who are skeptical, those who are negative, and most of all, those who seek to play on fears to divide us."

broadcast on Saturday. I can see the argument for having given the Newtists enough rope during his Hundred Days to hang themselves; but, now that the Hundred Days are over and people are beginning to read the fine print on the Contract,[*] it may be well to encourage and stimulate the inevitable backlash. Voters like fighting Presidents, especially when they feel the President is fighting for them. And people, on the whole, don't like Gingrich. He reminds them of the schoolyard bully who, when criticized, becomes the schoolyard crybaby.

You were kind enough to ask me to send a copy of my remarks,[†] which I herewith attach.

Best of luck in the stormy months ahead. Let me know if I can do anything to help.

Ever sincerely yours,
Arthur

To Herbert Kriedman[‡]

15 May 1995

[New York, New York]

Dear Professor Kriedman:

Forgive my inexcusable delay in answering your letter of some weeks back, but it has been a busy spring, and I have been out of the country.

Tom Wicker is an old and cherished friend (so I am sending him a copy of this letter), but I think he went badly off the rails in his review of Chomsky's *Rethinking Camelot* in *Diplomatic History*. Chomsky is no doubt a great linguistic scholar, but he is not much use as a historian. Years ago I

---

[*] The Contract with America, promulgated by Gingrich and the Republican Party during the 1994 congressional campaign, detailed actions Republicans promised to take if they became the House majority. Proposed legislation included a balanced budget requirement, tax cuts, term limits, welfare reform, new anticrime measures, and a missile defense system.

[†] Schlesinger quoted FDR's words of 1937: "The test of our progress is not whether we add more to the abundance of those who have much; it is whether we provide enough for those who have little."

[‡] Herbert Kriedman, Professor of history and political science at Nassau Community College in Garden City, New York.

exposed his use in one of his books of a fabricated Truman quotation in order to bolster his argument against Truman's foreign policy.[*]

I do not see how Tom Wicker can say that Chomsky made a "virtually irrefutable case" against the proposition that JFK was planning to withdraw American forces from Vietnam and that Chomsky "seems to me clearly right on his main point—that *the record* shows President Kennedy to have had no 'secret plan' for ending the war, or even a private impulse to do so."

Of course Kennedy had a secret plan for the withdrawal of the American advisers—secret at least until the publication of *The Pentagon Papers*. The plan can be found in the Gravel edition, II, 175–181. He did increase the number of American advisers because he thought the Saigon government should be given a run for its money. But he rejected every proposal that he send American combat units. He even brought General MacArthur to Washington to warn the military against the commitment of ground forces; and, as Maxwell Taylor says in his oral history in the Kennedy Library, whenever the JCS recommended the despatch of ground forces, "He'd say, 'Well, now, gentlemen, you go back and convince General MacArthur, then I'll be convinced.' . . . The last thing he wanted was to put in our ground forces. . . . It was really the President's personal conviction that US ground troops shouldn't go in." General Gavin has written, "I know he was totally opposed to the introduction of combat troops in Southeast Asia." And the first installment of a thousand advisers was withdrawn under the plan in October 1963.

Tom does not seem to be familiar with the evidence compiled in John Newman's[†] book *Kennedy and Vietnam* and in chapter 31 of my own *Robert Kennedy and His Times* (where I cite Mike Mansfield and Wayne Morse as well as the O'Donnell quotation[‡] you kindly sent me). Since Newman and I published, both McGeorge Bundy and Robert McNamara have said that

[*] See Arthur Schlesinger, Jr., *The Crisis of Confidence: Ideas, Power, and Violence in America* (Boston: Houghton Mifflin,1969), 90–92.

[†] John M. Newman (b. 1950). U.S. Army Intelligence, 1974–94; professor of international relations, University of Maryland, 1981–present; author of *JFK and Vietnam: Deception, Intrigue, and the Struggle for Power* (1992).

[‡] Kenneth O'Donnell once asked President Kennedy how he could pull out of Vietnam without damaging American prestige. "Easy," JFK replied. "Put a government in there that will ask us to leave." O'Donnell and David Powers, *"Johnny, We Hardly Knew Ye": Memories of John Fitzgerald Kennedy* (Boston: Little Brown, 1972), 18.

they believe Kennedy would have pulled out of Vietnam. Roger Hilsman[*] says in a (thus far unpublished) letter to the *Times* regarding the McNamara book: "McNamara does concede that President Kennedy would not have made Vietnam an American war. But Kennedy's view was much stronger than McNamara suggests. As Assistant Secretary of State for Far Eastern Affairs, I was the action officer on Vietnam, and Kennedy told me over and over again that my job was to keep American involvement at a minimum, so that we could withdraw as soon as the opportunity presented itself."

Chomsky seems to have the idea that Kennedy was a macho, victory-at-any-cost type. In fact, he was cautious and not inclined to make heavy investments in lost causes. His presidency was marked precisely by his capacity to *refuse* escalation—as in Laos, the Bay of Pigs, the Berlin crisis of 1961 and the Cuban missile crisis.

In short, Chomsky in this book seems to me as reliable as is his custom, and I am only sorry that he dragged Tom Wicker down with him.

Sincerely yours,
Arthur Schlesinger, jr.

To Mr. Tolson[†]

18 May 1995

[New York, New York]

Dear Mr. Tolson:

Veterans of earlier presidencies look on the recent development of speechwriting staffs with incredulity. In pre-Nixon days, speechwriters were persons, few in number, who had policy responsibilities and ready access to their presidents and for whom speechwriting was a secondary assignment. They were also professionally committed to anonymity and indeed were known as "ghostwriters," ghosts being notorious for invisibility. The now regular identification of the speechwriters in the next day's newspaper astonishes those of the old school who believe that the speech

---

[*] Roger Hilsman (b. 1919). Author and political scientist; OSS; assistant secretary of state for far eastern affairs, 1963–64; longtime professor at Columbia University.
[†] Mr. Tolson. Unknown correspondent.

belongs to the person who gave it. And the practice of consigning speech drafting to people who have no continuous contact with policy and no regular access to presidents no doubt accounts for the decline in quality of presidential speeches.[*]

The latter-day reliance on public opinion polls, focus groups, etc., also devalues the speech process. The one thing polls really prove is the volatility of public opinion. Polls register only what people think they think without having thought much about the question; but they are often ready to change their minds under the pressure of new considerations and of practical consequences. Polls are therefore chiefly of value in defining the challenge to presidential leadership and indicating what must be done to change people's minds.

Timing is essential too. FDR of course had a tremendous instinct for timing. In early 1935, Democrats and liberals had an unhappy sense that the administration was confused, drifting, in the doldrums. The strident voices of Huey Long,[†] Father Coughlin[‡] and General Hugh Johnson[§] dominated the headlines. People—among them Ray Stannard Baker,[¶] the biographer of Wilson, and my father, the liberal historian from Harvard—beseeched the president to regain command of the scene. FDR wrote Baker, "If since last November I had tried to keep up the pace of 1933 and 1934, the inevitable histrionics of the new actors, Long and Coughlin and Johnson, would have turned the eyes of the audience away from the main drama itself. Individual psychology cannot, because of human weakness, be attuned for long periods of time to a constant repetition of the highest note in the scale." He wrote my father, "I agree with you about the value of regu-

---

[*] See Robert Schlesinger, *White House Ghosts: Presidents and Their Speechwriters* (New York: Simon and Schuster, 2008).

[†] Huey Long, Jr. (1893–1935). Lawyer; Democratic governor of Louisiana, 1928–32; senator, 1932–35; leftist populist; promised to "share the wealth"; assassinated.

[‡] Charles Coughlin (1891–1979). Roman Catholic priest and political leader who used the radio to create a large following; established the National Union for Social Justice, 1934; expressed fascist sympathies; issued anti-Semitic commentaries.

[§] Hugh S. Johnson (1882–1942). U.S. Army brigadier general; businessman; head of FDR's National Recovery Administration, 1933–34, until FDR fired him; an admirer of Mussolini's national corporatist system; isolationist; as a columnist, criticized FDR harshly.

[¶] Ray Stannard Baker (1870–1946). Journalist; author; President Wilson's press secretary at Versailles.

lar reporting. My difficulty is a strange and weird sense known as 'public psychology.'" When the psychological moment came, FDR made the congressional session of 1935 as full of achievement as the hundred days of 1933.

Politics is in the end an educational process, and speeches are a vital instrument of presidential leadership. Speeches are also important within the executive branch as a means of forcing decisions, crystallizing policies and imposing discipline. Carol Gelderman[*] is absolutely right in arguing the necessity of "uniting important policymaking and speechwriting functions in one trusted adviser"—a Rosenman, a Clifford, a Sorensen, a McPherson.[†] . . .

[Sincerely yours,]
Arthur Schlesinger, Jr.

To Allida Black[‡]

3 September 1995

[New York, New York]

Dear Allida Black:

I have finally had a chance to read *Casting Her Own Shadow*. There is much to admire in the book. Your research is careful and thorough, and your judgments in the main temperate and thoughtful. I do, however, have some problems with the book. I think you quite understate Mrs R[oosevelt]'s rejection of American Communists. I wish you had quoted in full her comment in June 1945: "For years, in this country, they taught the philosophy of the lie. . . . Because I have experienced the deception of the American Communists, I will not trust them." When Jim Loeb told her of his plans to broaden the base of the Union for Democratic Action and asked whether

---

[*] Carol Gelderman. Author of *All the President's Words: The Bully Pulpit and the Creation of the Virtual Presidency* (1997); English professor, University of New Orleans.

[†] Harry McPherson, Jr. (1929–2012). Lawyer; longtime LBJ aide; White House counsel and presidential speechwriter, 1965–69.

[‡] Allida M. Black. Research professor of history and international affairs, George Washington University; editor of the Eleanor Roosevelt Papers; author of *Casting Her Own Shadow: Eleanor Roosevelt and the Shaping of Postwar Liberalism* (1995).

the bar against Communists should be retained, Mrs R. told him in the most definite way to keep the Communists out. I fear that younger historians who have never met a Communist tend to succumb to a romantic view of party members as honest if misguided idealists. The hard fact is that the Communists lied whenever it suited their convenience (or the party line); and it is always hard to work with congenital liars. Try it some time. Mrs R. felt personally betrayed and was unforgiving. A basic theme of your book, I take it, is the contrast between Mrs R. and "vital center" liberalism. Indeed chapter 5 is entitled "Confronting the Vital Center." But you misunderstand what the vital center was about. By "vital center" I meant democracy as between the two totalitarian faiths, fascism and communism (see the diagram on page 145). I definitely did not mean middle-of-the-road "consensus" (p 77) between the business community and the New Deal. I don't see how you can say that the vital center was "rejecting the anti-business sentiment [liberals] had embraced for half a century" when chapter 2 of the book is devoted to an attack on business-controlled government. Nowhere do I argue that "liberals had more in common with business than they had with radical reformers." I do say that liberals had more in common with businessmen than with Communists; but I did not (and do not) regard Communists as "radical reformers." Do you, really?

Also you seem to imply that vital center liberalism favored the "harsh restriction of political dissent" (170), threatened "the rights of Americans to join the Communist party" (201–2) and even favored outlawing the party (132). When, for example, did ADA ever take such positions? My chapter 9 in *The Vital Center* rejects proposals to outlaw the CPUSA. ADA consistently and vigorously attacked Joe McCarthy, and so did I and all vital center liberals (McCarthy attacked me in return in a nationwide radio broadcast in 1952). You say that I supported the Smith Act and that I said that Americans could only hold loathsome ideas in peacetime. That suggests that I believed that Communists should not be permitted to hold their loathsome ideas during the Second World War, which is of course ridiculous. My papers are in some disorder due to a fire in our house so I can't at the moment check your references, but I strongly doubt that I ever did the things you attribute to me on 155.

On page 5, you mention the "rapidity with which Adlai Stevenson, Schlesinger, and other liberals deserted Alger Hiss after his conviction." In fact, I thought Alger Hiss guilty well before his conviction because Jerome

Frank and Gardner Jackson, who had worked with Hiss in AAA, had told me that they believed him to have been a Communist (see also *The Coming of the New Deal*, 52–54).

I had hoped to be able to send the Columbia University Press some encouraging words about the book; but I fear that a blurb would imply an endorsement of what seems to me your misinterpretation of the vital center and of Mrs R.'s relationship to it. Anyway best of luck on the book. As the great Dutch historian Pieter Geyl* well said, "History is indeed an argument without end."

Sincerely yours,
Arthur Schlesinger, jr.

To Patricia Brooks[†]

13 July 1996

[New York, New York]

Dear Ms Brooks:

Two words on the lips of politicians that cause me to tune off at once are "values" (especially "family values" or "traditional values") and "compassion." I am not of course opposed to values or, heaven knows, to compassion, but I don't like to hear politicos righteously mouthing such words when they should be talking about the *policies* they propose to achieve their objectives. . . .

Sincerely yours,
Arthur Schlesinger, Jr.

---

* Pieter Geyl (1887–1966). Dutch historian; University of Utrecht.
† Patricia Brooks. Unknown correspondent.

To Bill Clinton

9 October 1996

[New York, New York]

Dear Mr President:

I wonder whether Dole's liberal-liberal-liberal litany might not be countered along these lines:

"I am not one for abstract labeling in politics. My approach is to identify concrete problems and do what I can to help people meet them. I like to think I am acting in the tradition of Franklin D Roosevelt, Harry S Truman and John F. Kennedy—and I don't think most Americans believe that is such a bad place to come from."

After all, polls show that FDR, Truman and JFK are the most popular Presidents of the century. A possibly useful Kennedy quote can be found on page 411 of his *Public Papers . . . 1963* when he rejects the idea of the national government as "an intruder, an adversary" and calls it "the people of fifty states joining in a national effort."

Also I wonder whether more might be done to use the widespread disgust over gridlock as an argument for electing a Democratic Congress. Something along these lines: "I know how much you share with me frustration and irritation over the gridlock in Washington. There is one sure way to overcome that gridlock and to get the country moving again. That is, to send people to Washington who can be relied on to work for our common goals of abundance and peace."

Ever sincerely yours,
Arthur

To Bianca Jagger[*]

18 October 1996

[New York, New York]

Dear Bianca:

It was a delightful luncheon—and here are the Yeats[†] poems that bear a bit upon our discussion.

THE GREAT DAY

Hurrah for revolution and more cannon-shot!
A beggar upon horseback lashes a beggar on foot.
Hurrah for revolution and cannon come again!
The beggars have changed places, but the lash goes on.

PARNELL

Parnell came down the road, he said to a cheering man:
"Ireland shall get her freedom and you still break stone."

Love,
Arthur

To Greg Klein[‡]

31 January 1997

[New York, New York]

Dear Mr Klein and the students in the World History Class:

Forgive my delay in responding to a most interesting and thoughtful set of letters, but it has been a demanding winter. I only wish I could answer

---

[*] Bianca Jagger (b. 1945). Human rights activist; former model and actress; married to rock star Mick Jagger, 1971–78. Bianca Jagger interviewed Schlesinger for German *Vogue* in 1993; he found her attractive, articulate, perceptive, open-minded, and good-hearted, and they became friends.

[†] William Butler Yeats (1865–1939). Irish poet and playwright; 1923 Nobel Prize winner; Schlesinger's favorite poet.

[‡] Greg Klein, history teacher, Littleton High School, Littleton, Colorado.

each letter individually. But in one's 80th year, time becomes the most precious of commodities (as you will discover around the year 2060), so I must answer you collectively.

I think that events around the world—the breaking of nations under the pressure of ethnic and religious antagonisms—are forcing people to consider with new urgency the question: What holds a nation together? Other countries break up because they fail to give ethnically diverse peoples compelling reasons to see themselves as part of the same nation. Now America has been a multicultural country from the start; yet, except for a terrible civil war, it has somehow cohered and endured.

What is it that, in the absence of a common ethnic origin, has bound Americans together over two turbulent centuries? The answer lies essentially in the creation of a common nationality and culture based on commitment to a common set of civic principles and ideals. Plainly there is no necessary incompatibility between fidelity to the unifying principles that hold us together as Americans and affection, as one wishes it, for one's ancestral or religious or gender group. It remains a vital part of America for people to cherish their own traditions, observances, rituals, creeds, customs, cuisines.

But it is also vital for Americans to be free to choose the group with which they wish to identify, and other loyalties may often be more important than ethnicity. Moreover, many, probably most, Americans are not members of a single ethnic group. Americans fall in love across ethnic, religious and, increasingly, racial lines, and most of us are of mixed ancestry.

Militant multiculturalism rejects the idea of a common culture, sees people as belonging irrevocably to one or another ethnic group and seeks to promote and perpetuate separate ethnic, racial and linguistic communities. A number of you are concerned about bilingualism. In so far as bilingualism is a means of facilitating movement into the English-speaking society, it is helpful; but, when it becomes (as it evidently has in some localities) a means of entrenching another language, it is a bad thing both for the young students and for society.

It is easy to denounce multicultural separatism. But separatism would not get very far if the white majority lived up to American ideals and really welcomed assimilation and integration. Minorities do not want to live in ghettos. They want to join the mainstream. Alas, too many whites still slam doors. Racism remains the curse of American life.

Recall words of Mahatma Gandhi that used to be seen on public posters in India, a country far more fiercely split than our own by racial and religious and linguistic and caste enmities. "We must cease," Gandhi said, "to be exclusive Hindus or Muslims or Sikhs, Parsis, Christians, or Jews. Whilst we may staunchly adhere to our respective faiths, we must be Indians first and Indians last." It is because India has abandoned these teachings of Gandhi that it is so bitterly divided today.

In the spirit of Gandhi, while we heterogeneous Americans may staunchly adhere to our respective traditions, let us never forget that we are members one of another, Americans first and Americans last, tied together, in Martin Luther King's phrase, in "a single garment of destiny."

All my best to you all,
Arthur Schlesinger, Jr.

PS I notice that three letters referred to *The Disuniting of America* as a novel! Hostile critics might agree, but I meant it as a work of non-fiction, not of fiction.

On February 3, 1997, Pamela Churchill Harriman suffered a massive brain hemorrhage at the Ritz health club in Paris, where she served as ambassador, and died the next day.

The Economist published an obituary on February 8, 1997, saying: "If you collect a dozen or so of Pamela Harriman's lovers and put them around a dinner table, you had the makings of a world government. . . . Mrs. Harriman's life was an astonishing tale of sex, money and—far sweeter than both these coarse commodities—power. . . . Doubtless she was expert between the sheets. . . . Was there not always, at the very back of her mind, just a nagging feeling that she was being laughed at, even scorned?"

Arthur found the notice vulgar and offensive and dashed off a letter in defense of his friend and her historical reputation.

To the Editor of *The Economist*

11 February 1997

[New York, New York]

To the Editor:

The Economist should be ashamed of itself. We had not realized over here that the scurrility of the London tabloids, the worst press in the English-speaking world, is beginning to corrupt 25 St James's Street. The obituary for Pamela Harriman is a masterpiece of cheapness and irrelevance.

You omit the salient fact that Pamela Harriman was a woman of considerable ability and public spirit, as her success as US ambassador to Paris demonstrated. When she was offered Paris, she asked for the best academic briefing and spent hours with Stanley Hoffman[*] of Harvard and Nicholas Wahl[†] of New York University. A woman who might well have passed her life at fashion shows and fashionable parties, she devoted herself in a conscientious and effective way to politics and government. Is it really an impeachment of character that she was among the first to spot the potentialities of Bill Clinton?

Sincerely yours,
Arthur Schlesinger, Jr.

To John Kenneth Galbraith

19 April 1997

[New York, New York]

Dear Ken:

You threw a considerable scare into all of us, and it is such a relief to know that you are on the road to recovery.[‡] When it appeared touch-and-go,

---

[*] Stanley Hoffmann (b. 1928). Harvard professor of international relations; chairman of Harvard's Center for European Studies, 1969–95.

[†] Nicholas Wahl (1928–96). Expert on postwar France; director of the Institute of French Studies at New York University, 1978–96.

[‡] In early April 1997, Galbraith, eighty-eight, tripped and fell, fracturing his pelvis and requiring emergency surgery. Travel and lecturing were now behind him, but his writing and commentary continued.

I began thinking how much your friendship has meant to me across the long years and how, given the restraints on communication between males of our generation, I have not tried to express it. I thought what a shame it would be if I never said anything to you; so, lest I be further shamed, I will say so now.

You are my closest and dearest (male) friend. I have learned a great deal from you not only substantively but stylistically. You have persuaded me, for example, that irony is far more effective than indignation when confronted by the parade of human folly—that a rapier works better than a saber. This has ended the ill-tempered explosions with which I used to spoil Cambridge dinner parties. You have also persuaded me, as Adam Smith[*] evidently persuaded you, that there is a lot of ruin in a country, which has discouraged any tendency toward apocalyptic prophecies. And you have contributed infinitely to the general joy of life.

Alexandra, who has no doubt that you have improved me greatly, joins in sending all love. We count on entertaining you and Kitty in our wonderful new place before too many months pass by.

Take care of yourself—and get well.

Yours ever,
Arthur

To the Children

13 March 1998

[New York, New York]

My dear children:

Friday the 13th!—an appropriate time to write this letter. As you probably know already, a series of tests show that I have prostate cancer. This is not so grave a matter as it sounds. Prostate cancer is not uncommon among men who have reached my advanced age. The saying among doctors is that more men die *with* prostate cancer than die *from* it.

---

[*] Adam Smith (1723–90). Scottish social philosopher and pioneering political economist; author of *An Inquiry into the Nature and Causes of the Wealth of Nations* (1776). As Smith remarked to a young man who bewailed the British surrender at Yorktown as the ruin of England, "Be assured, my young friend, that there is a great deal of ruin in a nation."

Catscan and bonescan inspections show that the cancer has not spread and is localized in the prostate. My doctor says that there are four courses from which to choose: do nothing (prostate cancer for octogenarians spreads slowly); stabilize it by monthly injections (among side effects: impotence); eradicate it by radiation (several times a week for six weeks, debilitating, with side effects); eradicate it by "seeds" (one time implantation; also side effects).

I am going abroad at the end of April; and, after discussion with the doctor, we decided that I should have a new test before I depart to see whether the cancer is growing. If the test shows cancer on the march, I will check it by the "seeds" operation on my return.

In short, there is no cause for worry, but I do want you all to know the situation. Prostate cancer brings with it no pain or discomfort, at least until the final stages. And, as Palmerston said on his deathbed, "Die, my dear doctor? That is the last thing I shall do."*

My love to all of you,
Daddy

To Joseph Nye, Jr.†

17 April 1998

[New York, New York]

Dear Joe:

I enjoyed the luncheon at the Century Club the other day, but I came away troubled by what appears to be the Kennedy School's enthusiasm over privatization, deregulation and devolution as the remedy for our social discontents.

It is surely naivete of the first order to suppose that the transfer of public functions to profit-making agencies will solve our problems. Profit-making agencies in their nature must put profits first; service to the public inevitably falls far behind. In their nature also, and especially under deregu-

---

* Schlesinger did nothing, and he died of a heart attack, not prostate cancer.
† Joseph ("Joe") Nye, Jr. (b. 1937). Author; political scientist specializing in international security affairs; served in Carter and Clinton administrations; dean of Harvard's John F. Kennedy School of Government, 1995–2004; wrote influential book, *Soft Power: The Means to Success in World Politics* (2004).

lation, they escape normal processes of accountability. The mismanagement, inefficiency and scandals of the great HMO experiment[*] represent the foredoomed fate of privatization. I am confident that the next years will see a massive recoil against the idea that private companies should make money out of public services.

A related fallacy is the enthusiasm for the transfer of national public functions to state and local government. Do take a look at the Center for Public Integrity's recent study of the Illinois legislature. History has long since refuted the Jeffersonian notion that government closer to the people is more responsive to the people. Local government is notoriously the government of the locally powerful. It has required the intervention of the national government to protect the interests of the powerless.

Privatization, devolution and deregulation are devices by which private business seeks to make money out of what should be public services. What is involved is essentially a shift in authority from Big Government, which is at least moderately accountable, to Big Business, which is hardly accountable at all. I am sorry to see the Kennedy School dressing all this up with pretentious verbiage about the "reconceptualization of government," "paradigm shifts," etc. . . .

All the best,
Arthur

To John Updike[†]

8 September 1998

[New York, New York]

Dear John:

That was a fine review of the Helen Keller book,[‡] but I must file a dissent with regard to the line about Mrs Roosevelt as "plausibly outed as a

---

[*] The market share of for-profit health maintenance organizations had reached 62 percent by 1997, even as the HMO industry was plagued by gross instances of financial fraud and poor patient care.
[†] John Updike (1932–2009). Prolific novelist, poet, critic, and short-story writer; author of *Rabbit, Run* (1960); two-time Pulitzer Prize for Fiction winner.
[‡] Dorothy Herrmann, *Helen Keller: A Life* (New York: Alfred A. Knopf, 1998).

lesbian." The person who has done the outing is Blanche Wiesen Cook,[*] a competent historian but a militant on the lesbian front. Geoffrey Ward[†] wrote an authoritative review of her book in the *New York Review,* and I have asked him to send you a copy. Mrs R., in the fashion of her generation and especially of the generation before her, was given to lush expressions of same-sex friendship; but if "lesbian" implies overt sexual acts, I doubt it.[‡]

Why does so much discussion these days end up in sex? At least that cannot be said about the history of the Academy!

All the best,
Arthur

---

[*] Blanche Wiesen Cook (b. 1941). Professor of history, John Jay College, City University of New York; author of *Eleanor Roosevelt: 1884–1933* (1992) and *Eleanor Roosevelt: 1933–1938* (2000).

[†] Geoffrey C. Ward (b. 1940). Author; historian; principal writer of the PBS miniseries *The Civil War;* FDR scholar.

[‡] In a publication of his collected essays and criticism, *More Matter* (1999), Updike qualified his comment on Mrs. R's sexuality in a footnote, writing, "Most surviving friends of the great lady doubt that the effusive warmth of her letters to [Lorena] Hickok was translated into physical action."

To Elia Kazan[*]

16 January 1999

[New York, New York]

Dear Gadge:

Warmest congratulations on the Academy award, however belated![†] The action a couple of years ago of those self-righteous pygmies of the AFI[‡] and the Los Angeles Film Critics was a disgrace, but your work and life will outlast idiots and idiocies.[§]

All the best,
Arthur

William F. Buckley, Jr., had written a book entitled The Redhunter: A Novel Based on the Life and Times of Senator Joe McCarthy *and wanted Arthur to write a blurb for it.*

---

[*] Elia ("Gadge") Kazan (1909–2003). Distinguished director, writer, producer; born in Istanbul of Greek heritage; member of the Group Theater in the 1930s; cofounded the Actors Studio, 1947; directed *A Streetcar Named Desire, Death of a Salesman,* and *Cat on a Hot Tin Roof* on Broadway; directed the movies *A Streetcar Named Desire, Viva Zapata, On the Waterfront,* and *A Face in the Crowd.*

[†] In 1952, Kazan appeared before HUAC and named eight of his friends from the Group Theater, along with himself, as members of the Communist Party in the 1930s. In 1999, the Academy of Motion Picture Arts and Sciences awarded him an honorary Oscar, dividing the Hollywood community; some still considered him a rat. "I did what I did because it was more tolerable of two alternatives that were, either way, painful, even disastrous, and either way wrong for me," Kazan wrote in his 1988 autobiography. He had quit the Communist Party after a year and a half, disenthralled, and HUAC already had the names he disclosed. The American Film Institute and the Los Angeles Film Critics Association had previously denied him a lifetime achievement award.

[‡] The American Film Institute and the Los Angeles Film Critics Association had vetoed giving Kazan a lifetime achievement award.

[§] Schlesinger, in a February 28, 1999, *New York Times* op-ed entitled "Hollywood Hypocrisy," wrote: "If the Academy's occasion calls for apologies, let Mr. Kazan's denouncers apologize for the aid and comfort they gave Stalinism."

From William F. Buckley, Jr.

February 24, 1999

[New York, New York]

Dear Arthur:

I do truly hope you won't just plain throw it away. It was practically written for you. I'd be grateful if you'd look at it and perhaps proffer a blurb.

Ken Galbraith read it and gave the following blurb: "To redeem even by fiction the career of Joe McCarthy is a challenging task for a truly brilliant writer. So it had to be William F. Buckley. All who marvel should read." Which was nice, and I'm grateful, but the book doesn't really try to "redeem" Joe as I hope you'll undertake to establish to your own satisfaction.

And Tom Reeves (Prof. Thomas C. Reeves)* author of *The Life and Times of Joe McCarthy, A Biography* [1982] has written for the jacket, "A splendid novel. There are things I would have put differently, but that doesn't matter. Buckley has produced a book that will attract the attention and applause of all serious students of the period. Equally important, it's hugely entertaining."

I do hope you'll read it.

Warmest,
Bill

To William F. Buckley, Jr.

9 March 99

[New York, New York]

Dear Bill:

I'm afraid you don't persuade me about Joe McCarthy. I still sing along with Dick Rovere. But I hope it is not too late to save you from an error that will delight unfriendly reviewers. On page 399 Wendell Willkie could not in 1954 have spoken the words you ascribe to him. Afterall, he had died in

---

*Thomas C. Reeves (b. 1936). American historian, University of Wisconsin–Parkside.

1944—unless of course he was speaking from the grave. (Also on p 403 I *opposed* the Communist Control Act, but Willmoore Kendall[*] often got things wrong.)

Anyway these references prove I read the book. And I hope it will at least inform new generations that there once was a Joe McCarthy![†]

We loved the picture of you and Ken in *Quest*.

All the best,
Arthur

Vice President Al Gore, Jr., planned to formally announce his candidacy for the presidency on June 16, 1999, in Carthage, Tennessee, his hometown, and asked Arthur for thoughts about the speech.

To Al Gore, Jr.

7 June 1999

[New York, New York]

Dear Mr. Vice President:

I am leaving the country on the 10th to deliver some talks in Italy. Because I am still working on the talks, I regret to say that I don't have time to provide much of use for Carthage. However, here are some random thoughts based on too many years as a free rider on presidential campaigns.

1. It is essential that a presidential candidate feel comfortable and at ease with himself and with what he is saying and doing. No amount of PR polishing can make people different from what they are. It is always a mistake to go out of character. I am not sure that the attempts to "humanize" Al Gore have always worked—the jokes, the macarena, etc.

---

*Willmoore Kendall (1909–68). Conservative writer and professor of political philosophy; OSS; Yale, 1947–61; the University of Dallas, 1961–67; cofounder of *National Review,* 1955.

† According to *The New York Times,* the novel portrayed Joe McCarthy as a "nice guy" who was pursuing a "noble cause" in his anticommunist crusade, but was hounded to death by blowhard journalists, vengeful Democrats, and Eisenhower machinations.

I would be especially careful about confessionals. You are a reserved and reticent man, I would judge, and you should be what you are. Can you imagine FDR speaking in public (or indeed in private) about the way polio changed his life? He won people's hearts by talking about them and their problems, not by talking about himself. So too JFK. You best project yourself by saying what you would like to do for others and for the republic. (But perhaps it is the age of Oprah, and I speak for another generation.)

2. The declaration of candidacy need not be technically specific about issues; but it must be clear about the "vision thing"—the direction in which the candidate proposes to take the country. As Henry Adams said, the President of the United States "resembles the commander of a ship at sea. He must have a helm to grasp, a course to steer, a port to seek." This is the part of the specch that you should write yourself, and out of your gut.

It is essential that a declaration be sufficiently specific to differentiate the candidate from his competitors, especially those in the opposite party. You should question any statement that might equally be given by George W Bush[*] or any other Republican. (It is more difficult for you to differentiate yourself from Bradley[†] since no one knows where he stands on anything.)

3. I think that a major problem in America today is the growing disparity in wealth and income. I well understand that anyone who makes a frontal issue of this is going to be attacked for waging class warfare, etc. But I wonder whether the issue cannot be approached in another way. Might it not be possible to congratulate the nation and its managers and workers for the booming economy of recent years and then say: we have moved wonderfully ahead, despite the Republican gloomers-and-doomers, but the economic revival is still incomplete. The job for the next administration is to build on the great gains of the last eight years and to "complete the economy" by helping the people left out of the boom, the farmers, the workers in sweatshops, the people who lose jobs

---

[*] George W. Bush (b. 1946). Republican governor of Texas, 1995–2000; forty-third U.S. president, 2001–9; son of President George H. W. Bush.

[†] William "Bill" Bradley (b. 1943). New York Knicks basketball player, 1967–77; senator (D-N.J.), 1979–97; candidate for the 2000 Democratic presidential nomination.

through global competition (inevitable as that may be), the people without health insurance, etc. . . .

Remember the words of the first president from Tennessee, Andrew Jackson: "When the laws undertake . . . to make the rich richer and the potent more powerful, the humble members of society—the farmers, mechanics, and laborers—who have neither the time nor the means of securing like favors to themselves, have a right to complain of the injustice of their Government."

COMPLETE THE ECONOMY would be a useful campaign theme for a variety of purposes. Among other things, steering more income to the hardworking poor would be the best way to enable working families to spend more time with each other, which I understand you have in mind as a major campaign theme.

4. Best of luck in Carthage on the 16th! And please give our affectionate regards to Tipper and to your mother.

Arthur

To Tina Brown[*]

8 July 99

[New York, New York]

Dear Tina:

Here it is.[†]

In the spring of 1993 the Clintons invited the Schlesingers to a farewell dinner for Pamela Harriman, the new ambassador to Paris. I happened to lunch that day with Jacqueline Onassis and mentioned that I had known Bill Clinton for a number of years but had never met Mrs Clinton. "I gather that she is a very intelligent young woman," I said, "but I imagine that she is awfully earnest and humorless, a real blue stocking." "You couldn't be more

---

[*] Tina Brown (b. 1953). British American journalist and author; editor of *Vanity Fair*, 1984–92; *The New Yorker*, 1992–98; *Talk* magazine, 1999–2002; *The Daily Beast*, 2008–present, and *Newsweek*, 2010–12.

[†] Brown had asked Schlesinger to write down his personal impressions of Hillary Clinton as a White House hostess.

wrong," Jackie said. "I saw something of Hillary during the campaign last year, and she is a delight, filled with fun and irony. You will have a jolly time."

That evening I found myself seated next to Mrs Clinton. I had a splendid time. Jackie, as usual, was quite right.

My only other dinner at the White House in the Clinton years took place last November. The occasion was the award to assorted dignitaries of National Medals for the Arts and for the Humanities. Once more I was placed next to Hillary. On her other side was Garry Wills, another historian and Humanities Medalist. Directly across the round table from Hillary was Gregory Peck,* an Arts Medalist. I said to her, "You have no idea what you are doing for the morale of scholars. Here you have seated yourself between a couple of historians when you could have had Gregory Peck." Without missing a beat, Hillary replied serenely, "Yes, but sitting here I can talk to both of you and look at Gregory Peck."

Affectionately, Arthur

John F. Kennedy, Jr., died in an airplane crash on July 16, 1999, at age thirty-eight.

To Caroline Kennedy Schlossberg†

25 July 1999

[New York, New York]

My dear Caroline:

It is one more bitter blow, and our hearts go out to you. I still can't believe that this wonderful young man and his charming wife are gone. John was graced with such decency and kindness, with so acute a mind, so generous a spirit, so merry a heart that he was irresistible. How proud his father would have been of him!

---

* Gregory Peck (1916–2003). Actor and Hollywood star; won an Academy Award for playing Atticus Finch in *To Kill a Mockingbird*.
† Caroline Kennedy Schlossberg (b. 1957). Lawyer, author, educator, Democratic Party activist; daughter of John F. Kennedy and Jacqueline Bouvier Kennedy; married Edwin Schlossberg, designer, author, artist, in 1986.

The national outpouring of grief was a tribute to his admirable personal qualities. It also, I think, sprang from a feeling that John represented something missing from our lives today—a determination to live beyond oneself, a readiness to serve the community and the nation, a passion to help the unlucky and the dispossessed to get a better break in life. I hope that *George** will be enabled to continue to spread the gospel that politics, and idealism, can be fun.

It was a beautiful service, and we loved your reading of the lines from *The Tempest.*[†] Alexandra joins in sending all sympathy and love at this terribly sad time.

My love to you, Arthur

To William F. Buckley, Jr.

12 August 1999

[New York, New York]

Dear Bill:

Thank you for your defense of the lifelong embrace of Jr (and for your nice words about JFK, Jr).

And add the following to your roster of lifelong Jrs: Adolf A Berle, Jr, Whitney Darrow, Jr,[‡] Henry Louis Gates, Jr, Robert F Kennedy, Jr, Maury Maverick, Jr,[§] FDR, Jr, George Stevens, Jr, Robert Wagner, Jr, Kurt Vonnegut, Jr.[¶]

Regards,
Arthur

* In 1995, JFK, Jr., founded *George,* a glossy, politics-as-lifestyle monthly magazine, which folded in 2002.

† Prospero's speech in act 4, scene 1, beginning, "Our revels now are ended. These, our actors, / As I foretold you, were all spirits and / Are melted into air, into thin air," and ending, "We are such stuff / As dreams are made on, and our little life / Is rounded with a sleep."

‡ Whitney Darrow, Jr. (1909–99). Longtime *New Yorker* cartoonist.

§ Maury Maverick, Jr. (1921–2003). Liberal Texas lawyer, political activist, and columnist.

¶ Kurt Vonnegut, Jr. (1922–2007). Novelist; leftist intellectual; wrote *Cat's Cradle* (1963) and *Slaughterhouse-Five* (1969); blended satire and science fiction.

To Warren Christopher

13 July 2000

[New York, New York]

Dear Chris:

Stimulated by the *Times Magazine* piece about the vice presidential search, I take the liberty of sending you some thoughts on the subject. As a historian, I have long been interested in the vice presidency (see ch 12 of *The Cycles of American History*,* "The Future of the Vice Presidency"—an essay somewhat overtaken by events but full of interesting historical data).

It is an illusion to suppose that the running mate always delivers his (her) own state. LBJ in 1960 was the glorious exception. In 1948 the Republicans put the most popular governor California ever had on the ticket (Earl Warren), and Truman carried the state. "The Vice President can't help you," said Nixon. "He can only hurt you." Few citizens decide their presidential vote on the ground of the vice presidential nominee.

Most voters are interested in the vice presidential choice only as a test of the judgment and taste of the presidential candidate. The elder Bush made a mistake in picking Quayle. Clinton did well in picking Gore. This standard, rather than alleged impact on the popular vote, should be controlling.

In 2000, the running mate who would inspire most confidence in the presidential candidate would be (in my view) George Mitchell.† He has a formidable record as judge, senator and diplomat; he is thoughtful and articulate; he has nice ironic humor; and, in case anything happened to the president, he would make an entirely convincing replacement. Also he is a little old to aspire to the presidency himself.

I wonder, by the way, why the *Times Magazine* article did not mention

---

*Arthur Schlesinger, Jr. *The Cycles of American History* (Boston: Houghton Mifflin, 1986).

†George J. Mitchell, Jr. (b. 1933). Lawyer; senator (D-Maine), 1980–95; Senate majority leader, 1989–95.

Chris Dodd* as a possibility. He is a far better man than his sanctimonious colleague† from Connecticut, whom the article does mention.

I do not envy you the task!—but I wish you all good luck.‡

Sincerely yours,
Arthur

On Monday, August 7, 2000, Gore named Senator Joseph Lieberman of Connecticut as his vice presidential choice. Arthur was outraged and thought momentarily he could not support the ticket. On August 12 at 12:50 a.m., Gore telephoned him from Rachel Carson's study in Springdale, Pennsylvania. Arthur said he was not happy about Lieberman and that there was little more insufferable than self-appointed guardians of the public morals. Gore said that Lieberman was fourth on his list and that he had almost named John Edwards,§ but he was excited by the selection of Lieberman as a blow against anti-Semitism. The reaction across the country, he said, was that it was "a bold choice, a gutsy choice." He asked Arthur for help on his acceptance speech.

---

* Christopher ("Chris") Dodd (b. 1944). Lawyer; representative (D-Conn.), 1975–81; senator, 1981–2011; presently chairman of the Motion Picture Association of America.

† Joseph Lieberman (b. 1942). Lawyer; Connecticut attorney general, 1983, 1986–88; senator, 1989–2013; onetime president of the Democratic Leadership Council (the Republican wing of the Democratic Party, according to Schlesinger); Democratic Party nominee for vice president, 2000. Lieberman failed to get his party's nomination for senator in 2006 and was reelected as an independent on a third-party ticket.

‡ Christopher replied almost at once, describing himself as "a longtime George Mitchell fan" and calling him "not only a fine man but a first-rate speaker."

§ John Edwards (b. 1953). Senator (D-N.C.), 1999–2005; Democratic nominee for vice president, 2004; involved in sex scandal.

To Al Gore, Jr.

13 August 2000

[New York, New York]

Dear Mr Vice President:

Here are a few thoughts along (I hope) the lines of our talk on Saturday. I doubt that they will be of much use; and, as a veteran in these matters, I know how irrelevant old-timers can be. There is no substitute for active participation to catch the rhythm of a presidential campaign. I well remember how useless the drafts produced by Sam Rosenman and Bob Sherwood were for Adlai Stevenson in 1952—and I am as much out of things today as they were half a century ago. Also I am not sure that I understand the gap in your argument that you thought I might be able to fill. And, because I must get in the corrected proofs of my new book today, I have not been able to give this assignment the time it deserves. So feel no misgivings about filing the enclosure in the wastebasket.

The choice of Senator Lieberman is obviously a political ten-strike (so far); so I wonder whether you should spend much time justifying it. You should simply say that you chose him because he seemed the best man for the job. Too much talk about a 'breakthrough' suggests you chose him to make a point about diversity or because you wanted to give representation to one or another group.

I do think you and Senator Lieberman should understand why, despite the adulation of the press, many of us are concerned about his designation. Americans respect religion but they distrust religiosity—holier-than-thou persons who wear their religion on their sleeves. Fundamentalists in particular, whether Christian, Jewish, Muslim or whatever, excite suspicion, and rightly so. Born-again people who claim to execute God's purposes reject the basic Christian insight into the unfathomable gap between sinful mortals and the Almighty. As Lincoln said in his Second Inaugural, "The Almighty has his own purposes." This is why so many of us are repelled by sanctimonious lectures from people who seem to think that they are more moral than the rest of us—Bill Bennett,* for example. Reflect on the sig-

---

* William J. ("Bill") Bennett (b. 1943). Conservative Republican pundit and politician; secretary of education, 1985–88; director of the Office of National Drug Control Policy, 1989–91.

nificance of the vote in Kansas last week overthrowing the fundamentalists and reinstating Darwin.

Anti-semitism is not involved. As a nation, we are over that, and any remaining anti-semites wouldn't vote Democratic anyway. Actually Senator Lieberman's religion protects him. If a southern Baptist had put on his performance at his designation, the press would have been merciless; but people refrain from criticizing Senator Lieberman lest they be suspected of anti-semitism.

All good luck on the speech and on the campaign, and Alexandra joins in love to Tipper and Karenna.

Warmest regards,
Arthur

There was uncertainty whether Gore or Bush won Florida—and thus the presidency—on Election Day, but a Democratic initiative to recount the Florida vote was thwarted by a phalanx of Republican Party lawyers, including Jim Baker, the former secretary of state.

To Al Gore, Jr.

29 Nov 2000

[New York, New York]

Dear Mr. Vice President:

I have been watching the proceedings in Florida with mingled disbelief and outrage. It is incredible that Republicans should accuse Democrats of "stealing" the election when the Republican effort has been devoted to stopping the counting of Florida votes. If Jim Baker really believed that a Florida majority voted for Bush, why would he not welcome and extend the vote recount in order to confirm that belief and put the result beyond question? And why does the press not make this point?

Your speech should be short, incisive and (despite the paragraph above) generous. I append a draft with different leads, one in case of victory, another in case of defeat. I couldn't use the two Washington quotes because I couldn't find the letters in the books at hand (the Library of America volume of Washington's writings and Saxe Commins's *Basic Writings of George Washington*), and I don't have a research assistant to look things up.

You have handled yourself with a dignity and restraint appropriate to a grave and difficult situation. Your father would have been proud of you.

All the best—and Happy Thanksgiving!
Arthur

DRAFT—

IN CASE OF VICTORY:

I thank the American people for the honor they have conferred on me, and I thank my valiant opponent for his generous words of concession. I look forward in the years to come to working with Governor Bush and his supporters in strengthening our democracy at home and in helping to bring peace to the world.

IN CASE OF DEFEAT:

I hasten to congratulate Governor Bush, and I call on all Americans to give our president-elect full acceptance and respect as he assumes his new responsibilities.

THEN:

In times of strain and stress, we can renew ourselves and our democracy by drawing upon the wisdom of those who founded this republic. There is nothing new about close and contentious presidential elections. In a dispute more bitter and divisive than this one, and after a far angrier election, it took 36 ballots in the House of Representatives before Thomas Jefferson was elected in 1800 as our third president.

Two weeks later in his inaugural address Mr Jefferson expressed the essence of our democracy. "This being now decided by the voice of the nation, announced according to the rules of the Constitution," he said, "all will, of course, arrange themselves under the will of the law, and unite in common efforts for the common good."

Speaking as the leader of what was then called the Republican party, Mr Jefferson continued: "Every difference of opinion is not a difference of principle. We have called by different names brethren of the same principle. We are all Republicans, we are all Federalists."

In the same spirit: I say today we are all Democrats, we are all Republicans. Let us unite in common efforts for the common good. Let no one among us go on about stolen elections or challenge the legitimacy of the outcome. Let us stand before the world as a splendid affirmation of democracy in action, negotiating a tricky passage through stormy waters and pulling up calmly and safely at our common destination.

Perhaps useful lessons can be drawn from our recent experience. A first lesson is the importance of voting. Long ago the great poet of democracy, Walt Whitman, urged young men "to enter more strongly yet into politics. . . . Always inform yourself; always do the best you can; always vote." Those who think that whether or not they vote makes no difference should study Florida in the year 2000.

A second lesson is the need for a review of the ways we vote. We can all agree that the times call for a modernization of electoral technology. I would like to think that we will never hear such words "chad" and "butterfly ballot" again! We must proceed to deal with the infirmities in our political process.

Above all, we must unite as Americans determined to affirm the values of democracy in a new century and a new millennium. The past is past, and we cannot allow it to poison the future. Let us work joyously and wholeheartedly together to fulfill the promise of American life.[*]

---

[*] On December 12, 2000, the Supreme Court by a vote of 5 to 4 decided to stop the Florida recount, giving Bush the state of Florida and victory in the electoral college. Gore, who won the popular vote nationwide by more than five hundred thousand, conceded on December 13.

To Frances Horowitz[*]

30 March 2001

[New York, New York]

Dear Frances:

I gather that the Schlesinger Chair is approaching realization, and I want to thank everyone involved in the process. The impending symposium and dinner on the fifth promise to be an occasion that will long live in my memory.

Since my name is to be attached to the new chair, I assume that its occupants will develop the historical areas in which I have particularly worked. The chair, I would hope, might be announced as the Schlesinger Chair in American Political, Diplomatic and Intellectual History. These fields may be somewhat out of fashion at the moment, but they are so central to an understanding of historical change that they are bound soon to be back in demand. There wouldn't be much point in naming the chair for me and then recruiting a scholar with quite different historical priorities.[†]

Once again let me express my unbounded gratitude to you and to the Graduate School for putting up with me for more than a third of a century!

With best regards,
Arthur

[*] Frances Horowitz. Child psychologist, author, president of the Graduate Center of the City University of New York, 1991–2005.

[†] The Arthur M. Schlesinger, Jr., Chair in American History was established at the CUNY Graduate Center in 2001 with Professor David Nasaw, biographer of William Randolph Hearst, Andrew Carnegie, and Joseph Kennedy, as its first occupant.

To Warren Christopher

12 May 2001

[New York, New York]

Dear Chris:

*Chances of a Lifetime** is one of the most attractive memoirs I have read for a long time—thoughtful, candid, modest, instructive and highly readable. It is a lasting contribution to the history of our times. I thank you for sending it and for that most generous inscription.

I thank you too for your kind words about my own book. I have been struck by the letters from our contemporaries describing parallel experiences and memories. I suppose that, as we approach the last hurrah, we are more disposed to remember, reconsider and recount the past.

Another subject: I hope that you will not feel constrained about speaking out on public issues. After a decent interval to let the new crowd get its bearings, the country will begin to welcome thoughts from persons of experience and wisdom. Or at least I hope so.

Best regards,
Arthur

To Marco Ermacora[†]

28 June 2001

[New York, New York]

Dear Mr. Ermacora:

. . . I read your letter with great interest and sympathy. Globalization in some form and at some pace appears irresistible, driven on as it is by high technology; but, in the absence of international regulatory mechanisms, globalization means new power to private international organization, whether corporate, criminal or terrorist, or even NGOs. Protests have their

---

* Christopher had written Schlesinger on April 17, 2001, praising his new book, *A Life in the Twentieth Century: Innocent Beginnings, 1917–1950,* and including a copy of his own new book, *Chances of a Lifetime.*

† Marco Ermacora. Unknown correspondent

place as a means of raising issues, but nutty or destructive protesting is likely to be counterproductive. Building international institutions is surely the long-term answer.

You ask how I can stay on good terms with people like Casey and Kissinger. I suppose it is partly because we have been through tough times together, like the Second World War (Casey) and various foreign policy crises (Kissinger); partly because as a historian I am naturally curious about the uses of power; partly because I do not quite believe that politics should determine friendships.

I thank you for your kind words about various of my writings and for your regard for the Kennedy legacy, and I wish you—and the world—all luck in the future.

Sincerely yours,
Arthur Schlesinger, Jr.

Fearing another Vietnam-like quagmire in Afghanistan, Arthur wrote Ted Kennedy, his friend and the liberal leader of the Senate, urging him to insist that the Bush administration focus exclusively on getting rid of al-Qaeda, not the Taliban, and once this was done, to depart Afghanistan promptly.*

To Edward M. Kennedy

4 November 2001

[New York, New York]

Dear Ted:

. . . The best way, it seems to me, to escape sending ground forces into another quagmire is to redefine—and narrow—our objectives.

Let us forgo specious rhetoric along the "who is not with us is against us" line and focus instead on the destruction of Qaida. This will enable us

---

* Al-Qaeda. "The Base," a global militant Islamist organization founded by Osama bin Laden in 1988; carried out the attack on September 11, 2001, that destroyed the twin towers of New York's World Trade Center and struck the Pentagon, killing more than three thousand people.

to claim victory and get out of Afghanistan once bin Laden[*] and his gang are captured or killed. In the meantime, let us try covert bribery and black-mail to persuade Taliban[†] leaders to betray bin Laden to us in order to get the heat off themselves.

Afghanistan is a riddle beyond our unilateral power or wisdom to solve; and, as we depart, we should turn it over to the UN. Of course, we would continue to pursue long-term police action against terrorism, pooling in-telligence on terrorism, identifying and uprooting terrorist cells, drying up sources of funds, etc.

If we do not narrow our objectives, we will, barring some stroke of un-predictable luck, go inexorably down the road to massive intervention in a terrain far more forbidding than Vietnam and in a famously unconquer-able country that has successfully repelled both the British Empire and the Soviet Union—also a country in which we have had no historical experi-ence and about which we have meager knowledge and expertise.

This is exactly what Bin Laden hopes we will do, and, if we do it, we are walking into the trap he is setting for us.

Yours ever,
Arthur

To George Kennan

14 February 2002

[New York, New York]

Dear George:

This letter (which requires no answer) brings Alexandra's and my most affectionate birthday wishes for health and happiness.

You have served the republic nobly—and it is hardly your fault if our government appears to be succumbing to those temptations of vainglory

---

* Osama bin Laden (1957–2011). Member of wealthy Saudi family; founded al-Qaeda; killed by U.S. special forces in Pakistan in 2011.

† The Taliban. "Students of Islamic Knowledge Movement," a militant Islamist politi-cal group that ruled Afghanistan from 1996 to 2001; ousted by U.S. military and Af-ghani opposition forces in December 2001; has proven highly resilient.

against which you have long warned with such eloquence and force. I sense a dangerous euphoria in Washington—a feeling that "we are on a roll." I fear that Colin Powell* as a military man is accustomed to carrying out his commander-in-chief's orders, even if he may personally disagree.

Anyway have a happy birthday—and give our love to Annelise. We love seeing Grace on her occasional visits to New York.

Yours ever,
Arthur

To Jimmy Carter

19 May 2002

[New York, New York]

Dear Mr. President:

I cannot withhold my admiration for your trip to Cuba.† You said the right things, did the right things and never set a foot wrong. It was a courageous and responsible performance, a diplomatic high-wire act, and you deserve the gratitude of two nations (rather than the abusive letters you are doubtless receiving). I have been to Cuba five times in the last fifteen years, and I know something of the atmosphere. I am glad that you saw Elizardo Sanchez, a brave and dedicated man. The US embargo in fact protects Fidel, giving him an all-purpose alibi for Cuba's economic troubles and enabling him to play the nationalist card before a proud people.

The best way to deal with the excesses of the revolution would surely be to flood Cuba with American tourists, American investors, American

---

*Colin Powell (b. 1937). Four-star U.S. Army general; national security adviser, 1987–89; chairman of the Joint Chiefs of Staff, 1989–93; secretary of state, 2001–5.

†Jimmy Carter visited Cuba May 12–17, 2002. He met with Fidel Castro and with students and dissidents. In a speech at the University of Havana, he called for the end of the U.S. economic embargo and for free elections and freedom of speech and association in Cuba.

consumer goods and American books and magazines. It is sad to see domestic politics dictating and corrupting US foreign policy.

Warmest congratulations on a most successful adventure.[*]

Yours sincerely,
Arthur Schlesinger, Jr.

To Lawrence Summers[†]

22 November 2002

[New York, New York]

Dear President Summers:

I was greatly relieved by the reinstatement of the invitation to Tom Paulin.[‡] Universities should be citadels of the First Amendment, and I was sad to see Harvard, the most influential of American universities, emerging as the champion of censorship.

Evidently some members of the Harvard community believe that people like Tom Paulin and David Duke[§] constitute so grave a threat to the intellectual chastity of the undergraduates as to forbid them to speak at Harvard. This is an extraordinary confession of lack of faith in the ability of the Harvard faculty to teach critical analysis. And it is also an extraordinary confession of lack of faith in the democratic idea itself.

---

[*] Carter replied in a handwritten note: "To Arthur, Thank you. It's a pleasure and honor to hear from you. Jimmy C."

[†] Lawrence Summers (b. 1954). Economist; Democratic activist; secretary of the Treasury, 1999–2001; president of Harvard University, 2001–6; director of the National Economic Council, 2009–10.

[‡] Tom Paulin (b. 1949). Irish poet and critic; lecturer in English literature at Hertford College, Oxford; author of the poem "Killed in Crossfire" with reference to "Zionist SS."; His invitation from the Harvard English department to lecture was rescinded on November 12, 2002, after protests concerning his views on Palestine. A week later, after Harvard Law School professors Alan Dershowitz, Laurence Tribe, and Charles Fried criticized the move in a public letter, the invitation was renewed.

[§] David Duke (b. 1950). Right-wing Louisiana political activist; onetime grand wizard of the Knights of the Ku Klux Klan.

Justice Brandeis summed up the problem in *Whitney v California* [1927]: "If there be time to expose through discussion the falsehood and fallacies, to avert the evil by the processes of education, the remedy to be applied is more speech, not enforced silence."

Yours sincerely,
Arthur

To George Kennan

15 February 2003

[New York, New York]

Dear George:

This is a belated letter, requiring no answer, of congratulations on your 99th, in which Alexandra enthusiastically joins. We count on your making a full century a year from now.

But what sad times are these for the republic! The shift from containment/deterrence to preventive war as the basis of our foreign policy is deeply disturbing, as is the absence of debate over the most solemn decision a free people are called upon to make—the decision of war or peace. . . .

Warmest thanks for the historic contributions you have made to political sanity over the last 99 years! And affections to Annaliese.

Yours ever,
Arthur

[Form letter]

I seem to have become in my old age a target for an endless flow of unsolicited manuscripts. Before 2003 is over, I will enter upon my 87th year, and at this point in life, as you will one day discover, time becomes the most precious of commodities. Wise old Benjamin Franklin observed that lost time is never found.

I don't doubt that I could learn much from your manuscript. But, since I am far behind schedule on a manuscript of my own, I trust you will forgive me if I take a pass on yours. Forgive me too for this form letter, but the flow is too endless to permit individual notes.

Yours sincerely,
Arthur Schlesinger, Jr.

To Nicholas D. Kristof[*]

6 August 2003

[New York, New York]

Dear Mr Kristof:

I applaud your piece on Hiroshima.[†] It was the most tragic decision any American president has ever had to make, but if President Truman had not brought the war to the speediest possible end, he would have been held personally responsible for every American death in the invasion of Japan (not to mention deaths in POW camps). When the American people discovered that Truman had the means to bring the war to a speedy end, a means developed at immense cost to the American taxpayer, and refused to use it, I believe he would have been impeached. . . .
Again congratulations on a bracing piece.

Yours sincerely,
Arthur

---

[*] Nicholas D. Kristof (b. 1959). Journalist; author; *New York Times* columnist.
[†] Nicholas D. Kristof, "Blood On Our Hands?" *The New York Times,* August 5, 2003. Kristof's answer was no: "The Japanese military ferociously resisted surrender even after the two atomic bombings on major cities. . . . The alternatives were worse."

To Edward M. Kennedy

19 September 2003

[New York, New York]

Dear Ted:

You ask what the value of oral history is for the historian. The value is very considerable, especially when oral history is professionally done.

Oral history is not a job for amateurs. The interrogator must be immersed in the career of the interrogatee and in the context of the times in order to ask useful and intelligent questions. You could not find a more professional team than the Miller Center at the University of Virginia, and I am delighted that you have decided to submit yourself to their ministrations.

Think how greatly history would be enriched if we had oral histories of the great senators of the past—Clay, Webster, Calhoun, La Follette, Norris, Wagner; or, for that matter, suppose we had oral histories of Shakespeare, Caesar, Socrates! You have played a considerable part in the history of our times, and historians in the future will be grateful to you and to the Miller Center. Best of luck on the oral history project.

Yours ever,
Arthur

To Jean Kennedy Smith

11 January 2005

[New York, New York]

Dearest Jean:

Alexandra and I read the news of Rosemary's death with sorrow. Perhaps you have forgotten that Rosemary was my first Kennedy. In the autumn of 1931 I went off to Exeter. I drew as a roommate a Swampscott boy named John O'Keefe, whose main interests were astrophysics (he later discovered the O'Keefe Asteroid) and religion. We spent the first term arguing about religion and playing a board game called (mystically) Camelot.

We were good friends, and during Christmas vacation in December

1931 John invited me to his parents' house for dinner. His father was a doctor, and his mother Ruth was an intelligent and attractive woman who had gone a quarter-century before to a convent in the Netherlands where her best friend was another girl from Massachusetts named Rose Fitzgerald.

You may remember the O'Keefes. They had two daughters, and the mothers, concerned over Rosemary's slow start, felt that a winter with the O'Keefe girls under the supervision of Dr. O'Keefe might be helpful to Rosemary. At any rate, it was in December 1931 that I met my first Kennedy. A couple of years later, when we were both at Harvard, John O'Keefe invited me to a dance. Rosemary was at the party, and my memory was that she insisted on leading me—probably rightly, since I was a bad dancer. I did not see her again for more than half a century until Thanksgivings at Bridgehampton.

The handicapped and retarded owe a great debt to Rosemary.[*] Hers was not a wasted life.

Love,
Arthur

To Art Buchwald

27 March 2006

[New York, New York]

Beloved Artie:

Alexandra and I are terribly impressed by the gallant way that you have confronted the ultimate decision.[†] It all reminds me of Ben Franklin, the

---

[*] Rosemary's condition became public after JFK's election when the newsletter of the National Association for Retarded Children mentioned that the president-elect "has a mentally retarded sister who is in an institution in Wisconsin." Rosemary's condition inspired her younger sister Eunice Kennedy Shriver to advocate for sick and disabled children, and in 1968 she founded the Special Olympics for mentally disabled athletes. Rosemary died in Wisconsin with her sisters and her brother Ted by her side.

[†] Arthur ("Art") Buchwald (1925–2007). American humorist, wrote a long-running column for *The Washington Post;* won Pulitzer Prize for Outstanding Commentary in 1982. Buchwald entered hospice care in early February 2006 when his kidneys failed

Art Buchwald of his day, who, dying, was queried by the president of Yale, a clergyman, about his religious views. Ben Franklin replied a few days before his death.

As to Christ, "I have some doubts as to his divinity, though it is a question I do not dogmatize upon, having never studied it, and think it needless to busy myself with it now, when I expect soon an opportunity of knowing the truth with less trouble." Your position is identical with Ben Franklin's— you stand on the threshold of the final mystery, and you make a joke.

In the meantime, you have brought across the weary years boundless pleasure and joy to boundless millions. And to your personal friends, you have given comfort, sympathy, love—and your friends compete in loving you. Alexandra and I deem ourselves in the magic circle of friendship. And you remind us all of human courage in face of death.

We love you, beloved Artie.
Arthur

To Catherine Galbraith[*]

8 May 2006

[New York, New York]

Dearest Kitty:

The world has been a black place since Ken died[†]—no acute observation, no witty commentary, no merry heart. He was my closest and best

---

as a result of diabetes. Doctors said that without hemodialysis every few days to cleanse his kidneys, he had only weeks to live, but Buchwald chose to discontinue the treatment. Yet he kept not dying and was healthy enough to receive scores of visitors, chat on the telephone, and write columns. On March 26, 2006, *The New York Times* published a story entitled "Washington's Hottest Salon Is a Deathbed." He was released from the hospice in June, his kidneys apparently functioning. He spent another summer on Martha's Vineyard and wrote a book about his situation, *Too Soon to Say Goodbye.* "So far things are going my way. I am known in the hospice as 'The Man Who Would Not Die,'" he wrote. "Dying isn't hard. Getting paid by Medicare is." He died on January 17, 2007.

[*] Catherine Atwater Galbraith (1913–2008). Married economist J. K. Galbraith in 1937.

[†] John Kenneth Galbraith died of natural causes on April 29, 2006, at age ninety-seven. Of his numerous honorary degrees, he liked to say, "My only rule in the matter is to have more honorary degrees than Arthur Schlesinger."

friend, and I miss him terribly. A thoughtful, kind and loving presence has irrevocably passed away. The Schlesinger family shares your grief and sends our collective love.

As I reflect on our friendship, it is evident that close contact with Ken changed my life. I loved him—and learned from him substantively and even more stylistically. No one reacted so intelligently; no one sparkled so brilliantly. His example persuaded me that irony is far more effective than indignation when confronted by the parade of human folly—that a rapier works better than a broadsword. This ended the ill-tempered explosions with which I used to spoil Cambridge dinner parties and prepared me for Washington in the Kennedy years and for the rest of my life. But I recognize that I am not the master ironist that Ken was!

Ken had a good long run, and I trust that his October 15 birth mate may do as well. All the Schlesingers mourn with all the Galbraiths.

Our love to you,
Arthur

Arthur died of a heart attack on February 28, 2007, while dining in a New York restaurant with his beloved Alexandra, his stepson, Peter, and Peter's fiancé, Claudia Chagall Ward. Despite Arthur's infirmities—including the onset of Parkinson's disease, which rendered his speech on occasion unintelligible—his mind remained as sharp as ever. He still cared deeply about his country. His last book, War and the American Presidency, *published in 2004, condemned the principle of preventive war so fervently embraced by George W. Bush.*

*Asked how an agnostic like himself faced death, he told an interviewer, "Paradise can't exist without an inferno. But I don't believe in either one. I believe that death is simply the end."**

---

* Antonio Monda, *Do You Believe? Conversations on God and Religion* (New York: Vintage Books, 2007), 147.

Postscript

Reviewing the Schlesinger letters collection proved to be a formidable task. The main repository of his correspondence is at the New York Public Library (a secondary archive is at the John F. Kennedy Presidential Library and Museum in Boston). The library provided us with a full fifty-nine page index of all the major items in the Schlesinger archives, placed in a series of numbered boxes carefully assembled over a two-year period and arranged in alphabetical order and by categories. This index allowed us to decide which set of the boxes we would ask for. We eventually selected 184 boxes that dealt exclusively with his correspondence from A to Z. Each box contained on average about two hundred or so letters. We estimated that, based on the box totals, Schlesinger must have generated at least a dozen letters a week over six decades, or some thirty-five thousand letters.

In hunting down the letters we desired, we abided by guidelines laid down by the library's archival division. The rules rigorously protect the valuable literary caches stored securely within the library's stalls. The specific regulations instruct on the use and handling of all archival materials. We received no special dispensation as the sons of the documents' donor. When we visited the library's Manuscript Room on the third floor to do our research, for example, we were asked to leave our overcoats, bags, briefcases, and pens in the building's cloakroom on the first floor. This was done so that no user could later possibly mark up files or even steal missives once inside the Manuscript Room. Each of our visits also required a sign-in slip. The research chamber supplied us with pencils so we could take notes. We were allowed to bring a laptop. Sometimes we brought sweaters, as the room was kept at a cool temperature to preserve the often fragile paper, parchment, or ancient documentation that was being examined.

Researchers sat at long wooden tables like those used in English boarding school dining halls. A light overhead and a chair marked each person's workstation. Each visitor, in his or her turn, ordered boxes in advance by numbers, sometimes four or five for a sitting. One was permitted to peer at only one box at a time and extract only one letter at a time, which meant that fishing a handful of correspondence out of a box was not permitted. Once a researcher selected a letter, he or she wrote down the letter's date and the box number on two different forms. One form was placed in the box next to the selected letter. The other was handed to the staff. Then the librarian took back the boxes and, using the forms as guidance, arranged for the chosen letters to be scanned. A few weeks later, upon the payment of a fee, the library emailed us the scanned letters. These elaborate steps ensured the library's archival treasures remained tightly safeguarded.

We would like to thank the archival staff for their help, particularly Tom Lannon, assistant curator of the Manuscripts and Archives Division, and Tal Nadan, reference archivist—and numerous others in the Research Division who were courteous and helpful to us at all times.

We owe a debt of gratitude as well to those individuals who granted us permission to use letters written to Arthur Schlesinger, Jr., by themselves or their family members. We would like to thank David Acheson, John Alsop, Christopher Buckley, Anthony Dolan, James K. Galbraith, Phil Gramm, Cynthia Helms, Hubert Humphrey III, Henry Kissinger, David Mortimer, Ann Rostow, Elizabeth Shannon, Adlai Stevenson III, Joan Buresch Talley, Elizabeth Winthrop, and Anna Wintour.

We would also like to cite our father's brilliant support staff, who made possible his legible, well-typed, and easily readable letters that make up this volume. The Schlesinger secretarial staff involved the following individuals: Julie Jeppson Ludwig, his secretary when he worked at Harvard University; Gretchen Stewart, his secretary and assistant when he was in the Kennedy White House and later when he taught at the City University of New York; and, after Stewart's death, Dianne Sikorski and Elizabeth Hogan, among others. With their superb help, he was able to dictate hundreds of missives in short amounts of time—besides those, of course, he composed himself without any office help.

Finally we want to thank Jon Meacham, our supremely talented editor at Random House, for his meticulous attention and assistance overseeing the editing of this book. From the moment the proposal for the Letters volume first landed on his desk, Jon showed an immediate interest in the project. He had his own personal stake in the endeavor as he and our father were close friends. Jon was an admirer of Arthur Schlesinger, Jr., as both a historian and as a literary figure. They had in common that each had written a biography of President Andrew Jackson for which each had earned a Pulitzer Prize. In all ways, our tie-in with Jon was immensely valuable for this undertaking. We want to thank Ben Steinberg at Random House, too, for his excellent labors on behalf of the book, and Dennis Ambrose for supervising the copy editing of the book's text.

Our gratitude, in addition, goes to our agent, Andrew Wylie, for recognizing the strength of this book idea from the start and for making certain that we found exactly the right publishing house for it. As always, Andrew and his formidable crew worked tremendously hard for the success of the venture. A shout-out, too, is in order for Jeffrey Posternak in the Wylie Agency, for his exemplary assistance.

In addition, Stephen would like to thank his wife, Judy, and his daughter, Sarah, for their constant love as well as unstinting backing for this enterprise. And we both are greatly obliged to members of our family for their various contributions in different ways to the book. Finally, we owe our greatest expression of appreciation to our father for the gifts he bestowed on the world in the form of these superb letters, which provide such intimate and personal insights into the ongoing struggles of American liberalism in our land over a sixty year period from 1945 to 2005.

Index

NOTE: ASJ refers to Arthur Schlesinger, Jr.

ABOUT THE EDITORS

ANDREW SCHLESINGER is the author of *Veritas: Harvard College and the American Experience,* and co-editor of *Journals: 1952–2000* by Arthur Schlesinger Jr. After his graduation from Harvard in 1970, he taught high school in Santa Fe, then worked as a staff reporter for the Nashville *Tennessean* and the *Rocky Mountain News.* In 1980, he joined ABC News in their documentary division, where his film scripts won two Emmy awards and a Writers Guild Award. He lives in Cambridge, Massachusetts.

STEPHEN SCHLESINGER is a Senior Fellow at the Century Foundation. He is the former director of the World Policy Institute. He previously served as a staff writer for *Time* magazine, speechwriter and foreign policy advisor to New York State's governor Mario Cuomo, and senior advisor to the UN's Habitat. A graduate of Harvard University and Harvard Law school, he is coauthor of *Bitter Fruit,* about the CIA coup in Guatemala, author of *Act of Creation,* about the founding of the United Nations, and coeditor of *Journals: 1952–2000* by Arthur Schlesinger Jr. He lives in New York City.